KALAMBO FALLS PREHISTORIC SITE

II

KALAMBO FALLS PREHISTORIC SITE

II

THE LATER PREHISTORIC CULTURES

J. DESMOND CLARK
University of California, Berkeley

WITH CONTRIBUTIONS BY

B. M. FAGAN
University of California, Santa Barbara

M. R. KLEINDIENST
Research Associate, Department of Anthropology
University of Toronto and
Department of West Asian Studies
Royal Ontario Museum

F. VAN NOTEN
Musée Royal de l'Afrique centrale, Tervuren

CAMBRIDGE
AT THE UNIVERSITY PRESS
1974

Published by the Syndics of the Cambridge University Press
Bentley House, 200 Euston Road, London NW1 2DB
American Branch: 32 East 57th Street, New York, N.Y. 10022

Library of Congress Catalogue Card Number: 68–25084

ISBN: 0 521 20009 1

Printed in Great Britain
at the University Printing House, Cambridge
(Brooke Crutchley, University Printer)

FOR BETTY

CONTENTS

The essence of their livelihood would have been related to the environment as is that of the indigenous animals whose ways they would have observed.

Desmond Vesey-FitzGerald

TABLES

FIGURES

PLATES

Frontispiece Wall painting on exterior of a hut in Mkamba Village.

The numbered plates appear on pages 257–409.

PREFACE

This volume contains the descriptions and discussion of the later prehistoric industries found at the Kalambo Falls, from the Iron Age to the Polungu Industry, the earlier stages of which belong in the later Pleistocene. It thus covers the period of technical and behavioural changes after 20,000 B.C. when the traditional 'Middle Stone Age' technology was being replaced by that of the 'Later Stone Age' based on the production of small blades and microliths. The book describes the partial excavation of an early second millennium hunters' camp; the settlement of the first metal-workers and agriculturalists to make their home at the Kalambo Falls in the fourth and fifth centuries A.D. and the subsequent establishment there of the present Bantu-speaking inhabitants. This whole period saw significant changes in the relationships between the human inhabitants and their use of the land and its natural resources.

This was a time when, throughout the continent, hunting and collecting activities were becoming more specialized and when, for demographic, technological or other reasons, the land was being exploited in greater depth than ever before. Social groups remained small and mobile until the coming of food producers with new domestic plants and animals, when larger and permanent settlements became possible.

The evidence to be presented is largely cultural and the absence of faunal remains at the Kalambo Falls is a limiting factor in its interpretation. However, this is partly compensated for by evidence relating to the plant communities and from ethno-botany, so making it possible to develop models for the life ways of the later hunter/gatherers and first farmers. Since the general topography, ecology and palaeo-ecology of the local basin, as well as the detailed stratigraphy of the sites, have already been described in Volume I, this should be referred to where necessary to amplify the summaries of the stratigraphic position and relationships of the various Archaeological Occurrences dealt with in this volume.

The excavations on which these chapters are based were undertaken between 1956 and 1966 and most of the analysis was carried out in 1962–3 in Livingstone or at the Kalambo Falls. The first drafts and analysis tables were prepared in 1966. These have now been completely revised and rewritten. Because of the great amount of material our aim has been to present the basic data to show the composition of the various Industries we recognize, together with the stratigraphic, chronological and classificatory evidence on which our identification of the entity has been made and some comparative and interpretative discussion relative to the industrial sequence in adjacent regions of east and southern Africa. Undoubtedly the material will lend itself to considerably more statistical analysis of morphological features in the future but we believe that what we have presented here provides an adequate basis for the definitions and interpretations that have been made. The excavated collections are all housed in the Department of Prehistory at the Livingstone Museum, Zambia and we believe it to be important that they should be kept together for future re-examination as greater refinement in analytical methods becomes available.

Since the publication of Volume I the township of Abercorn has been renamed Mbala and the new name has, therefore, been used in the present work. The Congo Republic also has now become known as Zaïre and the Congo river as the Zaïre river.

Metrical conversions for miles and feet to kilometres and metres have been given to the nearest round number except where the precise measurement is significant as, for example, with depths in an excavation.

It gives me great pleasure to record my very sincere appreciation and thanks to all those who have assisted in the publication of this work. The excavations were made possible by the Wenner-Gren Foundation for Anthropological Research, New York; the Boise Fund, Oxford; the National Science Foundation, Washington; and the Trustees of the Rhodes–Livingstone Museum (now the Trustees of the National Museums of Zambia); the National Science Foundation and the African Studies Center of the University of California at Los Angeles made possible the original analysis in 1962 and 1963; the first draft and some statistical analysis were undertaken in 1966 after the completion of Volume I and while a Research Professor of the Miller Institute, University of California, Berkeley. The book in its present form has been completed in 1971–2 while a Fellow of the John Simon Guggenheim Memorial Foundation, New York, to the Trustees of which I am deeply grateful for their generous support.

I wish to express my best thanks to Dr Brian Fagan for his analysis of the early Iron Age pottery; to Dr Francis Van Noten for contributing to Chapter 5; to Dr Sherburne F. Cooke for the phosphate and calcium analysis of soil samples from Site C; and to D. R. G. Kemp for the Petrographic Notes that follow Chapter 4.

I acknowledge a special debt of thanks to my friend and colleague Dr Maxine Haldemann-Kleindienst for her full comments on the draft text, for joining as co-author of Chapter 4 and for providing the statistical data on the aggregates from the Site A excavations that she analysed. Her thoughtful and careful comment has been invaluable and has considerably assisted in the formulation of my own opinions on many points that initially appeared obscure. Although we are very largely in agreement, I must, however, exonerate her from any responsibility for the conclusions arrived at for which I alone must be held accountable.

Various friends and colleagues have also read and commented on portions of the text and I gratefully acknowledge my indebtedness to them for their valuable advice and suggestions. In particular, I wish to thank Dr Elizabeth Colson, Dr Brian Fagan, Dr Glynn Isaac, Dr Monica Wilson and David Phillipson for their many cogent and helpful comments. I am much indebted also to L. D. F. Vesey-FitzGerald, formerly of International Red Locust Control, Abercorn, and now with the National Park Service of Tanzania, for valuable information concerning the game and useful plants of the Kalambo Falls area.

Plates 1–29 were drawn by my son John W. D. Clark; Plates 30, 31 and 34–42 by Dr Van Noten and Plates 32, 33, 43–54 by my wife. Their skill and generous help have added immensely to an understanding of the nature and variety of the cultural material. My best thanks also to Eve Kemnitzer who drew Figures 1–20, 22–27, 29 and 32; and to Judith Ogden for Figures 21, 28, 30, 31, 33 and 34.

My greatest debt is, as always, to my wife. Her constant help – in the field, with the typescript, calculations, illustrations and in many other ways – has not only been an indispensable source of inspiration and encouragement but has also considerably lightened the task of preparing this volume for the press.

At times the text may appear somewhat over full of metrical data and listings of artifact characteristics. I hope, however, that the discussions and interpretations that follow the descriptions of the various industries will show that such data are a necessary means whereby we may hope to identify the activities of the human groups whose tools are represented by the artifacts from our excavations. In this way we may arrive at an understanding of how these people reacted to and made use of the rich resources of the woodland savanna where they lived.

J. D. C.

Inverness, California
March, 1972

CHAPTER 1

Recent historical associations

The 1914–1918 War

The latest historical remains to be found at the Kalambo Falls date to the time of the East African Campaign during the First World War. The north bank of the river was German territory and a small strong-point, built of stone blocks, was sited on the hill immediately to the north of the Falls and overlooking the Gorge. Today this consists of one larger, but incomplete, and two smaller, low, roughly circular walls of dry stone with, in places, some ancillary walling and the remains of what are probably silted up trenches.

On the lower slopes of the eastward side of the ridge is the remains of a narrow trackway running north-west and connecting with the fortified boma at Kasanga. This track continued onto the lowest alluvial terrace in the basin and ends opposite Site A. A brass cartridge case was picked up and a number of very rusted and fragmentary 'bully beef' tins lie on the eroded slopes below the strong-point. Since the figures '1917' can be seen on some of the tins it is likely that they date to September 1919 when, after the Armistice, General von Lettow Vorbeck and his troops camped at the Falls on their way to embark at Kasanga for Ujiji and Dar-es-Salaam. On the same eroded slopes where the tins were found it is possible to find artifacts of every age from Sangoan upwards. The land rubble forming at the present time is a living example of the manner in which the rubbles were formed in earlier times.

At Site C on the Zambian side of the river was found evidence of occupation by British troops. Here in the top one foot (30 cm) of disturbed deposit overlying the Early Iron Age settlement investigated in the 1963 excavation, were found two regulation brass buckles and a brass end-piece with eyelet holes from British khaki webbing equipment.

The present Bantu inhabitants

The Bantu-speakers who live in the Kalambo valley nowadays number, perhaps, about 850 adults.[1] They are predominantly of Lungu tribal affinities and inhabit one large and six small villages. Three of these villages are situated on the Zambian and the others on the Tanzanian side (Figure 1). It is not known when the people arrived in the valley but they themselves say that the Fipa, now occupying the high grasslands of the Ufipa plateau to the north and east, were there before them.[2] If so, it would seem that the Fipa must have entered the valley some time after the eleventh century, perhaps in the sixteenth century, since up to the earlier date, if not later, it was occupied by the makers of the Kalambo Falls Industry who, though most probably of Bantu negroid stock, made a very different kind of pottery.

The Lungu[3] have a common origin and a common language with the Mambwe, Inamwanga, Iwa, Fipa and one or two smaller tribal groups that occupy the Lake Tanganyika/Lake Malawi (Nyasa) corridor country on either side of the territorial boundary (see Volume I, Figure 1 inset). They have been called the 'people of Mwika' by Monica Wilson from their place of origin which is said to be a mountain on the water-

[1] On the Zambian side of the river, the adult male population was estimated in 1966 at 280 adults for tax purposes by the Mbala (formerly Abercorn) Rural Council. I am indebted to Mr John Carlin for this information. Population figures are not available for the Tanzanian side but it is estimated that the population today on the north bank is quite double that on the Zambian side, thus giving a conservative estimate of 850 adults.

[2] There are clearly close and long-standing ties between the Fipa and the Lungu communities at the Kalambo Falls and in 1966 we found that a number of Fipa families from Ufipa had moved into the valley since 1963. These were settled either in the existing villages on both sides of the river or had formed new ones higher on the slopes of the valley to the north.

[3] *Ilungu* is the word for an iron smelting kiln in the Lungu, Mambwe, Fipa and Nyiha languages (Willis, 1966: 40).

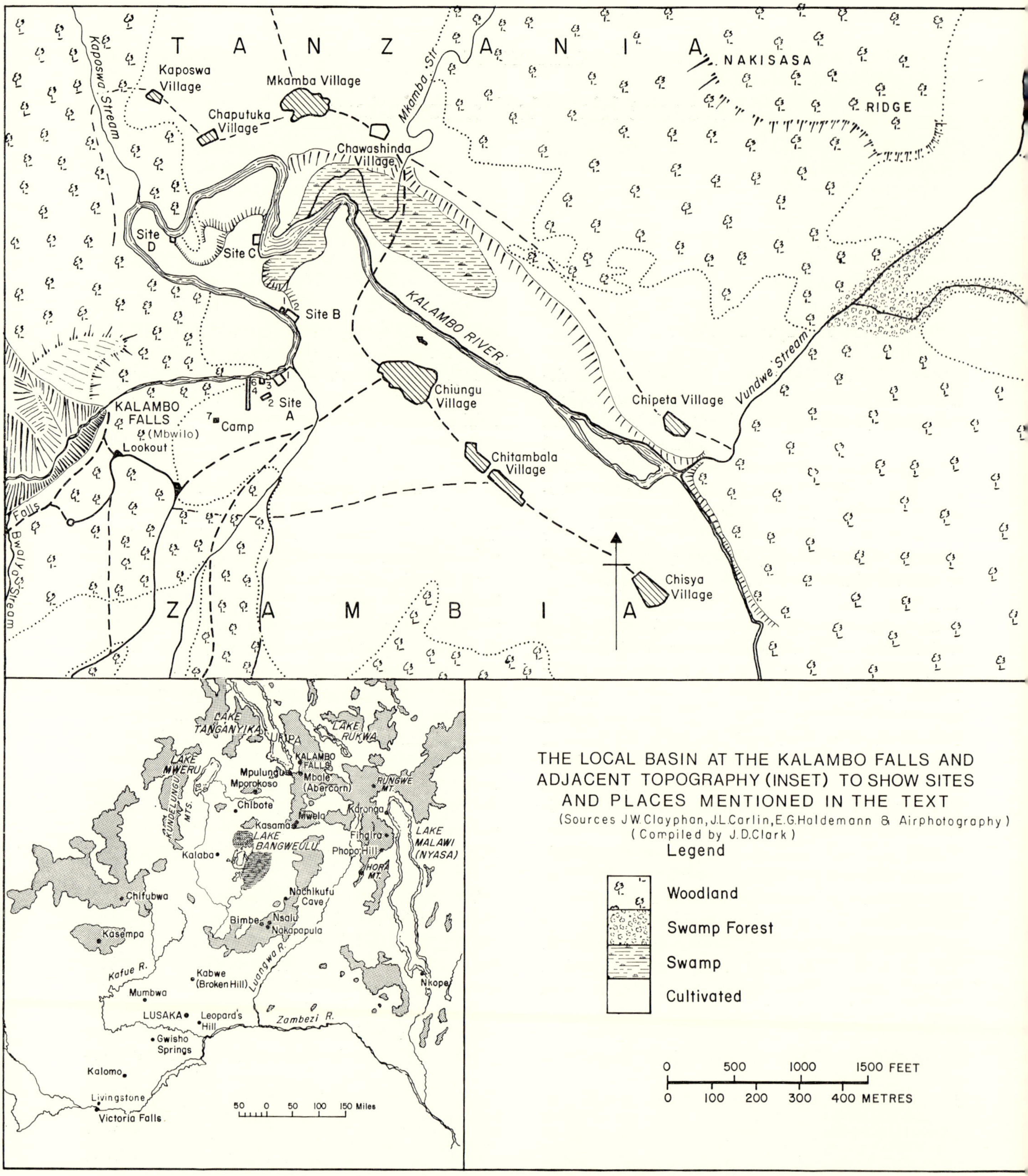

Fig. 1. The local basin at the Kalambo Falls and adjacent topography to show sites and places mentioned in the text. Darker areas denote land over 4,000 feet above sea level.

shed of the Chambezi and Saissi (Lechaptois, 1932: 24–5). Mwika may, however, be a secondary area of dispersal, for Watson (1958: 14) records a general tradition among the commoners of the Mambwe that they came from the northeast 'long ago' and lived where they are today until the coming of the chiefs.

The commoners of all these people claim a single origin and say that they lived for a long time without chiefs. Today, however, each of these tribes has a chiefly clan, the founders of which, it is claimed in the case of the Fipa, came from Rwanda-Burundi and of the Lungu and Mambwe, two from west of Lake Tanganyika and one from the Bisa country to the southwest.

The Lungu chiefs, the senior of whom is Tafuna living on the lake shore, probably established themselves in the seventeenth century (Brelsford, 1956: 67). In Ufipa, the ancestors of the royal house are thought to have arrived after A.D. 1700 (Wilson, 1958: 23). These chiefly houses introduced cattle, new food plants and improved methods of hunting and iron-working and established a central political system. These were, no doubt, the reasons why they were accepted by the peoples among whom they came.

Inheritance and descent are through the male line and the same clan names are found throughout these tribal groups. Originally, the people appear to have lived in small, open villages; to have cultivated finger millet (*eleusine*) and sorghum and owned sheep and goats. Cattle are said to have been introduced only after the arrival of the chiefs. This is also the tradition among the Nyakyusa (with whom the Mwika peoples share a number of cultural traits in common) north-west of Lake Malawi, east and south of Rungwe Mountain. However, tradition also speaks of the Kinga, who inhabit the top of the Livingstone Mountains, as being already established there and having cattle at the time of the arrival of the founders of the Nyakyusa royal house dated from genealogies at between 1550 and 1650 (Wilson, 1958: 47). Probably this event occurred at least a century earlier on the evidence of the radiocarbon date of A.D. 1410 ± 80 (UCLA 1236–540 ± 80) for the base of the occupation midden that is believed to relate to the establishment of the Ngonde chiefs on Mbande Hill (Robinson, 1966: 172–8; Fagan, 1969*a*: 161; Wilson, 1972). Wilson quotes the Nyakyusa as having a tradition that the forests on Rungwe Mountain were 'occupied by "little people" (*abatwa*) when their ancestors first arrived' and says that, from the physical types surviving in remote valleys in Nyakyusa country, it is apparent that these were of 'Pygmoid' rather than Bushmanoid stock (Wilson, 1958: 1).[1]

The earliest Bantu inhabitants of this corridor area of whom there is any record are the Kinga in the east, the Nyiha–Safwa[2] to the west and the Penja and Lugula (now absorbed by the Nyakyusa) to the north-west of the Malawi Rift. Some of the Nyiha claim affinities with the Kinga who themselves claim to have come from the north from central Tanganyika. If a fifteenth century date for the arrival of the first Nyakyusa chief is correct, both these peoples must have been established in the corridor well before the fifteenth century. The earliest inhabitants of the Nyakyusa valley were primarily hunters as the Mwika peoples are also said to have been. The first chief of the Inamwanga found this people living in forest country and subsisting on wild roots and game.

It would seem, therefore, that the initial, historical movement of Bantu peoples (Kinga and Nyiha) into the Corridor sometime prior to the fifteenth century, was followed by more than one subsequent migration of people of the same stock and cultural associations who have grown apart largely as a result of the isolation forced upon them by the very different nature of the habitats in which they lived. This isolation was reinforced by the difficulty of communication in this country of sharply changing relief, by the formerly more extensive areas of forest (Chapman and White, 1970: 31–3), by the belts of uninhabited country that usually separated one ethnic group from the next and by the general sparseness of the human population (Wilson, 1958: 2, 43). Such isolation was the means of preserving not a few of these groups from disappearance, either by absorption or annihilation by stronger and better organized tribes. They survived the Ngoni *impis*, though some of them only just! Those to the south, like the Nyakyusa, were largely off the line of the main Arab trade routes and the Lungu profited rather than suffered from their participation in the ivory and iron trade. The Mambwe were slowly being destroyed by the Bemba,

[1] In 1966 a survey of exposures and rock shelters on the western and southern sides of Rungwe Mountain, showed almost no evidence of human occupation until recent times. It appears likely, therefore, that, except for the craters and the temporary destruction of vegetation following eruptions and falls of pumice and ash – of which we recorded at least four separated by three brown palaeosols dating between A.D. 850 ± 400 and 5610 ± 140 B.C. (Clark *et al.* 1970: 316) – the mountain probably retained much of its evergreen forest cover until the nineteenth century when Nyakyusa and Safwa cultivators began to move up the slopes.

[2] The Safwa are included with the Nyiha (or Nyika) on account of their close linguistic and cultural connections (Harwood, 1970: 1).

raiding for slaves and acting as middlemen for the Arabs, and were only saved by the establishment of European colonial rule on the plateau in 1893.

Originally the villages had been small and unprotected but the raiding of the nineteenth century forced the Corridor tribes into large, stockaded villages of several hundred huts as their only effective defence. However, they have now once more gone back to the open village.

The Kalambo valley is to the west of the main line of movement across the Corridor country and it is likely that its population was little disturbed by the unsettled times of the nineteenth century, as there are no apparent signs of stockaded villages there.[1] For the most part, the people live in small villages, those on the Zambian side of the river (Chiungu; Chitambala; Chisya) being built now on the 'Older' and 'Younger' Boulder Beds (see Volume I: 54), although previously they were higher up the valley side to the south. On the Tanzanian side there are three small and one larger village (Mkamba) that line the cliff feature formed by the river's cutting into the 65 foot (19·8 m) terrace.

The houses are not grouped in any particular plan though formerly a circular layout was favoured. Generally today a family's dwellings, each with its grain bins and shelters, are spread out on one side or the other along the path leading to the next village. Apart from fowls, there is no stock in the valley, since this is a marginal tsetse fly area. Some villagers keep pigs, however, though this is probably a recent innovation, and some own cattle which they keep in Ufipa. Nowadays, the houses are mostly rectangular and may be made either of poles, plastered on both sides with daub (*daga*), or bamboo plastered only on the inside or of pisé brick, with a verandah and a pointed, thatched roof. Formerly, the huts were only of the first type but round, with conical roof of thatch; sometimes reeds or sorghum stalks will be substituted for poles in the wall construction. The floor of the hut and the verandah are raised slightly above the level of the surrounding ground by a puddled clay plinth (Plate 59). The mud plaster of the external walls may be painted, usually in grey and white from natural clays obtained in the basin, but sometimes yellow and red paint from ochre and haematite are added. Decoration is usually in bands of colour but occasionally the walls carry paintings of symbols and figures some of which are most lively renderings (frontispiece). The grindstone is set into a *daga* foundation built into the side of the verandah and its surrounds are plastered with mud. Cooking is generally done inside the hut, the round based cooking pot resting on three conical clay 'stones' with the fire between.

When a hut is destroyed on the death of an owner or for other cause, all the usable timbers, including the roof, are removed and the raised, circular, or rectangular pile of broken down *daga* does not take long to revert to soil again, unless it happens to be baked by a fire's passing over it (Plate 60).

Grain bins are constructed on a low platform of poles supported on short posts or upright stones. The bin itself is circular and consists of a coiled grass core plastered inside and out with clay. The top may also be plastered over and a removable, conical roof of thatch gives protection from the rains and allows access to the grain which is generally stored in the head. The old form of bin is a good deal taller than those made today and required the use of a ladder made from a notched palm stem.

By the side of the house is often a raised platform made for storing a variety of household utensils and impedimenta and for drying cassava and other food. Abutting upon the house itself may be one or two small, fenced enclosures in which vegetables are grown or firewood stored. A pole with a many-branched top may be set into the ground next to the house and will be hung with bags and gourds of various kinds and a spear or bow and arrows may be leaning against it. Chickens are housed at night in a conical shaped hen-house resting on poles about five or six feet above the ground. Outside the hut will be found cooking, relish or beer pots, baskets of various sizes and uses and a stool or chair and, sometimes, an upright wooden mortar for pounding grain.

Formerly, the characteristic dress was of skins, fore and aft, suspended from a belt but these are no longer seen and clothing is bought from the stores.

Lungu pots are made by the coil method from a carefully selected grey clay deposited during Sangoan times. They are made in two stages, the upper half being built up first. When this is dry it is turned over and the bottom of the pot added. Firing is done in an open fire with dry kindling to produce a rapid but intense heat. Depending on the size of the pot, firing takes from twenty-three to fifty minutes (Plate 94). Vessels are then given a black finish by beating and

[1] Unless the largest of the three stone structures ascribed to the German occupation west-northwest of the Falls in reality belongs to this time; the walling is more broken down than that of the smaller structures and from its appearance it might be older.

splashing them with bark strips that have been soaked in water (Fagan, 1961: 87–8).

Planted, apparently at random, in the village are mango, citrus and pawpaw trees and an occasional custard apple and there are small groves of bananas in the lower courses of the streams. Honey is another important food source and the Lungu of the Kalambo Falls use the hollow log type of hive, made from two half sections, which is set in the fork of a tree. Fish (small fry) are still available in small quantities in the river but large and small (*ndagaa*) fish are also brought from the lake shore.

The Lungu, Mambwe and Fipa peoples are renowned for their skill in working iron and so successful were the Fipa that in 1936 twenty kilns were still in use (Wilson, 1958: 25). Iron-working in this region has a long history for, judging by the quantity of slag associated with their occupation, the communities responsible for the Kalambo Falls Industry had smelted iron there in the earlier half of the first millennium. The Fipa (Greig, 1937; Wise, 1957), Nyiha (Brock and Brock, 1965), Mambwe (Giraud, 1890: 531–2), Lungu (Chaplin, 1961) and Iwa (Gouldsbury and Sheane, 1911: 279) furnaces and techniques have been described. They all used the tall, upright furnaces that induced their own draught and were used over a number of years (Plates 64–6). One reasonably complete furnace of this kind and several remnants of others are still standing near Mkamba village on the Tanzanian side (Plate 63) and were in use up to 1913–14. The ore was obtained from the iron oxide crust, or ferricrete, that is fairly universally to be met with below the infertile, sandy soils that overlie the quartzites and sandstones on the plateau.

The bow with poisoned arrows was the most important weapon both for hunting and for warfare (Plate 57). In war, each man also carried a spear and a battle axe together with a bag containing between twenty and thirty stones. These were not selected in any way except for convenience in throwing. Firstly, the stones were thrown, then, in closer fighting, the bow and arrows and spear came into play and, finally, the battle axe which was used to despatch a defeated enemy. My informants stated that only the Mambwe and Lungu used stones in war and not the Fipa or Bemba.

When hunting, a man would approach as close as he could to the animal he was stalking, if possible to within 25 yards (*c.* 22 m), before using his bow. Bows and arrows were still to be seen in the villages and we were fortunate in being able to record the full process of bow-making (Clark, 1958*a*), but they are now being replaced by the muzzle loading gun (Plate 58). Dead-fall traps are still made, their size depending on the size of the animal to be caught. For cane rats, reed fences are built on the river bank at right-angles to the water with three or four of these traps set in gaps left in the fence. Today a man may wait for a month or longer before an animal is caught in one of his traps. Noose traps are set in flimsy fences to catch guinea fowl, francolin and various small birds, and at one time wild pig were caught in pit traps.

The cultivated food plants are supplemented by wild relishes when in season. Specimens, with names, were obtained of thirty fruits and relish plants and of fifteen medicinal plants used by the Lungu at the Kalambo Falls and probably twice that number are still in current use (see Volume I, Appendix G). The staple food of the Lungu was finger millet (*eleusine*) supplemented with sorghum, pumpkins and various kinds of beans. Today, however, cassava is grown everywhere and is the most important crop, though maize and bananas are also grown where conditions are favourable.

The Lungu at the Kalambo Falls use swidden, or slash and burn, methods of cultivation and practice a combination of the grassland and woodland *chitimene* systems of the plateau – the former forced upon them, no doubt, owing to the need continually to recultivate the same ground. The *chitimene* gardens are now to be seen only on the Tanzanian side and there only on the upper slopes of the valley, since the south is now forest reserve and protected. The method entails the lopping of the branches from the trees in a selected area of woodland between July and September. These branches are piled into a circle and at the end of October the pile is fired. Millet and some sorghum is sown in the ash between the end of December and early January. Pumpkins and squashes are planted round the edge of the garden which then has to be protected with a substantial fence against the depredations of wild pig. The crop is harvested towards the end of May. By dint of growing a succession of other crops after the initial planting of millet, the garden remains productive for from three to five years.

On the alluvium in the basin, however, a modified form of the grassland system of crop rotation is practised. On the Zambian plateau and in Ufipa this system is employed by Fipa, Mambwe and Nyiha, while other Corridor peoples employ a related system

(Northern Montane System of Trapnell (1953: 78–9)) of grassland and mound cultivation near streams. It is thus possible to use the land for up to ten years before it has to be abandoned (Watson, 1958: 21; Willis, 1966: 23). In March, the ground is heaped up into mounds; later grass is cut and placed in circular piles on the field. When dry this is fired and pumpkins, beans and sweet potatoes are planted in the ash and gathered in May. In January, the main millet gardens are prepared by flattening out the dark, humic soil of the mounds in which the seed is sown. The millet gardens have to be protected from wild pig by long trenches, often associated with a fence, and these are laborious to construct. The deep gully joining the river upstream from Site A is said by one Agricultural Officer to have resulted from a ditch of this kind. As with the woodland *chitimene* gardens, a man will have four or five of these grassland-type gardens under cultivation at any one time, showing various stages of the rotation (Plate 56).

In June, the millet ripens and is harvested by the women. The finger-like heads are spread on low drying-platforms constructed near the fields and are there sun dried for some three to four weeks. The crop may then either be carried into the village and stored in the head in the grain bins or else threshed and winnowed near the garden and the drying-platform and then stored as grain. Millet is used extensively for beer of which the Kalambo Falls villagers brew a considerable quantity (Trapnell, 1953: 45–58). When beer is brewed, a little is always poured into the pot, the family shrine, for the ancestors (Watson, 1958: 18). Each village has its shrine dedicated to the ancestors of the headman and Watson records that, among the Mambwe, each family also has its own in the form of a small pot (*Katindya*), painted white and kept in the hut.

Threshing floors are a common feature of the valley. They are situated in the fields, measure about 20 feet (6 m) or more across and are circular or square in shape and often sunk a foot (30 cm) or so below ground level. The floor is compacted or clay plastered and kept clean by sweeping. The millet heads are beaten with sticks or pounded with a wooden pestle in a hole in the floor to free the grain which is then winnowed in a flat, circular basket, usually made from palm (*Borassus*) leaf (Plate 95). The garden is then left fallow until November when it is again worked into mounds and planted with beans, groundnuts, groundbeans, sorghum and maize. This rotation is repeated with variations until the ground is exhausted. Cassava is also now grown regularly on mounds and would today seem to be the staple for meal since it can be relied on even in famine years. The use of cassava has, thus, reduced the importance of millet and the wild vegetable relishes.

Evidence of Lungu occupation

In the archaeological excavations, Lungu pottery was always associated with the surface or sub-surface layer. In the vicinity of the Excavation Camp on the south side of the river were signs of former Lungu settlement. These took the form of graves – either low, oval mounds outlined with a circle of stones or a small pile of stones, with which would sometimes be associated one or more broken pots or an enamel bowl. Dish grindstones lie at random on these sites and a small settlement of some half a dozen huts had been recently deserted at the time of our first visit in 1953.

Other evidence of Lungu occupation were four shallow pits 1 foot to 1 foot 6 inches (30–45 cm) deep in the upslope end of the 1959 long trench excavation, A4, from just below the present surface (see Volume 1, Figures 28, 29) (see Plate 98). These had been dug into the red hillslope soil that contained the channel decorated pottery and were filled with black soil. Their use is unknown. They might have been storage pits but this seems unlikely since the Lungu do not build underground silos and they were probably dug to hold the large pots that are partly sunk into the ground in the vicinity of most homesteads and filled with water used to leach the cassava of its toxic properties before drying and cooking. However, one of the pits contained a quantity of ash and charcoal in the bottom and it is possible that this may have been a cooking pit of some kind. Further pits of this type were encountered in the Camp site excavation in 1966. Part of a *daga* floor with a small quantity of charcoal was found in grid square B-11 in the A4 trench at a depth of 6–9 inches (15·2–22·8 cm).

Other signs of recent Lungu occupation were found also in some sections in the Site A excavations where an undulating sub-surface contour can be seen, that is evidence of mound cultivation, probably for cassava but possibly for the indigenous Livingstone potato (*Plectranthus* (*Coleus*) *esculentus*) or the sweet potato.

With the Lungu occupation must be associated also the beads of blue and violet coloured glass from the superficial levels in some of the excavations as, follows:

Site A: One oblate of dark blue, translucent glass; no. A44/56. Site A1/1956, depth 2 to 4 inches (5–10 cm).
One oblate of dark blue, translucent glass; no. A17/59. Site A4/1959, depth 1 foot to 1 foot 6 inches (30–45 cm).
One oblate of dark blue, translucent glass; no. A/21/59. Site A4/1959, depth 1 foot 6 inches to 2 feet (30–61 cm). Plate 30: 2.

Site D: One annular bead of wound, violet coloured, translucent glass. D2/1956, depth 1 foot 6 inches (45 cm). Plate 30: 3.

These blue and violet oblates and annular beads are believed to be of nineteenth century date and were introduced most probably by the Germans at Kasanga or by the African Lakes Corporation at Katuta Bay. A Czechoslovakian origin may be suggested for the violet glass and the depth in the top-soil, rather than on the surface, is probably due to the mound method of cultivation practised by the Lungu.

From the surface layer at Site B an iron arrowhead of present-day Lungu pattern was found in 1963. This has a triangular head and a long tang on which the poison (*mwambane* and *isungwe*) is built up. It is illustrated at Plate 30: 1 for comparison with the arrowheads of the Kalambo Falls Industry at Plate 30: 12, 13. Such arrows (*lucheto*) were carried in a calabash and skin quiver (*munego*) and used with a one piece self bow (*ulapwa*) of *mukale* wood (*Thespia garckeana*), (Plate 57).

The Lungu pottery associated with old village sites and graves generally shows forms widely distributed over the Tanganyika plateau in northern Zambia (Plates 1: 1–3; 2: 3). Plate 2: 2 is an unusual form at the Kalambo Falls. The paste is very different and it is possible that this is a pot that was imported from another locality, perhaps from Ufipa, since there is much contact between the two areas. Plate 2: 1, on the other hand, would appear to preserve in some measure the tradition of the Early Iron Age Kalambo Falls Industry potters. The same applies to the bowl fragment at Plate 2: 4 but, since this is a surface sherd from Site C2, 1959, it is possible that it really belongs with the Kalambo Falls Industry though its state of preservation is different from that of the other sherds from this site.

The subsistence pattern of the present inhabitants of the valley cannot be greatly different from that of the Early Iron Age population except in so far as the reduction of game has probably curtailed the overall meat consumption and the Asiatic and American food plants have further modified the range of their diet. However, the inhabitants still supplement their basic diet of cassava, millet and bananas with a variety of wild foods and most of the essential requirements for supporting life still come from the valley itself and the surrounding woodland.

It is fortunate for archaeology that the isolation of the Kalambo valley and of the 'Corridor people' generally, has preserved their traditional way of life to a degree much less modified than that on the plateau to the south. To the north in Ufipa, European culture has had even less effect so that the technology and material culture of the existing populations here provide a most important basis for the reconstruction of that of the communities occupying the local basin at the Kalambo Falls during the earlier Iron Age.

CHAPTER 2

Iron Age occupation at the Kalambo Falls: the cultural remains

Introduction

The excavations at the Kalambo Falls revealed that the cultural remains of the earlier Iron Age population of the basin – described here as the Kalambo Falls Industry[1] – were distinct, both in pottery types and other characteristics, from those of the present-day inhabitants. Only the surface and the disturbed uppermost level of the excavations yielded sherds of recent Lungu type. Below this the pottery was different from anything found today among the population of the Northern Province of Zambia. It consists of globular pots and bowls and the most characteristic form of the decoration – by grooving and channelling[2] of the unfired clay together with hatching and stamping – shows it to be related, on the one hand, to the 'dimple-based' (Urewe Ware) and other Early Iron Age wares of east and central Africa and, on the other hand, to that named from Gokomere and other contemporary wares decorated by channelling and stamping from Zambia and Rhodesia. This relationship is confirmed by the radiocarbon dating.

The early agriculturalists who inhabited the basin may have spoken a Bantu language and the evidence for connecting these Early Iron Age pottery traditions with the spread of the Bantu has recently been reviewed by Huffman (1970). However, it is not possible to point to any very definite local associations between the present-day pottery and earlier wares, nor is there any very close resemblance between the Early Iron Age channel decorated Kalambo Falls Industry wares and those of the Nyiha, Safwa, Wanda and other small, independent groups living in the Tanganyika–Malawi corridor country.[3] Later population movements presumably underlie these differences. However, few ethnographic studies of these groups, except of the Safwa (Kootz-Kretschmer, 1929; Harwood, 1970) and of the Nyiha of Mbozi (Brock, 1966), have yet been published and, regrettably, very little is known of their pottery wares (Fagan and Yellen, 1968). There could, therefore, although this is unlikely, be more definite resemblances than appear at present.

Monica Wilson has summarized what is known of the Nyiha (Nyika) people (Wilson, 1958) and it seems probable that some of them, at least, are descended from the earlier inhabitants of this corridor country. Also a small group of sherds from the A4 excavation, 1959, and the Excavation Camp (A7) excavation of 1966 provided examples of a plain, thin ware associated with typical Kalambo Falls Industry sherds. This

[1] In Volume I the Early Iron Age aggregates from the Chiungu Member of the Kalambo Falls Formation and the settlement at Site C were described under the term 'Kalambo Industry'. At the time Volume I went to press we were unaware that Phillipson (1968*a*), in a review of the Early Iron Age in Zambia, had included these assemblages with others having the same pottery ware, in a regional variant which he designated 'the Kalambo group of the Early Iron Age'. Although a 'group' is differentiated on typology and geography, it is not defined further and so cannot be accommodated within the system of groupings that we have used to describe the prehistoric cultural entities at the Kalambo Falls. Phillipson's 'Kalambo group of the Early Iron Age' includes eleven sites distributed over a large part of the northern half of Zambia and it is apparent that this term relates to a higher order of abstraction – more equal to an Industrial Complex – than that of an industry as defined in the system we have adopted (see below p. 74). The Industry status of the Archaeological Occurrences that relate to the Early Iron Age is, therefore, retained but the grouping has been renamed *Kalambo Falls Industry* to indicate that it pertains only to the local basin. The term is given formal status by definition (see p. 68 below).

[2] Terms such as channelling (Summers, 1961; Fagan, 1963), grooving (Inskeep, 1962*a*; Phillipson, 1968*a*), channelling and grooving (Posnansky, 1967; Robinson and Sandelowsky, 1968: 119), deep grooving (Fagan, Phillipson and Daniels, 1969) and deep line incision (Huffman, 1970) have all been used to describe this characteristic form of decoration seen on Early Iron Age wares, probably from personal preference or from a desire to avoid the all-embracing term 'channel-decorated pottery', the use of which has now been discontinued. The term 'channelling' has preference and, as experiment shows, the technique of making such broad, shallow grooving almost invariably entails the removal of clay and does not – any more than 'grooving' – connote a wood-working technique, as has been claimed by one author (Huffman, 1970: 5; *Shorter Oxford Dictionary*, 1964: 291, 835); therefore the term 'channelling' is retained and used here synonymously with 'grooving'.

[3] For a synthesis and summary of ethnographic literature on these peoples see Willis, 1966.

could be representative of a pottery tradition transitional or interposed between that Industry and modern Lungu.

Iron Age remains – pottery, burnt clay from structures, grindstones, slag from iron-working and manufactured iron tools – have been found in the more recent levels in all the excavations, in the superficial layers of hillslope deposits, in swamp clays and on one settlement site. For particulars of the stratigraphic associations reference should be made to the detailed descriptions of the Site excavations in Volume I, pp. 85 *et seq.* Settlements were situated on the higher ground overlooking the swamp, the level of which was raised at that time by the temporary blocking of the outlet at the Spillway Gorge which created a situation similar to that to be seen in the nearby Ichianga basin today (Plate 55).

The cultural remains from the Chiungu Member of the Kalambo Falls Formation

(*a*) FROM HILLSLOPE AND CHANNEL SEDIMENTS

(Filling Phases F7, F7′ and F7″: see Volume I, p. 149)

Site A

Typical potsherds and other remains of the Kalambo Falls Industry are found in the top grey and red sandy soil on the upper slopes of the valley wherever these have been excavated (Phase F7). These were exposed in excavations A2 and A3 in 1956, A4 in 1959 and A7 in 1966. The uppermost 2 feet (61 cm) of this sandy soil is usually disturbed, probably due to the practice of making mound or pit gardens, as well as to the activities of burrowing animals. This has unfortunately led to a mixing of recent and earlier Iron Age remains. Since the greatest concentration of pottery at the upslope end of the A4 trench lies in this disturbed upper 2 feet (61 cm), little of stratigraphic value could be learned concerning the time and circumstances of the replacement of the Kalambo Falls Industry by that of the Lungu. Some better data were forthcoming, however, from the 1966 excavations, see below pp. 45–9.

Downslope erosion truncates the sediments exposed in the 65–70 foot (19·8–21·3 m) terrace feature formed by the Mkamba and Mbwilo Members of the Kalambo Falls Formation. Up to 13 feet (3·9 m) of red and grey clay and sandy clay of the Chiungu Member are found filling a former channel, the 'Older Channel' fill (Phase F7′), the base of which at this site (A1 excavation) is now some 10 feet (3 m) above low water level in the river. Kalambo Falls Industry sherds representing the scatter from a nearby occupation site are numerous in these clays (Plates 86, 89, 90). In the hillslope red, sandy loam of the A7 and A4 excavations, sherds are present at all depths down to 2 feet to 2 feet 6 inches (61–76 cm) while in the A1 excavation exposing the downslope channel deposits, they only begin to appear at a depth of 6 feet (1·8 m) from the surface, between which depth and 13 feet (3·9 m) they are common. The reason for this is that at both Sites A and B this 'Older Channel' fill has been cut out by later channelling and gullying which, in turn, has been filled with coarse grained and gritty red and red brown, sandy clay and sand ('Younger Channel' fill: Phase F7″) containing some derived potsherds and stone artifacts washed from the upper slopes and from the 'Older Channel' fill. This later period of gullying may be related to the formation of the low level ±6 feet (1·8 m) bench on the Tanzania side of the river and probably post-dates the Kalambo Falls Industry aggregates in view of the few abraded sherds that it contains.

This cutting and filling on the Zambian bank is probably related to an eastward shifting tributary of the main river, such as that seen today immediately upstream from Site A. The filling of the channels must have been a gradual rather than a rapid process. The fill was partly washed in from the catchment on the upper slopes and was partly from collapse of the walls so that the floor may have been available for temporary occupation at times, just as is the floor of the existing tributary near its junction with the main stream where it is used to plant bananas. The line of stones at between 6 and 7 feet (183–213 cm) may in part be artificial (Plate 67). The circular area of apparently burned and hardened clay, or *daga*, surrounded by stones and with a possible hearth area immediately to the north, encountered in grid squares B-1 and B-2 of A1 excavation at a depth of 9 feet (2·7 m) could, as suggested in Volume I (p. 97), represent the base of a small field shelter or hut (Plate 68). Also of artificial origin is the saucer shaped depression approximately 25 feet (7·6 m) in diameter and 7 feet (2·1 m) deep, found in grid squares B-19–14 in the A4 trench at the upslope end of the sandy Iron Age deposits.

The fill of this depression was more sandy and browner than the surrounding clays; its contents were no different except for a number of larger lumps of *daga* and small pieces of iron slag, so that its purpose is unknown. Pits of varying dimensions are recorded from a number of Early Iron Age sites in Zambia and Rhodesia (e.g. Summers, 1958: 26–49) and are still in use there today by some groups for storing vegetable foods (Phillipson, 1970*a*: 114). The same is the case in the Shire Highlands in southern Malawi where the pits are lined and used to store bananas (Personal observation, 1968). Some of the pots from the type sites for 'dimple-based' ware at Urewe and Yala Alego were found in circumstances suggesting burial in small, shallow pits (Leakey *et al.* 1948: 42). Saucer shaped depressions believed to be storage pits were seen also from the air in 1966 round several of the small Fipa villages in the more easterly parts of Ufipa bordering on the Rukwa Rift. It is, therefore, probable that the one at the Kalambo Falls may have served a similar purpose.

The only other feature located at Site A is a concentration of large stones together with a small pot and other sherds at the north end of the test excavation, A7, carried out in 1966. This exposed a sequence in the red, loamy hillslope adjacent to the Excavation Camp, the stone concentration perhaps demarcating the edge of a dwelling area. This excavation and the associated finds are described below (p. 45).

Site B

The 1956 and 1959 excavations at this site are situated on the very edge of the eroded bank of the ±30 foot (9·1 m) terrace (Mbwilo Member of the Kalambo Falls Formation) on which the makers of the Kalambo Falls Industry had one of their settlements. Here, however, the main part of the terrace lay to the west of the site but, due to the river's shifting its channel eastwards, it has been completely eroded away with the exception of a few yards of the lower levels of what had been the bank in Early Iron Age times. The Iron Age remains here, therefore, are found in buff to grey swamp clays (Phase F7′), having spilled down the slope of the old bank adjacent to the settlement.

At this site, however, a greater quantity of Stone Age cultural material occurs mixed with the pottery because the Iron Age bank truncated the Rubbles with Lupemban artifacts, even cutting into the levels containing Sangoan tools, and because the 'Later Stone Age' camp sites were located immediately beneath the Iron Age midden on the 30 foot (9·1 m) terrace. Numerous pieces of *daga*, iron slag and tuyère fragments also occurred in the excavations with the potsherds.

(*b*) FROM SOIL AT THE TOP OF THE MBWILO MEMBER

Site D

In 1956, a small area was excavated at this site which is situated on the east edge of the 30 foot (9·1 m) terrace (Figure 1). The grey sandy surface layers to a depth of 3 feet (91 cm) contained many flecks of charcoal, giving the deposit the appearance of a midden from which most of the organic remains had been removed by leaching. Besides the usual sherds, the excavation yielded one complete pot of the Kalambo Falls Industry with a most interesting decoration incised after firing (Plate 88); an oxidized fragment of iron and the usual number of pieces of iron slag and *daga*. It became apparent that this section probably lay close to or within the original settlement area but the need to concentrate work on the earlier cultural periods prevented further investigation of this site at this time.

The range of cultural material recovered in 1956 and 1959 from the clays of the 'Older Channel' fills and the earlier Iron Age swamp included everything from Acheulian hand-axes to Kalambo Falls Industry pottery. The contemporaneity of the pottery with anything older than the 'Later Stone Age' could, of course, be ruled out and most of this material was well abraded. It was, however, not so certain that a 'Later Stone Age' microlithic element might not have existed for a time contemporary with the pottery and iron technology of the Kalambo Falls Industry people. If this were so it might indicate, either that two contemporaneous but culturally distinct populations were present, or, alternatively, that the Iron Age inhabitants were themselves using stone for some purposes, since rare microliths, scrapers and a bored stone fragment were associated with the sherds.[1] The 1963 excavations, however, showed beyond any reasonable doubt that only some of the scraper forms and grinding tools were likely to have been used by the Iron Age population.

The stone assemblages from the clays of the Chiungu Member of the Kalambo Falls Formation

[1] Mambwe and Fipa believe that spirits reside in bored stones, which are sometimes kept under large trees near springs and used to divine causes of misfortune (Kleindienst, 1961*b*: 150). Similar ritual use in the Lake Rukwa Rift is recorded by Harding (1963) and among the Luapula peoples by Cunnison (1959: 221).

TABLE 1. *Analysis of lithic artifacts from the Chiungu Member of the Kalambo Falls Formation, Site A*

Level in feet (m)	Shaped tools											Utilized/modified							Waste												Total number of specimens
	Hand-axe	Cleaver	Pick	Core-axe	Chopper	Core scraper – large	Small scraper – core	Small scraper – flake	Microlith	Backed blade	Bored stone	Grindstone – upper	Grindstone – lower	Pestle stone	Burnishing stone	Pigment	Utilized piece	Hammer stone	Cores – 1 or 2 platform	Cores – proto biconical	Cores – disc	Cores – formless	Cores – microblade	Flakes – plain platform	Flakes – faceted platform	Flakes – point platform	Bladelets	Flake fragments	Chunks	Miscellaneous pebbles	
A1/56																															
0–1 (0–0·30)																															
1–2 (0·30–0·61)								1																							1
2–3 (0·61–0·91)																								1							1
3–4 (0·91–1·2)																															
4–5 (1·2–1·5)																	1														1
5–6 (1·5–1·8)												1					1							1				2	1		6
6–7 (1·8–2·1)												1	2											3				4	2		12
7–8 (2·1–2·4)													1								1			4	2	1		9	5		23
8–9 (2·4–2·7)		1															6				1	1		8	1			7	3		28
9–10 (2·7–3·0)																	2							8	5	5		15	9	1	45
10–11 (3·0–3·3)	1		1					2							1		3		1		1	1		36	12	4	1	14	7		85
11–12 (3·3–3·7)			1		1	1		1							3		1		1	1	1	4	1	17	13	6	1	18	1		72
12–13 (3·7–4·0)			1					2									2						1	2				1	1		10
13–14 (4·0–4·3)												1			1																2
Total A1/56	1	1	3	—	1	1	—	6	—	—	—	3	3	—	5	—	16	—	2	1	4	6	2	80	33	16	2	70	29	1	286
A2/56																															
0–2 (0–0·61)																								2	1			3	2		8
2–4[a] (0·61–1·2)												1						1						11	4	3		17	5		42
5–7 (1·5–2·1)			1												2		2				2			12	6	1		13	2		41
11–13 (3·3–4·0)																	1					1		1		1		1			5
Total A2/156	—	—	1	—	—	—	—	—	—	—	—	1	—	—	2	—	3	1	—	—	2	1	—	26	11	5	—	34	9	—	96
A3/56																															
1–2 (0–0·61)														Fresh hard quartzite > 10 cm in length 1																	1
A4/59																															
0–1 (0–0·30)	1						2	1	1						1		2	1	1		1		5	33	7	9	1	44	6		116
1–2 (0·30–0·61)					2			2				2		1	3	1 red ochre	6				1			33	12	9	4	30	8		114
2–3 (0·61–0·91)				1				2				1							1		1		1	22	6	11	1	37	5	1	90
3–4[a] (0·91–1·2)																								1	2			3	1		7
4–5 (1·2–1·5)				1	1												5		1		1			20	8	5	3	33	10		88
5–6 (1·5–1·8)																	1							5	2	3	2	6	1		20
6–7 (1·8–2·1)	1																3							3				19	1		27
Total A/59	2	—	—	2	3	—	2	5	1	—	—	3	—	1	4	1	17	1	3	—	4	—	6	117	37	37	11	172	32	1	462
Total Site A	3	1	4	2	4	1	2	11	1	—	—	7	3	2	11	1	36	2	5	1	10	7	8	223	81	58	13	276	70	2	845

[a] Below this level the artifacts occurred in the channel clays only.

TABLE I (*cont.*)

	Shaped tools											Utilized/modified							Waste											
	Hand-axe	Cleaver	Pick	Core-axe	Chopper	Core-scraper – large	Small scraper – core	Small scraper – flake	Microlith	Backed blade	Bored stone	Grindstone – upper	Grindstone – lower	Pestle stone	Burnishing stone	Pigment	Utilized piece	Hammerstone	Cores – 1 or 2 platform	Cores – proto biconical	Cores – disc	Cores – formless	Cores – microblade	Flakes – plain platform	Flakes – faceted platform	Flakes – point platform	Bladelets	Flake fragments	Chunks	Miscellaneous pebbles
Physical condition																														
Fresh																														
A1/56			1					5				3	3		5		12				1		2	23	4	6	2	21	6	
A2/56																	1							7	2			2		
A4/59					1		2	4	1								4	1	2		2		6	82	16	22	10	91	18	
Slightly abraded																														
A1/56																					1	2		2	5	2				1
A2/56																								2	3			30		
A4/59				1	1							3		1			7							14	5	5		35	4	
Abraded																														
A1/56	1	1	2		1	1		1									4		2	1	2	4		55	24	8		49	23	
A2/56			1									1					2				2	1		17	6	5		2	9	
A4/59	2			1	1			1									6		1		2			21	16	10	1	46	10	1
Patinated																														
A1/56																														
A2/56																														
A4/59				2				1									3				2		1	43	18	7	2	83	7	
Thermal fracture																														
A1/56																													1	
A2/56																														
A4/59																														
Raw material																														
Hard quartzite																														
A1/56	1	1	3		1	1						1			4		5			1				13	1	1				1
A2/56			1									1			2			1						2		1		5		
A4/59	2				2							3		1	4		3							16	2	4		5	5	1
Felspathic quartzite																														
A1/56																					1			1	2	1				
A2/56																														
A4/59																										1		1		
Quartz																														
A1/56																	1							2						
A2/56																														
A4/59																							1	4	2			1	1	
Chert																														
A1/56								6									10		2		3	6	2	61	30	14	2			
A2/56																	3				2	1		23	11	4		29	9	
A4/59				2	1		2	4	1								13		3		4		4	96	32	31	11	163	24	
Silcrete																														
A1/56																								3						
A2/56																								1						
A4/59								1									1											1		

Chalcedony																														
A1/56																														
A2/56																														
A4/59																						1	1	1	1		1			
Dolerite																														
A1/56											1																			
A2/56																														
A4/59																												2		
Sandstone																														
A1/56											1	3		1																
A2/56																														
A4/59																	1													
Length																														
> 10 cm																														
A1/56	1	1	3		1	1		1				2	3				1		1						2					
A2/56			1																					1					1	
A4/59	1			1	3							1		1			1							2		1		1	1	
10–5 cm																														
A1/56								3				1					8		1	1	4	1		47	18	8				1
A2/56												1					2	1			2			16	5	2		10	2	
A4/59	1			1			1	2				2			3		9	1	3		2		1	32	14	8		47	19	1
< 5 cm																														
A1/56								2									7					5	2	33	13	8	2			
A2/56															2		1					1		9	6	3		24	6	
A4/59							1	3	1						1	1	7				2		5	83	23	28	11	124	12	
Flake form																														
Irregular																														
A1/56																								72	22	12				
A2/56																	2							24	6	5				
A4/59																								99	24	34		170		
Long quadrilateral																														
A1/56																								1	2	2				
A2/56																														
A4/59																									3		4			
Short quadrilateral																														
A1/56																								6	4	1	2			
A2/56																	1							2	4					
A4/59																								15	6	1	7	1		
Triangular																														
A1/56																								1	3	1				
A2/56																									1					
A4/59																								3	2	1				
Elliptic																														
A1/56																									2					
A2/56																														
A4/59																									2	1		1		
Total number of specimens																														
A1/56	1	1	3	—	1	1	—	6	—	—	—	3	3	—	5	—	16	—	2	1	4	6	2	80	33	16	2	70	29	1
A2/56	—	—	1	—	—	—	—	—	—	—	—	1	—	—	2	—	3	1	—	—	2	1	—	26	11	5	—	34	9	—
A4/59	2	—	—	2	3	—	2	5	1	—	—	3	—	1	4	1	17	1	3	—	4	—	6	117	37	37	11	172	32	1

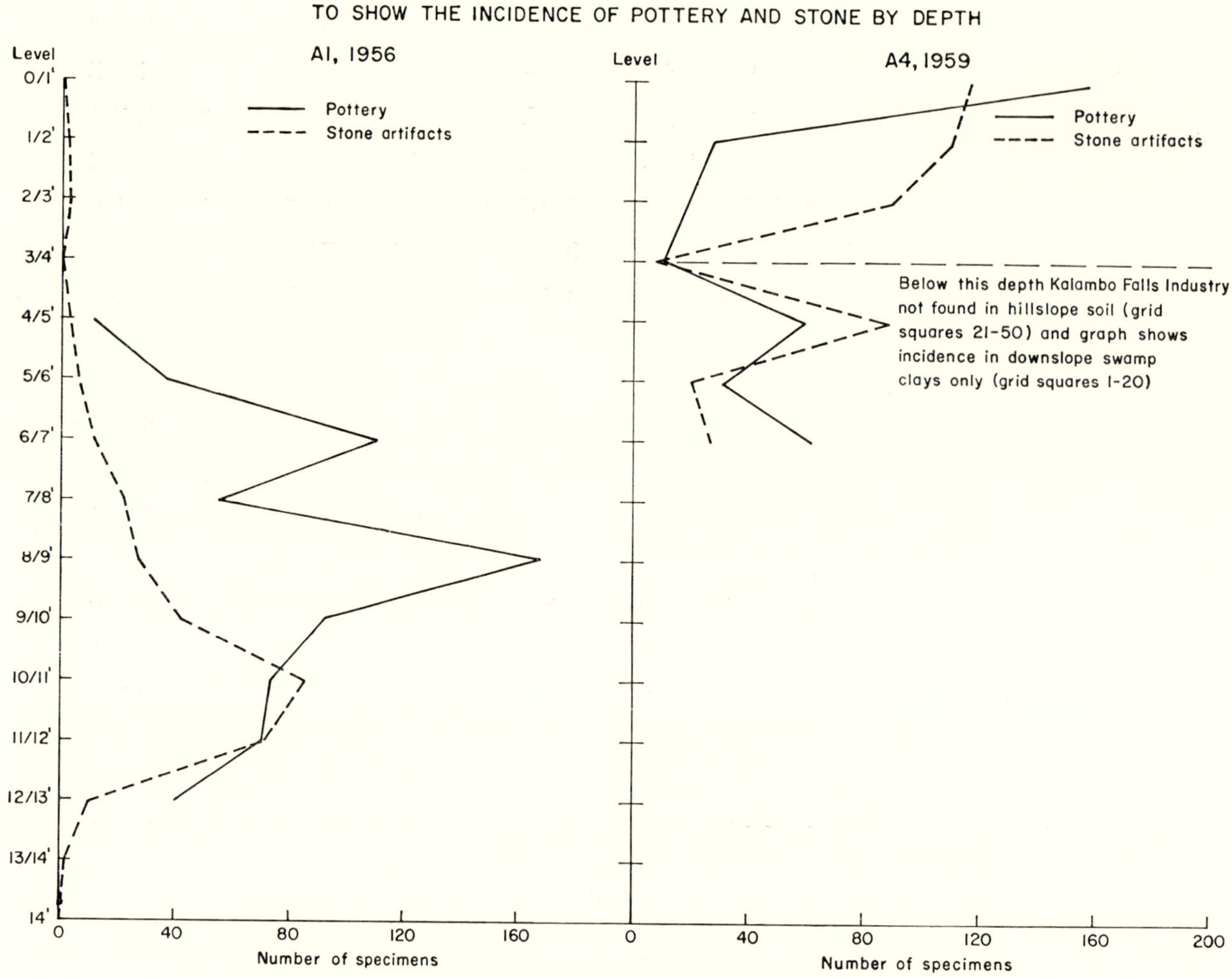

Fig. 2. Incidence by depth of pottery and stone in the clays and red loam of the Chiungu Member at Site A, A1 and A4 excavations.

have been analysed in Tables 1 and 2, both as to depth and attributes. The pottery is discussed and analysed at pp. 30–44 and in Tables 4–7, by Brian Fagan. The relationships of the worked stone to pottery in the channel fills at Sites A and B is shown in Figures 2 and 3. The graph for the stone and pottery incidence in the Chiungu Member at the A1 excavation (Figure 2) suggests that the stone artifacts are in general unconnected with the pottery for, while stone gradually increases with depth, reaching a maximum near the base of the channel at between 10 and 12 feet (3 and 3·6 m) where erosion has cut into the sands and rubble horizons of the Mbwilo Member, potsherds are common between 7 and 10 feet (2·1 and 3 m) and decrease below this.

The graph for the A4 excavation is less easy to interpret, however, probably due to the fact that it combines the data from both the hillslope loam and the red brown channel fill. The upper half of the graph reflects mostly the upslope incidence and shows the high percentage of sherds occurring down to 1 foot (30 cm) and the very small percentage that occur below 2 feet (61 cm), as opposed to the abundance of stone artifacts between 1 and 3 feet (30 and 91 cm). The data, taken mostly from the channel fill between 3 and 7 feet (91 cm and 2·1 m) in the A4 excavation, show a rhythmic increase and decrease of both stone and pottery which may, in view of the graph from the B1 excavations (see below), reflect depositional rates rather than cultural relationships.

Similar diagrams for Site B (Figure 3) show considerably more potsherds than stone artifacts, though both decrease with depth, as well as a comparable variability by depth that, again, suggests it may be an

TABLE 2. *Analysis of Lithic artifacts from the Chiungu Member of the Kalambo Falls Formation, Site B*

	Shaped tools											Utilized/modified						Waste												
Level in feet (m)	Hand-axe	Cleaver	Pick	Core-axe	Chopper	Core-scraper – large	Small scraper – core	Small scraper – flake	Microlith	Backed blade	Bored stone	Grindstone – upper	Grindstone – lower	Pestle stone	Burnishing stone	Pigment	Utilized piece	Hammerstone	Cores – 1 or 2 platform	Cores – proto biconical	Cores – disc	Cores – formless	Cores – microblade	Flakes – plain platform	Flakes – faceted platform	Flakes – point platform	Bladelets	Flake fragments	Chunks	Miscellaneous pebbles	Total number of specimens
B1/56																															
0–1 (0–0·30)												1				white clay	5							5		1		1	4	1	18
1–2 (0·30–0·61)							1					2		1			3	1					1	4		1	2	5	2		23
2–3 (0·61–0·91)									1			2			1		4							5		1		4	5		23
3–4 (0·91)–1·2)																	1							1		2		3	1		8
4–5 (1·2–1·5)															2		2							1	1				6	1	13
5–6 (1·5–1·8)	1								1			2				3								5		2	1	2			17
6–7 (1·8–2·1)															1		1							1		1	2	5			11
7–8 (2·1–2·4)			1													1									1				3		6
8–9 (2·4–2·7)											1					red clay												2	2		5
9–10 (2·7–3·0)																								1							1
10–11 (3·0–3·3)												1															1				2
11–12 (3·3–3·7)																								1					1		2
Total B1/56	1	—	1	—	—	—	1	—	2	—	1	8	—	1	4	4	16	1	—	—	—	—	1	24	2	8	6	22	24	2	129
B2/59																															
0–1 (0–0·30)							1		1	1		2		1	3	red ochre	4						1	5		1		11	7	2	40
1–2 (0·30–0·61)								1						2			1							2	1	2		6		1	16
2–3 (0·61–0·91)												2				1								22				14	6		45
3–4 (0·91–1·2)												2												2				2			6
4–5 (1·2–1·5)			1														2							1	1	1		6			12
5–6 (1·5–1·8)												1			1		1						1	1	1	1	1	1			9
Total B2/59	—	—	1	—	—	—	1	1	1	1	—	7	—	3	4	1	8	—	—	—	—	—	2	33	3	5	1	40	13	3	128
B3/59																															
0–1 (0–0·30)			1									1												1						1	4
1–2 (0·30–0·61)												1																1	1		3
2–3 (0·61–0·91)				1				1									1							6		3		14			26
3–4 (0·91–1·2)												1									2			2		1		4	1		11
4–5 (1·2–1·5)																								1	1	2		12	1		17
5–6 (1·5–1·8)																								2		2		3	1		8
6–7 (1·8–2·1)																								1			1		2		4
Total B3/59	—	—	1	1	—	—	—	1	—	—	—	3	—	—	—	—	1	—	—	—	2	—	—	13	1	8	1	34	6	1	73
Total Site B	1	—	3	1	—	—	2	2	3	1	1	18	—	4	8	5	25	1	—	—	2	—	3	70	6	21	8	96	43	6	330

TABLE 2 (*cont.*)

	Shaped tools											Utilized/modified							Waste											
	Hand-axe	Cleaver	Pick	Core-axe	Chopper	Core-scraper – large	Small scraper – core	Small scraper – flake	Microlith	Backed blade	Bored stone	Grindstone – upper	Grindstone – lower	Pestle stone	Burnishing stone	Pigment	Utilized piece	Hammerstone	Cores – 1 or 2 platform	Cores – proto biconical	Cores – disc	Cores – formless	Cores – microblade	Flakes – plain platform	Flakes – faceted platform	Flakes – point platform	Bladelets	Flake fragments	Chunks	Miscellaneous pebbles
Physical condition																														
Fresh																														
B1/56							1		2		1	7		1	1	3	16	1					1	23	1	7	5	21	24	1
B2/59							1		1			6		3			7						2	10		4	1	22	8	1
B3/59																												1		
Slightly abraded																														
B1/56	1											1				1								1	1	1	1			
B2/59			1							1		1					1							1	2	1		3	1	
B3/59																										2		14		
Abraded																														
B1/56			1																									1		1
B2/59								1																22	1			13	4	
B3/59			1					1									1				2			13	1	6	1	19	6	
Patinated																														
B1/56																														
B2/59																								1		2				
B3/59																														
Thermal fracture																														
B1/56												4					1											4	13	
B2/59																								1						
B3/59																														
Raw materials																														
Hard quartzite																														
B1/56			1									5			3		4							4	1	4		12	19	2
B2/59			1									5		1	4		2							1				2	3	1
B3/59			1	1								2												9		5		15	4	1
Felspathic quartzite																														
B1/56															1															
B2/59																								1						
B3/59																												1		
Quartz																														
B1/56																												1	1	
B2/59														1			1											2	1	1
B3/59																														
Chert																														
B1/56	1						1		2								12						1	20		4	6	9	3	
B2/59							1	1	1	1							5						2	31	3	4	1	34	8	
B3/59								1									1				2			4	1	3	1	17	2	
Silcrete																														
B1/56																									1					
B2/59																														
B3/59																														

Chalcedony																														
B1/56																														
B2/59																										1		1		
B3/59																												1		
Dolerite or schist																														
B1/56											1																		1	
B2/59														1														1		1
B3/59																														
Sandstone																														
B1/56												3		1				1												
B2/59												2																	1	
B3/59												1																		
Length																														
> 10 cm																														
B1/56	1		1								1	1		1			2						1	1				1		
B2/59			1									5					1													
B3/59																													2	
10–5 cm																														
B1/56												6			2		7	1						8	2	4		6	19	2
B2/59							1	1		1		2		3	3		4						1	22		1		11	7	2
B3/59			1	1				1				3									1			3		2		4		1
< 5 cm																														
B1/56									2			1			2	4	7							15		4	6	15	5	
B2/59							1		1						1		3						1	11	3	4	1	29	6	1
B3/59																1	1				1			10	1	6	1	30	4	
Flake form																														
Irregular																														
B1/56																								18		7				
B2/59																								29	1	5		33		
B3/59								1									1							11	1	6		30		
Long quadrilateral																														
B1/56																											2			
B2/59																														
B3/59																										1				
Short quadrilateral																														
B1/56																								5	2		4			
B2/59																								3	1			3		
B3/59																								2		1	1	4		
Triangular																														
B1/56																														
B2/59																								1	1			2		
B3/59																										1				
Elliptic																														
B1/56																								1						
B2/59																														
B3/59																														
Total number of specimens																														
B1/56	1	—	1	—	—	—	1	—	2	—	1	8	—	1	4	4	16	1	—	—	—	—	1	24	2	8	6	22	24	2
B2/59	—	—	1	—	—	—	1	1	1	1	—	7	—	3	4	1	8	—	—	—	—	—	2	33	3	5	1	40	13	3
B3/59	—	—	1	1	—	—	—	1	—	—	—	3	—	—	—	—	1	—	—	—	2	—	—	13	1	8	1	34	6	1

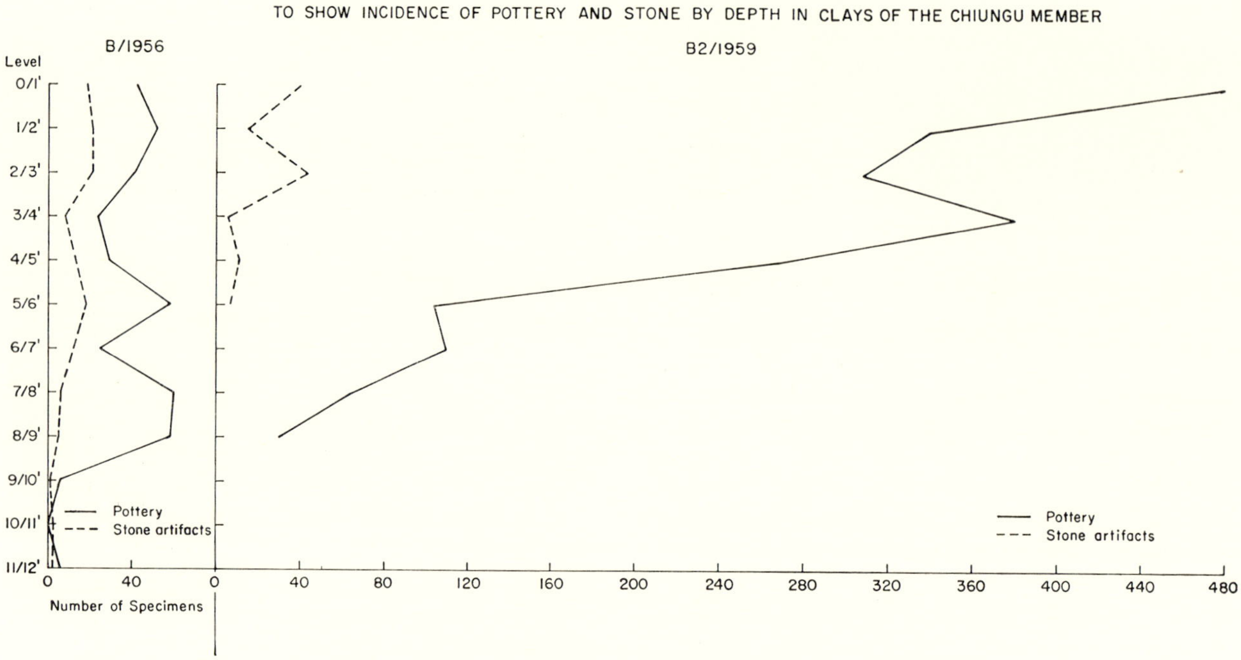

Fig. 3. Incidence by depth of pottery and stone in the clays and clay sands of the Chiungu Member at Site B, B1 and B2 excavations.

indication of variable factors of deposition. Being immediately adjacent to the Early Iron Age settlement, the results of the excavations at Site B reflect better the pottery/stone ratio for the time the Chiungu Member was being formed. The greater number of stone artifacts occurring in the upper part of the deposits can possibly be explained by the fact that they are derived from the immediately adjacent channel bank, composed here of sediments of the Mbwilo Member, in which are found 'Later Stone Age' microlithic aggregates including a bored stone fragment from a depth of 8 to 9 feet (2·4–2·7 m) and the pebble horizons with a mixed 'Middle Stone Age' aggregate. A greater concentration of artifacts is, therefore, to be expected in these levels and areas immediately adjacent to the exposure of the lithic horizon at the bank. The incidence of potsherds from the much larger B2 excavation and showing the greatest concentration between 3 feet and 5 feet (91 cm and 1·5 m) probably accurately reflects dispersal and scatter down the slope of the old bank from the Iron Age settlement situated on the surface of the terrace, the sherds becoming less numerous the lower and further into the swamp they occur from the edge of the settlement.

It appeared probable, therefore, at least from the pottery/stone incidence in the 1956 excavations, that the greater part of the lithic material is not connected or contemporary with the pottery. This could be confirmed by the technology and abraded physical condition of much of this material. It was, however, not until the 1963 excavation showed the 'Later Stone Age' camp floor with microlithic artifacts stratified immediately below the Iron Age midden that it was possible to establish that the microlithic elements were not contemporary with the Iron Age Industry. It then became possible to show that the microlithic material was older than that from the Iron Age and that, in addition to the abraded specimens from the earlier cultural stages, it was also derived.

There still remains, however, as Tables 1 and 2 show, a small number of stone artifacts recovered from the Chiungu Member clays that, by comparison with those recovered from the excavation of the settlement site in 1963, can be shown to belong with the Kalambo Falls Industry. These consist of the upper and lower grindstones, the pestle stones, burnishers and certain of the utilized, scraper-like tools, the thermally fractured fragments and, possibly, the pigment. These are set out in Table 3.

The utilized specimens and 'scrapers' have been included with the other artifacts here because they stand out in sharp distinction from the fresh microlithic elements, on the one hand, and the abraded

TABLE 3. *Kalambo Falls Industry stone artifacts from the Chiungu Member: Sites A, B, and D*

Class	A1	A2	A3	A4	B1	B2	D	Total
Grindstones – upper	3	1	—	3	7	7	1	22
Grindstones – lower	3	—	—	—	—	—	—	3
Pestle stones	—	—	1	1	1	3	—	6
Burnishers	5	2	—	3	4	4	—	18
'Scrapers'	5	—	—	7	1	2	1	16
Utilized pieces	12	3	—	8	16	8	1	48
Pigment	—	—	—	1	4	1	1	7
Thermally fractured stone	1	—	—	—	32	*	—	33
Total	29	6	1	23	65	25	4	153

* Not recorded.

'Middle Stone Age' artifacts, on the other. The quite fresh marginal scarring on one or more edges derives from use, not retouch, and is often found on an older patinated fragment or chunk thus giving the impression that any piece of stone might be used, provided it had a serviceable edge.

The Iron Age artifacts from the channel fills of the Chiungu Member are described below (p. 49 *et seq.*) and illustrated at Plate 32. The 'Later Stone Age' elements in these swamp and channel clays are examined at pp. 108–9 and a representative series is illustrated at Plate 33.

The Early Iron Age Settlement at Site C: the 1963 Excavation

BY J. D. CLARK AND F. VAN NOTEN

Introduction

This site is situated on the north edge of the 30 foot (9·1 m) terrace (Figure 1, Plate 56). In 1959 a small mound garden had been cleared on the eastward-facing sandy slope of the 30 foot (9·1 m) terrace, about 200 yards (183 m) north of Site B and close to the path leading to the old ferry by the 'Tanganyika Cliff' below Mkamba village. This clearing had exposed a number of potsherds and worked flakes and a surface grid collection was made by the late J. H. Chaplin. The sherds were of Kalambo Falls Industry type (Plates 3: 1; 9: 5) and are characteristic of those found in the 1963 excavations. The stone artifacts consisted of typical microlithic waste products together with some tools all in fresh, unpatinated chert. It was apparent from this that a settlement must exist somewhere on the 30 foot (9·1 m) terrace between the garden exposures and Site D and that the stratigraphic relationship of the pottery and the microliths could be demonstrated here.

During 1963, a further examination of the cliff at Site C was carried out on 17 July (see Volume 1, Plate 31). A naturally exposed section was revisited where, in 1959, sherds and occasional chert flakes had been observed in a black to grey soil at the top of the cliff. A considerable number of potsherds were found washed out by the river during the rains, through erosion and collapse of the cliff. These were concentrated mostly at river level. In the sand, that had slumped some 8 to 12 feet (2·4–3·7 m) below the top of the cliff, was also found one small complete pot (Plate 11: 3) and the greater part of two large, undecorated pots which appeared to have been intentionally broken. Both these pots seemed to be resting on stones – in the one case on two fragments of a large, thermally fractured grindstone and, in the other, on a complete, smaller, flat grindstone. The black earth at the top of the cliff appeared to be midden material and the circumstances in which the pottery occurred suggested the possibility of finding burials. It was decided, therefore, to excavate an area at the top of the cliff and Van Noten was placed in charge of this work.

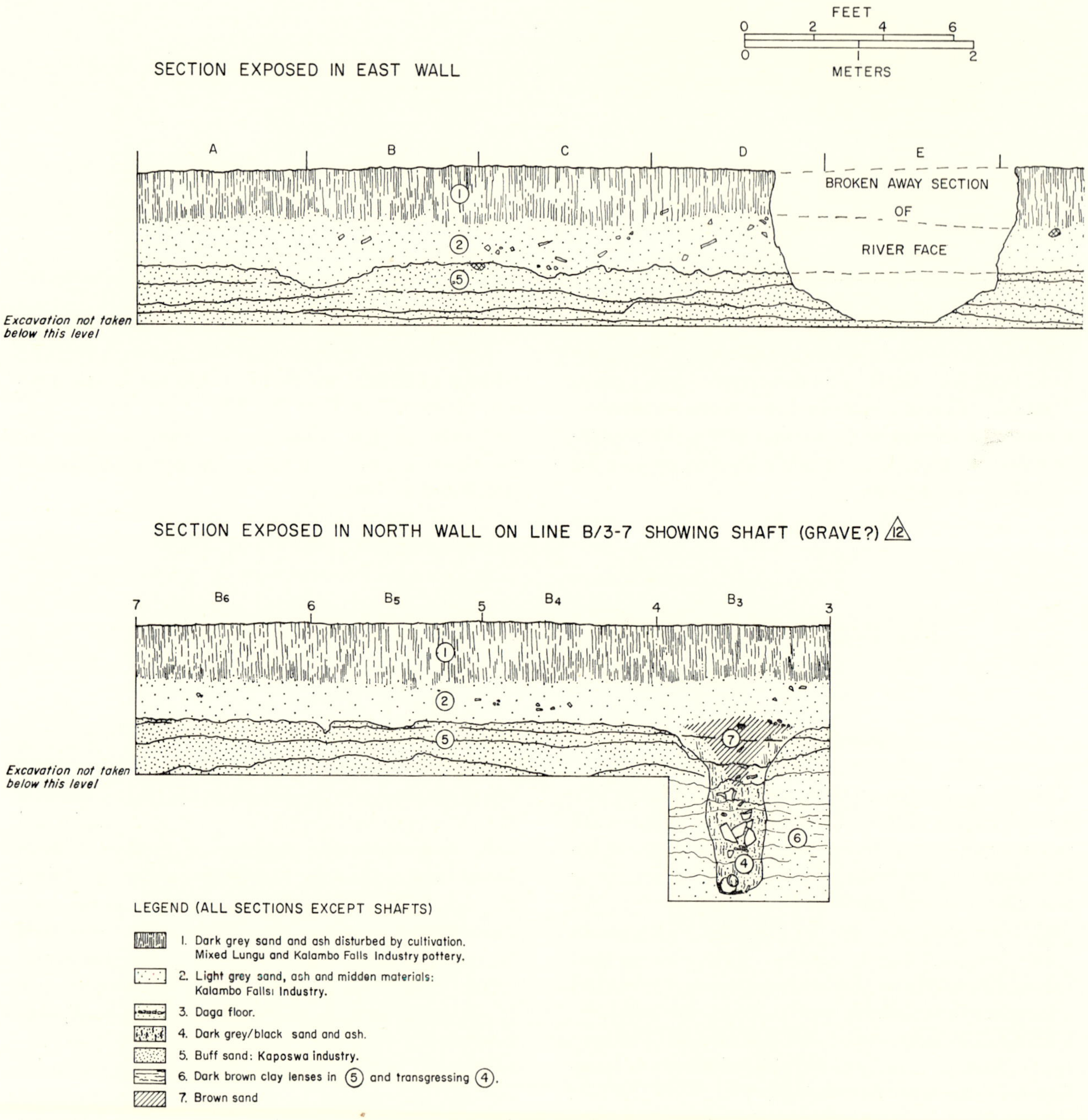
FEET
0 2 4 6
0 1 2
METERS
SECTION EXPOSED IN EAST WALL
A
B
C
D
E
BROKEN AWAY SECTION
OF
RIVER FACE
1
2
5
Excavation not taken below this level
SECTION EXPOSED IN NORTH WALL ON LINE B/3-7 SHOWING SHAFT (GRAVE?) 12
7
B6
6
B5
5
B4
4
B3
3
1
2
5
7
6
4
Excavation not taken below this level
LEGEND (ALL SECTIONS EXCEPT SHAFTS)
1. Dark grey sand and ash disturbed by cultivation. Mixed Lungu and Kalambo Falls Industry pottery.
2. Light grey sand, ash and midden materials: Kalambo Fallsı Industry.
3. Daga floor.
4. Dark grey/black sand and ash.
5. Buff sand: Kaposwa industry.
6. Dark brown clay lenses in 5 and transgressing 4.
7. Brown sand

Fig. 4. Site C excavation, 1963: sections of shafts.

SECTION EXPOSED ALONG BAULK-LINE D3-F3

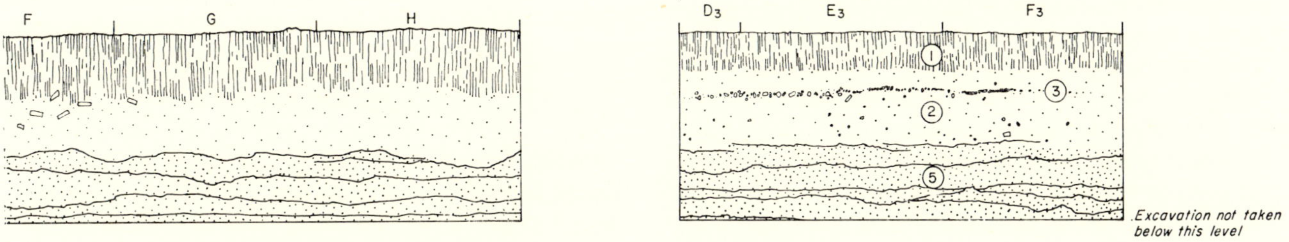

SECTIONS THROUGH SHAFTS (GRAVES?) 4-6 AND 8-11

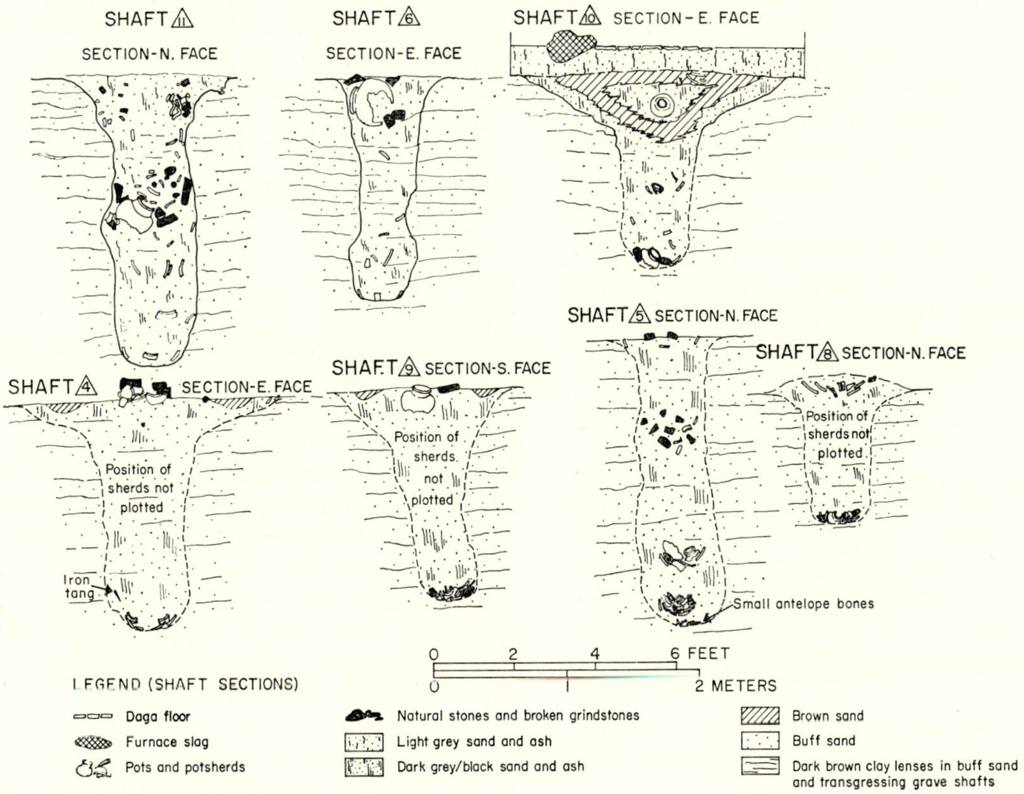

The surface of the 30 foot (9·1 m) terrace here is almost entirely flat and it is obvious that it must have formed an ideal location for a settlement overlooking the swamp and river. This terrace feature is now becoming more and more restricted as the river cuts into the fine, current-bedded sands of the Mbwilo Member that largely compose it. The terrace is now surrounded on three sides by the river but, during the earlier Iron Age, it may have extended back to the ridge separating the upper valley from the gorge. The site chosen for excavation was immediately adjacent to the cliff section at Site C and work was carried out between 20 July and 19 August in a near rectangular area 40 feet by 30 feet (12·2 × 9·1 m), laid out with a five foot (1·5 m) grid and dug in 6 inch and 12 inch (15 and 30 cm) spits.

Stratigraphy

Figure 4 shows the excavations at Site C and sections through the midden deposit exposed in them. From the surface down to a depth of 3 feet (91 cm) the deposits were homogeneous in composition and consistency, being composed of a fine sand and ash containing numerous potsherds and fire fractured pieces of stone. The top 1 foot to 1 foot 6 inches (30–45 cm), which was disturbed, was dark grey to black in colour due to the increased amount of humic matter in the soil. Surprisingly, very few modern Lungu sherds were found in the top one foot (30 cm) and it would seem that this had not been a village site since it was abandoned by the Early Iron Age inhabitants. The effect of rodents and, probably, of the heaping up of the soil for mound gardens, had been to mix the very few modern and the Kalambo Falls Industry sherds in the surface layer. From this level also were recovered the brass military equipment buckles from the 1914–18 war.

From 1 foot 6 inches to 3 feet (45–91 cm) the deposit was a homogeneous, midden soil containing an undisturbed sequence of channel decorated pottery. Below 3 feet (91 cm) there were only very occasional sherds concentrated in a shallow depression in grid square B-2. At this level also the deposit changes in a few inches to a buff to light grey sand with thin lenses of brown clay running through it. At this depth several circular areas of dark grey ashy deposit marked the top of pits or shafts that had been dug into the light coloured sand at the time the Iron Age midden began to form (Figure 5).

From depths of 3 feet 6 inches to 4 feet (106–122 cm), in a thin buff sand was found evidence of 'Later Stone Age' occupation which was concentrated in the area of grid squares H/G-2 into a camp floor with much charcoal. A single grid square, G-2, was excavated below 4 feet (1·2 m) and from here it was established that no 'Later Stone Age' implements occurred below 4 feet 6 inches (1·4 m).

The Kalambo Falls Industry occupation midden

Considerable quantities of pottery (see Table 7) were found between 1 foot and 3 feet (30 and 91 cm) in the midden, indicating that the site was fairly extensively occupied throughout this time. There were 1,169 potsherds, excluding those from the shafts. These were associated with 44 tuyère pipe fragments and numerous pieces of iron slag, *daga*, grindstone fragments and fire fractured stone, most of which was not kept. There can be little doubt that both iron smelting and smithing were practised near the village. Small pieces of charcoal were scattered throughout the deposit.

While heaps of *daga* abounded, in only one instance (associated with Shaft 10 and to be described below) was there evidence of a patch of this hardened clay material such as might have formed the floor of a hut. In grid squares D-3 to F-3 (Figure 5) a line of *daga* fragments clearly lay on a surface at a depth of 1 foot 6 inches (45 cm) but they had formed the wall plaster of some structure, perhaps a grain bin or hut, and not a floor. They lay on the buried surface in the way in which today, in any village, *daga* can be seen lying round a destroyed or abandoned hut (Plate 60). Much of the *daga* from the excavations shows the impressions of the poles or, rather, sticks that formed the framework of the structure against which the mud had been plastered. Normally, sun-dried mud does not survive unless it has been hardened by fire, but deserted village sites suffer repeated burning by bush fires during the dry season.

On the whole, the potsherds were well preserved by comparison with those in the swamp clays on Sites A and B, and the edges show little abrasion. The fire fractured stone – mostly quartzite – is such as can be found in every village today. It occurs in the form of irregular fragments and concavo-convex spalls that result from the too rapid cooling of a stone that has been in a fire. On the other hand, some of these fragments show clear signs of utilization.

A feature of the midden was the complete absence of any sign of a structure – other than the *daga*. It might have been expected that postholes would be encountered but, in spite of careful scrutiny, none could be seen. It would, therefore, appear either that no dwelling hut had been located in the area excavated or, and more likely, that if only a very shallow and narrow trench were necessary to support the pole or withy framework, as is the case with the now archaic *tutu* and *mwende* types of dwelling described below (p. 58), then little or no permanent record would be left in the grey, ashy sand of the midden.

At a depth of 3 feet (91 cm) a series of most interesting finds was made (Figures 4 and 5, Plates 69 and 70). These consisted of nine circular shafts, about 3 feet (91 cm) in diameter, which showed up clearly in plan as oval or circular patches of light or dark grey soil surrounded by clean, buff coloured sand. In four instances the circular shafts were surrounded by a narrow, 6 inch (15 cm) wide outer ring of the same dark soil. The upper 1 foot 6 inches (45 cm) of what appeared to be another such shaft, without any outer ring, was sectioned in grid square F-6, but not excavated through lack of time.

With the exception of no. 3, these shafts were dug to a depth of between 3 feet and 7 feet (91 cm and 2·1 m) from the surface at the 3 feet (91 cm) level, as far as could be judged. However, the top few inches of the shafts were indistinguishable from the surrounding and overlying midden soil and it was only where they had been dug through the undisturbed buff sand that they could be easily seen.

The tops or mouths of the shafts were funnel shaped but, below this, the diameter was usually fairly regular and varied from 2 feet 6 inches (76 cm) in some cases to 3 feet (91 cm) or a little more in others. Three of these shafts (nos. 6, 11 and 12) were sectioned and it was apparent that the walls were fairly regular and straight with no side chamber at the base. The filling of the shafts was composed of a dark grey to black sand and ash which was very like that forming the midden of the settlement, though generally blacker except at the base where the colour was browner.

Each shaft was distinguished at the top by one or two stones – either natural stones or pieces of grindstones that had been broken in a fire. With the stones there was sometimes a pile of potsherds or a nearly complete pot, always with the base missing. Sometimes, however, the sherds and pot lay a little way below the stones marking the shaft. Occasionally, also, on the outer circumference would be one or two small sherds placed upright in the soil as if to demarcate the shaft.

The shafts contained a varied assortment of potsherds (generally large), small pieces of *daga*, charcoal, tuyère fragments, iron slag and an occasional object of worked iron. The charcoal, tuyère fragments, *daga* and slag were similar in every respect to those spread ubiquitously throughout the midden into which the shafts had been dug and appeared simply to have formed part of the filling, indicating that this came directly from the midden itself. The large sherds and iron objects are a special part of the fill, however. Sometimes, midway down the shaft, would be a larger collection of sherds from nearly complete vessels together with more fire-broken stones. The lower parts and base of the shafts contained noticeably less pottery, although sometimes sherds from one or more nearly complete pot or bowl lay close together on or near the bottom. At the bottom of Shafts 6, 11 and 12 and, perhaps, of others also, three or four small sherds were found standing upright in the sand against the wall.

The only bone consisted of:

(1) Two small fragments of skull, one with a horn core, from a small antelope, probably a Blue Duiker (*Cephalophus monticolus*) or Sharp's Grysbuck (*Raphicerus sharpei*); an astragalus, mandibular fragment and isolated teeth, probably of the same animal, found in the bottom of Shaft 5.

(2) Occasional and minute fragments of calcined bone, not more than 5 mm or so in length. At first this was thought to indicate that cremation was practised but, in the absence of any other evidence to this effect, these small fragments must be considered to be part of the midden fill of the shafts.

Shafts 3, 5, 6, 8, and 11 had a simple, wide-mouthed profile and the plan of the top showed no surrounding ring. Shafts 4, 9, 10 and 12, on the other hand, had either an outer ring or, when seen in section, a Y-shaped area of buff-brown sand or soil filling the centre of the mouth and upper part of the shaft (Figure 4, Shafts 10 and 12). The junction between the buff and dark grey soil was nowhere clear cut and, at the surface, both became merged in the overlying midden material. There can, however, be little doubt that a considerable depression in the central part of the shaft had been intentionally filled with buff coloured sand that may have been somewhat heaped

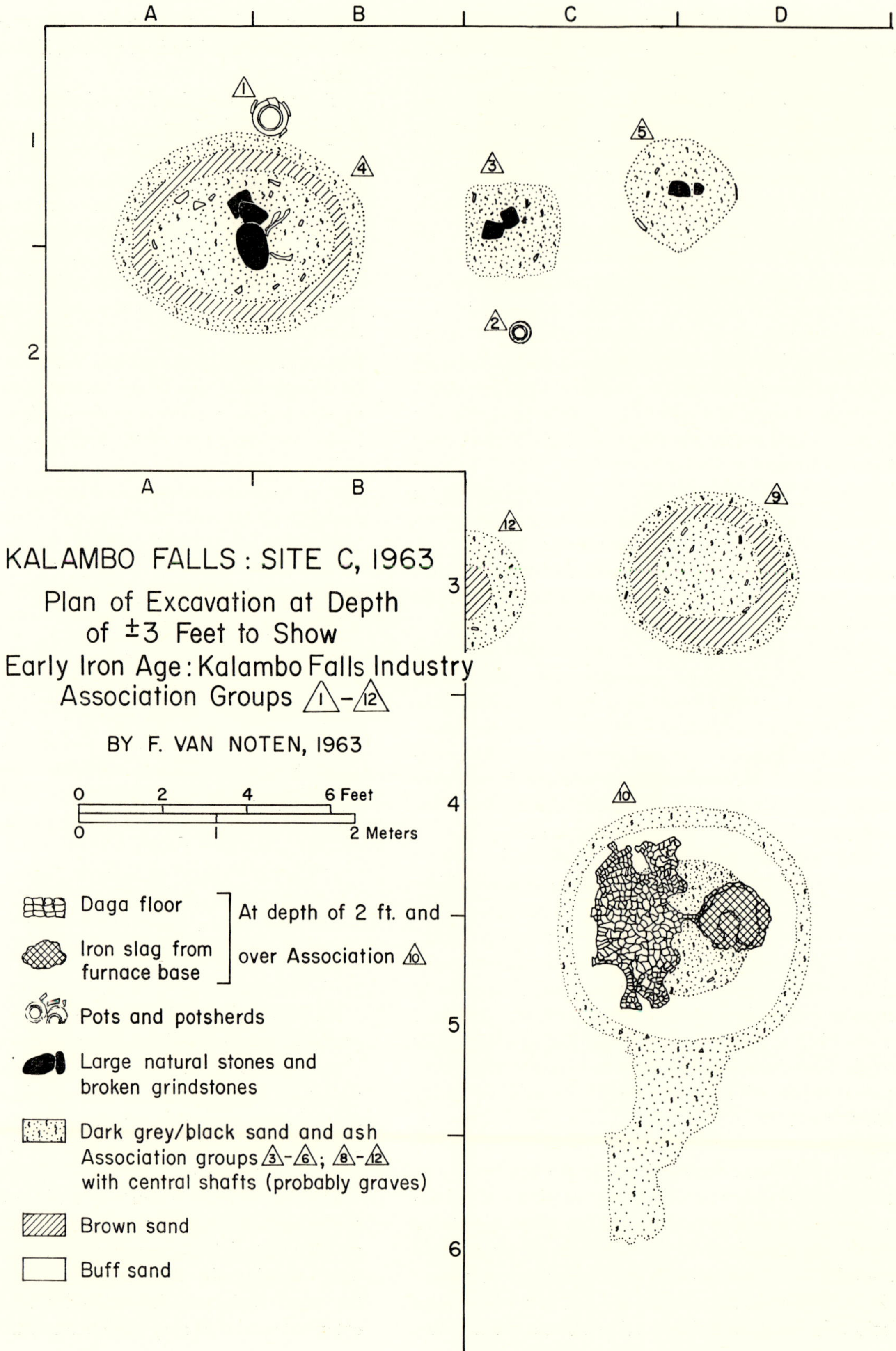
A
B
C
D
1
2
3
4
5
6
KALAMBO FALLS : SITE C, 1963
Plan of Excavation at Depth of ±3 Feet to Show
Early Iron Age: Kalambo Falls Industry
Association Groups 1 - 12
BY F. VAN NOTEN, 1963
0 2 4 6 Feet
0 1 2 Meters
Daga floor
Iron slag from furnace base
At depth of 2 ft. and over Association 10
Pots and potsherds
Large natural stones and broken grindstones
Dark grey/black sand and ash
Association groups 3 - 6; 8 - 12
with central shafts (probably graves)
Brown sand
Buff sand

Fig. 5. Site C Excavation, 1963: grid plan at depth of

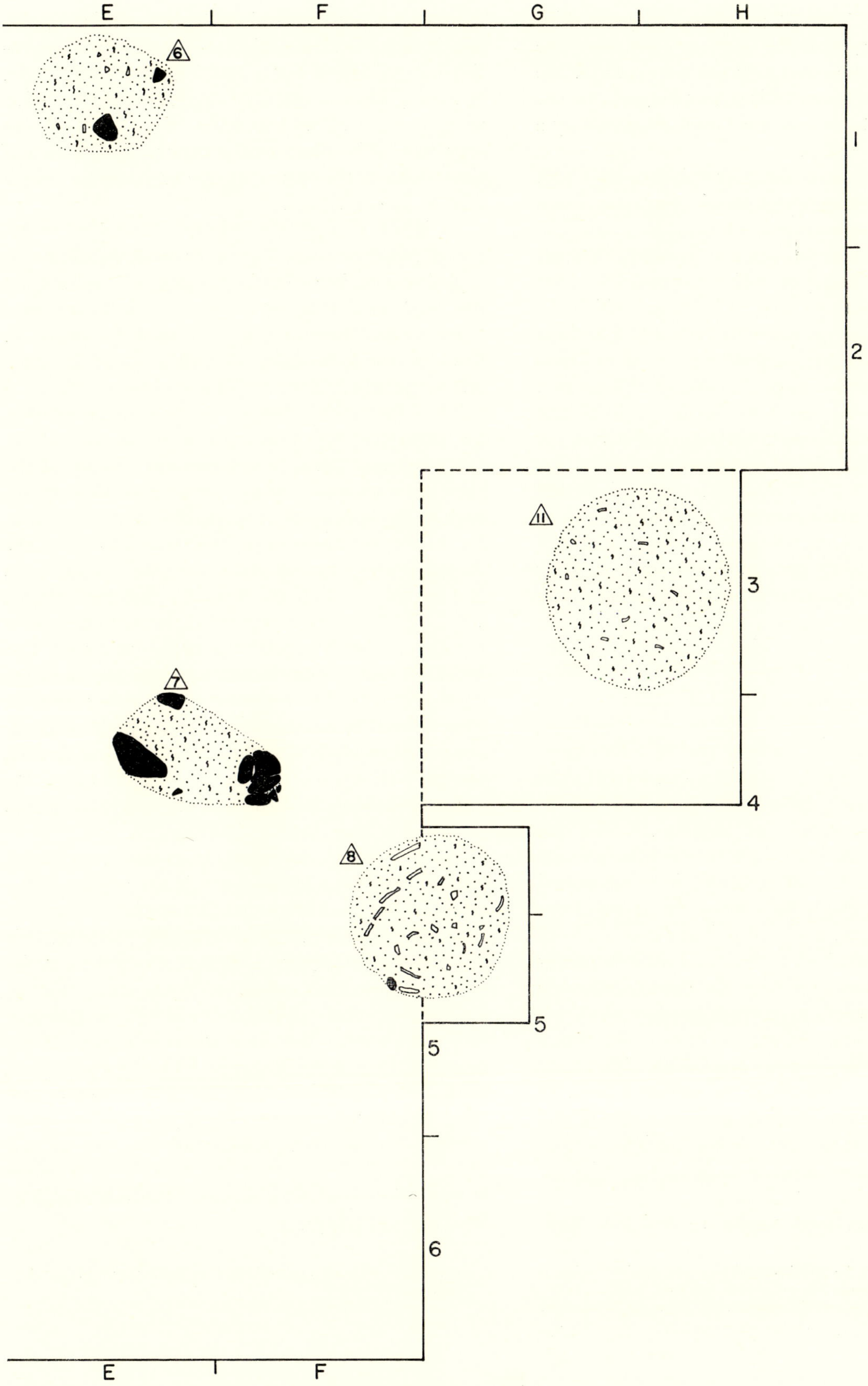

±3 feet (91 cm) to show Iron Age association groups 1–12.

up. In the case of Shafts 4, 9 and 10, a large pot with the base missing was found on or near the top. The clear outline of the outer ring and the fact that the buff sands had retained their colour suggest that the mouths of the shafts may have been protected by a structure of some kind.

At intervals of approximately 6 inches to 1 foot (15–30 cm), could be observed thin, irregular lenses or lines of dark brown clay, not more than 3 mm or so thick and running more or less horizontally through the buff coloured sand on which the midden of the settlement had accumulated and through which the shafts had been dug. It was at first thought that these lenses of fine clay were a phenomenon of the time when the sands and other deposits of the 30 foot (9·1 m) terrace were laid down. However, in several instances, they were observed to run right across the shaft, though they might be somewhat more depressed in the infilling than in the undisturbed buff sand. These irregular clay lenses, at least the topmost ones, must date to Iron Age times, therefore, and they are presumably to be associated with ground water phenomena, though how this could be is not immediately apparent.

Among the Bemba of Chinsali district, ritual demanded that when a village moved to a new site a *chishipa ca mushi* (pillar of the village) should be set up and this was the first official duty of the headman. The *chishipa* is a hole, some 5 feet to 6 feet (1·5–1·8 m) deep into which is sprinkled some of the blood of a freshly killed chicken. The 'planting' of the *chishipa* is done at night by the headman and his wife who place two horns in the hole as well as the chicken blood. The hole is then filled up and the top plastered with mud. Presumably the 'horns' are those of the female duiker killed in the ritual hunt that is always held to ensure that the new village site is favoured by the ancestors (Hoch, 1963: 97–8). Again, the Lunda *isoma* ritual (Turner, 1953: 50–2) performed to get rid of a spirit causing miscarriages in a woman, makes use of two four foot (1·2 m) deep holes with a connecting tunnel through which the woman crawls. At the end of the ceremony, food, a broken calabash and bark container with medicine, ashes and faggots from the fire are placed and thrown into the holes which are then abandoned but not filled.[1]

The writer has been unable to find that such customs were or are practised by the Corridor peoples but, if they were, this might have been the explanation for one or two shafts like those described above. It would, however, hardly explain the presence of so many in so small an area unless the settlement was regularly 'refounded' over an appreciable period of time or unless the area excavated had been the 'ritual centre' for the village.

As it was thought that phosphate analysis might reveal whether there had ever been much bony, organic matter in the shafts, samples were taken from the midden and from top to bottom and side to side of Shaft 11 and submitted to Professor Sherburne F. Cook of the University of California at Berkeley whose analysis is given at the end of the chapter.

The Iron Age midden at 3 feet (91 cm), which was the depth from which the shafts were dug, shows only 0·017 per cent phosphorus, whereas the top of the shaft gives a value of 0·094 per cent. Values remain high in the upper half of the shaft but at the bottom are little above those for the buff sand into which the shaft was dug. Since phosphorus travels downwards and is lost, it is to be expected that the original content of the lower part of the shaft would have been higher – probably equal to that of the upper part. The generally higher phosphorus values in the shaft are consistent with the suggestion that it once contained some animal substance, most likely a body, that has since disappeared. Whether the body was human cannot, of course, be determined, though the archaeological features of this and the other shafts suggest that they were burial places.

Since iron slag and tuyère fragments are common in the settlement and also occur in the infilling of the shafts, it has been suggested that the latter might be associated in some way with smelting furnaces. It is not uncommon for small holes or pits to be dug for medicines in the bottom of furnaces to ensure that the smelting will be successful, but I have been unable to find any evidence that such shafts were ever of the depth of those at the Kalambo Falls. Moreover, had these shafts been covered by furnaces, it would have been impossible for smelting to have taken place without leaving some substantial evidence to this effect. The shafts are, therefore, believed to be grave shafts, an interpretation supported by Cook's findings from the soil analysis.

[1] Another example of the association of pits with magical beliefs is found among the Safwa. For an ancestor rite two (?shallow) holes, 5 to 8 inches (127–203 mm) in diameter are dug at the head of the grave. Into these beer is poured and over them other rites take place (Harwood, 1970: 35).

Description of the individual shafts and their contents

(For the description of pottery forms and decoration, reference should be made to the section by B. M. Fagan beginning on p. 30.)

The individual features of the shafts and other complexes found in the Site C, 1963 excavation are recorded below. All finds are listed and the pottery classified in Table 7.

I. SHAFTS WITH NO SURROUNDING OUTER RING OF DARK SOIL AT THE TOP

(*a*) *Complex no.* 3 (Plate 11: 1)

Location: Grid squares C-1 to C-2.

Stratigraphic position and depth. This was the only shallow, circular hole found. The top was approximately 3 feet (91 cm) below the present surface and the base at 4 feet (1·2 m). Diameter: 2 feet 6 inches (77 cm).[1]

Description and Contents. A pot, complete except for the base was surrounded by six small stones and some large potsherds, irregularly placed. A larger stone lay over the pot. In all respects, other than the shallowness of its depth, this complex resembled the shafts.

(*b*) *Complex no.* 5 (Plates 14: 4, 5; 15: 1–7)

Location: Grid squares C-1 to D-1.

Stratigraphic position and depth. The top of the shaft appeared at 3 feet 6 inches (106 cm) below the present surface and the base at 10 feet (3 m). The shaft was, therefore, 6 feet 6 inches (2 m) deep. Diameter of mouth: 2 feet 6 inches (77 cm).

Description and contents. The top was marked by two stones lying in the middle of a circular area of dark soil. There were only two other stones from this shaft. At 7 feet 6 inches (2·3 m) were found several sherds, together; some large pieces of charcoal, a fragment of an iron tang, an arm-ring fragment and two pieces of worked iron, possibly from a spear or knife. At 9 feet (2·7 m) the broken remains of three large, decorated pots were encountered and lower still, close to the floor, were a number of other sherds, together with two cranial (one with a horn core) and one mandibular fragment and some isolated teeth of a small antelope, probably either Blue Duiker (*Cephalophus monticolus*) or Sharp's Grysbuck (*Raphicerus sharpei*). Both of these forms have been recorded from the Kalambo area (Ansell, 1960). Two very small fragments of burnt bone also came from this shaft. Three quartzite fragments from grindstones and one small piece of haematite were present.

(*c*) *Complex no.* 6 (Plates 15: 8; 16: 1 and 2; 83)

Location: Grid square E-1.

Stratigraphic position and depth. The top appeared at 3 feet (91 cm) from the surface and the bottom at 8 feet 6 inches (2·6 m). The shaft was, thus, 5 feet 6 inches (1·7 m) deep. Diameter of mouth: 2 feet 6 inches (77 cm).

Description and contents. The top of the shaft was marked by one large stone standing on end and by two smaller, fire-fractured stones with which were associated the upper two-thirds of a large pot, only the base being missing, lying on its side. Slightly lower was a used pebble, perhaps a hammerstone. Pottery was less common in this shaft than in most of the others. A large, isolated sherd occurred at 4 feet (1·2 m); smaller sherds elsewhere, and three small sherds were standing vertically against the wall at the bottom of the shaft.

(*d*) *Complex no.* 8 (Plates 16: 3–6; 17; 18; 19; 73; 74)

Location: Covered the four grid squares F-4/5 to G-4/5.

Stratigraphic position and depth. The top appeared at 3 feet 6 inches (106 cm) and the base at 6 feet 4 inches (1·9 m), the depth of the shaft, therefore, being 2 feet 8 inches (81 cm). Diameter of mouth: 4 feet (1·2 m).

Description and contents. The top was marked by a number of potsherds placed together one above the other and lying in a shallow depression. At 4 feet (1·2 m) the base of a pot and half a bowl were encountered and, immediately beneath these, an incomplete, decorated pot. Under this again, a broken, but complete vessel was resting on two broken stones.

[1] A similar pit with pottery is recorded from the Kisalian group cemetery at Sanga, Lake Kisale, Zaïre (Nenquin, 1963*a*: 59).

From the central portion of the shaft came an arrowhead, two finger or toe rings and a larger fragment of what was probably a child's armring. The greatest quantity of the pottery in this shaft lay at the top and in the upper, rather than in the lower part of the shaft. Ten grindstone fragments, two pieces of haematite and seven utilized fragments of quartzite complete the contents of this shaft.

(*e*) *Complex no.* 11 (Plates 23; 24; 25; 82)

Location: Grid squares G-3 to H-3.

Stratigraphic position and depth. The top was encountered at 3 feet (91 cm) from the surface and the base at 10 feet (3 m), the total depth being thus 7 feet (2·1 m). Diameter of mouth: 4 feet 6 inches (1·4 m).

Description and contents. The usual stone marked the top of this shaft but, apart from this and several small stones, most of the contents came from the central portion where an arrowhead and the tang of another iron tool were found. At 5 feet 6 inches (1·7 m) occurred, concentrated in a small area, the greater part of two large pots, some stone fragments and a number of large sherds from pots and bowls. Below this, the pottery gradually decreased and there were very few sherds in the lowest 1 foot 6 inches (45 cm). Again, however, the bottom of the shaft had three small sherds standing upright and marking, as it were, three of the cardinal points. This shaft was sectioned and a horizontal and vertical set of soil samples taken for phosphate and calcium analysis. Also from this shaft came a polyhedral hammer, two grindstone fragments, one flat stone used for grinding, a fragment of schist with one ground and rubbed edge, a piece of ?dolerite and a fragment of haematite. There was also a piece of stone provisionally identified as pumice. If this identification is correct it is of some interest since the nearest source of pumice must be ultimately the Rungwe volcanic massif some 200 miles (322 km) east-southeast of the Kalambo Falls, although pumice from Rungwe can also be found in the Upper Pleistocene lake sediments at the south end of Lake Rukwa.

2. SHAFTS WITH AN OUTER RING OF DARK GREY SOIL AT THE TOP

(*a*) *Complex no.* 4 (Plates 13: 2–7; 14: 1–3; 71; 72)

Location: Covering four grid squares A-1/2 to B-1/2.

Stratigraphic position and depth. The top of the shaft appeared at 3 feet 6 inches (106 cm) and the base at 9 feet 6 inches (2·9 m), the shaft thus having a depth of 6 feet (1·8 m). Diameter of mouth: minimum 3 feet (91 cm); maximum 4 feet 6 inches (1·4 m). Diameter of outer ring: minimum 4 feet 3 inches (1·3 m); maximum 6 feet (1·8 m).

Description and contents. At the top, the shaft was oval in plan with the long axis north and south and on the southeast side merged with the outer ring of dark soil. Parts of grindstones, other stone fragments and some decorated potsherds marked the central shaft. At a depth of 6 feet (1·8 m) below the surface, were found five large stones and three smaller ones surrounding several large sherds from bowls. A further concentration of sherds occurred in the lower levels and a large pot without a base was found close to the bottom. The tang of an iron tool came from the central part of the shaft. Of particular interest in this shaft were five stones used as hammers, an anvil stone and a sandstone pestle stained by red ochre, together with the usual grindstone fragments. The anvil and hammerstones look as if they had formed part of the equipment of a blacksmith.

(*b*) *Complex no.* 9 (Plates 20; 21; 75; 76)

Location: Grid squares C-3 to D-3.

Stratigraphic position and depth. The top was found at 3 feet (91 cm) and the bottom at 8 feet 3 inches (2·5 m) below the surface, the depth thus being 5 feet 3 inches (160 cm). Diameter of mouth: 2 feet 3 inches (68 cm). Diameter of ring: 3 feet 9 inches (114 cm).

Description and contents. The area of dark soil at the top of the shaft was oval in shape but 6 inches (15 cm) lower down the shaft it was circular and surrounded by an outer ring of grey soil. In the top levels only a few small sherds were found but, at a depth of 4 feet 10 inches (147 cm) below the surface was a large pot, again without a base, lying next to two grindstone fragments. A further collection of large sherds was encountered beneath this but the lowest part of the shaft contained only small stones. Rubbers, grindstones, hammer and pestle stones are also represented and this shaft yielded the second sherd found with a dimple base.

(*c*) *Complex no.* 10 (Plate 22; 78–80)

Location: Overlapping four grid squares C-4/5 and D-4/5.

Stratigraphic position and depth. The top of the shaft was encountered between 2 feet 10 inches and 3 feet (86 and 91 cm) below the surface and the base at 7 feet (2·1 m). The shaft was, thus, approximately 4 feet 2 inches (127 cm) deep. Diameter of mouth: 3 feet 8 inches (112 cm). Diameter of ring 6 feet (1·8 m).

Description and contents. This shaft was unique in that at approximately 1 foot (30 cm) above the top occurred a large, round-based and circular mass of iron slag and bloom that had clearly been in the bottom of a smelting furnace (Figure 5). It lay at a slight angle against an irregular area of burnt clay, buff to red in colour, that was part of a floor such as might have formed the surface on which a fire had been built. The top of the iron bloom lay only 1 foot 6 inches (45 cm) below the surface and the upper side of this thin burnt clay floor at 2 feet (61 cm). Ordinary, ashy, midden deposit appeared to separate the top of the shaft from the bloom and burnt clay area. Although there was apparently no direct connection between the bloom and the shaft, yet the fact that the latter lay directly beneath the former suggests that the two may probably be related. Again, at the top of the shaft, the outer ring of dark soil is present and an irregular area of grey soil immediately to the west of it. The ring and the hearth-like area confirm the impression that some structure covered the shaft and the floor.

After the clay floor and the bloom had been removed, the central area at the top of the shaft yielded several sherds, small pebbles and a little burned bone with, below the bloom, some larger pieces of charcoal. In the centre of the shaft at a depth of 3 feet 6 inches (106 cm) a large, incomplete pot was encountered with a grindstone and boulder immediately adjacent.

The brown soil filling that formed the conical plug in the mouth of the shaft showed a more complicated structure than that in the other shafts of this sort. It is considered likely that this 'plug' was made up of a layer of brown soil, a layer of grey and a final layer of brown, though it is possible that the central shaft continued right through the plug of lighter coloured soil.

This shaft produced a considerable number (370) of sherds, but there was no great concentration of pottery below the large pot and, again, the lowest part of the shaft produced little. In addition to the pottery were two haematite fragments (one showing two rubbing facets), quartzite hammer, pestle and grindstone fragments and six utilized pieces of quartzite – four battered and two split pebbles with slight evidence of use, perhaps as scrapers.

(*d*) *Complex no.* 12 (Plates 26; 27; 28: 1–3; 84; 85)

Location: Grid squares B-3 to C-3.

Stratigraphic position and depth. The top of the shaft was found at 3 feet (91 cm) from the surface and the bottom at 8 feet (2·4 m). The depth of the shaft was, thus, 5 feet (1·5 m). Diameter of mouth: 3 feet (91 cm). Diameter of ring: 4 feet (1·2 m).

Description and contents. The appearance of the top of this shaft was of a continuous circular area of dark grey soil but a few inches below this the plug of brown to buff sandy soil was visible and the plan form was of a central circular shaft surrounded by another ring of dark soil. It appeared that the lighter coloured soil may have been heaped up somewhat above the surface of the shaft. Near the top of the shaft was a large, waterworn, quartz boulder and three smaller stones lay a few inches above it. At 4 feet 6 inches (1·4 m) occurred a concentration of large potsherds and more broken stone fragments. The sherds have been reconstructed into an incomplete pot and a deep, undecorated bowl. On the floor of the shaft was a further concentration of pottery including one small complete and unbroken pot which was the only unbroken vessel to come from any of these shafts. Once more, one or two smaller sherds were standing vertically against the walls. Noteworthy among the contents of this shaft were fifteen pieces of haematite.

3. COMPLEXES NOT ASSOCIATED WITH SHAFTS

(*a*) *Complex no.* 1 (Plates 12; 87)

Location: Grid squares A-1 to A-2.

Stratigraphic position and description. At a depth of approximately 2 feet (61 cm), were found several sherds with the rim facing down which, on reconstruction, proved to form approximately two-thirds of an undecorated bowl. The wall of this bowl had been pierced in two places, 3 inches (76 mm) apart, with a rotary drill, probably for the insertion of a fibre or string handle since, if they had been intended for binding to seal a crack, the holes would have had to be close to each other on either side of the crack. Below these bowl sherds and with its base resting on midden ash and soil at 2 feet 8 inches (81 cm) was a small, nearly complete channel-decorated pot placed on its base. Further sherds lay inside this pot. No evidence was preserved in the homogeneous, ashy soil of the midden to indicate whether these vessels had been buried in a shallow pit, although it is suspected that this may have been so, in which case it must have been dug from the 1 foot 6 inches to 2 feet (45–61 cm) level.

(*b*) *Complex no.* 2 (Plate 13: 1).

Location: Grid square C-2.

Stratigraphic position and description. This complex consisted of a single, channel-decorated, shouldered pot, again resting on its base and a decorated rim sherd from a globular pot. Three channelled lines bevel the rim; below it are two bands formed by a double row of triangular impressions producing false relief. It was apparent that the pottery must have lain in a shallow pit which, at the base, was approximately rectangular with rounded corners.

(*c*) *Complex no.* 7 (Plate 77).

Location: Grid squares E-4 to F-4.

Stratigraphic position and depth. The top was at a depth of 2 feet 6 inches (76 cm) and the base at 3 feet (91 cm).

Description and contents. This complex comprises a group of stones and must belong to the earliest period of midden formation since the base rested on the buff coloured sand. One large stone that had been used for grinding was associated with three further grindstone fragments that had been broken by fire, a large piece of *daga*, a single potsherd and some fragments of sandy quartzite that probably represented the remains of a rubber. There was no sign of a pit of any kind and this complex would seem to represent rather the base of some feature – perhaps a grinding place or a base for a small storage bin or jar.

The Early Iron Age pottery from the Kalambo Falls

BY BRIAN M. FAGAN

The Early Iron Age pottery collection from the Kalambo Falls is of particular interest since it is one of the largest assemblages of such ware from Zambia. Furthermore, the cultural sequence spans most of the first millennium A.D., a period when there were major changes in pottery traditions over much of Zambia. The Kalambo Falls sequence, indeed, is one of the longest known from sub-Saharan Africa.

Sources of the clay

The Early Iron Age pottery, like modern Lungu ware, was made from clay of immediately local origin. During the excavations, Lungu women collected clay from the spoil heaps as well as making use of the deposits of grey and white clay exposed in the banks of the river. The Pleistocene lake beds were, in all probability, the source of potting clay throughout the Iron Age. In general, the clay from these beds is fine with coarse grit inclusions, thus rendering the use of a temper unnecessary under most normal circumstances.

Paste and construction

The paste of the Early Iron Age industry has a sandy texture, relieved by quartz, quartzitic or other inclusions. As stated above, the use of temper was normally unnecessary but a few sherds show that a mixture of crushed potsherds was sometimes used. The paste of modern Lungu pottery is coarser, with more gritty inclusions; the colour of vessels after firing is almost invariably grey or black.

It has not been possible to deduce with clarity the methods used to make the vessels. Some doubtful coil breaks were observed but not any certain examples. Both the coil method and the working up of a pot from a lump of clay were practised near the Kalambo Falls in modern times (Fagan, 1961; Foran, 1937: 148) and it is probable that both these methods were used by the makers of the Early Iron Age ware. Wall thicknesses vary from 0·2 inches (5·1 mm) to 0·6 inches (15·2 mm) or more.

The presence of considerable numbers of flattened rims indicates that a proportion of the vessels were constructed in an inverted position.

Both the inner and outer surfaces of vessels were smoothed with grass or fingers, but little else was done to them. A fine pebble burnish is found on the exterior of a good number of vessels[1] and waterworn pebbles of a suitable shape for burnishing came from the deposits.

All decoration was applied to vessels before firing, except for the exotic motif illustrated at Plate 6: 6 which was executed after firing (Plate 88).

The degree of firing appears to have been variable and the observed phenomena are consistent with burning over an open fire. An account of modern Lungu methods has been published elsewhere (Fagan, 1961). Some sherds are baked a brick red colour throughout the wall thickness; others show the characteristic sandwich effect of rapid and imperfect firing. As a result of these firing methods surface colours vary from orange to yellow through pale red, bright red or light brown to grey or a patchy black.

Vessel forms

The basic forms of the Kalambo Falls ware are simple but precise classification is difficult, the main types of vessel tending to merge into each other. The following broad classes of vessel are distinguished, percentages being based on the samples as shown below:

Class no.	Vessel form	No.	%
1	Hemispherical bowls	221	37·0
2	Spheroidal bowls	30	5·1
3	Shouldered pots	275	46·1
4	Globular pots	47	7·9
5	Straight-sided pots	22	3·6
6	Gourd-shaped vessels	2	0·3
	Total	597	100·0 %

These vessel classes are illustrated at Plates 3–28, as listed below:

1. *Hemispherical bowls*
   Plate 3: 1, 2, 4, 5, 6.
   Plate 4: 1, 2, 3.
   Plate 10: 1, 2, 5, 10, 11, 13.
   Plate 11: 2.
   Plate 12: 2.
   Plate 13: 4, 6, 7.
   Plate 15: 2.
   Plate 16: 2, 4, 5.
   Plate 18: 2.
   Plate 21: 5.
   Plate 22: 7, 10.
   Plate 27: 4, 6.

2. *Spheroidal bowls*
   Plate 4: 4, 5, 6, 7, 8, 9.
   Plate 5: 1.
   Plate 24: 5.
   Plate 28: 2.

3. *Shouldered pots*
   Plate 5: 2, 3, 4.
   Plate 6: 1–8.
   Plate 7: 1–3.
   Plate 8: 1, 3, 4.
   Plate 10: 3, 4, 12.
   Plate 11: 1, 3.
   Plate 12: 1, 3.
   Plate 13: 1, 3, 5.
   Plate 14: 1, 2, 4, 5.
   Plate 15: 1, 3, 4–7.
   Plate 16: 1, 3, 6.
   Plate 17: 1–4.
   Plate 18: 1, 3, 4.
   Plate 19: 1–4.
   Plate 20: 2.
   Plate 21: 2, 4.
   Plate 22: 2–5, 8.
   Plate 23: 1, 2.
   Plate 24: 1–4, 6.
   Plate 25: 1, 2, 4, 5.
   Plate 26: 1–3.
   Plate 27: 1–3, 5, 7, 8.
   Plate 28: 1, 3.

4. *Globular pots*
   Plate 9: 1, 5, 6, 8, 9.

[1] Unfortunately, owing to the weathered state of the sherds from the channel clays, it is impossible to give an accurate count.

Plate 13: 2.
Plate 14: 3.
Plate 15: 8.
Plate 20: 1.
Plate 22: 1, 6.

5. *Straight-sided pots*
Plate 8: 6.
Plate 9: 7, 10, 11.
Plate 21: 3.

6. *Gourd-shaped vessels*
Plate 8: 5.
Plate 10: 7.

Dimple based sherd
Plate 21: 1.

Miscellaneous forms
Plate 3: 3.
Plate 5: 5.
Plate 8: 2.
Plate 9: 2–4, 12, 13.
Plate 10: 14.
Plate 19: 5–7.
Plate 25: 3.

1. HEMISPHERICAL BOWLS (e.g. Plates 3: 1, 2, 4–6; 4: 1–3; 10: 1, 2, 5, 10, 11, 13).
These shallow vessels have either nearly straight or curved sides (e.g. Plate 4: 1–3). The rims may be simple (e.g. Plate 22: 7); flattened (e.g. Plate 3: 1 and 4); or rolled over as at Plate 10: 1. Although the shapes of the bowls vary considerably, clear cut subdivisions cannot be made and are, therefore, not attempted. At one extreme the vessels are almost saucer-like (e.g. Plate 3: 6), or, at the other, deep, with convex or straight sides (e.g. Plate 27: 6). Just under eighty per cent of these simple vessels are undecorated; this high incidence of undecorated bowls can be taken as characteristic of the Kalambo Falls Industry. Rims may be bevelled (e.g. Plate 10: 2) and the vessels sometimes decorated with horizontal channelled lines, incised zigzag or false relief impressions (e.g. Plate 11: 2). Diameters vary between 10 inches (25·4 cm) and 4½ inches (11·4 cm) and heights between 4½ inches (11·4 cm) and 3 inches (7·6 cm).

2. SPHEROIDAL BOWLS (e.g. Plates 4: 4–9; 28: 2)
These are little more than a variant of the hemispherical form. They are distinguished by their more convex walls, which give a narrow opening to the vessel. Once again, there is considerable variation in form from almost completely subspherical shape (e.g. Plate 4: 9) to the convex-sided, more hemispherical type which is near to Class 1 (e.g. Plate 4: 5). Rims are simple; decoration is invariably found. Dimensions are as for Class 1.

3. SHOULDERED POTS (e.g. Plates 5: 2–4; 6; 7; 17; 27: 1–3, 5–8)
This form is a major element in the industry. Once again there is great variation in shapes and sizes but clear cut subdivision is impossible for, as with the bowls, the different shapes of shouldered pots merge into each other. At one extreme there is the small, concave necked pot with a pronounced rolled over rim and globular body (e.g. Plate 6: 1 and 7). Somewhat similar vessels are known from both the Machili sites (Clark and Fagan, 1965) and Samfya (Fagan and Van Noten, 1964). The plates show the range of variation and the most common form is that of the vessel at Plate 12: 1.

The neck is almost invariably concave, although merging into a form with a more gradually sloping neck and a more globular body which approaches Class 4. Rims may be everted, rolled over, squared off, bevelled by means of channelled lines or inclined. Most Class 3 vessels bear some form of decoration, normally confined to the rim, neck or sometimes the shoulder. Dimensions are: height *c.* 15 inches (37·6 cm); rim diameter *c.* 10 inches (25·4 cm).

4. GLOBULAR POTS (e.g. Plates 9: 1, 5, 6, 8, 9; 15: 8)
These are characteristically found at Site C, 1963, in the shafts although isolated sherds occur at Sites A and B. The body is globular, the small orifice of the pot being demarcated by a straight neck (e.g. Plate 15: 8), or by a short, vertical or everted rim (Plate 9: 8, 9). This form passes imperceptibly into Class 3. Presumably these pots were used for carrying and storing liquids. A typical specimen (e.g. Plate 22: 1) has a rim diameter of 6·8 inches (17·3 cm) and is *c.* 15 inches (37·6 cm) high.

5. STRAIGHT-SIDED POTS (e.g. Plates 9: 7, 10, 11; 21: 3)
Once again, these are a variant of Class 1. At one extreme one finds the convex-sided form (e.g. Plate 9: 11) and at the other a deep, straight-sided

vessel, often with thin walls (e.g. Plate 9: 7). There is also a concave-sided form (Plate 9: 10). The more straight-sided examples tend to be undecorated; some are almost deep bowls (e.g. Plate 21: 3). Dimensions vary: height – over 6 inches (15 cm); rim diameter – *c.* 6–8 inches (15–20·3 cm).

6. GOURD-SHAPED VESSELS (Plates 8: 5; 10: 7)
This class is represented by two large sherds and a few doubtful examples.[1] The illustrated specimens can, perhaps, be taken as indirect evidence for the cultivation of the gourd (*Lagenaria vulgaris*). Gourds were probably grown by several contemporary Iron Age communities, amongst them the Leopard's Kopje people from Rhodesia (Robinson, 1959: 8) and the Ingombe Ilede folk in the middle Zambezi valley (Fagan, Phillipson and Daniels, 1969: 85).

In general this industry can be divided into two broad classes of vessel: firstly, Classes 1, 2 and 5; secondly, Classes 3, 4 and 6. As the sherds are sometimes fragmentary, it is impossible to subdivide the various classes metrically and the question of accurate definition arises. In the absence of more complete vessels, the distinction between the two groups is best made by referring the reader to, for example Plate 3: 1 and Plate 13: 1 which show the extremes of Classes 1 and 3 respectively. It is unfortunate that no more satisfactory definition can be formulated, in the absence of an attribute analysis.

Rims

Based on a count of 272 rims the following rim types occur:

1. *Rounded* – (53·31 per cent, 145 examples). A simple, rounded profile (e.g. Plate 21: 1).

2. *Squared* – (4·04 per cent, 11 examples). The rim has a flattened top (e.g. Plate 16: 5).

3. *Rolled over* – (2·94 per cent, 8 examples). The rim is thickened and then rolled over (e.g. Plate 24: 2).

4. *Everted* – (15·07 per cent, 41 examples). The rim is turned outwards with the fingers (e.g. Plate 26: 1).

5. *Inverted* – (1·47 per cent, 4 examples). The rim is turned inwards (e.g. Plate 4: 2).

6. *Bevelled* – (12·05 per cent, 34 examples). Bevelling is achieved by the use of longitudinal, channelled lines on the rim surface (e.g. Plates 19: 2; 25: 1). Other types of rim are sometimes decorated with stamped or incised motifs (e.g. Plate 13: 7).

7. *Inclined* – (4·04 per cent, 11 examples). The rim is flattened and then inclined at an angle inwards or outwards as the case may be (e.g. Plate 27: 4).

8. *Rim bands* – (6·62 per cent, 18 examples). The outside edge of the rim is raised to form either a convex or flat band around the pot (e.g. Plate 5: 1).

Projecting features

Lugs, spouts, studs and handles are unknown in this industry. One Class 2 vessel bears a decorated rib below the rim. Until the 1963 season it was thought that *dimple bases* did not occur at the Kalambo Falls. In that season, however, two typical examples were found at Site C, one from Pit 9. Both had been made by a thumb imprint (see Plate 21: 1). Dimple bases are commonly found in east Africa but not on Early Iron Age pottery from Zambia.

Decoration

With the one exception already referred to (i.e. Plate 6: 6), all decoration was applied to the damp clay before firing and the range of techniques was apparently limited. The methods used were:

(*a*) CHANNELLING
This is the most characteristic technique of the industry and was executed by channelling the clay with a spatulate object (e.g. Plates 4: 2; 7: 1–2; 25: 1). It was either applied in bands as a bevelling effect on a rim (e.g. Plate 17: 1) or in rows of parallel lines (e.g. Plates 4: 1–5; 18: 1), or used to delineate boundaries to other motifs (e.g. Plate 27: 2). The width of the channelling varies from as much as 0·2 inches (5·1 mm) to 0·05 inches (1·25 mm). Horizontal bands of channelling, the most characteristic motif of

[1] Two further decorated sherds with rim profile similar to that at Plate 10: 7 were recovered from collapsed midden deposit at the foot of the cliff at Site C in 1966.

TABLE 4. *Synopsis of finds (excluding stone and metal) and the incidence of vessel forms and decorative motifs in the Kalambo Falls Industry, Early Iron Age (B. M. Fagan)*

	Synopsis of finds					
	Pottery		Other finds (not stone or metal)			
Excavation	Decorated or rimsherds	Undecorated body sherds	*Daga*	Slag	Tuyères	Total
A1, 1956	71	649	242	44	—	1006
A2, 1956	6	88	22	78	2	196
A3, 1956	3	82	17	3	—	105
A4, 1959	39	549	23	77	4	692
B, 1956	8	443	285	250	—	986
B2, 1959	360	1965	62	137	16	2540
C2, 1959	54	45	9	13	2	123
C (Midden) 1963	336	1861	232	594	101	3124
C (Complexes) 1963	412	2301	248	754	75	3790
D2, 1956	24	198	13	7	3	245
Totals	1,313	8,181	1,153	1,957	203	12,807

	Vessel forms								
Excavation	Hemispherical bowls 1	Sub-spherical bowls 2	Shouldered pots 3	Globular pots 4	Straight-sided pots 5	Gourd-shaped vessels 6	Total of classified pots	Unclassifiable	Total of decorated and rim sherds
A1, 1956	17	9	31	3	3	1	64	7	71
A2, 1956	—	—	—	—	—	—	—	6	6
A3, 1956	—	—	—	—	—	—	—	3	3
A4, 1959	12	2	9	4	3	—	30	9	39
B, 1956	3	—	3	—	—	—	6	2	8
B2, 1959	42	5	42	8	3	—	100	260	360
C2, 1959	7	1	12	1	1	—	22	32	54
C (Midden) 1963	47	11	49	19	5	1	132	204	336
C (Complexes) 1963	93	2	129	11	7	—	242	170	412
D2, 1956	—	—	—	1	—	—	1	23	24
Totals	221	30	275	47	22	2	597	716	1313
Percentages of classified pots	37·0	5·1	46·1	7·9	3·6	0·3	100		

TABLE 4 (*cont.*)

Excavation	Decorative motifs											
	Dimple bases	Channelling only	Channelling with bands of incised cross-hatching	Channelling with stamped motifs	Stamped lines, chevrons, panels	Comb-stamped zone	Stamped false relief (with notched decoration)	Plain undecorated	Incised motifs	Total of identifiable motifs	Unidentifiable	Total of decorated and rim sherds
	1	2	3	4	5	6	7	8	9		10	
A1, 1956	—	12	5	10	—	—	—	17	2	46	25	71
A2, 1956	—	—	—	—	—	—	—	—	—	—	6	6
A3, 1956	—	—	—	—	—	—	—	—	—	—	3	3
A4, 1959	—	4	4	1	—	—	—	4	4	17	22	39
B, 1956	—	—	—	2	1	—	—	3	—	6	2	8
B2, 1959	—	4	—	6	18	1	2	47	1	79	281	360
C2, 1959	—	1	1	3	6	1	—	7	1	20	34	54
C (Midden) 1963	—	15	13	8	23	—	8	55	21	143	193	336
C (Complexes) 1963	2	7	38	42	48	6	9	105	11	268	144	412
D2, 1956	—	—	—	—	—	—	—	1	—	1	23	24
Totals	2	43	61	72	96	8	19	239	40	580	733	1313
Percentages of decorative motifs	0·36	6·8	10·5	12·24	16·8	1·3	3·4	41·7	6·9	100		

this technique, are subject to zigzag (Plate 4: 2), triangular (e.g. Plate 6: 4), loop (e.g. Plate 18: 4), diagonal (e.g. Plate 5: 3), or chevron (e.g. Plate 13: 1) variations.

(*b*) INCISION

There is a difference between this method of decoration (e.g. Plate 12: 1) done with a sharp point or blade and the U-shaped lines which are the result of channelling, also on the same, illustrated vessel. Incision of variable quality of execution and fineness appears in a number of forms: as a zigzag motif on a rim (e.g. Plate 9: 5), as a series of short, diagonal, horizontal or vertical lines (e.g. Plate 8: 5), or in cross-hatched bands with channelled motifs (e.g. Plate 5: 3).

(*c*) STAMPING OR IMPRESSED DECORATION

Here both techniques can be classified in the same group for much of the decoration is made by impressing a single stamp into the clay. True comb-stamping, i.e. fine stamping applied with a comb-like implement, is rare (e.g. Plates 3: 4, 6; 13: 3) and is normally used to produce bands of obliquely stamped lines or chevrons (e.g. Plate 7: 1) and also to fill in occasional triangles (e.g. Plate 9: 10). Most commonly, a single, triangular, semicircular, rectangular or circular stamp is used and applied in lines, horizontal bands, zigzags or chevrons (e.g. Plates 14: 2; 19: 5; 24: 2).

MOTIFS

The basic motifs of decoration on the Kalambo Falls Industry pottery are simple. Channelling is the foundation upon which many of the motifs are based. A zone of horizontal, channelled lines may occur by itself, or it may be elaborated with a chevron pattern (e.g. Plate 13: 1), loops (e.g. Plate 19: 1), zigzags (e.g. Plate 3: 6) or by directing the lines downwards and starting a new series against them (e.g. Plate 25: 2).

Such bands of channelling are associated with bands of cross-hatched incision (e.g. Plate 5: 3), a characteristic motif at the Kalambo Falls. Channelling is also found with lines of false relief stamped decoration (e.g. Plate 11: 1, 2) or with comb-stamping (e.g. Plate 7: 1). The stamped and incised motifs which occur in association with channelling are also found by themselves.

TABLE 5. *Stratigraphic analysis of Early Iron Age finds (excluding stone) from Sites A, C2 and D, 1956 and 1959 (B. M. Fagan)*

Site A4, 1959 — Depth in feet	Distribution of finds: Pottery — Rims and decorated	Undecorated	Other finds — *Daga*	Slag	Tuyères	Totals
0–1	16	141	6	44	2	209
1–2	5	22	4	9	1	41
2–3	1	17	—	4	—	22
3–4	—	15	—	—	—	15
4–5	1	1	57	3	—	61
5–6	2	32	—	—	—	34
6–7	3	60	7	4	—	74
Stepping back	11	205	3	16	1	236
Totals	39	549	23	77	4	692

Site D2, 1956 — Depth in feet	Distribution of finds: Pottery — Rims and decorated	Undecorated	Other finds — *Daga*	Slag	Tuyères	Totals
0–1½	2	38	3	1	1	45
1½–2	5	35	2	—	—	42
2–2½			No sherds			
2½–3	1	—	—	—	—	1
3–3½			No sherds			
3½–4	3	9	—	—	—	12
Stepping back	13	116	8	6	2	145
Totals	24	198	13	7	3	245

Site A3, 1956 — Depth in feet	Distribution of finds: Pottery — Rims and decorated	Undecorated	Other finds — *Daga*	Slag	Tuyères	Totals
0–1	—	9	2	3	—	14
1–2	1	37	5	—	—	43
2–3	2	20	10	—	—	32
3–4	—	16	—	—	—	16
Totals	3	82	17	3	—	105

Site A2, 1956 — Depth in feet	Distribution of finds: Pottery — Rims and decorated	Undecorated	Other finds — *Daga*	Slag	Tuyères	Totals
0–1	1	1	5	—	1	8
1–2	1	—	—	2	—	3
2–3	2	1	—	2	1	6
3–7			Sterile			
7–8	—	81	11	72	—	164
8–11			Sterile			
11–12	2	2	3	1	—	8
12–16			Sterile			
16–18	—	3	3	1	—	7
Totals	6	88	22	78	2	196

Surface site C2, 1959	Distribution of finds: Pottery — Rims and decorated	Undecorated	Other finds — *Daga*	Slag	Tuyères	Total	Vessel shapes: Pottery Classes 1	2	3	4	5	Unclassifiable	Total	Decorative motifs: Pottery-Classes of decoration 1	2	3	4	5	6	7	8	9	10	Total
Total	54	45	9	13	2	123	7	1	12	1	1	32	54	—	1	1	3	6	1	—	7	1	34	54

TABLE 5 (*cont.*)

Site A1, 1956	Distribution of finds: Pottery		Other finds				Vessel shapes: Pottery – Classes								Decorative motifs: Pottery – Classes of decoration										
Depth in feet	Rims and decorated	Undecorated	*Daga*	Slag	Tuyères	Totals	1	2	3	4	5	6	Unclassifiable	Total	1	2	3	4	5	6	7	8	9	10	Totals
1–0						—																			
1–2						—																			
2–3			9	12		21																			
3–4			19	8		27																			
4–5		11	17	5		33																			
5–6	1	36	38	4		79							1	1										1	1
6–7	4	105	47	2		158			1		1		2	4	—	2	—	1	—	—	—	—	—	1	4
7–8	2	55	36	6	Not counted	99	1	—	—	—	—	—	1	2	—	—	—	—	—	—	—	1	—	1	2
8–9	15	158	15	2		190	4	3	5	2	—	1	—	15	—	2	—	—	—	—	—	3	1	10	15
9–10	14	83	13	2		112	4	3	7	—	—	—	—	14	—	4	2	1	—	—	—	1	—	6	14
10–11	7	60	10	—		77	2	1	3	—	1	—	—	7	—	3	1	1	—	—	—	2	—	—	7
11–12	15	59	—	—		74	4	2	8	1	—	—	—	15	—	1	1	4	—	—	—	4	1	4	15
12–13	8	32	38	3		81	1	—	6	—	1	—	—	8	—	—	1	1	—	—	—	5	—	1	8
13–14	5	50	—	—		55	1	—	1	—	—	—	3	5	—	—	—	2	—	—	—	1	—	2	5
Totals	71	649	242	44	—	1,006	17	9	31	3	3	1	7	71	—	12	5	10	—	—	—	17	2	25	71

Stamped decoration may be used in single, double or triple lines (e.g. Plate 16: 3), immediately below or on the rim (e.g. Plate 21 : 2) or on the neck or shoulder of a pot (e.g. Plate 5: 2). A characteristic stamped pattern is a zigzag, false relief formed by the careful juxtaposition of two lines of triangular stamping (Plates 11: 2; 14: 1; 21: 4; 22: 4). This motif is a widespread feature on Rhodesian Iron Age pottery (Phillipson, 1968*a*, *b*) and also occurs on modern Lungu ware (e.g. Plate 2: 1).

Incised motifs are confined to cross-hatched bands (e.g. Plates 9: 2; 18: 3) with or without vertical borders and zones of oblique, vertical or zigzag lines (e.g. Plate 8: 3).

Occasional bands of oblique comb-stamping complete the common motifs (e.g. Plate 26: 5).

A striking feature of the Kalambo Falls collection is the high number of plain, undecorated vessels, especially among the bowls (e.g. Plates 3: 5; 16: 2, 4, 5; 18: 2; 21: 5; 22: 7).

The proportions of the different motifs in the various excavations are shown in Table 4. Plain, undecorated vessels (41·1 per cent) dominate all other types. Channelling, either alone or in combination, accounts for 29·5 per cent of the decorated sherds. This is made up of 6·9 per cent of channelling only, 10·5 per cent of channelling with bands of incised, cross-hatching and 12·24 per cent of channelling with stamping. Stamped lines, zigzags, panels or chevrons represent 16·8 per cent and comb-stamped motifs 1·3 per cent. Sherds showing incised motifs only comprise 6·9 per cent. Thus, the channelled and the plain undecorated sherds represent more than 70 per cent of the total. It can be said, indeed, that the pottery of the Kalambo Falls Industry is remarkable for its standardized decorative motifs.

Correlation of motifs and vessel forms

As has been mentioned above, just under 80 per cent of the hemispherical bowls are without decoration; undecorated, shouldered pots also occur but these vessels are characteristically adorned with bands of channelling, with or without zones of incision or impressed decoration. Otherwise motifs are well distributed, the bevelled rim and channelled bands appearing on hemispherical bowls and on deeper pots.

Functional uses of the pottery

The pottery of the Kalambo Falls Industry can be divided basically into two halves – the bowls and the pots. It is probable that the two groups had different functions and, on analogy with modern practice, it is likely that the deeper vessels played a more important role in storage than the bowls.

TABLE 6. *Stratigraphic analysis of Early Iron Age finds (excluding stone) from Site B, 1956 and 1959 (B. M. Fagan)*

Site B2, 1959	Pottery		Other finds				Pottery – Vessel shapes							Pottery – Decorative motifs										
							Classes							Classes of decoration										
Depth in feet	Rims and decorated	Undecorated	*Daga*	Slag	Tuyères	Totals	1	2	3	4	5	Unclassifiable	Totals	1	2	3	4	5	6	7	8	9	10	Totals
0–1	71	416	9	60	3	559	8	—	9	—	—	54	71	—	—	—	—	4	—	—	8	—	59	71
1–2	40	301	6	35	2	384	3	2	5	2	1	27	40	—	1	—	1	3	—	—	4	—	31	40
2–3	48	258	9	13	1	329	10	—	5	5	2	26	48	—	—	—	1	4	—	2	12	—	29	48
3–4	58	323	17	16	5	419	9	2	13	1	—	33	58	—	2	—	1	4	1	—	8	—	42	58
4–5	41	230	10	7	3	291	4	1	4	—	—	32	41	—	—	—	1	1	—	—	4	1	34	41
5–6	29	75	4	4	—	112	1	—	—	—	—	28	29	—	—	—	—	—	—	—	1	—	28	29
6–7	18	92	7	—	—	117																		
7–8	22	56	—	2	1	81	7	—	6	—	—	40	53	—	1	—	2	2	—	—	10	—	38	53
8–9′ 3″	13	19	—	—	—	32																		
Stepping back	20	195	—	—	1	216	—	—	—	—	—	20		—	—	—	—	—	—	—	—	—	20	20
Totals	360	1,965	62	137	16	2,540	42	5	42	8	3	260	360	—	4	—	6	18	1	2	47	1	281	360

Site B, 1956	Pottery		Other finds			
Depth in feet	Rims and decorated	Undecorated	*Daga*	Slag	Tuyères	Totals
0–1	1	42	8	21	—	71
1–2	—	52	12	80	—	144
2–3	—	42	25	39	—	106
3–4	—	24	14	5	—	43
4–5	—	30	11	5	—	46
5–6	—	59	18	18	—	95
6–7	—	26	36	20	—	82
7–8	2	58	72	—	—	132
8–9	2	57	28	48	—	135
9–10	—	6	2	—	—	8
10–11	—	—	—	—	—	—
11–12	—	6	—	—	—	6
Stepping back	3	42	59	14	—	118
Totals	8	443	285	250	—	986

Stratigraphical changes

Studies of the typological development of the Kalambo Falls Industry are hampered by the small stratified samples and the fragmentary and weathered state of the potsherds. The stratigraphy can be studied from three areas: A1 excavation, 1956; B2 excavation, 1959; and the Site C (settlement) excavation, 1963. The counts of the vessel forms and motifs are given in Tables 5–7 and the following observations are made:

(*a*) A1, 1956 (Plates 86, 89)
No identifiable and stratified sherds are present above a depth of 6 feet (1·8 m). In the lower half of the sequence all vessel forms are represented, albeit sporadically. Both hemispherical bowls and shouldered pots are found at every level, the latter predominating over the bowls. Channelled bands and cross-hatched, incised motifs are almost universal and are presumably present as a result of the abundance of the shouldered pots. Undecorated vessels occur in each level.

No conclusions can be drawn from this incomplete sequence.

(*b*) B2, 1959
Hemispherical bowls occur throughout the Iron Age

levels and, with shouldered pots, are the most abundant vessels in the excavation. Shouldered pots are also ubiquitous and appear to be in roughly the same proportions as the bowls. Classes 3, 4 and 5 occur sporadically in the middle levels; this may be due to chance rather than to stratigraphical change.

Plain, undecorated vessels are in overwhelming numbers in this excavation. Stamped motifs are also more frequent than usual. Channelled bands are not abundant, although fragments of channelled vessels are common amongst the unidentifiable specimens. Once again, there appear to be few major changes in the pottery sequence.

(*c*) SITE C, 1963

There is a rise in the number of shouldered pots in level 2, plain, undecorated bowls are common in both the main horizons. Only four identifiable vessels come from level 3. Spherical pots are more common in this excavation and are a feature, also, of the shaft complexes.

Incised motifs are more frequent; stamped lines are also well represented but, here again, plain, undecorated vessels are common (41 per cent of the total).

No major changes in vessel forms can be detected from these figures. The small numbers of identifiable sherds which are stratified make it impossible to draw any unassailable conclusions on the development of the Kalambo Falls Industry wares but there appear to have been few major innovations during the six hundred or so years of the Iron Age occupation at the Kalambo Falls.

This report was originally drafted before the advent of statistical techniques of pottery analysis to Zambian archaeology. It has not been possible to re-analyse the pottery or to apply multivariate analytical techniques to the Kalambo Falls material at this stage.

Discussion

The Early Iron Age of Zambia is still imperfectly known after more than a decade of research, but an increasing number of sites have been located in recent years. David Phillipson (1968*a*) has recently distinguished several, provisional, regional variants of the earliest pottery tradition north of the Zambezi, formerly known as 'channelled ware' or 'channel-decorated' pottery, terms that are now no longer used. Most of his sites are concentrated around the main centres of population in the Central and Western Provinces. The large tract of *Brachystegia* woodland country lying to the north and west of the line of rail is still very imperfectly known from the Iron Age point of view. Phillipson (1968*a*: 197) recorded eleven Early Iron Age sites in this area, most of them scatters of potsherds from the upper levels of rockshelters. The Kalambo Falls Iron Age sequence remains one of the longest in southern Africa, and a yardstick against which we can study other sites.

As we have seen, the Kalambo Falls pottery is dominated by shallow bowls and necked pots, with many undecorated vessels. Simple decorative techniques predominate, while channelled decoration is the basis for most motifs. False relief chevron designs are found and decorated and bevelled rims, often thickened externally, are common. As far as can be established, at least some of these motifs and vessel forms are repeated at other sites in northern Zambia. The Early Iron Age sherds from Chipya Forest near Samfya, Lake Bangweulu (Fagan and Van Noten, 1964) bear channelled bands and cross-hatched, incised zones as decorative motifs, somewhat resembling the Kalambo Falls material. False relief chevron stamping and chevron patterns on rim bevels are found at Nakapapula rock shelter near Serenje (Phillipson, 1968*a*: 199; 1969), as are fragmentary vessels with channelled or grooved decoration. Early Iron Age pottery has also been found at Mwela Rocks near Kasama and in Late Stone Age levels at Bimbe and Nsalu (Clark, 1950*a*: 117), while, nearer the Kalambo Falls, the Itimbwe rock shelter near Mbala, as well as a site in the Uningi pans, have yielded similar material.

The eleven sites from this northern area of Zambia come from a region where soils are less fertile and the terrain more thickly wooded than in southern Tanzania or near the Copperbelt. The chances for more permanent settlement were slim, with the apparent result that village sites were moved more frequently than in the south, where mound villages are not uncommon (Fagan, 1965). Archaeological evidence for early agricultural settlement is correspondingly thinner but Phillipson (1968*a*: 197–200) has used the Kalambo Falls pottery as a basis for a provisional definition of his 'Kalambo group of the Early Iron Age' in which he includes both the Kalambo Falls Industry itself, and the material from the other sites mentioned above. Unfortunately, finds are too scanty for an accurate definition of the Kalambo Falls Industry or for detailed comparisons

TABLE 7. *Kalambo Falls Industry, Site C Excavation, 1963.*

1. *Analysis of finds from the midden by depth and grid square*

	Distribution of finds														Pottery – Vessel shapes								Pottery – Decorative motifs										
	Pottery		Stone						Other finds						Classes								Classes of decoration										
Depth in feet	Rims and decorated sherds	Undecorated	Rubbers	Utilized pieces	Fragments	Thermal fragments	Pebbles and un-worked stone	L.S.A. waste derived	*Daga*	Slag	Tuyères	Brass	Iron	Totals	1	2	3	4	5	6	Unclassifiable	Totals	1	2	3	4	5	6	7	8	9	10	Totals
*0–1½	51	409	8	—	25	59	10	19	34	125	19	3	—	756	20	4	15	8	3	—	1	51	—	6	7	3	4	—	2	20	9	—	51
1½–3	252	1,419	54	26	17	159	26	52	176	369	82	—	1	2,624	26	6	32	11	2	1	174	252	—	7	6	5	18	—	6	33	10	167	252
3–4	33	33	3	—	—	—	—	4	22	100	—	—	—	195	1	1	2	—	—	—	29	33	—	2	—	—	1	—	—	2	2	26	33
Totals	336	1,861	65	26	42	218	36	75	232	594	101	3	1	3,575	47	11	49	19	5	1	204	336	—	15	13	8	23	—	8	55	21	193	336

* This includes 6 illustrated pots from collapsed midden material on the River face.

Distribution of finds 1 foot 6 inches–3 feet

Pottery – rims and decorated. Total – 252

	A	B	C	D	E	F	G	H
1	31	3	9	16	7	4	13	12
2	18	13	12	12	5	3	15	12
3			9	10	4	7		
4			5	1	3	3		
5			2	2	4	8		
6			2	2	1	4		

Pottery – undecorated. Total – 1,419

	A	B	C	D	E	F	G	H
1	133	45	30	151	58	48	46	61
2	73	104	82	65	32	48	47	120
3			32	16	7	7		
4			18	27	2	25		
5			8	14	28	36		
6			5	4	26	21		

Daga. Total 176

	A	B	C	D	E	F	G	H
1	26	10	1	24	4	3	4	4
2	10	15	8	6	3	17	12	10
3			3	3	3	2		
4						1		
5			2	2		1		
6					1	1		

Slag. Total 369

	A	B	C	D	E	F	G	H
1	31	9	4	11	11	10	10	17
2	11	21	5	23	3	3	18	18
3			26	14	1	9		
4			11	12	8	11		
5			11	22	4	6		
6			5	15	1	8		

Tuyère fragments. Total 82

	A	B	C	D	E	F	G	H
1	9	2	4	2	4	1	2	2
2	6		3	3	2	7		9
3			3	3	2	3		
4			3	1	4			
5				1		2		
6			1	2	1			

2. *Distribution of finds from shafts and other complexes*

	Pottery																		
	Decorative motifs											Vessel forms							
Complex	1	2	3	4	5	6	7	8	9	10	Total of rims and decorated sherds	1	2	3	4	5	Unidentified	Undecorated body sherds	Total pottery
No shaft																			
1	—	—	2	2	—	—	—	2	1	1	8	2	—	4	—	—	2	43	51
2	—	—	—	2	—	—	—	—	—	—	2	—	—	1	1	—	—	—	2
7	—	—	1	—	—	—	—	—	—	—	1	—	—	—	—	—	1	—	1
Shallow shaft																			
3	—	—	3	3	1	—	1	1	—	3	12	—	—	9	—	—	3	53	65

Shaft with no outer ring																			
5	—	1	4	7	4	—	1	13	2	12	44	5	—	16	4	2	17	227	271
6	—	—	2	—	2	—	1	1	—	2	8	2	—	2	1	—	3	68	76
8	1	1	9	6	3	1	—	10	2	15	48	12	—	16	1	1	18	362	410
11	—	3	9	7	9	2	1	22	2	26	81	23	—	21	1	1	35	417	498
Shaft with outer ring																			
4	—	1	4	6	7	1	2	28	1	22	72	23	—	22	—	3	24	320	392
9	1	—	1	3	—	—	—	8	—	24	37	8	1	8	1	—	19	245	282
10	—	—	1	2	12	2	—	12	1	22	52	11	—	13	2	—	26	338	390
12	—	1	2	4	10	—	3	8	2	17	47	7	1	17	—	—	22	228	275
Totals	2	7	38	42	48	6	9	105	11	144	412	93	2	129	11	7	170	2,301	2,713

	Worked iron						Other finds															
												Stones and stone fragments										
Complex	Arrowheads	Spear or knife fragments	Tangs	Arm rings	Finger rings	Total of worked iron	*Daga*	Iron slag	Tuyères	Rubber/Upper grindstones	Lower grindstones	No thermal fracture	Thermal fracture	Pestle stones	Hammerstones	Anvil stones	Other utilized stone	Haematite	Bone fragments	L.S.A. artifacts (derived)	Totals of other finds	Totals of all finds
No shaft																						
1							—		—	—	—	—	—	—	—	—	—	—	—	—	—	51
2							—		—	—	—	—	—	—	—	—	—	—	—	—	—	2
7							1	†	1	2	5	—	1	—	—	—	—	—	—	2	12	13
Shallow shaft																						
3							3	5	1	—	—	9	1	—	—	—	—	—	—	—	19	84
Shaft with no outer ring																						
5	—	2	1	1	—	4	16	—	4	—	3	5	—	—	—	—	—	1	6	17	52	327
6	—	—	—	—	—	—	3	20	3	—	—	19	—	—	1	—	—	—	—	14	60	136
8	1	—	—	1	2	4	29	108	6	—	10	14	12	—	—	—	7	2	—	20	208	622
11	1	—	1	—	—	2	81	226	22	—	3	61	—	—	1	—	1	1	—	15	411	911
Shaft with outer ring																						
4	—	—	1	—	—	1	45	184	17	2	76	17	11	1	5	1	4	—	—	8	371	764
9							26	98	8	2	5	12	8	1	2	—	1	1	—	20	184	466
10							44	113	13	2	4	33	8	1	2	—	6	2	—	20	248	638
12							†	†	†	—	—	8	—	—	—	—	2	15	—	66	91	366
Totals	2	2	3	2	2	11	[248]	[754]	[75]	8	106	178	41	3	11	1	21	22	6	182	1,656	4,380

† Not recorded.

with other regional variants from central or eastern Zambia. Four Early Iron Age sites have been described from the Eastern Province, three of these – Makwe and Thandwe rock shelters and an open site at Kamnama – have been dated, the last of them having been occupied in the fourth century (Phillipson, 1968*a*: 197; 1971). The Chondwe group of Early Iron Age wares from the Copperbelt Province, dated to the ninth century at the type site, shares many features with the Kalambo Falls Industry (Phillipson, 1968*a*: 196–7). Most of the sites are open localities where sherds with broad grooving are found, somewhat similar to the Kalambo Falls examples. Chondwe vessels are distinguished from the Kalambo Falls vessels by the large quantity of comb-stamping, used to fill gaps in bands of horizontal grooving. Bevelled rims are also absent. One has a preliminary impression of differences of typological detail rather than of a major cultural nature.

The Kalambo Falls pottery lies well within the limits of variation of the earliest Iron Age pottery tradition of south central Africa. The Kalambo Falls vessels display a general lack of sophistication which is characteristic of Zambian Early Iron Age pottery as a whole, but the two dimple bases and some emphasis on bevelled rims serve to show some links with east African Early Iron Age wares. Unfortunately, comparative material is scanty as few sites have yet been investigated in the east African interior.

The nearest Tanzanian Iron Age site to the Kalambo Falls which has been excavated is the Ivuna salt pans (Fagan and Yellen, 1968), some 150 miles (241 km) to the northeast in the Rukwa Rift. A multicomponent sequence of Iron Age culture was excavated from dumps around the salt pan at Ivuna, which has been radiocarbon dated to between the thirteenth and sixteenth centuries A.D. generally later than but, perhaps, in part contemporary with the Kalambo Falls sequence. Grooved or channelled pottery was collected at the pans as early as 1952, and has been compared on occasion with the Kalambo Falls sherds. But the excavations showed that the vessels in component Alpha, at the base of the sequence, which might be in part contemporary with the Kalambo Falls Industry, were of quite different shape, predominantly undecorated or cord-impressed and often graphite burnished. The contrast to the wares of the Kalambo Falls Industry is striking and the pottery tradition quite different, even if the later Ivuna vessels were decorated with some grooved motifs.

The Ivuna pottery has no connections with the earliest Iron Age pottery tradition of eastern Africa, while the Kalambo Falls Industry vessels do. In east Africa, as in regions to the south, the earliest Iron Age pottery tradition appears to have been broadly similar over a large geographical area. The dimple-based (or Urewe) ware of the central Nyanza Province, Kenya, was first described in 1948 by the Leakeys (Leakey, *et al.* 1948). As originally defined 'dimple-based' ware is characterized by elaborate bevelled rims and scrolled, grooved or channelled decoration combined with incised motifs. Vessel forms range from a wide variety of shallow bowls to shouldered, or more elaborate pots. More recent work has extended the distribution of dimple-based wares from Nyanza into the coastal regions of Kenya and northern Tanzania (Soper, 1967*a*, *b*) as well as into Uganda (Posnansky, 1961*a*), and Rwanda (Hiernaux, 1960), as well as at Uvinza in western Tanzania (Sutton and Roberts, 1968). Sutton's sites are the nearest localities to the Kalambo Falls yielding Early Iron Age pottery. The Uvinza salt pans were an important centre of salt trade in prehistoric times and a long sequence of Iron Age culture was obtained from Sutton's small scale excavations. The earliest Uvinza wares probably belong with the Sandaweland group of the Early Iron Age. Bevelled rims and false relief chevrons, also characteristic of the Kalambo Falls Industry wares, are found at the Uvinza localities, but there are closer connections with Uganda Early Iron Age sites, such as Nsongezi (Sutton and Roberts, 1968: 55), as well as, of course, with the pottery from Sandaweland (Smolla, 1956; Sutton, 1968).

No one has yet published a detailed analysis of the differences between the east African Early Iron Age pottery tradition and that of the Kalambo Falls Industry of Zambia. Most of the east African sites have been investigated since the descriptive part of this report was prepared in 1963 and the writer has had no opportunity to make a detailed comparison of the two pottery groups. In any case, the evidence is still too inadequate for comprehensive, multivariate investigation. But there is already general agreement that the Kalambo Falls pottery belongs to the same broad pottery tradition as the 'dimple-based' ware, even if there are numerous differences in sophistication, vessel form and decorative technique. My impression is that the differences between the Kalambo Falls wares and the east African vessels are about the same as those between the Gokomere pottery of Rhodesia (Robinson, 1963) and the Kalundu group of southern Zambia (Phillipson, 1968*a*).

A decade or less ago, when less was known of the distribution and dates of the east African Early Iron Age wares, there was considerable agreement that the Kalambo Falls Industry wares and 'dimple-based' pottery were related to each other and that Early Iron Age people entered south central Africa from the north (Fagan, 1965: 50–1). The channelled Zambian pots were regarded as either devolved (Posnansky, 1961*b*: 134) or evolved versions of 'dimple-based' ware, depending on the closeness with which one examined the material. Iron Age radiocarbon chronology has been revised so drastically in recent years that the theories, or rather intelligent guesswork, of the past decade are no longer tenable. Early Iron Age culture seems to have appeared in both south central and eastern Africa at about the same time. The type locality for 'dimple-based' ware at Urewe in the Nyanza Province of Kenya is now dated to A.D. 270 ± 110 (N-435), A.D. 320 ± 110 (N-436) and A.D. 390 ± 95 (GX-1186), (Soper *in* Fagan, 1969*a*: 157) while the Kwale site near Mombasa, yielding related pottery, dates to A.D. 270 ± 110 (N-291) and A.D. 260 ± 110 (N-292). Two sites close by (Kwale Forest Site and Kwale Ditch Site) with similar pottery date to A.D. 120 ± 115 (N-483) and 160 ± 115 (N-484) (Phillipson, 1970*b*: 14–15) respectively. The earliest pottery from Uvinza in eastern Tanzania dates to A.D. 420 ± 160 (N-463) (Pwaga) and A.D. 520 ± 200 (N-465) (Nyamsunga) (Sutton and Roberts, 1968). Early Iron Age settlement was widely established in eastern Africa by the third century A.D., if not earlier, while 'dimple-based' ware was still being made at Nsongezi in Uganda as late as the eleventh century (Posnansky, 1961*a*: 185).

Robinson and Sandelowsky (1968) have recently suggested that the Early Iron Age pottery of Malawi is closely related to the east African Iron Age wares. The Phopo Hill site in central Malawi has yielded early pottery and iron tools, the former having in its vessel forms and decorative motifs some links with 'dimple-based' wares. The settlement has been dated to A.D. 295 ± 95 (SR-128), A.D. 205 ± 170, and A.D. 505 ± 170 (SR-161) (Robinson *in* Fagan, 1969*a*: 160; Phillipson, 1970*b*: 15). Similar pottery has been found further south in Malawi at Lumbule Hill (A.D. 565 ± 100 (SR-170)) and Nkope Hill at the south end of Lake Malawi (A.D. 360 ± 120 (SR-174) and A.D. 775 ± 110 (SR-175)) (Phillipson, 1970*b*: 6, 15). Detailed comparisons between the Phopo pottery and that from the Kalambo Falls remain to be made (Robinson and Sandelowsky, 1968: 119), and the writer has yet to examine the Phopo material. However, the vessel forms and decorative motifs of the Malawi pottery, while bearing some generalized resemblances to the Kalambo Falls pottery, appear to be more elaborate at Phopo, on examination of the drawings in the preliminary report on the Malawi site. Once again, one has the impression that the Malawi pottery is another variant with a broad cultural continuum. The arrival of Iron Age culture in Malawi appears to be generally contemporaneous with the same event at the Kalambo Falls and in Zambia as a whole.

The Kalambo Falls Iron Age dates span a time scale from A.D. 345 ± 40 (GrN-4646) and A.D. 430 ± 40 (GrN-4647) to a date somewhere between the late tenth and eleventh, perhaps as late as the thirteenth centuries[1] (Clark *in* Fagan, 1969*a*: 523). Radiocarbon dates from elsewhere in Zambia are broadly contemporary with the Kalambo Falls readings. Early Iron Age pottery at Kapwirimbwe, near Lusaka, dates to the fifth and sixth centuries (Phillipson, 1968*b*: 92), while the lowest levels of the Kalundu mound in southern Zambia yielded a date of A.D. 300 ± 90 (SR-65) (Phillipson, 1968*a*: 202). The well known date of A.D. 96 ± 212 (C-829) from Machili on the borders of the Western (formerly Barotse) Province is now regarded as suspect pending further research (Phillipson, 1968*a*: 208), but is not much earlier than the Kalundu date, or some readings from south of the Zambezi.

Rhodesian Early Iron Age dates cover most of the first millennium with Ziwa ware from eastern Rhodesia dated to as early as the fourth century (Fagan, 1965: 62) and a second century date from Mabveni (Robinson, 1961) associated with Gokomere-type pottery, also found in the basal levels on the Acropolis at Zimbabwe (Summers, Robinson and Whitty, 1961), assigned to earlier than the fourth century A.D.

More and more Early Iron Age radiocarbon dates are released every year. None of them are earlier than the second century A.D. and many within the third and fourth centuries throughout the enormous area of east and south central Africa. Iron Age technology and economy seem to have appeared within a short period of time over much of eastern Africa at the beginning of the Christian era. Radiocarbon dating is not a sufficiently accurate chronological material to allow us to work within such narrow margins as a

[1] A complete list of the Kalambo Falls Iron Age radiocarbon dates is given in Volume I, Appendix J, p. 236; see also pp. 165–6.

century at the beginning of the first millennium A.D. Not, therefore, until a more accurate method of time measurement is developed are we likely to be able to establish the detailed chronology of Iron Age settlement in the savanna woodlands of eastern Africa. Most authorities now agree, however, that the initial spread of Iron Age culture into the area was connected with the dispersal of Bantu-speaking peoples throughout much of sub-Saharan Africa, some two thousand years ago, perhaps from a dispersal area to the west of Lake Tanganyika. Unfortunately, however, the archaeology of that particular region is almost unknown (Nenquin, 1963*b*; Phillipson, 1968*a*: 209; Oliver and Fagan, in preparation).

The Kalambo Falls Industry pottery falls within the accepted range of variation of Early Iron Age wares in east and central Africa, and remained in use for a period of over 650 years during a time when basically similar pottery forms were in use over a wide area of eastern Africa. Further discoveries and future research will demonstrate more clearly the exact relationship between the important Kalambo Falls sequence and its neighbours to the north and south of the Zambian frontier.

Modern Lungu pottery

BY BRIAN M. FAGAN

(Plates 1 and 2)

Isolated sherds of Lungu ware are mingled with channel-decorated fragments to a depth of 3 feet (91 cm) in the disturbed areas of the Chiungu Member clays and numbers of sherds and more or less complete vessels have been found on isolated graves and in the cassava gardens around the basin. The techniques of manufacture and firing of Lungu pottery have previously been described (Fagan, 1961) so that only a brief account is given here of the salient features of the modern vessels (see Plates 1 and 2).

Paste and manufacture

The paste is normally black or grey with coarse inclusions from the lake clays. Reddish paste colours also occur; sandwich effects are common and it is known that the pottery was fired in an open hearth.

Both the coil and 'single lump' method of manufacture have been used near the Kalambo Falls within living memory. Pebble burnish is common and vessels are artificially blackened (Fagan, 1961).

Vessel types

The range is shown in Plates 1 and 2. Shouldered pots are characteristic (Plates 1: 2, 3; 2: 2) and probably the most common type, followed by the shouldered bowl, which can either be shallow (Plates 1: 1; 2: 3) or deep enough to merge into the pot group. Occasional plain, undecorated deep or shallow bowls (Plate 2: 4) are also found. In addition to these more common forms, the writer has seen in the villages, straight-sided vessels, a gourd-shaped pot and carinated forms (Plate 1: 1).

Techniques and motifs of decoration

Incision and coarse stamping are the most common techniques. Channelled decoration is almost unknown and cannot be regarded as a persistent feature of the industry.

Rims are sometimes adorned with lines of 'nicks' or incised dashes (Plate 2: 3). Other decoration normally occurs on the neck or shoulder; zigzag motifs (Plate 1: 1 and 3), semicircular panels of cross-hatched incision are also characteristic (Plate 1: 2). Undecorated vessels are not infrequent. Occasionally a pot bears a band of more elaborate decoration on the neck. The shouldered pot at Plate 2: 2 has four parallel bands of comb-stamping on its neck.

Conclusions

It is clear that there are many points of difference between the Kalambo Falls Industry ware and modern Lungu pottery. Carination, shouldered bowls and cross-hatched, semicircular bands of incision are not found in the Kalambo Falls ware. The modern vessels tend to be thinner and black pots are common.

There are, however, points of resemblance. The shouldered pots have occasional rolled-over rims and rim bands; inclined rims also occur but, in general, the rims are thinner in the modern pottery and tend to be everted. Plain, undecorated vessels of the Kalambo Falls ware form are made (Plate 2: 4) but this generalized type is almost universal in Zambia.

It can be said, therefore, that Lungu ware is substantially different from the earlier industry. As can only be expected, however, there are minor points of resemblance which may, perhaps, be attributed to a long tradition of Kalambo Falls Industry ware that has survived into the later centuries of the Iron Age. No Lungu sites have been investigated which predate the nineteenth century and, until they have, we can say little about the antecedants of modern Lungu pottery.

Kalambo Falls Industry pottery (possibly a later phase) from Site A, Excavation A7, 1966

BY J. D. CLARK

During our stay at the Kalambo Falls in October, 1966, a small rubbish pit was excavated immediately adjacent to the camp beneath the large fig tree. This pit, dug to a depth of 2 feet 3 inches (68·6 cm), yielded potsherds, *daga*, fractured stone and charcoal and it was decided to make a small excavation close by in order to prove the extent and nature of the archaeological horizon and its contents. Accordingly, a rectangular area 15 feet by 10 feet (4·6 × 3·0 m), marked in grid squares A and B 1–3, was laid out immediately west of the rubbish pit and 40 feet (12·2 m) from the base of the fig tree. Mr Joseph Siantumbu was placed in charge of the excavation which was carried out with six labourers from 18 to 27 October.

The ground level sloped gently down towards the north and west as can be seen in the section drawings (Figure 6), as did also the red and brown sandy loam exposed by the excavation. This was dug in spits of 6 inches (15 cm). All finds are listed at Table 8.

The uppermost deposit was a dark brown soil with some humic matter, some 7 inches (17·8 cm) deep at the south end, thickening to approximately 12 inches (30 cm) at the north end. It contained a number of potsherds, fragments of iron slag and other artifactual waste. Beneath this the deposit became more loam-like and red/brown in colour, especially at the northwest side of the excavation where some 9 inches (22·9 cm) of this red/brown coloured, loamy soil was present, grading into the underlying red coloured loam similar to that encountered upslope in the A4 excavation.

Over the rest of the excavation (grid squares A-1/3 and B-1/2), the change from the dark brown surface soil to the red loam was more abrupt, although there was no stratigraphic break. The red loam showed no evidence of bedding and no certain signs of artificial disturbance though it will be necessary to check this, so far as the northwest corner is concerned, by further excavation at a later date. In the upper levels, from the surface down to between 3 feet and 3 feet 2 inches (91 and 106 cm) the archaeological material belonged to a 'Later Stone Age' microlithic aggregate similar to that described from Site C; the excavation was not taken below this depth. Scattered charcoals were present at all levels and a large fragment of completely charred wood was found at a depth of 2 feet (61 cm) from the surface in grid square A-2.

The table of finds shows that the Iron Age material (i.e. potsherds, iron slag, worked iron and *daga*) is most common above the 1 foot 6 inches (45 cm) level. On the other hand, percussion flaked stone, in particular microlithic waste and tools, only became abundant below 3 feet 2 inches (96 cm). Fire fractured stone, mostly quartzite fragments, are a feature of the Iron Age occupation, as the table shows.

There is no apparent difference in the composition of the pottery in the dark brown, the red/brown and the top of the red loam but sherds, together with other non-lithic artifacts, gradually decrease with depth. Further excavation may well show that

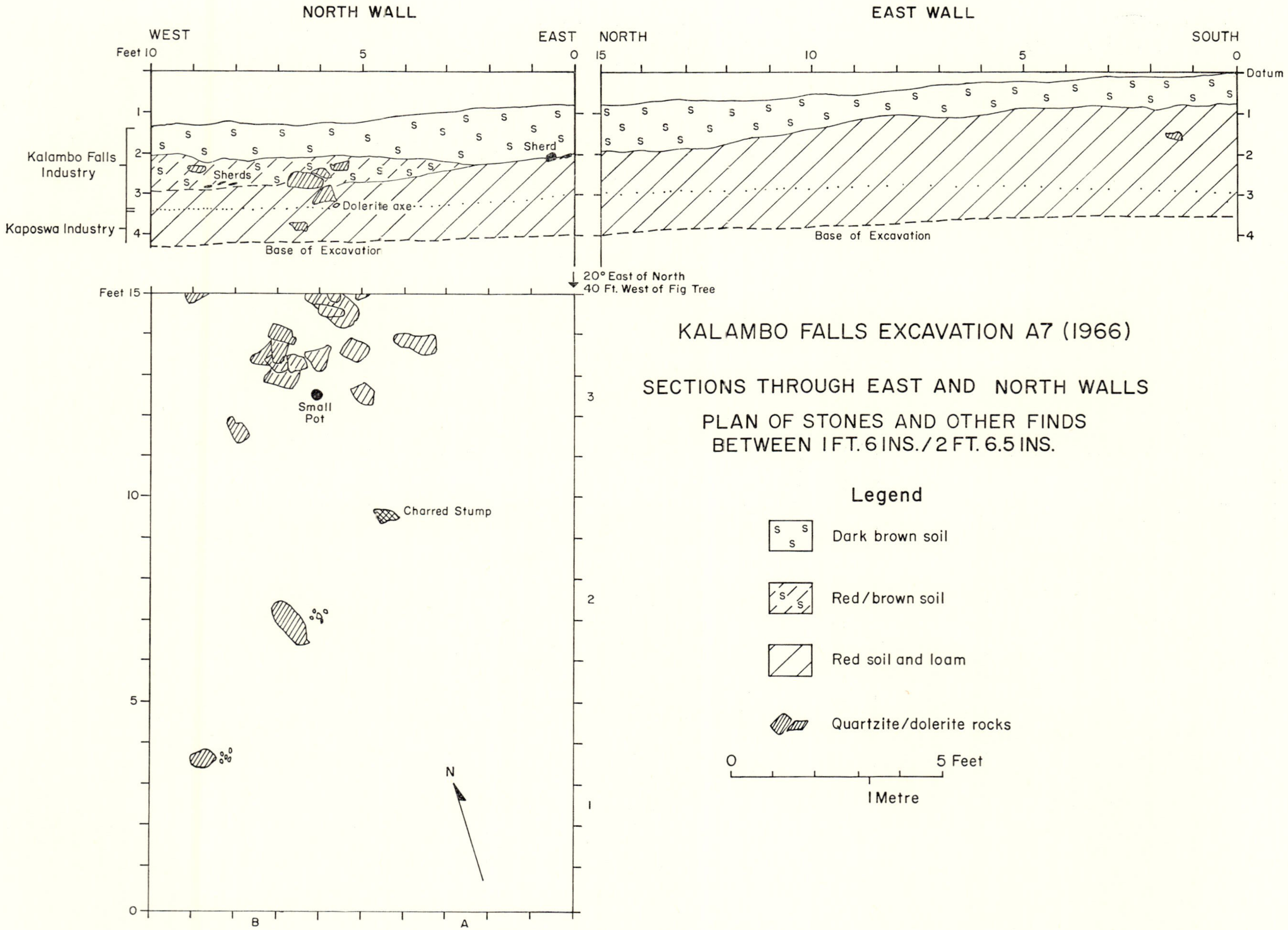

Fig. 6. Plan and sections of Excavation A7, 1966.

TABLE 8. *Analysis of finds by depth, A7 Excavation*, 1966

Depth: Feet	(cm)	Pottery: Black ware: Decorated and rim	Black ware: Undecorated	Red ware: Decorated and rim	Red ware: Undecorated	Buff/brown ware: Decorated and rim	Buff/brown ware: Undecorated	Vessel type when determinable: 1	2	3	4	5	6	Rim form: Rounded	Square	Rolled over	Everted	Inverted	Bevelled	Inclined	Rim bands
0–0·5	(0–15)	2	27	2	117	2	7	2	—	—	—	1	—	1	3	1	—	—	—	—	—
0·5–1·0	(15–30)	20	103	3	114	—	9	3	—	3	—	—	—	8	7	1	3	—	1	1	—
1·0–1·5	(30–45)	3	10	3	45	—	5	2	—	1	—	—	—	1	—	—	1	—	—	1	—
1·5–2·0	(45–61)	—	6	2	5	—	8	1	—	1	—	—	—	—	1	—	1	—	—	—	—
2·0–2·5	(61–76)	2	9	—	4	1	9	—	—	2	—	—	—	2	2	—	—	—	—	—	—
2·5–3·0	(76–91)	1	23	7	9	—	—	1	—	2	—	—	—	—	2	—	—	—	1	—	1
3·0–3·5	(91–106)	—	—	—	4	—	1	—	—	—	—	—	—	—	—	—	—	—	—	—	—
Total		28	178	17	298	3	39	9	—	9	—	1	—	12	15	2	5	—	2	2	1
		563																			

Depth: Feet	(cm)	Pottery: Decorative motifs: Plain undecorated (8)	Incised motif (9)	Stamped punctate (5)	Comb-stamped (6)	Channelling (3)	Shallow grooving	Mamillated	Burnish	Other finds: *Daga*	Slag	Worked stone: Shaped and utilized	Worked stone: Waste	Fire fractured stone	Worked iron	Shell	Pebbles	Tuyère fragment	Bone	Total all objects
0–0·5	(0–15)	4	1	1	—	—	—	—	17	3	24	1	11	6	2	3	2	1	1	211
0·5–1·0	(15–30)	18	—	—	2	1	3	—	26	16	27	1	17	89	27	2	1	—	—	429
1·0–1·5	(30–45)	2	1	—	—	1	—	1	2	1	3	1	13	5	—	—	—	—	1	90
1·5–2·0	(45–61)	2	—	—	—	—	—	—	8	—	2	1	36	10	—	—	—	—	1	71
2·0–2·5	(61–76)	2	—	—	—	—	—	—	7	—	5	1	15	7	—	—	—	—	4	57
2·5–3·0	(76–91)	3	—	—	—	3	1	—	4	—	1	—	34	—	—	—	4	—	6	85
3·0–3·5	(91–106)	—	—	—	—	—	—	—	—	—	—	11	268	—	—	—	2	—	1	287
Total		31	2	1	2	5	4	1	64	20	62	16	394	117	29	5	9	1	14	1,230

quantitative differences do, in fact, exist but the finds from the present excavation are too few and too incomplete for any significant changes to be distinguished.

It is, however, of significance that the Iron Age artifacts and the microlithic 'Later Stone Age' are both present in the same red, hillside soil and are stratified one above the other with no evidence of any stratigraphic break between them. This suggests that the local circumstances favourable to the formation of hillslope soil remained unchanged at least over the initial period when an iron technology replaced the use of stone. The profile exposed in the upper part of the section is interpreted as a normal soil profile showing A and B horizons with some modification due to the accumulation of organic material from human occupation.

Only in grid square B-3, where the red loam is overlain by the red/brown loamy soil layer, is there evidence for a possible occupation surface (Figure 6). At the junction of the two deposits, a scatter of large stones (the 'stone pile') was found, as well as a number of potsherds which may be associated with a 'floor'. The stones were unmodified blocks of local sandy quartzite; they were mostly found to rest one upon the other over a vertical depth of 12 inches (30 cm), between 1 foot 6 inches and 2 feet 6½ inches (45 and 77·5 cm) from the surface, suggesting that they had been intentionally placed in position. The majority occur at depths between 1 foot 10 inches (55·9 cm) and 2 feet 3 inches (68·6 cm). The lowest blocks are seated in the red loam while those above are either in the red/brown loam or at the junction of the dark brown soil and red loam. It seems probable, therefore, that the surface of the red loam represents a settlement horizon which belongs in time to that of the Kalambo Falls Industry, on the evidence of the pottery.

The pottery consisted mostly of undecorated body sherds but, at a depth of 2 feet (61 cm) in grid square B-3, was found the lower half of a small, round based pot, the whole of the upper half and rim being missing. The lower part of this pot has a diameter of 82 mm and a vertical height of 64 mm. It is 4–6 mm thick and is composed of a grey–black, gritty paste, the outside being unburnished. In addition this grid square produced several rim sherds and the greater part of another, diminutive pot at a depth of 2 feet 6 inches to 3 feet (76–91 cm). This small, malformed pot is reminiscent of a child's first attempts at potmaking.

The red loam was quite undisturbed beneath the 'stone pile', the other half of which lay to the northwest outside the excavation. Although the function of such a pile cannot be determined, it does show that, when a larger area of the site is excavated it may yield other structural evidence.

Description of finds

1. *Pottery*. Since there were comparatively few decorated rim and body sherds and because it was thought that more than one ware might be present, the collection was first divided according to the external appearance and the general colour of the paste. On this basis it was thought possible to distinguish:

(*a*) a ware with a dark grey to black paste and black, usually burnished exterior finish. Some of these sherds are thinner than

(*b*) a generally thick ware with red to red/brown interior paste and mostly red exterior finish;

(*c*) a ware with buff/brown exterior finish.

The (*b*) ware is typical of the Kalambo Falls Industry ware with channel decoration. The (*a*) and (*c*) wares are less typical although they do occur, notably in the hillslope soil at Site A (Plate 6: 2 and 6).

Vessel form is equally divided between hemispherical bowls and shouldered pots with one straight-sided pot.

Rim forms are the same as those of the Kalambo Falls Industry but with a proportionately larger number of square or flattened rims.

The great majority of the vessels are undecorated, as is the case at the other sites. The range of decorative motifs is more limited, however, and incised cross-hatching, horizontal channelling broken by chevrons or dragged lines and false chevron relief are absent. If the excavated area had been larger, however, there is no reason to suppose that these motifs would not have occurred. A representative sample of the pottery from the A7 excavation is illustrated at Plate 29 for comparison with that from the Site C settlement and the other sites. This collection clearly belongs with the Kalambo Falls Industry but, in view of the minor differences in decoration that appear to exist, the increased number of dark grey ware sherds from thinner walled vessels, relative to the typical red ware pottery, and the association of all three wares at all levels with the Iron Age horizon, it is possible that the occupation at A7 may be a somewhat later expression than that at the settlement at Site C. It may date to a time when innovations were entering the local basin introduced either by trade or new immigrants.

2. *Worked Iron*. Twenty-six small, flat fragments of much oxidized iron from a depth of 6 inches (15 cm) and one fragment from 2 inches (51 mm) higher, all came from grid square A-2. These could have come from the same object, perhaps a hoe blade.

3. *Daga and slag*: small, typical pieces.

4. *Shell*: fragments from freshwater mussel (*Unio*

sp.), one fragment showing possible rubbing of an edge such as results from use as a pot smoother.

5. *Stone.* The greatest concentration of fire fractured and reddened stone occurs at the same level as the greatest concentration of pottery. Of the nine small pebbles clearly introduced to the site, those from the Iron Age level may have served as burnishing stones for pottery; the ones from the microlithic horizon probably represent raw material for flaking.

The greater number of the percussion flaked stone artifacts are in silicified mudstone (chert) and come from the red loam below the three foot (91 cm) level. Unmodified waste predominates, mostly diminutive flakes, bladelets and fragments. There is one micro-core with two striking platforms in different planes and one possible micro-burin spall. Two small flake fragments showed utilization and two haematite fragments attest to the use of pigment. Shaped tools consist of 4 small scrapers (1 double ended, 2 notched and 1 single, straight), one convex backed blade, one straight backed bladelet and two lunates. Of particular interest is a dolerite axe, bifacially flaked by percussion, possibly preparatory to edge grinding (see p. 114). This was found in grid square B-3 at a depth of 2 feet 6 inches (76 cm), immediately under a large quartzite boulder lying on what is believed to be the surface of the microlithic horizon. The microlithic component of the red loam is identical with that from the occupation floor below the Early Iron Age occupation at Site C (see pp. 109, 125). By contrast, the five shaped tools from above the 2 feet 6 inches (76 cm) horizon associated with the pottery are non-microlithic, informal scraping tools showing minimal modification; four are in hard quartzite and one in chert.

The discovery of bone and buffalo teeth close to the base of the Early Iron Age layer is of importance since it holds out the possibility of obtaining sufficient faunal material when excavation is resumed at this site, to be able to reconstruct the nature of the exploitation of wild and domestic animals.

Metal, stone and other cultural remains from the Early Iron Age

BY J. D. CLARK

The numbers in brackets refer to the total number of finds from all excavations.

(a) Metal (20) (Plate 30)

(i) IRON OBJECTS (18)

Surprisingly little manufactured iron was found in the excavations when one considers the quantity of slag. It seems probable, therefore, that much of it has been destroyed by the acid nature of the soil which is also perpetually moist at all sites except the settlement midden at Site C. Those pieces which have survived are greatly oxidized and usually incomplete. Finds comprise the following:

1. *Spearheads or knives* (?3)

The greater part of a tanged and barbless spearhead or knife blade from Site C, 1963 midden, grid square C-1, at a depth of ±2 feet (60 cm) (C-27-63). The blade is lenticular in section with no sign of a mid-rib. The section of the tang was probably circular (Plate 30: 17).

Two fragments of broad-bladed tools were recovered from the shaft of Complex 5 but are too incomplete for it to be possible to reconstruct the original shape (Plate 30: 11 and 16).

An additional iron tool, a thin blade, was found by Dr Glen H. Cole on 8 November 1966, embedded in a block of brown/grey midden soil that had fallen from the top of the cliff face at Site C. The same block also contained one straight-backed microlith. The iron blade is much oxidized and sand grains adhere in places forming a coating to the metal. It is a tapering blade, probably for an adze or light, ceremonial axe; the former is more likely, as, when seen in profile view, the specimen has a very slight curvature. One half of the working edge is missing but the remainder is convex and splayed and shows a recent break, probably from the time of the collapse of the block in which it was found. The tang, instead of tapering to a point, as is usual, shows some slight broadening and thickening towards the proximal end that was inserted in the shaft. The proximal end itself is missing and the break is old. The section of the blade is flat without any central rib or ridge. The length of the complete blade and tang is unknown but the specimen measures 114 mm in present length; the estimated width of the blade from shoulder to shoulder of the convex cutting edge is 44 mm. The minimum width of the tang is 12 mm and the width at the broken, proximal, end is 15·5 mm; average thickness is 4 mm (Plate 30: 18). (Not included in count.)

2. *Arrowheads* (2)
A broad-bladed, barbless arrowhead came from the shaft of Complex 8. The section across the blade is flat and that through the tang circular (Plate 30: 13). A barbless iron point, somewhat flattened at the tip and with one edge sharpened, came from the shaft of Complex 11 (Plate 30: 12). If it is an arrowhead, then this is an unusual type for central Africa today, though heads somewhat similar to this are known from among the Hadza and from Zaïre (the Congo) where they are used with poison. Alternatively, this specimen might possibly be a needle or awl of some kind used for matting or basketry.

3. *Tangs* (3)
All three were from incomplete iron tools. The first, from the shaft of Complex 11 (Plate 30: 15) was a fairly thick, circular-sectioned tang, perhaps from a spearhead. The second, also circular-sectioned but from a less substantial tool, came from the shaft of Complex 4 (Plate 30: 14). The third, with an approximately circular section, was much oxidized at both ends and came from a depth of 1 foot 6 inches to 2 feet (45–61 cm) on Site D, 1956 and is illustrated at Plate 30: 9.

4. *Conical fragment* (1)
This is the lower end of what must have been a heavy and substantial iron tool. It could have come from a heavy spearhead such as might have been used with a fall trap for elephant or, alternatively, it might be the pointed end of a blacksmith's spike anvil. It came from a depth of 9 to 12 feet (2·7–3·7 m), probably from the later Iron Age channelling, when stepping back Site A1, 1956 (Plate 30: 10).

5. *Arm or leg rings* (4)
A fragment of an asymmetric, circular-sectioned ring of solid iron, with an approximate internal diameter of 7·8 cm came from the shaft of Complex 8 (Plate 30: 5). A similar fragment (internal diameter *c.* 4·6 cm) came from the shaft of Complex 5 (Plate 30: 4). The small diameter of this ring suggests that it belonged to a child rather than to an adult. A curved iron fragment, believed to be from an armring, was found in the B2 excavation, 1959, grid section H, at a depth of 1 foot 6 inches to 2 feet (45–61 cm) (No. B-28-59). Another fragment of iron ring from Site B (B2, 1959) came from a depth of 2 feet 6 inches to 3 feet (45–61 cm) in grid section G.

6. *Finger or toe rings* (2)
From the shaft of Complex 8 came a ring of solid iron, with sub-rectangular section, made from a strip of rod bent into a circle but with the ends not welded together. The internal diameter is 21 mm (Plate 30: 7). Half a ring of solid iron with sub-rectangular section and internal diameter of 19 mm was also found (Plate 30: 8).

7. *Miscellaneous* (3)
These consist of two fragments of worked iron recovered from a depth of 4 feet 9 inches to 5 feet 3 inches (1·4–1·6 m) in swamp clays at Site B (B2 excavation, 1959) (No. B-79-59); a small ring of flat iron pierced twice for attachment to a holder that came from a depth of 4 inches (102 mm) at Site A4, 1959, grid square B-1. It is probably the band from the top of the shaft of a spear used to prevent the tang of the head from splitting the shaft and it is very likely to be of recent Lungu origin.

(ii) COPPER OBJECTS (2)
Only two specimens of worked copper were found and, from their depth in the red loam at the upslope end of the A4 excavation at Site A, there is no reason to disassociate them from the Kalambo Falls Industry.

1. A bracelet or anklet of thin copper rod, with asymmetric, circular section, bent round in a circle with the ends left open. The shape has been distorted by burial and the metal is oxidized. It comes from a depth of 2 feet to 2 feet 6 inches (61–76 cm) in grid square B-49 in the A4 long trench, 1959 (No. A-22-59) (Plate 30: 6).

2. A small, hollow, conical object made from thin copper sheet with a loop of metal at the pointed end. Regrettably, when the collections were studied in

1962 in the Livingstone Museum, the specimen could not be found. Its shape is recorded in the field notebook in the accompanying sketch. It measured approximately 30 × 12 mm and was identified by some of our African workmen as an earring. Mambwe–Lungu ear ornaments are large, oval discs of wood or ivory, now no longer worn. While this specimen could, indeed, have been an earring, it might equally well have been part of the decoration on a belt or charm. It is, however, of interest that similar ear ornaments of copper occur in the eleventh century cemetery at Katoto on the Lualaba, Zaïre, and the same type is today made in Rwanda and worn by warriors (J. Hiernaux, personal communication).[1]

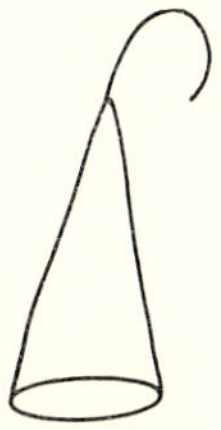

(b) Grindstones (205, mostly fragments)

The material used was sandstone or hard quartzite. While very few complete grindstones were found, there were numerous fragments, believed to have been purposely broken, associated with the shaft complexes at the Site C settlement.

(i) UPPER GRINDSTONES AND RUBBERS (94, MOSTLY FRAGMENTS) (Plate 91 (left), 92 (left))
One good example of a bun rubber type of upper grindstone, used on both faces, was recovered from the clays in the A1, 1956 excavation at a depth of 6 feet 6 inches to 7 feet (1·9–2·1 m). It is circular, measures 15 × 15 × 7·5 cm, is made of sandstone and illustrated at Plate 91 (left). The flat, double sided example (Plate 92 (left)) is of the kind used by some Bantu peoples today for grinding tobacco, leaf relishes, etc. The majority of upper stones are, however, smaller, often less regular in shape and thicker, without the evidence of continuous use shown by this specimen. These others can best be described as rubbers and are often only represented by fragments. A well-made example is illustrated at Plate 32: 14. It is on a flat, oval pebble of quartzite with one flat rubbing surface, has been used as a hammer or pestle at one end and may have been used also for burnishing.

(ii) LOWER GRINDSTONES (111, MOSTLY FRAGMENTS)
None of these is of the dish variety, showing that they were neither in as continual use as are the grindstones of the present-day populations, nor were they roughened with a spherical stone sharpener. At best the Kalambo Falls Industry stones show only a very shallow grinding surface – the striations being usually parallel to the long axis of the stone (Plate 91 (right)).

Several smaller grindstones were found and one, from A1, 1956 at a depth of 7 feet to 7 feet 6 inches (2·1–2·3 m) (no. A-1/27) is particularly interesting since it shows sharply incised cuts near one end, clearly made by a metal tool (Plate 92 (right)).

Three flat grinding stones approximately 1 foot 6 inches (45 cm) square by one inch (25·4 mm) thick were recovered. One was associated with the greater part of the large pot at the base of the channel cut in the River Face section on Site A in 1959; one, with a nearly complete pot from collapsed earth at Site C, the 1963 cliff section; and the third came from the shaft of Complex 11 in the settlement. Again, the grinding faces are shallow and the stones are similar to those used by some Bantu-speaking peoples for grinding relishes, tobacco and ochre (personal observation).

(c) Pestle stones (9)

For the most part these are elongate or irregular pebbles or pieces of sandstone and quartzite with one or more broad, battered, convex surface but with few, if any, irregularities and there is usually no sign of heavy battering, such as is present on hammerstones. The upper grindstone or rubber at Plate 32: 12 has also been used as a pestle and shows the characteristic pecking and smoothing at both ends of the tool.

(d) ?Burnishing stones (21)

These were commonest in the clays of the Chiungu Member in the A and B excavations and are small, smooth pebbles of quartzite and quartz. They do not appear to be a natural component of the gravels in the local basin and were, therefore, introduced. They are similar to the stones used today for smoothing and burnishing pottery vessels (Plate 32: 10).

[1] Comparable, but not identical, are the seven conical 'bells' of rolled sheet copper forming a 'rattle' said to have come from a grave at Sanga, Lake Kisale (Nenquin, 1963*a*: 233–4).

(e) Hammerstones (14)

These are oval or elongate pebbles (Plate 32: 11) as well as less regular, weathered lumps of quartzite which show clear evidence of bruising and battering of one or more edges or ends. Particularly worthy of note are those found in the shaft of Complex 4 which are most probably smith's hammers. They show pitting and bruising at the end and one specimen also has a battered edge. Three are irregular cobbles, battered and bruised on one or more faces. The remaining two are more cylindrical in shape. One exhibits much heavy battering and concoidal pitting at one end. The bruising on the working end of the second specimen forms a more regular, convex surface and the angle of intersection with the cortex, forming the wall of the cylindrical cobble, is sharp. Such hammers are still in use today among the Fipa and other Bantu-speaking peoples for working iron.

(f) Anvil stones (1)

Only one definite anvil stone was found, associated with the hammers in Complex 4. It is large, roughly spherical and with two flattened faces. Two of the edges are battered and have had small flakes removed from two faces. One face shows a smooth, oval area that has become gently concave from pounding.

(g) Informal, utilized stone tools (125)

It is of considerable interest that it has been possible to distinguish a number of specimens that have clearly been utilized. They occurred both in the swamp and channel clays of the Chiungu Member at Sites A and B and in the settlement at Site C and it should be generally recognized that for some purposes the earlier Iron Age populations continued to make use of stone – in fact, for two purposes it was used into very recent times by some of the Corridor tribes.

These artifacts are irregular-shaped pieces of stone, mostly hard quartzite, but chert (especially for scrapers) and sandstone were also used. The chert was mostly patinated fragments or, more rarely, flakes of abraded 'Middle Stone Age' type. Sometimes fresh quartzite flakes were used but more generally the fragments are typical fire-fracture, concavo-convex heat spalls. The utilized and fractured areas are always quite fresh and unpatinated. Four types of these informal tools can be recognized:

(i) NOTCHED AND STEEP SCRAPERS (Plate 32: 1–4, 6, 7, and 9)
These are in quartzite and chert and the fractures resulting from use are always fresh showing, if the material is chert, the natural blue-black or green colour. The edge, however, may sometimes be dulled by use. Except for the formation of notches, there has been no attempt at intentional shaping of the specimen and it is apparent that controlled percussion flaking to improve the shape was a technique unknown to the users. As is to be expected in totally unskilled stone working, the edges are steep.

These tools may have been used to smooth down wooden shafts for spears, bow staves, throwing clubs and similar tools and weapons in every day demand, for such is still their use today. An elderly resident of Mkamba village gave a demonstration of the use of stone for this purpose and of other techniques besides, in the course of manufacturing a bow stave (Clark, 1958*b*). Today, bottle glass is used in preference to stone; metal files are rarely seen in the Kalambo Falls villages. Any sharp piece of stone was used and informants stated that, if no naturally sharp pieces were available, stone was broken thermally.

(ii) FRAGMENTS AND FLAKES WITH CHIPPED EDGES (Plates 31: 1–3, 7–9; 32: 5)
These may have been cutting tools. Two 'Later Stone Age' microlithic flakes derived from the immediately underlying horizon showed fresher serration of the edges indicating that they may have been used as saws.

(iii) FRAGMENTS WITH RUBBED AND DULLED EDGES (Plate 31: 4, 6)
These vary in size from small fragments to split sandstone pebble sections which have had one or more edges or an end rubbed smooth by use. Such stones might have been used for scraping skins to remove the fat before curing.

(iv) MISCELLANEOUS
This category includes an irregular fragment of hard quartzite used as a chopper (Plate 31: 5); the broken upper half of an edge-ground axe of dolerite, most probably derived from the immediately underlying 'Later Stone Age' horizon (Plate 34: 2) and a spherical, dolerite grindstone sharpener (Plate 32:

15). However, since this was the only specimen of its kind found in the excavations and it came from the surface at Site B, it is possible that it may be more recent and of Lungu origin. A small, truncated, near-ellipsoidal pebble with concave grooving on the truncated face (Plate 32: 8) was recovered from the Chiungu Member clays in the A1 excavation. It is difficult to know to what use such a tool can have been put.

(h) **Pigment** (28) (Plates 31: 10; 32: 13)

This includes both white clay and haematite for red ochre. Some of the specimens have rubbed facets and it would seem probable that the paint was mixed with oil and used on the body – a practice widespread in the Nyasa–Tanganyika Corridor in earlier times.

(i) **Natural stones** (858)

This constitutes by far the largest group of stone material from the settlement site and must all have been carried in. Since many show heat spalling and have been broken, it is possible that they were hearth stones, while others could have been used as foundation supports.

(j) **'Later Stone Age' artifacts** (257, Site C, 1963, only)

In addition to the edge-ground axe fragment referred to under (*g*) (iv) above, each of the shaft complexes produced microlithic factory waste and an occasional microlith. These were derived from the top of the buff sand through which the shafts had been dug and, with the debris of the Iron Age midden, formed part of the soil filling of the shafts.

(k) **Iron slag** (1956) (Plates 78 and 89)

This was ubiquitous throughout the Iron Age levels in all the excavations and, in most cases, only a representative sample was retained. It is less common in the lowest part of the channel and swamp clays of the Chiungu Member at Sites A and B. It usually occurs as small, irregular pieces approximately one inch (25·4 mm) in greatest length and, except where oxidized, preserves a smooth, glossy black exterior. Occasional, larger pieces were recovered and of special interest was the bloom from the complete base of a small furnace, 1 foot 6 inches (45 cm) across and 8 inches (20·3 cm) high. It has a flattish top with a convex underside conforming to a shallow, saucer-shaped depression that must have been present in the floor of the furnace (see the description of Complex 10 on p. 29).

A sample of Kalambo Falls Industry slag from the red clays from the 1956 excavation at Site A1, was analysed by the Geological Survey, Lusaka, with the following result:

$S:O_2$ %	Fe_2O_3 %	Fe %	CaO + MgO %
19·2	74·7	52·2	2·8

Lab. Rep. No. 1397/1401, dated 7 January 1961.

A sample of the bloom associated with shaft complex no. 10 from the settlement at Site C gave the following results:

	Iron metal (Fe) %	or	Iron oxide (Fe_2O_3) %
Slag	53·1		73·3
Sands	1·3		1·7

Lab. Rep. No. 1874, dated 25 March 1964.

The two samples agree closely in iron metal and iron oxide composition. The sands are typical reddened surface sands of immediately local derivation.

(l) **Tuyère pipe fragments** (203) (Plate 90)

No complete tuyères were found, although several substantial sections and many smaller pieces were recovered from all depths in the Iron Age deposits. Except for one fragment, all appear to come from parallel-sided, cylindrical pipes, the end that was facing the interior of the furnace showing a mass of vitreous slag and fused silica. Some of the fragments show parallel veinings in the interior, indicating that they were made on a stick in the way that most central African Bantu-speaking iron-workers make their tuyères (Plate 28: 4, 6). These are generally considered to be tuyères for use with smelting furnaces similar to the larger types built until recently (Plates 63, 64).

One large fragment of tuyère from the settlement area on Site C – the exception referred to above – shows tapering sides and a splayed or bell-shaped lower end (Plate 28: 5). This kind of tuyère is more generally used with small furnaces or to protect the bellows of the smith. This particular specimen is fired to a brick red colour while many of the parallel-sided tuyères have been fired to an even buff or white. This colour difference may have resulted from the use of different types of clay or, perhaps, anthill, in the manufacture of the tuyères or from a variation in the amount of heat induced in the furnace.

(m) **Daga** (1153) (Plate 90)

Again, this material was common in all Iron Age levels although the fragments rarely exceeded 2 inches (50·8 mm) in length. Pieces came from two kinds of structures: one group preserved the impressions of sticks or poles which showed that they came from a living hut or a storage bin, one side of the fragment being smooth and the other showing the 'wattle' marks (e.g. Plate 90). The other group is not nearly so common and was best seen at Site C in the settlement, 1963. These are pieces of *daga* one inch (25·4 mm) or more thick, smooth on both faces and gently curved. They may have come from the type of food storage pot that is still used today by the Valley Tonga (Reynolds, 1968: 19–20), and made by the Kisi on the lake shore at the foot of the Livingstone Mountains (personal observation). Alternatively, they may, perhaps, have formed part of a wall of a smelting or refining furnace.

Faunal remains

Buffalo, cane rat and the smaller antelope are all hunted and eaten today by Bantu-speakers and, with other wild game, they provide an important supplementary source of meat to that supplied by domestic animals. The acid nature of the soil in the local basin has generally precluded the survival of bone and those specimens that can be associated with the earlier Iron Age are minimal.

SITE A

A small number of unidentifiable fragments were recovered from the A2 excavation at a depth of 1 to 2 feet (30–61 cm) in the red, sandy loam of the hill slope. In 1966 a further unidentifiable fragment was found in the grey–brown soil of the A7 excavation at a depth of 1 foot to 1 foot 6 inches (30–45 cm) in grid square B-2 and, in the red brown loam below this at a depth of 2 feet 10 inches (86·4 cm) in grid square B-3, occurred parts of four molar teeth and two fragments of long bone from a large bovid associated with characteristic channel-decorated pottery. These have been identified by C. K. Brain as from the lower jaw of a young adult buffalo; all probably from the same individual. Since this was only a small, trial excavation, the prospects would seem to be good for recovering more bone with the Kalambo Falls Industry in this area.

A very few fragments of shell, probably *Unio* sp. were found. One piece of burnt shell occurred at a depth of 5 feet 6 inches (1·7 m) in the grey, silty clay of the Older Channel Fill (F-7) at Site A, 1956 and further fragments were found in the hillslope soil at Site A, 1966 (see p. 48).

SITE B

A little, very fragmentary fauna was found in 1959 in the top one foot (30 cm) of the grey sand of the B2 excavation. Although this is probably to be associated with the Lungu rather than with the Early Iron Age occupation, the possibilities of finding identifiable bone with the Kalambo Falls Industry are better than was thought at first, in view of the bone fragments recovered from the shaft of Complex 4 in the 1963 excavations at Site C.

The following species have been identified by C. K. Brain, R. F. Ewer and B. M. Fagan: Cane rat (*Thrynomys swiderianus*) two mandibles, a maxilla and limb fragments; Black backed jackal (*Canis* cf. *mesomelas*) two mandibles; and, possibly, domestic cattle (*Bos taurus*) molars, the proximal end of a radius and other limb bone fragments.

Cane rat is still present in the basin and is a sought-after item of food with the inhabitants. The black backed jackal is not yet recorded from Zambia, previous identifications now being referred to *Canis adustus* (Ansell, 1960: 111). It occurs, however, in Tanzania and it is possible that the Kalambo Falls lie near the southern limit of the range of the east African form. Ewer, who has examined the Kalambo Falls specimens, confirms that they are not *Canis adustus*. If the bovid remains are of domestic cattle and not buffalo, they may imply that the local basin at the Kalambo Falls was for a time free from the tsetse fly that at present precludes the keeping of cattle there.

SITE C

Cranial and mandibular fragments of Blue Duiker or Sharp's grysbuck were recovered from the shaft of Complex 5 (see p. 27).

This completes the description of the finds that can be associated with the makers of the Kalambo Falls Industry and in the following chapter an attempt will be made to reconstruct the culture of which these finds represent only the more imperishable material part.

Report on chemical tests on Iron Age soil samples from the Kalambo Falls

BY SHERBURNE F. COOK[1]

The tests for phosphorus and calcium performed on the 18 samples taken from the Iron Age midden and shaft Complex no. 11 at the Kalambo Falls Site C, 1963 in northern Zambia, give us an unusual opportunity to study on a microscale the value of such analysis in determining the extent and type of human occupation. Ordinarily, chemical investigation embraces large areas, such as a village, or even a province; here we are concerned with only one small area. Was, or was not a body buried in what appears to have been a grave? The answer may lie in the vertical and horizontal distribution of the two elements most likely to have been deposited by the decomposition of a human body: phosphorus and calcium.

Three consecutive series of samples were taken. The first (5 samples) extended from the surface of the ground through the midden to a depth of 48 inches (1·2 m). The second started at the east side of

TABLE 9. *Chemical tests on Iron Age soil samples from the Kalambo Falls*

Sample no.	Position	% phosphorus	% calcium	Ca/P ratio
	Series 1 – Midden series			
1	Line B/C 4, ground level	0·061	0·057	0·934
2	Line B/C 4, 12 inches (30 cm)	0·066	0·009	0·136
3	Line B/C 4, 24 inches (61 cm)	0·032	0·007	0·218
4	Line B/C 4, 36 inches (91 cm)	0·017	0·006	0·352
5	Line B/C 4, 48 inches (1·2 m)	0·013	0·007	0·538
	Series 2 – Pit no. 11, horizontal series			
6	East side of shaft, 51 inches (1·3 m) below surface of ground	0·015	0·007	0·466
7	3 inches (7·6 cm) outside east wall of shaft	0·014	0·006	0·428
8	In the east side of shaft	0·049	0·049	1·000
9	In the centre of the shaft	0·042	0·082	1·952
10	At the west edge of the shaft	0·021	0·007	0·333
11	Outside the west wall of the shaft	0·015	0·009	0·600
	Series 3 – Pit no. 11, vertical series			
12	At centre and top of shaft, 36 inches (91 cm) below surface of ground	0·094	0·144	0·531
13	12 inches (30 cm) below no. 12; 48 inches (1·2 m) below surface	0·046	0·084	1·826
14	24 inches (61 cm) below no. 12; 60 inches (1·5 m) below surface	0·028	0·051	1·821
15	36 inches (91 cm) below no. 12; 72 inches (1·8 m) below surface	0·058	0·024	0·413
16	48 inches (1·2 m) below no. 12; 84 inches (2·1 m) below surface	0·044	0·037	0·840
17	60 inches (1·5 m) below no. 12; 96 inches (2·4 m) below surface	0·035	0·013	0·371
18	68 inches (1·7 m) below no. 12; 104 inches (2·6 m) below surface	0·018	0·002	0·111

[1] Professor of Physiology, University of California, Berkeley. Acknowledgement for financial assistance is made by the writer to the Nationa Science Foundation, grant no. G-16112.

Complex no. 11, crossed horizontally through its centre and ended beyond its west wall (6 samples). The third started at the centre and at the top of the shaft and extended downward at 12 inch (30 cm) intervals (7 samples) to a depth of 104 inches (2·6 m) below the surface of the ground, or a depth of 68 inches (1·7 m) below the top of the shaft. The tests were carried out according to the customary methods of soil analysis and the results expressed as per cent of the element by weight in the sample.

The first series (see Table 9) shows a relatively high concentration of phosphorus and calcium at the surface (due, probably, to the activity of the local plant cover), diminishing sharply with depth. This is entirely in conformity with the normal distribution of these elements, as seen in soil studies throughout the world. It also establishes the expected level of phosphorus at about 0·015 per cent and of calcium at 0·007 per cent in the subsoil in the area where the shaft occurs. The second series shows the normal quantity of both elements as existing to the east and to the west of the walls of the shaft. However, the values rise to many times the normal levels at and in the shaft itself. The third series starts with a very high concentration of both calcium and phosphorus at the centre and top of the shaft, falling steadily and significantly on descending by 12 inch (30 cm) intervals, until the concentrations reach the minimum values found in the first and second series.

The high concentrations of calcium and phosphorus in and around the shaft can be explained as due to the former presence of a human body. Any other source of such quantities would be very difficult to find, but a human body could have supplied the amounts found, particularly from the bones. Incidentally, there is evidence of some downward leaching. The high, but diminishing values which persist to a depth of 96 inches (2·4 m) may safely be ascribed to movement of calcium and phosphorus from a body, rather than to any increments originating at the surface of the ground.

If the percentages of calcium and of phosphorus in the second and third series are correlated with each other, the magnitude of r, $+0{\cdot}83$, indicates a high degree of significance. In turn a common source in the ground is implied for the two elements. The calcium–phosphorus ratio is low (less than 1·0) for all those samples not in immediate contact with, or directly below the shaft, whereas it is higher (1·0–2·0) at and just below the burial. A low ratio is normal and expected for undisturbed soil of the sandy, acid type found in this area. A high ratio implies a compound of the two elements such as tricalcium phosphate, or the spatite fraction of bone.

The evidence is, therefore, very strong that the shaft under consideration is a grave that once contained a human body and that the body has decomposed and disintegrated physically since burial, leaving *in situ* a substantial residue of calcium and phosphorus.

April 1964

CHAPTER 3

Iron Age occupation at the Kalambo Falls: interpretation and reconstruction

Radiocarbon dates show that the makers of the Kalambo Falls Industry appear to have arrived in the valley about A.D. 300 and to have remained in possession for 600, perhaps even for 1000 years. While the lower limit of the occupation can be shown to be fairly accurately defined by radiocarbon dating, further dates are needed to determine the upper limit (see Volume I, Appendix J).

Charcoals from near the base (9 feet 6 inches to 10 feet (2·9–3 m) of the 'Older Channel' fill of the Chiungu Member at Site A, date to A.D. 550 (L-395C 1400 ± 150). Another sample from a depth of 6 feet 6 inches to 7 feet (1·9–2·1 m) in these clays dates to A.D. 870 (L-395B 1080 ± 180). From the same site at a depth of 3 feet 6 inches to 4 feet (107 cm–1·2 m) charcoal from weathered, red-brown clays with Kalambo Falls Industry pottery, dates to A.D. 890 (L-395A 970 ± 150). At Site B, a sample from the B2 excavation at a depth of 7 feet (2·1 m) in the 'Older Channel' fill, dates to A.D. 1020 (GrN-3580 930 ± 40). A second sample from this excavation at a depth of 2 to 3 feet (61–91 cm) from the base of the red clays of the 'Younger Channel' fill give a date of A.D. 1580 (GrN-3189 370 ± 50), though, due to the known variation in C14 content of the atmosphere during this time, an age of about A.D. 1350 is also possible. Since, however, these clays contain only rare channel-decorated sherds and they are lithologically similar to those at Site A1 which cut out the grey and grey-brown clays and clay sands of the 'Older Channel' fill where most of the pottery occurs, they are considered to post-date the Kalambo Falls Industry. If this is so then this Early Iron Age tradition had already been replaced by the end of the sixteenth century A.D.

The best dating evidence comes from the shaft complexes at the Site C settlement area where charcoals from Shafts 11 and 8 have given results of A.D. 430 (GrN-4647 1520 ± 40 B.P.) and A.D. 345 (GrN-4646 1605 ± 40 B.P.) respectively. All these results show good agreement and indicate that the makers of the Kalambo Falls Industry were settled in the local basin at the Kalambo Falls by the middle, if not the beginning of the fourth century A.D. or perhaps later. As yet, as has been noted, we have little knowledge of the culture of the peoples who followed but we may know more about this when more extensive excavations have been carried out in the camp area at Site A.

The Early Iron Age inhabitants probably lived in villages composed of a number of extended family units, as the present Lungu population do today and two such settlement areas (represented by Sites B, C and D on the 30 foot (9·1 m) terrace and Site A on the southern flank of the valley) are known. The settlements overlooked the swampy central part of the basin and the rubbish from the villages spilled down the banks and became incorporated in the stream channels and swamp. When these communities first arrived, the floor of the valley and the water level were several feet higher than they are today and continued to rise for approximately a further 12 feet (3·7 m) due, presumably, to the blocking of the spillway gorge. The extent of the settlement areas cannot yet be estimated except to say that the one on the remnant of the 30 foot (9·1 m) terrace centred on Site C must have covered at least 9·4 acres (3·8 hectares).

There is, as yet, no evidence to show that these settlements were defended by a stockade and ditch or in any other way, and everything points to their having been peaceful communities of cultivators who probably lived a semi-independent existence under their own headman or group of elders.

The only other Early Iron Age open settlements in Zambia and Malawi for which it is possible to obtain a very approximate estimate of the extent of the occupied area are Kamnana in the Eastern Province of Zambia – 12·36 acres (5 hectares) (Phillipson,

1971) and Nkope – 39·54 acres (16 ha) (Robinson, 1970: 16), Phopo Hill – more than 1·74 acres (0·7 ha) (Robinson and Sandelowsky, 1968: 114) and Mwavarambo (several acres) (Robinson, 1966: 185) in Malawi. The depth of occupation is generally shallow – 1 foot (30 cm) at Nkope but deeper at the Kalambo Falls site and at Phopo Hill where some 31·5 inches (79 cm) of midden was found. It is of interest that the thickness of the occupation layer was greater where the available area was limited by natural features: the river cliffs in the case of the Kalambo Falls site and the hill and stream in the case of Phopo Hill. In contrast, Nkope is an open, lake shore site and Kamnana is on the bank of a dambo. In general, depth of midden suggests more intensive occupation at the Kalambo Falls and Phopo Hill and, if it was the custom of the Early Iron Age communities to rebuild on the same site, the greater depth of occupation debris might be only a reflection of the more limited acreage available at these two sites.

Of interest in this connection is the method of fixed cultivation traditional to the Nyakyusa and Ngonde peoples. Wilson (1958: 15) records that this was preferably on old village sites, where also the new village was built every generation – not on the identical but on an overlapping site. In this way the same site was used for generations. Cultivation was by the *matuta* and *fyungu* methods of parallel ridges and mounds (see Sutton, 1969: 4–8) and the disturbance to the topsoil caused by the construction of these ridges, *c.* 1 foot 6 inches (45 cm) high, would effectively destroy evidence of most features surviving from former village sites. The same would be the case with the form of grass mound cultivation practised by the Lungu and Mambwe on the Zambian plateau (see pp. 5–6). The absence of features or definite horizons, which is a common condition at Early Iron Age sites, might, therefore, be the outcome of a similar pattern of settlement and cultivation.

If the area excavated at Site C is typical, dwellings may have been generally insubstantial for, if the huts had been as permanent as those in use in the valley today, evidence of post holes or shallow trenches should have been preserved in the underlying, sterile buff sand, unless these had later been destroyed by cultivation. They are nowhere found except for the shallow trench circling some of the shaft complexes noted above. If the *daga* area and stone surround found in the clays of the A1 excavation (see p. 9) is indeed a field hut or shelter floor, then the diameter was little more than 4 feet (1·2 m) and the structure was of insubstantial material – withies and thatch, for example – with no wall plaster. However, the diameter of the circular *daga* covered area in the D-3/F-3 grid squares of the Site C settlement excavation, is *c.* 8 feet (2·4 m) and suggests a different type of structure. Unfortunately, it was not possible to determine whether the *daga* had been applied on the inner, outer, or both sides of the wooden framework. Since there is no discernible mark of trenching or post holes, the dwellings could have been rather similar to those at one time in common use among the peoples of southern or western Tanzania in the earlier years of the century, and still to be found in parts of the Ufipa highlands. This type of dwelling is reported as still having been occasionally built in the 1930s by the Nyiha in Ufipa (Popplewell, 1937) and by the Ha (Moffett, 1939) north of the Malagarasi river.

In 1966, the writer observed two different kinds of traditional hut still in use in Ufipa west of Sumbawanga and was able to arrange for and record the construction of similar huts at the Kalambo Falls, the details of which will be published elsewhere. These dwellings were built by two elderly brothers in their seventies who had recently come to settle in the valley from Ufipa. Both dwellings are traditional forms in the Ufipa highlands although they have been largely replaced today by the vertical walled hut of pole and *daga* with conical or gabled roof.

The commoner form of the two was the *tutu* hut[1] – circular in plan and beehive in section, made of a number of thin, pliable branches that are bent over and secured at both ends in the ground (Plate 61). To these are lashed horizontal rails or ribs of similar branches, this framework then being completely thatched with grass down to ground level where the lower ends are buried in a shallow trench 2 to 3 inches (50·8–76·2 mm) deep. The diameter of the floor space varies with the wishes of the builder – the example built for us had a diameter of 9 feet (2·7 m) and was 6 feet (1·8 m) high at the centre. During the rains the thatch will be plastered over with *daga* by the women, except for a small area at the apex and such a hut is said to remain serviceable for five years and is very simple to construct.

The second type is the *mwende* hut which is built either as protection against lions or to keep out the cold (Plate 62). It is constructed by the men who set

[1] This type of hut is also known by the name *ipala*. It is possible that the name *tutu* derives from that of a group of hunters, the WaTutu, related to the Pimbwe, living in Ufipa. This group turned to raiding and occupied Kasanga for a time in 1874 (Foran, 1937: 147).

a number of short poles close together in a circle leaning inwards so as to come together at the apex some 5 feet 6 inches (1·7 m) above the centre of the floor space, so that the section is triangular. The lower ends of the poles rest in shallow holes dug into the ground and the upper ends are tied together with bark string. The example built for us had a six foot (1·8 m) diameter floor space and sixty-six poles were used. The floor was dug down a few inches with a hoe so that it was slightly below the outside ground level. Any gaps between the poles were filled in with thinner poles and the whole outer face was then covered with supple branches or grass. Earth was then thrown up against the walls for two thirds of their height and the remaining one third was thatched. I was informed that, as an alternative to earth, *daga* may be used to seal the outside of the hut. There is a specially constructed doorway and door made of individual slats of wood. The *mwende* hut as built by the Nyiha in the Ufipa highlands is illustrated by Lechaptois (1932) (see Plate 62).

Both *tutu* and *mwende* types of hut can be shown to have been widely distributed formerly in the corridor country between Lakes Tanganyika and Malawi. As *chitutu* (or *senje*) and *toro* respectively, they were in regular use among the Phoka of the Livingstonia and Nyika plateaux (Robinson and Sandelowsky, 1968: 121). It can further be seen that the *tutu*, at least, was very widely spread in central and southern Africa in the past where it is known from Rhodesia, on the one hand from an eleventh century archaeological context (Robinson, 1968) and, on the other hand, from sites in northeast (Luembe river, Dundo district) and also southwest Angola where it has been observed by the writer as still in use for a temporary dwelling by the people of the Huila plateau. Monica Wilson informs me that similar beehive huts were also in use among the Nguni peoples in southeast Africa up to the last century, and that they still appear every season for boys' initiation shelters in the Transkei and the Ciskei. The now unpopular *minkunka* hut made by the Ambo of the Luangwa valley, is built of poles, like the *mwende* hut, bound with withies and covered with grass (Stefaniszyn, 1964: 25). In southwest Angola the Himba use the *mwende* hut (Lopes Cardoso, 1967) and a modified form is used by the Lambya north of Nyale in Chitipa district of northern Malawi, and also by the Bisa/Bemba in the Muchinga escarpment near the Chitambo Mission in northern Zambia (personal observation). Goats are kept in unplastered *mwende* type huts in southwest Angola (A. Cruz, *in lit*,) and in the Gwembe valley (Reynolds, 1968: 21–3). Robinson (1966) also has clear evidence for this type of hut from a thirteenth century context Early Iron Age village site near Karonga in the Malawi Rift.

The branch and pole impressions of the fragments of *daga* preserved in the Chiungu Member of the Kalambo Falls Formation and the absence of any deep post holes or clear disturbance of the ground in the settlement area suggest that a structure of the *tutu* and also, though less certainly, of the *mwende* form of hut, was in general use by the makers of the Kalambo Falls Industry in the local basin. Huts with vertical walls and a steep, conical roof, like those built by the Safwa (Kootz-Kretschmer, 1929: 168) would have left more extensive evidence in the record. Hut floors at the Site C settlement were not made of specially puddled clay, though that of the hearth area became fired and hardened; but clay was used, presumably both for hut walls and for grain storage containers. There were no fragments that might have come from grain storage bins with a coiled grass frame, like those made by the modern Lungu. If large bins were constructed, they must have had a withy frame but smaller, thick-walled, clay jars may also have been made.

The large grindstones, typical of those found with early food-producing cultures, show that the inhabitants were cultivators. The small number of bun-type rubbers or grindstone sharpeners and the absence of dish querns, seem to suggest, however, that the settlements never remained long in one place since, if they had done so, the grindstones should show signs of more extensive use, as do the deep dish querns for sorghum on the early Tonga sites on the southern plateau of Zambia (Fagan *et al.* 1969, Plate 126). The suitability of the site and the time scale established by excavation show, however, that the Site C settlement area must have been occupied for a long time. This apparent anomaly can be explained if finger millet was the cereal most extensively grown, as it still is today in this area. This crop is not ground on a grindstone but may either be pounded in the gardens with a short pestle in a mortar that consists of a cylindrical hole let into the ground near one side of the threshing floor and lined with clay (Plate 95), or else in a wooden mortar back at the village. The grindstones found with the Kalambo Falls Industry more closely resemble the thinner, slab-like stones used by a number of Bantu-speaking peoples for preparing relishes, both vegetable and animal, as well as for grinding pigment and may, therefore, have been used for a similar purpose.

No carbonised food remains were found nor were any grain impressions seen on the potsherds examined. The crops grown cannot have differed greatly from the present-day crops of the region, except for the introduced American and Asiatic food plants. They would probably, therefore, have consisted of finger millet (*Eleusine corocana*), perhaps sorghum (*Sorghum caffrorum*), Livingstone potato (*Plectranthus* (*Coleus*) *esculentus*), cow-peas (*Vigna unguiculata*), ground beans (*Voandziaea subterranea*), perhaps sesame (*Sesamum orientale*), palm oil (*Elaeis guineensis*), cucumbers (*Cucumis* sp.) and gourds (*Lagenaria vulgaris*), the presence of the last named being attested by the presence of gourd-shaped pottery vessels (Plates 8: 5; 10: 7).[1] Moreover, many kinds of wild vegetable relishes and other foods would have been collected and eaten. Some of these, still available and used in the valley today, are listed at Appendix G of Volume I.[2] It may be expected that some system of crop rotation was practised within the confines of the Kalambo Falls local basin and both flat gardens for millet and sorghum on the higher slopes and mound and pit gardens for Livingstone potatoes on the edge of the swamp, were probably made.

In the virtual absence of faunal remains, it is not possible to know what domestic stock may have been owned although cattle are recorded from Kapwirimbwe in a fifth century context (Phillipson, 1968*b*) and sheep/goat from the ninth century mound settlement at Isamu Pati (Fagan, 1967: 681), both these in southern Zambia. Among the bone from the surface levels on Site B, 1959, domestic ox is tentatively identified, but the remains are too fragmentary to be certain. Even if the identification is confirmed by further finds it does not necessarily mean that cattle were kept in the basin by the Kalambo Falls Industry makers. Fly precludes their presence there today, but some of the local inhabitants keep cattle in Ufipa and will ocasionally bring an animal down to the valley to slaughter. Tradition among the Mwika peoples of the Corridor indicates that their original stock consisted of sheep and goats and that they obtained cattle only after they had acquired their chiefs in the sixteenth century or later. The Safwa seem to have been hunters pure and simple and the Nyiha in Ufipa were also renowned hunters, living mainly by this means. The Kinga, however, and probably some of the other Nyiha also, owned cattle as well as small stock before the coming of the Nyakyusa chiefs in the fifteenth century.

It seems likely that the makers of the Kalambo Falls Industry kept some small stock, including the domestic fowl[3] but, even if they also had cattle, they must, like all the Corridor peoples, still have obtained the greater part of their meat by hunting. Their weapons were the bow and arrow and a light spear, the knife, and no doubt also, a wooden throwing club. The Safwa used hunting nets, the Nyiha in the grasslands of the Ufipa plateau preferred to drive the game by firing grass (Popplewell, 1937) and both these methods, as well as hunting with dogs, could have been available to the Early Iron Age population at the Kalambo Falls. Traps of various kinds can be expected to have been in regular use and honey would have been important as a food source and for beer. Small fish were probably caught by poisoning or in earth dams by women using drag and plunge baskets, or by dragging a festoon-like bundle of reeds and creepers through the shallow water (Stefaniszyn, 1964: 89).

Hunting was of much greater importance in pre- and early colonial times than it is today since many areas have now been denuded of all but very small game. The quantity of large and small game of many

[1] Carbonized remains of sorghum (*Sorghum* cf. *caffrorum*) have been found at Ivuna in the Rukwa Rift in a horizon dated to A.D. 1425±100 and domestic ox, goat, dog and fowl also occur in the earliest horizons here dating to A.D. 1235±100 (Fagan and Yellen, 1968: 12, 13). Sorghum, and, possibly, *Pennisetum typhoides* were identified from the Karonga Industry settlement at Mwamasapa's at the north end of Lake Malawi, dating to A.D. 1190±80 (Robinson, 1966: 180). Further south, cow-peas are reported from Nkope at the south end of the lake in an eighth-century context (Robinson, 1970: 121) and sorghum is also found at the Kalomo group site of Isamu Pati dating between the seventh and the thirteenth centuries, A.D. (Fagan, 1967: 681). At Inyanga in Rhodesia, ground beans, cowpeas, and a cucurbit are found in a ninth century Ziwa context and again with sorghum, bullrush millet and finger millet in a sixteenth century and later context (Summers, 1958: 175–7; 1967: 692).

[2] Extensive use is still made of wild relishes by the south central Bantu. The following examples are given since any or all of these would certainly have been used by the earlier Iron Age population. Those collected by the Ushi in Fort Rosebery district include 39 species of edible mushrooms, numerous insects, especially 19 edible caterpillars, more than 20 different varieties of fruit, especially *mpundu* (*Parinarii mobola*), *masuku* (*Uapaca kirkiana*) and *mfungo* (*Anisophylleae* sp.), various roots and numerous edible beans, some herbs (mainly medicinal) and honey (Kay, 1964: 51–4). Among the Ambo of the Luangwa valley, leaves of 16 wild plants, 13 edible mushrooms, 8 insects, caterpillars, grubs and flying ants, 5 roots and some 26 wild fruits are collected and eaten (Stefaniszyn, 1964: 46–51). The Valley Tonga in the middle reaches of the Gwembe (Middle Zambezi) valley, similarly make regular use of collected wild foods, in particular leaf relishes of which 18 are listed by Scudder (1962: 204–5). The same authority cites also 7 species of flowers and fruits and one species each of tubers and mushrooms, also honey, pigs, small rodents, termites, caterpillars and grasshoppers, land and water turtles.

[3] Present at Isamu Pati and Kalundu on the Tonga plateau in first millennium contexts (Fagan, 1967: 681) also at Ivuna (Fagan and Yellen, 1968).

different kinds that abounded in the plateau country up to the early years of the present century accounts for the emphasis placed upon hunting in tribal tradition, the special place and respect reserved for the hunter in the village community, the number of hunters' shrines and the highly prized nature of wild meat. The indications are, thus, that a great deal more of a man's time was spent on hunting than is the case today and that, indeed, most of the meat eaten was the produce of the chase.

Methods used, with or without the aid of dogs, covered individual hunting with bow and arrows; driving of game, either by individuals or by firing the grass, towards a group of hunters armed with bows and arrows or spears and clubs with, perhaps, nets; driving elephants towards trees from which, as they passed beneath, they were speared by hunters already hidden in the branches; bird lime and traps of several different kinds – pit traps, fall traps for large and medium sized animals, spring traps for medium and small animals, nooses for small animals and birds. These methods would have ensured a regular supply of wild meat for any village in the Corridor country.

The time spent in hunting activities would naturally vary with the season and the composition of the wild fauna of the area. Quantitative data on hunters and collectors as, for example, among the Bushmen (Lee, 1968) and Hadza (Woodburn, 1968*a*), indicate that much less time is spent on hunting than used to be thought and that a community will account for less than fifty large animals in a year. The habitats in which these people now survive are impoverished in comparison with the many more favourable ones in southern Africa now occupied by Bantu-speakers and it is to be expected that the Early Iron Age cultivators of the Zambian plateau and southern Tanzania, using spears and arrows with iron heads, exploited the wild meat resources to a considerably greater degree, even though such hunts were still on a small scale and unlike the large organized *chila* drives of the Ila when over two hundred buffalo may be killed in one day's hunt (Read, 1951: 66) or the *maonga* fence drives of the Lozi which, in one day, accounted for over five hundred wildebeeste and other game (Cambell, 1950: 21).

Little or no reliable data exist that could provide even an approximate estimate of the amount of time a young man would have spent in hunting activities in pre-colonial times or on the numbers of the male population who engaged in hunting. Tradition, ritual and the respect paid to hunters generally, suggest that the professional hunters in any one community may have been few in number; many more, in fact all, the young males would have engaged in driving and communal hunting activities. Possibly some estimate may be arrived at on the basis of information collected by Kay from Chief Kalaba's (Ushi) village in Fort Rosebery district in 1959–60 (Kay, 1964: 68).

The Ushi are essentially cultivators and not cattle-keeping people, because of the presence of tsetse, while sheep, goats and chickens, though present, are not numerous. The working time of the young men was divided between miscellaneous activities (domestic chores, food preparation, craft industry and building) 34·5 per cent, agriculture 39·9 per cent, collecting 1·8 per cent, fishing 2·4 per cent, paid employment 13·5 per cent and hunting 8·4 per cent. Assuming that hunting activities would increase and others (e.g. domestic chores and food preparation) would decrease if the larger animals were there to hunt, it might be suggested that the time spent on miscellaneous activities could be halved and the other half of that devoted to hunting. Since also, in pre-colonial times, there was no paid employment as such, a young man would, at a minimum estimate, have spent over 10 per cent of his time hunting and he may well, in individual cases where choice and skill were deciding factors, have devoted over 40 per cent of his time to hunting activities of one kind or another for both large and small game.

No doubt, also, some very variable amount of time would have been spent on fighting and warfare though, except in cases where the tribal organization was on a para-military basis, inter-group fighting is not likely to have interfered seriously with hunting and agriculture. Time spent on collecting and fishing for both men and women is not likely to have varied very much except that, if the agricultural technology and range of plants was less efficient or complete than it is today, less time might have been devoted to agriculture and more to collecting. Such an assumption is not too far off the mark and, using Kay's figures for the percentage distribution of work done by all adult members of the village as a basis (and discounting the time spent in paid employment which would not apply to the earlier community) it may be suggested that for the earlier Iron Age cultivators living in the *Brachystegia* savanna of south central Africa and not extensively engaged in stock raising, the working time may have had some approximation to that set out in the following table:

Category of work	Chief Kalaba's village: Adults (46)	Chief Kalaba's village: Young men (13)	Hypothetical equivalent: earlier Iron Age community All adults
Miscellaneous activities	46·4	34·5	39·8
Agriculture	40·6	39·9	40·6
Collecting	4·6	1·3	4·6
Fishing	4·3	2·4	4·3
Hunting	1·6	8·4	10·7

The traditional clothing, like that of the Mwika (Wilson, 1958: 25) and Safwa (Kootz-Kretschmer, 1929: 101) must surely have been skins which were scraped clean with a stone – the Safwa method (Kootz-Kretschmer, 1929: 184). The absence of spindle whorls shows that weaving was unknown.

The white and red pigment was probably used for decorating the body. White was much used as a body paint by the Corridor peoples until recent times, both for ceremonial occasions and for identification in war (Kootz-Kretschmer, 1929: 108).[1] It would have been prepared with pestles and rubbers on flat grindstones. The only evidence of personal ornaments that has survived is arm and/or leg rings, finger or toe rings and a copper earring. The absence of any imported glass beads or other exotic trade goods implies that the area lay outside any regular trade routes to and from the coast but the presence of copper ornaments is evidence of local trade, perhaps with the Katanga, where copper was extensively worked in the eighth and ninth centuries. It should be noted also that one occurrence of Early Iron Age pottery with dimple bases is recorded from the southern Kasai (Nenquin, 1959). The most likely route by which the copper could have reached the Kalambo Falls is across the Tanganyika plateau north of Lake Bangweulu and across the Luapula. The only other area from which the copper might have come is a small copper deposit in the extreme north of Malawi in Chitipa district. Relations with this area are suggested by the pumice fragment from Shaft Complex No. 11. Pumice is, of course, an excellent burnishing agent for iron or steel.

The absence of shell beads is somewhat surprising and may be explained either by the possibility that the customary form of adornment was strips of hide or bands of woven grass or, perhaps, that the acid soil has destroyed the shells – only one small fragment of *Unio* shell was found in any of the deposits in the valley (see p. 54).

Each household would have used baskets of various kinds and large and small globular and shouldered pots and bowls would have served for storing water and beer, or for drinking and cooking. The pottery is well made, though on the whole, poorly preserved in the swamp clays. Probably – although it is not possible to be certain – it was made by building from a lump of clay rather than by coiling. Building would seem to be a long established method in this part of the plateau. It was observed near the boundary of the Lungu and Tabwa country at the south end of Lake Tanganyika by Cameron in 1874 (Foran, 1937: 148) and is the method used by the Safwa (Kootz-Kretschmer, 1929: 183).

If the large globular and shouldered pots suggest water and beer storage, the numbers of both decorated and undecorated, wide-mouthed bowls suggest the importance in the economy of meat and other relishes and perhaps also of milk if domestic cattle or goats were kept.[2] In this connection it is of interest to note the dependance of the Nyakyusa and the Ngonde on milk and their skill as herdsmen (Wilson, 1958: 14).

No close parallel with present-day pottery is apparent in the Kalambo Falls Industry sherds. Certain minor points of resemblance to modern Lungu pottery have already been noted (pp. 44–5). The form of some of the Safwa pots is reminiscent of the shouldered and globular pots from the Kalambo Falls (Kootz-Kretschmer, 1929: Volume I, Plate 5; Volume II, Plate 5) but the only decoration I have seen on a Safwa pot consisted of finger impressions on the rim. Pottery with channelling on the neck has been found at Ivuna, a site where salt has been extracted for many centuries, near the southeast corner of Lake Rukwa, though it shows no close resemblance to that of the Kalambo Falls Industry (Fagan and Yellen, 1968). As might be expected, the pottery of the Kalambo Falls Industry is clearly, though distantly related to that of the Early Iron Age Sandaweland group from the salt pans by the mud 'volcanoes' at Uvinza in the valley of the Malagarasi in western Tanzania and the decorative motifs common to both have been described by Fagan (p. 42).

I have been unable to obtain details of Fipa pottery

[1] Nyakyusa also use black (charcoal), yellow (yellow earth) and red pigment, the last from a root traded from the Kinga (Wilson, 1964: 59).

[2] Among present-day peoples in Zambia and Malawi, the cooked relish is served for eating in shallow bowls and dishes. Deeper bowls are used for cooking relish and wide-mouthed pots for cooking porridge (*nsima*).

or of that of the Nyiha in the Ufipa highlands. However, while travelling by landrover between Lake Rukwa and Sumbawanga in 1966, we found a complete pot some six miles south of the village named Upper Muse, situated to the south again of the road up the Rukwa escarpment. The pot was half filled with dried *mpundu* fruits and had apparently been abandoned sometime prior to the previous rainy season. It is a shouldered, asymmetric pot with an everted rim and, although of inferior craftsmanship, is nevertheless of interest since it has a dimple base (Plate 93). The rim is not thickened but is obliquely flattened and in one place a shallow drawn line is present. An interrupted band of oblique incisions or impressions, perhaps done with a fingernail, is the only decoration of the neck. On the shoulder, an equally crude attempt at a chevron pattern has been made with a double pointed stick drawn over the clay when it was still wet. At one place is a horizontal line and, to the left of this, the chevron design passes over what looks like an older attempt at a decorative motif. The pot is made from a fine, gritty paste, well fired and crudely burnished on both surfaces. The dimple in the base, which has a diameter of 65 mm, is flattish and depressed 4 mm. The wear on the base of the pot round the circumference of the dimple shows that it had been in use for some time before it was discarded or lost.

Although, as an example of the potter's art, this specimen has little to commend it, its shape and the dimple at least suggest that it would be important for a study to be made of modern pottery of Ufipa, since the possibility exists that survivals of the channel-decorated pottery tradition may be present here. Local informants identified Karonga ware from sites near Karonga on the shore of Lake Malawi as 'Nyiha pottery'. Possibly, therefore, Karonga ware may later be found to be related to that of the Nyiha on the plateau (Robinson, 1966: 182). The Ivuna pottery components appear to show features in common – vessel forms, ribs and bosses, comb stamping (often in loops) on the neck and rim – with some of the later wares of northern Malawi (Fagan and Yellen, 1968; Robinson, 1966; Robinson and Sandelowsky, 1968). Since the first inhabitants of the Ivuna area are also said to have been Fipa (Fagan and Yellen, 1968: 29), the possibility should also be borne in mind that this tradition may have had a wide distribution in the corridor country after the beginning of the second millennium. At Ivuna also, the persistence of bevelling, rather crude channelling and meandering lines suggests a possible continuation in modified form of the Early Iron Age tradition as seen in the Kalambo Falls pottery after the beginning of the thirteenth century.

On the Tanzanian side of the river at the Kalambo Falls there are almost unlimited deposits of ferricrete that cap and cement the deposits of the 65 foot (19·8 m) terrace and this is probably the reason for what must have been a prosperous iron-working industry at the Kalambo Falls. There are two types of furnace in use by the Corridor peoples: the large, upright, permanent type with self-induced draught, 8 to 12 feet (2·4–3·7 m) high with internal diameter of 3 to 6 feet (0·9–1·8 m), as once used by the Fipa, Nyiha and Mambwe–Lungu (Greig, 1937; Cline, 1937); and the small type of furnace as typified by that formerly used by the Kinga and Lala (Plates 63–65). This stood 70 cm high with an internal diameter of 40 cm and was used for one smelting only and then broken down (Fülleborn, 1906: 166). Although the large furnace was in use at the Kalambo Falls in 1914 (Plate 63), it is not known when or from where it was introduced to the southern part of the central plateau. Since the chiefs of the Nyakyusa and other Corridor people are credited with introducing iron tools[1] it is possible that this large type of furnace is a sixteenth century introduction and that the original type was the small variety used by the Kinga and similar to one of the refining furnace forms used in Ufipa (Greig, 1937) and by the Mambwe (M. R. Kleindienst, personal communication). Alternatively, tall, upright furnaces could also have formed part of the iron technology of the Kalambo Falls Industry people since they are associated with dimple-based wares at two sites in Rwanda dated to A.D. ±100 and A.D. 300±80, respectively (Fagan, 1969*a*: 155). Judging by its size, the bloom from above Complex 10 might be the product of one of the larger kinds of furnace; its dimensions exceed those of the bloom obtained after an eight hour smelt in a small, upright furnace by Kaonde smiths at Solwezi in 1960.

Furnaces need not have been further from the village than the outskirts, for the taboos and ritual usually associated with iron smelting among tribal groups of Congo origin do not seem to have been so numerous or so strict among the Corridor people.

[1] The Nyakyusa did not smelt but obtained their iron and iron tools from BuKinga, and these were then worked up into various objects by Nyakyusa smiths (Wilson, 1964).

Sheane describes how, at night, in an Iwa village, 'the tall, red-hot kilns make an impressive sight, standing sentinel, as it were, round the outskirts of the village with their cylindrical pillars of flame' (Gouldsbury and Sheane, 1911: 279).

Smithing would have been done in the village under an open shelter. Hammers, tongs and clamps of iron belong with more sophisticated metal-working techniques (Lala smiths still use bark tongs) and the hammers used at this time are likely to have been of stone of various weights. In fact they were probably like those which occur in the shaft of Complex 4, and those recently, or still in use among the Fipa (Lechaptois, 1932), (Plate 66). The finishing process can be expected to have been done with small iron bar hammers on a stone or iron spike anvil. Products are known to have been spear and knife blades, arrowheads, bracelets and smaller rings. With the addition of axe and adze blades, and probably also razors, matting needles and awls for skin sewing, the iron equipment of the Kalambo Falls Industry people was probably complete.

Iron is unlikely to have been used for hoe blades until much later and cultivation was most probably by means of wooden hoes or digging sticks. If more metal was produced than was required for domestic use, it may have been traded to peoples such as the Safwa or the lakeside fishermen in Tanzania, neither of whom are known to have smelted, in exchange for some commodity, such as salt or fish, in the same way that iron implements were traded from Ufipa into the Rukwa Rift (Fagan and Yellen, 1968: 13).

The enigmatic shafts at the settlement site (C, 1963) look in every way to be graves except that they contain no bodies. If the acid nature of the soil were the only explanation for the total absence of skeletal remains, then it would surely also have destroyed the antelope bone fragments in Shaft 5. There are, however, a number of characteristics which point to the shafts' having been graves, viz. the marking of the top with stones, a broken pot or sherds; the putting of pottery from intentionally broken vessels in the infilling; the looser nature of the fill and the smaller number of sherds in the lower part of the shafts which suggest that this part once contained some perishable object now disappeared.

The body, if these were, indeed, graves, must have been placed upright in a sitting position – a not uncommon practice for burial among many of the southern Bantu-speakers – for there would not have been room for a body to lie on its side. The shafts must have been dug by means of a digging stick, hoe blade or a shovel of some kind and not with a hafted hoe, since the diameter of the hole is too narrow. At least four of the shafts exhibit indications that some kind of small structure was built over the mouth, similar to the miniature huts commonly to be seen marking graves or shrines. When seen in section, the oblique angle of the trench that surrounds the shaft, if this trench was, indeed, the footing for a circular wall, shows that this would have sloped outward at the top away from the centre of the hut, similar to one of the two traditional forms of dwelling built by the Nyakyusa; this is perhaps a unique method of construction in southern Africa but is rarely seen today (Fülleborn, 1906).

Among most of the Bantu-speaking peoples of the Corridor, chiefs' graves are usually together in special groves, while commoners are buried anywhere inside or outside the village. The shafts at the Kalambo Falls, if indeed they were graves, were inside the settlement and there are at least nine of them (including the one not excavated) that constitute what might be called a cemetery. Among the Corridor people, only the Inamwanga are known to bury their dead in cemeteries while their chiefs, as in the case of the other Mwika peoples, are buried in their huts. The children of Inamwanga chiefs are buried together in a large, round hole or grave which is not filled with earth but, instead, covered with a wooden roof over which soil is heaped and a hut built over the top (Kootz-Kretschmer, 1929: 308–9). The graves of Mambwe commoners are also circular but with a side niche in which the body is placed on a mat with grave goods. Gifts of bracelets and rings from the mourners are thrown into the grave as it is filled in.

The spirits of Mambwe chiefs are believed to be reincarnated in lions which come out of the grave, which again is circular with a niche to one side at the bottom to hold the body. The chief is buried in a sitting position with grave furniture and from his right ear projects a hollow reed reaching above the surface of the ground. It is from out of this that the spirit is said to come (Gouldsbury and Sheane, 1911: 188). Among the Fipa chiefs a similar belief relates to pythons (Boileau, 1899: 587). Among the Safwa, chiefs but not commoners, are buried close together in the same place and a large stone buried at the head of the grave which is, however, elongate. The body is placed lying on its left side facing east. All clothing and ornaments are removed from the corpse and placed at random in the grave. An offering of a sheep, a cow or a hen, depending on the status of the dead person, is buried with the body.

The Nyiha custom is to bury chiefs' families together and Nyiha graves are round, with the bodies placed in a sitting position. The graves may or may not be in the village (Kootz-Kretschmer, 1929: 308–10).

The absence of a body in the Kalambo Falls 'graves' might be partially explained by the curious habit among some Corridor people of digging up the body. The hill Safwa will dig up and carry away the body of a relative who has died and been buried away from his village and rebury it where the deceased had lived (Kootz-Kretschmer, 1929: 309).

Although the Nyakyusa–Ngonde people dig oblong, oval or round graves (depending on the clan to which they belong) with the corresponding niche for the body in a reclining or sitting position, among one of these groups – the Ndali – they dig up the bones a year or two after burial and pile them up off the ground, if members of the family have fallen ill after the kinsman's death (Wilson, 1957: 249–50). The Fipa similarly used to dig up the bones of a corpse if the spirit was deemed to have been responsible for misfortune or sickness to the community or to a kinsman (Lechaptois, 1932: 260).

Among some Bantu-speaking peoples the relatives carry out a ritual form of burial for a kinsman who dies far from the village. It was a custom among the Kalanga of Mashonaland (Willoughby, 1928: 29) and among the Venda of the northern Transvaal (Stayt, 1931: 163), who buried the usual grave goods with a sheep's head identified as the body of the dead person. Such, indeed, would seem to be the interpretation of the so-called 'beast burials' at K-2, Bambandyanalo (Gardner, 1963: 54–9).[1] In fact, there are several features in common between these K-2 'beast burials' and the Kalambo Falls shaft complexes, though they differ in the shallowness of the pits at Bambandyanalo (6-18 inches (15–45 cm)). Stones marked the pits, vessels were broken and the sherds piled together, often upside down; some sherds were placed on and round the circumference of the pit and rings and bracelets were a feature of the associations, though at K-2 they were made of copper. The antelope remains in the shaft of Complex 4 at the Kalambo Falls recalls the almost equally fragmentary animal remains in the K-2 burials. At K-2, however, there can never have been a body associated with the pits and animal bones.

Fear of dying in a strange country far from home was very great also among the Nyakyusa, 'If I die far from home I shall never reach my ancestors, for people will not bury me properly' (Wilson, 1957: 18). The Nyakyusa rituals connected with death are rigidly laid down by traditional custom and the fear of the misfortune that would follow the anger of a dead kinsman for whom the rituals had not been exactly carried out ensured their continuance by each new generation. The Nyakyusa bury in the open space surrounding the huts and the earth of the grave is stamped flat, leaving no outward sign of its presence (Wilson, 1957: 15). Among other Corridor peoples different burial customs exist, as has been noted, but among all the neglect of ritual is one of the greatest sins. It is, therefore, likely, though this has seldom been recorded, that in earlier times the rituals for a kinsman who died in a strange country would have been observed as rigorously as they would for those who died and were buried at home.

It has also been suggested by Jean Hiernaux (personal communication) that it might have been a foetus that was buried in each of these shafts at the Site C settlement area. This would explain the absence of any human skeletal remains since any bony parts would be unlikely to survive, and also the phosphorus and calcium values for the filling of the shaft that are associated with a body's having been buried in it. However, the number of shafts would need to be explained on the basis of ritual burial or of the use of a recognized communal burying place for unborn or newly born infants.

Another possible explanation, although it does not account for the high calcium/phosphorus ratio, is that it may have been the general custom to expose rather than to bury and that only some of the belongings or perhaps an effigy of the dead person, were actually buried. Such a practice is preserved in the *ako* funeral ceremonies for chiefs in the Nigerian forests today and it has been cited as one possible explanation behind the burial of the bronze heads at Ife which may have been mounted on wooden bodies and buried in grave pits in the sacred grove to ensure the continuity of the chieftaincy (Willett, 1967: 26–7). If it can subsequently be shown that the burial pits at Site C are restricted to the immediate area round the 1963 excavation, a similar ritual explanation for the Kalambo Falls Industry shafts might be acceptable. As yet, only fragmentary skeletal remains have been

[1] These remains are very fragmentary and represent only a small part of the animal buried with the pots. The term 'beast burial' is, therefore, incorrect.

found in association with Early Iron Age pottery, though in both instances they appear to have been buried in a grave (Robinson, 1963; Phillipson, 1970*a*).

Whether the Kalambo Falls shafts represent ritual burials without a body or whether they are graves from which the bodies have subsequently been disinterred or destroyed by the acidity of the soil, cannot as yet be determined. Ethnographic example exists for any of such possibilities but it seems reasonable to suppose that the shafts and their contents, as also the pots of Complexes 1 and 2 in shallow pits, formed a part of the mortuary rites of the Early Iron Age population at the Kalambo Falls. The curious engraving incised on the complete, otherwise undecorated pot from Site D (Plate 6: 6) may possibly have been intended as a reproduction of a burial in a round grave such as the shaft complexes are believed to have been. Unfortunately, however, too much of the burnished surface of the pot has been destroyed by acidity in the soil to be certain of this interpretation.

This, then, is the little that can be inferred concerning the culture of the Early Iron Age population at the Kalambo Falls. It is conspicuous for the conservative nature of its pottery for, since it lasted at least six hundred years, it might have been expected to show some distinctive development which is not readily apparent from the collections recovered so far. A general relationship seems to be established between the pottery of the Early Iron Age groups in Zambia and the 'dimple-based' and other wares of east Africa and Rwanda, at least so far as the Kalambo Falls Industry is concerned. The vessel forms of the globular and shouldered pots and bowls, the bevelled and everted rims, the channelling on the rims, the combination of channelling, or deep grooving and incised hatching and of comb-stamping and channelling on the neck and shoulder and other decorative motifs, as well as the dimple base and the generally fine paste of the sherds, link it with the Early Iron Age wares of east Africa. The radiocarbon dating is a further indication of their general contemporaneity (Fagan, 1966).

Kalambo Falls Industry pottery shares with the Early Iron Age wares of east Africa, the thickened, bevelled and channelled rims and, although it is rare at the Kalambo Falls, the dimple base. In the use of punctate decoration and the false relief chevron motif, it resembles more the pottery from the other Zambian groups. In its relationship with Gokomere ware it shares, as does the other Zambian pottery, a more frequent use of the impressed stamp. These and other more specific differences in the decorative motifs and variability in pot and bowl forms have been well demonstrated by Huffman (1970). Because of its closer proximity, a nearer relationship might be expected with the Early Iron Age Mwavarambo ware from northern Malawi which dates between 220 ± 115 and 270 ± 115 at Phopo Hill. In fact, it appears to have no more traits in common, however, than it does with the other Early Iron Age pottery from Zambia. One form of decoration which in Zambia is unique to the Kalambo Falls, does, however, occur also at Phopo Hill, namely a series of parallel, channelled lines broken by chevrons or dragged lines (Robinson and Sandelowsky, 1968, Figure 14). This form of decoration is reminiscent of the channelling broken by concentric loops or semi-circles present on the east African pottery (which is, however, more sophisticated) and the Kalambo Falls motif was at one time considered by the writer to be a possible derivative form which would thus support a northern origin for the pottery of the Kalambo Falls Industry. Huffman (1970), however, has now shown that all these nearly contemporary Early Iron Age wares can more convincingly be viewed, not as a continuum spreading from north to south or south to north, but rather as two early traditions – a Northern and a Southern – that radiated out from a 'co-tradition' or common source culture, to be followed shortly after by the Zambian traditions. Recent concepts concerning the origin of the Bantu-speaking peoples and the inferred relationship of these Early Iron Age wares with the Bantu, locate, therefore, the co-tradition culture in the west, presumably in the southern part of the Congo Basin.

Some time subsequent to the channelling and clay filling of the Chiungu Member with Kalambo Falls Industry pottery, the water level in the basin was again lowered due to the partial removal, presumably from natural causes, of the barrier at the Spillway Gorge. The low terrace at 8 feet (2·4 m) above the present river level on the Tanzania side of the river opposite Sites A and B may represent a period of stable water level in the basin or, perhaps, a temporary rise due to reblocking of the spillway. Although it seems unlikely that the makers of the Kalambo Falls Industry practised any form of irrigation, it should be remembered that this is by no means unknown from Tanzania. It is practised by the Nyakyusa today, as in the past, and bean gardens are said to have been made by the valley Safwa on the banks of rivers and 'the water of the stream led into them' (Kootz-Kretschmer, 1929: 158). The central part of the basin would have been suited to cultivation of the ridge and ditch type known as *fyungu* in the Southern Highlands of Tanzania (Sutton, 1969: 7–8), the ditches serving to drain the fields of surplus water. Such a possibility could indirectly have been responsible for the sudden lowering of water level, though, in the absence of any concrete evidence to the contrary, a natural cause seems to be more likely.

Whether the Kalambo Falls Industry and its characteristic pottery was replaced suddenly or gradually is as yet unknown, since the period between the end of the first millennium A.D. and the present day is only very imperfectly known from the stratigraphy of the excavated sections. No evidence of a complete cultural break has been found; in fact the A7 camp site excavation of 1966 suggests that the replacement of the Kalambo Falls Industry wares by Lungu pottery was more of a gradual than a rapid process. This is perhaps borne out by the continuation of certain Early Iron Age features in the modern pottery (see p. 45 and Plate 2: 1) and, if this interpretation is later substantiated, it would suggest that it was not so much a replacement of population and technology that was effected as a changed pattern brought about by the appearance of new groups of people with certain cultural innovations of sufficient importance to modify the traditional forms. Such newcomers would have to have been small in numbers also otherwise it is to be expected that the Kalambo Falls pottery tradition would have been completely replaced.

The Lungu, organized on a clan basis with small chiefdoms, were already in occupation of their present territory east and south of the lake by A.D. 1600 since they lost part of this to the Bemba sometime shortly after that (Vansina, 1966: 90). The ancestors of the present chiefs are said to have arrived in uLungu at the end of the seventeenth century from west of the lake (Brelsford, 1956: 67) and it is certain that close links existed with the Fipa after, if not also before this time since the ancestors of the Fipa royal line remained for a long time with the Lungu, according to Lechaptois, on condition that the 'Fipa chief came to seek his royal stool in uLungu' (Wilson, 1958: 20–2). It seems probable, therefore, that the stylistic differences that can be seen in the recent wares at the Kalambo Falls were initiated at the time of reorganization and emergence of the Fipa, Lungu and other 'Mwika' peoples as separate tribal entities sometime before A.D. 1600. Tribal differentiation would have been intensified by the changes that were brought about in administration and technology with the coming of the chiefs at the end of that century. The modern Lungu pottery certainly forms part of a tradition widely distributed in the northern part of Zambia and having relationships with the Lunda/Luba wares in Zaïre. Such a link, together with the tradition that derives the Lungu chiefs from Zaïre also, may perhaps be used to support the suggestion made above for earlier contacts, which may have already been established between the copper producing areas of the Katanga and uLungu by the eleventh century A.D. in Early Iron Age times.

It seems probable that Kalambo Falls pottery spread widely over the Tanganyika Plateau in northern Zambia during the first millennium A.D. and that the populations associated with this tradition were the earliest food-producers and metal-workers to establish themselves there. Whether they were eventually annihilated in war, lost their independent identity through absorption by stronger groups as have the Penja[1] and Lugulu among the Nyukyusa, or preserved it and survive today within the clan structure of the Nyiha and other small, independant tribal groups now living there, will not be known until we have ethnographic studies of the Nyiha of the kind that are of special significance to the archaeologist and that can be used to link directly with the evidence from systematic investigation of archaeological sites in the region. In this way, by working from the present into the immediate and thence into the more distant past, the sequence of events that makes up the history of these peoples will be elucidated and it will be possible to know more precisely the importance of the part played in this by the makers of the Kalambo Falls Industry.

[1] The Penja made pottery and traded it to the Nyakyusa before the Kisi trade expanded (Wilson, 1964: 58). Since sherds of Kisi pottery are found with Mbande Hill ware at Mbande Hill, Mpata, dating to A.D. 1410±80, and probably also with Karonga ware at Mwamasapa and Mwenepera Hill dating to A.D. 1240±80, both on the west side of Lake Malawi, it is possible that the Kisi pot trade has been established for a long time. Penja pottery might, therefore, preserve traits of a tradition of some antiquity and it would be of interest to study this ware.

Definition of the Kalambo Falls aggregates: Kalambo Falls Industry

STRATIGRAPHY

(i) A settlement site situated on the 30 foot (9·1 m) terrace and within *c.* 3 feet (91 cm) of brown–grey, fine, slightly coherent sand and midden debris and resting on the yellow, medium to fine sand (F6) containing a microlithic aggregate and forming the top of the Mbwilo Member of the Kalambo Falls Formation at Site C.

(ii) Within Filling Phases F7, F7′ and F7″ of the Chiungu Member of the Kalambo Falls Formation: F7 – red brown to brown clays (Excavations A4 and A3); F7′ – the grey silty clays and fine gravel filling the 'Older Channel'; F7″ – red sandy and silty fill of the 'Younger Channel' (Sites A and B). The Kalambo Falls Industry artifacts within Phase F7″ are probably derived as are the Stone Age implements also.

(iii) Within the upper 2 feet (61 cm) of grey to red sandy soil and slopewash on the upper slopes of the valley, in particular at Site A, where it directly overlies (A7) a horizon with a microlithic aggregate.

RADIOCARBON DATING

(i) *Site C Settlement*

Charcoal from shaft of Complex 11 – 1520 ± 40 B.P. A.D. 430 GrN-4647.

Charcoal from shaft of Complex 8 – 1605 ± 40 B.P. A.D. 345 GrN-4646.

(ii) *'Older Channel' Fill: Chiungu Member*

Site B2, Charcoal in grey clay and silt, *c.* 17 feet (5·2 m) above river level – 930 ± 40 B.P. A.D. 1020 GrN-3580.

Site A1, Charcoal in grey clay and silt, *c.* 17 feet (5·2 m) above river level – 1080 ± 180 B.P. A.D. 870 L-395B.

Site B2, Charcoal in grey sandy silt *c.* 14 feet (4·3 m) above river level – 1400 ± 150 B.P. A.D. 550 L-395C.

(iii) *'Younger Channel' Fill: Chiungu Member*

Site B2, Charcoal in red clay, *c.* 17 feet (5·2 m) above river level – 370 ± 50 B.P. A.D. 1580 GrN-3189.

Site A1, Charcoal in red/grey clay, *c.* 20 feet (6·1 m) above river level – 970 ± 150 B.P. A.D. 980 L-395A.

Radiometric time range – A.D. 345 ± 40 to A.D. 1020 ± 40; possibly, but improbably, extending to A.D. 1580 ± 50.

CULTURAL CHARACTERISTICS

Settlement area

Occupation debris covers the whole surface of the surviving area of the 30 foot (9·1 m) terrace, i.e. *c.* 9·4 acres (3·8 hectares) and extended also an unknown distance to the west, having been subsequently cut out here by the Kalambo river. No evidence of ditch or other defensive work and the settlement was probably an open one.

Settlement plan

Unknown: no evidence available of interrelated dwelling or other structures.

STRUCTURES AND PITS

(*a*) Roughly circular 'floor area' 4 feet (1·2 m) in diameter of hardened, red clay and grit surrounded by several large stones; at depth of 9 feet (2·7 m) base of the 'Older Channel' cut: Site A1.

(*b*) Area, *c.* 8 feet (2·4 m) in diameter of collapsed *daga* with pole and stick impressions. Possibly from wall or roof of a dwelling or storage structure. At depth of 1 foot 6 inches (45 cm) in the settlement area excavation at Site C.

(*c*) Irregular area of hardened and ?burned earth *c.* 4 feet (1·2 m) in diameter and possibly the floor of a small working-shelter since a large mass of bloom from an iron-smelting furnace rested on this floor overlying the top of Complex 10.

(*d*) Pits:

(i) Saucer shaped pit, 25 feet in diameter (7·6 m), about 3 feet (91 cm) below the surface and *c.* 7 feet (2·1 m) deep. A4. Possible storage pit for vegetable produce.

(ii) Shallow pit (Complex 3) 2 feet 6 inches (76 cm) in diameter and 1 foot (30 cm) deep, the top marked by stones, a pot and potsherds. Site C settlement excavation.

(iii) Four straight-walled pits or shafts with no surrounding trench; average diameter at mouth 3 feet 4 inches (102 cm), average depth 5 feet 6 inches (168 cm). Shaft contents: pots and potsherds, grindstone fragments, iron objects and slag. Complexes 5, 6, 8 and 11, Site C, settlement excavation.

(iv) Four straight-walled pits or shafts with surrounding trench, possibly evidence of superstructure. Average diameter at mouth 3 feet 2 inches (96 cm); average diameter of surrounding trench 4 feet 9 inches (145 cm); average depth 5 feet 1 inch (155 cm). Shaft fillings as for (iii) above. Complexes 4, 9, 10 and 12, Site C, settlement excavation.

IRON AND IRON-WORKING

1. Numerous small and some larger fragments of iron slag from smelting furnaces. From Channel Clays of the Chiungu Member, Hillslope Soil, Site A and the Site C settlement. Complete bloom from base of furnace (diameter: 1 foot 6 inches (45 cm), height 8 inches (203 mm).

2. Numerous tuyère fragments, with one exception from straight-walled pipes. One only with flared end. From Channel Clays, Chiungu Member at Site C settlement.

3. Eighteen manufactured iron artifacts: spearheads or knives (3), arrowheads (2), arm and leg rings (4), finger and toe rings (2), miscellaneous (7). From Shaft Complexes, Site C settlement.

COPPER

One bracelet or anklet, 1 conical ?earring of rolled sheet copper. From Hillslope Soil, Site A.

STONE

111 lower grindstones and fragments with only minimal dishing of the grinding surface.

94 upper grindstones and fragments, mostly without signs of extensive use.

9 pestle stones, some stained from grinding ochre.

21 stones for ?burnishing pottery.

14 hammerstones, five coming from shaft of Complex 4 and believed to be smith's hammers.

1 anvil stone from shaft of Complex 4.

125 informal artifacts with evidence of utilization for scraping, cutting and rubbing. Chiungu Member clays, Hillslope Soil and Site C settlement.

PIGMENT

White clay and red ochre with and without rubbed surfaces and striae. Chiungu Member and Site C settlement.

POTTERY

Paste and external finish. Fine, sandy clay with quartz inclusions; both inner and outer surfaces generally burnished and oxidized.

Vessel forms. These comprise hemispherical (37 per cent) and spherical (5·1 per cent) bowls, shouldered pots (46·1 per cent), globular pots (7·9 per cent), straight-sided pots (3·6 per cent) and gourd-shaped vessels (0·3 per cent).

Rims are mostly rounded (53·31 per cent) and everted (15·07 per cent), being thickened externally; but bevelled (12·50 per cent), squared (flattened) (4·04 per cent), inclined (4·04 per cent), rolled over (2·94 per cent), rimbands (6·62 per cent) and inverted (1·47 per cent) rims also occur.

Bases. All are rounded except for two pots with finger impressed dimple.

Handles and lugs are absent but hour-glass piercing of the wall for attachment of a handle, as well as for mending cracked bowls, occurs rarely.

Decoration was applied before firing in the form of channels, grooves, incision, stamping and impressed punctate designs. Decoration confined to above the shoulder and *Bowls* commonly undecorated. *Pots* generally decorated on and above the shoulder.

Motifs – bands of parallel, horizontal channels interrupted by chevrons and loops. Oblique, incised hatching and cross-hatching on neck and shoulder; lines of stamp impressed decoration and lines of triangular punctate impressions in particular to form false relief chevron pattern.

FAUNA

(i) *Association certain:*

Synceros caffer A7 1966 teeth.

Cephalophas monticolus or *Raphicerus sharpei* C 1963 Complex 5 cranial and mandibular fragments.

(ii) *Association uncertain:*

Bos taurus B2 1959 teeth; radius and other limb fragments.

Canis cf *mesomelas* B2 1959 two mandibles.

Thrynomys swiderianus B2 1959 two mandibles, maxilla and limb fragments.

RECORDED DISTRIBUTION OF POTTERY SIMILAR TO THAT OF THE KALAMBO FALLS INDUSTRY

Recorded from eleven sites in the Northern Province of Zambia; from Uningi Pans and Itumbwe, east and southeast of Lake Tanganyika; from two sites at the southwest end of the Lake; from Samfya at the southwest side of Lake Bangweulu and from four sites in the Muchinga Escarpment southwards to Nakapapula between Mpika and Serenje.

Approximate area of known distribution 375,000 square miles (97,125 km^2).

A possible structural model for Early Iron Age communities

Early Iron Age social and economic patterning in south-central and east Africa might have been similar to the following model that can be constructed on the basis of the available evidence.

The population lived mostly in open village settlements of *c.* 20–30 families, situated within the immediate vicinity of their cultivated lands. New villages were built adjacent to the old, the abandoned sites being later brought into regular cultivation. Thus, although individual portions may only have been used for a relatively short period of time, the same area was inhabited for many generations and today the debris covers *c.* 10–40 acres (4–17 ha) giving the appearance that the settlement was large. There were few, if any permanent structural features but both light, impermanent (beehive) and semi-permanent (conical) dwellings of pole and *daga* may have been built, together with ancillary structures such as food bins of sun-dried clay and covered pits for the storage of vegetable foods.

Some system of fixed cultivation would need to have been practised, perhaps including green manuring and the construction of mounds, ridges and ditches in favourable localities on hill slopes and in valley bottoms.[1] Crops grown on these mounds might have included sorghum, cow-peas, ground beans, Livingstone potato, cucurbits and, perhaps, an indigenous aroid. Finger millet and, perhaps, bullrush millet would have been grown in small, circular 'ash gardens' cut from the adjacent forest or woodland and often including large termite mounds.

Some small stock – sheep/goats, dogs, domestic fowl – may sometimes have been kept, though initially there was probably no cattle except among those living in proximity to pastoral Neolithic groups in east Africa. Hunting was a major activity and thus the main source of meat. Relations between settlements and indigenous hunting groups appear to have been cordial, resulting in free exchange of manufactured goods and produce. Concentration rather than dispersal of food-producing activities, low population density and the absence of competition for existing resources were probably important factors contributing to symbiotic relationships.

Political control may have been in the hands of village headmen and elders without any unified political authority. Ethnic unity of groups of settlements may, perhaps, be inferred from identical pottery traditions which may also imply common customs and linguistic affinities. Adjustment for normal population increase was by colonization.

Communities lived in semi-isolation, except where special geographical features dictated otherwise and settlements were separated from each other by wide tracts of undeveloped woodland or forest. Contact may, however, have been maintained by short distance trade of certain commodities, carried on because of economic need but also and, perhaps more especially, because of the necessity for maintaining and fulfilling social obligations. Commodities traded probably included salt, beeswax, arrow poison (*Strophanthus* sp.), pottery, iron artifacts, pigments and dried fish. 'Short distance' trade of this kind is well attested in recent and historical times in south-central Africa (Trapnell, 1953: 120–1, 132–3; Wilson, 1958: 32; Fagan and Yellen, 1968; Fagan, 1969*b*).

Copper and in some cases also salt should more probably be classed as 'long distance' trade commodities from the beginning. Exotic trade items from the east coast began to make their appearance at Early Iron Age sites in south-central Africa from the middle of the fifth century and probably represent the beginnings of 'long distance' trade with the coast. The chief raw materials exported were probably gold, copper and ivory.

Political, social and economic changes modifying and transforming Early Iron Age culture were probably related to the proximity of trade routes, control of raw materials and the interaction which such trade produced among these independent, semi-isolated communities.

The above model is but one of several that might be constructed from the little evidence at present available and it rests with future investigators to show whether it has any validity.

[1] It might be thought that the systems of fixed cultivation in use in northeastern Zambia and the southern highlands of Tanzania evolved from one based on small circle agriculture (*chitimene*) but, as Allan (1967: 72) suggests, it is equally likely that the change was in the other direction and that these systems are of some antiquity.

CHAPTER 4

The Stone Age cultural sequence: terminology, typology and raw material

BY J. D. CLARK AND M. R. KLEINDIENST

One of the primary objectives of every archaeologist is to be able to reconstruct the pattern of settlement and range of activities that are reflected by the cultural remains of the past population he is excavating. For the Iron Age in Africa this is made easier by the present day survival of behavioural traits and technologies that archaeology and other sources show to have had a long history in the continent. For the Stone Age, interpretation is rendered more difficult because the greater time depth involved has removed everything except the least perishable elements of the material culture and because the technology of hunter/gatherers is in general less elaborate than that of agriculturalists. Survival is reduced to a minimum for the Pleistocene where the material remains rarely include more than the stone artifacts and sometimes associated bone implements and the debris from food waste.

At the Kalambo Falls, the acid nature of the soils has precluded the survival of bone with even the latest Stone Age aggregate and thereby a very important source of economic evidence has been lost. However, the vegetable remains and wooden tools that have survived with the earlier cultural units provide an almost unique opportunity for examining the kinds of stone tools or groups of artifacts with which these are more generally associated. Whether this was of more than local significance must await similar studies at other sites where vegetable remains are preserved. However, when our results are compared with those obtained from a study of associated bone or shell artifacts elsewhere, interesting points of difference emerge.

With the exception of the aggregates from the Rubbles, the cultural remains from the long stratified sequence at the Kalambo Falls in most cases occur on temporary surfaces or horizons that were exposed and so available for occupation for only a limited period of time before being covered with further sediments by the aggrading river. Generally, however, the artifacts that compose these aggregates are in fresh condition with sharp edges. This freshness and the pattern of their distribution on the occupation floor show that any disturbance or movement which they may have suffered from natural or other causes subsequent to abandonment by their makers, was probably minimal. Particular attention has, therefore, been given to the precise positions and associations of artifacts on occupation floors and so to any observed groupings of the artifact classes that are apparent from these floor plans. If, as we believe, the form of an implement is directly related to its function, then the associations on the occupation floors have special importance for any attempt to connect significant clusterings with the activity or activities to which they once related.

In the belief that groups of artifacts with the same attributes will reflect the prevailing technological preferences and abilities, as well as the particular requirements of the individuals who made them, aggregates have been analysed on a typological basis recognizing a number of categories and classes. Artifacts that tend to share a cluster of specified attributes, regarded by the investigators as significant, constitute a *class* and certain major classes or *categories* are recognized according to the degree of secondary modification and retouch which their component artifacts have undergone. This procedure follows largely from the assumption that the more a piece is modified the more clearly it will show the design principles formerly incorporated in the culture of the Stone Age craftsmen. This is standard practice in the analysis of lithic assemblages and has not been departed from here except to give greater emphasis to the morphological attributes which relate to modification by usage. At present these provide the best means of distinguishing meaningful differences which are believed to result from the preparation of an artifact for a particular purpose and from the manner of its use. It must be emphasized, however, that the terms used here bear no functional implications but are those in current usage to describe particular classes of artifacts recognized by reason of the attributes they have in common.

We did not find it to be a useful procedure, in analysing the Kalambo Falls aggregates, to attempt to establish a large number of closely defined classes and sub-classes of artifacts. Such a practice seems to confuse rather than clarify understanding in sub-Saharan Africa where informality predominates over formality in tool morphology and where gradations, rather than sharp boundaries between classes, are more commonly met with. The more minutely detailed the typology, the more room there is found to be for inconsistency between individual workers unless these have been closely associated in their use of the system. We believe, therefore, that the smaller number of classes employed here partially compensates for the wide range of variability and overlap shown by almost all classes of stone artifacts in Africa, provides a better opportunity for distinguishing true, or intrinsic, morphological sets from arbitrary type categories and, at the same time, reflects more realistically the limitations in the range of activities associated with the hunting and gathering way of life. It should also be borne in mind that analysis of the stone tools in use among present-day, stone-using peoples suggests that such groups recognize a minimal number of tool categories (Gould, 1968; White, 1968*a*; MacCalman and Grobbelaar, 1965).

Every artifact from an occupation floor, occupation surface, horizon or rubble was classified, measured and attributes of primary and secondary flaking, raw material and physical condition recorded. Where aggregates contain large quantities of unmodified waste, its technological characteristics have sometimes been shown here by sampling, using the contents of grid squares which were not specifically selected.

The unmodified products of stone flaking have been analysed equally with the trimmed and utilized pieces, since waste products of stone working provide evidence of technical skill, traditional associations and the industrial level, as well as of rates of change and innovation, when the results from several stratified aggregates are compared. On the other hand, the trimmed and utilized pieces provide information concerning the range of activities practised and the living pattern of their makers.[1]

Nomenclature, classification of archaeological units and terminology

The terminology used here is that laid down by international agreement for sub-Saharan Africa, namely that adopted at the joint meeting of the South African and British Associations for the Advancement of Science in Johannesburg in 1929 (Goodwin and Van Riet Lowe, 1929; Goodwin, 1953) with special reference to the recommendations for greater precision in nomenclature made in 1965 by the Wenner-Gren Symposium 'Systematic investigation of the African Later Tertiary and Quaternary' (Bishop and Clark, 1967) and to decisions by the Commission on Nomenclature and Terminology of the Pan-African Congress on Prehistory and Quaternary Studies in Nairobi (1947) (Leakey and Cole, 1952), Livingstone (1955) (Clark and Cole, 1957) and Dakar (1967).[2]

Classification of archaeological units follows that recommended by the 1965 Symposium, as further agreed at a meeting to discuss the east African Acheulian held in April, 1971, in Urbana, Illinois (Keller and Isaac, 1971). These definitions, as we interpret them, together with those used here for other non-classificatory terms, are set out below:

1. *An artifact* is an object of any material that can be shown to have been made or used by man. This includes not only retouched, modified and utilized pieces but unmodified waste as well as materials which, although bearing no obvious evidence of utilization (e.g. natural stones and pieces of bone or wood) yet, by reason of their associations, must have been carried onto the occupation site by man; these last have been termed 'manuports' by M. D. Leakey (1967: 420).

[1] The analyses of stone artifacts were carried out in the field and in Livingstone in 1959, 1960, 1962, 1963 and 1966. Microlithic aggregates and the Polungu aggregate (see p. 153 *et seq.*) were analysed by J. D. Clark in 1963. Lupemban aggregates were analysed as follows: Site A1: C. M. Keller and J. D. Clark, 1962 and 1963; other Site A aggregates by M. R. Kleindienst and C. M. Keller, 1959, 1960 and 1963; Sites B and D by J. D. Clark, 1963; Site C by C. M. Keller, 1963. Sangoan aggregates were analysed: Site A by M. R. Kleindienst, 1959 and 1963; Site B by J. D. Clark. Acheulian aggregates: Site A1 by C. M. Keller and J. D. Clark, 1962; Sites A4 and A5 by M. R. Kleindienst, 1963; Site A6 by J. D. Clark, 1963; Site B by J. D. Clark, 1962 and 1963. It must be noted that the importance of some attributes was observed in the course of the investigation and that these were consistently recorded only after 1959. A high degree of consistency was maintained between the three of us by frequent reference, discussion and cross-checking.

[2] At the time of writing the recommendations of the Dakar Congress remain unpublished. The volume has just appeared dated November, 1972! Edited by H. J. Hugot.

2. *An aggregate* is a number of artifacts, whether large and representative or small and unrepresentative, that are associated in geological context irrespective of whether they belong to a single archaeological unit or to several. Where it can be demonstrated that the artifacts comprising an aggregate all belong within a single brief period in time, and have suffered no visible redistribution, they are considered to be in *primary context*. Where no such contemporaneity can be established or where geological or other agencies have redistributed the artifacts, these are considered to be in *secondary context*.

3. *An Archaeological Horizon* or *Archaeological Occurrence* is the smallest cultural stratigraphic unit that can be defined at any one place. The concept includes both the natural context and the artifacts that together form the aggregate(s) within this context. Specific kinds of Archaeological Horizons or Occurrences recognized at the Kalambo Falls are:

(i) *An occupation surface:* a particular stratigraphic horizon, either temporary or of longer duration (e.g. where soil forming processes may be evident), that provided a land surface on which single artifacts or aggregates occur and attest to human occupation, whether or not the artifacts are in primary or secondary context.

(ii) *An occupation floor:* an area of limited but variable extent on an occupation surface where artifacts in primary context are concentrated on what the distribution pattern of the aggregate suggests was a former camping place or workshop of prehistoric man.

(iii) *A rubble:* an accumulation of angular, subangular and/or rounded stones, resting disconformally on the surface of the underlying deposits. On the higher flanks of the valleys such rubbles are in the nature of a talus scree; lower and nearer the centre of the basin, the stones are sub-angular and rounded showing that water action played a greater part in their accumulation. Such rubbles usually contain artifacts of several industrial stages, derived and contemporary. In some cases the aggregates from the rubbles probably relate to streamside activities and have not been much disturbed (Volume I: 185–6). In other cases, some distance of transport is indicated by the degree of abrasion.

4. *A component* is a term we have found necessary to introduce here to define the content abstraction of several aggregates from one or more Archaeological Horizon(s) at a single site, which are in secondary, disturbed, context but which share a common typology and technology and can be shown to be broadly contemporary. A component is, therefore, recognized on the basis of artifact sets showing consistently common attributes and forms an entity from which limited palaeo-cultural inference can be made. The meaning given to the term here is thus different from that in wide use among New World archaeologists (Willey and Phillips, 1958: 21–2) in that it relates specifically to artifact sets or aggregates in disturbed contexts. Since this term has not yet been discussed or received official recognition from the Commission on Nomenclature of the Pan-African Congress on Prehistory and Quaternary Studies, it is accorded only informal status here.

5. *An assemblage.* Where the aggregate from an Archaeological Occurrence is in primary archaeological context and the constituent artifacts can be shown to be contemporary or nearly so, as well as to have spatial relationship, as may be the case on an occupation floor, surface or workshop horizon, the associated set of artifacts is defined as an *assemblage.* Recognition of an assemblage carries with it, therefore, the inference that the artifacts were made and used by a single cultural unit and that the content represents a significant fraction of the stone working products of that unit. Such usage is similar to and follows that proposed by Marks (1971) but, since it has not yet received official recognition, its status, as here, remains informal.

6. *A Phase* is a grouping of similar artifact assemblages from Archaeological Occurrences that can be shown to be related by typology, technology or recurrent associations and which have also specific spatial and temporal limits. In cases where similar artifact aggregates, believed to relate to a single cultural stratigraphic entity, are contemporaneous such groupings are considered to be *facies* and may represent 'activity variants'.

7. *An Industry* is 'represented by all the known objects that a group of prehistoric people manufactured in one area over some span of time' (Bishop and Clark, 1967: 893). This classificatory category is further defined as 'comprising groups of related artifact aggregates,[1] whether or not sub-divided into Phases, which share a large number of technical and

[1] Either assemblages or components.

typological features in recurrent associations, but which are more diversified than the members of a Phase' (Clark *et al.* 1966: 118). The Archaeological Occurrences that compose this basic cultural unit usually have limited stratigraphic and spatial distributions. Phases can only be formally named after the definition of an Industry.

8. *An Industrial Complex* is defined as a grouping of industries considered to have cultural entity by reason of their having specific traditions in common. We regard them as referring to general developmental or adaptive stages achieved by early man. They are, therefore, comparable to the techno-complex as defined by D. L. Clarke (1968: 357).

Terms such as Earlier, Middle and Later Stone Age and First and Second Intermediate, as adopted at the Third Pan-African Congress on Prehistory in Livingstone in 1955, which are neither purely cultural content terms nor time-stratigraphic in usage, have not been employed as formal nomenclature. These terms represent a level of abstraction above that of Industrial Complex and have, as yet, no place in the hierarchical system of graded units employed here. Since they have received wide usage in the literature and carry connotations that still remain useful and as we anticipate that they may in time acquire sufficiently precise definition and usage to receive acceptance as formal nomenclature, we have, accordingly, retained them and shown them as having informal status, indicated by the use of quotation marks.

On the basis of comparative, quantitative studies, it is sometimes possible at the Kalambo Falls to assign groupings of Archaeological Occurrences to already recognized and defined Industrial Complexes and to give them formal status here. Within these broad, generalized entities, other groupings are recognized and have been given the status of an Industry and named after a relevant locality or topographic feature within the immediate area of the local basin. Although the Kalambo Falls prehistoric site is one of the very few known from the northern end of the Zambian plateau and the only one to have been investigated in any detail, we feel that the archaeological richness and long record of settlement shown by the many aggregates contained within the sedimentary succession, make this a unique locality and justify the introduction of these new terms at the industrial level.

The graded groupings and units recognized and employed in our work at the Kalambo Falls are set out and discussed below:

1. No formal definition exists of the 'Central African Iron Age' and, in the present state of knowledge, probably could not be made. Although later and earlier (or Early) cultural entities at the level of an Industry have been described from central Africa, no higher order of definition and names has yet been proposed.

In Zambia, Phillipson (1968*a*) has identified several regional variants which all fall within the chronological period known as the 'Early Iron Age'. These are believed to form distinct geographical and typological 'groups', that from the northern part of the country having been informally described as the 'Kalambo group' after the locality that has yielded the most complete knowledge of this entity, as previously stated (p. 8, footnote (1)). In 1969 (Volume I of this series) we described the cultural unit we had identified at the Kalambo Falls as being within the 'Early Iron Age', under the name 'Kalambo Industry', being then unaware of the term applied to it by Phillipson. Since, at the time, no formal definition of the 'Kalambo Industry' was given, it might seem preferable to use Phillipson's earlier term 'Kalambo group of the Early Iron Age'. However, 'group' is a new term which has not yet been defined, nor has it received official recognition and its probable status within the hierarchical system acknowledged by the Commission on Nomenclature and Terminology of the Pan-African Congress is unclear. Since the eleven sites producing this related pottery ware are spread over a large part of the northern half of Zambia (Phillipson, 1968*a*: 192), the entity described as the 'Kalambo group of the Early Iron Age' would, within the system employed here, have the status of an Industrial Complex. As more sites are located and knowledge of the aggregates within each locality increases, it seems likely that several sub-groups will become apparent. The aggregates within the local basin at the Kalambo Falls clearly represent a more closely related unit in time and space than can be accommodated within the entity envisaged by Phillipson. In the system we have used, as here described, we have given these aggregates the status of an Industry and, on the evidence put forward in this volume, we believe there is justification for formal use of this term.

However, we recognize that the term 'Kalambo Industry' implies that it is found throughout the catchment basin of the Kalambo river which, as has been shown (Volume I, Figure 4), is quite extensive. This may later be shown to be the case but, in order to avoid ambiguity and to show that the spatial extent of the Industry, as at present known, does not extend beyond the limits of the local basin, the name of the entity is now amended to *Kalambo Falls Industry*. As defined here, the Kalambo Falls Industry can be seen to be one of several local entities within the 'Kalambo group of the early Iron Age'.

2. The microlithic aggregates at the Kalambo Falls cannot be identified on the basis of the stone artifacts with any of the Industries or Industrial Complexes previously described from south central Africa. They are known from five sites within the local basin but only one of these has been systematically investigated. They are defined here under the name *Kaposwa Industry* from the name of the tributary stream that joins the main river at the northwest corner of the local basin on the Tanzania bank, opposite the 30 foot (9 m) terrace at Site C and the microlithic living floor.

3. The aggregates contained within the hillslope deposits that overlie Rubble I at Site A, Excavation A4, and the latest and typologically most advanced of the group of aggregates contained within and just above Rubble I (Mbwilo Member) at Sites A, B, C and D have previously been referred to as a local expression of the 'Magosian' (Volume 1). Re-excavation of the type site in Uganda by Cole (1967*a*) has shown that the original Magosian concept of aggregates that fall chronologically and typologically in a 'Second Intermediate Period' between the 'Later' and the 'Middle Stone Age' was based upon a mixture of two temporally distinct aggregates. The use of the name 'Magosian' can, therefore, no longer be justified. The two groups of aggregates at the Kalambo Falls that have been included within the entity previously referred to as 'Magosian' have been renamed the *Polungu Industry*, the name being taken from the prominent hill at the end of Siszya Ridge immediately to the south and overlooking Site A. Since no occupation floors belonging to this unit have yet been found, the two groups of aggregates are further distinguished as the *Hillslope component* (that from Excavation A4, 1959 and 1963) and the *Rubble component* from Rubble I (Mbwilo Member). The latter is stratigraphically older and exhibits close technical and typological connections with the Siszya Industry of the Lupemban Industrial Complex that forms the main cultural constituent of Rubble I. However, the presence of certain tool classes not found with the Siszya Industry and the absence of others that are characteristic, when taken together with the degree of variability, small though it is, shown by the unmodified waste, suggest that the artifact sets defined here as the Rubble component have sufficient individuality to require distinctive treatment. Since, in the shaped tool categories, these artifact sets also show resemblances with the Hillslope component and on the understanding that reclassification may be necessary when homogeneous assemblages are discovered in primary context, we have referred this component to the Polungu Industry where it best appears, at present, to belong and of which we believe it to constitute an earlier Phase.

4. *Lupemban Industrial Complex*. Introduced by Breuil (1944), re-employed by Mortelmans (1962), the term has since been applied to Archaeological Occurrences in east Africa (Kleindienst, 1967: 844) and used to define entities in South Africa (Mason, 1962: 290–7), South West Africa (MacCalman and Viereck, 1967), Rwanda and Burundi (Nenquin, 1967*a*) and Angola (Clark, 1963). The term *Lupemban* has received wide recognition and usage within the Zaïre (Congo) Basin (Clark, 1971) but precise definition of the entities in the Lower Zaïre and the type area of the Kasai is lacking. However, the entities recognized in the northern part of the Lunda Province of Angola relate to the same eco-system and stratigraphic units are removed by less than 150 km from the type site at Lupemba. From the material we have seen and examined from Lupemba and the other Tshikapa mines, the artifact aggregates at the type site appear to be significantly similar to those of the Angola sites, for the latter to be used, in effect, as 'para-types'.

The aggregates from the Archaeological Occurrences at the Kalambo Falls which have a composition similar to those from southern Zaïre and which, therefore, fall within the Lupemban Industrial Complex are contained within the Red Rubble Bed and Rubble Bed (Rubble I) of the Mbwilo Member and in the Pits Channel Fill and Rubble Bed (Rubble II) of the Mkamba Member. These aggregates include a large number of tools and unmodified waste. Each of the excavations at sites A, B, C and D produced the same range of artifacts from Rubble I; aggregates from Rubble II and the Pits Channel Fill were exposed in Excavation A4. Analysis shows all of these aggregates to relate to a common tradition, within which temporal divisions can be recognized on stratigraphic, typological and technical grounds.

Two industries within the Lupemban Industrial Complex are distinguished. The earlier is represented by Archaeological Occurrences associated with Rubble IIa, IIb and II composite, distinguished here as the *Nakisasa Industry*. The name is taken from that of the high ridge bounding the local basin on the north and east, referred to as 'Burnt Ridge' by the Gordon–Gallien expedition (Cornwall, 1929). This entity was referred to as '?Lupemban' in Volume I (Appendix K, p. 239) and is in some respects similar to those called 'Sangoan/Lower Lupemban' in the Angola sites (Clark, 1963, Chapter VI).

A later entity represented by the Archaeological Occurrences from the Pits Channel Fill, the Red Rubble Bed, and Rubble I (a, b, c and composite) is named the *Siszya Industry*. The name is taken from the high ridge that bounds the local basin on its south side with, at its southern end, Siszya Forest, the dry *mushitu* relict of the old forest type containing representatives of both the west African lowland forest species and others found in the higher altitude montane forests (Volume I: 59–60). These plant communities have particular relationship to the time when the Siszya Industry was being made at the Kalambo Falls. Two components have been recognized within the aggregates of the Siszya Industry on the basis of typology and technology. The artifacts assigned to *component A* are less evolved technologically (and often more abraded) than those of *component B*, which is considered to be the later of the two.

5. *Sangoan Industrial Complex.* The Sangoan was first described by Wayland (1923) from the type site at Sango Bay on Lake Victoria and further defined by O'Brien (1939) and Van Riet Lowe (1952) from the Nsongezi area, all in Uganda. The term has, at the same time, been more loosely applied in many widely separated regions of the continent, from the Upper Nile to west Africa, the Congo Basin, Zambia, Rhodesia and South Africa (see Kleindienst, 1967). It has, however, recently been more strictly defined from the Kagera region of Uganda by Cole (1967*b*) who has drawn comparisons with some entities described as Sangoan from other regions, amongst them aggregates from the Kalambo Falls where the entity present within the local basin shows close relationships typologically and technically with those described from Angola, Uganda, Zambia and Rhodesia though minor differences of a regional nature can be distinguished.

At the Kalambo Falls, the local industry that belongs within the Sangoan Industrial Complex is found within the Ochreous Sands and Grey Clay Beds of the Mkamba Member at Sites A and B. These are channel deposits consisting of discontinuous spreads of fine gravel that represent the surfaces of sand bars and the bottom of shallow channels and the aggregates usually occur in relation to these. The artifacts are generally slightly abraded but they have not been moved very far, if at all, from their original position. There is one occupation surface within the Ochreous Sands at Site B2, 1959.

The local industry has been named the *Chipeta Industry* after the village of that name situated on the Tanzania bank of the river approximately 150 m northwest of the confluence of the Vundwe stream and the main river (Volume I, Figure 5). Occasional core-axes and other artifacts of Sangoan type were collected along the exposed slopes of the Mkamba Member between this point and the 'Tanganyika Cliff' at Mkamba Village (Volume I: 203).

It should be recorded that almost all those archaeological units that have been described as Sangoan from sub-Saharan Africa, have also a basically similar ecology in that they relate to the high rainfall and thicker vegetation cover and climate of Equatoria and outliers of this equatorial environment. As with the Lupemban and Upper Acheulian Industrial Complexes recognized at the Kalambo Falls, there is no implication of relationship between the many lesser groupings (Industries, etc.) within the vast region where these Industrial Complexes have been shown to occur, other than that which results from analogous social and technological responses to similar environmental conditions.

6. *The Upper Acheulian Industrial Complex.* The degree of variability within the Upper Acheulian that is found at a single site or locality and in different ecological regions, is attested from a number of detailed descriptions and definitions. Some of these for east and south central Africa are summarized by Kleindienst (1961; 1967).

The Archaeological Occurrences that belong within the cultural expression of the Upper Acheulian Industrial Complex in the local basin at the Kalambo Falls have been shown to differ in a number of respects from those at other sub-Saharan sites such as Isimila (Howell *et al.* 1962), Olorgesailie (Isaac, 1968), Kariandusi (Kleindienst, 1961) and Nsongezi (Cole, 1967*b*) in east Africa; Baia Farta in Angola

(Clark, 1966); Broken Hill in Zambia (Clark, 1959*c*) and the Cave of Hearths in the Transvaal (Mason, 1962), Montagu Cave (Keller, 1966; 1970) and Amanzi (Deacon, 1970) in South Africa. To distinguish the cultural expression of the Upper Acheulian Industrial Complex found at the Kalambo Falls, we have used the name *Bwalya Industry* from the small stream entering the Kalambo gorge on the south side approximately 400 m west of the Kalambo Falls. The Industry is here represented by six living floors at Site A and four at Site B. Two Phases are recognized: the *Inuga Phase*, represented by the aggregates from the topmost Acheulian occupation floor yet recovered (Floor IV) at Site A1, 1956 and A5, 1963 which is stratigraphically above and younger than the *Moola Phase* that comprises the aggregates from all the occupation floors below Floor IV.[1]

We are applying the Burg Wartenstein categories agreed at the 1965 Wenner-Gren Symposium (see p. 72 above) as a means of communicating what we believe to be the technological and typological affinities of artifact aggregates at the Kalambo Falls prehistoric site with the following reservations as to the definition of *Industry* quoted above. We regard the assumption that the aggregates assigned to an Industry were made by the same 'group of prehistoric people' as unwarranted, except in the broadest sense of conceiving 'a group' as having had a similar environmental setting and the possibility for direct connections; that is, the aggregates are not so separated in time and/or space as to make connections between the makers inconceivable. Whether or not the people who made the artifacts assigned to an Industry did have sociological or genetic ties must at present be regarded as not proven.

The Archaeological Horizons and the artifact aggregates from them at the Kalambo Falls prehistoric site have been listed at Appendix K in Volume I and this should be consulted for easy reference as to their stratigraphic relationships. The terminology employed here and the cultural and stratigraphic successions are summarized in Table 10, together with the characteristic artifact composition of the archaeological units and other details.

[1] Since there are comparatively few appropriate locality names known to us from the local basin, these two Phases have been named after two of the more important wild fruit trees growing there today and associated also with the Upper Acheulian occupation floors. *Inuga* (*Syzygium guineense*) a component of fringing forest, is well represented in the pollen spectra and *Moola* (*Parinari curatellifolia*), a species of savanna woodlands, is represented by wood and seeds belonging either to this species or to *P. excelsa*.

Measurement and morphology
(Figures 7–15)

In view of the differences that exist among archaeologists working in Africa in basic measurement usage and methods of presentation of taxonomic analysis, and in order to reduce possible misunderstandings, we have set out below the system used to analyse the Kalambo Falls lithic aggregates.

Where possible, the principles of systematic typological analysis adopted follow the usage set out in classificatory systems having wide, current usage such as the *Typologies* of F. Bordes (1961), D. de Sonneville-Bordes and J. Perrot (1954–6), Tixier (1963) and de Heinzelin (1962). Reference has also been made to Brézillon (1968). However, much of the lithic material from Africa south of the Sahara cannot readily be accommodated within these *systèmes* and we have, therefore, chiefly used typologies devised specifically for the more precise definition of sub-Saharan African culture units: for example M. D. Leakey (1967) (Oldowan and Developed Oldowan Industries), M. R. Kleindienst (1962) (East African Acheulian constituents), J. D. Clark (1963) (Sangoan, Lupemban and Tshitolian Industries) and Mason (1957) (Plan Forms of flakes and 'Middle Stone Age'). Our typology for the microlithic aggregates is closely comparable to that compiled by Miller (1969) which is in part based on that used here. Where equivalence or near equivalence exists with 'types' defined in other classificatory systems, this has been indicated in the text.

DEFINITIONS AND DESCRIPTIVE TERMS
(Figure 7)

Length. The length of an artifact is that of the shortest rectangle into which the specimen can be fitted. In the case of a flake, however, this is always measured with the striking platform orientated along the base line.

Breadth. The breadth of an artifact is the width of this rectangle.

Thickness. Unless otherwise stated, the thickness is the maximum measurement at right-angles to the

TABLE 10. *The cultural sequence at the Kalambo Falls: summary of aggregate composition, stratigraphy and dating of the main archaeological units*

Developmental chrono-stratigraphic terms	Industrial complex	Industry	Phase	Component	Main artifact classes	Sites and stratigraphy: Archaeological Occurrences	Radiocarbon dates
Iron Age	(Late)				Not positively identified before Lungu settlements. This volume, Plates 1 and 2.	Surface and sub-surface hillslope soils.	? <350 B.P. (<A.D. 1580 ± 50)
	(Early)	Kalambo Falls			Open settlements, permanent occupation but few permanent structural features. Storage pits, ?grave shafts and furniture. Iron working tools and personal ornaments. Copper (rare). Grindstones, pigment, pots and bowls with bevelled rim, hatching, stamping, parallel channelling, grooving and false relief chevron decoration. ?Cattle and wild fauna. This volume, Plates 3–32.	Site C *Settlement* (1963). Hillslope soil, Site A7 (1966). Chiungu Member channel clays, Sites A and B, 1956–1963.	930 ± 40 B.P. (A.D. 1020 ± 50) 1905 ± 40 B.P. (A.D. 345 ± 40)
'Later Stone Age'		Kaposwa			*Flakes:* long and short quadrilateral, irregular. Mostly parallel, convergent and irregular dorsal scar patterns. Plain or point striking platforms. Micro-burin variant spalls. *Cores:* single (especially pyramidal) and two platforms; formless; bipolar. *Utilized/modified:* small flakes, bladelets, fragments, etc. *Outils esquillés*. Anvils (dimple scarred). Rubbers, grindstones, pestles, hammerstones, pigment. *Shaped tools: large cutting* – none. *Heavy duty:* percussion flaked and ground and polished stone axes, bored stones. *Light duty:* mostly microlithic – backed bladelets and flakes; lunates, trapezes, triangles; shouldered and truncated forms; small scrapers (mostly short end and side), pieces with burin blow. This volume, Plates 33–42.	Occupation floor. Top of sands (Mbwilo Member) of ±30 foot (9 m) terrace, Site C, 1959, 1963. Surface, Chitambala Gravel Beds.	3850 ± 40 B.P. (1900 ± 40 B.C.) 3920 ± 40 B.P. (1970 ± 40 B.C.)
Second Intermediate'		Polungu		Hillslope component	*Flakes:* all forms, especially blades and short triangular. Parallel, convergent and radial dorsal scar patterns. Plain, faceted and point striking platforms. *Cores:* single and two platforms; bipolar; formless; Levallois and discoid. *Utilized/modified:* block anvils, rubbers, pestles, hammerstones, pigment, *outils esquillés*; flakes, blades, etc. *Shaped tools: large cutting* – none. *Heavy duty:* irregular core-axes and convergent picks (rare); core-scrapers; choppers (rare); retouched cores (?adzes). *Light duty:* backed and truncated bladelets; backed flakes; unifacial (short triangular) points; small convex scrapers; burins (rare); proto-burins. This volume, Plates 43–47.	Hillslope deposits A4 Excavation, 1959 and 1963.	
				Rubble component	*Flakes:* all formes especially elliptic, quadrilateral and triangular. Plain, faceted and point striking platforms; all forms of dorsal scar pattern. *Cores:* single platform (especially pyramidal); two platforms; bipolar, Levallois and discoid. *Utilised/modified:* flakes, blades, fragments, etc. Block? and cobble anvils; rubbers; grindstones; pestles; hammerstones, pigment; *outils esquillés*. *Shaped Tools: large cutting* – none. *Heavy Duty:* convergent and parallel-sided core-axes (rare); core-scrapers: chisels and choppers (rare); ?Bored stone. *Light Duty:* backed flakes and blades; truncated flakes and blades; unifacial and bifacial points; small scrapers (most forms); *becs* (rare); burins; borers; discs (later form). This volume, Plates 48–54	Surface of rubble at northern end of Excavation A2, 1956. Bed 7, Excavation A4, 1959. Rubble 1, (a, b, and composite), Sites A, B, C, and D: Mbwilo Member.	9550 ± 210 B.P. (7600 B.C.)
'Middle Stone Age'	Lupemban	Siszya		Component B	*Flakes:* all forms; plain, faceted and point striking platforms. All dorsal scar patterns. *Cores:* single and two platforms; formless; proto-biconical and biconical (rare); Levallois (all types) discoid. *Utilized/modified:* block anvils; split cobble anvils; rubbers; grindstones; pigment.	Mbwilo Member. Red Rubble Bed and Rubble I (*a*, *b*, *c* and composite). Sites A, B. C and D, 1956, 1959, 1963, 1966.	

					Shaped tools: large cutting – Lanceolates. *Heavy duty:* parallel (later forms) divergent and convergent (later) core-axes, earlier convergent forms (rare); picks (round-ended); core-scrapers; chisels; choppers. *Light duty:* backed flakes and blades; truncated flakes and blades; trapezes; unifacial and bifacial points; small scrapers (all forms); *becs*; borers.		27,500 ± 2300 B.P. (25,500 ± 2300 B.C.)
				Component A	*Flakes:* irregular, elliptic, quadrilateral (large blades characteristic), triangular. Radial, parallel and convergent dorsal scar patterns. Plain and faceted striking platforms. *Cores:* single platform (normal and angle); two platforms; form less; proto-biconical and biconical; Levallois (flake and blade); discoid. *Utilized/modified:* flakes, large blades, cores, fragments and chunks. Block anvils. Hammerstones. *Shaped tools: large cutting* – lanceolates, large scrapers. *Heavy duty:* convergent and parallel sided (earlier form) core-axes; picks (convergent and round ended); core-scrapers; chisels; choppers; polyhedrals. *Light duty:* points (unifacial); small scrapers (most forms); *becs*; burins (dihedral, single blow); proto-burins; pointed tools; discs (earlier form); backed blades (large).	Mbwilo Member. Rubble I(*a*, *b*, *c* and composite). Sites A, B, C, D, 1956, 1959, 1963.	30,500 ± 2000 B.P. 28,550 ± 2000 B.C.)
		Nakisasa			*Flakes:* mostly irregular, elliptic, short and long quadrilateral, short triangular with radial, parallel and convergent dorsal scar patterns. Plain and faceted striking platforms. *Cores:* single platform (normal and angle); two platforms; formless; proto-biconical and biconical; Levallois and discoid (rare). *Utilized/modified:* flakes, blades, fragments, chunks and core forms. *Shaped tools: large cutting* – handaxes and cleavers (rare); large scrapers. *Heavy duty:* core-axes (convergent and parallel sided); picks (pointed); polyhedrals; stone balls; choppers; chisels; core-scrapers. *Light duty:* small scrapers (most forms); proto-burins; pointed tools; *becs*.	Mkamba Member. Rubble II*a*, II*b* and II – composite. Site A, Excavation A4 and ?A2.	31,660 ± 600 B.P. (> 29,710 ± 600 B.C.)
'First Intermediate'	Sangoan	Chipeta			*Flakes:* mostly irregular with plain striking platforms: quadrilateral flakes with parallel dorsal scar patterns (rare). *Cores:* single platform (normal and angle); two platforms; formless; proto-biconical; biconical. *Utilized/modified:* flakes, cores, fragments and chunks; block anvils. Possibly modified wooden artifact. *Shaped tools: large cutting* – handaxes and cleavers (rare) large scrapers; knives. *Heavy duty:* core-axes (convergent, irregular and truncated forms); picks (convergent and round ended); core-scrapers; chisels; choppers; polyhedrals. *Light duty:* small scrapers (all forms except micro-convex); *becs*, burins (single blow, dihedral, polyhedral); proto-burins; pointed tools; discs (earlier form).	Mkamba Member: Ochreous Sands and Grey Clay Beds Site B Occupation surface (B2: Bed 20*b*) and channel deposits. Excavations B1 and B2, 1956 and 1959. Site A Excavations A1, A4, A5. Channel deposits.	37,900 + 1500 − 1200 B.P. (35,950 B.C.) 43,000 ± 3300 B.P. 42,000 ± 3000 B.P. (40,550 B.C.) 40,600 ± 1300 B.P. (38,650 ± 1300 B.C.) 46,100 + 3500 − 2400 B.P. (44,150 B.C.)
'Earlier Stone Age'	Upper Acheulian	Bwalya	Inuga Phase		*Flakes:* mostly irregular with plain and pseudo-faceted striking platforms. Handaxe trimming flakes. *Cores:* single platform (normal and angle); two platforms; formless; proto-biconical; biconical. *Utilized/modified:* flakes; cores; fragments and chunks; block anvils; dimple-scarred hammerstones and grindstone (rare). Wooden artifacts modified by scraping and sometimes by the use of fire.	Mkamba Member: White Sands and Dark Clay Beds. *Site A.* Archaeological Horizons: IV (Excavations A1 and A5)	> 60,000 B.P.
			Moola Phase		*Shaped tools: large cutting* – handaxes; cleavers; knives; large scrapers. *Heavy duty:* picks (convergent and parallel); round ended bifaces; core-scrapers; chisels; choppers; polyhedrals; stone balls. *Light duty:* small scrapers (all types except small convex); *becs*; burins (single blow, dihedral); proto-burins; pointed tools; discs (earlier form).	*Site A.* Archaeological Horizons: V (A1); VI (A1) and 1, 2 and 3 (A6). *Site B.* Archaeological Horizons: V (B1 and B2); VI (B1 and B2); VII (B2) and VIII (B2).	

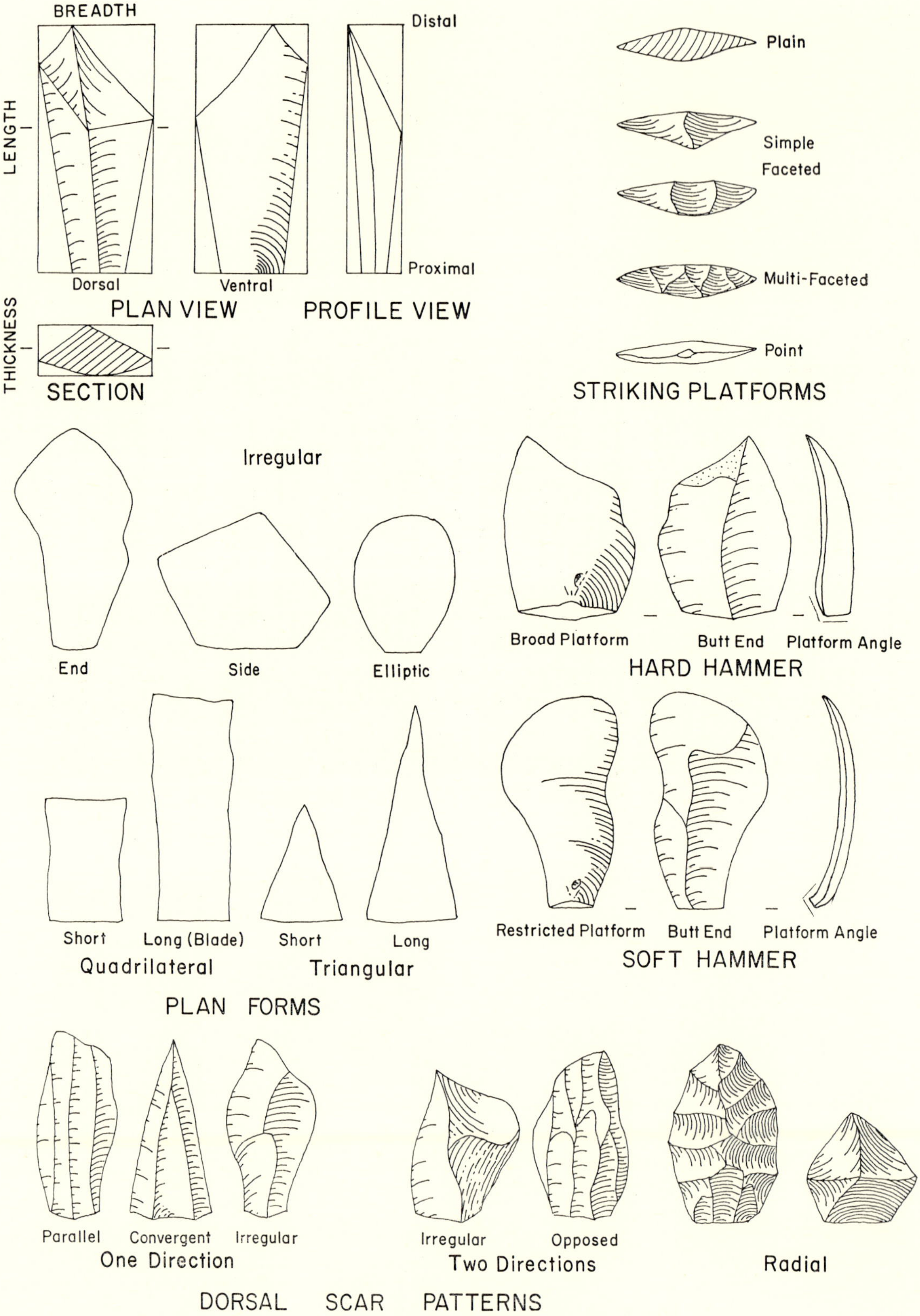

Fig. 7. Characteristics of flakes.

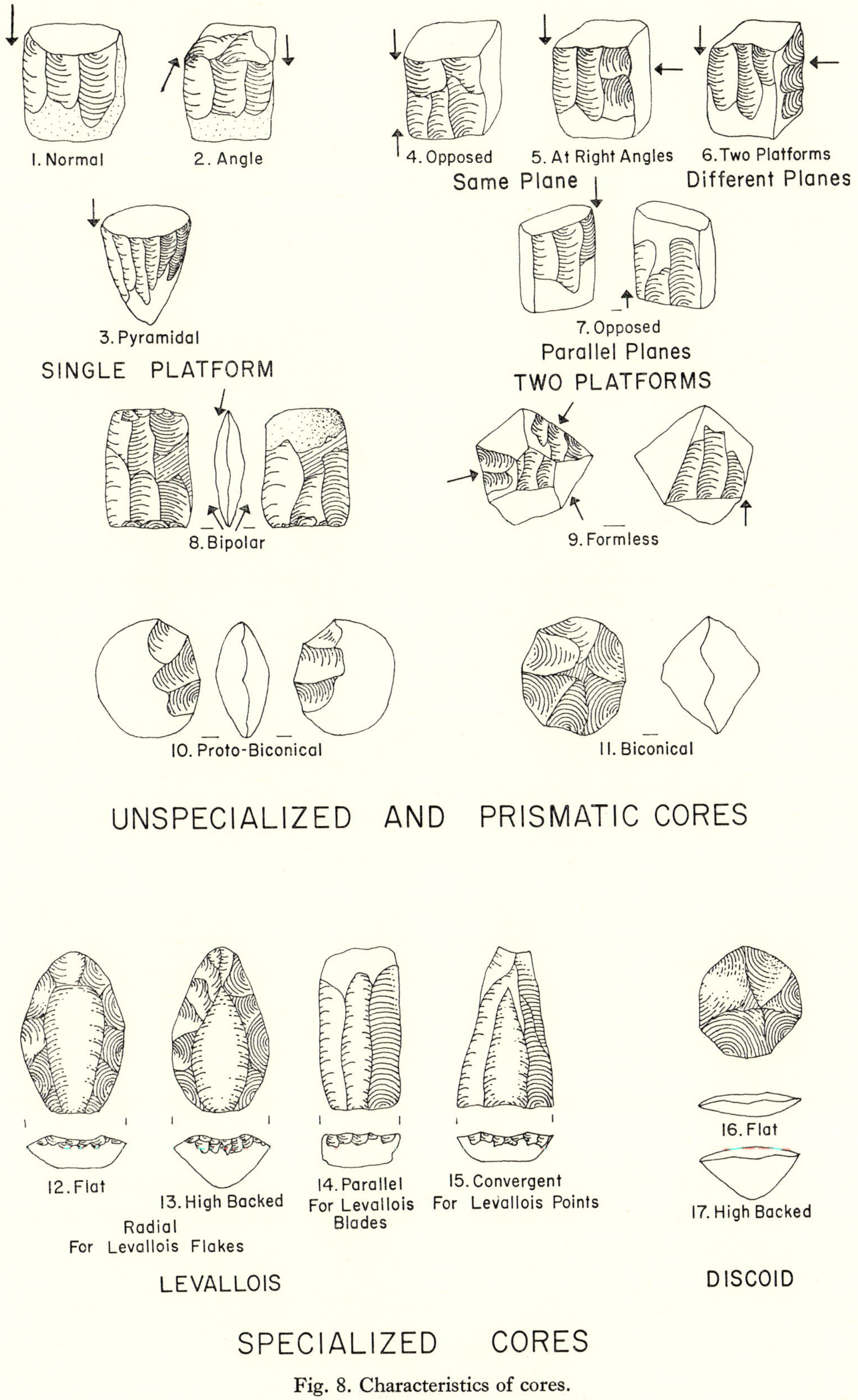

Fig. 8. Characteristics of cores.

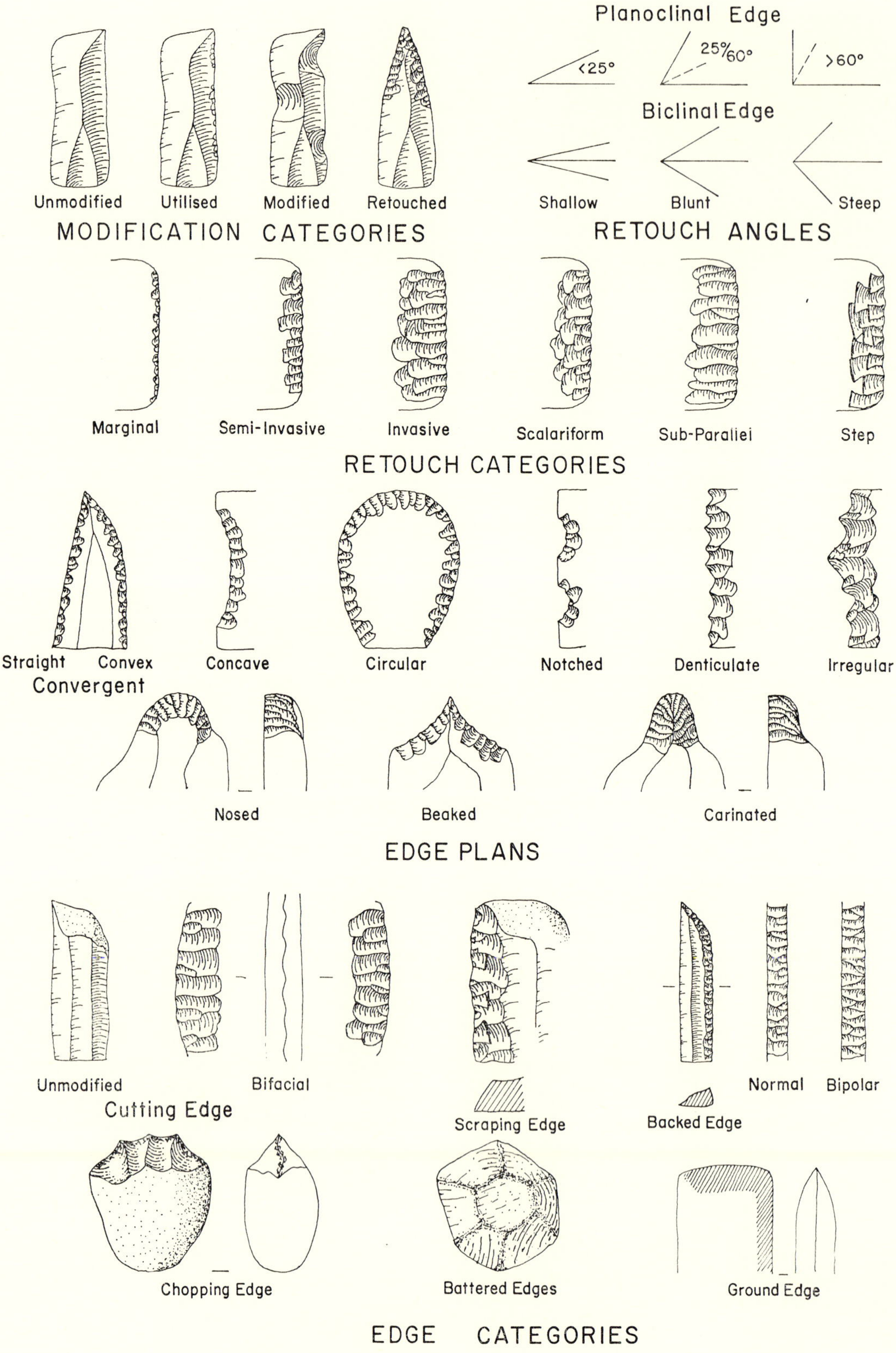

Fig. 9. Modification and retouch categories.

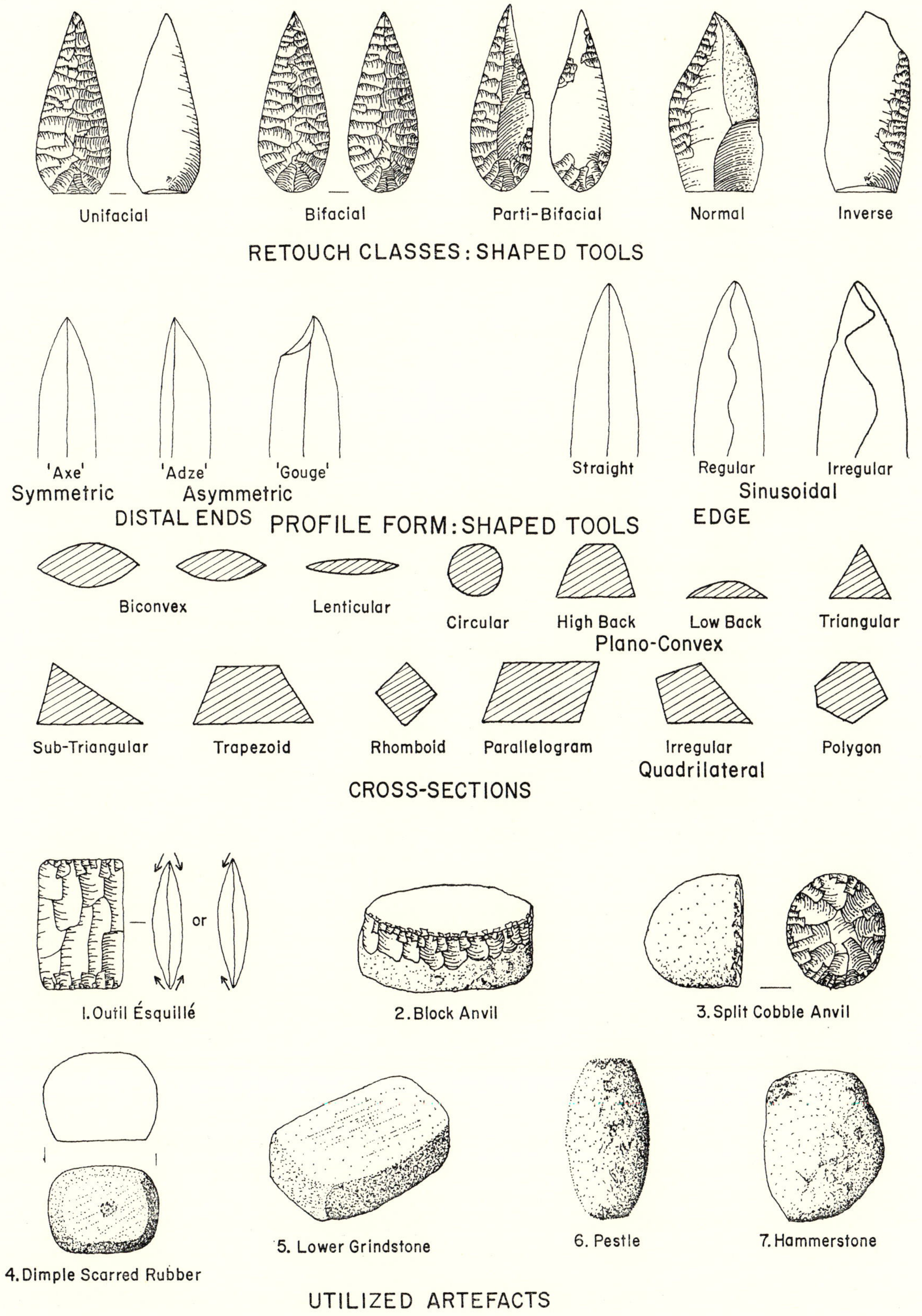
Unifacial
Bifacial
Parti-Bifacial
Normal
Inverse
RETOUCH CLASSES: SHAPED TOOLS
'Axe'
'Adze'
'Gouge'
Symmetric
Asymmetric
DISTAL ENDS
Straight
Regular
Irregular
Sinusoidal
EDGE
PROFILE FORM: SHAPED TOOLS
Biconvex
Lenticular
Circular
High Back
Low Back
Plano-Convex
Triangular
Sub-Triangular
Trapezoid
Rhomboid
Parallelogram
Irregular
Quadrilateral
Polygon
CROSS-SECTIONS
or
1. Outil Ésquillé
2. Block Anvil
3. Split Cobble Anvil
4. Dimple Scarred Rubber
5. Lower Grindstone
6. Pestle
7. Hammerstone
UTILIZED ARTEFACTS

Fig. 10. Retouch and utilization.

plane of measurement of length and breadth, between the opposite faces of an artifact.

Classes of artifacts that generally have the greatest dimension equal to or more than 100 mm have been classed here as 'large', those under 100 mm as 'small'.

Plan view. This is the view of the artifact when orientated in the horizontal plane, i.e. when flat on the table. The *plan form* is the shape of the artifact when seen in plan view.

Profile form is the shape of the artifact when seen at right angles to the plan view.

Face or surface. An artifact orientated in the horizontal plane (plan view) has two faces – a *ventral*, or lower face and a *dorsal*, or upper face. In the case of a flake or a tool made from a flake, blade or fragment of these, the ventral face is always the *main flake surface* or *main release face*. In cases where it is not possible to distinguish the main release face, the flatter of the two faces has been selected as the ventral face.

Cross-section. Unless otherwise stated, the cross-section is the section across the short axis of the artifact midway down and at right-angles to the long axis. Cross-sections, which may be symmetric or asymmetric, are classified as – biconvex, lenticular, circular, plano-convex (high-backed and low-backed), triangular and sub-triangular, trapezoid, rhomboid, parallelogram, irregular quadrilateral, polygon (Figure 10).

Edge. The line where the dorsal and ventral surfaces intersect at the perimeter of the artifact; also, where the artifact is a polyhedron, the line at which any two of the surfaces intersect is termed the edge. The number of edges on an artifact is, thus, determined by the number of angular intersections that can be observed when it is orientated in plan view and, when the artifact is a polyhedron, in both plan and profile views.

Edge plan (Figure 9). This is the line of the edge after modification by retouch or utilization. On artifacts where such a distinction can usefully be made, we may refer to the right or left *lateral edge* and to the *ends*. Edge plans are classified as straight, convex, concave, circular, notched, denticulate, irregular. Where only one edge is modified, the artifact is said to be 'single'; where two edges show retouch it is 'double' and so on.

Proximal and distal ends (Figure 7). The *proximal* or *butt end* of an artifact is that bearing the striking platform or, where no evidence of the striking platform is preserved, it is the end opposed to that showing the most sign of utilization or retouch. The *distal end* is that opposite to the proximal end or butt. In cases where the lateral edges converge at a low angle this intersection is known as *the point*. Proximal and distal ends may also be in the plane of, oblique to or vertical to the main axis. Retouched ends may be straight, convex, concave, carinate, nosed, beaked, convergent or irregular. They may also be straight or oblique to the main axis.

When retouch is concentrated on an edge or end so that it is apparent that this was the main operative part of the tool, it is referred to as the *working edge* or *working end*.

Profile view of retouched distal end (Figure 10). Such views of the retouched distal ends of tools are classified as *symmetric* ('axe-ended'), *asymmetric* ('adze-ended') and *concavo-convex* ('gouge-ended').

Profile views of unifacially and bifacially retouched edges are classified as straight, regular sinusoidal or irregular sinusoidal.

CATEGORIES OF MODIFICATION (Figure 9)

Four categories are recognized:

1. *Unmodified:* (*a*) An artifact of any material, carried onto a site by human agency, that shows no evidence of modification; such artifacts are also called *manuports* (M. D. Leakey, 1967). (*b*) Products of intentional primary flaking of stone that show no evidence of secondary trimming or utilization.

2. *Utilized:* an artifact of any material with no intentional trimming to produce modification but with minor fracturing, bruising and crushing, battering or nibbling damage to one or more edges[1] or faces.

3. *Modified:* an artifact that has been minimally trimmed, shows no patterned shaping and does not fit

[1] Although systematic edge damage studies were not carried out at the time the Kalambo Falls aggregates were analysed, it is certain, because of the primary contexts in which many of the aggregates occur, that such studies would provide significant additional evidence of functional differences. Use-wear has been recorded where this was noted.

into any of the shaped tool classes. Some workers classify such artifacts as miscellaneous trimmed/retouched pieces, others as 'utilized'.[1]

4. *Retouched or trimmed:* An artifact that shows significant, patterned flaking with the apparently deliberate intention of altering the form of the piece is said to be retouched or trimmed.[2]

Following Isaac (1968, Figure VIII: 3) retouch is classified as:

Marginal, when confined to the edge of the artifact.

Semi-invasive when it extends half way across the surface of the tool between two edges.

Invasive when retouch extends across more than half of the surface of the tool between two edges.

An edge is said to be *planoclinal* when it shows a 'bevelled margin, asymmetric to the "horizontal" plane of the piece'; such edges, modified or retouched, are characteristic of scrapers. The edge is *biclinal* when both edges show a symmetric bevel, as with handaxes where both faces on the same edge have been retouched (Isaac, 1968, Figure IX: 2–3).

Unifacial retouch is that which is directed from one face, or part of one face, only of an artifact; at the Kalambo Falls such retouch is more usually marginal or semi-invasive. Fine marginal retouch approximates that known as *retouche Ouchtata* in north Africa (Tixier, 1963: 48).

Retouch (Figures 9 and 10) is generally from the ventral onto the dorsal face and is then known as *normal*; when on the ventral face it is known as *inverse* retouch.[3] If retouch on the same edge comes partly from the ventral, partly from the dorsal face, it is said to be *alternate*. Where the retouch is normal on one edge and inverse on the opposite edge, it is here termed *opposed*.

Bifacial retouch is directed from both the ventral and dorsal faces, is often – though not necessarily – invasive and may cover the greater part of both faces of the tool.

Parti-bifacial retouch is used to describe retouch that occurs on both faces of a tool but which is restricted to a particular portion(s) only of one or both faces.

The angle of retouch is the average angle formed at the edge of a tool between the dorsal and the ventral faces and measured with a goniometer; one or both faces of the tool may be retouched. The angle of retouch is most meaningful where flake tools are concerned. Angles have been described as:

(*a*) shallow: under 25°;
(*b*) blunt: 25°–60°;
(*c*) steep: 60°–90° or over.

The angle of retouch is believed to be directly related to the functional purpose of the tool and to the amount of usage and retrimming it has undergone.

Edges (Figure 9) of shaped, modified and utilized artifacts are also classified in accordance with the attributes of what is believed to be the operational or functional part of the tool, as follows:

Cutting edge. This is a long, thin and relatively sharp edge, straight in profile view which may, or may not, be retouched. The angle formed by the intersection of the two faces is usually not more than 45°.

Scraping edge. A planoclinal edge retouched unifacially, generally from the main release surface. The angle of retouch may be shallow but is most commonly blunt or steep.

Backed edge. This is an edge formed by either unifacial or bifacial trimming to produce a steep angle of retouch of approximately 90°. In the case of microliths it is believed that this is designed to facilitate hafting. The term *backing* is also used to describe intentional blunting of this kind. Backing may be *normal* (from the ventral face) or *bipolar* from both faces (*sur enclume*, Tixier, 1963: 87).

Chopping edge. In profile view this is an irregular or sinusoidal edge which may be formed by unifacial, though more commonly by bifacial flaking and often shows bruising or fracture from heavy use. The angle formed by the intersection of the two faces is usually greater than 45°.

[1] J. D. Clark and C. M. Keller have not distinguished between 'utilized' and 'modified' pieces in the analyses and have included both in the 'utilized' category.

[2] Some workers distinguish between a greater amount of and more regular secondary flaking (retouch) and a smaller amount with less regularity. Others again use 'retouch' to denote less and 'trimming' to imply more secondary work. We intentionally make no distinction here.

[3] Inverse retouch along one, sometimes two lateral edges and associated with the Howieson's Poort and later industries in the eastern Cape Province in South Africa has been termed 'Kasouga retouch' after the river of that name near which characteristic artifacts were first found.

Battering or hammer edge. This is the type of bruised and pounded face seen on spheroids and polyhedral stones, anvils and hammerstones.

Other edge types. These may be, for example, pecked or ground edges and edges smoothed by rubbing; also faces smoothed by pecking or rubbing.

FLAKING TECHNIQUES (Figure 7)

The following techniques are recognized as having been used at different times by the prehistoric inhabitants of the local basin at the Kalambo Falls. This recognition is based on comparative studies between the prehistoric artifacts and the products of controlled experiment (carried out both by acknowledged experts in lithic technology such as Bordes, Crabtree and Tixier, and also by ourselves) and ethnographic data concerning extant stone-working techniques. It is, however, necessary to emphasize that, while the products of certain techniques are sufficiently distinctive to preclude their having been made by other flaking methods, this is not always the case and, it must be appreciated, it has been shown that there is nearly always more than one way of producing the same result.

The initial process of fracturing stone for the purpose of obtaining pieces for subsequent use and/or modification is known as *primary flaking*. The broad and heavy flakes used for the manufacture of hand-axes, cleavers and other large cutting tools are distinguished here as *large primary flakes*.[1] The process of altering significantly the form of the by-product by intentional retouch is known as *secondary flaking*.

By-products of primary and secondary flaking are *flakes* (or *blades*) and other forms (see below p. 89). Primary flakes are struck from *cores* which may or may not show evidence of special preparation for determining the shape of the flake(s) produced from them.

A complete flake or blade will exhibit a *striking platform* (or *talon*) which is the portion of the striking platform of the core remaining on the proximal end of the flake after removal; a *main release surface* on the ventral side exhibiting a bulb or semi-cone of percussion and sometimes also concentric rings, bulbar scar and shatter lines resulting from the blow that removed the flake from the core. The dorsal face preserves either a varying degree of cortex (the original, weathered surface of the stone) or the partial or complete scars resulting from the previous removal of flakes from that surface of the core.

Striking platforms are either *plain* – showing cortex or a portion of a simple fracture face; or *faceted* – showing portions of two or more scars indicating previous preparation of the core platform. Where it exhibits not more than four facets a striking platform is *simple faceted* (S/faceted or S/F in the tables) and when five or more facets are present it is *multi-faceted* (M/faceted or M/F in the tables).[2] Where the detaching blow has been struck so close to the edge of the core that only a bulb of percussion without any striking platform results, the product is termed a *point platform*.

When the measurement of the striking platform between the two shoulders (i.e. its length) is equal to half, or more than half the flake breadth it is said to be *broad*. When this measurement is less than half, the platform is *restricted*. The *thickness* of a striking platform is the maximum measurement at right angles to that between the shoulders; in the case of restricted platforms, this measurement is generally also low.

The *platform angle*, in our usage, is that formed by the intersection of the surface of the platform and the proximal end of the main release surface of the flake.

FLAKING BY PERCUSSION (Figure 7)

A. Hard Hammer

1. *By hammerstone.* Together with the direct anvil method, this is probably the commonest way of working stone. Flakes are removed from the artifact being shaped by means of a stone hammer held in the hand. The resulting flakes generally show a broad, plain striking platform, a prominent bulb or semi-cone of percussion and are thick and wide relative to their length. This is equivalent to the term 'Clacton technique' in use in Europe.

2. *By direct anvil* (formerly 'block-on-block', see Bishop and Clark, 1967: 898). Flakes are removed by striking the piece against a stationary anvil. This method most readily produces large, thick flakes especially where the raw material occurs in the form of boulders or large blocks. The method was also

[1] M. R. Kleindienst used the term *trimming flake* to distinguish the ordinary debitage products of primary flaking.

[2] M. R. Kleindienst has included 4 facets with the multi-faceted unless the platform is very broad relative to the number of scars. On subsequent reflection, a better way of assessing faceting is probably as an expression of the number of facets relative to the length of the platform.

used to break up large boulders of quartzite and other hard rock, by striking one against the other with considerable force until one or other (or both) fractured, producing by repeated blows a number of large flakes and blocks (cf. the Acheulian Industry at the Kalambo Falls). From these by-products a selection was made for trimming into hand-axes, cleavers, knives and other large tools.

Study of flaking products in the many hard rocks used in Africa by the makers of the Acheulian in relation to our own experiments with these materials, has led us to believe that the finely made *large cutting tools* (see below p. 95) are more likely to have been produced from such materials by the direct anvil method than by a hand-held, soft hammer. By using an anvil with a rounded striking surface and by varying the angle and force of the blow, as well as the area of contact between artifact and anvil, it is possible to remove flakes of these hard rocks that exhibit all the characteristics obtained by soft hammer technique. Our experiments have led us to believe that a hand-held hammer of bone, horn or wood (antler was not available to prehistoric man in Africa south of the Sahara) is not of sufficient hardness to work easily such intractable rocks. So far as we are aware from the published literature, the experimental work of acknowledged experts in lithic technology has been carried out using relatively 'soft' and homogeneous rocks – for example, flint, fine-grained quartzites and volcanic rocks, obsidian and other crypto-crystalline stone – which fracture comparatively readily when struck with a 'soft', hand-held hammer. Clearly, further experiment using the 'hard', tough rocks – hard quartzites, basalt, dolerite, andesite, gneiss or granite, for example – favoured so often by Lower Palaeolithic man in Africa and India, can be expected to improve understanding of what can and cannot be achieved by the 'hard' and 'soft' hammer techniques. It should also be borne in mind that, besides stone, hard wood or a large bone might have served effectively as an anvil.

3. *By indirect anvil.* The edge to be flaked is rested on the anvil and the piece is struck by a hand-held hammer on the upper and opposite face. If the angle made between the platform on the lower edge of the piece and the anvil is correct, a flake or flakes will be removed from this edge. Thick or thin, broad or narrow flakes can be removed by varying the angle between the artifact and the anvil, the contact area formed by the platform and the force of the blow. *Anvils* may be: (*a*) *spherical* or *sub-spherical* or (*b*) *block*. Block anvils exhibit at least one flat face of which one or more edges have a scar pattern of persistent fracture with much step flaking and evidence of crushing and battering.

We believe also that many of the Levallois flakes and blades found with aggregates at the Kalambo Falls were removed by some kind of rest or indirect anvil technique. A number of the cores show a small, battered area on the base, to one side of the axis of the flake removal and this would appear to be directly related to the method of removing the flake. Our own experiments for detaching such flakes, directly by means of a stone hammer or indirectly with the core reversed and the prepared platform resting on the edge of the anvil, were never very successful and the flake generally shattered or hinged out. However, a greater degree of success is possible if the core is first wrapped with bark or leather before it is struck. This permits the force behind the detaching blow to be diffused over the release surface and greatly reduces shattering. Among the Highland populations of New Guinea, where the bipolar technique is used, one method of working the core is first to wrap it with bark. This results in longer and thinner flakes, permits the use of smaller pieces of stone as cores and keeps all the flakes neatly together (White, 1968*b*: 661 and Plate 1). It seems possible that the wrapping of cores may have been widespread in antiquity when the necessity arose for more blade-like flakes.

Where flakes are removed from both ends of a vertically held piece by the indirect anvil method, the resulting core is said to be *bipolar* and to result from *bipolar technique*.

Indirect anvil technique is probably that most commonly used to produce the backing on microliths and perhaps for striking bladelets and micro-flakes from diminutive cores such as those found with the microlithic Kaposwa aggregates at the Kalambo Falls.

B. Soft hammer

Because it is softer, a hammer of antler, bone or hard wood will 'give' on striking the stone. This penetration of the hammer by the stone diffuses the force more shallowly over the face of the artifact than is the case with hard hammer technique. Since also the blow is generally directed so that only the very edge of the artifact comes into contact with the hammer, the striking platform of the resulting flake is usually minimal. Besides being thinner, flakes are generally more sinuous, longer in relation to breadth, concavo-convex in profile view and often have a shallow bulb and lip to the sharply inclined striking platform, which may be *pseudo-faceted* when the tool being retouched is a biface. Such flakes are common on the Acheulian occupation floors at the Kalambo Falls prehistoric site and have been termed *hand-axe trimming flakes* (see p. 89 below). While they have generally been considered the characteristic products of soft hammer technique, it must be stressed that flakes with precisely similar attributes can be obtained by the anvil method, as has been pointed out above.

As discussed above, while it seems probable that the tools made of hard rocks were the result of controlled flaking by the direct anvil method, tools made from feldspathic quartzite, silicified mudstone or chert, are more likely to have been the products of conventional soft hammer technique which lends itself to the production of thinner and more shapely tools. Crabtree's experiments using wooden billets and other hammers (Crabtree, 1970) have also shown that these characteristic, thin, flat flakes can be produced by more than one kind of fabricator and technique. The differences in the products of hard and soft hammer techniques have recently been well demonstrated by Newcomer (1971).

C. Punch

Punch technique employs the intermediary of a punch of soft material, the lower end being rested on the prepared platform edge of the core. When the upper end of the punch is struck with a hammerstone, a flake or blade is removed from the flaking face of the core. Flakes or blades removed by punch technique show a small but prominent, nipple-like bulb and a very restricted, or negligible striking platform. Diminutive step flaking and bruising on the dorsal face of the blade at the proximal end are the result of careful preparation of a regular edge on the platform which, experiment has shown, is essential for the successful use of punch technique for the manufacture of blades. The platform edges of micro-cores commonly show this kind of preparation. This technique has been demonstrated and more fully described by Bordes (1967: 42–5).

Punches are likely to have been made of horn, bone or hard wood in Africa. In our own experiments the best results were obtained by using a horn punch.

An interesting survival of punch technique for the manufacture of gunflints is known from the southern part of the Congo Basin (Clark, 1963: 171–83). The artifact or core is held between the heels of the seated worker who thus has both hands free for using the punch and bar hammer (Plate 97). A modification of this method is still practised in the Western Province of Zambia (Phillipson, 1969*a*). The end-products of these techniques are not easily distinguishable from those of pressure-flaking, but the primary flakes exhibit the attributes produced by punch technique except that they are generally shorter and broader.

As with soft hammer technique, thinner and more shapely tools can be obtained by the punch method, since the precise point on the platform edge can be selected prior to removal of the flake. There is clear evidence of punch technique with the Kalambo Falls facies of the Lupemban and later aggregates.

D. Flaking by pressure

There is no very good evidence of pressure flaking in the industries at the Kalambo Falls but it is possible that some of the small points with the Polungu aggregates were retouched by this method since some of them exhibit very small, flat, sinusoidal and sub-parallel scars. Microliths may also sometimes have been backed by pressure though the steep backing these exhibit can better be produced by the indirect anvil method.

CATEGORIES OF RETOUCH (Figure 9)

The scar patterns resulting from secondary flaking that are found at the Kalambo Falls are: *scaled* (*retouche en écaille*), *sub-parallel* (*retouche sub-parallèle*) and *step* (*retouche écailleuse scalariforme*) (Bordes, 1961: 8–9). Step flaking is most common on small scrapers and other small tools with Acheulian and Sangoan aggregates and scaled and sub-parallel retouch are more generally associated with the Lupemban and Polungu aggregates, as also with the retouched distal, or working ends of core-axes.

Artifact typology

The major categories of stone artifacts are as follows:

A. Unmodified waste (flaking debris; debitage). Flakes, flake fragments, chunks and cores which are by-products of intentional flaking but which show no evidence of utilization or further modification.

B. Utilized. Pieces that exhibit damage or wear on an edge or edges, or on a face or faces, such as very minute and marginal flake scars, bruising, crushing, battering and rubbing, that show no regular pattern and which experiment indicates to result from use (see also p. 84 above).

C. Modified. Miscellaneous, informal pieces that show no patterned flaking but which exhibit a few scars resulting from deliberate modification (see also p. 84 above).[1]

D. Shaped tools. All artifacts that show regular, patterned retouch which significantly alters the original shape of the piece.

A. UNMODIFIED WASTE

I. Flakes (Figure 7)
Sub-divided on the basis of plan form (see p. 84 above) into:

(i) *End-struck* – any flake in which the length, when measured perpendicular to the striking platform (see p. 77 above) exceeds or equals the breadth.

(ii) *Side-struck* – any flake in which the length, when measured perpendicular to the striking platform, is less than the breadth i.e. less than the axis parallel to the striking platform (see Isaac and Keller, 1968).

Unmodified flakes having the greatest dimension over 100 mm are also referred to as *large primary flakes.*

The plan forms of flakes are described as:
(*a*) irregular (end-struck and side-struck – 'end' and 'side' in the tables);
(*b*) short quadrilateral (S/Q in the tables);
(*c*) long quadrilateral or *blade* (in the tables L/Q or Blade) having the length greater than twice the breadth or equal to twice the breadth. *Bladelets* are diminutive blades with the length less than 50 mm;
(*d*) triangular (long and short);
(*e*) elliptic.

Dorsal scar patterns.[2] (*a*) Flaking from one direction only (one directional) which may be (i) convergent, (ii) parallel or (iii) irregular. (*b*) Two-directional flaking, either (i) irregular or (ii) opposed. (*c*) Multi-directional or radial flaking.

Flakes which were produced by the working of prismatic blade cores and those produced by the working of Levallois or disc cores are referred to as *specialized flakes* (formerly 'prepared' flakes). They are recognized on the basis of their dorsal scars, shape and platform characteristics. The blade and Levallois cores recovered suggest that it is not always possible to differentiate the flakes which came from prismatic blade cores and those from Levallois blade cores with parallel or convergent trimming (see also p. 91 below).

Striking platforms (see p. 86 above). Any or all of the plan forms, dorsal scar patterns and striking platforms may be found associated with most core forms recognized. However, the multi-directional and one-directional, convergent, primary preparation and multi-faceted striking platforms are more commonly associated with cores that have been specially prepared.

Special flake forms (Figure 7)

1. *Hand-axe/cleaver trimming flakes* (*éclat de taille de biface*). Flakes possibly removed by 'soft hammer technique' in the later stages of shaping a biface. For attributes see p. 88 above.

2. *Core-axe utilization or resharpening spalls.* In a number of cases the working ends of core-axes have been removed by blows struck on one or other of the faces or side edges of the tool. It is possible that these ends may have been fortuitously removed though the number found makes it more probable that the removal was intentional in order to resharpen the end of the tool after it had become blunt. In several cases the scars left on the core-axe bear unmistakable indications of re-use (Clark, 1964).

Some Lupemban core-axes have been made on what appear to be flat, sub-rectangular cores, trimmed bifacially. From these there have sometimes been removed one or more long, thin quadrilateral flakes or blades having characteristics very suggestive of punch technique (see p. 88 above) and showing evidence of a radial scar pattern on the dorsal face. If, as is believed, these artifacts were the blades of axes or adzes

[1] The original form of an artifact has sometimes also been modified by *pecking* or hammering with or on another stone. This crushes small areas of the stone and leaves minute concoidal fracture scars. Spheroids not infrequently show such modification, though whether intentionally or incidentally from use, which is more probable, cannot yet be shown. Intentional pecking is clearly present, however, on some of the ground stone axes/adzes associated with the Kaposwa microlithic aggregates and it is apparent that this was, by that time, a regular method of modifying the original form of the stone in conjunction with grinding. Such artifacts are, therefore, classified with the Shaped Tools.

[2] At the time our analyses were carried out no routine count was made of the number of dorsal scars so that this attribute is recorded only in specific instances.

and not simply a special kind of core, then the blade-like flakes derived from them could either have been intended for re-sharpening a blunt working end or have been due to fortuitous fracture resulting from over zealous use.

3. *Core rejuvenating spalls.* When the platforms of unprepared or angle cores (see below p. 90) become too battered by use, the whole or part of an old platform may be removed. When struck at right angles to the flaked surface, the rejuvenating flake bearing the old platform is either broad – removing the whole of the platform face – or long and triangular in section – removing only the edge. The retouched edges of core-scrapers have also sometimes been resharpened in this way (e.g. Plate 39: 24, 36–38; Plate 45: 6, 7).

II. Cores (Figure 8)
Cores are those nuclei that remain after flakes and blades have been intentionally removed and flakes and cores can be correlated by means of the scars on the latter. Cores are divided into:

(*a*) *Unspecialized cores* classified according to the number and nature of the striking platform(s); and

(*b*) *Specialized* (*formerly 'prepared'*) *cores* where the flake release face or faces and also sometimes the striking platform may show special preparation. It has proved useful and necessary, for some purposes, to include the products of prismatic blade, Levallois and discoidal techniques of flake production at the Kalambo Falls, under one heading. In many cases, which technique produced a given flake cannot be determined with any certainty, although it can be associated with this range of techniques. A number of cores intergrade, technologically and typologically, and it appears likely that all of these techniques might have been applied by the same artisan. It has been generally recognized that these techniques have important advantages over those employing cores which we designate as unspecialized. These advantages are an increased complexity in the manufacturing process resulting in greater predictability of the attributes of the end-product; and consequently more efficiency, as less effort and less raw material are needed, particularly in the case of blade technology. The application of these techniques effectively increased the range and quantity of raw materials available for use and we, therefore, regard them as *specialized.* As defined here, specialized cores are sub-divided into:

(i) *Prismatic cores for the production of quadrilateral flakes.* Such cores show a parallel (sometimes convergent) scar pattern on the flake release surface(s) and may have more than one striking platform.

(ii) *Discoid or Levallois cores.* These exhibit a parallel, radial or convergent scar pattern on the specially prepared release surface(s) and are designed for the removal of one or more 'prepared' flakes.

Specialized prismatic blade and unspecialized cores have been classified according to the number of striking platforms and the positions in which they occur on the specimen. Sub-classes (i)–(iv) below may all include prismatic blade core forms but these are most commonly represented by (i) single platform cores (including the pyramidal form),[1] (ii) two platform cores (in particular the type with opposed platforms) and (iii) bipolar cores for the production of micro-blades.

(*a*) *Unspecialized cores and prismatic blade cores.* These are usually on chunks or angular fragments, less commonly on cobbles. In general, the younger the aggregate the more regular are the scar patterns on the associated cores.

(i) *Single platform.* Either a single striking platform, more usually unfaceted, from which flakes/blades have been removed from one flaked surface; or a single platform from which flakes have been struck in two directions using as platform the scar of the previous detachment. These last have been called *Angle Cores* by Kleindienst (1962: 99) since the flaking surfaces are often at right angles. When found with the Acheulian they produced only flakes.

A special form of single platform, prismatic core in which the striking platform is circular, or nearly so, with the scars of the flakes/blades removed from it meeting at the apex of an inverted pyramid is termed a *pyramidal core*, or, more strictly speaking, a conical core.[2]

[1] Occasionally cores are struck from a single platform in parallel planes.

[2] We distinguish between cores designed primarily for the production of blades and those producing only flakes. Although blade cores may also produce flakes the reverse is not the case. At the Kalambo Falls, blade cores make their appearance in Rubble II. They are recurrent with the Siszya aggregates and usually show some preparation of the striking platform. At first this usually takes the form of faceting of the platform surface and later of the more regular preparation of the platform edge. Pyramidal and other single platform prismatic cores for the production of blades and bladelets by punch technique also make their appearance with the Siszya aggregates.

(ii) *Two platforms.* These platforms may be either at right angles or at opposite ends of the core, struck *in the same plane on the same face*. When the platforms are struck in *parallel planes*, they may be at right angles or at opposite ends of the core on *opposed faces*.

(iii) *Bipolar cores* are a special form of opposed platform core and are the products of the bipolar flaking technique (see p. 87 above). Flakes/blades may be removed from both platforms on one or both faces. More rarely, the scar pattern shows fracturing from only one platform, in which case battering at the opposite end of the core provides evidence of its having been rested on the anvil. Scar patterns show step flaking and splintering; where the flaking is bifacial, the platform is a ridge and the by-products show only a point platform (see p. 86 above). Such cores are not uncommon with the microlithic aggregates and grade into the splintered pieces known as *outils esquillés* or *outils écaillés* (see p. 92 below).

(iv) *Two platforms on two faces in different planes.* These are generally chunky cores and the flaking faces to which the platforms relate are usually contiguous. Occasionally, prismatic cores have more than two platforms struck in different planes.

(v) *Formless cores* are polyhedral nuclei (equivalent to Isaac's 'irregular polyfaceted cores' (Isaac, 1968: x, 4)) showing more than two striking platforms and have often been casually struck, only a small number of flakes having been removed from each platform. 'Bashed chunk' cores (Kleindienst, 1962: 98) are a less worked class of formless core, equivalent to Isaac's 'casual cores' (Isaac, 1968: x, 5).

(vi) *Proto-biconical cores* are angular chunks or cobbles that have been flaked from one face or alternately from opposite faces to produce a sinuous edge round not more than half the periphery. These are synonymous with the radially trimmed 'pebble' and 'chunk' cores of Kleindienst (1962: 98) and are regarded as partially worked biconical cores. They grade into angle cores and are sometimes of large size.

(vii) *Biconical cores.* Angular chunks or cobbles that have been flaked alternately on both faces using the previous platform on the one face for the removal of the next flake from the opposite face. Approximately circular in plan form, these cores show radial flaking on each face converging at the centre and they always have a rhomboid or thick, biconvex section, though frequently one face is flatter than the other. Sometimes they are of large size.

The above cores, with the possible exception of some of the later 'pyramidal' cores, show no preparation of the flaking surface or striking platform which may be plain or simple-faceted. However, the later flakes removed, in particular from proto-biconical and biconical cores, will show simple faceted striking platforms, but this is pseudo-faceting and does not represent preparation of the striking platform. Some of the single and two platform blade cores associated with the Lupemban aggregates do, however, show intentional preparation of the striking platform.

(*b*) *Specialized (formerly 'prepared') cores.* There are two main classes of dorsally prepared cores: (i) Levallois cores and (ii) disc cores. It is often difficult, if not impossible to distinguish between the two where no flake has been removed from the prepared surface. In such cases the cores are termed *unstruck* and those which have had the flake or flakes removed are termed *struck* cores.

(i) *Levallois cores.* These are cores which have been specially prepared, generally for the removal of a single large flake or blade of predetermined form. Preparation of the flaking surface is generally again necessary before a further flake/blade is removed. Striking platforms are often simple- or multi-faceted but may also be plain. The angle between the prepared surface and the platform is steep (see pp. 85 and 86 above), often a right angle. Plan forms may be oval to circular, in which case the prepared face generally shows radial preparation; sub-triangular with either radial or convergent preparation; or sub-rectangular with parallel or convergent flaking from one or both ends. In the last instance, the core is classified as Levallois only if the striking platform shows preparatory faceting. The flakes removed from the above cores have much the same shape as the cores themselves.[1]

Certain cores (e.g. Figure 8: 14), generally of small size, that show one-directional or opposed dorsal preparation and usually careful faceting of the striking platform have been classified here with *Levallois blade cores.* However, since at least some minimal, radial dorsal preparation appears to be characteristic of the Levallois blade cores illustrated by Bordes (1961: Plate 104) and Brézillon (1968: 89), these Kalambo Falls cores are not strictly comparable and, although Levallois-related, they lie technically between the Levallois and prismatic blade cores.

[1] Some 'para-Levallois cores' – those struck across the long axis (de Heinzelin, 1962: 9) – occur but they have not been counted as a separate type.

Since they are associated with the Polungu Industry, and for clarification, it might be preferable to refer to them as 'Polungu cores'.[1]

(ii) *Disc* (*or discoid*) *cores*. These are radially prepared cores for the removal, from round the periphery, of several flakes from one or both faces. As flakes are removed, the diameter is reduced and the core will be discarded when it becomes too small to yield flakes of the size required.

Levallois cores grade into disc cores following continual use as we were recently able to demonstrate in Malawi (Clark *et al.* 1970: 341). When, therefore, a core is too small to produce Levallois flakes, it is often worked as a disc core until this, in turn, becomes too small for the removal of useful flakes and is finally discarded.

Levallois and disc cores may both show either asymmetric biconvex or lenticular sections; the former are referred to as *high-backed* and the latter as *flat*. Disc cores may be distinguished from biconical cores in that they have at least one flattened flake release surface, and often retain cortex on the ventral face.

III. Flake and blade fragments

Incomplete fragments of flakes/blades, including chips, from which the original measurements of the piece cannot be reconstructed. Proximal ends have sometimes been counted separately to show the ratio of faceted to non-faceted striking platforms.

IV. Chunks

These are irregular pieces of stone, the by-products of artificial fracture, other than broken fragments of flakes or blades. Some authors classify fragments and chunks together as *angular waste*.

B. UTILIZED (Figure 10)

Utilized pieces are artifacts showing one or more of those evidences of modification believed to result from utilization and not from any intentional alteration of the primary form (see p. 88 above).

(i) *Flaked pieces* – flakes, blades, flake or blade fragments, chunks or cores – that have been utilized are classified according to the plan and edge forms, in the same way as are small scraping tools. Cores that show evidence of utilization have been classified with 'cores' for purposes of artifact counts.

These forms grade into the retouched category through classes that some authors have called 'trimmed and utilized' flakes, blades, etc. In these cases the discontinuous marginal trimming generally shows a shallow angle of retouch. Such artifacts, if they show any regular pattern of retouch, have been classified here as shaped tools.

Artifacts showing utilization can now be seen to form a significant part of all lithic aggregates from living sites and a recent study of a 'Later Stone Age' occupation site on the Zambian Copperbelt indicates that '...of all the work done with stone artifacts at the site, only 6·3 per cent was done with artifacts which would normally be classed as implements. The remaining 93·7 per cent was done with artifacts conventionally classed as waste' (Phillipson and Phillipson, 1970: 53–4). The disproportion between retouched and utilized pieces is never so great at the Kalambo Falls. In part this may be accounted for by the general difficulty of distinguishing between utilization and other forms of edge wear at an open site of this kind. Various agencies such as trampling by men and animals, soil and scree creep, rubble formation, weight of overburden after burial, will fracture edges by pressure. Even minor redistribution of artifacts on an occupation surface by gentle water action with fine sediment in suspension will dull or smooth an edge. Furthermore, there is as yet no sure means of distinguishing edge damage due to utilization from that resulting from simultaneous damage and fracture as the piece is detached in primary flaking; from that which results when flakes fall on stony as distinct from soft ground; or the kind of flaking necessitated by the modification of the edge of a core preparatory to flaking. Our counts for artifacts showing flaking by utilization/modification clearly err on the low side, therefore.

(ii) *Outils esquillés* (less correctly *outils écaillés*): generally small or microlithic forms, sub-rectangular in plan form and often with lenticular section. One or both ends show splintering and step flaking, usually on both faces of the piece, of the kind that results from the shock of sudden resistance following several sharp blows. The ridge-like edge, or edges, are generally straight or, more rarely, gouge-shaped when observed from above. They can be distinguished from bipolar cores only by the more regular form of the faceted edges. Since this class grades into bipolar cores and

[1] This kind of core, though of larger dimensions, is also not uncommon with 'Middle Stone Age' assemblages from southern Africa and the Aterian in the central Sahara.

White (1968*b*) has shown that, in the New Guinea Highlands, *outils écaillés* are solely the product of the bipolar flaking method, it may be that the pieces here classified as *outils esquillés* are, in fact, only cores. However, since the characteristic splintering is sometimes found also on flake fragments, thus suggesting its derivation from some special kind of utilization, as a wedge or adze blade, for example, we prefer, for the present, to classify these artifacts separately from cores.

(iii) *Rubbers:* cobbles, pebbles and sub-angular fragments, generally oval or circular in plan form, that exhibit one or more faces which are worn, smoothed and striated by rubbing and grinding. Two types occur at the Kalambo Falls – one with and one without dimple scarring in the centre of the rubbing plane. These may have been used either by themselves or sometimes in conjunction with a lower grindstone (see (iv) below). Not infrequently the circumference of the specimen, at right angles to the grinding surface, will show regular bruising and pounding resulting from use as a pestle.

(iv) *Grindstones:* larger, usually flat stones with one or more faces striated and worn smooth by grinding and rubbing. These surfaces may sometimes show a high gloss which may result from the materials with which the stone was used. The earliest grindstone is found with the Acheulian at the Kalambo Falls.

(v) *Pestle stones.* These are roughly cylindrical cobbles or pebbles having one or both ends used for pounding and showing a regular convex surface or surfaces formed by minute concoidal pitting. They make their first appearance with the Lupemban – the Siszya Industry.

(vi) *Anvils.* Those at the Kalambo Falls are of two kinds: on blocks or boulders and on the halves of split cobbles or pebbles.

(*a*) *Block anvils* have no regular form and the edges of one or more flat faces may have been used. Such edges show evidence of heavy battering, scarring and crushing from one direction.

(*b*) *Split cobble* anvils are a special form associated with the Siszya Industry aggregates and it is likely that they may be connected with some special method of striking flakes and blades by the Levallois technique. Specially selected, usually oval cobbles are centrally split across the short axis and the flat face so formed shows the heavy usage associated with anvil edges, round part or all of the circumference. The pebble cortex forms the striking platform and the direction of the blows is towards the centre of the flat fracture surface.

(vii) *Hammerstones.* These are polyhedral chunks, cobbles or pebbles of a size easily held in the hand and of no regular shape, that show bruising and battering on one or more faces or edges such as results from the hard hammer technique of tool manufacture. Occasionally, hammerstones are dimple scarred and these have been found with the Bwalya Industry (Inugu Phase).

(viii) *Pigment.* Small pieces of rock, usually soft, which, when rubbed, produce a powder suitable for use as paint. At the Kalambo Falls, these materials include haematite (red and purple); limonite and weathered dolerite (yellow); kaolin (white); and ferruginous schists (red and yellow); specular iron was also carried into the valley. In most cases, the pieces of pigment included in the tool lists are those that show rubbing facets and striations resulting from use.

C. MODIFIED

Flaked artifacts – chunks, flakes or fragments – that show minimal but intentional modification as defined above (p. 89). These are invariably informal pieces, unifacially or bifacially flaked, showing no attempt at organized flaking or refinement.

D. SHAPED TOOLS (Figures 11–15)

Shaped tools are artifacts that show deliberate retouch which substantially alters the primary shape of the piece. This category is divided into three subcategories following Kleindienst (1962). Intended originally for use with east African Acheulian assemblages, these sub-divisions are generally applicable to most time periods. However, while these groupings help to distinguish the different 'types' of edge and usage they are not intended as an attempt to define the *method of use*. The three sub-categories are:

1. *Large cutting tools* – hand-axes, cleavers, knives, lanceolates – usually more than 100 mm long and with regular and sharp edges.

2. *Heavy duty tools* – core-axes, picks, choppers, spheroids, core-scrapers, etc. These tools may be more than or less than 100 mm in length and there is no *regular* standardization of the shape of the tool by

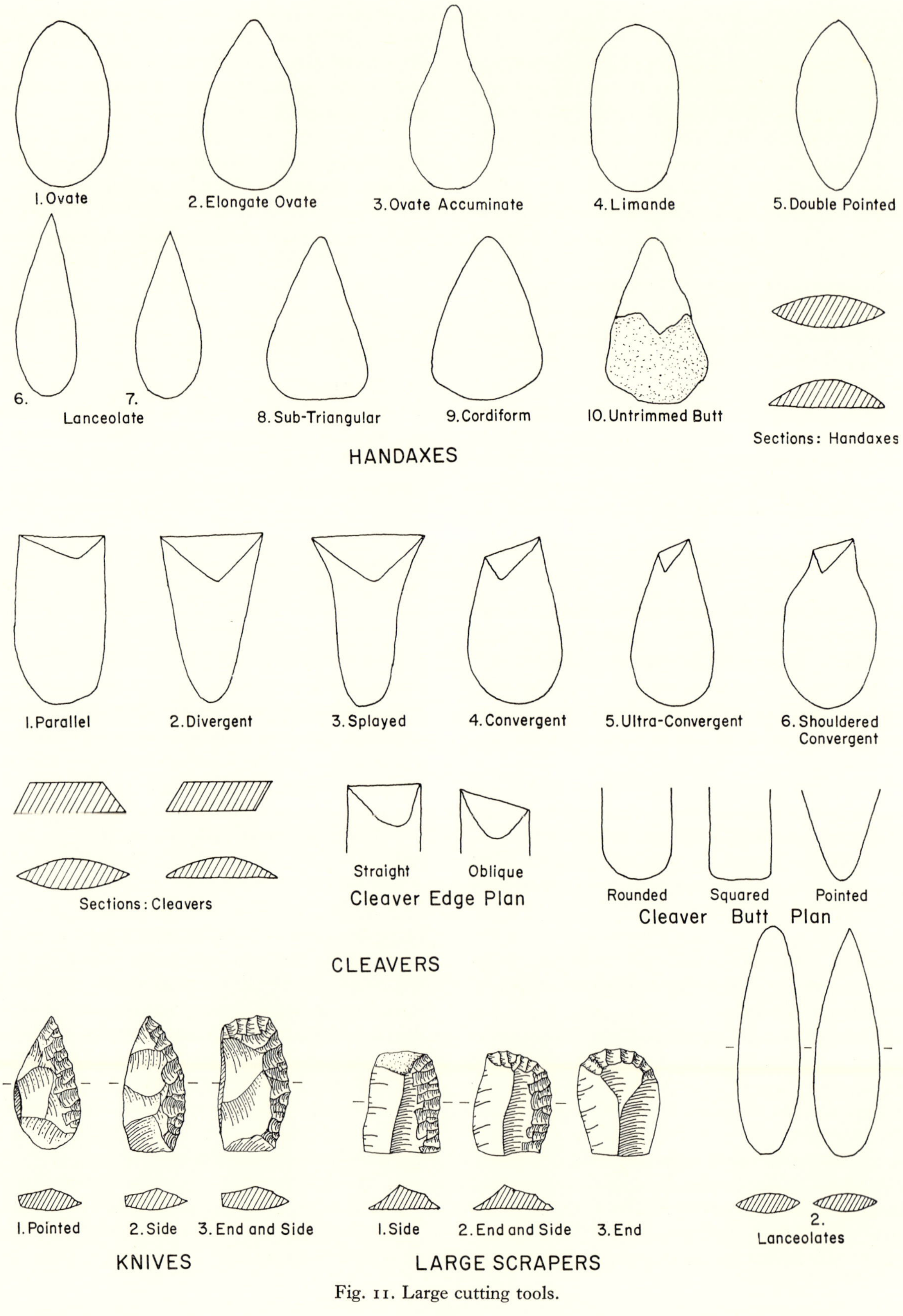

Fig. 11. Large cutting tools.

retouch. The working parts appear to be designed for heavy usage of which they often bear evidence.

3. *Light duty tools* – scrapers, points, awls, burins, microliths, etc. Usually less than 100 mm long, these tools are often made on flakes and blades.

1. *Large cutting tools* (Figure 11)

(*a*) *Hand-axes.* These are generally bifacially retouched but, more rarely, unifacially worked. They are characterized by a flat, biconvex or plano-convex cross-section and a cutting edge around the whole circumference except, sometimes, at or near the butt. The forms found at the Kalambo Falls are classified as follows:

Ovate (*biface ovalaire*)[1]
Elongate ovate (*biface cordiforme allongé* or *biface amygdaloïde*)
Ovate acuminate (*biface micoquien*)
Limande
Double pointed (*biface naviforme*)
Lanceolate (*biface lancéolé* or *ficron*)
Sub-triangular
Cordiform.

Both symmetric and asymmetric forms occur. Hand-axes are found with Acheulian, Sangoan and Lupemban aggregates. Those with the Sangoan and Lupemban appear to have been made by a different technique from that of the Acheulian examples and are thicker with broader and deeper flake scars and rarely show fully invasive retouch.

(*b*) *Cleavers.* Usually made on a large flake (*hachereau sur éclat*) cleavers are generally worked down the side edges and butt and have a cutting end formed by the intersection of one large flake scar on the dorsal face with the main flake, or ventral surface. This cutting end may be straight (approximately at right angles) or oblique to the long axis of the tool and at the Kalambo Falls seldom shows evidence of utilization or damage. The following sub-types are found at the Kalambo Falls:

Parallel edges (Types 1, 2 and 5 of Tixier, 1957);
Convergent edges;
Divergent edges (Types 3 and 4 of Tixier, 1957).

The butts or proximal ends of cleavers are classified as round, square or pointed. Special forms of parallel and divergent edged cleavers have splayed ends and some convergent cleavers may be shouldered and ultra-convergent (*hachereau biface*).[2]

As with hand-axes, cleavers may be both symmetric and asymmetric. In most examples the side edges are bifacially trimmed. Examples retouched only on the dorsal face are termed *cleaver flakes*. The cross-sections are commonly biconvex, trapezoid and parallelogram.

Cleavers are found with Acheulian and, very rarely, with Sangoan and Lupemban aggregates.

(*c*) *Knives:* a term proposed by Kleindienst (1962: 89) for tools having the whole or part of one edge blunted by retouch or naturally 'backed'.[3] The opposite, or cutting edge may show bifacial, unifacial or no retouch. Three sub-classes are represented – pointed; end and side; and side.

Bifacially flaked knives approximate to the forms known as *racloir à retouche biface*: *types – ordinaire et Quina.*

Knives are found with Acheulian and Sangoan aggregates.

(*d*) *Lanceolates* (*biface foliacé* or *pic foliacé*). These are long, bifacially, or parti-bifacially retouched tools with parallel or tapering side edges. One end (distal) is generally more pointed than the other (proximal). The cross-section is symmetrically biconvex and the side edges in profile view are usually straight or regular sinusoidal. These edges, as well as the point, appear to be functional parts of the tool. There are two sub-classes: parallel sided and convergent sided.

Lanceolates occur with Siszya Industry aggregates.

(*e*) *Large scrapers.* Certain large flake scraper forms, found generally with the Acheulian but also with the Chipeta and Nakisasa aggregates, and having predominantly shallow angles of retouch have also been classified among the large cutting tools. The sub-classes are: side; end and side; and end.

(2) *Heavy duty tools* (Figures 12 and 13)

(*a*) *Core-axes* (Figure 12). The earlier forms are usually heavy tools with convergent or parallel edges,

[1] Unless otherwise stated the French equivalents are taken from Bordes, 1961 or de Sonneville-Bordes and Perrot, 1954–6.

[2] Ultra-convergent cleaver forms are also classified as chisel (*biseau*) ended hand-axes by some authors (Chavaillon, 1964: 211 – *biface à biseau terminal*).

[3] Isaac and G. Cole express a preference for splitting the class between hand-axes and cleavers and regard backing as a secondary attribute (personal communication: Urbana Acheulian Meeting, 1971).

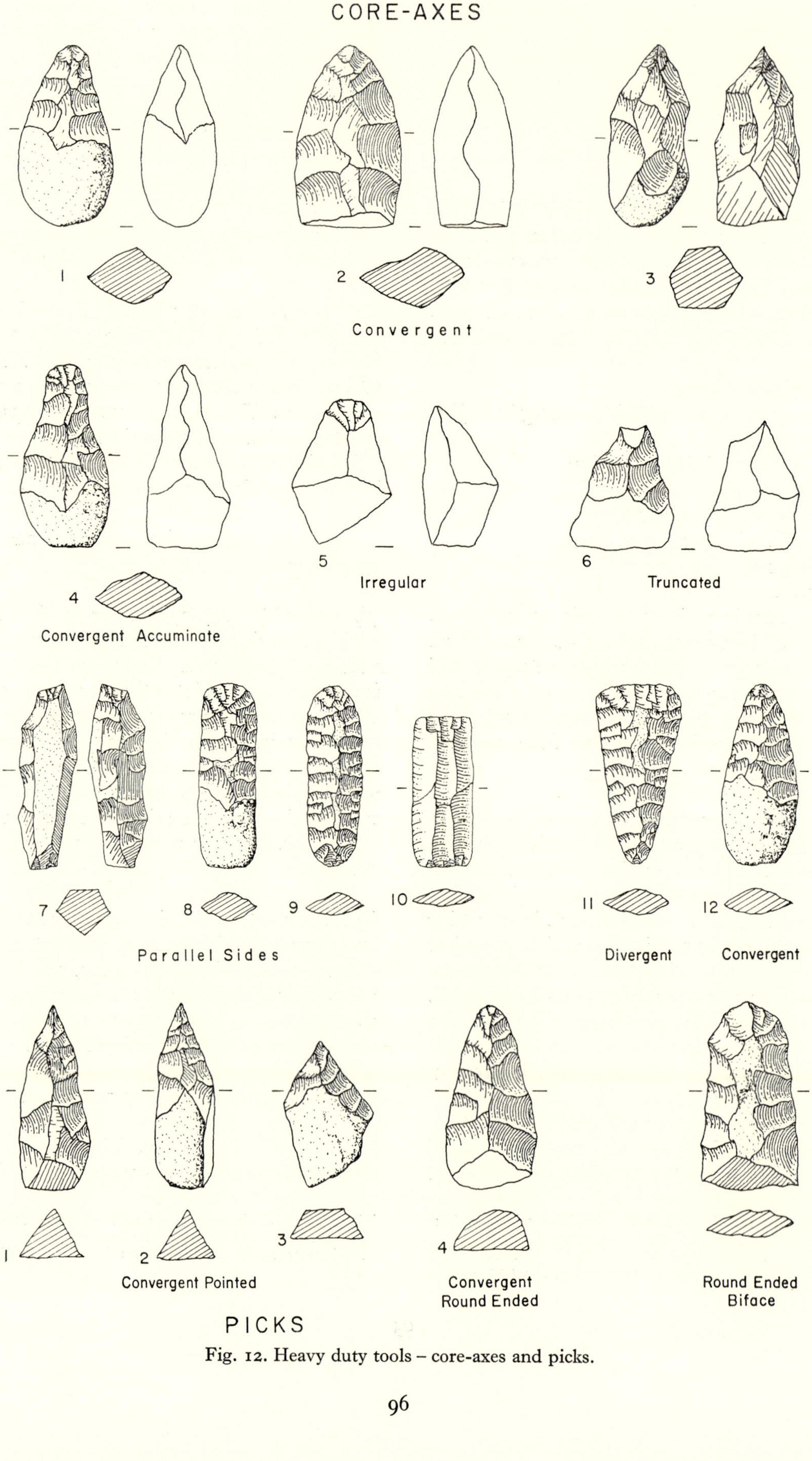

Fig. 12. Heavy duty tools – core-axes and picks.

Fig. 13. Heavy duty tools – scrapers, choppers, etc.

made on blocks, cobbles or thick flakes. They are bifacially, more rarely unifacially, trimmed by hard hammer technique and, when viewed in profile, the side edges are irregular. The butt is most often left completely unworked, so providing added weight to the tool when in use. The cross-section is usually thick. The main functional part of the tool is the distal end opposite to the butt and this always shows more careful retouch. In some examples this end is 'twisted' towards the vertical in relation to the horizontal plane. Sometimes also the proximal end has been retouched as a core-scraper, chisel or a second core-axe end.

In the past, these tools have been described as 'picks' or 'long, bifacial tools'. Although differing, often considerably, in plan view, they all have certain characteristics in common, namely a blunt, but tough working end, minimal modification (by primary, hard hammer flaking) of the surface of the original block or cobble and their weight.

The later forms are appreciably more symmetrical, more carefully retouched, sometimes over most or all of both faces, less thick in relation to their breadth, of smaller size and lighter in weight. Usually the distal but sometimes the proximal end also has been trimmed to give the tool a symmetric (axe), asymmetric (adze) or concavo-convex (gouge) edge profile. In earlier publications these implements have been described as chisels or gouges. Although it is probable that many of these later core-axes were hafted, there can be little doubt from the similarity of both earlier and later forms, that their functions were similar and that they represent the same basic kind of tool.

The plan forms of core-axes found at the Kalambo Falls are: convergent edged; convergent acuminate; pointed; divergent; parallel sided; irregular and truncated. The cross-sections are mostly biconvex, high-backed, plano-convex, triangular, rhomboid and irregular quadrilateral.

At the Kalambo Falls, the larger and heavier convergent and parallel-sided forms are associated more particularly with the Chipeta Industry (Figure 12, sub-classes 1–6), although they may occur with the Nakisasa Industry and with any of the stages of the Siszya Industry also. Synonym – *biface, pic.* The large parallel and some convergent forms are those associated more specifically with the Nakisasa Industry (Figure 12, sub-class 7), while the smaller and lighter forms with more elaborate retouch and regular section are characteristic of the Siszya Industry (Figure 12, sub-classes 8–12). Synonym – *ciseau-gouge.* Certain examples have been made on blade cores, cf. the sub-class 10 with opposed parallel and radial flaking. Examples have sometimes been truncated to form either chisel or gouge-type ends and may be found with all the above cultural stages.

(*b*) *Picks* (Figure 12). These are heavy, pointed, sometimes round-ended tools with a minimum of unifacial primary flaking or retouch, even at the distal end. They always exhibit a high-backed, plano-convex or triangular cross-section, the ventral face being usually unflaked. If the ventral face is flaked, the artifact is a trihedral pick (*biface trièdre*). Picks may be single or double ended. (Synonyms – *pic, rostro-caréné.*) The following sub-classes are found at the Kalambo Falls: convergent sided; parallel-sided and rregular.

(*c*) *Round-ended biface* (Figure 12). This is a large tool with minimal trimming and a bifacially retouched end, showing, however, neither the retouch characteristic of the core-axe class nor signs of having been used for chopping, although that is the most closely related class.

(*d*) *Core-scrapers* (*rabot; grattoir nucléiforme* (Tixier, 1963)) (Figure 13). High-backed tools, characterized by steep retouch, usually from the flat, ventral face, along some part or parts of the circumference to form a scraper edge. Continued use and trimming sometimes result in the undercutting of this edge. Most of this class are large tools (i.e. longer than 100 mm) but smaller specimens also occur. Some examples have the ventral face formed by two fracture planes intersecting at an angle (bevel-based) (sub-class 4). Others have several scraping edges in different planes and each opposed to a flat, ventral face. Core-scrapers at the Kalambo Falls may be one edged, two edged in the same plane, two edged in different planes, three edged in different planes; end ('push plane') and end and side edged, round or circular.

(*e*) *Chisels* (Figure 13). These tools are generally large, informal and bifacial with minimal primary flaking and retouch and a sharp, chisel or *biseau* proximal end or edge. This edge may be formed by the intersection of part or the whole of two main flake surfaces or it may be further retouched unifacially or bifacially. Cross-sections are thick and the working end is wedge shaped in profile. Chisels may be straight ended or gouge ended.

(*f*) *Choppers* (Figure 13). Often these tools do not have a regular plan form but are characterized by chopping edges with irregular sinusoidal profiles and showing evidence of heavy usage. They are usually bifacially flaked ('chopping tools') and may be single side; double side; end; end and side or round. Where the battered edge is absent, such artifacts grade into single platform (unifacial flaking) and proto-biconical (bifacial flaking) cores.

(*g*) *Spheroids* (Figure 13). More or less spherical artifacts of which two sub-classes are recognized – the polyhedral stone (*sphéroïde à facettes* (Balout, 1955)) and the stone ball (*bola*, see Balout, 1955: 152). The first type shows numerous intersecting facets and appears to have been shaped more as a result of use than by purposeful design. The second type often began as a polyhedral but has been battered, whether deliberately or by use, to form a regular surfaced, near spherical ball.

Three further classes of heavy duty tools are associated with the Kaposwa aggregates (*h, i, j*) and with the Polungu (*j*) (Figure 13):

(*h*) *Percussion flaked axe/adze*. Weathered fragments or thick flakes of dolerite appear to have been selected for the manufacture of these tools. They have been percussion flaked round most or all of the periphery by hard hammer technique to form a biface with limande, ovate, or sub-rectangular plan form and flat biconvex section. One end, or more rarely both, will show evidence of step flaking or splintering due to hard usage; sometimes the proximal end may be thick and untrimmed but show evidence of battering and some polishing from use. The profile views of the 'working ends' may be symmetrical ('axe-edged') or asymmetrical ('adze-edged'). This class grades into:

i) *Ground stone axe/adze*. The primary shaping may be by direct percussion or by pecking or by a combination of both. Plan forms are similar to (*h*) above. The working end and a variable part of the remaining area show regular planed and striated surfaces on both faces of the tool resulting from intentional grinding and rubbing on an abrader. Edges are symmetric or asymmetric and may also show polish due to use. The grinding and polishing exhibited by these tools may be minimal or it may be extensive, covering most of both faces. Dolerite weathers easily in the acid soil of the Kalambo Falls local basin so that it it is difficult to determine the full extent of grinding on some of these specimens.

(*j*) *Bored stones*. These are rare at the Kalambo Falls and only broken examples have been recovered from the excavations. They are made from softish rock – mudstone, sandstone or sandy quartzite – all of which are available locally. Plan forms are circular to oval and sections are flattened elliptic. The bore is hourglass in section being made by pecking with a pointed stone tool from both faces and later being enlarged by reaming. Irregularities on the circumference and surfaces of the tool have been reduced by pecking and grinding.

(3) *Light duty tools* (Figures 14 and 15)

(*a*) *Microliths*[1] (Figure 14). These are small, 30 mm or less in length and are usually made on bladelets or diminutive flakes. They are characterized by generally steep retouch down one side edge, the opposite edge being sharp and formed by the intersection of dorsal and ventral flake scars. More rarely, both edges of the tool may exhibit backing. Microliths occur only with the Kaposwa and Polungu aggregates and the following forms are recognized at the Kalambo Falls:

Backed blades – convex (*lamelle à bord abattu arqué*)
– straight (*lamelle aiguë à bord abattu*)
Lunates (*segment demi-cercle*)
Trapezes
Triangles
Shouldered (*pointe à cran*)
Double backed (*mèche de foret*); probably some form of drill.

(*b*) *Truncated flakes/blades*[1] (*pièces à troncature(s)*) (Figure 14). These may be of microlithic proportions or larger. The primary flakes and blades on which this retouch occurs appear mostly to have been obtained by the punch method. The trimmed edge is plano-clinal and the retouch angle steep or blunt. The truncation is usually oblique to the long axis. This class occurs with component B of the Siszya Industry, with the Polungu and also, in microlithic proportions, with the Kaposwa Industry.

(*c*) *Trapeziums* (Figure 14). These are non-microlithic forms measuring between 30 and 50 mm and having usually oblique, steep truncation at both ends. They

[1] French equivalents from Tixier, 1963.

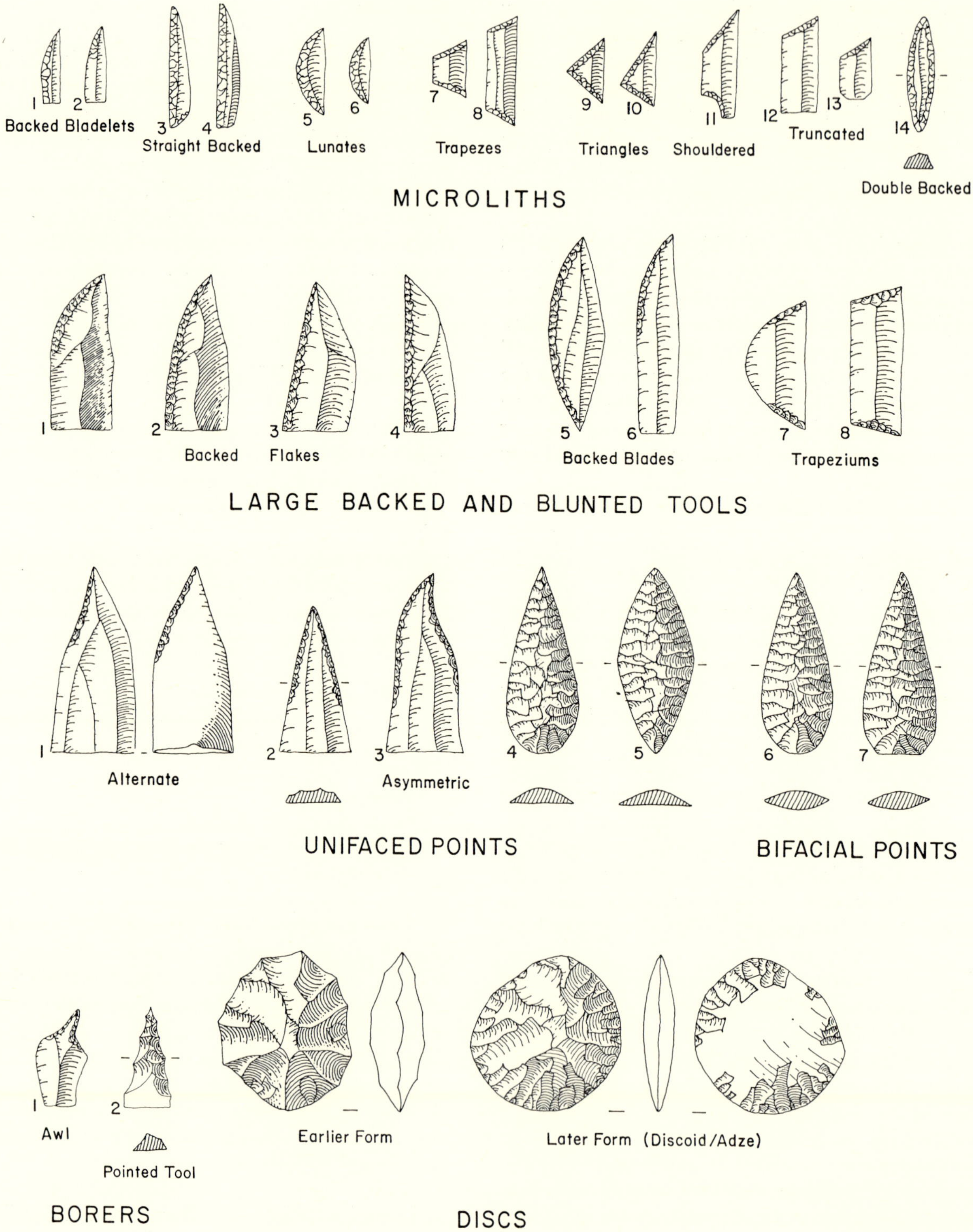

Fig. 14. Light duty tools – microliths, points, discs.

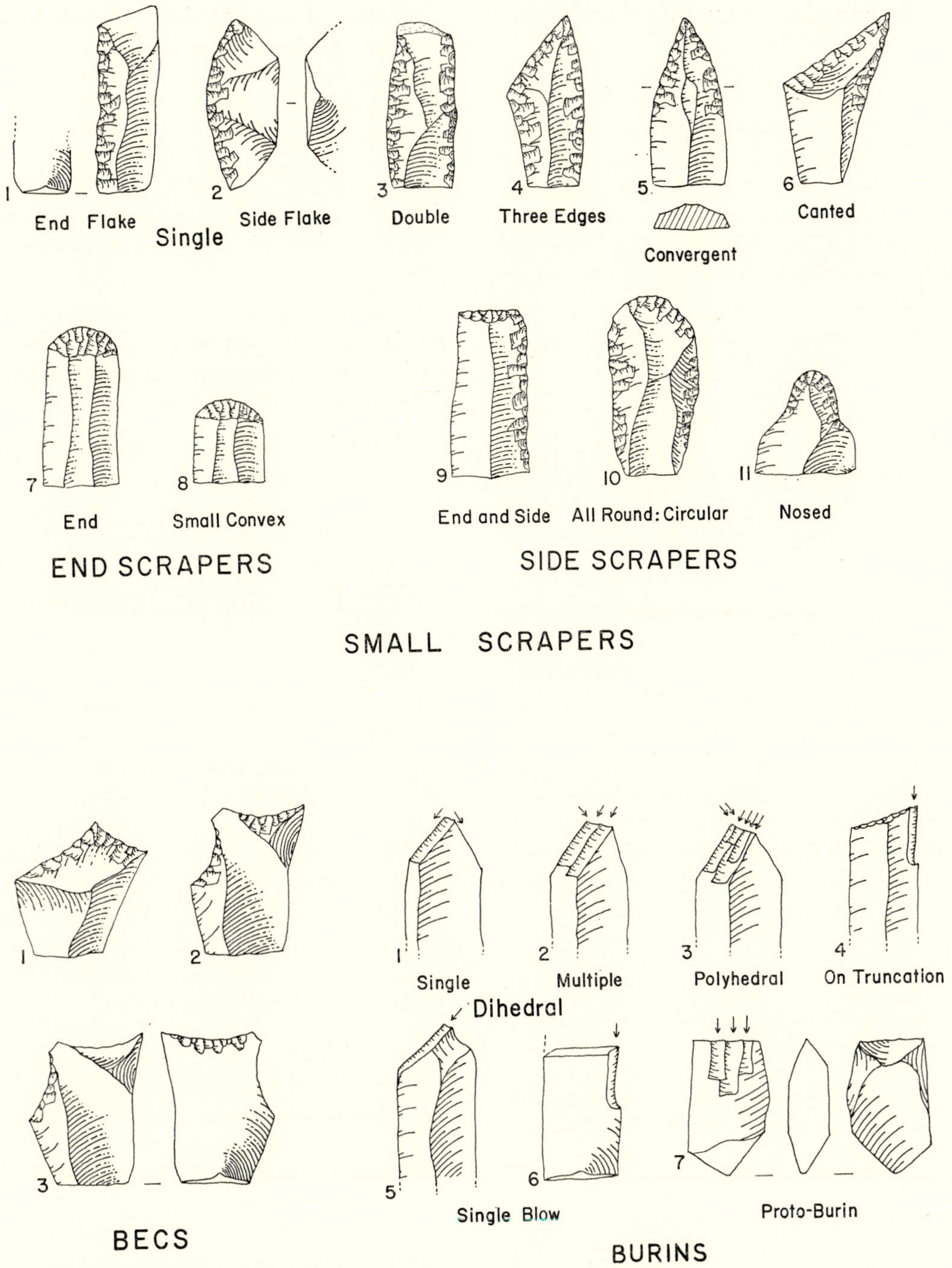

Fig. 15. Light duty tools – scrapers, burins, etc.

are associated with the Siszya Industry (component B) as also in microlithic form with the Kaposwa Industry.

(*d*) *Backed flakes* (*éclats à bord abattu arqué et partiel*)[1] (Figure 14). These are usually triangular flakes with faceted striking platforms that have been unifacially backed down the whole or part of one edge; the backing may be blunt or steep. They are associated with component B of the Siszya Industry. The class of 'naturally backed flakes' has not been used in the Kalambo Falls analyses but, where evidence for utilization is present on cortex backed flakes, these have been classified in the utilized category.

(*e*) *Backed blades* (*lames à bord abattu arqué et partiel*)[1] (Figure 14). These are outside the range of microliths and are associated with the Siszya Industry (mainly with component B) and with the Polungu aggregates. The retouch may be shallow, blunt or steep.

(*f*) *Points* (Figure 14). Made on flakes, these are generally lanceolate or triangular in plan form and may be bifacially, parti-bifacially or unifacially retouched. The extent of the retouch varies considerably and, on unifacial specimens, is often confined to the edge margins and point of the tool. The Kalambo Falls forms are usually made on triangular primary flakes and the striking platform, which is often faceted, may or may not have been removed by trimming. Sections are lenticular or flat, plano-convex; retouch angles are shallow and, more rarely, blunt.

Points are sub-divided into:

unifacial – (*pointe à face plane; pointe levallois retouchée* or *pointe moustérienne*).
bifacial – (*feuille de laurier*).

(*g*) *Small scrapers* (Figure 15). These are planoclinal tools less than 100 mm in greatest length and are divisible into several sub-classes according to the nature of the retouched edge or end, to the plan form and to other attributes. They are made on flakes, chunks, flake fragments or cores and are classified as follows:

one side (*racloir simple; racloir transversal*)
two sides (*racloir double*)
three sides (*racloir déjeté double*)
end (*grattoir*)
end and side
convergent (*racloir convergent*)
circular (*grattoir sur éclat; grattoir circulaire*)
nosed (*grattoir à museau*)
beaked
angled (*racloir déjeté*)
small convex

The above sub-classes have also been classified according to the nature of the edge plan, e.g. convex, concave, straight, notched, denticulate, irregular, etc.

(*h*) *Burins* (Figure 15). Tools with a characteristic burin facet or facets formed on the thickness of the artifact, which is generally a flake or flake fragment. The burin types present are:

dihedral – single facet (sub-class 1) (*burin dièdre droit*)
– multiple facets (sub-class 2) (*burin dièdre d'angle*)
polyhedral (sub-class 3) (*burin dièdre caréné*)
single blow – sub-class 5 (*coup de burin*); sub-class 6 (*burin d'angle sur cassure*)
burin on truncation (*burin sur troncature*)

(*i*) *Proto-burins* (Figure 15). These are small tools usually not more than 100 mm in length, made on thick flakes, fragments or chunks. One or several small flakes may have been removed from the end of one face which is opposed to a flake or fracture scar on the opposite face. This small 'chisel-like' edge also shows fracturing and bruising due to use. Both straight and gouge ended forms are found. They differ from burins in that the working end is broader and in the horizontal plane or oblique to the horizontal plane rather than in the vertical.

(*j*) *Becs* (Figure 15). Small tools on flakes or fragments having a flat beak or *bec* formed by the intersection or near intersection of two trimmed notches. These latter may be flaked from the ventral face and also alternately, one from the ventral and one from the dorsal face. Where the notches intersect, the tool equates with the *bec* in the *système Bordes* (1961: 32). Where a small chisel-like area (formed by the intersection of a remaining portion of a dorsal primary scar with the main release surface) separates the two notches, the tool approximates to the *bec burinant alterne* (Bordes, 1961: 37) except that the notches are both more often formed by flaking from the ventral face.

[1] French equivalents from Tixier, 1963.

(*k*) *Borers* (Figure 14), *Pointed Tools* (sub-class 1). Various forms of small tools on which a rough point has been prepared. They occur mostly in the Acheulian and Sangoan aggregates but also in more refined form with the Rubble component of the Polungu Industry. Synonym – *pointe de Tayac*. *Awls* (*perçoirs*) (sub-class 2). Occasional tools occur that appear to have had a point worked, either unifacially or bifacially, for piercing or boring, but this is a rare and atypical artifact at the Kalambo Falls.

(*l*) *Discoids* (Figure 14). Small circular artifacts, usually radially flaked bifacially and with a flat, biconvex or lenticular section. The later forms as found with the Siszya (component B) and Polungu aggregates, show regular retouch round most of the circumference. These tools may have been hafted as the blades of adzes or used as circular knives.

For ease of reference, the way in which the different artifact classes defined above combine in each of the archaeological units recognized at the Kalambo Falls is set out in Table 10.

Physical condition

In cases where artifacts derived from more than one industrial unit are found together, as they are in the Rubble horizons of the Mbwilo Member, we have attempted to distinguish between the different cultural entities these represent by comparing the technical and typological attributes of the individual artifacts and relating these to a study of physical condition and the raw material preference.

Three degrees of natural attrition by stream action and/or weathering have been recognized – abraded, slightly abraded and fresh. We attempted to maintain consistency in classification by constant reference to the standard set.[1] In general the most abraded were also the most heavily patinated. The natural expectancy is that the oldest artifacts in a secondary context aggregate of the kind found in the Rubbles, will be the most abraded. While this is probably true for the upslope parts of the Rubbles, it is not so where they rest in channels cut into the sediments of the Mkamba Member. For example, the lowest of the Rubbles which rest disconformably in channels cut into the Ochreous Sands, have sometimes incorporated Sangoan artifacts which, because they have suffered only minor movement before redeposition, generally show a slighter degree of abrasion than younger ingredients of the same Rubble.

Raw Material

The great majority of the rocks used for making stone tools occur in the area of the Kalambo Falls local basin. The Plateau Series metamorphosed sedimentaries provide an excellent range of materials from hard and tough rocks to homogeneous, siliceous stone capable of producing very sharp edges and taking fine retouch. The available supply and size of these rocks was unlimited so far as prehistoric man was concerned.

The commonest materials are hard and soft quartzites and silicified mudstone, or chert, but there is considerable variation in texture and hardness in each of these groups. Judging by the very large quantity of artifacts found in the valley, the debris left on the mining and factory sites must have been considerable but these have not yet been located though it seems clear that they must lie at the south and southwest end of the basin.

Petrographic notes on the rocks used by the prehistoric populations in the local basin at the Kalambo Falls are set out in Appendix A.

HARD QUARTZITE

Thick bands of quartzites and quartzose sandstone can be seen in section in the cliffs on either side of the Falls but it seems probable that prehistoric man made use of the large boulders and angular blocks of this rock that can be found on the higher slopes of the basin. These were broken by striking one boulder a number of times with another until eventually one would split and could then be more easily dealt with.

Several variations of hard quartzite are distinguishable: grey, light brown, greenish, pink and red in colour. The finest textured variety is a banded purple and red colour and appears to have been especially selected. Tools made from these rocks were

[1] Although we attempted to minimize the problem with a standard set, we found that consistency in assessing the degree of natural abrasion upon artifacts was generally good but not exact. Some artifacts recorded as 'slightly abraded' by Kleindienst or Keller would probably be regarded as 'fresh' by Clark. A count by M. R. K. on 272 artifacts grouped into the three abrasion categories by M. R. K. and J. D. C. independently gave the following results: same abrasion category 79·8 per cent, J. D. C. placed 14·7 per cent in a lower abrasion category and 5·5 per cent in a higher abrasion category than did M. R. K. This can probably be accepted as a fair measure of consistency since these are gradational categories and only 9·2 per cent is systematic error (J. D. C. tending to a lower category than M. R. K.).

usually, but not invariably, large and would take an edge that could stand up to rough usage on resistant materials.

FELDSPATHIC QUARTZITE

This, again, varies considerably in texture and hardness, showing gradations between sandstone and quartzite. It is more fine grained and more easily fractured and it will take a more finely retouched edge than the hard orthoquartzites. This rock is grey to creamy white in colour and some of it is very fine textured. The stone has, however, become less hard with weathering of the feldspar and in some instances specimens made of it have become completely desilicified and will break easily. In general, it is more subject to both abrasion and weathering than the hard quartzites.

It was not possible to locate any outcrops or large erratics of this rock in the vicinity but it occurs so commonly that it is certainly local and it is probable that the main source lies buried under the sediments of the 70 foot (21 m) terrace. Judging from the large flakes that were used by Acheulian and Sangoan man, it occurred in the form of boulders as well as outcrops. Usage of both feldspathic quartzite and hard orthoquartzite decreases in the more recent industries.

SILICIFIED MUDSTONE OR CHERT

Thin bands or veins of this rock some 3 to 6 inches (7·5–15 cm) thick can be seen interbedded with marly sandstones at the western end of the Spillway Gorge and on the southern flanks of the main Kalambo gorge. It is well jointed and cleaves more or less readily along the lines of weakness, forming slabs or prisms that, in some cases, constitute ready-made blanks for blade cores. This tendency does impose some limitation on the size of usable raw material which may explain why it was not consistently chosen for larger tools. It is the finest grained rock in the valley and some extremely elegant tools of all size ranges were made from it. The main varieties are green and yellow in colour but a black, indurated, form which outcrops in the Bwalya stream a quarter of a mile (*c.* 400 m) southwest of the Falls, was also used, especially in later times. A highly silicified whitish or purple variety was used for making some artifacts of the Siszya Industry from Excavation A1, 1956.

Some of the Siszya (Rubble I phase, component B) aggregates from the water-sorted rubble lines have a rather 'greasy' feel and appearance that is suggestive of heat treatment of the stone by the method outlined by Crabtree (1964). This appears unlikely, however, both because of the 'washing' and slight degree of abrasion from fine, silty sands that these artifacts have often undergone, which can also produce a similar 'greasy' surface texture. There is also no evidence of any heat treated material with the later – Kaposwa – microlithic aggregate on the living floor at Site C, where it might be most expected.

DOLERITE

A sill or dyke of this rock is present on the southern side of the valley where it has been cut through by the tributary gully entering the main river between Sites A and B. It is difficult to judge to what extent dolerite was used by early man in the area since it has completely weathered to a white, soft, clay-like consistency in the waterlogged horizons and can easily be cut through with a trowel. Dolerite produces a hard and resistant edge, but was not nearly so commonly used, apparently, as was hard quartzite, though handaxes and cleavers in it were recovered by casting the clay remnants in 1963 in Site A trench A5. It was favoured by the later peoples for making ground stone axes.[1]

'SILCRETE'

During the Lupemban a very fine grained quartzite, silcrete or siltstone, was used, often in connection with the prepared core technique. The source of this material is not certainly known but there can be no doubt that it is local to the valley. It is usually cream or light purple in colour.

SANDSTONE

Some of the sandier, more friable quartzose rocks may be classified as sandstone and were used chiefly for rubbers or grindstones.

The following raw materials are found in very small quantities on the occupation sites and must have been brought from the plateau into the valley:

(i) *Quartz*. A few flakes and tools, including quartz crystal burins, occur with the Polungu and Kaposwa

[1] Due to the fact that in the Mkamba Member dolerite is completely weathered to clay, artifacts made in this material may not have been recovered in fair proportions. This is particularly likely in the case of heavy duty tools (polyhedrals, choppers, etc.) for which – based on evidence of selection of raw materials at other Acheulian occupation sites – dolerite may even have been the favoured raw material.

aggregates. As quartz is sometimes found as veins in the Plateau Series quartzites, it could also be a local material but crystal quartz has not been found locally.

(ii) *Chalcedony*. This is another rock that is believed to be associated with the Pre-Cambrian sediments on the plateau, the nearest available source being several kilometres distant from the Kalambo Falls. Like quartz, it occurs very rarely in the Polungu and Kaposwa aggregates but some fine tools are made in it. There are also a few artifacts in chalcedony from the Red Rubble that probably belong with the Siszya Industry.

(iii) *Pot-hole pebbles of hard quartzite*. Ovoid to spherical pebbles are sometimes met with on the living floors and in particular were used for split cobble anvils. It is possible that they are local to the valley though Bond considers that they were probably carried in from outside (Volume 1: 208). They occur from the Acheulian onwards but are never common. If they are, indeed, derived from an outside source, the nearest place might be upstream at the Sansia Falls, or, perhaps, at the base of the Kalambo Falls themselves. Another possibility is that they were carried in from the shore of Lake Tanganyika at the mouth of the Kalambo River and gorge. If this could be shown to be, indeed, the case, it would be evidence that the inhabitants of the local basin were also in contact with the lake.

(iv) *Occasional fragments of sericitic schist*, which probably derive from outside the areas of the Plateau Series outcrops, were found as exotic materials in the clays of the Chiungu Member in Trench A4.

Details of raw material are noted for each aggregate and it can be seen that the trend, as elsewhere in Africa, is towards the more exclusive use of the homogeneous materials – from hard and feldspathic quartzites towards chert and silcrete and some fine grained, homogeneous stone imported into the valley.

In the analysis lists the different raw materials have been designated by the following abbreviations:

Hard quartzite	H/Q
Feldspathic quartzite	F/Q
Sandstone	SSt
Silcrete	Sil
Silicified mudstone or chert	Ch
Dolerite	D
Chalcedony	Chal
Quartz	Qz
Other	O

Appendix

Petrographic Notes

Specimen(s): 20 hand-axes, etc. for petrographic notes on rocks utilized.
Submitted by: Dr E. G. Haldemann, Geologist, Dodoma.
Locality: Kalambo. D.S. 68 SW.
Degree Square: 68 SW.
EGH A1, B2, D3, D4 Slides missing.
EGH A2 *Orthoquartzite* Sub-rounded quartz grains (*c.* 0·3 mm) with interstitial chert and sericite.
EGH A5 *Feldspathic sandstone* Sub-angular quartz grains (*c.* 0·3 mm) with microcline and chert.
EGH B1 *Orthoquartzite* Sub-rounded to rounded quartz grains (*c.* 0·4 mm) with chert and interstitial sericite.
EGH D1 *Feldspathic sandstone* Sub-rounded quartz grains (*c.* 0·2 mm) with microcline, chert and sericite.
EGH D2 *Feldspathic sandstone* Sub-rounded to rounded quartz grains (*c.* 0·3 mm) with sericitized feldspar and chert; interstitial sericite; and accessory muscovite and zircon.
EGH D5 ?*Silicified mudstone* Quartz, albite, chert, sericite and chlorite grains in a fine grained silicious groundmass. Diagenetic sericite flakes in parallel orientation.
EGH E *Silicified mudstone* with grains of chert; also sericite and a little epidote.
EGH K *Silicified mudstone* with sericite.
EGH KM *Chert* Veined by chalcedony and stained by limonite.
EGH S2 *Orthoquartzite* Sub-rounded to rounded quartz grains (*c.* 0·5 mm) with chert and interstitial sericite.
EGH S4 *Orthoquartzite* Sub-rounded quartz grains (*c.* 0·4 mm) with chert and interstitial sericite.

EGH S5 *Orthoquartzite* Sub-rounded quartz grains (*c.* 0·5 mm) with chert and interstitial sericite and carbonaceous material.

EGH S6 *Orthoquartzite* Sub-rounded quartz grains (*c.* 0·6 mm) with chert and interstitial sericite.

EGH S7 *Silicified mudstone* (quartz proved by X-ray powder photograph No. 1534) with sericite, chlorite, limonite and carbonaceous material.

EGH S8 *Orthoquartzite* Sub-angular to sub-rounded quartz grains (*c.* 0·3 mm) with chert and interstitial sericite and carbonaceous material.

EGH S9 *Orthoquartzite* Sub-rounded quartz grains (*c.* 0·4 mm) with a few chert grains.

Note: All the quartzites show signs of strain. Each has a silica cement in optical continuity with the quartz grains. Classification from F. J. Pettijohn, *Sedimentary Rocks* (New York: Harper and Row, 1957), p. 291.

(Signed) D. R. C. Kemp
Geologist

Tanganyika, Department of Geological Survey Laboratory Service. Ref. No. X/6905/2.

Dodoma,
5 September 1961

CHAPTER 5

The Later Stone Age: the Kaposwa Industry

Stratigraphic position

For a long time, remains dating to the 'Later Stone Age' appeared generally to be very scarce in the local basin and any living sites that might have existed, successfully eluded the investigators. Although surface collections had been found in 1953 on the southern shoulder at the Falls, it was not until the 1963 season that it was possible to date accurately any of the microlithic aggregates.

Artifacts of types associated with the microlithic aggregates occurred at all levels in the swamp clays of the Chiungu Member together with Early Iron Age pottery of the Kalambo Falls Industry and derived lithic material of different ages. However, in the long trench A4 in 1959, the lowest 2 to 3 feet (60–90 cm) of these clays, here light grey and very sandy (Bed 7: Phase F7), contained no pottery and only a very few microlithic artifacts, so that it is possible that the earliest of these clay aggradations may pre-date the Early Iron Age.

At the end of the 1959 season, surface scatters of waste and a few tools were found in the sandy topsoil of the boulder bed in the vicinity of Chitambala's and Dominico's villages towards the eastern end of the basin. The Chitambala Gravel Beds are probably contemporary with the formation of the 30 foot (9·1 m) terrace of sandy sediments at the western side of the local basin (Volume I: 54) so that the aggregates from the topmost levels in the cliff face and from the cassava garden at the south end of Site C are likely to be contemporary with the artifacts on the surface of the Chitambala Gravel Beds.

When this occupation began, the local base level of the Kalambo river was generally some 30 feet (9 m) higher at the western end than it is today. However, the river must already at that time have begun to cut down from this level, or the localities would hardly have been suitable for habitation. It would, therefore, seem that the microlithic aggregates here either directly predated or were contemporary with the erosion that preceded the filling of the basin during the period of the Early Iron Age settlement. The locality must have been very much as it is today with the river cutting steep banks in the angles of the meanders and depositing sand bars in time of flood.

The 1963 excavation in the Site C Early Iron Age settlement brought to light part of a camping area immediately underlying the midden soil containing the aggregates of the Kalambo Falls Industry. From here came a most important collection of tools and waste giving the first precise knowledge of a microlithic tradition based, not upon quartz as is usual in Zambia, but on chert from the Plateau Series rocks.

In 1966 the small excavation in the hillslope soil at A7 adjacent to the camp site and overlooking the earlier excavations at this locality (Figure 6) provided further evidence for the greater age of the microlithic aggregates. As will be apparent from the list of finds by levels (Table 8) and the description of this excavation (pp. 45–9), the main concentration of microlithic artifacts occurs at the 3 feet to 3 feet 6 inches (91–106 cm) level, whereas the greatest density of sherds and other artifacts of the Kalambo Falls Industry was found between the surface and 1 foot (0–30 cm). From the distribution of sherds, slag and bone, there is reason to think that the Early Iron Age occupation continued down for a further 1 foot 6 inches to 2 feet (45–60 cm) and that, allowing for local disturbance, the base of this occupation occurred at 2 feet 6 inches to 3 feet (75–90 cm). Some unmodified microlithic waste is present in the levels above 3 feet (90 cm) but there are no microliths and the number of pieces is more consistent with their having been derived from former exposed scatters of workshop waste further up the slope than with there having been any appreciable overlap in time.

The stratigraphic evidence is, therefore, strongly suggestive that the microlithic waste and artifacts found mixed with the Early Iron Age pottery in the previous seasons' excavations in the clays of the Chiungu Member, belonged to an earlier cultural stage and that there was no overlapping in time between the Early Iron Age (Kalambo Falls Industry) and the manufacture of the microlithic aggregates.

Dating (See Volume I, Appendix J)

The occupation floor at Site C partially excavated in 1963 has been dated to the beginning of the second millennium B.C. by two samples of scattered charcoals associated with the lowest part of the concentration of lithic material in Grid Squares G–H/1–2. The results obtained were as follows:

GrN 4225	3850 ± 40 B.P.	1900 ± 40 B.C.
GrN 4224	3920 ± 40 B.P.	1970 ± 40 B.C.

A further sample from this site within the top of the brown/yellow sand immediately below the Early Iron Age midden soil, was dated to 2730 ± 40 B.P. (780 ± 40 B.C.) (GrN 4223). This suggests an appreciable period of time, approximately 1200 years, between the abandonment of the site by the occupants of the microlithic camp and settlement by the makers of the Kalambo Falls Industry. This period was long enough for processes of soil formation to become apparent.

Radiocarbon dates for the Early Iron Age traditions in east and southern Africa suggest that they make their first appearance shortly after the beginning of the present era so that it is to be expected that hunting/gathering Stone Age peoples continued to occupy the basin until their replacement by agriculturalists in or before the fourth century A.D. (see p. 57 above). As yet, we can only presume this to have been the case since we have no occupation sites from this period unless some of those on the surface soil over the Chitambala Gravel Beds belong to this time. Evidence from further south in Zambia (Miller, 1969; Phillipson, 1969*a*) and Malawi (Robinson and Sandelowsky, 1968; Clark *et al.* 1970: 349) shows that some hunting and gathering groups persisted throughout the first millennium B.C. and subsequently established a successful symbiotic relationship with Iron Age cultivators.

The Kaposwa Industry

It was to be expected that the composition of the microlithic assemblages at the Kalambo Falls would conform to some extent to that of one or more of the Industries of the partly contemporary Nachikufan Industrial Complex, which is generally distributed over the northern and central parts of the Zambian plateau (Miller, 1969). However, as will become apparent when these aggregates are compared, there are considerable differences which make it impossible, on the basis of the lithic technology, to include the aggregates from the local Kalambo basin within any of the Nachikufan archaeological units. The Kalambo Falls aggregates resemble even less those of the Tshitolian in the Congo basin and insufficient is known about the comparable units in the eastern part of the Katanga Province. They cannot, therefore, as yet be placed within any of the known Industries or Industrial Complexes of the 'Later Stone Age' in south-central Africa. Accordingly and for ease of reference as well as to distinguish them from other and older aggregates that also contain microliths, they have as stated above (p. 75) been defined as 'the Kaposwa Industry' – named after the small stream that joins the Kalambo River at the northwest corner of the local basin on the opposite side of the river from Site C which has yielded the main microlithic occupation floor.

A. Derived, in the clays of the Chiungu Member

Artifacts of this time found in the clays of the Chiungu Member are always fresh or slightly abraded and unpatinated and, with the exception of an occasional rubber and one bored stone fragment, are all microlithic. They can, therefore, easily be distinguished from the Siszya Industry (Lupemban) and earlier, artifacts which are almost invariably abraded and patinated. In Tables 1 and 2, the relevant specimens can be identified with reasonable certainty by their microlithic, or semi-microlithic proportions, fresh condition and matt finish; however, for ease of reference they have been extracted and are shown on p. 109.

The figures given are minimum, being based only on those specimens that can, with absolute certainty, be ascribed to a microlithic aggregate. In addition, it is probable that one should include some, if not all,

	Flakes (mostly plain platform)	Bladelets	Micro-blade cores	Micro-liths	Bored stones	Totals
A1, 1956	43	2	2	—	—	47
A4, 1959	120	10	6	1	—	137
B1, 1956	19	5	1	2	1	28
B2, 1969	14	1	2	1	—	18
Total	196	18	11	4	1	230

of the rubbers with dimple scarring made on pebbles as well as at least nine of the informal, utilized specimens and one chopper.

A small series of tools and waste from the clays is illustrated at Plate 33 for comparison with those from the occupation floor on Site C, 1963 (Plates 34–42). Precisely the same microlithic types and factory waste are represented at all these sites although the larger tools in hard quartzite (Plate 33: 21 and 23) from the clays at Site A could be derived and have been reused, as was a chopper found at Site C (Plate 35: 8).

Of special interest are the bored stone fragment (Plate 33: 22) and the double-sided, dimple-scarred anvil which, on one face, also shows initial use as a rubber (Plate 33: 20). The bored stone is typical of the flat examples found with the Nachikufan Industry on the Zambian plateau south of the Corridor country.

B. Sites on the Chitambala Gravel Beds

1. CHITAMBALA'S VILLAGE

Quite fresh artifacts were found eroding from a surface covered by 1 foot (30 cm) or so of loose grey to buff coloured sand that rested directly on the Chitambala Gravel Beds. They were scattered over a distance of some 30 feet (9 m) near the northern edge of the terrace on the outskirts of the village.

The raw material was almost exclusively chert, obtained from exposures of gravel with older artifacts, presumably on the hill slopes further to the west, and carried up to the terrace for use. Two waste fragments are in chalcedony and one in quartz. A small percentage of the specimens are lightly patinated due, probably, to longer surface exposure. The inventory of the tools is set out in Table 11. The microliths include one large triangle (35 × 20 × 7 mm), somewhat reminiscent of the Tshitolian *tranchets* from the Congo basin. The number of steep scrapers on cores or chunks at this site can probably be related to one particular type of activity. A short quadrilateral flake with a single blow burin facet and signs of utilization was also found.

This site has not yet been excavated and the extent of the occupation area is not known, but the absence of any concentration of waste suggests that it was either small or the main area still remains to be uncovered.

2. CHIUNGU (DOMINICO'S) VILLAGE

Here the artifacts occur as a small surface scatter covered by a thin spread of sand over the Chitambala Gravel Beds. The few implements recovered confirm, however, the relationship of the Kaposwa aggregates to this terrace-like feature and are generally typical of the microlithic aggregate from Site C; of special note is a scraper with three concave working edges. For the inventory, see Table 11.

3. SITE A: EXCAVATION A7, 1966

The small assemblage from a depth of 3 feet to 3 feet 6 inches (91–106 cm) in the red loam is analysed in Table 12. It is predominantly microlithic, made mostly from chert and differs in no essential way from the much more complete aggregate from the Site C, 1963 excavation to be described below. Two lunates (20 × 7 mm and 15 × 6 mm), two straight backed microliths and a backed blade (33 × 10 mm) occur. These are regularly retouched and contrast with the informal scraper classes. Utilized artifacts comprise a flake with marginal scarring on one edge and a notched chunk. The core is chunky and shows two platforms at right angles and in different planes for the removal of micro-flakes and blades (42 × 37 mm). Among the flake fragments is one spall resulting from a modified micro-burin technique of sectioning bladelets.

Also ascribed to the microlithic aggregate is a percussion flaked axe made from dolerite. This is weathered with a thick, ochreous patina and has been

TABLE 11. *Site C, 1963: inventory of finds from the excavation including material from Site C, 1959 and Chitambala's and Dominico's villages*

Kaposwa Industry	Raw material										Dimensions												
											Length				Breadth				Thickness				
Artifact classes	Total Site C Excavation, 1963	Chert	H/Q	F/Q	Qz	Chal	SSt	Dol	Mudstone	Pigment	> 100 mm	100–> 50 mm	50–30 mm	< 30 mm	> 100 mm	100–> 50 mm	50–30 mm	< 30 mm	> 50 mm	50–20 mm	< 20–10 mm	< 10–5 mm	< 5 mm
Shaped tools																							
Axes																							
Ground and polished	4[a]							4			2					2			2				
Percussion flaked	1							1			1				1				1				
Choppers	3		2					1			2	1				3				3			
Microliths																							
Lunates	100	99				1								100				100			1	4	95
Triangles	29	29												29				29					29
Trapezes	9	9												9				9					9
Shouldered	11	11											2	9				11					11
Backed bladelets, convex	66	66											3	63				66				5	61
Backed bladelets, straight	15	15											3	12				15			1		14
Obliquely truncated	36	36											2	34				36					36
Broken	42	42																					
Scrapers																							
On flakes and flake fragments	30	30										1	10	19			7	23		2	6	5	17
On cores and chunks	36	36										12	22	2		1	27	8		23	12	1	
Total shaped tools	382	373	2			1		6			5	14	42	277	1	6	34	297	3	28	20	15	272
Utilized/modified																							
Flakes and flake fragments	130	128	2								1	2	75	52		5	23	102		7	5	8	110
Blades and blade fragments	36	36										1	19	16			2	34			3	3	30
Chunks and cores	52	43	3		3		1	1	1		2	10	36	4		5	33	14	1	33	15	3	
Outils esquillés	6	3			3								3	3			2	4			2	3	1
Rubbers	9		9								1	6	2			7	2		6	2		1	
Anvils																							
Dimple scarred	3		3								3					3			3				
Other	5	1	4								2	3			2	3			4	1			
Pestles	1	1									1						1			1			
Abraders	2		2								2				1		1		1	1			
Hammerstones	4		4								1	3				4			2	2			
Pigment																							
Red	184									184													
Yellow	7									7													
White	4									4													
Miscellaneous	24	19	1	2	2																		
Total utilized/modified	467	231	28	2	8	—	1	1	1	195	13	25	135	75	3	27	64	154	17	47	25	18	141
Unmodified waste																							
Flakes																							
Irregular, end-struck	1,357[b]	1,308	42	1	5	1					1	7	143	296	1	1	47	398	1	4	23	115	304
Irregular, side-struck	560[b]	526	28	3	1			2				1	22	163		3	49	134		2	15	49	120
Short quadrilateral	83	80	3										22	61			2	81			3	18	62
Triangular	24	22		2									10	12			5	17			1	9	12
Long quadrilateral	407[b]	406	1									2	63	60				125			5	15	105
'Micro-burins'																							
Distal end	106	106												106				106					106
Proximal end	47	47												47				47					47
Cores																							
Single platform, short/broad	24	24										3	19	2		23		1		9	15		
long/narrow	3	3										1	2			1	2			1	2		
Pyramidal	12	12										1	11				11	1		12			
Two platforms, bipolar	8	8											7	1			6	2		3	5		
at right angles	18	18										1	17			1	17			16	2		
Proto-biconical	3	2				1						1	1	1			2	1		2	1		
Biconical	5	4	1									2	3				5			5			
Discoid	2	2											2				2				2		
Formless	11	11										3	8				11			11			
Flake and blade fragments	7,546[b]	7,306	157		80		1	2					51	1,912									
Chunks	1,084[b]	575	349	7	103	2	15	20		13		8	36	112									
Pebbles	30		8		21		1					1	1	28									
Total unmodified waste	11,330	10,640	589	13	210	4	17	24		13	1	31	418	2,801	1	29	159	913	1	65	74	206	756
Total all artifacts	12,179	11,064	619	15	218	5	18	31	1	208													

[a] 2 are fragments. [b] Full data recorded for sample only.

TABLE 11 (*cont.*)

Striking platform: Type – Plain	Striking platform: Type – Faceted	Striking platform: Shape – Broad	Striking platform: Shape – Restricted	Striking platform: Angle – Inclined	Striking platform: Angle – Right angle	Point	Dorsal scar pattern – 1-direction	Dorsal scar pattern – 2-direction	Dorsal scar pattern – Multi-dir.	Dorsal scar pattern – Unclassified	Other sites – Site C, 1959 total	Other sites – Chitambala's village – total	Other sites – Dominico's village – total	Other sites – Total other sites
												2	1	3
												1	1	2
												1		1
												4		4
											3	2		5
											8		1	9
												6	1	7
											11	16	4	31
												7	1	8
												3		3
											11	2	1	14
											2	3		5
											13	15	2	30
281	17	206	92	264	34	149	376	68	3		54	34	14	102
114	23	113	24	108	29	49	154	31	1		3	48	17	68
50	8	46	12	53	5	25	78	5			3			3
18	1	18	1	14	5	3	19	3			1			1
56	5	33	28	55	6	64	120	5			6	24	6	36
											2			2
												1		1
												1	1	2
												1		1
											1			1
											22	90	12	124
											8	24		32
519	54	416	157	494	79	290	747	112	4	—	100	223	50	373

TABLE 11 (*cont.*)

Kaposwa Industry	Kaposwa Industry, Site C, 1963: analysis by grid squares																			
Artifact classes	A1	A2	B1	B2	C1	C2	C3	C4	C5	C6	D1	D2	D3	D4	D5	D6	E1	E2	E3	E4
Shaped tools																				
Axes																				
Ground and polished																1				
Percussion flaked																				
Choppers												1				1				
Microliths																				
Lunates				1									1					7		2
Triangles																		2		
Trapezes																				
Shouldered																	1	1		
Backed bladelets, convex											3		1				1	8		3
Backed bladelets, straight				1		1												4		1
Obliquely truncated									1								1	3		1
Broken																		5		
Scrapers																				
On flakes and flake fragments											2	1					1	1		2
On cores and chunks				1										1				2		2
Total shaped tools				3		1			1		5	2	2	1		2	4	33		11
Utilized/modified																				
Flakes and flake fragments			1	1							2			1			5	8	1	2
Blades and blade fragments								1			2	3	1				3	2		
Chunks and cores											1		1		1	2		3		2
Outils esquillés				1														3		
Rubbers					1	1										1	1			
Anvils																				
Dimple scarred																				
Other						1											1			
Pestles																				
Abraders																1				
Hammerstones					1											1				
Pigment																				
Red				4	1	2			1	5		1			3	6	2		35	12
Yellow																				
White																				
Miscellaneous						2														
Total utilized/modified			1	6	3	6		1	1	5	5	4	2	1	4	11	12	16	36	16
Unmodified waste																				
Flakes																				
Irregular, end-struck				3	1	5			4	1		39	8	11	3	7	39	84	3	57
Irregular, side-struck			1	2		4		1	2	1	7	15	1	1	2	2	6	34	5	20
Short quadrilateral			2	4	1			1	1	2	6	3		1		2	1	16	4	2
Triangular			1								2						1	5	2	
Long quadrilateral			1		1	1		3	1	2	5	15			1	4	11	26	2	11
'Micro burins'																				
Distal end										1			2				1			
Proximal end																				
Cores																				
Single platform, short/broad									1	1								2		
long narrow																				
Pyramidal						1														
Two platforms, bipolar																		1		1
at right angles																	1	1		
Proto-biconical																			1	
Biconical																				
Discoid																				
Formless																		3	1	
Flake and blade fragments		1	8	8	6	16		4	9	15	38	26	34	28	9	22	20	571	68	237
Chunks		1	1	2		8		3	7	4	30		7	10	13	7	19	22	6	50
Pebbles								1												
Total unmodified waste		2	14	19	9	36		13	25	27	88	98	52	51	28	44	99	765	92	378
Total all artifacts	—	2	15	28	12	43	—	14	27	32	98	104	56	53	32	57	115	814	128	405
	A1	A2	B1	B2	C1	C2	C3	C4	C5	C6	D1	D2	D3	D4	D5	D6	E1	E2	E3	E4

TABLE II (*cont*).

Kaposwa Industry, Site C, 1963: analysis by grid squares

E5	E6	F1	F2	F3	F4	F5	F6	G1	G2	G3	G4/5	H1	H2	H3/4	G2 4 feet–4·5 feet	G3 4 feet–4·5 feet	Total
			1		2												4
							1										1
													1				3
	1	6	7	15	5	3	6	5	22	6		5	5	2		1	100
		3	2	5		1		4	3		1	2	5			1	29
		1	1	1					2	2	1		1				9
			4	2	1		1							1			11
		7	13	5	2		1	3	3	2	2	5	6	1			66
		4	1	1	1							1					15
			1	1	4		1	1	14		1	3	4				36
		7	7	7					9	3	1	3					42
		7	1	1			1	4	4	1			2	1		1	30
		3	1	6	1	1		6	8			2		2			36
	1	38	39	44	16	5	11	23	65	14	6	21	24	7		3	382
3	1	12	36	6	7	2	5	9	4	3	4	6	3	2		6	130
	1	2	5	1				3	5	2	1	1	2		1		36
1	3	3	3	2			3	5	13	4			3	2			52
								1					1				6
	1	1												3			9
			1	1								1					3
								1				1	1				5
									1								1
						1											2
							1		1								4
2	8	3	9	9	8	8	19		16	8	6	2	4	4		6	184
							1	1	1		1					3	7
									4								4
		2	2	1			4	1	1	3		2	5	1			24
6	14	23	56	20	15	11	33	21	46	20	12	13	19	12	1	15	427
22	13	114	136	51	57	41	21	28	244	63	38	82	98	37	5	42	1,357
16	18	44	37	56	36	14	4	48	65	18	10	33	37	8	2	10	560
1		3	1	2	1	1		3	20			1	4				83
		1	1	1					8			2					24
5		26	24	46	7	7	6	39	57	13	8	28	27	10	1	19	407
	3			6	6	1		13	45	9	7		10		1	1	106
				11				11	18		1	1	5				47
		1		3	1			3	7			1			1	3	24
		1		1												1	3
		1		3	1			1	4			1					12
	1			1				1	2	1							8
1		3		1	1			3	4			2					18
					1				1								3
								1	2			1	1				5
				1					1								2
		4						1	2								11
69	3	515	896	919	243	530	70	528	1,202	287	100	384	476	77	22	105	7,546
17	22	71	65	99	60	46	31	49	139	80	26	76	50	14	15	34	1,084
		1		2	1		4		1	17		2			1		30
131	60	785	1,160	1,203	415	640	136	729	1,822	488	190	624	698	146	48	215	11,330
137	75	846	1,255	1,267	446	656	180	773	1,933	522	208	658	741	165	49	233	12,179
E5	E6	F1	F2	F3	F4	F5	F6	G1	G2	G3	G4/5	H1	H2	H3/4	G2 4 feet–4·5 feet	G3 4 feet–4·5 feet	

8

CKF

TABLE 11 (*cont.*)

Site C, 1963, Kaposwa Industry: Analysis of scrapers and utilized/modified pieces

Artifact classes	Total	Plan form: Irregular	Long quad.	Short quad.	Triangular	Elliptic	Worked edges: Single	Double	Side and end	3 edges	End	Circular	Edge form: Straight	Convex	Concave	Notched	Denticulate	Burin-type	Edge angle: Shallow	Blunt	Steep
Shaped tools																					
Scrapers																					
Flake	30	20		10			12				18		10	6	2	11	1			27	3
Core	36	16		11		9	10	1	5	3	11	6	10	18		3	5			20	16
Total scrapers	66	36	—	21	—	9	22	1	5	3	29	6	20	24	2	14	6	—	—	47	19
Utilized/modified																					
Flakes and flake fragments	130	106	2	17	4	1	112	11	1		6		62	27	10	30		1	112	14	4
Blades and blade fragments	36	4	8	24			29	7					30		1	3	2		35	1	
Chunks[c]																					
Burin type	9	9					9											9			9
Other	40	38		1	1		34	2			4		13	9	3	14	1		8	17	15
Outils esquillés	6	1		5			2	4					6						6		
Total utilized/modified	221	158	10	47	5	1	186	24	1	—	10	—	111	36	14	47	3	10	161	32	28
Total all artifacts	287	194	10	68	5	10	208	25	6	3	39	6	131	60	16	61	9	10	161	79	47

[c] Does not include 3 unclassified, utilized chunks.

bifacially flaked round the circumference by hard hammer technique. The flake scars are sub-invasive, the plan form is elliptic, the section biconvex and it measures 126 × 77 × 38 mm. It shows no evidence of pecking or grinding. This axe was found at a depth of 2 feet 6 inches (75 cm) on or immediately above the surface of the horizon with the Kaposwa aggregate. Such axe/adze tools, together with the edge-ground class, are a regular constituent of 'Later Stone Age' industries in south central Africa although they are never found in any number at any one site. The flaked tools from the 2 feet 6 inches to 3 feet (75–90 cm) level consist of 4 irregular micro-flakes and thirteen flake fragments – all in chert; seventeen chunks, mostly quartzite and four pebbles, also quartzite.

4. MISCELLANEOUS SURFACE FINDS

Four surface finds of complete bored stones have been made in the local basin by others than ourselves and can with confidence be ascribed to the 'Later Stone Age'.[1]

One sub-rectangular, ground stone axe was found by the writer in October 1966, eroding from the roadway approximately 50 yards (48 m) south of the rondavel above the lip of the Falls. It is weathered and has a greenish patina which suggests that the material may be dolerite or, at least, foreign to the immediate area of the local basin. This specimen measures 105 × 81 × 21 mm. The form was initially blocked out by percussion but the scars have been mostly obliterated by grinding over both faces. The lateral edges are straight and the distal parts of these, together with the working edge itself, show polish presumably from use subsequent to grinding. One face of this end shows one large and three small flake scars such as could have resulted accidentally from use.

A small spheroid (54 × 52 mm) made from soft, weathered ?phyllite or mudstone may also date to this time. It was found by another of our workmen while digging a latrine at Dominico's (Chiungu) village and, if it does indeed date to this time, must have come from the Chitambala Gravel Beds.

[1] One was found at the 'View Point' on the southern rim of the Falls by Dr Hans Bredo, then of International Red Locust Control, Mbala; one by Father Fürstenberg of the White Fathers' Mission, Mbala from 'near Kalambo with wood through the middle'; one was found in 1943 by D. G. Lancaster then of the Northern Rhodesia Game Department, again from the 'View Point' at the Falls and was associated with a scatter of flaked stone artifacts in chert. This last specimen is in the collection in the Livingstone Museum. It is made from an irregular, flat, quadrilateral slab of mudstone and shows the usual hourglass perforation but without any attempt to modify the irregular shape of the piece. The fourth specimen was found in 1966 by one of our workmen, Lion Kalimawa, on top of Polungu ridge overlooking our camp. This is made from sandstone and is roughly circular with hour-glass perforation. It measures 152 × 133 × 48 mm and weighs between 5 and 6 pounds (2·3–2·7 kg).

TABLE 12. *Inventory of artifacts of the Kaposwa Industry from the horizon at 3 feet to 3 feet 6 inches (91–106 cm) in hillslope soil at Site A7, 1966*

		Raw material				
Artifact classes	Total	Ch	Qte	Qz	D	Other
Shaped tools						
Microliths						
Lunates	2	2	—	—	—	—
Straight backed	2	2	—	—	—	—
Convex backed	1	1	—	—	—	—
Scrapers						
Single edge (straight)	1	1	—	—	—	—
Double edge (straight/concave)	1	1	—	—	—	—
Notched/concave	2	2	—	—	—	—
Utilized/modified						
Flake	1	1	—	—	—	—
Chunk	1	1	—	—	—	—
Unmodified waste						
Flakes						
Irregular, end-struck	35	34	1	—	—	—
Irregular, side-struck	13	13	—	—	—	—
Long quadrilateral	7	7	—	—	—	—
Cores – two platforms, blade	1	1	—	—	—	—
Flake fragments	134	116	15	3	—	—
Chunks	76	22	45	4	5	—
Pebbles	2	2	—	—	—	—
Haematite	2	—	—	—	—	2
Totals	281	206	61	7	5	2

C. Site C

1. 1959 SURFACE COLLECTION

A scatter of stone tools and waste mixed with Early Iron Age potsherds of the Kalambo Falls Industry came from the surface of a mound garden dug for cassava. The garden was situated on the upper part of the slope at the south end of the 30 foot (9 m) terrace, approximately 300 yards (275 m) south of the 1963 excavation at Site C. An area some 175 feet × 60 feet (53 × 18 m) was marked out as a grid by J. H. Chaplin and a small series of artifacts was obtained from it. This occurrence helped to concentrate our search for stratified microlithic aggregates at Site C and to show that at least one other small concentration from a camp site exists on the 30 foot (9 m) terrace. Table 11 shows the inventory of these artifacts. Of interest are two good examples of straight-backed bladelets (Plate 36: 77 and 78).

2. 1963 EXCAVATION

The base of the ash and sandy soil of the Early Iron Age settlement midden occurs at a depth of 3 feet (91 cm) and rests on a brown, ?sterile sand which gradually changes over a depth of 5 inches (12·7 cm) to a clean, buff to white alluvial sand. This was loosely compacted and comprised the uppermost bed in the Mbwilo Member exposed in the cliff face.

The microlithic industry was concentrated at a depth of 3 feet 6 inches to 4 feet (106–122 cm) and the distribution pattern is shown by Van Noten in Figure 16. Above 3 feet 6 inches (106 cm) artifacts were less frequent and at 3 feet (91 cm) were mixed with occasional sherds or slag that had worked down from above. Early Iron Age material was scarce at this level, only 30 undecorated sherds, 25 pieces of iron slag, 4 lumps of *daga* and 1 tuyère fragment being encountered. Below this it was totally absent except where the shafts had been dug into the sand. These facts suggest the unlikelihood of there having been

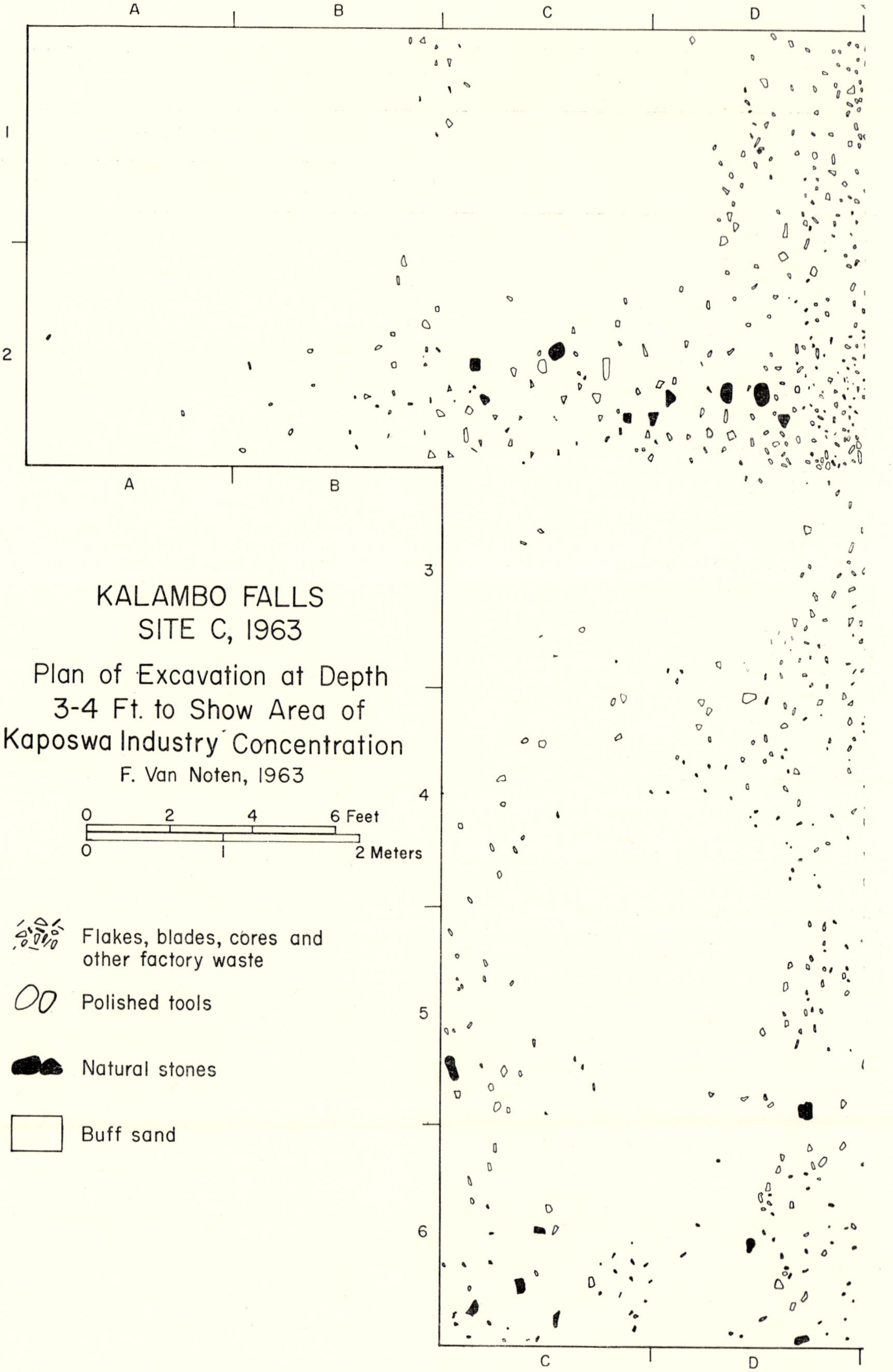

Fig. 16. Site C, 1963: Plan of excavation at depth of 3 to 4 feet (91–122 cm) to show area of 'Later Stone Age'

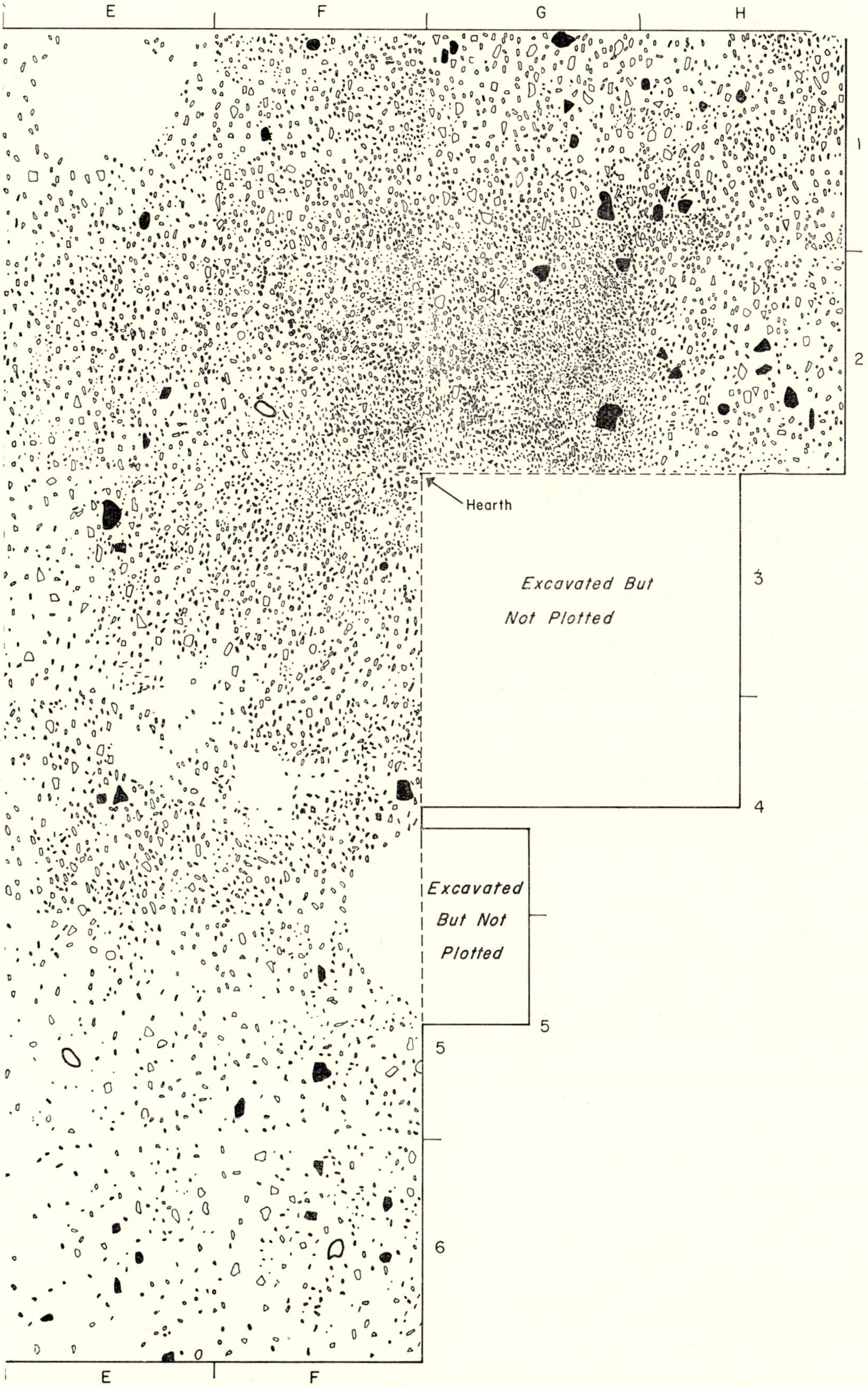

concentration (F. Van Noten). (See over the page for an enlargement of the top right-hand corner.)

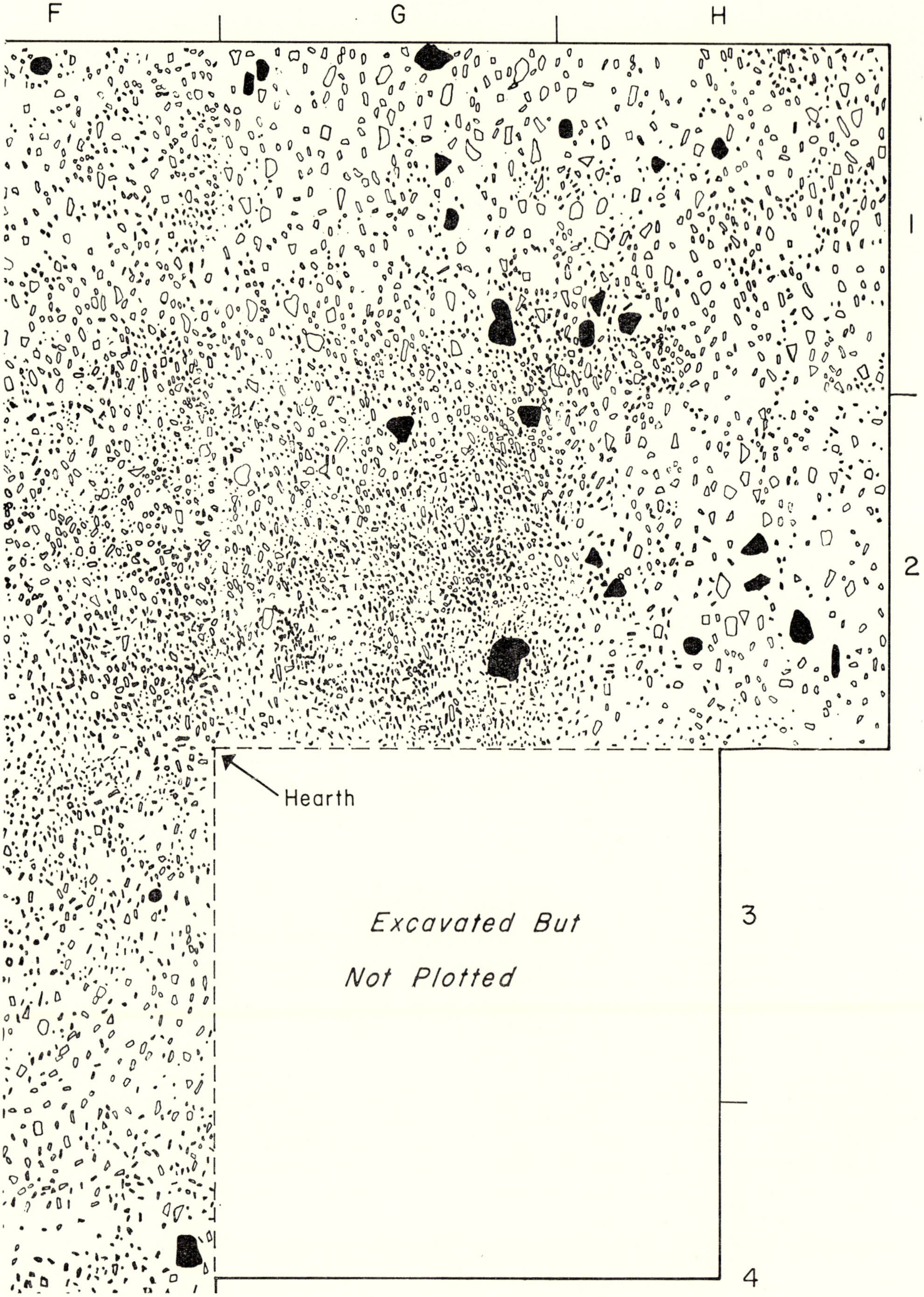
F
G
H
1
2
3
4
Hearth
Excavated But
Not Plotted

any overlapping of the two industrial traditions and the comparatively small numbers of microlithic artifacts from the midden itself more probably arrived there through the activities of the shaft diggers.

At the 4 foot (122 cm) level there was a marked falling off in the number of artifacts. The two grid squares G–2 and G–3 were excavated below this to a depth of 4 feet 6 inches (137 cm). Between 4 feet and 4 feet 6 inches (122 and 130 cm) square G–2 contained 49 specimens, all except one of which were factory waste; and square G–3, 233 specimens of which only 3 were shaped and 15 utilized. Between 4 feet 3 inches and 4 feet 6 inches (130 and 137 cm) the sand was found to be sterile.

Confirmation for this concentration of the microlithic industry between 3 feet 6 inches and 4 feet (106 and 122 cm) was found when sectioning shafts 6, 11 and 12. While derived material was sometimes found in the shafts themselves, none occurred in the undisturbed sand below a depth of 4 feet 6 inches (137 cm).

Figure 16 shows that the maximum concentration of artifacts occurred in the three grid squares F–1 and 2 and G–2 and also, possibly, in G–3 although the count from this square is incomplete due to disturbance by the shaft of Complex 11. The scatter was somewhat less concentrated and more evenly distributed in squares E–2, F–1 and G and H–1. Beyond these it thinned out rapidly and the remaining grid squares contained very few specimens, most of which were waste. Even though the Iron Age shafts have destroyed much of the distribution over the northern part of the excavation, it is clear that the density of artifacts here was decidedly much less. The greatest density occurs, therefore, in a small oval area measuring approximately 6 feet (1·8 m) in diameter and *c.* 28 square feet (2·6 m^2) in area; around this is a larger area of *c.* 70 square feet (6·5 m^2) where the concentration is less dense. By far the greater number of tools were found within this smaller area.

The river sand at the top of the Mbwilo Member on the flat top of the 30 foot (9 m) terrace, provided a soft and loose surface on which to camp and the normal trampling and range of group activities connected with this kind of occupation can be expected to have caused some downward movement of artifacts into the top 3–4 inches (75–100 mm) of sand and perhaps even deeper. Outside the area of maximum concentration the artifacts are more evenly scattered over the southern part of the excavation. When considered in relation to the vertical distribution of the artifacts within the top of the sand, such a pattern is not inconsistent with the suggestion that it reflects fairly regular occupation of the site which would thus bring about a redistribution of the debris of previous occupations. If this were so, then the heavy concentration in the southeast corner of the occupation floor would represent the debris of the final occupation which remained undisturbed except by minor natural agencies. Such an interpretation rests on the belief that in tropical Africa, hunting/gathering groups, the composition of which often varies from day to day, did not generally reoccupy the abandoned dwelling structures of previous years but built a new camp close by; such is the practice among the !Kung Bushmen, for example (Lee, 1968: 35).

The aggregate analysed includes all the artifacts found within the uppermost 6 inches (152 mm) of the buff/white sand beneath the brown sand that underlies the Early Iron Age midden soil. The few artifacts obtained from the 4 feet to 4 feet 6 inches (122–137 cm) level in grid squares G–2 and 3, have also been included in the analysis total. Since no evidence of stratification was present in the sand at this level, the artifact aggregate has been treated as a single unit. It should be borne in mind, however, that it is as likely that the aggregate represents the debris from a number of distinct and temporary re-occupations, as it is that it results from a single occupation of longer duration. Further excavation with precise recording of artifact depths might show whether there is any significant shifting of the areas of maximum concentration and associations of various artifact classes between the bottom and top of the cultural horizon such as would imply multiple occupations. The distribution plots (Figure 17) show no very obvious separate clusterings of artifact classes, neither does the range of tool classes show any observable vertical change within the horizon, as might also be expected where several separate occupations are present. Absence of these features would still not necessarily preclude an interpretation of multiple occupations but, if this were so here, it would be necessary to accept that the activities and range of tools these required were similar at each ensuing visit. Such may well have been the case where limitations existed on the available suitable floor space, as in some caves and rock shelters and Sampson (Sampson and Sampson, 1967: 17, 53–70) has recently demonstrated this at Riversmead Shelter in the middle Orange basin where the activities centred at the eastern side of the shelter because the lowness of the roof of the western

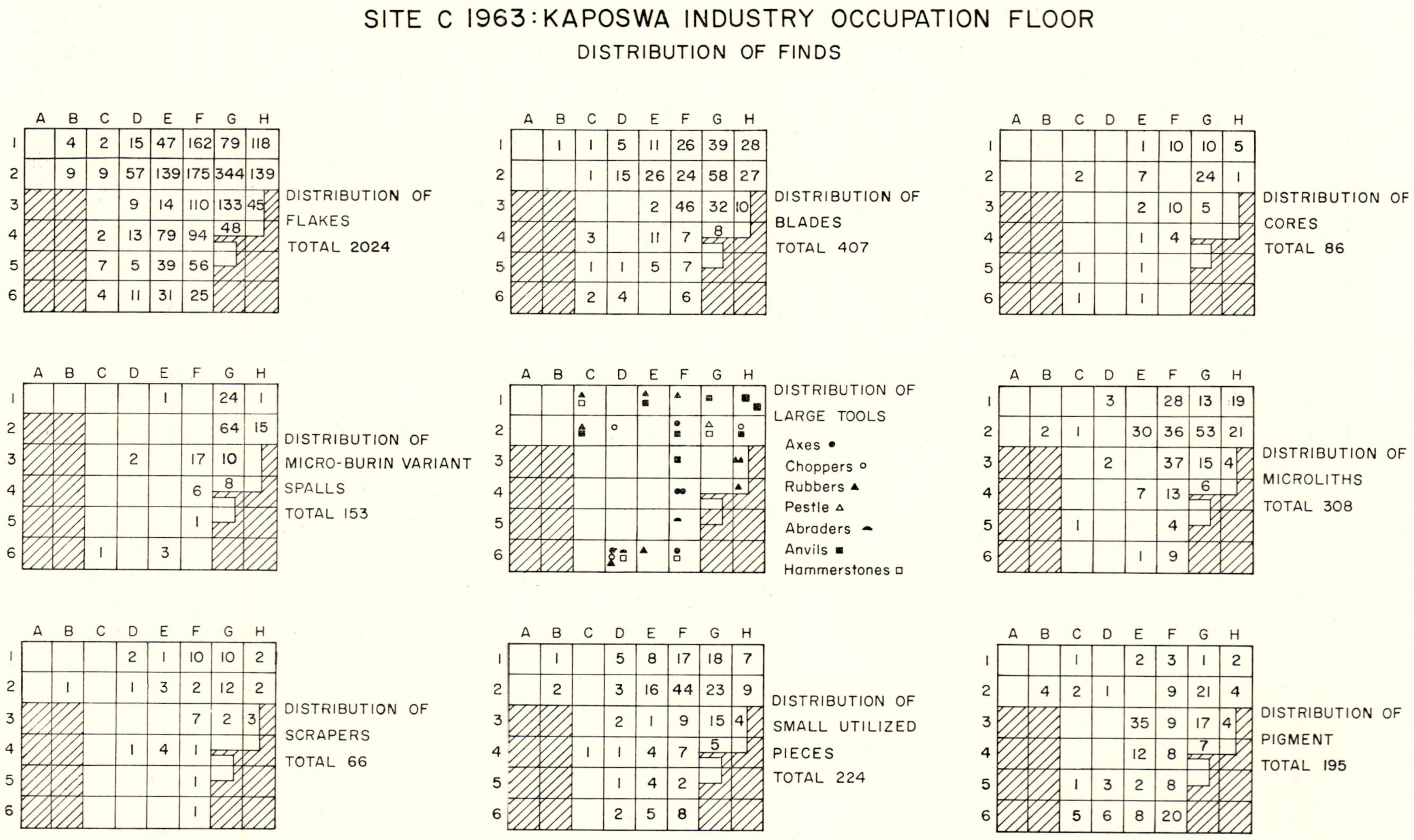

Fig. 17. Site C, 1963: 'Later Stone Age' living floor: distribution of finds by grid squares.

half and the rock rubble on the floor made this area uninhabitable. Open sites would have had fewer such inhibiting features, though the presence of a favourable shade tree may well have influenced the siting of the camp and re-occupation of the same area for a period of several years. No evidence was found to show whether this might have been so at Site C.

In sum, therefore, and until further evidence is forthcoming, we prefer to interpret this distribution pattern as representing a single occupation of more than purely transitory duration. This was probably sited within a traditional camping area the surface of which had, through time, acquired some general scatter of debris from stone flaking.

Associated with the percussion flaked and rubbed artifacts were a number of medium sized natural stones (quartzite and sandstone) scattered at random. All are manuports that had been carried onto the site although the majority preserve no indication of the use to which they had been put. A few show fracture by fire and at least one sandstone specimen in grid square C–2, had been used as an anvil and shows battering on three faces. They must all have had some special purpose or they would not have been carried into the camp. Some, no doubt, served as hearth stones, others as anvils or pounding stones, and others, perhaps, as weights to help keep in place the framework of the dwelling structure.

No intentional grouping or alignment of these stones is apparent although this is hardly surprising on an open site of this kind where, observation shows, the larger stones generally suffer some displacement after abandonment and exposure (Clark, 1969: 46–7 and Plates 7, 8). Each subsequent re-occupation of such a site would further dislocate any original plan their grouping may once have preserved. The outer edge of the concentration of flaked stone artifacts is, however, fairly clearly defined in the floor plan and forms a rather irregular semi-circle within grid squares F–H/1–2 with a 'tail' of artifacts extending to the west in grid square F–3. This is not unlike the kind of scatter that has been observed associated with the entrance or pathway giving access to a dwelling or homestead.

Also of considerable interest was the discovery of a concentration of fairly large charcoals in the middle of this area of maximum density of artifacts. Scattered charcoals were found throughout grid squares A–D/1 and 2 and E–H/1 and 2, between 3 feet and 3 feet 6 inches (91 and 106 cm) but these might, perhaps, have been derived from the overlying midden. Between 3 feet 6 inches and 4 feet (106 and 122 cm) in grid squares H–1 and 2 and G–1 and 2, a heavier scatter occurred and in F–2 was found a concentration that was believed to be a hearth and here also there was a boulder that had been broken into three pieces by fire.

It would seem, therefore, that activities at this prehistoric camp site were carried out in close proximity to the hearth. Among the Bushmen, the hearth is invariably located across the front of the windbreak, thus affording warmth, light and protection at night. 'Life takes place for the most part outside them (the windbreaks) beside the fire. The fire is the home' (Marshall, 1960: 344). The concentration uncovered by our own excavation might, therefore, be interpreted as the hearth and working area of a single family adjacent to its shelter, one of the main activities carried on close to this hearth being the manufacture of microliths. Fire would have been necessary for the shaping of wood by charring and scraping or by bending and hardening, but it is not clear why stone should have been worked in such proximity to the fire. The reason might, perhaps, have been the necessity for the stone to be at the right temperature and to have the correct moisture content to obtain the best results, or it might simply have been the attraction of a fire for the hunter during the cold of the dry season (the advantages of which were readily appreciated by archaeologists in a later period) and the fact that the fire was, indeed, the home.[1] Plate 96 shows such a shelter and activity area round the hearth at a Hukwe camp in southwest Zambia.

Further excavation is expected to reveal whether this concentration is an isolated example or, as appears more likely, was one of several. Until, therefore, the full extent of the occupied area is known, no estimate can be made of the probable size of the nomadic group that camped there.

The aggregate analysis

The composition and attributes of the Kaposwa Industry aggregate from Site C, 1963, are summarized in the bar diagrams (Figure 18) and in Table 11. Further details of range and mean measurements and other statistical data on microliths, scrapers, flakes and blades are given at Table 13. The distribution by

[1] Possible heat treatment of the chert can be eliminated because of the matt surface texture of all artifacts.

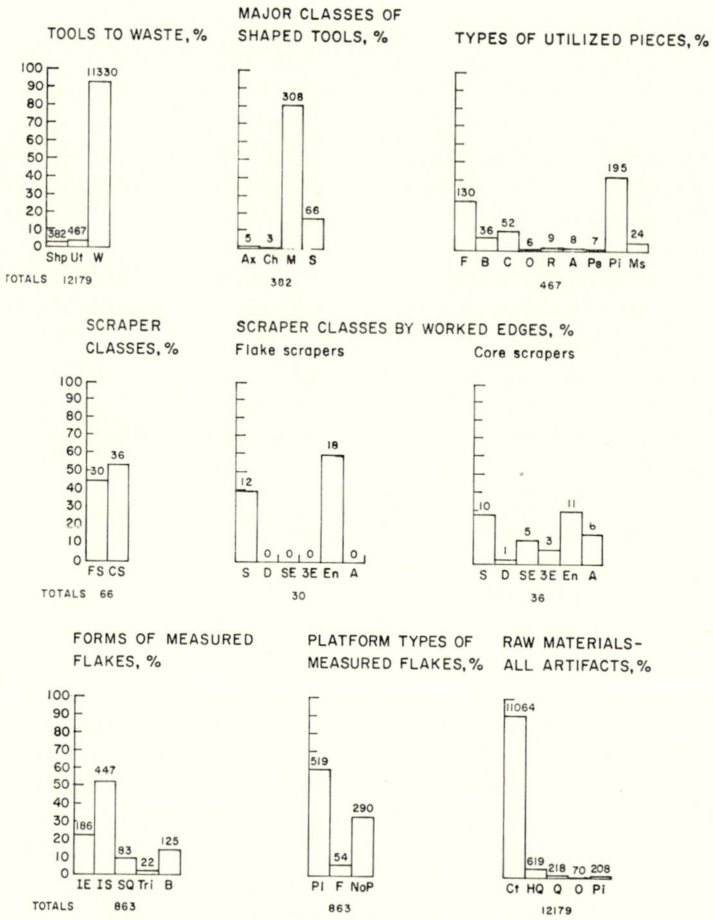

Fig. 18. Site C, 1963: Analysis of Kaposwa Industry – bar diagrams.

Key:

Tools to waste
Shp = Shaped tools
Ut = Utilized/modified
W = Unmodified waste

Utilized/modified pieces
F = Flake and flake fragment
B = Blade and blade fragment
C = Chunks and cores
O = *Outils esquillés*
R = Rubbers
A = Anvils
Pe = Pestles, abraders, hammerstones
Pi = Pigment
Ms = Miscellaneous

Scraper classes
FS = Flake scrapers
CS = Core scrapers

Flake scrapers
S = Single side
D = Double side
SE = End and side
3E = Three edges
En = End
A = Angled

Shaped tool classes
Ax = Stone axe
Ch = Chopper
M = Microlith
S = Scraper

Flake form
IE = Irregular end-struck
IS = Irregular side-struck
SQ = Short quadrilateral
Tri = Triangular
B = Long quadrilateral (blade)

Platform types
Pl = Plain
F = Faceted
NoP = Point

Raw materials
Ct = Chert
HQ = Hard quartzite
Q = Quartz
O = Other
Pi = Pigment

TABLE 13. *Measurements of certain tool classes of the Kaposwa Industry, Site C, 1963*

Artifact class	Measurement in mm	Number in sample	Range: Min.	Range: Max.	Mode(s)	Median	Mean ±	S.D.
All microliths	Length	240	7·5	35 = 27·5	15	17·5	18·5 ± 0·35	5·44
	Breadth	240	2·5	20 = 17·5	7·5	7·5	8·1	
	Thickness	108	< 2·5[a]	12·5 = 10·5	2·5	2·5	2·9	
	B/L ratio	100	0·2	1·5 = 1·3	0·4	0·4	0·45 ± 0·019	0·19
Flake scrapers < 50 mm long	Length	21	10·0	47·5 = 37·5	30	30	28·2 ± 2·3	10·45
	Breadth	21	10·0	40·0 = 30	15, 30, 40	20	24·1	
	Thickness	19	2·5	17·5 = 15	2·5	5	8·4	
	B/L ratio	21	0·5	1·2 = 0·7	0·9	1·0	0·8 ± 0·03	0·14
Core scrapers < 50 mm long	Length	20	15·0	50·0 = 35	50	40	38·5	
	Breadth	20	10·0	45·0 = 35	22·5	23·75	27·0	
	Thickness	18	7·5	25·0 = 17·5	17·5	17·5	17·2	
	B/L ratio	20	0·4	1·3 = 0·9	0·5	0·7	0·68	
Scrapers > 50 mm (1 flake 60 × 55 × 20) (12 core)	Length	13	57·5	85·0 = 27·5	60	65	60·1	
	Breadth	13	40	60·0 = 20	40, 50	45	48·6	
	Thickness	12	25	47·5 = 22·5	25	27·5	28·5	
	B/L ratio	13	0·57	0·9 = 0·33	0·6, 0·7, 0·8	0·7	0·73	
All scrapers	Length	54	10	85 = 75	40	40	39·5	
	Breadth	54	10	60 = 50	40	30	30·7	
	Thickness	49	2·5	47·5 = 45	2·5	17·5	14·7	
	B/L ratio	54	0·4	1·3 = 0·9	0·6, 0·7, 1·0	0·75	0·77	
Flakes	Length	338	10	70 = 60	25	25	26·1 ± 0·58	10·76
	Breadth	338	5	72·5 = 67·5	12·5, 20	20	20·0	
	Thickness	338	< 2·5[a]	20 = 18	2·5	2·5	4·1	
	B/L ratio	100	0·25	2·4 = 2·15	0·6	0·8	0·79 ± 0·04	0·41
Blades	Length	56	15	52·5 = 37·5	30	31·5	31·4 ± 1·19	8·9
	Breadth	56	2·5	25 = 22·5	10	12	12·6	
	Thickness	56	< 2·5[a]	12 = 10	< 2·5[a]	2·5	3·3	
	B/L ratio	56	0·13	0·5 = 0·37	0·35	0·36	0·38 ± 0·02	0·15

[a] For calculation purposes regarded as 2 mm.

grid squares of the main artifact classes is seen at Figure 17 and will be discussed later.

Unmodified waste from stone flaking and manufacture of microliths comprises 93 per cent (11,330 specimens), only 3·1 per cent (382 specimens) are intentionally retouched shaped tools and approximately the same percentage (3·9 per cent: 467 specimens) show evidence of utilization and minimal modification. Such a percentage of unmodified waste is high but not unusual and, since it is mostly of microlithic proportions, it emphasizes the role of the microlith and the equipment and activities with which it is associated, at this site.

RAW MATERIAL

The material from which most of the artifacts were made was carefully selected. Overwhelming preference (11,064 specimens) was given to a green coloured chert (silicified mudstone) with excellent cleavage properties. The stone occurs locally in bands in the Plateau Series sediments and must have been available in unlimited quantity since only small pieces were required. In addition, hard quartzite (619 specimens) and sandstone (18 specimens) were used, mostly for rubbers and anvils and in the form of flakes or other tools required for heavy work. Dolerite (31 specimens) was used in the same way for heavier artifacts. Although only 5 artifacts were made of chalcedony, this was a preferred material on the plateau where it was more readily available (cf. at Chulungoma, near Mbala), but never abundant. It is not local to the Kalambo basin and so must have been carried in for a distance of several miles. The same applies to some, at least, of the 218 quartz specimens since, although some of this material may have been obtained locally from veins in the Plateau Series rocks, the crystals must have been brought in from further afield.

A. Shaped tools (382: 3·1 per cent)

LARGE TOOLS ('HEAVY DUTY')

Although small flaked tools predominate (97·8 per cent: 374 specimens) in the shaped tool category there is also a significant but small number (2·2 per cent: 8 specimens) of large stone tools. The thirteen scrapers (one on a flake and twelve on chunks) that measure more than 50 mm have been classified with the remainder of the scrapers since in our system they are not regarded as large tools. The utilized category reflects a similar situation with 44·5 per cent of the total (208 specimens out of 467) representing artifacts on small percussion flaked pieces, 3·4 per cent (16 specimens) on larger (50–100 mm) flaked pieces and only 5·2 per cent (24 specimens) being heavy equipment. The remaining almost 47 per cent is composed of pigment (195 pieces) and some two dozen miscellaneous items.

Of the larger artifacts – axes/adzes, choppers, grinding stones, rubbers, bored stones – it is rare to find more than a very few on most single unit occupation sites of the 'Later Stone Age'. As a consequence, it has been the tendency among prehistorians to treat them as unusual or miscellaneous constituents while giving most emphasis to the smaller flaked specimens, the quantitative analysis of which has provided the main basis for making meaningful comparisons. However, the role of this 'large' element cannot have been inconsiderable and there is reason to think that these were indispensable items of equipment at the camps where they are found. It can be expected also that some of them were left on the site when the group moved and regularly re-used at each visit, in the same way that grindstones remain permanently on the camp sites of some Bushmen and Australian groups (R. B. Lee, personal communication; Thomson, 1964; Gould, 1969: 77). Hadza pounding stones are not usually carried about but left by the side of the hollow in the flat rock where the pounding is done (Woodburn, 1970: 40).

The axe/adze with its carefully prepared cutting and chopping edge, is the only formal item of 'heavy duty' equipment on the 'Later Stone Age' occupation sites in this woodland–savanna country, though it is supplemented by the use of informal choppers and scraping tools. Experiment shows that the preparation of a tough, ground edge of the axe/adze type on such hard rocks as those of which the specimens are made required considerable time and labour. Similarly, with a bored stone, the perforation and reaming of the hole and the further shaping of the piece also require time and, as with the axe/adze some continual usage is to be expected in return. The wear to be observed on the grinding and rubbing stones is clear evidence of their regular usage and analagous ethnographic contexts show them to be essential equipment for the preparation of food by hunter/gatherers. Every family group can be expected to have possessed one or more of these specialized activity tools which would have to have been replaced only rarely, when they were lost or broken. This equipment is clearly not expendable to the same extent as were the microlithic artifacts, if one may judge by the quantities in which these last were produced. This heavier equipment, it is believed, was indispensable at all 'Later Stone Age' general purpose camps in the south central African savanna and probably throughout the sub-continent as a whole and it was certainly an integral part of the toolkit at the Kalambo Falls.

Axes (5: 1·4 per cent)

(*a*) *Ground and polished* (4) (Plate 34: 1–4). Two are complete specimens and two broken fragments. Dolerite was the material used, no doubt for its resistant qualities. The two complete specimens were probably made from flakes struck from boulders and worked to shape by direct percussion. The cutting edge was formed by grinding and rubbing, probably on sandstone. No attempt was made to produce a uniform finish over the whole tool and the scars resulting from the primary flaking are easily seen. The main functional part of these tools was the tough, but not particularly sharp, ground edge. This, and their weight, suggest that they were heavy duty tools.

One of the two broken specimens was found near the base of the Iron Age midden in grid square B–1, at a depth of 2 feet 8 inches (81 cm) and is illustrated at Plate 34: 2. It is the same type of edge-ground axe made in dolerite and can with confidence be considered to be derived from the underlying microlithic occupation floor; it may have been turned up by the makers of the Kalambo Falls Industry in the course of digging shafts 3 or 4.

(*b*) *Percussion flaked* (1) (Plate 34: 5). The working end of this tool is missing so that it is not possible to be sure whether or not it was polished. It is made from a large piece of dolerite shaped by percussion.

It is possible that specimens such as this, which have been flaked only and not ground, are 'roughouts' or incomplete tools. However, they occur unassociated with the edge-ground forms at Hora Mountain and Fingira Hill in Malawi and one example from Fingira shows extensive polishing from use. It would seem, therefore, that edge-grinding was not an essential attribute of these axe/adze tools.

Choppers (3: 0·8 per cent) (Plate 35: 8, 10 and 11)
These are informal tools and show the minimum amount of retouch on one or both faces. The bruising and battering due to use are very apparent. The large end-scraper at Plate 35: 7 has also been used as a chopper at the upper end. That choppers were sometimes more regularly retouched can be seen from the example illustrated at Plate 33: 23 which was found in the hillslope soil on Site A, Trench A4, 1959.

Bored stones
Although no example was found *in situ* in the excavated area, it is certain that the bored stone was known and manufactured in the local basin. Besides the surface examples listed above (p. 114) one broken specimen was recovered by us from an earlier horizon (Rubble I) at Site B and one broken example was recovered from the clays of the Chiungu Member at Site B in 1956 (Plate 33: 22) where it occurred with a similarly derived microlithic element. One broken and incompletely bored specimen was found also in the collapsed sand at the Site C river face close to the excavation in 1963 (Plate 41: 1). This is made of sandstone and in its small size it resembles the small examples found with the Nachikufan Industrial Complex on the plateau to the south. There can be little doubt that this specimen comes from the microlithic occupation floor. The same applies to a second complete specimen found in the collapsed sand of the cliff face at Site C in 1966 (Plate 33: 24). This is sub-rectangular in plan form, is made from a flat piece of mudstone, has an hour-glass perforation and measures 110 × 82 × 32 mm.

The large examples from the Kalambo Falls are all flat, with no very regular plan form, and hour-glass perforation. In this they also resemble the bored stones found with the Nachikufan, and those from southern Tanzania (Kleindienst, 1961*b*; see also p. 10 above), the Katanga and the Lunda Province of Angola (Clark, 1968: 167–79). The small, incompletely bored specimen also suggests that the range of sizes and uses may be the same at the Kalambo Falls as at the Nachikufan sites, though the comparatively small number known from the local basin would indicate that the bored stone was not in such regular use there as at some of the sites further to the south in the Northern Province of Zambia.

SMALL TOOLS ('LIGHT DUTY')

Microliths (308: 80·5 per cent. Includes 42 broken specimens) (Plate 36)
Characteristic are the well made lunates, trapezes and triangles for these forms are not generally the most numerous classes found with microlithic industries in south central Africa. The great majority are made from triangular sectioned, or wedge shaped fragments of bladelets and flakes. In approximately one third of these tools, the dorsal face consists of part of a single scar. The remainder generally, though not invariably, show two or more parallel flake scars on this face. The broken examples have been excluded from the percentage counts in the sub-classes since it is not possible to be sure to which of these they belong.

(*a*) *Lunates* (100: 37·6 per cent) (Plate 36: 1–30). These are the commonest form of microlith and are all diminutive, that is less than 30 mm in length and the majority are less than 20 mm. Sections are always triangular or wedge shaped. The backing is steep and usually normal (i.e. directed from the main flake surface only). Opposed backing occurs less commonly and is generally confined to one or both ends of the convex back of lunates. The cutting edge or cord may be straight (Plate 36: 6), concave (Plate 36: 7) or, rarely, convex (Plate 36: 1) and in no instance does it show any sign of utilization, notching or retouch.

(*b*) *Triangles* (29: 10·9 per cent) (Plate 36: 31–47). The backing is steep and similar to that on lunates.

Both scalene (Plate 36: 33, 38, 41, 45 and 46) and equilateral (Plate 36: 31, 32, 34–37, 39, 40, 42–44 and 47) forms occur. Again the cutting edge shows no sign of use.

(*c*) *Trapezes* (9: 3·4 per cent) (Plate 36: 52–56). These are intermediate between triangles and lunates and are probably atypical. One heavier specimen occurs (no. 56). The backing is blunt and steep.

(*d*) *Shouldered microliths* (11: 4·1 per cent) (Plate 36: 48–51 and 75). These are broken blades, lunates or triangles with a notch, or shoulder, worked by steep, concave backing at one end. This is probably the result of the technique used for the manufacture of the microliths rather than an attempt to produce a special sort of microlith. The technique is seen by comparing the specimen at Plate 36: 75, where the retouch on the shoulder is not yet complete and the artifact resembles a *lamelle à piquant trièdre*, with Plate 36: 48 where the retouch is complete.

(*e*) *Backed bladelets*[1] (81) (Plate 36: 57–68, 77 and 78). The backing may be either convex (66: 24·8 per cent) (Plate 36: 57–60, 62 and 64–68), or straight (15: 15·6 per cent) (nos. 61, 63, 77 and 78). The former is considerably the more common and these two sub-classes are the most characteristic forms found with the microlithic aggregates from the more southern parts of Zambia (e.g. at Mumbwa Caves and Gwisho Springs). The great majority are under 30 mm long but a few longer and cruder examples occur (cf. Plate 36: 57 and 60). The straight-backed class is rare in the excavated material but two typical specimens came from the southern end of the site in 1959 (Plate 36: 77 and 78) and examples were also found in the A7, 1966 excavation and at Chitambala's village.

(*f*) *Obliquely truncated microliths* (36: 13·6 per cent) (Plate 36: 69–72 and 76). Mostly these are the distal ends of bladelets that show oblique truncation. They may have been used as they are or have been further reduced by snapping and then trimming of the opposite edge to form a triangle or trapeze. One atypical specimen has been truncated at right angles to the long axis by notching (Plate 36: 76).

It is well seen from the illustrations that the above sub-classes of 'geometric' microliths grade into each other.

Scrapers (66: 17·3 per cent) (Table 11 gives the analysis as to plan form and type of edge retouch and quantitative data are shown at Table 13)

This is in general an atypical class of tool at the Kalambo Falls. Included in it are one flake scraper and 12 on cores that are larger than 50 mm, otherwise they possess the same attributes as the remainder of the class.

(*a*) *Flake scrapers* (30: 45·5 per cent of scrapers) (Plate 37: 1–8 and 16). These are on whole flakes or fragments of flakes and bladelets and are either irregular or short quadrilateral in plan form. The only modification is at the working edge which exhibits a blunt or steep retouch angle. The majority (18) are small end-scrapers with a straight or notched working end and others are worked on one lateral edge only. They conform to no regular dimensions or plan form. Some of the short end-scrapers exhibit parallel dorsal flaking but the greater number show two- or three-directional flake scars on the dorsal face.

(*b*) *Core-scrapers* (36: 54·5 per cent of scrapers) (Plate 37: 9 and 11–15). These scrapers, worked on chunks and having a steep retouch angle, are the second most typical tool form in the collection. It is often difficult to decide whether a core should be classified as a core-scraper or simply as a core, since the amount of trimming is very variable and at least some of this would seem to have been produced by the normal preparation of the edge of the platform before the removal of flakes and blades. Only those cores, therefore, that show bruising and blunting of the edge as well as retouch have been classified as core-scrapers. Some of these tools (e.g. Plate 37: 11 and 12) resemble the *grattoir caréné* and *grattoir à museau* (Plate 37: 9 and 15) forms of scraper from the Upper Palaeolithic of Europe and the Levant and the Epi-Palaeolithic of the Maghreb. Besides being made on cores they were not infrequently made on tabular chert. The retouch is blunt or steep. The commonest plan forms are end (Plate 37: 13), side (Plate 37: 14), end and side (nos. 9, 12 and 15) and circular, or all round (no. 11). One of the larger forms is illustrated at Plate 35: 7. The commonest edge forms are straight and convex but there is also a significant number of denticulated and notched examples.

[1] This class includes forms made on both micro-blades and micro-flakes. No attempt has been made to separate these as in many cases it is not possible to be certain of the primary form.

Burins

It will be noted that no 'burin class' has been included with the shaped tools, in spite of the occurrence of artifacts and the quartz crystal (Plate 36: 74) which show the *coup de burin*. Technically, these are all burins and the presence of minute scars on the burin edges of a few of them perhaps indicates that some may be true burins as distinct from technical burins.

In 1963, at the time this analysis was carried out, no such burin scars were observed on any of the flakes, blades or flake and blade fragments that occurred in such abundance, with the exception of the burin on a split flake or flake fragment (*burin à coup diamétral* or *burin moustérien*) which is a product of primary flaking and the micro-burin and micro-burin Krukowski which are products of the technique of making microliths and are described below. Some bladelet cores might be described by some workers as *burins nucléiformes* but they grade into examples which could never be mistaken for burins and, accordingly, all have been classified here as cores (e.g. Plate 40: 7).

If true burins had been present, it was to be expected that they would be made on flakes and blades rather than on chunks and so those burin scars that did occur were considered to be more likely 'technical' and the unintentional product of flaking.

I have recently re-examined a total of 646 flakes and flake fragments from grid square H–2, amongst which eight specimens were found which might be classed as burins although they were all questionable examples made on snapped flake fragments. Five of these are single blow burins, the burin blow either on a vertical or horizontal snapped edge, one is dihedral and two are multiple dihedral burins (i.e. one with two scars and one with four, opposed to a snapped edge). There is also a specimen which might be considered a burin on a truncation, although the latter shows a minimal number of scars. All of these artifacts are likely to be fortuitous (i.e. technical) burins though there is doubt whether they should even be classified as technical. It is considered, therefore, that the burin is only doubtfully present in the Kaposwa microlithic aggregates at the Kalambo Falls.[1]

B. Utilized pieces (467: 3·9 per cent)

Utilized flakes and flake fragments (130: 28 per cent) (Plate 38: 1, 2, 3, 9, 10, 12 and 14)

See Table 11 for classification by plan and edge form.

After microliths, these constitute the next largest class of tool. The great majority are irregular flakes and fragments that have been used or modified along the whole or part of one or more lateral edges. This utilization takes the form of minute marginal flake scars or nibbling, edges that are notched or denticulated or bear evidence of some incipient retouch. Most specimens have only one edge utilized in this way. Such tools may have served as knives and saws as well as for scraping and are a significant element in the Kaposwa Industry.

Utilized blades and blade fragments (36: 7·7 per cent) (Plate 38: 3, 11 and 15)

See Table 11 for analysis. There is no essential difference in the nature of the utilization and edge wear between these and the utilized flake forms above.

In both these classes of utilized pieces, the degree of modification and utilization of the edge or edges grades from examples with minimal edge wear to others that show a more consistent pattern of utilization and some discontinuous marginal retouch resembling 'Ouchtata retouch'. They, therefore, grade up to the class of retouched, backed and truncated bladelets though they never show the regular trimmed and blunted edges of the retouched classes.

Utilized chunks and cores (52: 11·2 per cent) (Plate 38: 16–19)

See also Table 11. These are mainly irregular chunks showing one utilized edge (Plate 38: 17) and, more rarely, two such edges (no. 16).

Three chunks of hard quartzite have one or more edges that show blunting due to rubbing rather than to percussion or pressure. Such dulled and rubbed edges can be shown by experiment to result from scraping wet hides or cleaning the sinew and meat off bones and these specimens may have been used for a similar purpose. They cannot be classified in the same way as the other utilized chunks and so have been grouped separately.

[1] The two most convincing burins come from Chitambala's village and are on a flake fragment and blade (classified as Utilized in Table 11). The first might be described as a *burin plan*, the second is technically a transverse burin and shows also concave marginal modification of one lateral edge.

The small group of artifacts that have been classified as technical burins (Plate 38: 19) have been referred to at p. 127 above. They exhibit one or more burin-like facets on the thickness of a chunk and sometimes show minute scarring of the 'burin' facet or facets, presumably from utilization. They resemble proto-burins rather than true burins and may be representative of a class of tool that occurs throughout the earlier cultural succession at the Kalambo Falls.

Outils esquillés (*écaillés*) (6: 1·3 per cent) (Plate 38: 5–8)

These are conspicuous at the Kalambo Falls by their rarity when compared with the numbers often associated with the 'Later Stone Age' aggregates from the areas to the south and east in Zambia and Malawi where quartz was the raw material used. The Kalambo Falls examples mostly show straight, opposed *esquillé* edges, the splintering affecting both faces of the artifact. They are usually on chunks and so are more probably worked out bipolar cores into which class they imperceptibly grade (cf. Plate 36: 73). Three examples are made on thick flake fragments.

It is probable that the rarity of this artifact in the local basin is directly related to the kind of raw material used. In the writer's experience, the *outil esquillé* (or *écaillé*) is particularly common where the material used is quartz. Quartz, especially the semi-crystalline varieties, splinters readily and, where the selection of the most suitable kinds of material, including quartz crystal, means using pieces and pebbles of quite small size, as is not infrequently the case, the only technique that could be effectively employed is the bipolar one. In view of the recent finds of White (1968*b*) concerning the by-products of this technique in the New Guinea highlands and again of Logsdon (1971) there is now reason to consider most, if not all, of these *outils esquillés* as the by-products of bipolar technique. If this is the case, then the small number of these artifacts and of bipolar cores found with the Kaposwa aggregates suggests that this technique was not the usual method employed to flake the chert used at the Kalambo Falls.

Rubbers (9: 1·8 per cent) (Plate 34: 6. See also Plate 33: 20)

These are made on quartzite pebbles and both whole and broken (3) specimens are found. The essential feature is one (or more) rubbed and finely striated faces. Not infrequently, however, such tools have served also as hammers, pestles or anvils, so that they have been classified here by whichever appears to have been the predominant use. Plate 34: 6 combines three of these uses but preserves one well worn rubbing face. Dimple scars in the centre of a rubbing face are often associated with 'Later Stone Age' rubbers of this kind. In ethnographic use the dimple serves to retain a portion of the substance being ground – wild seeds, for example – and helps to ensure that it is properly ground instead of being pushed off the grindstone.

No large lower grindstones were found, such as are associated with the Iron Age cultures and it seems probable that the rubbers may have been used in pairs, one serving as the upper and the other as the lower stone. On the other hand, these hard stones show a considerable amount of use wear and their comparatively small size and weight may indicate that they were carried round with the group as it moved. Any large flat stone, or even a log with a convenient flat face, could be used on which to pound and grind, as occasion required.

Anvils (8: 1·6 per cent)

Three good examples of dimple-scarred anvils were found, made on quartzite pebbles and showing an irregular area of battering, forming a shallow dimple on one or more of the faces. The rubber at Plate 34: 6 shows one of the side faces with dimple scarring of this irregular, anvil-type which should be compared with the more regular and deeper scarring and pitting associated with rubbing faces, as is present also on the same specimen. Plate 34: 7 is a dimple-scarred anvil pitted in five separate places and having also one rubbing face. Plate 35: 5 is a dimple-scarred stone on three faces and is well hammered at both ends.

The class of block anvil with a much battered edge or edges is represented by five specimens (Plate 35: 6 and 9; Plate 41: 7). These may have acquired their battered edges from use with the indirect anvil technique (see p. 87 above).

Pestles, abraders and hammerstones (7: 1·4 per cent)

(*a*) *Pestles* (1) (Plate 35: 1). A long quadrilateral pebble of chert shows bruising at both ends from use as a pestle.

(*b*) *Abraders* (2) (Plate 35: 2 and 3). These interesting tools are made on large chunks of sandy quartzite. In each case one end shows extensive rubbing and abrasion, very different from the concoidal fracture associated with pounding and hammering stone against stone. This type of wear could have resulted from use of the tool for working a soft material – cleaning a skin, for example – by means of an abrasive such as moist sand, or from pounding gritty vegetable materials. Three small utilized chunks showing slight evidence of rubbed edges have already been noted but the specimens illustrated at Plate 35: 2 and 3 show much greater evidence of such wear. This is a type of tool that may occur with other 'Later Stone Age' aggregates in south central Africa but awaits more general recognition.

(*c*) *Hammerstones* (4) (Plate 35: 4). Irregular cobbles and pebbles exhibiting one or more areas of battering.

Pigment (195: 42 per cent) (Plate 41: 2, 3 and 6)
A considerable number of small fragments of haematite were scattered over the surface of the camping floor but only a few of these show the typical rubbing facets that result from being ground to provide powder for pigment. Besides haematite, a red, ferruginous schist or ochre was also used. Four small pieces of white kaolin clay were found in grid square G–2 and within the area of greatest concentration were seven pieces of yellow ochre and much weathered dolerite with thick, yellow patination. One of these fragments shows rubbing facets. All this colouring material was undoubtedly carried onto the site and was presumably used for body paint and for decorating equipment and clothing.

Miscellaneous (24: 5 per cent)
Included here are certain manuports, older and derived artifacts that were presumably collected and brought back, perhaps for use as raw material. They include 3 flakes from prepared cores; a flake fragment, a core fragment, a core-axe of ?Lupemban or later Sangoan type and a core-axe resharpening flake. The core-axe is little abraded and there may have been an attempt to re-use it. It was possibly derived from Rubble II in the middle levels of the Mkamba Member.

Also included in this miscellaneous class are: 1 quartz crystal burin illustrated at Plate 36: 74; 1 irregular, end-struck flake with bifacial (Quina-type) retouch on one convex edge (Plate 37: 10); 1 irregular end-flake with inverse retouch along one edge (Plate 38: 13); 1 pebble unifacially flaked on one edge and possibly used as a chopper or core-scraper; 1 small, plain platformed, sub-triangular flake with marginal utilization and minimal retouch on both edges which might be classified as a 'micro-point'; 1 poorly made borer; and 11 steeply trimmed edge fragments from flake scrapers or perhaps from large backed blades.

C. Unmodified Waste (11,330: 93 per cent)

Flakes and blades (2,431: 22·4 per cent)
These comprise less than a quarter of the unmodified waste and details of plan form and measurements are set out in Tables 11 and 13. A range of typical forms is illustrated at Plate 39.

Flakes (2,024: 83·6 per cent) predominate over blades (407: 16·4 per cent), are mostly under 50 mm and generally microlithic. In plan form the majority (1,357) are irregular, end-struck flakes although there is a significant number (560) of side-struck forms. The dorsal scars show flaking almost entirely from one direction and a parallel or convergent pattern. Striking platforms are generally plain, broad and inclined at a low angle to the main release surface. Dihedral platforms and occasional examples with more than two facets also occur but are not common. They are generally derived from proto-biconical, biconical and discoid cores or are the result of resharpening or rejuvenating the flaking edge of single platform cores. The type of faceted striking platforms associated with the Levallois and discoid core techniques does not occur.

Flakes grade into bladelets and all except two of these latter are less than 50 mm in length with practically half being under 30 mm long. The blades almost invariably show parallel, one directional flaking from the platform end. The platforms are mostly plain, broad and gently inclined. Significant is the number of bladelets that exhibit a point platform. This is accompanied at the proximal end on the dorsal face by a number of very small step flakes and splintering which results from the preparation of the edge of the core – straightening out irregularities in the plan view of the edge and ensuring the correct angle between the striking platform and the fabricator. These features and the small, nipple-like bulb that is generally present are characteristic of flake/blade removal by means of a punch which was, therefore, probably the main method used here.

'*Micro-burins*' (153: 1·4 per cent)
These are discussed below with the description of the technique used at the Kalambo Falls.

Cores (86: 0·75 per cent) (Plate 40; Plate 41: 4 and 5)
For details of core forms and attributes see Table 11. Although cores constitute only a small percentage of the unmodified waste, the number found is sufficiently large to make it possible to reconstruct the techniques of which they are the product. The great majority of these cores have the greatest measurement between 90 and 50 mm; only 12 examples are longer than 90 mm and only 4 were less than 30 mm in length. This is in agreement with the size of the majority of the flakes and bladelets, the lengths of which lie under 50 mm, so that there are virtually none that are too large to be accounted for by the cores as found.

The most characteristic forms are single platform cores. These may be long and flat with straight platform edge (Plate 40: 1), i.e. where the length of the core at right angles to the striking platform exceeds the breadth (the length of the striking platform) or they may be thick and broad (Plate 40: 2) in which case the breadth exceeds the length. A characteristic form is the prismatic, pyramidal core (Plate 40: 6 and 9–11) of which 12 examples were found. These are designed for the removal of bladelets. 'Chunky' cores with two platforms at right angles to each other on different faces or on the same face (Plate 40: 3; Plate 41: 4) are found with almost all 'Later Stone Age' aggregates, as is the formless class of core with three or four platforms (Plate 41: 5). Three small proto-biconical and 5 biconical cores (Plate 40: 5) and two discoid cores (Plate 40: 8) complete the range of core forms found. By reason of the radial flaking on the dorsal face, these last resemble, though only superficially, the disc cores of the 'Middle Stone Age'; they and the biconical forms are not typical of this microlithic aggregate.

Cores were resharpened by removing the whole or part of the platform edge by a blow directed at right angles to the flaking surface (Plate 39: 24, 30 and 36–38 are typical examples of such resharpening flakes). Platform rejuvenating flakes of this kind are not uncommon and generally show a battered or jagged ridge on the dorsal face which represents the worked out edge of the striking platform.

The proportion of flakes and bladelets to cores is just under 30 to a core. The average number of flake scars on a core is between 6 and 9 so that it might at first appear as if some of the flakes had been carried in. Since, however, the scars preserved on the cores constitute only the evidence of the final flaking prior to their being discarded, such a proportion is not incompatible with all the flaking's having been done in and around the concentration area.

Flake and blade fragments and chunks (7,546: 65·5 per cent; 1,084: 9·6 per cent)
The number of fragments is high but this is in accordance with what might be expected from a flaking floor of this type where a large number would undoubtedly have broken in the course of primary flaking. In view, also, of the modified micro-burin technique used for making microliths, the number of butt ends, middle and end fragments would be considerably increased. There are, perhaps, fewer chunks of chert (575) than might have been expected and a large number of the chunks (349) are quartzite lumps that probably result from pounding and hammering equipment.

Pebbles (30: 0·25 per cent)
With one exception, these call for no special comment and represent raw material awaiting use. In grid square G–3 occurred 17 diminutive, round quartz pebbles, each less than 10 mm in diameter and with a fairly high surface polish. Since all the pebbles must have been carried onto the site and these are well below the average core size, it seems possible that this little group must have been intended for some other purpose, perhaps for rattles, in the same manner that Bushmen and Bantu use small pebbles in various kinds of leg rattles for dancing. Alternatively, Dr Kleindienst has suggested that they may have been counters, similar to those used today to play *chisolo* or *bau* while the absorption of the present-day Hadza male with gambling (Woodburn, 1968*a*: 53) raises the possibility of their having been gaming pieces.

Primary flaking techniques

The preponderance of specialized, prismatic, single platform and pyramidal cores, often with marginal preparation of the release face of the platform edge to reduce irregularities; the number of edge rejuvenating flakes; the absence of any consistent evidence of bruising and scarring of the end of the core opposite the platform; and the scarcity of bipolar cores – all strongly suggest that some form of punch was used to work these cores. Many of the flakes and bladelets also show the characteristics of punch technique, as stated above, in particular the point platform and incipient scarring and bruising at the proximal end which formed part of the trimmed edge of the platform before detachment from the core.

There was virtually no restriction on the size of the pieces of chert available for working, which is probably another reason why a punch rather than the bipolar technique was preferred. The punch technique is, moreover, a flaking method that can be shown to have been present since the time of the Siszya Industry in the local basin.

The writer has experimented with hard wood, bone and horn punches and has found the last to be much the most satisfactory. Experimental reproduction of Lupemban- and Tshitolian-type artifacts by the Chokwe gunflint maker, Mwambumba, at Dundo in northeast Angola in 1963 and 1968, showed that, in the hands of a skilled worker, the horn punch used with a bar hammer of wood was nearly as effective for flaking as was the soft iron punch and bar hammer that were his normal tools. The horn did not splinter or show evidence of undue wear except as a result of my own, less skilled, efforts! The technique has been described elsewhere (Clark, 1963: 171–83) and the flaking waste analysed and illustrated (Clark, 1963: Plates 79 and 80). Plate 97 shows the method of holding the core between the heels and the position of the punch ready for striking with the hammer. The method is pertinent to the Kaposwa microlithic aggregates since the flakes and bladelets resemble those resulting from the Chokwe method. In both there are broad as well as narrow flakes, plain, broad and inclined striking platforms and preparation of the platform edge before striking a flake. It is suggested, therefore, that the method most commonly used to manufacture the microliths and other small flaked tools at the Kalambo Falls may have been similar to that used by the Chokwe worker.

The bipolar technique, where the core is rested on a stone anvil and struck at the upper end with a stone hammer, was certainly also used but the small number of bipolar cores shows it to have been uncommon. Splintering (*esquillé* flaking) is not, moreover, characteristic of the Kaposwa aggregates and this also can be interpreted as indicating that the bipolar method of using a stone hammer and stone anvil was very rarely used. If a wooden anvil were substituted for the stone one, this would eliminate most of the indirect flaking from the lower end of the core but would hardly affect that at the upper (i.e. the hammerstone) end. If, however, the dimple scarring observed on the three artifacts classified as 'dimple-scarred anvils' was, indeed, the outcome of their having been used as anvils (and not, in fact, as handstones for pounding and grinding seeds and nuts) then their presence on the occupation floor needs to be accounted for. A possible explanation is that they were used in conjunction with a punch of hard wood, bone or horn, the lower end of the core, held by the heels, resting on the anvil. We have not yet experimented with such a possibility but it is relevant that at Cambay in Gujerat on the west coast of India, micro-blades are still removed from fluted cores for the production of hexagonal, chalcedony beads by resting the platform on the end of a metal spike anvil and striking the upper end with a flexible, hafted, soft stone hammer (Sankalia, 1964: 33). A pointed anvil is not easily come by in stone and, although an edge anvil might produce some results, it is more probable that the small bladelets at the Kalambo Falls were produced without a hard, resistant rest, such as a stone anvil. If such an anvil were used and became pitted in this way, then the lower ends of the cores should also show some bruising and crushing and this is not the case. A study of the micro-wear patterns on all these kinds of pitted stones is long overdue.

Van Riet Lowe identified average sized cobbles of quartzite used as anvils and hammers in his original description of the bipolar anvil technique with the Coastal Smithfield Industry in Natal (Van Riet Lowe, 1946: 243) and he demonstrated that both anvils and hammerstones showed dimple scarring. Similarly, Logsdon (1971) has shown by experiment that the hammerstone will become more pitted than the anvil when the latter is made from hard material. Stones with one or more grinding surfaces and pitted areas are the regular form of handstone in use among Bushmen (e.g. Dunn, 1931: 68 and Plate 10) for cracking nuts and grinding seeds. The bipolar technique is also known in ethnographic context from New Guinea (White, 1968*a*) and among the Ova-Tjimba of South West Africa (MacCalman and Grobbelaar, 1965: 12). Cobbles were fractured by bipolar technique in western North America – in the Great Basin, Northern California and British Columbia – as well as in Argentina (Holmes, 1919: 300–2; Ellis, 1957: 22–5). It is clearly important to show how the handstones and anvils differ and may be distinguished and also the extent to which the same stone may be used for both purposes.

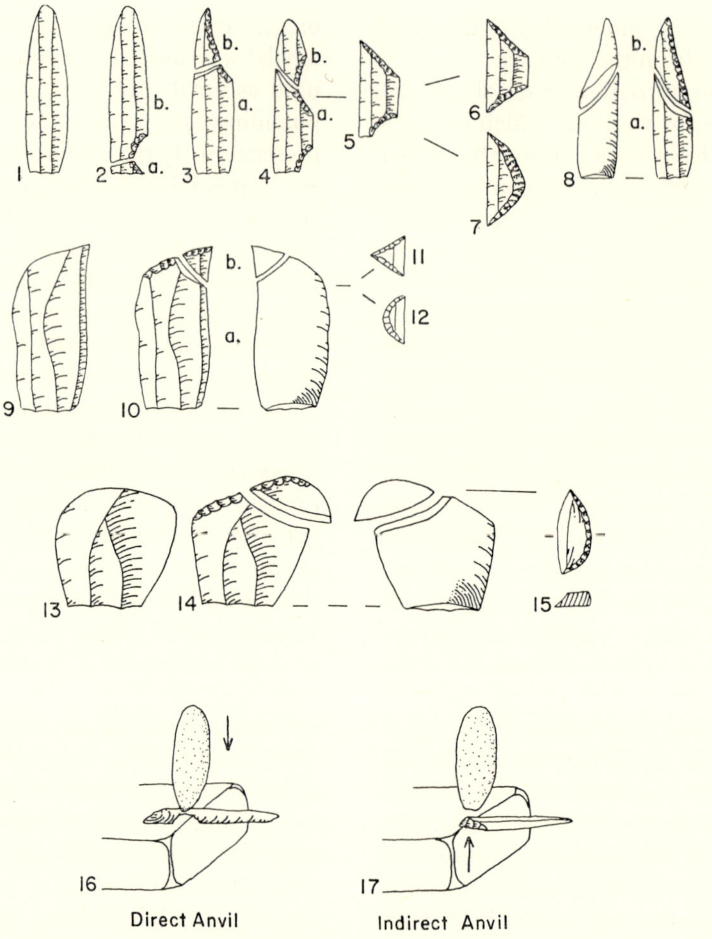

Fig. 19. Diagrammatic interpretation of the methods used for making microliths in the Kaposwa Industry at the Kalambo Falls.

Nos. 1–8 *on narrow bladelets*

1. Primary bladelet.
2. Bladelet with proximal notch and fracture to produce:
   (*a*) proximal 'micro-burin' spall; and
   (*b*) distal 'micro-burin' from which microlith was made.
3. Truncated/notched bladelet that has fractured to produce:
   (*a*) proximal; and (*b*) distal 'micro-burins'. A triangle can be produced from 3(*b*) by retouch on the snapped edge.
4. Bladelet from which the proximal (butt) and distal ends have been removed by notching and snapping. The fracture at the distal end of 4(*a*) forms a trihedral point (*piquant-trièdre*); 4(*b*) is a distal 'micro-burin'.
   From 4(*a*) can be produced:
5. a shouldered microlith;
6. a trapeze;
7. a lunate.
8. Fortuitous fracture while truncating and backing a bladelet sometimes results in (*a*) a snapped proximal end (*micro-burin raté*) and (*b*) a 'Krukowski burin'.

Nos. 9–12 *on broad bladelets*

9. Unmodified bladelet.
10. Bladelet, steeply trimmed at the distal end on the dorsal face as for shaping a scraper and intentionally fractured, on the edge of an anvil by a blow with a hammerstone, struck on the ventral or dorsal face to produce a triangular segment (10(*b*)). The piece (10(*a*)) from which this segment is removed shows steep trimming over one half of the distal end and a triangular scar as with the *piquant-trièdre* over the other half. Further trimming of the fracture edge of the segment will produce:

The manufacture of microliths by a modified micro-burin technique

Although microliths were made from suitable small bladelets or flakes that required no prior modification before being retouched by the indirect anvil method, the platform and bulb being removed in the normal course of the trimming, approximately 69 per cent of those with the Kaposwa aggregates were made from middle or distal fragments which appear to have been obtained in several different ways. A certain number of such fragments will always become available from fortuitous splitting in the course of removing the flakes and bladelets from the cores. The number produced in this way depends on the texture of the raw material, the method of flaking used and the hardness of the ground onto which the pieces fall in the course of the work. In this instance, the floor of the flaking area was sand so that few fractures can be expected to have occurred due to impact with the ground. Experiment with the chert used as raw material produced no higher percentage of fractures as the flakes and blades were removed than is normally to be expected. From the significant number of flaking by-products showing consistent patterns of breakage, it is clear that the great majority of the fragments used for making into microliths were intentionally broken. Confirmation is provided by the mean length of flakes (26 mm), bladelets (31 mm) and microliths (18·5 mm) from which it is evident that the primary forms were intentionally segmented, in particular to remove the proximal end with the bulb and striking platform.

Many bladelets and flakes were snapped by a direct blow on the centre of one or other face, possibly with the artifact rested on an anvil.[1] Fracture of this kind results in the formation of a small lip on the fracture surface parallel to the face opposite to that on which the blow was struck. The point of impact itself and sometimes also the point or points at which the artifact touched the anvil, will show microscopic evidence of scarring and crushing. Plate 42: 1 shows the butt end of a bladelet snapped across the short axis in this way. The plan and section form and the backing characteristics of the microliths, as well as certain other by-products in the aggregate, suggest the use of another sectioning method that resembles, but is not identical with, the 'micro-burin' technique as described by Tixier (1963: 39–42). At the Kalambo Falls it was not only bladelets and short quadrilateral flakes that were modified in this way for the manufacture of microliths but broad and irregular flakes also. When the primary piece is a bladelet, the by-products of the method most resemble those from the micro-burin technique. The inferred method of producing microliths from the primary forms by this method is set out diagrammatically in Figure 19.

The initial stage was to form a notch on one edge of the flake, bladelet or fragment, by means of a hammerstone and anvil (such as the one illustrated at Plate 41: 7) using the direct method as reconstructed by Tixier (1963: 40) (Figure 19: 16). When the notch is deepened sufficiently, the specimen will fracture at the deepest point of the notch or just to one side of it. This fracture may produce on the proximal (butt) end, a micro-burin scar (*micro-burin proximal ou 'de base'*) (cf. Plate 42: 4) or a snapped fracture surface usually

---

11. a triangle; or
12. a lunate.

Nos. 13–15 on flakes

13. Unmodified primary flake.
14. Flake trimmed at the distal end as for shaping a scraper and intentionally fractured to remove a segment as with 10 above. In this case the segment is obtained by resting the dorsally trimmed edge on the anvil and striking on the ventral face with a hammerstone. If the resulting fracture face of the segment is steep, then this is the edge that will be trimmed. If, however, the angle is right the fracture will be oblique, not vertical, to the long axis and can be used to form the cord for:
15. a lunate which is completed by further trimming of the convex edge.
16. *Direct method of producing a notch on a bladelet* (after Tixier, 1963). The bladelet is placed across the edge of the anvil with the dorsal face down and the notch is formed on this face by light blows with the hammer at the place where the bladelet crosses the edge of the anvil. When the notch is deepened sufficiently, the bladelet will fracture, usually at the deepest point of the notch.
17. *Indirect method of trimming or retouching a bladelet or microlith.* The bladelet is placed ventral face down with the edge to be trimmed resting on the edge of the anvil. Light blows with the hammerstone on the dorsal face will remove very small flakes from the edge of the ventral face that rests on the anvil. The backed edge produced by this indirect anvil method is generally steep or at right-angles to the face.

[1] Intentional snapping of blades for tool manufacture begins at the Kalambo Falls in the Siszya Industry.

connecting with the notch (*micro-burin raté*) (cf. Plate 42: 2 and 3; Figure 19: 2*a* and 3*a*). At the Kalambo Falls, the second is the more common, perhaps on account of the particular fracturing properties of the raw material.

The distal end resulting from this notching shows part of the trimming of the notch. However, because of the generally more irregular plan form of the primary artifact and the frequency of snapped fractures in the place of micro-burin scars, it resembles less closely the regular form with the triangular sectioned point (*lamelle à piquant-trièdre*) from which the microliths were made in north Africa. The commoner form at the Kalambo Falls, therefore, is seen in Figure 19: 3*a*, although the *piquant-trièdre* does sometimes occur (Figure 19: 4*a*; Plate 36: 75). Examples of distal ends removed by notching resemble those shown in Figure 19: 3*b* and 4*b* and are illustrated at Plate 42: 5–13. Plate 42: 5–9 are distal micro-burins and resemble the *micro-burins distal ou 'de pointe'* of north Africa. Plate 42: 10–13 and Plate 36: 75 resemble the *lamelle à piquant-trièdre*, although more in its *raté* than in its *typique* form. This 'atypical' nature of the Kalambo Falls examples can most probably be ascribed to the shorter length and more irregular form of the primary flakes and bladelets used there which required the initial edge trimming or notching to be positioned closer to one of the ends of the piece. Plate 42: 5 is an example where the notching was positioned close to the proximal end and striking platform. Plate 42: 14 is an example where the trimming was commenced at the distal end but the bladelet has not fractured and the proximal end has not yet been removed; typologically, therefore, this specimen is an obliquely truncated bladelet. It was from the distal ends such as those illustrated in Figure 19: 3*b* and 4*b* and at Plate 42: 5–13 that the shouldered, trapeze, triangle and lunate microliths illustrated at Plate 36 were made.

Some examples (Figure 19: 8; Plate 42: 15–19) represent the distal ends of bladelets that appear to have been fortuitously fractured in the course of completing or modifying the backing of the tool. They may be classified as 'Krukowski burins' and were probably not intentionally produced.

A variation on the above method of notching, trimming and snapping was adopted where broad blades and flakes were used. This is shown diagrammatically in Figure 19: 9–15. The frequency with which both proximal parts and distal segments occur suggests that this kind of fracture is not fortuitous but deliberate. It is possible to regard these as unintentional fractures produced in trimming or retrimming an end-scraper and, if end-scrapers had been a distinctive class of tool at the Kalambo Falls, this would have added weight to such an interpretation. However, the flake scrapers found with the Kaposwa aggregate at Site C, 1963, are not a large class (30 specimens). They are generally small and grade into the class of truncated blade microlith with squared truncation. Some are more typically short end-scrapers but the small percentage of the shaped tool category that they comprise and the less regular nature of the retouch they exhibit, suggests that they are different and distinct from the short, broad blades and flakes that show retouch over approximately one half of the distal end and a *piquantt-rièdre* fracture scar on the other half. Examples of these last are illustrated at Plate 42: 20, 22, 23 and 25. The corresponding distal segments removed from such examples are seen at Plate 42: 21 and 24. Usually the fracture plane forms a steep angle with the surviving portion of the ventral face and requires trimming to make the fragment into a microlith. Sometimes, however, the fracture plane is at a more oblique angle as in Plate 42: 24. In this case, continuation of the trimming on the convex edge carried out on the original piece prior to fracture, will form the lunate. This is shown schematically at Figure 19: 15. Since the primary form of the flakes so treated is generally irregular, the segments removed in the course of the trimming are also irregular and have to be further modified by retouch.

The distal segments show that the trimming on this end of the original piece had not always been carried across the whole of the end before the fracture took place. Some doubt must remain as to whether the fracture was accidental to the trimming of the end, in the same way that 'Krukowski burins' are believed to be accidental to the backing of bladelets. Probably some belong in this category but it is more probable that the majority were intentionally detached, particularly in view of the scarcity of end-scrapers. If the left side of the distally trimmed end of the end-scraper illustrated at Plate 37: 7 had been removed by fracture, there would have resulted a typical wedge shaped segment ready for backing to form a microlith.

So far as the writer is aware, this is the furthest south that any modified micro-burin technique has been recorded. In east Africa, it is found with the 'Kenya Capsian' of Gamble's Cave (*c.* 6500–6000 B.C.) (Leakey, 1931: 156–7) and the later facies from the Naivasha Railway Rock Shelter (Leakey, 1942: 172) and other sites. The raw material was obsidian from which blades and bladelets were readily produced and similarly had to be broken down. The micro-burin also probably occurs on microlithic sites in central and southern Somalia (Clark, 1954: 281) where the raw material was chert or flint. Elsewhere in east Africa where small pebbles or crystals provided the raw material, the micro-burin is absent (e.g. Nelson and Posnansky, 1970: 142; Van Noten, 1971: 56–8). In central and southern Africa, the micro-burin makes only a fortuitous appearance. There microlithic industries were generally manufactured from quartz or pebbles of chert, chalcedonies and other crypto-crystalline rocks, so that the mean lengths of the primary products were generally less and the flakelets and bladelets often broader, as the comparative bar diagrams and graphs show (Figure 20).

In the Congo basin, the Tshitolian is not primarily a microlithic tradition, although microliths occur. The tranchets (generally over 30 mm long) were produced from snapped sections of broad, end-struck flakes where the material used was a fine-grained quartzite (*grès polymorphe*) (Clark, 1963: 159–60); when quartz provided the raw material the tools are most frequently of microlithic proportions (Clark, 1963: 155; 167–70 and Plates 36 and 37).

The 'micro-burin' technique, therefore, in the opinion of the present writer, directly relates to the size range and texture of the raw material used. Its distribution, both in time and space, is sufficiently wide to show that it was one of several basic techniques which appeared towards the end of the Pleistocene and were adopted in Eurasia and Africa wherever and whenever the need arose. That it was adopted at the Kalambo Falls is, therefore, due solely to the nature of the raw material used and carries with it, in the writer's opinion, no genetic or ethnic connotations or implicit industrial associations. At the Kalambo Falls it is not a typical micro-burin technique but it may be considered a closely allied and simpler variant of the general method.

Distribution of finds on the occupation floor

Figure 17 shows the distribution by grid squares of the main artifact classes. The greatest concentration of flakes and bladelets is found in grid square G–2 and those squares immediately adjacent. Cores, though far fewer in numbers, show the same general scatter as the flakes and bladelets with the greatest number in grid square G–2 and the next most frequent counts in F–1, G–1 and F–3. There are approximately twice as many flakes, bladelets and cores in square G–2 as there are in the other grid squares. There are just over two and one half as many 'micro-burin' spalls in square G–2 as there are in G–1 which has the next highest number.

Within the main concentration, the greatest number of blades and 'micro-burin' spalls lies in an arc formed by grid squares G–1 and 2 and F–3, while the greatest flake concentration is more widely spaced in squares F–1, E–2, G–2, H–2 and G–3 and does not include the squares F–3 and G–1. The core distribution conforms more, though not completely, to that for blades and 'micro-burins'. The significance of this slight difference in distribution cannot be determined, though it may relate to the number of stone workers, the techniques they employed and the positions round the hearth in which they operated. It does, however, show quite clearly that the stone working was concentrated in one small area in the southeast corner of the excavation.

This was also the area where the microliths were manufactured. Again, the greatest number is found in grid square G–2 but they concentrate also in those adjacent squares immediately to the north – E–2, F–2, F–3. The sub-classes of microliths also show minor differences of distribution: the greatest number of backed bladelets is in grid squares E–2, F–1 and F–2; the majority of obliquely truncated bladelets occurs in square G–2; lunates concentrate in squares G–2 and F–3 and trapezes and triangles are more evenly distributed. This general distribution is consistent with the number of 'micro-burins' in squares G–2 and F–3 but is not fully consistent with the numbers of microliths in squares E–2, F–1 and F–2. However, it is these grid squares that have the greatest number of backed bladelets and flakes or non-geometric microliths which do not require 'micro-burin' technique.

It is of some interest that the anvils found with this flaking workshop are situated more on the periphery than in the centre of the concentration. If the method of primary flaking had been dependent on the use of an anvil, it might have been expected that at least one would have been found in grid square G–2. Experiment shows that punch flaking with heel-held cores results in a fairly tight concentration of waste and

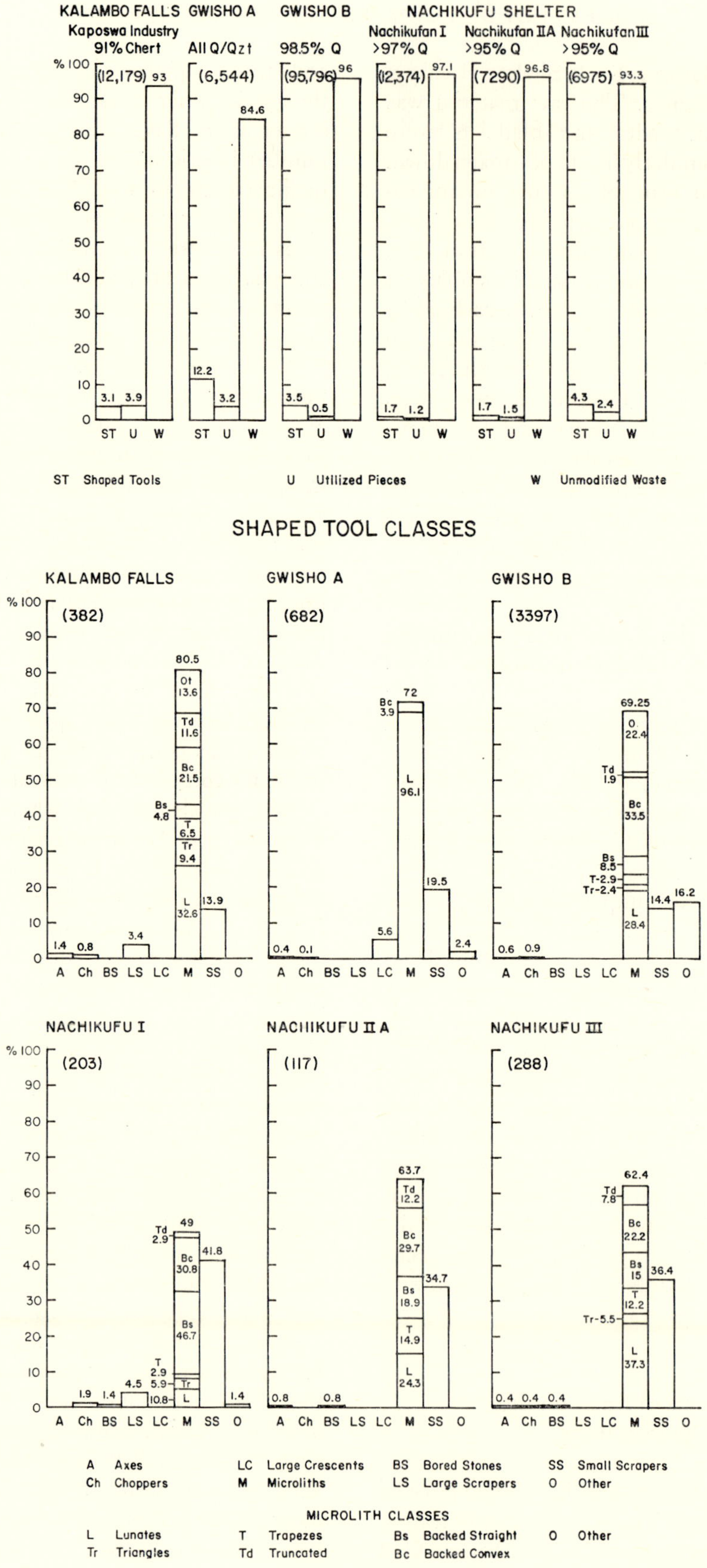
KALAMBO FALLS Kaposwa Industry 91% Chert
GWISHO A All Q/Qzt
GWISHO B 98.5% Q
NACHIKUFU SHELTER
Nachikufan I >97% Q
Nachikufan IIA >95% Q
Nachikufan III >95% Q
(12,179)
(6,544)
(95,796)
(12,374)
(7290)
(6975)
ST Shaped Tools
U Utilized Pieces
W Unmodified Waste
SHAPED TOOL CLASSES
KALAMBO FALLS (382)
GWISHO A (682)
GWISHO B (3397)
NACHIKUFU I (203)
NACHIKUFU II A (117)
NACHIKUFU III (288)
A Axes
Ch Choppers
LC Large Crescents
M Microliths
BS Bored Stones
LS Large Scrapers
SS Small Scrapers
O Other
MICROLITH CLASSES
L Lunates
Tr Triangles
T Trapezes
Td Truncated
Bs Backed Straight
Bc Backed Convex
O Other

Fig. 20 (i)

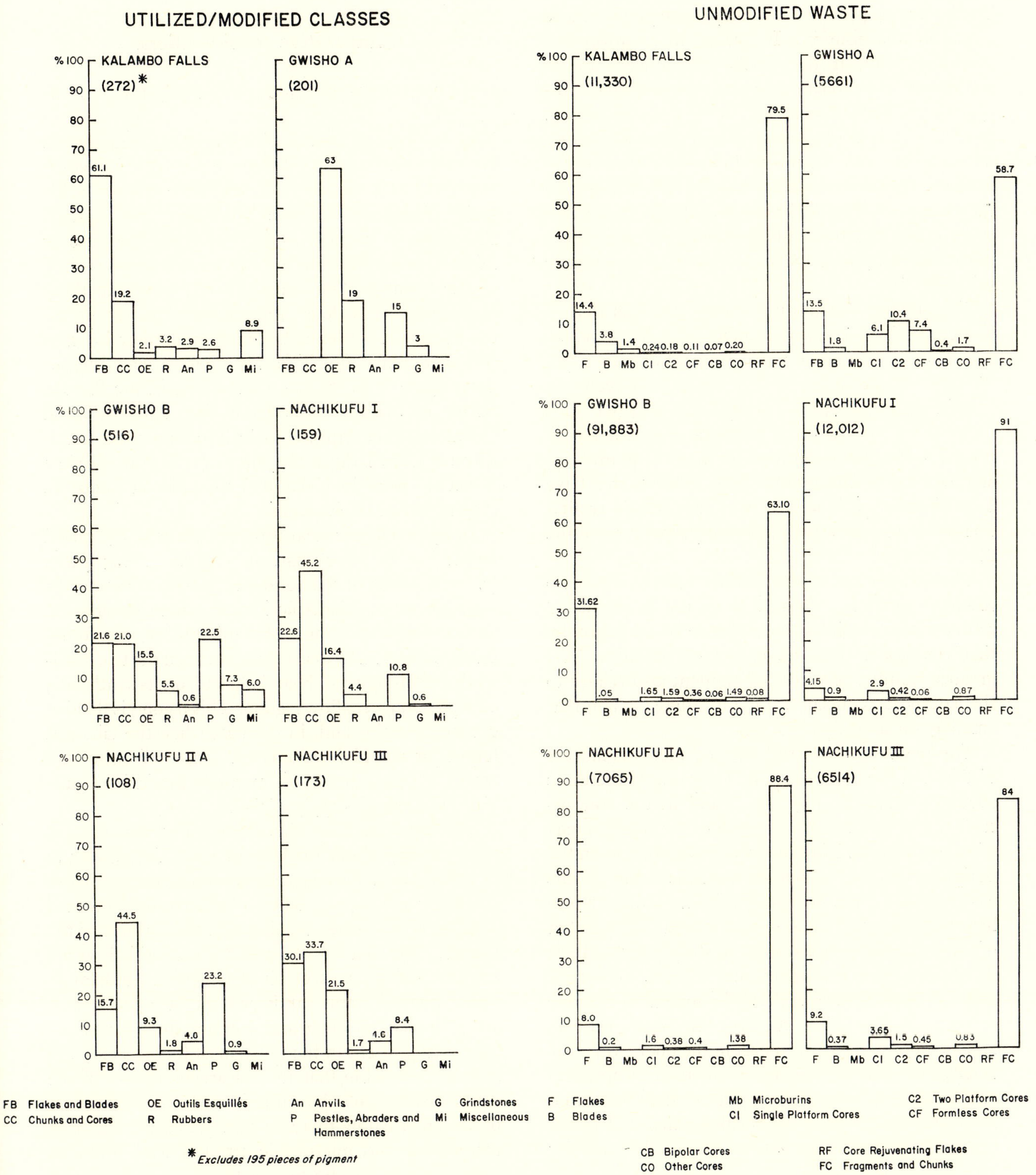

(ii) (iii)

Fig. 20. Bar diagrams showing the comparison of the percentage composition of certain 'Later Stone Age' aggregates with that of the Kaposwa Industry from Site C, 1963.

bipolar flaking produces a similar but somewhat more scattered distribution. It seems more probable, therefore, that, if the anvils are, indeed, to be associated, they relate more to the secondary retouching of shaped tools than to the primary flaking. Such a view is not inconsistent with the distribution of microliths and 'micro-burin' spalls. If this was the case, then it is possible to suggest that at least two individuals or two different periods of flaking are represented which would agree with the differences in the distribution of 'geometric' and non-geometric microlith forms.

The scraper distribution closely parallels that of the cores. The greatest number of flake scrapers occurs in F–2 (7 specimens), G–1 (4) and G–2 (4). The core scrapers are complementary and concentrate in grid squares F–3 (6), G–2 (6) and G–3 (8). This distribution of the core scrapers, particularly in regard to the maximum number in grid square G–3, suggests the possibility that those artifacts that have been classified as 'core-scrapers' here are, in reality, no more than cores that exhibit re-preparation of the platform edge.

The distribution of small utilized pieces shows no essential difference from that of the other flaked artifacts and confirms the evidence of ethnography that the hearth was the centre of activities. The greatest number of pieces of pigment also relates to the southeast concentration but there is another, smaller concentration in F–6.

The few large tools and utilized pieces again are distributed more peripherally. Only one of the three ground stone axe/adzes was found in the concentration area and the others relate to the western part of the excavation. Most of the rubbers are also on the periphery and seven out of the nine occur in the eastern half of the occupation floor. Choppers and hammerstones are randomly distributed. The number of these large tools is too small to show whether their distribution has any significance relative to activity areas, though it may tentatively be suggested that one activity, necessitating the use of hand rubbers relates more to the eastern part of the floor, while the small group of axes, rubbers, hammerstones, abraders and a chopper on the western edge of the excavation, associated as it is with the relative paucity of flaked tool waste there, may relate to yet another activity area.

Comparative considerations

1. AGGREGATES FROM MPULUNGU, LAKE TANGANYIKA

The nearest aggregates with which to compare the Kaposwa Archaeological Occurrences and for which statistical data are available, are those of the Nachikufan Industries in the Northern and Central Provinces in Zambia and those from the sites at Mumbwa and Gwisho Springs in the southern half of the country. The material from which all these aggregates are made is predominantly quartz, unlike the Kaposwa implements which are largely in chert (silicified mudstone). The only other excavated aggregates made from the chert occurring in the Plateau Series sediments come from two Archaeological Occurrences at Mpulungu in Zambia on the south shore of Lake Tanganyika some 25 miles (40 km) in a direct line from the Kalambo Falls and over 1,000 feet (305 m) lower in elevation.

In 1953, a small excavation was made in the raised beach bar at Mpulungu at a place *c.* 125 yards (*c.* 115 m) west of the boundary beacon at the northwest corner of Niamkolo Estate, where waterworn, unmodified waste, some of it microlithic, was found on the surface. The beach runs between the two headlands of Polungu and Niamkolo and, on its south side, cuts off a long, shallow lagoon. This lagoon is flooded during the rains and, in the past when the lake was higher, it would have formed a natural backwater where trapping and other methods would have provided a plentiful supply of fish.

The top of the beach here was at an average height of *c.* 5 metres above the level of Lake Tanganyika in October, 1953. The excavation was carried to a depth of 6 feet 7 inches (2 m) when it had to be discontinued because of the water seeping into the bottom of the trench. The bar is composed of stratified beach cobbles and pebbles of chert (silicified mudstone), shale, quartzite and sandstone set in a calcareous, sandy matrix. Broken and comminuted shell fragments are present in the uppermost foot (30 cm) and it seems probable that the calcareous nature of the sandy matrix beneath results from the decomposition of the shell below this one foot (30 cm) level. Both macrolithic and microlithic artifacts were found to occur from top to bottom of the excavation though they were more numerous in the uppermost two feet (61 cm).

The artifacts show variable degrees of water rolling

and it is quite clear that, during the time that the bar was being built up, it was sporadically occupied by a population making microliths and other tools. Although this aggregate is not in primary context, it probably represents the scatter from temporary camps redistributed within a limited area by the rising water of the lake. The excavation and aggregate are to be described in detail elsewhere, but the artifact composition is summarized here.

Tools comprise nearly 27 per cent of the artifacts, the remainder being unmodified waste.[1] Microliths make up 14·2 per cent of the shaped tool classes – not a large proportion. Of these, most (36·5 per cent) are backed bladelets and flake segments with, in addition, 23·3 per cent of straight backed bladelets. Narrow lunates (17·3 per cent) also occur; 13·4 per cent are truncated and 7·6 per cent are double backed microliths or drills. There is also one proximal end, 'microburin' spall. The backing on the microliths is normal and often the full length of the primary bladelet has been used with no attempt to remove the proximal end by snapping or notching.

The remainder of the shaped tools comprise single-blow burins on flakes (0·8 per cent) and the same percentage of core-scrapers. Choppers, initially, probably, cores, comprise 3·5 per cent. However, most of the shaped tools (64·3 per cent) are scrapers made on non-microlithic flakes and flake fragments. The majority of these are concave and notched forms but nosed, side, end, convergent and denticulate forms also occur. These scrapers show no regular plan form being made on any convenient piece of shale or quartzite and, in a number of cases, more than one edge shows trimming. Miscellaneous, informal artifacts make up the remainder of the shaped tools.

Of the unmodified waste, 28·7 per cent is represented by whole flakes; 29·1 per cent by flake fragments; 40·2 per cent by angular waste and 3 per cent by cores. A small number of these cores are chunky with two opposed platforms on the same face. Together with specialized, prismatic, single platformed cores, these produced bladelets and small flakes. The larger triangular flakes were struck from formless cores (the largest class represented), angle, biconical and high-backed discoid cores. Not surprisingly, the number of micro-blade cores in the aggregate is small and the cores in general are made from water-rolled lumps of chert and quartzite.

In a measured sample of 50 indiscriminately selected flakes, 58 per cent have lengths between 20 mm and 40 mm. Although 56 per cent are end-flakes, all of them are broad, irregular and short quadrilateral flakes, except for one specimen which is a bladelet.[2] Of the 44 per cent of side-flakes, one example only had the breadth more than twice the length; the remainder are closer to 1:1 than to 1:2.

The second site at Mpulungu is a shallow shell midden on the neck of rock at the foot of Polungu Hill on the east side and about 70 feet (21 m) above the lake. The midden itself is composed mainly of two species of lake snail, the shells being set in a dark grey, ashy and sandy soil. The midden dates to the Iron Age since it contained fragments of pottery and a burial with glass and shell beads in addition to a sparse stone industry similar to that from the beach bar except that the microliths are less regularly retouched. The two commonest shells of the midden are two varieties of *Neothauma tanganyicense*; the bivalve *Iridina spekii* occurs less frequently. The two former are found in shallow, sandy bays with some mud and the latter in a similar habitat down to depths of 5–10 metres in water with some movement. These shells are commonly used as bait by fishermen along the lake shore and, although the modern Lungu people do not use them as food, they are apparently eaten in Zaïre (Capart, 1949).

The midden is underlain by a thin soil, on the surface of which and in what appears to be a shallow artificial pit in the mudstone bedrock, is an earlier aggregate. This consists of a small number of well made microliths – lunates and convex backed bladelets – together with a range of utilized larger flakes and flake scrapers of chert and quartzite, more specifically comparable to those from the beach bar excavation. In the main microlithic layer, a number of water abraded flakes show that the group were collecting these and reworking them. One with backing is an indication that the midden aggregate may be later than the beach. On the whole, the microliths are less well made than those in the beach and are generally smaller. Narrow lunates and straight backed bladelets and flakes all occur; there are a number of broken examples. The backing is steep or blunt,

[1] No utilized pieces are recorded because, due to the abraded nature of the aggregate, it was not possible to distinguish these. For the same reason, the high percentage of Shaped Tools to waste may be due to our having counted some of the artifacts as tools which are, in reality not so.

[2] It might have been expected that wave action during the building of the bar would have caused some fracturing of these delicate artifacts but the number of fragments of broken blades was not great and confirms the low percentage of bladelets in general.

sometimes with evidence of bipolar working. Cores are generally formless, angle and single platform, yielding mostly irregular flakes.

Although none were found in the excavation, a number of whole and fragmentary bored stones have been collected in the immediate vicinity of the beach at Mpulungu and from the spoil of the drainage ditch adjacent to the midden excavation.

It is apparent that these aggregates differ in a number of significant respects from the Kaposwa Industry notably in their high percentages of flake scrapers and utilized flakes and also in the choppers at Mpulungu. The microliths from the beach bar show a closer relationship to those from the Kalambo Falls and it is probable that this aggregate is in part contemporary with the Kaposwa Industry. On account of the iron, pottery and beads and the much better preservation of the shells in the Mpulungu midden, the aggregate from here is likely to be later, suggesting that some stone-using groups persisted here in the hunting and gathering way of life after the coming of the Early Iron Age agriculturalists.

The specialist nature of the Mpulungu aggregates and their direct connection with Lake Tanganyika suggests that they represent the stone tool-kit associated with fishing activities – the working of reeds for fences, weirs and traps; the manufacture of fish spears and the scaling, gutting and smoking of fish. The comparatively small number of microliths suggests the probability that these were not particularly connected with the specialist activities taking place at these camps. It seems likely, however, that they were used in connection with the hunting of aquatic mammals – cane rats and hippopotamus, for example. It would clearly be of interest to make a close comparative study of one or more lake-side camps of this kind, preferably at the mouth of the Kalambo river, since seasonal transhumance from the lake to the local Kalambo basin and back seems not impossible at this time.

The level of Lake Tanganyika is controlled largely by the rock shelf at the Lukuga outlet. When this is blocked by vegetation and sand the level of the lake rises and is lowered when the barrier is breached. In the early 1960s the outlet became blocked and the lake level rose. The seasonal rise has increased from 30 inches (76 cm) in 1956/57 to 42 inches (107 cm) in 1963/64. In 1963/64, the water level was 4·34 metres above the height of the rock shelf at the outlet (J. L. Carlin: personal communication). In 1874, the lake level was below the level of the Lukuga gap and the river was blocked. Three years later the water was level with the lowest point in the gap and the next year the bar was breached and the water level fell again. It continued to fall and five years later was 16 feet (4·9 m) below the previous level (Haldemann; Volume I: 35). Fluctuations in lake level are, therefore, controlled in part by the build up and breaching of the outlet and also in part by the longer term effects of changes in the rainfall and evaporation rates in the area of the lake catchment.

It is difficult to see how the Mpulungu beach bar could have been built up in the course of a few years only. It is not an isolated occurrence and beach sediments that show evidence of no tectonic deformation occur at a number of other localities within the basin at a height of ± 6 metres above the water level of 1946/47 (Capart, 1949). The excavations at Mpulungu show this bar to have been contemporary with a microlithic industry having some affinities with that from the Kalambo Falls which is dated to the beginning of the fourth millennium B.C. It is tempting to see this extension of the lake in late prehistoric times as being due to increased run off in the catchment affecting the balance between intake and evaporation during the post-Pleistocene hyperthermal. It will be remembered that erosion in the local basin at the Kalambo Falls was also probably taking place at this time. Without further studies, however, one cannot discount the possibility of its having been the result of seismic activity in the Ruwenzori valley to the north which controlled the outflow from Lake Kivu into Lake Tanganyika.

2. NACHIKUFAN INDUSTRIES

The three Industries that make up the Nachikufan Industrial Complex are defined by Miller (1969) from seven sites in northern and central Zambia that were excavated by the present writer and Mrs L. E. Hodges between 1948 and 1958. Nachikufu Cave itself, 240 miles (386 km) to the south in the Muchinga mountains, and Mwela Rocks Shelter on the plateau at Kasama, 120 miles (193 km) south, are the two closest to the Kalambo Falls. Two other sites (Nsalu Cave and Bimbe wa Mpalabwe) are at no great distance from Nachikufu Cave; the other sites are further away on the Zambezi–Congo watershed near Solwezi (Chifubwa Stream Shelter) and at Leopard's Hill 30 miles (48 km) east of Lusaka.

The Nachikufan represents a long developing tradition covering some 12,000 years or more. The aggregates belonging with the earlier Industries are more closely comparable with those from the Kalambo Falls than are the later ones, in which the differences may represent a closer adaptation to the local habitats made possible by a more efficient technology.

Nachikufu I is at least as old as 12,000 B.P. and its first appearance may date to more than 16,000 B.P. It is characterized by very small retouched and utilized bladelets and microliths, small convex scrapers, a large number of bored stones and an important heavy scraper element. The microliths are often made on quartz crystals. The core types compare with those of the Kaposwa Industry except as to size and the greater number of bipolar cores. The Nachikufan Industry has a larger number of *outils esquillés*.

Nachikufu II is sub-divided into two phases, an earlier IIA, which is dated at Mwela Rocks and Leopard's Hill to early in the tenth millennium B.P. Narrow bladelets are superseded by a greater use of flakes and numbers of broad backed microliths. The ground stone axe/adze is present together with a low percentage of flake and heavy duty scrapers and bored stones. For Nachikufu IIB the earliest date is the middle of the seventh millennium B.P. at Nachikufu and there is a date also in the early fifth millennium from the same site. The characteristic microliths are broad lunates, trapezes, backed and truncated forms. There are a number of concave, notched and strangulated scrapers which form 25·5 per cent of the small scraper classes. Bored stones and ground stone axes/adzes are also present.

The earliest date for Nachikufu III from any of these sites is at the beginning of the second millennium B.P. from Nachikufu. Well made small lunates replace the broad lunates, trapezes and other broad microliths of Nachikufu IIB. The concave and notched scraper forms increase and the same range of heavy duty tools occurs. The later stages of Nachikufu III, late in the first millennium A.D., have pottery and evidence of iron working associated. At Nakapapula Shelter, also in the Muchingas, the first appearance of pottery is dated to A.D. 770 ± 100 (Phillipson, 1969*b*).

The Kaposwa Industry falls in time almost midway between Nachikufu IIB and Nachikufu III, which may in part explain its dissimilarity with both of them. Phillipson identifies the aggregate which he excavated at Nakapapula with a late phase of the Nachikufan Industrial Complex. It is in part contemporary (980 ± 85 to 3280 ± 90 B.P.) with the Kaposwa Industry and thus might be expected to show some similarity. It comprises microliths (lunates, backed and truncated bladelets) which account for 39·1 per cent of the shaped tools. Scrapers (convex and concave) constitute 23·6 per cent and *outils esquillés* 13·0 per cent of the tools. The site also yielded five bored stones, a ground stone axe, two dimple-scarred rubbers or anvils and eleven grindstones, and the excavation documents very satisfactorily the changes effected by the entry of agriculturalists into northern Zambia.

In northern Malawi, several aggregates from the plateau and the Lake Malawi Rift have been excavated by the University of California Expedition to Malawi between 1965 and 1967. Here again the microlithic artifacts are made in quartz (and sometimes in quartzite at the sites in the Rift) and they relate more with the Nachikufan than they do with the Kaposwa Industry (Sandelowsky and Robinson, 1968: 2).

The sites of Mumbwa Caves and Gwisho Springs A and B in southern Zambia have produced aggregates with which it is possible to make comparisons. Mumbwa is located north of the Kafue Flats in the administrative district of that name. The 'Later Stone Age' aggregate there, excavated by the present writer in 1939, was named 'Northern Rhodesian Wilton' (Clark, 1942) and is as yet undated.

3. GWISHO SPRINGS

At Gwisho, on Lochinvar Ranch on the south side of the Kafue Flats in Monze district, a line of hot springs has provided a focal point for hunting/gathering groups since at least the middle of the fifth millennium. The camping places were situated immediately adjacent to three of these springs and have yielded a large quantity of animal bone and plant remains together with burials and a unique collection of wooden implements associated with a prolific stone industry.

Gwisho A was excavated by Gabel (1965) in 1960–61; Gwisho B and C were excavated by Fagan and Van Noten (1971) in 1963–64. Gwisho has provided a considerable amount of economic data that makes it possible to estimate the degree to which the hunting population was exploiting the local resources. At least three vegetation communities and the animal life they contained were available and made use of – the grasslands of the Kafue flood plain, the mixed swamp and woodland of the site itself and the *Brachystegia* woodlands of the plateau. The Gwisho sites belong in the fifth and fourth millennia B.P.

(4785 ± 70 to 3660 ± 70 at Gwisho B), the later occupation levels being contemporary with the Kaposwa occupation floor.

Gabel (1965: 62) and Fagan and Van Noten (1971: Tables 26 and 27) have compared the Gwisho aggregate with that from Mumbwa and have shown that they are clearly similar although not entirely so. At Gwisho, there are 20 per cent more lunates and backed blades and the grinding and pounding equipment there is certainly more numerous. Grinding equipment associated with the collection and preparation of plant foods is a regular occurrence with all the aggregates of the Nachikufan Industry and those from the Gwisho sites. The hand rubbers generally show dimple scarring and it is clear that at Nachikufu, as at Gwisho, plant foods were a normal part of the diet.

4. GENERAL COMPARISONS

The bar diagrams and graph in Figures 20 and 21 compare the constituents of the Kaposwa aggregates with those from Gwisho A and B and the Nachikufu Industries from the excavation in the shelter part of the Nachikufu Cave[1] based on data from published and unpublished literature.

Comparing the percentages of shaped tools, utilized/modified and waste, the only significant difference lies in the greater values for tools and utilized pieces at Gwisho A which are difficult to explain unless the fragments and chunks were omitted from the count for the waste. The values for the other sites are usual for Central Africa where the site represents both a settlement and a stone working area. It is of interest to note that these values are broadly the same whether the raw material was chert (91 per cent at the Kalambo Falls), or quartz 98·4 per cent at Gwisho B and more than 95 per cent at Nachikufu).

All tool classes, both large and small tools, have been included in the diagrams comparing the shaped tools. In each aggregate the commonest are the microliths but the two Gwisho sites (with 72 per cent and 69·25 per cent respectively) most nearly resemble the Kalambo Falls (80·5 per cent); in particular Gwisho B, if the large crescents are counted with the microliths. The highest percentage for microliths at Nachikufu is found with the Nachikufu IIA (63·7 per cent) while the lowest occurs with Nachikufu I (49 per cent).

In the small scraper classes, again, Gwisho is closer to the Kalambo Falls and the values for each of the Nachikufu Industries differ significantly from those of the Kalambo Falls aggregates. Nachikufu I has nearly three times as many small scrapers; Nachikufu IIA has just under two and a half times as many and Nachikufu III has just over two and a half times as many as the Kaposwa Industry. Moreover, these show more regular retouch and plan form and the steep, concave, notched and strangulated scrapers of 'Smithfield-N' type are not represented at the Kalambo Falls, where the artifacts in the 'large scraper' category also are not comparable with the heavy duty core-scrapers found with the Nachikufu I. The small number of axes and choppers appears to be a general characteristic of 'Later Stone Age' aggregates in central Africa as do also the bored stones. At Nachikufu, however, there are a greater number of these last with the Nachikufu I, IIA and B. In particular the number of broken halves and incomplete examples (> 50) shows that the cave was probably a place where these stones were manufactured. The only site known to the present writer yielding a comparable number of specimens is at Mitwaba in the north of the Kundelungu Plateau in the Katanga, associated with an industry of quartz flakes, where they have been recovered from the basal gravel in the stream during mining operations (Mortelmans, 1947).[2]

Turning to the utilized category, the greatest divergence is between the 61·1 per cent – more than twice as many – utilized flakes and bladelets at the Kalambo Falls and the other industries, which are generally similar to each other except at Gwisho A where utilized flake and chunk fragments were not counted. On the other hand, the percentage of utilized chunks and cores shows general agreement between Kalambo Falls and Gwisho B, with significantly larger percentages at Nachikufu – twice as many for Nachikufu I and IIA. *Outils esquillés* are significantly represented in all the aggregates with the exception of the Kalambo Falls, reaching 21 per cent with Nachikufu III. The high value of 63 per cent for Gwisho A is due perhaps (as well as to the omission of the utilized flake and blade fragments which lowers the total) to the inclusion of a number of pieces that might be classified as bipolar cores by other workers; the lower percentage of bipolar cores (4·2 per cent) recovered from Gwisho A tends to confirm this.

The large equipment in the utilized category –

[1] At this site, Nachikufu I occurs in the dark earth: Nachikufu IIA in the lower part of the brown earth and Nachikufu III in the green-brown earth.

[2] Included in the miscellaneous classes are borers/drills (also called double backed microliths) a small significant class with the Nachikufu as also at Gwisho B. The higher value for the 'Other' category at Gwisho B is due to the inclusion here of 'notched pieces', 'retouched flakes and chunks' and 'composite tools'.

dimple-scarred hand rubbers, pestles, lower grindstones and anvils – represent a small but significant percentage of all the aggregates. The absence of lower grindstones at the Kalambo Falls and in the Nachikufu III is probably to be explained as an accident of distribution within the excavated areas. At Gwisho the increased percentage of grinding/pounding equipment is likely to be due to the larger areas excavated while a similar increase at Nachikufu Cave is probably because it had been a regular place of settlement over a long period.

In the category of unmodified waste, the greatest percentage is represented by angular fragments and chunks. The Kaposwa aggregate and those from Nachikufu show the same high percentage which is interesting in view of the different raw materials used. At Gwisho, there is less angular waste which is surprising since quartz usually produces a considerable amount when shattered; it could be due to the nature of the quartz, a difference in the method of making the microliths or to different counting procedures.

There are appreciably more unmodified flakes (31·6 per cent) at Gwisho B than at any of the other sites. Kalambo Falls compares more closely with Gwisho than it does with the Nachikufan although the lowered percentages of unmodified flakes with the latter may not be significant.

It is in the bladelets that the Kaposwa Industry waste differs from that at the other sites, with 3·8 per cent blades, compared with a maximum of 0·9 per cent at Nachikufu and Gwisho B. At Gwisho A, 1·8 per cent have been classified as blades but Gabel's description of these (1965: 42) indicates that they are more specifically quadrilateral flakes.

Spalls of 'micro-burin' type are present only at the Kalambo Falls and the reason for this is believed to lie in the greater dimensions in which the chert there was available and to its texture, both of which made possible the production of more blade forms. The Kaposwa Industry cores are 50–100 mm long (mean 56 mm) while those at Gwisho A[1] average 26·5 mm and those with the Nachikufu I 38·8 mm, Nachikufu II 36·7 mm and with the Nachikufu III 24·7 mm.

The Kaposwa Industry also has the lowest percentage of cores but the range of forms is generally the same. The commonest class at all sites, except Gwisho A, is the single platform core, followed by the two platform class. Unfortunately, Miller does not distinguish a bipolar core class and her definition shows that these have been included as one sub-group of her blade/bladelet core class. The other sub-class 'approximates the single-platform cores'. For the purposes of this comparison, therefore, her blade/bladelet cores have been grouped with the single platform class but, since the breakdown of the two sub-groups is not available, the bipolar cores are necessarily also included in the percentage for this class. Gwisho A again shows differences from the other aggregates in that there are a greater number of chunky, two platformed and formless cores than of other types. The differences between the two Gwisho aggregates may perhaps be idiosyncratic since there is no difference in the raw material.

Figure 21 compares the mean lengths of microliths (all classes), small flake scrapers and unmodified flakes and bladelets. Microliths at Gwisho A are somewhat longer (22·5 mm) than at the other sites and, when compared with the mean flake/bladelet length (26 mm) it can be seen that the whole flake/bladelet was used and backed with no attempt to modify the length by snapping or notching. The same is the case at Gwisho B (17·8 mm and 20·7 mm). With the Nachikufu I, the mean length of microliths is about the same as that of the flake/bladelet mean (18·4 mm, 18·7 mm) while the corresponding figures for Nachikufu III show the mean for the microliths as being somewhat larger than that of the primary forms which is due to the 13·2 per cent of side flakes. However, Nachikufu II A shows a significant difference from the other aggregates in that the primary flake/bladelet forms are over a third as long again as the microliths. The great majority here are end-struck flakes and it would appear that these may have been intentionally broken to produce the deep crescents that make their appearance with this industry. Similarly, the means of the microliths and the flake/bladelets suggest initial modification before backing. The small scrapers on flakes and fragments at Gwisho A and the Kalambo Falls have a generally comparable mean size but, since this exceeds the mean for flakes and bladelets, the primary form must have been selected. Those from Nachifuku are shorter but were also, it would appear, made from selected larger blades and fragments.

The diagram (Figure 21) on which have been plotted the mean breadth/length ratios for the three artifact classes – microliths, scrapers and flake/blades – with each of the six aggregates, shows best, perhaps, the differences between them. The Kaposwa

[1] Figure for Gwisho B not available.

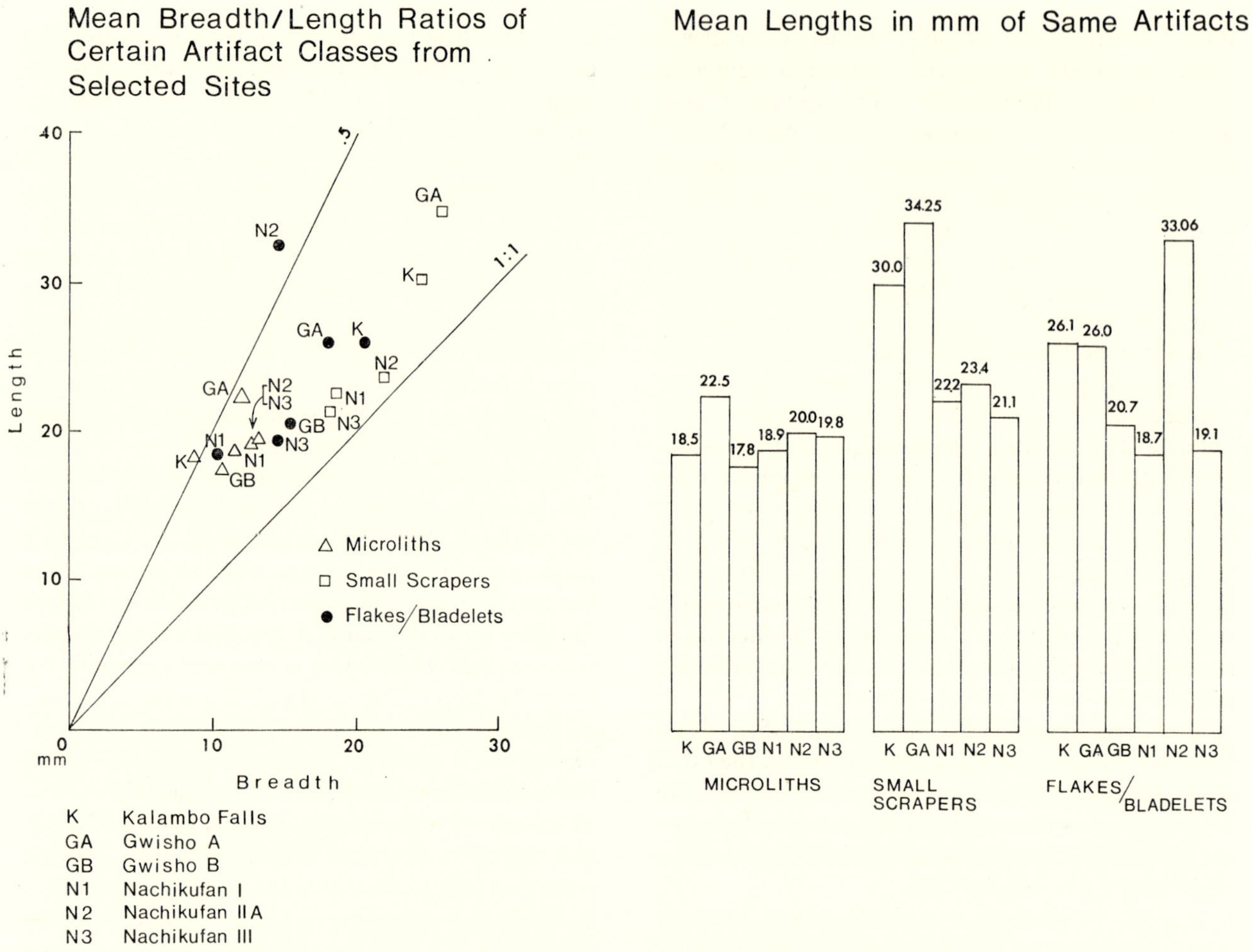

Fig. 21. Graph showing comparative breadth/length ratios and bar diagrams of lengths of certain tool classes from selected sites.

Industry microliths are narrowest (more blade-like), followed by Gwisho A, Nachikufu I and Gwisho B. The broadest are Nachikufu IIA and, if Nachikufu IIB had been included, these would have been even broader. The same relationship between the unmodified primary form and the microliths is shown by the bar diagrams of mean lengths (Figure 21), for the Kaposwa and the Nachikufu IIa Industries, while it is apparent that little or no modification of the primary form was practised at Gwisho and in the Nachikufu II and III. The manufacture of 'deep crescents' or semi-circular microliths from snapped fragments of flakes is similar to that used to make the Tshitolian trapezes and other forms in northeast Angola (Clark, 1963: 158–60). The mean for small scrapers with the Kaposwa, Nachikufu I and III and Gwisho A,[1] all fall outside that for the mean flake/bladelet length. This suggests that, besides some selection for large primary forms, the cores were also being worked more specifically for other forms of tool, in particular for the manufacture of backed microliths.

5. CONCLUSIONS

In summary it can be said that the Kaposwa Industry differs from the Nachikufu Industries and the Gwisho Springs aggregates with which it has been compared, in the frequency of its narrow lunates and virtual absence of broad ones and the way in which the bladelets and flakes were segmented, in the casual nature of most of the scrapers and the absence of the concave and strangulated scraper forms, in the scarcity of *outils esquillés* and burins and the absence of the double backed microlith or drill and the heavy duty core-scraper forms of the Nachikufu I. It

[1] Figure for Gwisho B not available.

resembles the Nachikufu and Gwisho aggregates in having small percentages of trapezes and triangular microliths.

Raw material could account for the differences in the microliths and the method of making them, as well as for the correlation between *outils esquillés* and quartz. It can, however, hardly explain the absence of the concave scraper class or of the drills which can be better explained as being related to some activity or activities not carried on at the Kalambo Falls site. Where the Plateau Series outcrop these scraper forms are made in chert. The aggregate from Mporokoso, 150 kilometers to the southwest of the Kalambo Falls on the Zambia plateau and also in *Brachystegia* woodland, shows a preponderance of scraper forms (93 per cent) of which 76·8 per cent are concave, notched and strangulated and the remainder core-scrapers. Microliths, however, formed only 2·4 per cent of the shaped tool category and there were two bored stones (Clark, 1958*a*). The collection from Chibote Mission, Luwingu district, not yet described, is similar to that from Mporokoso, and the surface collection made by D. G. Lancaster on the southern rim of the Kalambo Falls during the Second World War also contains some of these concave scrapers. The collection from Glendale, north of Salisbury in Rhodesia, is composed almost entirely of these concave and strangulated scrapers. There is reason to believe that these scrapers may be connected with wood working (Clark, 1958*a*: 64–6), in which case, this was not one of the activities carried out on the excavated part of the Kaposwa settlement.

'Later Stone Age' sites in south central Africa generally contain a small number of heavy duty tools – axes/adzes, bored stones, grinding and pounding equipment – and in this the Kaposwa Industry, and the others with which it is compared, is no exception. This equipment is usually durable and not readily expendable and must be considered as essential to the exploitation of the resources of the woodland habitat. Typological differences in the flaked stone artifacts of the various regional industries of the central African woodland savanna can be interpreted as being traditional to relatively local groups and to be due in no small part to their use of different, preferred, raw materials. The similarities in the tool-kits and the range of activities these represent, imply an economy and social structure that probably differed in no major way throughout the whole region of extensive deciduous *Brachystegia–Julbernardia* woodlands of south central Africa. Each of these local populations can be seen as existing in near isolation, which, as we have already seen, extended into historic times among the peoples of the Corridor country (Wilson, 1958: 5). In such circumstances, divergence is to be expected in the developing traditions as independent invention and diffusion introduced new and more efficient or more attractive techniques which local societies interpreted and used in different ways to improve their general way of living. These variations are manifested in the different industrial entities that have been recognized such as the 'Nachikufu', 'Kaposwa', 'Zambian Wilton' and other, as yet unnamed entities, from Zambia, Malawi, the Katanga and adjacent regions.

The origins of the Nachikufu Industrial Complex have been shown to extend back to 12,000 B.P., perhaps to 16,000 B.P. and it is now known that a microlithic technology was widely dispersed in Equatoria about this time, on evidence from the Munyama Cave on Buvuma Island in Lake Victoria (14,480 ± 130: 14,925 ± 80 B.P.) (Van Noten, 1971), from Calonda 3 in northeastern Angola (12,970 ± 250 B.P.) (Clark, 1963: 155, 167–70 and Plates 36 and 37), from the Nakuru/Naivasha Rift in Kenya (13,300 ± 220 B.P.) (Isaac, Merrick and Nelson, 1972) and in central Tanzania at the Kisese rock shelter (18,190 ± 306 B.P.) (Inskeep, 1962*a*). The local microlithic tradition at the Kalambo Falls, of which the Kaposwa Industry represents only one temporal entity, can be expected to have had an equally long history though, as yet, any ancestral entities have either not been identified or are imperfectly known.

The same is the case with the later aggregates, between 2000 B.C. and the beginning of the Early Iron Age with the coming of the Kalambo Falls Industry in the fourth century A.D. It is clear from oral tradition and from radiocarbon dates from Zambia and Malawi, that hunting/gathering groups continued in some localities until as recently as two or three hundred years ago. The majority, however, became assimilated at various times into the agricultural population or succeeded in making the change themselves from a hunting/gathering to a cultivating and stock-breeding economy. Traditions of hunting people are particularly strong among the tribal populations of the Eastern Province of Zambia (Bruwer, 1956; Clark, 1950*b*) and in central Malawi (Nurse, 1967; Rangeley, 1963) but they are present also in a number of other parts of south central Africa (e.g. on the Tonga Plateau (Colson, 1964)) and some of this evidence has been summarized recently by Miller (1969). Whether and for how long the hunters were able to maintain their way of life, was dependent, presumably, on the time when effective occupation of the country by Iron Age peoples began. The watershed country of Rhodesia and southern Zambia or parts of southern Malawi have been permanently occupied by agriculturalists since the Early Iron Age. Other regions, notably large parts of northern Zambia where the soils are poor, appear to have been occupied effectively only in the closing stages of the first millennium. Although enclaves of earlier cultivators persisted in particularly favourable localities, as in the local basin at the Kalambo Falls, for example, their influence on the aboriginal hunting populations must have been equally local and so enabled some of these to maintain their independent way of life to a relatively recent date.

Technology and economy of the makers of the Kaposwa Industry at the Kalambo Falls

The 'Later Stone Age' hunter/gatherer population in the local basin at the Kalambo Falls was probably never a large one, else more prolific evidence of its activities would have been forthcoming. Probably the camps were sited in a few naturally favourable localities at the western end of the basin – on the 30 foot (9 m) terrace, on the hillslope above Site A, on the Chitambala Gravel Beds – and they may have alternated between them as do the Lungu inhabitants today.

The portion of the occupation floor excavated at Site C in 1963 represents the greater part of a single occupation of more than purely temporary duration, probably relating to one family group, with the greatest density of flaked artifacts centred round a hearth area towards the southeast corner of the excavation; the evidence suggests a situation similar to that shown in Plate 96. Taking the hearth as the approximate centre of occupation, as the distribution scatter in Figure 16 suggests it to be, the activities of the group required roughly 70 square feet (6·5 m^2) of floor surface. However, if the hand rubbers, heavy duty and pounding equipment on the western and eastern peripheries are evidence of two other activity areas, then the habitation space is increased to *c.* 450 square feet (42 m^2). This may be compared with a !Kung Bushman camp of 8 family fires (32 persons) occupying an area 40 feet × 20 feet (75 m^2) (Marshall, 1960: 343).

The relationship between the workshop waste, the tools and utilized artifacts shows that all of these were manufactured on the site and used there also. Only the large, heavy duty tools appear to have been made elsewhere and carried in. The distribution of hand rubbers at the eastern side of the occupation floor and of axe/adzes and other heavy duty tools at the western side, is probably suggestive of two additional activity areas.

The properties of the fine grained chert selected for making the microliths and other small flaked tools resulted in a significant proportion of larger flakes and bladelets which were intentionally broken into segments by a method of notching, trimming and sectioning the primary forms that resembles, but is not identical with, the 'micro-burin' technique as found in north and east Africa.

Microliths are the most characteristic of the flake tools and the 'geometric' forms (lunates, triangles, trapezes) predominate over the non-geometric forms (backed bladelets). No evidence was obtained as to the manner of use of these tools although data from ethnographic and later prehistoric sources, as well as from Pre-Dynastic and Dynastic Egypt, indicate that one of the main uses was as barbs and transverse heads for arrows. The barbs were attached to wooden points by means of mastic and the head, with or without a foreshaft, was mounted directly into the shaft which was generally of reed.

The wooden points found with the near-contemporary Gwisho B aggregate from Gwisho Springs (Fagan and Van Noten, 1971, Figures 12 and 13) are made from hard wood and were worked to a fine point. Others which are shorter, thicker and blunter suggest use as linkshafts. Similar wooden points are reported from Pomongwe Cave in Rhodesia (Cooke, 1963: 108, 111). The unbroken specimens from Gwisho closely resemble those found in early Dynastic sites in Egypt where the microliths were mounted either transversely or on either side of the point, as in historic Bushmen arrows from the western Cape (Goodwin, 1945; Clark, 1959*a*: 223). The microliths were mounted in mastic and in the region of Mbala an efficient mastic is made from the tip leaves of *Gardenia imperialis*. These are chewed and form a gum which hardens on exposure but which can be made malleable again by heating and working with the hands. This mastic is still used today by the Lungu and Mambwe peoples for mending leaks in pots and for a number of other purposes. I am indebted to Miss Hope Gamwell for bringing this mastic to my attention and for furnishing me with a supply with which to experiment (Clark, 1958*b*: 151).

Tools for the manufacture and repair of the wooden points (the ends of which were probably equally as expendable as the microliths) as well as for the manufacture of other wooden and bark equipment must have been an essential part of the tool-kit also. The axe/adzes and choppers represent the heavier equipment while the finer work would have been carried out by means of the small flake and core scrapers, if these were used in a manner similar to that in which the Australian aborigine uses such tools. The many small flaked artifacts with evidence of marginal wear and minimal retouch would have furnished, whether mounted or not, effective knives for cutting and sawing.

Although the stone equipment comprises only a small number of tool classes, there is reason to think that these are generally representative of everything in this material that was necessary for supporting the 'Later Stone Age' economy. Heavy and light duty tools for chopping, cutting and scraping, for working wood, bark, fibre and, perhaps, bone; pounding and grinding equipment for the preparation of food; abraders and sharp flakes, possibly associated with the working of skins. Microliths imply the use of the bow and arrow for hunting and bored stones may have served as the weights of digging sticks as in South Africa. However, the bored stones found with 'Later Stone Age' aggregates in south central Africa vary greatly in size and weight and so must have had other uses in addition to the possible one of weights for digging sticks. One of these, ethnographic evidence suggests, may have been as an essential part of the mechanism of certain spring traps (Cabu and Van den Brande, 1938; Robertson, 1961; and the present writer's personal observation in southern Malawi in 1968).

Another possible use of bored stones in south central Africa may have been as pot-boilers. More elongated forms made from soapstone with a hole pierced near one end, through which a stick is passed, are kept and used by the population of the Luangwa valley for reconstituting flat beer, the stone being heated in the fire and plunged into the beer. Any convenient stone, even unpierced (a quartzite cobble, for example) will also be used for the same purpose. In this case it is removed from the fire and dropped into the beer by means of a split bamboo stick (Brelsford, 1938: 61; and the collections of the Livingstone Museum in Zambia). Such a practice suggests also a use for some of the natural stones brought onto the occupation floor at Site C.

Different coloured pigment indicates that the inhabitants were not lacking in artistic ability and the small, smooth, quartz pebbles suggest dancing also. Finally, the introduction of small quantities of chalcedony and quartz crystal and the surface find of the ?diorite axe show that the group in the local basin at this time and whose territory included the Kalambo Falls, also ranged over a wide area of country.

It is unfortunate that the sediments in the local basin which are younger than the later part of the Mbwilo Member, do not appear to contain any pollen. However, a core studied by Livingstone (1971) from Ishiba (Shiwa) Ngandu, 175 miles (282 km) south of the Kalambo Falls in Zambia and with the same *Brachystegia* woodland vegetation, shows no significant change in the pollen assemblage over a period of 22,000 years except at *c.* 3000 B.P. when some decline occurred in moist and dry evergreen taxa, perhaps, Livingstone suggests, coincident with the introduction of agriculture. Other localities in east Africa confirm this evidence from Ishiba Ngandu (Livingstone, 1971). If, therefore, climatic changes during this time were insufficient to bring about any major readjustment in the vegetation cover of northern Zambia, then ethno-botanical studies will have particular relevance for establishing models for better understanding the basis for the prehistoric collecting economy. It is, therefore, of interest to attempt to determine what vegetable, as well as animal, resources would have been available to the late prehistoric hunter/gatherers at the Kalambo Falls. So far as the vegetable resources are concerned, we have the ethno-botanical data obtained by us in the local basin itself (see Volume I, Appendix G) and the botanical check-list of trees and shrubs occurring in the vicinity of the Kalambo Falls compiled by Mrs Mary Richards (Volume I, Appendix F). When checked against the known nutritional and technological value of the species found, as reported in Williamson *Useful Plants of Nyasaland* (1955), it is apparent that a wide range of edible and serviceable species would have been available.

The following trees and shrubs occurring in and in the immediate proximity of the local basin provide edible fruits or pods of which the pulpy flesh and/or the seeds are eaten: *Anisophyllea pomifera*; *Bauhinia petersiana*; *Borassus aethiopium*; *Brachystegia allenii* (the leaves also); *Bridelia micrantha*; *Celtis durandii*; *Ficus* spp.; *Grewia* sp.; *Isoberlinia angolensis*; *Landol-*

phia kirkii; *Lannea discolor*; Liliaceae; *Parinari curatellifolia*; *Parkia filicoidea*; *Pseudolachnostylis maprouneifolia*; *Randia kuhniana*; *Sclerocarya caffra*; *Strychnos innocua*; *Syzygium guineense*; *Thespesia garckeana*; *Trichilia roka*; *Uapaca kirkiana*; *Uapaca pilosa* (the leaves also); *Uvariastrum hexabloides*; *Vitex doniana*; *Vitex madiensis*; *Ziziphus abyssinica*; *Ziziphus mucronata*.

The most important of all the wild plant relishes eaten by the southern African Bantu today are leaf relishes. The leaves of the following species are still collected and eaten as relish at the Kalambo Falls or on adjacent parts of the plateau. However, they are generally cooked and this poses the question as to what kind of container would have been used before the introduction of pottery, unless, of course, they were eaten raw: *Afzelia quanzensis*; *Boscia* sp.; *Commelina* sp.; *Gynandropsis gynandra*; *Sesamum angolense* (the seeds also); *Solanum* sp. (the fruits also).

The most important of these wild relishes is certainly the annual *Gynandropsis*, which is not infrequently cultivated round the villages today and is probably the most popular of all the wild leaf relishes.

Clearly, this is a very incomplete list due to our failure to make any proper collection or to record the herbaceous plants in the local basin. For example, at least two species of *Hibiscus* also occur there although we did not collect specimens. The leaves are cooked and the fibre used for rope making. At times when there was open water and the local basin was more swampy than today (like the Ichianga basin in Plate 55, for example), various swamp grasses, including *Panicum* sp.; *Echinochloa* sp., and the water lily (*Nymphaea calliantha*) may be expected to have appeared. The two former, with grains of other wild grasses of the woodlands and dambos, are used as famine foods in the Luangwa and Zambezi valleys. The corms of perennial grasses might also have been used to a greater extent even than was their grain (L. D. F. Vesey-FitzGerald: personal communication). The bulb, head of the flower stalk and the seeds of the water lily are also an important food source in times of scarcity in many parts of the continent and form the chief vegetable food of Batwa fishermen in the Kafue Flats in the closing part of the dry season. Potash is derived from burning *Cyperus* reeds and 'salt' manufactured from them; the bulbils of *Cyperus usitatus* are still extensively eaten. Several species of mushroom are available during the rains and may be dried in the sun after boiling and kept as a reserve source of food. In central Malawi we recorded twenty-three different kinds of mushrooms that are collected, dried and stored for long periods.

The flowers of *Dissotis* and of *Dracaena reflexa* are collected and the gum of *Albizzia antunesiana* and *Acacia albida*, both present at the Kalambo Falls, could have been eaten as well as used for other purposes. The fermented fruits of *Sclerocarya* produce a strong beer.

A number of other useful species are also present: some are used for making rope and string or for binding – *Brachystegia spicaeformis*; *Cissampelos mucronata*; *Cryptosepalum exfoliatum*; *Dombeya* sp.; *Piliostigma thonningii*; *Terminalia sericea* and *Sansevieria* sp. In addition, rope and bark cloth are made from the bark of *Brachystegia allenii* and *Pseudolachnostylis maprouneifolia* produces a dye used for bark cloth.

Two of the hardest woods suitable for arrow points are *Afrormosia angolensis* and *Erythrophloeum guineense* – the bark of the latter also yielding the famous *mwavi* poison used in ordeals and the wood of the former being used for making pestles and hoe blades when iron was scarce at the time of the Ngoni raids. A softer, much used wood is *Pterocarpus angolensis*. *Lannea* is commonly used for poles and *Uvariastrum* wood is used for game traps. Latex is produced by three species: *Diplorhynchus condylocarpon*, *Ficus* sp. and *Landolphia* sp. that of the first two being used for bird lime. Some species of *Ficus* have rough leaves that were used at one time as sandpaper.

Thespesia garckeana is widely used for making bows and the shafts of arrows are made from the *Phragmites* reed which grows abundantly in the modern swamp. The latex of *Diplorhynchus* would also have been available for fixing the heads of the arrows into the shaft as it is so used today in Malawi.

The arrow poison used was almost certainly, as today, made from the seeds of *Strophanthus kombe* which is commonly seen growing on the woodland slopes overlooking the valley. *Combretum* sp., also present, is another species that yields a poison; this is made from powdered parts of the tree and is used as a fish poison.

For mats and baskets the split leaves of *Raphia* and *Borassus* palms growing in the valley provide an unlimited supply of material and *Phragmites* reeds, the tough stalks of elephant grass (*Pennisetum purpureum*) and *Hyparrhinia* grasses are generally used to construct temporary shelters and as thatch.

The pods of *Trichilia roka* are an important source of body oil and also yield a variable amount of fat that can be used for cooking; a sweet drink is made from the liquid extracted from the arils. *Piliostigma thonningii* is another source of oil.

Small containers that could be used for carrying and perhaps also for cooking are provided by the hard rind of the *Strychnos* fruits, the Raphia palm and the Baobab fruits (*Adansonia digitata*), the last available along the shore of Lake Tanganyika. It seems very probable also that the *Lagenaria* gourd was available, since it occurs in east Africa in an early first millennium B.C. context (Leakey and Leakey, 1950: 38) and at Gwisho in the second millennium (Fagan and Van Noten, 1971: 49, 50). An indigenous bamboo (*Oxytenanthera abyssinica*) is also found on the plateau from which containers, such as those of the Nyakyusa, could be made.

From the above it is apparent that the local basin and the immediately surrounding woodland-covered ridges provided a rich supply of vegetable foods and plants to meet most of the essential needs of a hunting/gathering group. The !Kung Bushmen consume all food within forty-eight hours of its collection (Lee, 1969: 50) and generally similar behaviour is to be expected of hunting/gathering groups in the woodland and savannas. Sun dried caterpillars, mushrooms, seeds and fruits as well as dried meat and smoked fish may be kept for various periods of time as is done by Bantu-speaking groups in the region today. If, however, any significant quantities of food were stored, more permanent occupation of the camp is to be expected, with a correspondingly greater accumulation of occupation debris; this is, moreover quite unsupported by the available evidence.

Many of the more important fruits become ripe towards the end of the dry season and in the beginning of the rains – October to December. Others, such as *Bridelia micrantha* and *Parkia filicoidea*, became available during the rains from December onwards; while the fruits of *Ziziphus* ripen in April to May. It would, therefore, seem probable that the 'Later Stone Age' inhabitants converged on the local basin in the later part of the dry season or the first part of the rains, moving out onto the surrounding ridges and the plateau and perhaps down to the lakeshore in the later part of the rains and first part of the dry season when the resources of these areas were again abundant. Among the most important of these resources would have been the game animals, if the high percentage of microliths with the Kaposwa Industry is indicative of hunting with the bow and arrow.

For the following information concerning the species and habits of the edible game animals in the Kalambo Falls area, I am much indebted to L. D. F. Vesey-FitzGerald, formerly of International Red Locust Control at Abercorn. The available species include elephant, buffalo, roan antelope, greater kudu, Lichtenstein's hartebeest, zebra, waterbuck (*defassa*), sitatunga, reedbuck (*arundinum*), bushbuck, common duiker, blue duiker, greysbok, klipspringer, bushpig and aardvark. The grazing regimen in the woodland catena is strictly seasonal: during the wet season the animals are dispersed through the woodland; during the dry season they are concentrated on the dambos. Certain animals are associated with special habitats as, for example, the klipspringer with rocky hills, the sitatunga with wet *mushitu* thickets and swamp or the blue duiker with dry *mushitu*. Changes in the relative abundance of the species are directly related to changes in the plant catena. In this kind of country a population of about ten animals of hartebeest size per square mile could be expected. By local and limited movements within this plant catena, hunting-gathering populations, like the animals, would have obtained all they needed from their habitat, adapting themselves successively to seasons of plenty and stress without either having to store food or starve. Termite swarms and fruiting trees would form highlights in their life as with birds and other animals today (D. Vesey-FitzGerald: personal communication). Moreover, the favourableness of the habitat for game can be expected to increase with human occupancy and the use of fire.

Although now indiscriminate hunting has eliminated or made most of the larger animals scarce, it is clear that as recently as the turn of the century they were particularly abundant in the Corridor country generally. 'Hardly a *nyika* (grassy plain) can be visited without several head of roan, reedbuck, hartebeeste, eland and zebra being found upon it...' (Gouldsbury and Sheane, 1911: 193). Elton (1879) makes reference to large herds of elephant, eland and buffalo north and west of Lake Malawi. Twenty years later Boileau (1899: 582) reported that the rinderpest epidemic had caused the buffalo almost to disappear from the plateau, although he reported seeing their tracks along the Kalambo river and in a comparatively short time the game had recovered again. His report of game fences three to four miles (4·8–6·4 km) long with various sorts of traps at intervals of about 30 yards (27 m) and the very large numbers of game caught in these by the big drives in which a whole village would participate, shows something of the abundance of animal life in this part of Africa at that time (Boileau, 1899: 583).

Such elaborate drives were both unnecessary for the needs and probably beyond the ability of the late prehistoric hunters, but most of the other hunting methods in use on the Zambian plateau in the early part of the present century (Gouldsbury and Sheane, 1911: 201–2) are likely to have been employed. Driving by burning grass, hunting nets, game pits, snares, fall traps, 'box traps' and, perhaps, even the harpoon for hippo. Among the Safwa (Kootz-Kretschmer, 1929: 144), as among the Fipa, elephants were killed with a spear with a specially strong shaft and broad blade. Although not perhaps as efficient, a hardwood spear would no doubt have been adequate for thc task. Small carnivores, such as genet and serval cats, as well as vervet and blue monkeys, are hunted with bows and arrows and trapped to provide meat; in addition, the skin, when removed from the body in one piece, serves as a container. Cane rats (*Thryonomys*) were once abundant on the river banks and swamps at the Kalambo Falls and are a preferred source of meat, the animals being taken in fall traps set in fences. Hares and a range of smaller rodents, especially *Steatomys*, *Arvicanthis*, *Pelomys* and rodent-moles *Cryptomys* and *Heliopholius*, are also available and regularly eaten. Another preferred food are the two varieties of large lizard *Varanus* sp. and the python. Eggs and nestling birds are collected and men and boys regularly catch birds such as guinea fowl, francolin, doves and pigeons and also smaller birds, with bird lime or in snares. One such trap is depicted in a late prehistoric rock painting near to the Mwela Rocks Shelter at Kasama in Zambia (Clark, 1959*b*, Figure 46 (3): 176).

Besides being a source of food, game provided skins for clothing, containers and thongs; sinew and gut for binding, nooses and bow-strings; bone for awls and points and horn for small containers, decoy whistles and various other purposes. The shell of a tortoise is also a common food container among both Bush- and Bantu-peoples.

Honey is readily available and was the main source of sugar until the introduction of sugar cane. The sugary juice of *Echinochloa stagnina* may have also been used as a source of sugar or to make a sweet drink as is done in the Niger valley of west Africa (Busson, 1965: 462–3).

Termite mounds are ubiquitous in the local basin and on the hill slopes and termites would have been a valuable source of protein. They are regularly collected and eaten today when the young queens fly at the first rains and an ingenious trap for catching them is used among the peoples of northern Zambia and Malawi. The termites are roasted or stewed and salted and used as relish. In the *Brachystegia* woodland, in particular, a number of edible grubs, larvae of wood boring beetles, *Cerambycidae*, caterpillars and large grasshoppers *Cyrtacanthacris* and *Ornithacris* are to be found, becoming available during the rains or early in the dry season. They are usually sun-dried and provide the people of the Corridor country with an important source of fat and protein.

The local basin can never have been an important source of fish although small species are found there in abundance and caught in basket traps. It is, however, unlikely that the much more important large fish fauna of the lower Kalambo river where it enters the lake would have gone untapped. Fishing, as at the present time, was probably done there by weirs and simple basket traps made from *Phragmites* reeds as the flood water receded after the rains. Besides fish, frogs are likely to have been eaten, in particular the bull frog, as it is today. The large land snail *Achatina* sp. although not eaten by the eastern Bantu or those in Zambia, is commonly eaten in Nigeria and Zaïre and may have been more regularly collected by prehistoric hunter/gatherers.

Bearing in mind the probability of low density of the hunting/gathering population per square mile and the comparatively few game animals killed in a year by the groups still living in Africa today, as well as the abundance of animal and plant resources, it becomes apparent that the local basin at the Kalambo Falls was among the richest and most favourable habitats in the continent in 'Later Stone Age' times.

The physical type of the population

As has already been suggested, the Site C occupation floor at the Kalambo Falls may be interpreted as the seasonal camp of a single family group. The remains were centred round the hearth and three activity areas are provisionally recognized relating to the making of microliths, the working of ?wood with ground stone axes and choppers and the grinding and pounding of foodstuffs. It is likely that this working area, covering approximately 450 square feet (42 m^2) of floor space, was one of several such family units making up the group whose territory included the local basin above the Kalambo Falls in the early part of the second millennium B.C.

The physical character of the 'Later Stone Age' population in south central Africa is known as yet from only a few burials and fragmentary remains. The best preserved are those from Hora Mountain (Wells, 1957) and Fingira Cave (Brothwell and Molleson, unpublished report), both in northern Malawi. They indicate an essentially Bushman physical type though more robust, approximating to the 'large Khoisan' group but with some non-Bushman characteristics. Wells sees these as relating, on the one hand, perhaps, to the negro and, on the other, to an Afro-Mediterranean or Erythriote stock. However, whether these differences are due to genetic divergence in isolated environments or to hybridization with other ethnically distinct populations, remains to be determined though, in the opinion of the present writer, the former is the more likely.

It would not be unexpected also to find some Pygmy characteristics in the central African physical type and this may be the explanation of the remains classified as pygmoid from Chipongwe Cave (Toerien, 1955) and of the description of the hunting groups whom the Nyakyusa (Wilson, 1958: I, 8) and people of the Luapula (Cunnison, 1959: 34–5) found in occupation of the country on their arrival. The valuable evidence from the late prehistoric population at the Gwisho sites (Gabel, 1965; Brothwell, 1971) and also at Mumbwa (Wells, 1950: 145–8) confirms the genetic relationship of the southern Zambia groups with the 'large Khoisan' physical type. The greater robustness they share with those from the north can be seen as a general characteristic widely spread in Equatoria since it appears again in the skeletal remains from the waterside fishing and hunting settlement at Ishango on Lake Edward dated to the seventh millennium B.C. (Twiesselmann, 1958). This robust 'large Khoisan' race persisted in some regions after the introduction of agriculture, for it is attested in some of the earlier Iron Age populations in Zambia (Tobias, 1961), Rhodesia (Tobias, 1958; Colson, 1964) and the Transvaal (Galloway, 1959). It helps to explain the element of continuity that is one of the most characteristic features of African culture south of the Sahara.

Further north in the Malawi–Tanganyika Corridor country, proto-negroid (or pygmoid) characteristics may have been more apparent if the Luapula (Clark, 1950*b*) and Nyakyusa (Wilson, 1958: I, 8) traditions can be accepted. Physically, so tradition says, these people were small statured and squat, very black and robust featured. This physical type can still be seen among the Nyakyusa, where its origin is clearly recognized (Wilson, 1958). The Nyiha groups in Ufipa, the Safwa and other of the Corridor peoples, also presumably combined in their gene pool elements of the earlier hunting populations. The Safwa, in particular, state that at one time they lived only by hunting and tradition speaks of meat's having been eaten raw in former times and of the late introduction of fire-making, in this sense, presumably, in connection with the cooking of food. The Hehe in the southern highlands of Tanzania speak of aboriginal hunters – the VaMia – whom they found in occupation when they entered Uhehe (Worsley and Rumberger, 1949: 42–6), while the Twa, a fishing people inhabiting the Malagarasi swamp in western Tanzania are said to be pygmies (Gulliver, 1959: 74).

The following Safwa folk tale (Kootz-Kretschmer, 1929, II: 101–3) may, perhaps, be based upon an integration story of this kind where a hunting group is admitted into the society of an agricultural community.

The girls in the cave

Ten girls once said to each other, 'Sisters, let us go and cut grass' (needed for thatching). So they took their knives and went into the bush and looked for (good) grass which they found and began to cut.

It began to rain and they said to one another, 'Sisters, let us go and shelter in the caves'. So they ran to find the caves and went inside and when they were all inside the cave it closed up so that they had to remain there.

Some time later a woman said, 'I am going to cut grass'. She went off, found good grass and cut and cut until she noticed, lying on the ground, grass which had been cut some time before and she said, 'Who has been cutting grass here?' She cut further and came to the cave. When the girls heard someone cutting grass they sang a song which said:

'A man from Urizya is playing the drum, owe!
Let him bring a sacrifice of a cow to set us free, owe!
Let him bring a sacrifice of a goat to set us free, owe!
Let him bring a sacrifice of a hoe to set us free, owe!
Let him set us free.'

The woman returned to the village with her grass. She spoke to the others in the village and said, 'Friends, I found the grass that someone had cut, it lies there outside the cave. And I heard them singing a song in the cave. They said – – –' and she repeated the song.

The next day they all went and came to the cave. One of the old women cut grass and the other men and women stood nearby. Then the girls in the cave sang their song again.

Then the people said, 'These are our children who were lost'. They brought cattle and goats and hoes and piled them up before the entrance to the cave. Then the cave opened, the girls all came out, they went to the village and their mothers embraced them.

CHAPTER 6

The Polungu Industry: the Hillslope component

Introduction

In spite of repeated attempts to recover primary context assemblages representative of the cultural stages immediately prior to the microlithic Kaposwa Industry, we have to date been unsuccessful. However, in 1959 and 1963, aggregates stratigraphically ante-dating the microlithic and later than those referred to the Lupemban Industrial Complex were recovered in disturbed context from the hillslope soil at Site A and from Rubble I at various sites in the local basin. At the time this material was studied and analysed in 1959 and 1963, it was unanimously ascribed to the Magosian. However, since this is no longer a valid concept, it becomes necessary to determine what, if any, entity (or entities) is represented by these aggregates, particularly since a number of differences are apparent between those from the two sets of sediments.

At the time when the hillslope soil in which the later of the 'Magosian' entities occurs, was being accumulated, the Kalambo river was aggrading and the local base level rose nearly 40 feet (12 m), due to the building up of the sediments and vegetation that formed a natural dam blocking the exit at the Spillway Gorge. The central part of the local basin must have been unsuitable for occupation at this time for the upper and middle levels of the yellow/brown, bedded sands below the occupation floor with the Kaposwa Industry at Site C, and above Rubble I at the base of the Mbwilo Member, have nowhere yielded any cultural material. The more favourable areas for human settlement would, therefore, have been on the hillslopes to the south below Polungu Hill and Siszya Ridge and on the gently sloping surface of the Mkamba Member on the north side of the river. On the Tanzania side few natural exposures exist so that the extent of occupation there at this time is unknown.

On the Zambian side, however, the A4 Trench, downslope from the Camp, produced Archaeological Occurrences stratigraphically and typologically older than the Kaposwa Industry and younger than the latest component that can be isolated in Rubble I. The stratigraphic relationship of these Occurrences to those in the different rubble horizons and other sedimentary deposits in Excavation A4, 1959, is shown in Fig. 22. The aggregates are distributed within the hillslope soil (Bed 4) (Plate 98; Figure 22 and Volume 1: 125) and grey, sandy clay (Bed 11) (Figure 22 and Volume 1: 125–6), immediately south of the channel filled with sediments of the Mbwilo Member, with, at the base, the erosion surface on which rests Rubble I (Volume 1, Plate 20). A few artifacts of the same, or closely related form have also been found in a fresh and slightly abraded condition in the light grey, sandy clay (Bed 7; Figure 22 and Volume 1: 125–6), immediately downslope in the same excavation. This may have filled a channel contemporary with the formation of Beds 4 and 11 and their cultural aggregates, or it may be later and the aggregates derived.

Other archaeological aggregates that are stratigraphically earlier but show some, though no close, typological and technical relationship with those from the hillslope soil at Site A occur:

(i) in association with discontinuous pebble lines at the base of the bedded sands of the Mbwilo Member at Site A1, 1956 and Site B1, 1956;
(ii) both on and in the Rubble Ia, Ib and I (composite) at Sites A–D; and
(iii) where channelling prior to the aggradation of the bedded sands of the Mbwilo Member has re-exposed a rubble believed to date to a late stage of cutting and filling (Pits Channel Fill) seen at the top of the Mkamba Member, as at Excavation A2, 1956 (Volume 1, Figures 25 and 26); a small and typologically related aggregate was found on the surface of this rubble at the eastern end.

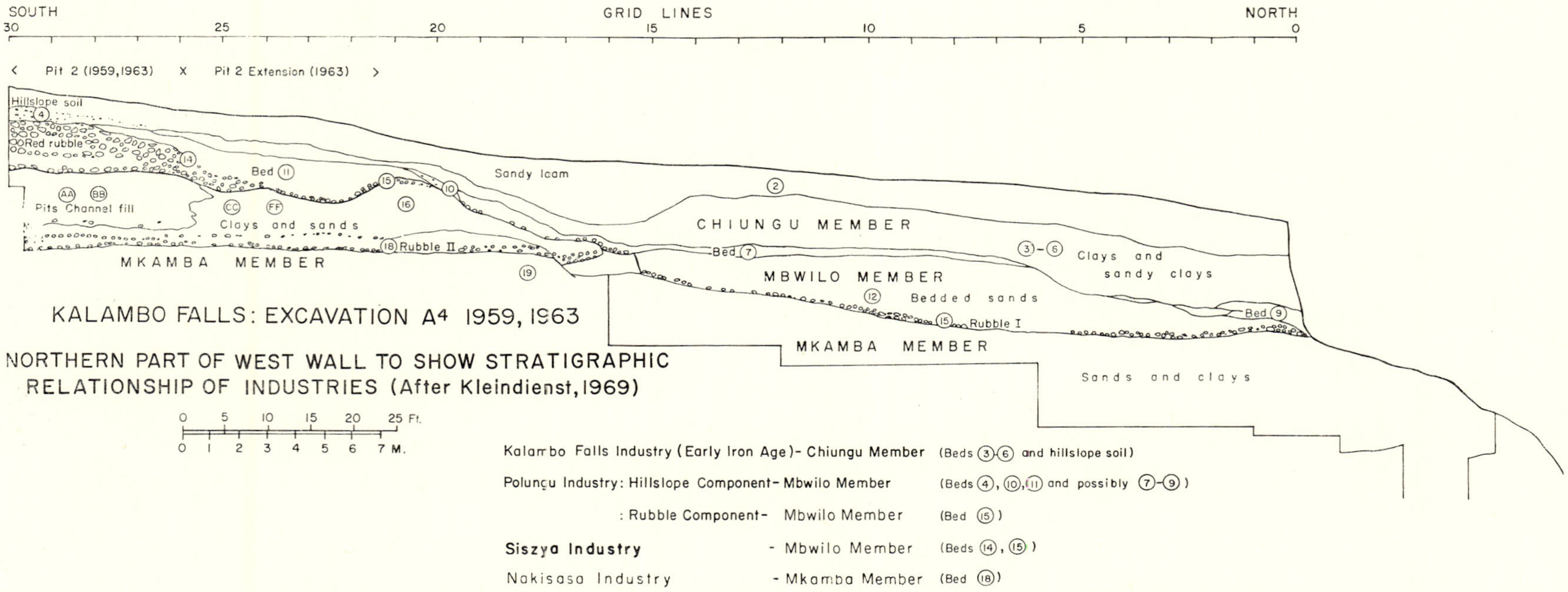

Fig. 22. Section showing stratigraphic relationship of Hillslope and Rubble components of the Polungu Industry, Excavation A4, 1959 and 1963, and other industrial entities. (After Kleindienst, 1969).

Although the artifacts in these rubbles are not in primary context, the physical condition of a small percentage of them is fresh or only very slightly abraded, usually with a matt patina, suggesting that they have not been moved very far, if at all, from the place where they were made or used. The series of artifacts in fresh condition are never large and often too small for statistical significance, but the common attributes they share indicate that they form a constituent which is distinct from that to which the great majority of the artifacts in Rubble I and the Red Rubble Bed upslope in Excavation A4, 1959, belong, while being different again from that in the hillslope soil. The unmodified waste with this fresh and latest artifact constituent of Rubble I has traditional relationships, on the one hand, with the earlier industrial constituents from this horizon but also, on the other hand, with the lower levels of the hillslope soil at Site A, in which technological modification and innovation has been taken a step further. An intermediate position is suggested also for this constituent by the persistence of some traditional, shaped tool forms in association with others that are present in the aggregate from the hillslope soil, but which make their first appearance here.

The fresh and slightly abraded artifact content of the hillslope deposits (Beds 4 and 11) in the A4 Trench has, accordingly, been distinguished here as the *Hillslope component* and the latest, fresh constituent of Rubble I and the overlying sands as the *Rubble component*. Since continued usage of the term 'Magosian' can no longer be justified, these components have been grouped as the Polungu Industry (see p. 75).

Dating

The Rubble component is associated with one charcoal sample dated by radiocarbon to 9550 ± 210 years B.P. (7600 ± 210 B.C.) (Lamont L395D). This sample was composed of small scattered charcoals from Site A3, 1956, Rubble Ia. At the south end of this excavation, Rubble Ia immediately overlay the main composite Rubble Ib and c with which it merged over the northern half of the excavated area. This sample dates the beginning of the aggradation of the current bedded sands (Aggradation Phase F6) of the Mbwilo Member overlying Rubble Ia at Site A. It has also been taken to provide a *terminus post quem* date for the Rubble component of the Polungu Industry. Whether this assumption is justified, only further investigation will show since there is, as yet, no way of knowing the length of time that the surface of the various rubbles remained exposed and so available to the makers of the Polungu Industry, before being buried by the overlying sands. The artifacts of the Rubble component of the Polungu Industry occur within, as well as on the surface of the rubble so that the first appearance of the industry may be contemporary with the later stages of rubble formation. The fresh or very nearly fresh condition of the artifacts suggests that the time involved may have been short for, if the Rubble component had continued to be made over a very long period, a greater degree of weathering might be expected; even so, the time it covers may still have been considerable.

For dating the Rubble component, it is significant that a bored stone fragment was found within Rubble Ia at Site B2, 1959. Bored stones have been reported with the Umgusan[1] (formerly 'Magosian') from Khami, Rhodesia (Cooke, 1957) which, in Pomongwe Cave (Cooke, 1963: 146–50), is dated to 15,800 ± 200 B.P. (S.R. 11). One complete bored stone was found with a 'proto-L.S.A.' aggregate in the lowest layer at the Leopard's Hill Cave, sealed under stalagmite and dated to 21,550 ± 950 (GrN, 957) (Miller, 1969: 316, 495). They also occur in quantity at the type site with the Nachikufu I industry which, at Leopard's Hill, is dated to 16,715 ± 95 B.P. (S.R. 138) and at the Mwela Rocks Shelter to 10,820 ± 340 B.P. (Y. 808) (Miller, 1969). The later accumulation of Rubble I could, therefore, be as old as 20,000 years B.P. though they might equally well be younger.[2]

[1] The Rhodesian Stone Age and Iron Age terminology was revised in 1966 and the terms, e.g. Umgusan, used here are those set up by definition at that time (Cooke, Summers and Robinson, 1966). The table published subsequently by Cooke (1968: 6) further revises the terminology but without redefinition. In the table, the Bambata Industry is shown as being sub-divided into two Phases – Bambata and Tshangula. The second of these replaces the term 'Umgusan' and the occurrences previously defined as falling within this entity are reclassified and given Phase status. Thus, the aggregates from Rhodesia formerly described as 'Magosian' and in 1966 revised to the 'Umgusa Industry' would, by the 1968 revision, be classified as the 'Tshangula Phase of the Bambata Industry'. These revisions have informal status pending formal redefinition of the entities concerned. Similar revision is suggested for the 'Later Stone Age' entities from Rhodesia, the 'Matopo Industry' and the 'Pfupi Industry' being replaced by 'Rhodesian Wilton Industry' sub-divided into three Phases – Khami, Pfupi and Dombozanga.

[2] More recently, fragments of three bored stones have been found with a late phase of the Bambata Industry at Zombepata Cave, Mashonaland (Rhodesia) (Cooke, 1971), associated with a radiocarbon date of 40,720 ± 1620 B.P. If this sample can be taken as dating the associated lithic industry which has a significant proportion of small blades and triangular flakes, it raises the possibility that Rubble I could be of comparable age, in which case there may be some factor, such as the organic content of the groundwater in the local basin, which might be responsible for giving generally

The age of the Hillslope component falls between 9550 ± 210 B.P. and 3920 ± 40 B.P. (the earlier date for the Kaposwa Industry). As yet, no more precise dating is possible but the component occurs through at least 2 feet 6 inches (76 cm) of deposit and some technological development is discernible between the earlier and later levels and it may well, therefore, have continued to have been made for some 5,000 years. The dating of the Rubble component is even less satisfactory. Its age lies somewhere between 9550 ± 210 B.P. and ± 20,000 years B.P., if we accept the evidence for the age of the bored stone in central Africa. An age as early as 20,000 years B.P. for the formation of Rubble Ia at Site B is in agreement with the radiocarbon age of the charcoal sample from the older Rubble Ic(iii) in Excavation A1, 1956 (30,500 ± 2000 and 27,500 ± 2300 B.P. (L. 3991)). It had previously been suggested that the charcoal which gave this date had been redeposited from earlier sediments but now it appears perhaps more probable that it is, in fact, contemporary with the formation of Rubble Ic(iii). If this is so (and this rubble contained no artifacts that clearly belong with the Polungu Industry) then it would provide a date for the latest aggregates in the rubble which are those of component B of the Siszya Industry. The sediments immediately over Rubble Ic fall within the cold stadial known as the *Mount Kenya Hypothermal* (*c.* 18–22,000 B.P.) (see Van Zinderen Bakker, Volume I: 74). It is tentatively suggested, therefore, that the Rubble component may have lasted for some 10,000 years, *c.* 10,000–20,000 B.P., and that the Polungu Industry as a whole covers a considerable period of time.

The Polungu Industry – Hillslope component

SITE A, EXCAVATION A4, 1959 AND 1963, BEDS 4 AND 11 (TABLES 14–19; FIGURES 23, 24; PLATES 43–47)

Stratigraphy and details of excavated units

Artifacts occur in the compact, red, sandy hillwash soil and fine gravel (Bed 4) in grid squares 21–50 – that is to say, in the upslope half of the excavation (Plate 98; Figure 22 this volume and Figure 28 Volume I). In grid squares 32–50, the material is more often associated with thin concentrations of fine, angular, hillwash gravel such as is often present in localities where there is little or no humus and the surface cover of vegetation has been removed. Such fine concentrations where, also, the deposit takes on a yellower colour, were best seen between grid squares 43–50 and 35–39. Downslope, the amount of natural gravel becomes appreciably less until, in squares 32–21, there is very little above the Red Rubble Bed and the sandy white soil is replaced by a mottled, clay sand with ferruginous pisolites (Bed 11) (Figure 22 this volume; Figure 28 Volume I).

The main concentration of artifacts lies in grid squares 20–35. At a depth of 3 feet to 3 feet 6 inches (91–106 cm) *c.* 94 per cent of the artifacts were found to occur in grid squares 21–37; between 3 feet 6 inches and 4 feet (106–122 cm) *c.* 84 per cent were between squares 21 and 34; between 4 feet and 4 feet 6 inches (122–137 cm) *c.* 81 per cent came from squares 23–43 and *c.* 90 per cent lay between squares 20–34 at the 4 feet 6 inches to 5 feet (137–172 cm) level. The industry makes its appearance at an average depth of 3 feet (91 cm) below the surface and the artifacts occur scattered over a vertical range of approximately 2 feet 6 inches (76 cm) to a depth of 5 feet 6 inches (1·68 m), at which depth the cultural content of the deposit is negligible. Although there are no clearly discernible surfaces or floors on which the artifacts lie, they are noticeably more concentrated at depths between 3 feet 6 inches and 4 feet (106–122 cm). In the 1963 excavation that extended Pit 2 (grid squares 21–26), a small number of artifacts were dispersed within the clayey sand (Bed 11), which here sloped from east to west and south to north.

Immediately beneath the mottled and ferruginous clay sand (Bed 11) in grid squares 25–28 is a rubble which represents the downslope end of the Red Rubble Bed (Bed 14) (Figure 22 this volume and Figure 28 Volume I), exposed in thickness upslope in Pits 1, 2 and 3 (Volume I, Plate 21). This Red Rubble contains fresh and abraded artifacts belonging to the Siszya Industry of the Lupemban Industrial Complex. The deposits have been cut out by channelling immediately north of gridline 20 and the floor of the channel is formed by more rubble. This probably correlates with Rubble I but it is possible that this horizon may have been re-exposed here by erosion that is either contemporary with the Polungu aggregate or later, as it is overlain downslope by light grey,

younger dates for the Kalambo Falls samples. On the other hand, the extent to which dispersed charcoals in occupation deposits in caves can become redistributed upwards and downwards through human, animal or geological agencies, still remains to be investigated. Further discussion of the radiocarbon chronology is reserved for Volume III.

sandy clay (Bed 7) (Figure 22 this volume and Figure 28, Volume 1) of the Chiungu Member. In grid squares 6 to 16 these sands are overlain by 1 to 2 feet (30–60 cm) of the light grey, sandy clay (Bed 7). This bed may, therefore, have formed the lower part of a clay band within the sands (Bed 12) over Rubble I, though it seems more probable that it is the base of the overlying clay sands in which the Early Iron Age Kalambo Industry occurs. As, however, no potsherds or other Iron Age artifacts were found in Bed 7 and it did contain a small number of very slightly abraded and patinated artifacts of Polungu Industry type that had been incorporated by slopewash down the bank of the channel, it is possible that Bed 7 could represent the base of a fill contemporary with Beds 4 and 11 that contain the Polungu Industry upslope.

The Hillslope component can, therefore, be seen to represent the dispersed scatter of artifacts from a settlement area adjacent to the bank of the river channel and not far removed from those parts of the deposits uncovered in the excavation. That it was also a traditional locality for settlement, revisited over a longish period of time, is indicated by the thickness of the cultural layer and minor but definite technological developments shown by the artifacts from the bottom and top of this Archaeological Occurrence.

1. *A4* 1959 *Excavation*

Throughout the main cultural layer in the red hillslope soil, artifacts are almost all in fresh condition and show most commonly a thin, reddish-brown to buff patina, less often, a light green patina. The raw material consists almost entirely of angular chunks of chert though, more rarely, abraded pieces of the same rock were used. An indurated black and an olive green variety predominate and are, respectively, responsible for the variable patination colour. Other materials are much less common. There is a small percentage of hard quartzite and some chalcedony which, as in the case of the Kaposwa Industry, must have been brought from several miles away.

Associated with the fresh material is a variable number of derived artifacts all well patinated and abraded. At depths below 5 feet (152 cm) in Pits 1 and 2, they are almost the only artifacts in an otherwise sterile horizon. In the main Polungu Industry level (3 feet 6 inches to 4 feet 6 inches (106–137 cm)) they constitute only a very small percentage of the total number of artifacts and, presumably, are either naturally derived from upslope or may have been brought to the site as raw material by the makers of this industry.

The aggregate has been analysed by 6 inch (15 cm) levels, i.e.

Level 1 – 3 feet to 3 feet 6 inches (91–106 cm)
Level 2 – 3 feet 6 inches to 4 feet (106–122 cm)
Level 3 – 4 feet to 4 feet 6 inches (122–137 cm)
Level 4 – 4 feet 6 inches to 5 feet (137–152 cm)
Level 5 – 5 feet to 5 feet 6 inches (152–168 cm).

The result is recorded in Table 14. Artifacts have been grouped as fresh, slightly or fully abraded. In almost every case, the artifacts of the slightly abraded group can, on technical and typological grounds, be seen to belong with the Polungu Industry. Attributes of shaped tools, together with the unmodified waste have been recorded in Tables 14–19 and further details are given in Figures 23 and 24.

From Table 14 it will be immediately apparent that the Hillslope component contains comparatively few retouched tools and that most of those that are found are informally trimmed and conform to no regular plan form. The significance of this is discussed more fully below (p. 190) but it may be noted here that this paucity of shaped tool classes could be explained by the inferred peripheral position of the aggregate in relation to the main concentration or occupation floor where the full range of artifacts can be expected. Alternatively, it is possible that this aggregate is fully representative, in which case, it belongs with an industrial stage with a minimal number of formal stone tool classes. No such doubt can exist, however, in regard to the debitage from the workshop floors and representative samples were obtained from each of the levels, except the lowest which showed a significant fall in the number of fresh artifacts.

It was important to know whether any significant changes in technique or shaped tool classes could be distinguished between the bottom and top of the cultural layer. Table 14 shows that no fundamental changes in tool classes or technique are represented in the contents of the five levels and this is confirmed by the following general observations on the five artifact collections.

Level 1. 3 feet to 3 feet 6 inches (91–106 cm). The only tools are five rather crude, irregular scrapers, one of the only two small, convex forms recovered and two burins (simple and single blow). Noticeable among the waste is the small number of blades and the large number of flakes, mostly irregular. Under

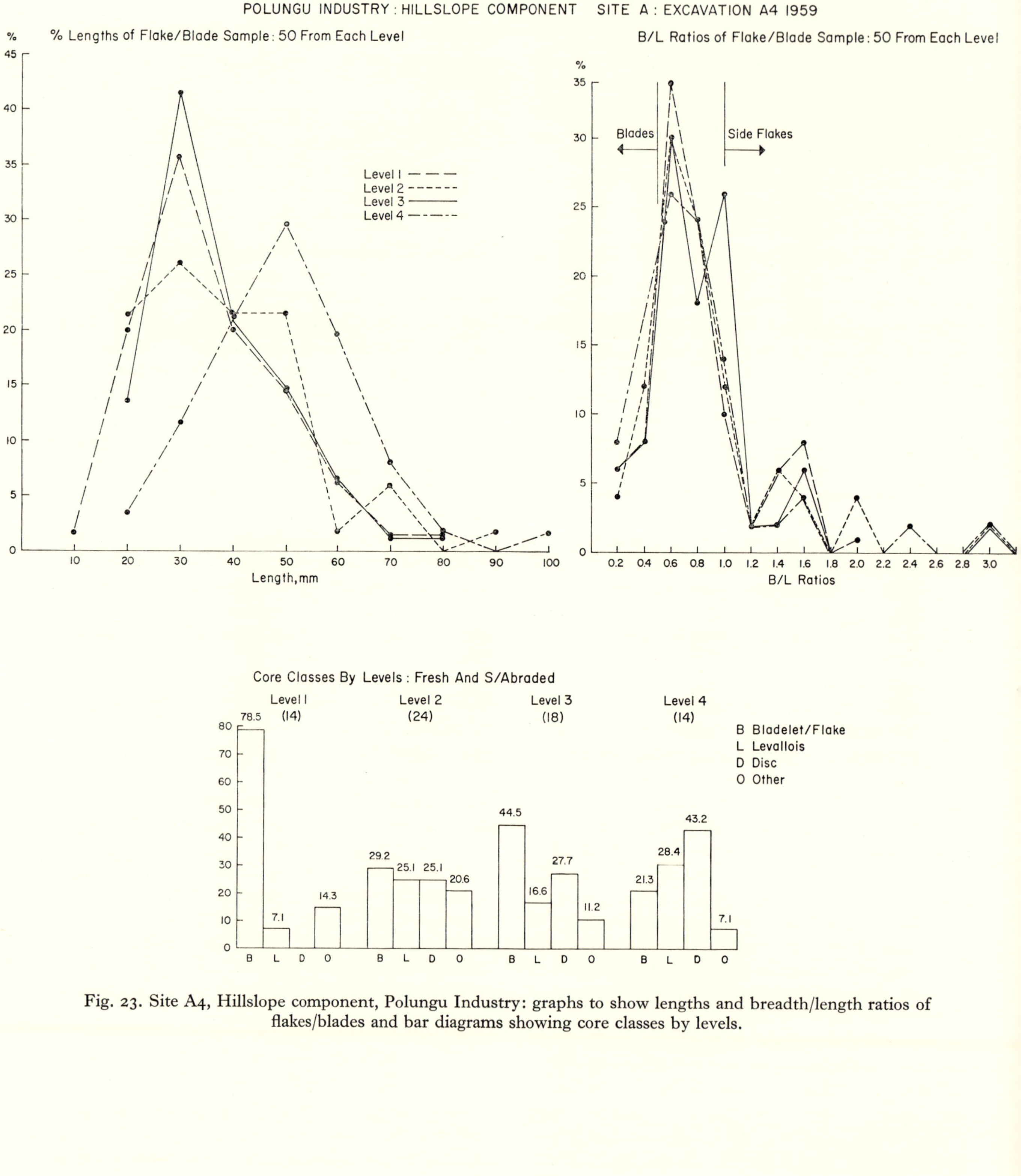

Fig. 23. Site A4, Hillslope component, Polungu Industry: graphs to show lengths and breadth/length ratios of flakes/blades and bar diagrams showing core classes by levels.

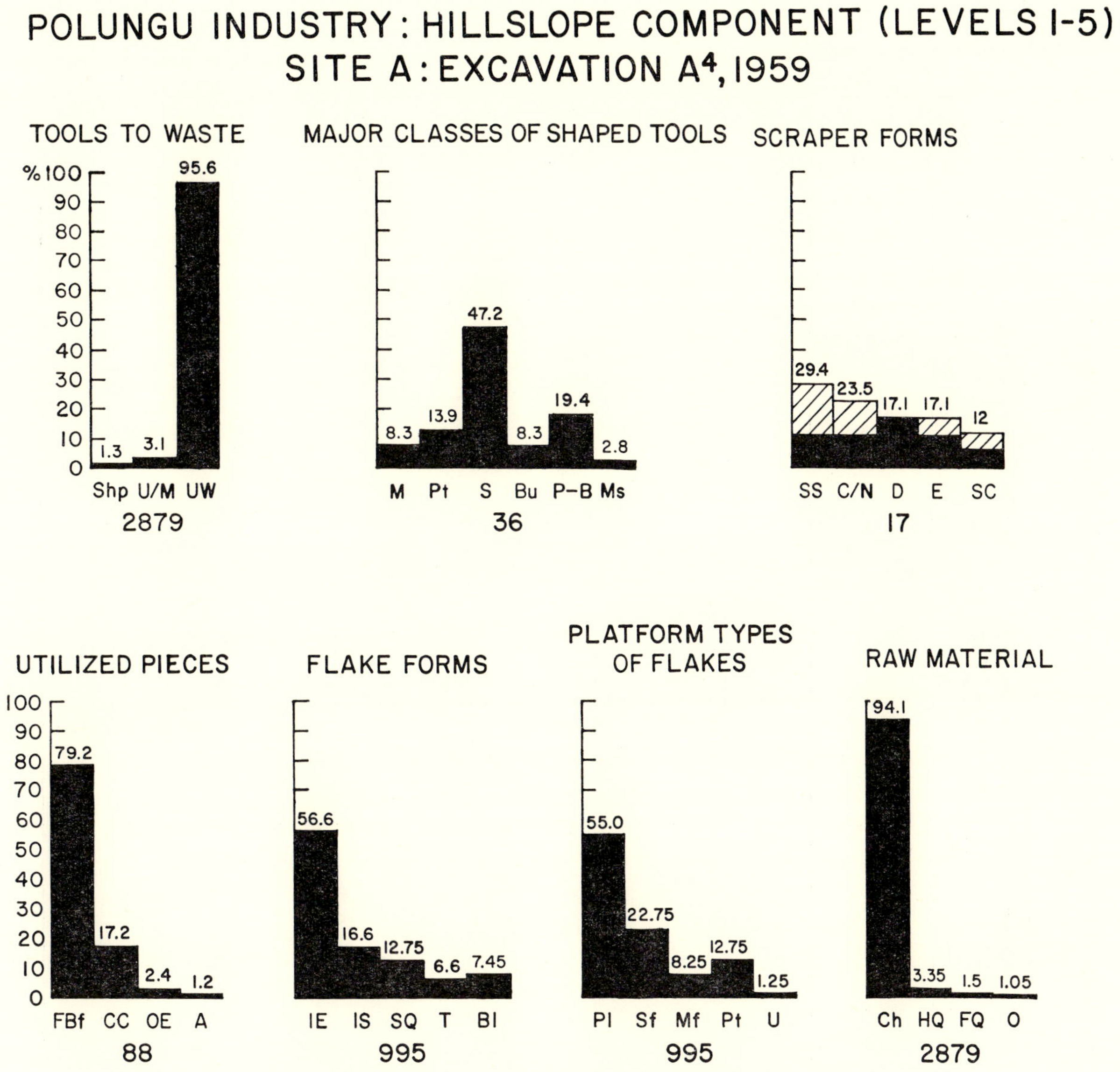

Fig. 24. Composition of Polungu Industry, Hillslope component (Levels 1–5), Site A, Excavation A4, 1959.

Key:

Tools to waste
- Shp = Shaped tools
- U/M = Utilized/modified
- UW = Unmodified waste

Major classes of shaped tools
- M = Microliths
- Pt = Points
- S = Scrapers
- Bu = Burins
- P-B = Proto-burins
- Ms = Miscellaneous

Scraper forms
- SS = Side, single
- C/N = Concave/notched
- D = Denticulate
- E = End
- SC = Small convex
- Hatched portion = made on chunks or cores
- Black portion = made on flakes or fragments of flakes

Utilized pieces
- FBf = Flakes, blades and fragments
- CC = Chunks and cores
- OE = *Outils esquillés*
- A = Anvils

Flake forms
- IE = Irregular end-struck
- IS = Irregular side-struck
- SQ = Short quadrilateral
- T = Triangular
- Bl = Blades/long quadrilateral

Platform types
- Pl = Plain
- Sf = Simple faceted
- Mf = Multi-faceted
- Pt = Point
- U = Unclassified

Raw material
- Ch = Chert
- HQ = Hard quartzite
- FQ = Feldspathic quartzite
- O = Other

TABLE 14. *Excavation A4, 1959: Bed 4; Artifact classes by levels of the Hillslope component of the Polungu Industry (fresh and slightly abraded categories only)*

Level 1, 3 feet–3 feet 6 inches (91–107 cm)

Artifact classes	Total all artifacts	Physical condition			Raw material						Dimensions in millimetres: Length				Dimensions in millimetres: Breadth				Dimensions in millimetres: Thickness				Flake platforms					Dorsal scar pattern				Core platform	
		Fresh	S/Abraded	Abraded	Chert	H/Q	F/Q	Qz	Chal	Sil	>100	100–>50	50–30	<30	>100	100–>50	50–30	<30	>50	50–>20	20–10	<10	Plain	S/Faceted	M/Faceted	Point	Not recorded	1-Directional	2-Directional	Multi-Dir.	Unrecorded	Plain	Prepared
Shaped tools																																	
Microliths																																	
Points – unifacial																																	
Scrapers																																	
On flakes and flake fragments	1	1			1								1					1			1						1	1					
On cores and chunks	2	1	1		1	1					1	1				2			2									1	1				
Small convex	1	1			1									1				1			1						1	1					
Burins	2	2			2							1	1					2			1	1					2				2		
Proto-burins																																	
Choppers																																	
Miscellaneous																																	
Total shaped tools	6	5	1		5	1					1	2	2	1		2		4	2		3	1					4	3	1		2		
Utilized/modified pieces																																	
Flakes and flake fragments	18	14	3	1	14	2			1	1		3	14	1		1	7	10		2	12	4	11	2		5		11	3	4			
Blades and blade fragments	3	2	1		3							1	1	1			1	2			1	2		1		1	1	2	1				
Chunks and cores																																	
Dimple scarred anvil																																	
Outils esquillés																																	
Total utilized/modified	21	16	4	1	17	2			1	1		4	15	2		1	8	12		2	13	6	11	3		6	1	13	4	4			
Unmodified waste																																	
Flakes																																	
Irregular, end-struck	126	104	16	6	120	4	2					13	87	26		6	43	77		4	99	23	80	18	4	24		74	31	17			
Irregular, side-struck	40	32	5	3	38	2					1	1	11	27	1	1	23	15		2	6	32	22	10	1	7		21	8	11			
Short quadrilateral	35	32	2	1	34					1		4	24	7			7	28			11	24	26	3	4	2		27	5	3			
Triangular	10	8	1	1	10							1	7	2			4	6			4	6	5		5			9		1			
Long quadrilateral	11	11			11							4	6	1				11		1	3	7	6	2		3		10	1				
Cores																																	
Single platform	10	10			10							1	9				10			9	1										10	7	3
2 platforms, opposed	1	1			1								1				1			1									1			1	
2 platforms, 2 planes																																	
Pyramidal	1			1	1							1					1		1												1	1	
Formless	1	1			1								1				1			1										1		1	
Proto-biconical	1	1			1								1				1			1									1			1	
Biconical																																	
Specialized Levallois/discoid	5	1		4	5							1	4				5			3	2								1	4			5
Flake and blade fragments	281	264	9	8	273	5	2	1					270	11																			
Chunks	100	96	1	3	90	7	2	1				3	96	1																			
Miscellaneous	12			12	12								12																				
Total unmodified waste	634	561	34	39	607	18	5	2		1	1	29	529	75	1	7	96	137	1	22	126	92	139	33	14	36		141	48	37	15	11	8
Total all artifacts	661	582	39	40	629	21	6	2	1	2	2	35	546	78																			

Level 2, 3 feet 6 inches–4 feet (107–122 cm

Shaped tools																																
Microliths	2	2			2								2				2				2					2	2					
Points – unifacial	3	2	1		3							2	1			1	2			2	1		1	2			1	2				
Scrapers																																
On flakes and flake fragments	3	2		1	3					1		1	1	1		1	1			2	1	1	1			1	1	1		1		
On cores and chunks	4	1	1	2	3	1				2	1	1			2	1	1	2	2								3			1		
Small convex																																
Burins																																
Proto-burins	5	5			5							4	1			3	2		4	1							2	1		2		
Choppers	1			1	1						1				1				1									1				
Miscellaneous	2	1		1	1	1				1		1		1			1	1			1	1							1	1		
Total shaped tools	20	13	2	5	18	2				4	2	9	5	2	3	6	9	3	7	5	5	2	2	2		3	9	5	1	5		
Utilized/modified pieces																																
Flakes and flake fragments	23	20	1	2	20	2		1			5	17	1		1	13	9		1	14	8	7	4	2	10		4	9	4	6		
Blades and blade fragments	6	6			5		1				2	4				1	5		1	2	3	5	1				5	1				
Chunks and cores	6	6			6							6				5	1		4	2							4		2			
Dimple scarred anvil	1	1				1					1					1			1													
Outils esquillés	1	1			1							1					1			1						1		1				
Total utilized/modified	37	34	1	2	32	3	1	1			8	28	1		1	20	16		7	19	11	12	5	2	10	1	13	11	6	6		
Unmodified waste																																
Flakes																																
Irregular, end-struck	234	213	11	10	217	9	6			1	17	164	52		2	48	70		6	33	81	119	50	22	37	6	52	42	24	2		
Irregular, side-struck	83	71	5	7	79	3	1					57	26		3	38	41		2	17	63	30	23	9	21		32	32	15	3		
Short quadrilateral	58	56		2	56	1	1				3	44	11			9	38			10	37	30	16	7	5		31	12	4			
Triangular	28	26	1	1	27							16	12			2	16			2	16	9	7	11	1		15	1	2			
Long quadrilateral	28	28			28						4	24				1	11			5	7	12	2		2	12	10	2		16		
Cores																																
Single platform	5	5			5						1	4				5			4	1							1	4			1	4
2 platforms, opposed	2	2			2							2				2			2									2			2	
2 platforms, 2 planes																																
Pyramidal																																
Formless	1	1			1							1				1			1									1				1
Proto-biconical	3	3			3							3				3			3									3			3	
Biconical	1	1			1						1					1			1													1
Specialized Levallois/discoid	12	12			11				1		2	10			2	10			8	4								1	3	8		12
Flake and blade fragments	593	589		4	563	22	5		3		72	521																				
Chunks	101	93		8	79	17	2	3			27	74																				
Miscellaneous	8			8	8							8																				
Total unmodified waste	1,157	1,100	17	40	1,080	52	15	3	7	1	127	928	101		7	120	176		27	72	204	200	98	49	66	18	141	100	48	29	6	18
Total all artifacts	1,214	1,147	20	47	1,130	57	16	4	7	5	137	965	107																			

Table 14 (*cont.*)

Level 3, 4 feet–4 feet 6 inches (122–137 cm)

Artifact classes	Total all artifacts	Physical condition: Fresh	S/Abraded	Abraded	Raw material: Chert	H/Q	F/Q	Qz	Chal	Sil	Dimensions in millimetres: Length: >100	100–<50	50–30	<30	Breadth: >100	100–>50	50–30	<30	Thickness: >50	50–>20	20–10	<10	Flake platforms: Plain	S/Faceted	M/Faceted	Point	Not recorded	Dorsal scar pattern: 1-Directional	2-Directional	Multi-Dir.	Unrecorded	Core platform: Plain	Prepared
Shaped tools																																	
Microliths																																	
Points – unifacial																																	
Scrapers																																	
On flakes and flake fragments	3	3			3							1	2				2	1			3		3					1	2				
On cores and chunks	2	1		1	2								1	1			1	1		2								2					
Small convex																																	
Burins	1	1			1								1					1				1				1		1					
Proto-burins	1	1			1								1				1				1							1					
Choppers	1			1		1					1					1			1												1		
Miscellaneous																																	
Total shaped tools	8	6		2	7	1					1	1	5	1		1	4	3	1	2	4	1	3			1		5	2		1		
Utilized/modified pieces																																	
Flakes and flake fragments	11	10	1		11							1	9	1			9	2		1	7	3	9	2				3	1	6	1		
Blades and blade fragments	2	1		1	2								2					2				2		1		1		1			1		
Chunks and cores	6	5		1	6							1	4	1			3	3		1	5							1	1	2	2		
Dimple scarred anvil																																	
Outils esquillés	1	1			1								1					1				1					1		1				
Total utilized/modified	20	17	1	2	20							2	16	2			12	8		2	12	6	9	3		1	1	5	3	8	4		
Unmodified waste																																	
Flakes																																	
Irregular, end-struck	143	121	1	21	136	5	2					10	100	33		1	89	53		7	108	28	85	29	8	21		38	31	23	8		
Irregular, side-struck	26	24		2	23	1	1			1		3	14	9		3	22	1		1	16	9	24	1	1			11	9	5	1		
Short quadrilateral	22	22			22								17	5			2	20			3	19	13	3	3	3		15	6	1			
Triangular	15	15			14	1						1	13	1			8	7		2	8	5	3	7	5			7	1	1	6		
Long quadrilateral	12	11	1		12							2	9	1			4	8			6	6	8	2		2		7	1		4		
Cores																																	
Single platform	5	5			5							1	4				5			5								5				1	4
2 platforms, opposed	1	1			1							1				1			1										1			1	
2 platforms, 2 planes	2	2			2								2				2			1	1								2			2	
Pyramidal																																	
Formless																																	
Proto-biconical	1	1			1								1				1				1								1				1
Biconical	1	1			1								1				1			1										1			1
Specialized Levallois/discoid	9	8		1	9							1	7	1		1	7	1		3	4	2						1		8			9
Flake and blade fragments	279	258		21	270	4	4			1			274	5																			
Chunks	52	42		10	43	8		1				24	28																				
Miscellaneous																																	
Total unmodified waste	568	511	2	55	539	19	7	1		2		43	470	55		6	141	90	1	20	147	69	133	42	17	26		84	52	39	19	4	15
Total all artifacts	596	534	3	59	566	20	7	1		2	1	46	491	58																			

Level 4, 4 feet 6 inches–5 feet (137–152 cm)

Shaped tools																														
Microliths																														
Points – unifacial	2	1	1		2				2					1	1			2		2								2		
Scrapers																														
On flakes and flake fragments	2			2	1		1		2					2				2						2				2		
On cores and chunks	4	3		1	3	1		1		3		1		3		1	3								2			2		
Small convex	1	1			1					1					1			1						1	1					
Burins																														
Proto-burins	2	1		1	2					2				1	1		2											2		
Choppers	1			1		1		1					1			1												1		
Miscellaneous																														
Total shaped tools	12	6	1	5	9	2	1	2	4	6		1	1	7	3	2	5	5		2				3	3			9		
Utilized/modified pieces																														
Flakes and flake fragments	13	5	3	5	12	1			6	7				8	5			11	2	2	4		1	6	2	3		8		
Blades and blade fragments	3	2	1		3					3					3				3	1			2		1			2		
Chunks and cores	5	4		1	5					5				4	1		1	4							4			1		
Dimple scarred anvil																														
Outils esquillés																														
Total utilized/modified	21	11	4	6	20	1			6	15				12	9		1	15	5	3	4		3	6	7	3		11		
Unmodified waste																														
Flakes																														
Irregular, end-struck	105	89	4	12	99	6			4	96	5	recorded for sample only								46	44	2	11	2	10	11	9	71		
Irregular, side-struck	34	23	3	8	28	4	2	1	9	24										21	12		1		7	3	4	20		
Short quadrilateral	18	13	1	4	16	1	1		2	16				10	8			9	9	13	2	2	1		10	6	1	1		
Triangular	14	13	1		13	1			1	14				10	4		1	8	5	5	6	3			8	3	1	2		
Long quadrilateral	24	21	1	2	23	1			9	14	1									10	11		3		4	7		13		
Cores																														
Single platform	2	1		1	2				1	1				2			2								1			1	1	1
2 platforms, opposed																														
2 platforms, 2 planes	1	1			1					1				1			1									1			1	
Pyramidal																														
Formless	1		1		1				1					1			1										1		1	
Proto-biconical																														
Biconical																														
Specialized Levallois/discoid	19	10		9	19				8	11			2	17			14	5								6	7	6	5	14
Flake and blade fragments	339	300		39	332	6	1		200	139																				
Chunks	42	35		7	38	4			38	4																				
Miscellaneous																														
Total unmodified waste	599	506	11	82	572	23	4	1	273	319	6		2	41	12		19	22	14	95	75	7	16	2	40	37	23	114	8	15
Total all artifacts	632	523	16	93	601	26	5	3	283	340	6																			

Table 14 (*cont.*)

Level 5, 5 feet–5 feet 6 inches (152–168 cm)

Artifact classes	Total all artifacts	Physical condition: Fresh	S/Abraded	Abraded	Raw material: Chert	H/Q	F/Q	Qz	Chal	Sil	Dimensions in millimetres: Length: > 100	100–>50	50–30	<30	Breadth: >100	100–>50	50–30	<30	Thickness: >50	50–>20	20–10	<10	Flake platforms: Plain	S/Faceted	M/Faceted	Point	Not recorded	Dorsal scar pattern: 1-Directional	2-Directional	Multi-Dir.	Unrecorded	Core platform: Plain	Prepared	Totals: Fresh	S/abraded	Abraded	All artifacts
Shaped tools																																					
Microliths	1		1		1								1					1				1					1				1			2	1		3
Points – unifacial																																		3	2		5
Scrapers																																					
On flakes and flake fragments	1		1		1								1					1			1						1	1						6	1	3	10
On cores and chunks																																		6	2	4	12
Small convex																																		2			2
Burins																																		3			3
Proto-burins																																		7		1	8
Choppers																																				3	3
Miscellaneous	1			1	1							1					1				1						1				1			1		2	3
Total shaped tools	3		2	1	3							1	2				1	2			2	1					3	1			2			30	6	13	49
Utilized/modified pieces																																					
Flakes and flake fragments	4			4	4							1	3			1	2	1			4		3		1			1	1	2				49	8	12	69
Blades and blade fragments																																		11	2	1	14
Chunks and cores																																		15		2	17
Dimple scarred anvil																																		1			1
Outils esquillés																																		2			2
Total utilized/modified	4			4	4							1	3			1	2	1			4		3		1			1	1	2				78	10	15	103
Unmodified waste																																					
Flakes																																					
Irregular, end-struck	14	1	2	11	13			1				1	13				11	3		1	12	1	10	3			1	6	4	3	1			528	34	60	622
Irregular, side-struck	9	1	3	5	8		1					2	3	4			6	3			6	3	5	2			2	3	2		4			151	16	25	192
Short quadrilateral	4		1	3	4							2	2			1	1	2		1	2	1	2	2				2	1	1				123	4	10	137
Triangular																																		62	3	2	67
Long quadrilateral	1	1					1				1					1				1					1					1				72	2	2	76
Cores																																					
Single platform																																		21		1	22
2 platforms, opposed	1	1					1					1				1				1											1	1		5			5
2 platforms, 2 planes																																		3			3
Pyramidal																																				1	1
Formless																																		2	1		3
Proto-biconical																																		5			5
Biconical	1			1		1						1					1			1											1	1		2		1	3
Specialized Levallois/discoid																																		31		14	45
Flake and blade fragments	23			23	20	3						11	12																					1,411	9	95	1,515
Chunks	3		3		1	2						3																						266	4	28	298
Miscellaneous																																				20	20
Total unmodified waste	56	4	9	43	46	6	3	1			1	21	30	4		3	19	8		5	20	4	17	7	1		3	11	7	5	7	2		2,682	73	259	3,014
Total all artifacts	63	4	11	48	53	6	3	1																										2,790	89	287	3,166

Abrasion categories: percentage by levels

Category	Level 1	Level 2	Level 3	Level 4	Level 5
Fresh	88·04	94·49	89·61	82·76	6·34
S/abraded	5·91	1·64	0·50	2·53	15·87
Abraded	6·05	3·87	9·89	14·71	77·79
Number of artifacts	661	1214	596	632	63

'miscellaneous Waste' are 12 specimens that are broken flake and blade fragments showing various stages of abrasion and steep, irregular retouch of the edges. These represent natural fracture as a result of surface exposure, movement and probable trampling by animals.

Level 2. 3 feet 6 inches to 4 feet (106–122 cm). (Plates 44 and 45.) There are approximately half as many artifacts again in this level as there are in those immediately above and below. Microliths and points are present as well as the usual scraper forms and a fairly large number of utilized pieces. There is also a full range of cores and it is apparent that the most significant are the small, discoid, sub-triangular, Levallois specialized forms and the flake and blade cores with single platform. 1,143 of the artifacts from this level are fresh and only 17 slightly and 40 fully abraded. Again, there is a small number of naturally fractured pieces classified as 'miscellaneous waste'.

Level 3. 4 feet to 4 feet 6 inches (122–137 cm) (Plate 46). There is a noticeable decrease in the number of fresh specimens and an increase in the proportion of abraded specimens derived from earlier contexts. Again, the only tools are informal scrapers and utilized pieces. The reduction in the number of specimens is at the expense of the irregular flake forms.

Level 4. 4 feet 6 inches to 5 feet (137–152 cm) (Plate 47). The largest number of tools and utilized pieces below 3 feet 6 inches to 4 feet (106–122 cm) come from this level. There is a comparatively smaller number of irregular, end-struck flakes and a correspondingly larger number that are broad and side-struck. There is also a sharp increase in the number of abraded, derived specimens.

Level 5. 5 feet to 5 feet 6 inches (152–168 cm). The greatly reduced number of artifacts from the fifth level and, of these, the small number that are fresh as compared to abraded, shows that the main aggregate comprising the Hillslope component comes from above this level. This can be clearly seen when the percentage of artifacts in the three abrasion categories is compared by level.

At the southern, upslope end of Trench A4 (Pit I) the red, stony soil rests directly on the surface of the Red Rubble Bed. Further downslope, however, in the area of Pits 3 and 2, the grey, sandy clay with iron pisolites (Bed 11) is interposed between the soil and the Red Rubble. A small number of artifacts was obtained from this pisolitic, sandy clay in Pit 2 (grid squares 27–30) in 1959 but the archaeological content of this layer can best be seen from the somewhat larger sample recovered in 1963 from the excavation of Pit 3 and the extension to Pit 2. The collection from the pisolitic, sandy clay (Bed 11) found in 1959 will, therefore, be described below with those from the 1963 excavations.

2. *A4, 1963 Excavation*

Small additional series of fresh Polungu Industry artifacts were obtained in 1963 from the red, ferruginous soil (Bed 4) and grey clay sand (Bed 11) in the following sections of the upslope end of the A4 trench:

(*a*) *Pit* 1 (grid squares 45–47) (Figure 28 Volume 1). Artifacts were found in the red soil in the course of stepping back the east and west walls 2 feet (61 cm) horizontally down to the Red Rubble (Bed 14) at 3 feet (183 cm) below the surface. From the upper 6 feet (91 cm) came 28 potsherds. From the stepping back as a whole, in addition to slightly abraded, abraded and derived Siszya Industry tools and waste, came the following fresh, light brown or brown patinated artifacts belonging to the Hillslope component of the Polungu Industry:

Waste flakes

Irregular, end-struck	7
Irregular, side-struck	3
Short quadrilateral	4
Triangular	–
Long quadrilateral	3
Total	17

Nine of these artifacts were made of chert and eight of hard quartzite. The former are all small with lengths between 50 and 20 mm and the latter range in length between 45 and 130 mm. This sparse scatter shows that this part of the trench was outside the main concentration further downslope where Pits 3 and 2 are located.

(*b*) *Pit 2 Extension* (grid squares 22–26). In 1963, the artifacts were obtained from that part of the 4 feet to 5 feet (122–152 cm) level, not excavated in 1959. They were found to be scattered sparsely throughout the base of the red soil and top of a consolidated, pisolitic sand, which might be a lens in the top of Bed 11 and they were not related to any occupation horizon. The base of Bed 11 rests on a rubble which rises steeply to the south in grid squares 24–26 to merge

Pit 2	Pit 2 Extension, 1963, Red Soil (grid squares 22–23 and 24B) Consolidated Pisolitic sand (grid squares 25–26) 4 feet to 5 feet (122–152 cm)	Pit 2, 1959, Pisolitic Clay (grid squares 26–28) 5 feet to 6 feet (152–183 cm)	Pit 2, 1959, Pisolitic Clay (grid squares 27–30) 6 feet to 6 feet 6 inches (183–198 cm)
Shaped tools			
Burin (Qz. XL)	1	—	—
Utilized/modified			
Flake	—	—	1
Rubber	1	—	—
Anvil	—	—	1
Unmodified waste			
Flakes			
Irregular, end-struck	21	3	19
Irregular, side-struck	3	2	3
Short quadrilateral	9	—	2
Triangular	7	1	—
Long quadrilateral	4	1	1
Cores			
Specialized disc/triang:	3	—	2
2 platforms opposed	1	—	—
Bashed chunks	2	—	—
Proto-biconical	—	—	2
Flake fragments and chunks	38	—	7
Totals	90	7	38
Fresh	61	—	—
Slightly abraded	21	2	7
Abraded	8	5	31
Chert	74	4	35
Hard quartzite	7	1	1
Feldspathic quartzite	7	—	—
Sandstone	—	2	1
Quartz	2	—	—
Chalcedony	—	—	1

with the Red Rubble Bed. The artifact composition of this small collection is given above, together with that obtained in 1959 from the underlying pisolitic, grey clay between depths of 5 feet and 6 feet 6 inches (152–198 cm). Of interest from the 1963 excavation in the red soil and consolidated, pisolitic sand are the broken quartz crystal with burin facet similar to those recovered from other Zambian and Rhodesian sites (Clark 1942: 177; Cooke, 1963: 97, 136) and also the single rubber. Thirty-eight of the flakes and all the blades are in chert, the remaining six flakes being in hard and feldspathic quartzite. One of the triangular flakes is a diminutive Levallois point – short and broad with multi-faceted platform. This small collection differs in no essential ways from that obtained during the 1959 season.

From the grey, pisolitic clay in Pit 2 (1959) between 5 feet and 6 feet (152 and 183 cm) came only seven artifacts among which are one sub-triangular, Levallois flake in chert, heavily abraded, and a long quadrilateral flake, broken, with parallel dorsal scar pattern, made from sandstone and lightly abraded. The collection from between 6 feet and 6 feet 6 inches (183 and 198 cm) is larger but the preponderance of abraded artifacts and absence of fresh material suggests that these are mostly, if not all, derived from the Red Rubble. There are three complete, specialized flakes with parallel dorsal scar pattern and five butts in addition to two mid-sections of other flakes. Both the specialized cores are unstruck, high-backed and made from chert. One is sub-triangular and the other a disc; the two proto-biconical cores are made on pebbles.

(*c*) *Pit 2* (grid squares 27–30). A further number of artifacts in fresh condition were found when clearing collapsed deposit preparatory to beginning excavation in 1963. They are believed to be derived from the ferruginous grey clay (Bed 11) and, if so, they belong with the Hillslope component of the Polungu Industry. Their fresh condition distinguishes them from a larger number of abraded and slightly abraded specimens derived from earlier horizons. Seventy-three of the flakes and blades are made from chert; ten from hard quartzite; seven from feldspathic quartzite and one from chalcedony. The core-axe is biconvex and pointed (*limace*-like) in plan form and is unifacial except where the bulb and platform have been removed by retouch; the section is plano-convex and the specimen measures 110 × 60 × 30 mm. It is made from feldspathic quartzite, is in fresh condition and could, therefore, belong with the Polungu Industry. If so, it is as yet the only example of the *limace* from the Kalambo Falls to be associated with this Industry. The Lupemban core-axe, a characteristic tool of the Siszya Industry in Rubble I, appears to have been replaced by this time by the finely retouched discoids with attributes suggesting use as some kind of adze-blade or knife.[1] The retouched blade is a long, core-trimming flake, triangular in section, that shows subsequent casual retouch at the distal end of the trimmed edge. The small scrapers are typical. Among the utilized pieces, the discoid core with straight, bifacially worked adze-edge should be noted. The utilized flake is a short quadrilateral (50 × 33 mm) with simple faceted platform and parallel flaking on the dorsal face. It shows casual retouch on the distal end of one convex edge; if this retouch had been continued, the artifact would have been classed as a backed flake.

Shaped tools	
Core-axe, double pointed	1
Retouched blade (?)	1
Small scrapers – single side	1
convergent	1
Utilized/modified	
Flake, one edge (part) convex	1
Blade, butt end, convex	1
Specialized, flat discoid cores: with adze edge	1
: notched	1
Unmodified waste	
Flakes	
Irregular, end-struck	54
Irregular, side-struck	4
Short quadrilateral	8
Triangular	18
Long quadrilateral	7
Cores	
Specialized, discoid flat	2
Single platform, irregular, plain	8
Chunks and fragments	46
Total	155

[1] Kleindienst has pointed out that it is possible that a unifacial, heavy duty element may form part of the Rubble component of the Polungu Industry and represent some form of high-backed scraping tool. The possibility should, therefore, not be excluded that some of the heavy duty tools from Rubble I classified as unifacial core-axes may post-date the Siszya Industry and belong with the Rubble component of the Polungu Industry. Examples would be the two such tools from Excavation A1, 1956, Rubble Ib; one of the 'core-axes' from A3, 1956, Rubble Ib and c (composite); and one or more of those from A4, Rubble I, composite. Another example with more certain relationship with the Rubble component of the Polungu Industry, is the specimen from between Rubbles Ia and Ib in Excavation B2, 1959, illustrated at Plate 53.

TABLE 15. *Excavation A4, 1963: Pit 3 (grid squares 34 and 35). Artifact classes (fresh and slightly abraded only) of the Hillslope component of the Polungu Industry, from the Red Soil (Bed 4) and the Pisolitic Sandy Clay (Bed 11)*

	Physical condition			Total all	Raw material							Flaking platform			
Artifact classes	Fresh	S.A.	A.	artifacts	Chert	H/Q	F/Q	Qz	Sil	Chal	Other	Plain	S/F.	M/F.	Point
					Red Soil (Bed 4) 4 feet 6 inches–5 feet 6 inches (137–168 cm)										
Shaped tools															
Core-axe/scraper, unifacial															
Discoid/adze															
Chopper															
Point, unifacial															
Small scrapers															
End	2			2	2										
Single side		1		1					1						
Double side															
Truncated bladelet	1			1	1										
Backed flake		2		2	2							1			1
Burin	1			1				1							
Proto-burin															
Total shaped tools	4	3		7	5			1	1			1			1
Modified/utilized pieces															
Flakes and flake fragments	3	3	1	7	6				1			1			
Chunks	1		1	2	1	1									
Anvils															
Pigment															
Total utilized/modified	4	3	2	9	7	1			1			1			1
Unmodified waste															
Cores															
Single platform, flake															
Single platform, blade															
Double platform, blade			1	1	1										
Biconical		1		1					1						
Formless	1			1		1									
Discoid, high-backed		1		1	1										
Discoid, flat		1		1	1										
Flakes															
Irregular, end-struck	17	10	8	35	26	3			6			22	7	1	5
side-struck	9	7	2	18	14	1			3			11	3	3	1
Short quadrilateral	2			2	2							2			
Triangular															
Long quadrilatera	4	1	1	6	5	1						1	3	1	1
Flake fragments	38	33	21	92	77	7	3		5						
Chunks	8	16	5	29	20	8			1						
Total unmodified waste	79	70	38	187	147	21	3		16			36	13	5	7
Total all artifacts	87	76	40	203	159	22	3	1	18						
					5 feet 6 inches–6 feet 6 inches (168–198 cm)										
Shaped tools															
Core-axe/scraper, unifacial															
Discoid/adze															
Chopper		1		1	1										
Point, unifacial															
Small scrapers															
End	1			1		1						1			
Single side															
Double side	1			1	1										
Truncated bladelet															
Backed flake															
Burin															
Proto-burin	1			1		1									
Total shaped tools	3	1		4	2	2						1			
Modified/utilized pieces															
Flakes and flake fragments	4	2		6	6										
Chunks	2			2	2										
Anvils			1	1	1										
Pigment	2			2							2				
Total utilized/modified	8	2	1	11	9						2				
Unmodified waste															
Cores															
Single platform, flake	1			1							1				
Single platform, blade															
Double platform, blade															
Biconical															
Formless															
Discoid, high-backed	2	3		5	4				1						
Discoid, flat	1	1		2	2										
Flakes															
Irregular, end-struck	21	15	8	44	32	9			3			20	6	6	12
side-struck	6	5	5	16	9	5			2			9	4	1	2
Short quadrilateral	5	3		8	6	1				1		2	5		1
Triangular	1			1	1									1	
Long quadrilateral		2		2	2							1	1		
Flake fragments	37	66	15	17	8	98	15		5						
Chunks	7	13	12	32	22	9			1						
Total unmodified waste	81	108	40	229	176	39			12	1	1	32	16	8	15
Total all artifacts	92	111	41	244	187	41			12	7	3				

Table 15 (*cont.*)

Artifact classes	Physical condition			Total all artifacts	Raw material							Flaking platform			
	Fresh	S.A.	A.		Chert	H/Q	F/Q	Qz	Sil	Chal	Other	Plain	S/F.	M/F.	Point
Pisolitic Sandy Clay (Bed 11) 5 feet 6 inches–6 feet 6 inches (168–198 cm)															
Shaped tools															
Core-axe/scraper, unifacial															
Discoid/adze	1			1	1										
Chopper															
Point, unifacial															
Small scrapers															
End															
Single side	1	1		2	2										
Double side															
Truncated bladelet															
Backed flake															
Burin															
Proto-burin															
Total shaped tools	2	1		3	3										
Modified/utilized pieces															
Flakes and flake fragments	2			2	2							2			
Chunks															
Anvils															
Pigment															
Total utilized/modified	2			2	2							2			
Unmodified waste															
Cores															
Single platform, flake															
Single platform, blade	1			1	1										
Double platform, blade															
Biconical															
Formless															
Discoid, high-backed	1			1	1										
Discoid, flat															
Flakes															
Irregular, end-struck	11	1	2	14	12	1			1			8	2	2	2
side-struck	2		1	3	3							3			
Short quadrilateral	2	1		3	3							3			
Triangular	1			1	1								1		
Long quadrilateral	1			1	1							1			
Flake fragments	7	5	1	13	8	1			4						
Chunks	5	1	2	8	6	1				1					
Total unmodified waste	31	8	6	45	36	3			5	1		15	3	2	2
Total all artifacts	35	9	6	50	41	3			5	1					
6 feet 6 inches–7 feet 6 inches (198–229 cm) Squares 36A and B and 35B															
Shaped tools															
Core-axe/scraper, unifacial		1		1		1									
Discoid/adze															
Chopper															
Point, unifacial			1	1	1							1			
Small scrapers															
End	1		1	2	1	1							1		
Single side	1	1	1	3	2	1						2			
Double side		1		1	1								1		
Truncated bladelet															
Backed flake															
Burin															
Proto-burin															
Total shaped tools	2	3	3	8	5	3						3	2		
Modified/utilized pieces															
Flakes and flake fragments		1		1	1							1			
Chunks															
Anvils															
Pigment															
Total utilized/modified		1		1	1							1			
Unmodified waste															
Cores															
Single platform, flake															
Single platform, blade															
Double platform, blade			1	1	1								1		
Biconical															
Formless															
Discoid, high-backed															
Discoid, flat															
Flakes															
Irregular, end-struck	2	1	4	7	4	2	1					5	1		1
side-struck		4	1	5	5							3	2		
Short quadrilateral	2	1		3	2	1						1			
Triangular		1	1	2	2							1			1
Long quadrilateral															
Flake fragments	5	3	8	16	8	8									
Chunks															
Total unmodified waste	9	10	15	34	22	11	1					10	4		2
Total all artifacts	11	13	19	43	27	14	2								

TABLE 15 (*cont.*)

Artifact classes	Physical condition: Fresh	S.A.	A.	Total all artifacts	Raw material: Chert	H/Q	F/Q	Qz	Sil	Chal	Other	Flaking platform: Plain	S/F.	M/F.	Point
				Pisolitic Sandy Clay (Bed 11) 7 feet 6 inches–8 feet 6 inches (229–259 cm) Squares 35 and 36A											
Shaped tools															
Core-axe/scraper, unifacial	1			1		1									
Discoid/adze															
Chopper															
Point, unifacial															
Small scrapers															
End	1	1		2	2										
Single side															
Double side															
Truncated bladelet															
Backed flake															
Burin															
Proto-burin															
Total shaped tools	2	1		3	2	1									
Modified/utilized pieces															
Flakes and flake fragments			1	1	1							1			
Chunks															
Anvils															
Pigment															
Total utilized/modified			1	1	1							1			
Unmodified waste															
Cores															
Single platform, flake															
Single platform, blade															
Double platform, blade															
Biconical															
Formless															
Discoid, high-backed															
Discoid, flat															
Flakes															
Irregular, end-struck	1	2	3	6	5	1						5	1		
side-struck		1	2	3	2	1						2	1		
Short quadrilateral	2	2	2	6	4	1	1					5	1		
Triangular		1	1	2	2							2			
Long quadrilateral			1	1	1							1			
Flake fragments	1	6	5	12	9	3									
Chunks															
Total unmodified waste	4	12	14	30	23	6	1					15	3		
Total all artifacts	6	13	15	34	26	7	1								

S.A. = S/Abraded A. = Abraded S/F. = S/Faceted M/F = M/Faceted

(*d*) *Pit* 3 (grid squares 35 and 36/A and B). Pit 3 was excavated with a view to linking up the stratigraphy in Pit 1 with that in Pit 2 and the extension excavation. The work was supervised by Miss Barbara Anthony. The Red Rubble (Bed 14) thins out downslope and the depth of ferruginized red hillslope soil (Bed 4) that remained unexcavated from the 1959 season was *c.* 1 foot 6 inches to 2 feet (46–61 cm); below this the grey, sandy clay (Bed 11) reaches a depth of *c.* 3 feet (91 cm) and rests directly on the rubble. On the south side of the Pit, the Red Rubble thickens, coming closer to the surface and Bed 11 begins to lense out upslope. The Polungu Industry tools in this bed show the same buff to brown patina and are sometimes coated with ferruginous incrustations. The contemporary Polungu Industry and derived artifacts contained in these deposits are listed at Table 15, the artifact content of Beds 4 and 11 having been kept separate in the table.

From 4 feet 6 inches to 5 feet 6 inches (137–168 cm) in the red to buff hillslope soil (Bed 4) came a total of 203 artifacts. The shaped tools comprise a truncated bladelet and two parti-backed flakes (all less than 30 mm long) and a single-blow burin on a quartz crystal. The utilized flakes are irregular and end-struck – one shows use on the distal end, two are used down one lateral edge, two have both lateral edges used; one is notched and one is a flake fragment broken in excavation which might be the retouched end of a truncated flake. The two specialized discoid cores have been utilized, one is notched and the other flat with an adze edge. An unused quartz crystal was not included in the lists though it must be a manuport.

The level from 5 feet 6 inches to 6 feet 6 inches

(168–198 cm) in the red hillslope soil (grid squares 36A and B and ?35A) yielded 244 artifacts. The shaped tools include a diminutive, end-chopper, an end-scraper and a double, concave side-scraper. The last shows a shallow angle of retouch and is made from a blade-like spall struck from what appears to be a core-axe of Lupemban type: it has been retouched as a scraper, the lower half of the flake having been removed by snapping. Although the retouched scraping edges are fresh, the rest of the artifact is very slightly abraded and so must be an older and derived piece. One very typical example of a proto-burin with a gouge-type edge is also present. Of the utilized flakes, three have one edge used, two have two edges used and one is notched. One small, flat piece of haematite and a fragment of specularite, though they show no evidence of use, must clearly have been obtained from a source outside the local basin and were probably intended for use as pigment and for hair decoration. Of the specialized cores, three are radially prepared Levallois cores, each having had a single, large flake removed; two others are discoid and have marginal retouch probably for use as adze blades.

A total of 50 artifacts were recovered from between 5 feet 6 inches and 6 feet 6 inches (168–198 cm) in the pisolitic, sandy clay (Bed 11; grid square 35B). Over the southeast side of the Pit the red hillslope soil is replaced by the ferruginous, sandy clay (Bed 11); this contained only three shaped tools the most interesting of which is a flat discoid that has been retouched on one convex edge and used as an adze. The specimen is made on a chunk, shows opposed, two-directional flaking and has, in addition, two notches formed by retouch at the proximal end. The other two tools are, one, a single, concave and the other a notched, side-scraper. The two utilized flakes are also notched. One example of a short, triangular flake with broad, simple faceted striking platform and a one-directional dorsal scar pattern was also recovered and resembles the characteristic form found with the Hillslope component of the Polungu Industry from the immediately overlying bed.

From 6 feet 6 inches to 7 feet 6 inches (198–229 cm) in the pisolitic, sandy clay (Bed 11) grid squares 30A and B and 35B, 43 artifacts were recovered. Among the eight shaped tools, the quartzite core-axe (230 × 100 × 70 mm), with converging lateral edges and rounded point is lightly weathered and must be considered as derived or reused. It shows a biconvex to triangular section with semi-invasive, bifacial retouch and the butt has been steeply trimmed to form a core-scraper edge. The point (50 × 31 × 8 mm) is broken at the distal end and shows marginal trimming on the right lateral edge at the butt; it is made on a Levallois point flake with parallel dorsal preparation. The two small end-scrapers are on chunks and have steep retouch. One of the single edge side-scrapers is made of feldspathic quartzite and shows a sinuous edge with blunt retouch angle; one is a transverse scraper in hard quartzite with denticulate edge. The single scraper with two retouched edges is convergent, made on a specialized, sub-triangular flake and shows alternate trimming. There are two specialized, quadrilateral flakes with parallel dorsal scars and sections of three others. The core is discoid for the removal of Levallois blades; it shows two opposed platforms which are multi-faceted and it may have been struck by bipolar technique.

Thirty-four artifacts were recovered from grid squares 35A and 36A in the pisolitic, sandy clay (Bed 11) between 7 feet 6 inches and 8 feet 6 inches (229–259 cm). The quartzite core-axe (120 × 60 × 60 mm) is fresh and so might be considered to be contemporary with the aggradation of Bed 11. It is asymmetric, biconvex in plan form, bifacially trimmed except at the point which is carinated with a flat ventral face. The two short end-scrapers are made on chert chunks with steep retouch angles; one is fresh and one abraded. Among the unmodified waste are two Levallois flakes with radial trimming, one slightly, the other more heavily abraded; there are six specialized flakes with parallel dorsal scars. At this depth over grid squares 35 and 36B, the grey sandy clay is replaced by the Red Rubble and the artifact content of the bed shows an increase over that in Bed 11.

Comparison of the lithic aggregate from Levels 1–4, A4 Excavation, 1959

In order to determine whether any significant trends can be recognized in the unmodified waste, a comparison was made of the core and flake/blade forms from each level except the lowest (Level 5) which contained too few tools for such an analysis. Only fresh and slightly abraded artifacts have been included in the study, the abraded and derived specimens being omitted. The graphs at Figure 23 compare the lengths and breadth/length ratios of samples of 50 flakes/blades, indiscriminately selected, from each of the four levels. The graph of the length shows that approximately one third of flakes in all but

TABLE 16. *Numbers of specialized and radially prepared flakes: Polungu Industry, Hillslope component, A4, 1959*[a]

	Striking platforms									Per cent of total of fresh and s/abraded flakes
	Multi-faceted			Simple faceted		Plain				
	1-Dir.	2-Dir.	Radial	1-Dir.[b]	Radial	1-Dir.[b]	Radial	Point Radial	Totals	
Level 1										
Ir/SQ	5	—	—	—	5	—	15	8	33	10·9
Triang.	3	—	2	1	—	3	—	—	9	4·3
									42	15·9
Level 2										
Ir/SQ	6	4	7	—	12	—	21	4	54	13·1
Triang.	10	1	2	1	—	10	—	—	24[c]	6·0
									78	19·1
Level 3										
Ir/SQ	9	2	1	—	4	—	19	5	40	18·7
Triang.	5	1	—	—	1	2	—	—	9	4·2
									49	22·9
Level 4										
Ir/SQ	2	1	1	—	6	—	3	—	13	7·6
Triang.	3	—	—	5	—	2	1	—	11[d]	6·5
									24	14·1

[a] Does not include irregular or short quadrilateral flakes unless radially prepared or with faceted platforms.
[b] Triangular flakes only recorded.
[c] Does not include flakes that do not fall into the categories specified in the table, i.e. one simple faceted/2-directional and one point/1-directional flake.
[d] Does not include flakes that do not fall into the categories specified in the table, i.e. 3 plain/2-directional flakes.

the deepest level (Level 4) have lengths of 30 mm (35·5 per cent in Level 1, 25·6 per cent in Level 2 and 41·5 per cent in Level 3). Levels 1 and 2 also have, respectively, 20·0 per cent and 21·6 per cent of flakes/blades that are 20 mm long. These levels are, therefore, generally comparable except that Level 2 has a greater number of specimens that are 50 mm (21·6 per cent) and 70 mm (5·8 per cent) long. In Level 4 the flakes/blades tend to be longer, the majority (29·6 per cent) having lengths of 50 mm and 11·6 per cent are between 70 mm and 80 mm in length. There is, therefore, a general tendency for the flake forms to become smaller through time and for the long quadrilateral forms to be bladelets.

Turning to the graph of the breadth/length ratios, Levels 1–3 show values of 14 per cent, 16 per cent and 14 per cent respectively for blades/bladelets but in Level 4 these increase to 24 per cent. The greatest percentage of blade-like flakes (i.e. those with ratios of 0·6) occur in Level 1 where they reach 34 per cent, followed by Levels 2 and 3 with 30 per cent each and Level 4 with 26 per cent. Most of the flakes from all the levels are short quadrilateral and irregular, end-struck forms. Levels 1 and 2 each have 18 per cent of side-flakes compared with 12 per cent in Level 3 and 16 per cent in Level 4. Comparing the two graphs, therefore, it is apparent that the flake/blade forms show no essential changes except for a tendency for the blades to be longer in Level 4 than in Level 1.

The bar diagram of core classes shows, perhaps, a more definite trend to increasing percentages of blade/bladelet cores (single, opposed and two platforms at right angles) from Level 4 to Level 1 and, less certainly, a decrease in the percentages of specialized Levallois and disc cores. If the number of cores in the analysis had been greater, the 78·5 per cent of blade cores (10 single platform and 1 opposed platform) in Level 1 and 71·6 per cent of prepared cores (4 Levallois, 6 discoid) in Level 4 would have been significant. In Level 2, which has the largest

TABLE 17 *Comparison of aggregates from Red Soil, Grey Clay and Red Rubble Beds, Excavation A4, 1963, Pit 3 (M.R.K. and J.D.C.)*

Excavated spit	Chips and chunks			Flakes			Specialized flakes (whole)	Cores			Tools and utilized			Total	Total excluding chips and chunks	Cubic feet of deposit	Artifacts per cubic foot excluding chips and chunks
	F	S/A	A	F	S/A	A		F	S/A	A	F	S/A	A				
Red soil 4½ feet–5½ feet (137–167 cm)	46	49	26	32	18	11	/5/	1	3	1	8	6	2	203	82	100	0·82
Red soil 5½ feet–6½ feet (167–198 cm)	44	79	27	33	25	13	/10/	4	4	—	11	3	1	244	94	75	1·25
Pisolitic clay 5½ feet–6½ feet (167–198 cm)	12	6	3	17	2	3	/4/	2	—	—	4	1	—	50	29	25	1·16
Pisolitic clay 6½ feet–7½ feet (198–229 cm)	5	3	8	4	7	6	/2/	—	—	1	2	3	4	43	27	100	0·27
Pisolitic clay 7½ feet–8½ feet (229–259 cm)	1	6	5	3	7	9	/7/	—	—	—	2	1	1	35	23	50	0·46
Red rubble (top) 7½ feet–8½feet (229–299 cm)	2	6	8	—	3	29	/9/	—	1	—	—	—	7	56	40	50	0·80
Red rubble (middle) 8½ feet–9½ feet (259–289 cm)	3	26	24	4	22	42	/18/	—	3	6	1	6	12	149	96	100	0·96
9½ feet–10½ feet (289–320 cm)	1	7	11	2	10	19	/7/	—	2	5	1	7	3	68	49	100	0·49
Red rubble (lower) 10½ feet–11½ feet (320–350 cm)	18	13	16	40	52	33	/30/	5	—	8	3	10	11	209	162	100	1·62
11½ feet–12½ feet (350–381 cm)	13	8	11	17	43	31	/15/	2	1	2	7	5	3	142	110	50	2·20
Green clay (top 3 inches)	3	3	—	4	3	3	/3/	—	—	1	1	—	1	19	13	33·2	0·39

number of cores, the proportion of specialized cores is still as much as 50 per cent.

The numbers of specialized Levallois and radially prepared flakes in each of the four levels are not greatly different when considered in relation to the total number of artifacts in each level (see Table 16). Blades show plain or point platforms except for two from Level 2 which have simple faceted platforms. If the sample from Level 4 is discounted as being inadequate, the figures of 22·9 per cent for Level 3, 19·1 per cent for Level 2 and 15·2 per cent for Level 1, suggest a gradual decrease in the number of specialized flakes from the earlier to the later levels. The most characteristic flake form is certainly the short, triangular flake with broad, multi-faceted striking platform. This is a diminutive Levallois point and, although never common, it occurs in approximately the same percentage in all four levels.

It is apparent from the comparisons made above that no very significant changes are discernible in the artifact content of the four levels. Blade technology increases in Level 1 where there is a tendency towards more and smaller blade forms. By contrast, the specialized flakes and cores appear to show some slight increase with depth. Level 1 could, therefore, be more directly ancestral to the Kaposwa Industry while the aggregate from Level 4 is, perhaps, closer to those aggregates comprising the Rubble component of the Polungu Industry.

Comparison of the red soil and grey sandy clay aggregates

It remains to be seen to what extent the aggregate from the grey, sandy clay (Bed 11) is different from that from the red soil (Bed 4). Table 17 compares the aggregates by level in the lower 2 feet of the Red Soil, the Grey Sandy Clay and the Red Rubble in Pit 3, Trench A4, 1963. The artifact content of the clay is significantly less than is that of the other two deposits. The incidence of fresh artifacts, of specialized flakes, cores and tools, all decrease from top to bottom in the sandy clay bed while the overall number of artifacts per cubic foot also decreases. The incidence of artifacts, as also of specialized flakes and cores, increases

TABLE 18. *Excavation A4, 1959, Pit 2, artifact incidence: Red Soil, Pisolitic Clay, and Red Rubble Beds (M.R.K. and J.D.C.)*

Spits	Number of artifacts (excluding chips and chunks)	Number of cubic feet of deposit	Artifacts per cubic foot	
Red soil				
−4′–5′ (122–152 cm)	99	100	0·99	
Pisolitic clay				
−5′–6′ (152–183 cm)	7	50	0·14	
−6′–6′ 6″ (183–198 cm)	39	25	1·56	
Total	46	75	0·61	
Red Rubble (top)				
−5′–6′ (152–183 cm)	61	50	1·22	
−6′–6′ 6″ (183–198 cm)	73	25	2·92	
Total	134	75	1·79	
Red Rubble (base[1])				
−6′ 6″–7′ (198–213 cm)	173	100	1·73	
−7′–7′ 6″ (213–229 cm)	200	100	2·00	
Total	373	200	1·86	Arbitrary break based on artifact incidence
Red Rubble (base[2])				
−7′ 6″–8′ (229–244 cm)	76	100	0·76	Abrasion and patination indicate same natural deposit
−8′–8′ 6″ (244–259 cm)	32	100	0·32	
−8′ 6″–9′ (259–274 cm)	82	100	0·82	
−9′–9′ 6″ (274–289 cm)	64	100	0·64	
Total	254	400	0·64	
Total base	627	600	1·04	

again in the Red Rubble. The lowest density of artifacts per cubic foot occurs between 6 feet 6 inches and 7 feet 6 inches (198–229 cm) in Pit 3 and a slight increase is apparent in the basal layers.

When this evidence is compared with that from the Red Rubble for Pit 2 (provided by M. R. Kleindienst) (Table 18) the volume of artifacts in the clay and the upper part of the Red Rubble can be seen to be closer than is that between the top and lower parts of this rubble. This might indicate a lateral downslope shift in the centre of occupation, also that rubble derived from the Red Rubble upslope continued to form for a time after deposition of the grey, sandy clay had begun and, perhaps, too that the artifact composition of the aggregate from the clay might be comparable to that from the upper part of the Red Rubble.

Turning to the upper end of the sequence in the clay, the incidence of artifacts per cubic foot in the 4 foot to 5 foot (122–152 cm) level in the 1963 extension to Pit 2 (0·90 per cubic foot) shows again that the main aggregate forming the Hillslope component lies in the red soil.

The relationship of the aggregate in Bed 11 to that in the Red Rubble or resorted Red Rubble bed in the extension to Pit 2, will be discussed in Volume III but it can be stated here that they are not the same. Any differences between the aggregates in the red soil and those in the grey, pisolitic, sandy clay can be expected to show more clearly, perhaps, in percentages and the dimensions of the unmodified waste and some comparisons between unspecialized and specialized flake forms are made in Table 19. When the percentages of fresh and slightly abraded whole flake classes in the red soil (Bed 4) and grey clay (Bed 11) are compared there is little observable difference between the aggregates:

	Red soil: levels 1–5		Grey clay: pits 2, 2 extn. and 3	
	No.	%	No.	%
Irregular, end-struck	562	56·6	39	44·31
Irregular, side-struck	167	16·6	24	27·27
Short quadrilateral	127	12·75	10	11·36
Triangular	65	6·6	5	7·95
Blades	74	7·45	8	9·05
Totals	995	100	88	99·94

The same is also the case with the specialized flakes if the sample from the clay provides a true indication of the position:

Specialized flakes – radial and parallel trimming:				
Irregular/quadrilateral	140	14·07	14	15·68
Triangular	53	5·32	2	2·27
Totals	193	19·39% of flakes	16	17·97% of flakes

Turning now to Table 19. Although the results for the aggregates from the red soil are based on a larger number of unspecialized flakes, there is no reason to suppose that they would have been very much different if a larger sample had been available from the grey clay. Dimensions for Levels 3 and 4 from the soil have been compared with those for the aggregates from the base of this bed and the consolidated pisolitic sand (?top of the clay), and of the clay proper, since this can best be expected to show the pattern of any changes that may have occurred. No major differences are apparent but there is a slight shift in the dimensions of unspecialized flakes as between the sample from Level 4 in the red soil and that from the pisolitic sand and grey clay. However, these last are very little different from the values for Level 3. Values for specialized flakes remain very similar but it is unfortunate that there is not a larger sample to confirm whether flake lengths really become somewhat shorter in the clay. Again the differences in breadth/length ratios of both flake categories are not great and do not appear to be significant.

TABLE 19. *Flake lengths and breadth/length ratios: fresh and slightly abraded artifacts from Red Soil and Grey Clay Beds, Excavation A4, 1959 and 1963 (Pit 2 Extension) (J.D.C. and M.R.K.)*

	Total no.	Range Min.	Range Max.	Mode	Median	Mean	S.D.
Red Soil (Level 3)							
Lengths all flakes	79	10	60 = 50	30	40	40·5	11·31
Lengths specialized flakes	29	20	60 = 40	50	40	41·5	12·16
B/L ratios all flakes	79	0·16	3·0 = 2·84	1·0	0·66	0·73	0·34
B/L ratios specialized flakes	29	0·25	1·0 = 0·75	0·4	0·4	0·56	0·17
Red soil (Level 4)							
Lengths all flakes	75	20	80 = 60	50	45	46·4	12·31
Lengths specialized flakes	25	35	70 = 35	40	50	48·8	10·60
B/L ratios all flakes	75	0·28	2·5 = 2·22	0·4	0·6	0·7	0·43
B/L ratios specialized flakes	25	0·25	1·0 = 0·75	0·4	0·5	0·53	0·21
Red soil/base of Consolidated Pisolitic sand, Pit 2 Extn. 4′–5′ (122–152 *cm*)							
Lengths all flakes	37	5	80 = 75	28	35	36·8	20·04
Lengths specialized flakes	5	36	59 = 23	—	51	49·6	—
B/L ratios all flakes	37	0·3	3·1 = 2·8	0·6, 1·5	0·9	1·04	0·58
Grey Clay, Pit 2							
Lengths all flakes	25*	20	152+ = 132	35	37	30·92	35·37
Lengths specialized flakes	10*	30	152+ = 122	30	44	60·3	37·93
B/L ratios all flakes	22*	0·3	1·75 = 1·45	0·6	0·7	0·79	0·33
B/L ratios specialized flakes	10	0·3	0·75 = 0·45	0·5	0·54	0·55	0·12

* Approximate length only recorded for one flake and no breadth recorded for three others.

Although it produced so few artifacts, Bed 11 here contains a very similar collection of implements to that in the overlying layer with a slight, but noticeable decrease in the average size of the flakes and in the number of broken flake fragments. There is also a noticeable increase in the percentage of abraded artifacts when compared with the aggregate from Bed 4. Because the collection is so small, it is not possible to be certain whether the degree of variability that can be seen is such as can be expected within aggregates comprising the Hillslope component of the Polungu Industry. More probably this collection should be given separate status for it is clearly older than that from the downslope part of the red soil and would, thus, form an earlier aggregate of this component. If a more complete sample had been available it would have been possible to see more clearly its precise relationship to the aggregates from the Red Rubble and also that which it bears to the Rubble component of the Polungu Industry. Such limited comparisons as are possible suggest that they have little in common.

Although the flake classes from the grey, pisolitic clay (Bed 11) show no very significant differences from those excavated in 1959 from the lower levels in the red soil (Bed 4), the trimmed and utilized artifacts recovered do, however, extend the known range of the utilized category to include the dimple-scarred rubber and pigment (haematite and specularite). The *limace*-type core-axe from the collapsed deposit in Pit 2 is another possible, though less likely addition.

Only the more complete aggregates from the five levels in Bed 4 excavated in 1959 have been used, therefore, for the description of the Hillslope component of the Polungu Industry.

THE AGGREGATE FROM THE A4 EXCAVATION, 1959, BEDS 7 AND 9 (FIGURE 22; SEE ALSO VOLUME I, PLATE 20)

Bed 7, exposed in grid squares 6–21, is a light grey, very sandy clay (or clayey sand), the sand content increasing at the north end of the excavation. It forms the basal deposit in an erosion channel cut down into the ferruginous, cross-bedded sands of Bed 12 which, in turn, overlies Rubble I. No discordance was noted between Bed 7 and the overlying brown clays containing pottery and other Early Iron Age artifacts but the contact with the underlying sands is abrupt and may represent an erosion surface, though it might equally well be conformable on the sands (Volume I: 125). Upslope to the south, Bed 7 either grades into the grey, sandy clay or clayey sand with the Polungu artifacts (Bed 11) or is banked against it. No direct contact was observed, however, since the buff sand (Bed 10) is interposed: Bed 10 is believed to be contemporaneous with Bed 11 of which it forms a lateral facies.

In grid squares 6–16, Bed 7 is found at from 10–12 feet (3–3·7 m) below the surface. In squares 17–21, where it overlies the bank of the old channel, it lies between 10 feet (3 m) at the lower and north end, rising at the south end to 5 feet 6 inches (168 cm) below the surface at grid square 21. Intermediate in age between Bed 7 and Bed 12 appears to be a sandy, gritty layer (Bed 9) and a lens of grey clay (Bed 9′) at the north end of the excavation in grid squares 2 to −2; this sand also contains a small number of stone artifacts.

Bed 7 was at first thought to be the basal deposit of the mottled brown clays and sands of the Chiungu Member. Since, however, this grey, sandy clay contained no pottery and was of a somewhat lighter texture than the overlying clays with the Iron Age artifacts, it seems probable that it may have been either contemporary with the final stage of the Polungu Industry in the red soil upslope or be later but pre-Iron Age in date. The number of artifacts contained in Bed 7 falls off sharply north of grid line 17 and the majority are found in the grey, clayey sand and buff-white sand (Bed 10) into which this grades near the top of the channel bank. The white sand in grid squares 20–21 contained 33 artifacts in the 5 foot 6 inches to 6 foot (168–183 cm) level and 9 between 6 feet and 6 feet 6 inches (183–198 cm). In the next three grid squares to the north, the grey, clayey sand and white sand contained 37 artifacts at a depth of 5 feet 6 inches to 6 feet (168–183 cm). Between 6 feet and 6 feet 6 inches (183 and 198 cm), the number was 21 and between 6 feet 6 inches and 7 feet (198 and 213 cm) there were 12. North of grid line 17 only two stone artifacts are recorded from Bed 7; one at 6 feet to 6 feet 6 inches (183–198 cm) and the other at 12 feet 6 inches to 13 feet (3·7–4·0 m). The artifacts contained in these beds are shown in Table 20. The artifacts are not in primary context and the majority are abraded and derived from earlier beds higher up the slope and belong with older cultural entities. The few slightly abraded and fresh artifacts are generally representative of those found in Beds 4 and 11 belonging to the Polungu Industry. They are classified as follows:

Shaped tools	
Unifacial point	1
Unmodified waste	
Flakes	
Unspecialized – irregular end-struck, plain platform	13
Specialized – Levallois point, faceted platform, one-directional flaking	3
Levallois flake, S/Q, faceted platform, one-directional flaking	1
Levallois flake, Irr/end, faceted platform, one-directional flaking	2
Levallois flake, Irr/end, faceted platform, radial flaking	2
Levallois blade, faceted platform radial flaking	1
Blade fragments	3
Cores	
Blade, one-directional flaking	2
Formless, two platforms	1
Flake fragments	1
Chunks	1
Total	31

All but two of the unspecialized flakes are less than 50 mm long; the Levallois points are 50, 38 and 35 mm long, respectively; the short quadrilateral is 76 mm and the other two Levallois flakes have lengths of 62 mm and 30 mm.

Besides the small Levallois points with simple and multi-faceted platforms, the most interesting artifact is the finely retouched, asymmetric, unifacial point (Plate 49: 1) in chert from a depth of 5 feet 6 inches to 6 feet (168–183 cm) in grid squares 20–21. The retouch is marginal to semi-invasive, scalar with some step flaking at the proximal end; on the left, lateral edge this retouch is inclined at a high angle for the greater part of the length. This tool is unabraded and measures 63 × 24 × 8 mm. It is longer than the mean flake length for retouched tools and utilized pieces and the retouch is more regular and elaborate than that found with the Hillslope component. In these attributes it compares more closely with the component from Rubble I and it could be derived from this where it was exposed at the base of Beds 7 and 10 in these grid squares.

The abraded series from Beds 7 and 10 comprise 44 irregular flakes with plain striking platforms, one triangular flake, 4 radially prepared, Levallois flakes and 6 with parallel flaking; 6 bladelet fragments, 5 blade cores and 6 specialized cores, 5 with radial flaking the other a Levallois point core; 4 chips and chunks. Shaped tools consist of one 'Sangoan-type' hand-axe in feldspathic quartzite, a stubby pick on a block of hard quartzite, a bifacially trimmed flake and a thick, bifacial point, both in chert.

At the north end of the A4 Trench, several abraded and a few slightly abraded to fresh artifacts were found in the fine, brown, gritty sand (Bed 9). Together with some 20 abraded flakes was one triangular-sectioned pick. One longitudinally split and broad, end-struck flake in hard quartzite and three broken bladelets in chert are fresh as also is one diminutive Levallois point with multi-faceted striking platform and steep to blunt marginal retouch at the proximal end of the two lateral edges (Plate 49: 2). This type of retouch has already been noted as being present in the Hillslope component; it has not yet been found with the Rubble component in this form unassociated with more elaborate modification on other parts of the tool and may, therefore, be more characteristic of the later component.

The composition of the Hillslope component of the Polungu Industry

Figure 24 shows the composition of this component when the counts for all fresh and slightly abraded artifacts from Levels 1–5 in Bed 4 are combined. Abraded and derived artifacts have not been included and the only tools in the abraded group calling for comment – all large – are three choppers, one in chert and two in hard quartzite; a very abraded core-scraper, also in hard quartzite; and a convergent-ended core-axe of Sangoan type in the same material which would appear to be a manuport. There is no appreciable difference in the percentages of raw materials used between the abraded and fresh/slightly abraded groups, namely:

	Fresh and slightly abraded (%)	Abraded (%)
Chert	94·1	85·5
Hard quartzite	3·35	10·9
Feldspathic quartzite	1·5	1·9
Quartz	0·4	0·3
Chalcedony	0·05	—
Silcrete	0·6	1·4

TABLE 20. *Artifacts, mostly from Grey, sandy clay (Bed 7) and underlying sands (Beds 9 and 12) above Rubble I, A4 Excavation, 1959*

		Fresh condition													
		Raw materials					Lengths in mm				Flake platforms				
Artifact classes	Total no.	Ch	Qz	F/Q	SSt	O	<31	31–60	61–90	>90	Pl	S/F	M/F	None	?
SHAPED TOOLS															
Large cutting/scraping															
Hand-axes															
Cleavers															
Knives															
Lanceolates															
Large scrapers															
Total															
Heavy duty															
Chisels															
Picks															
Core-axes															
Choppers															
Round-ended biface															
Core scrapers															
Spheroid															
Total															
Light duty															
Microliths															
Truncated flakes/blades															
Backed flakes/blades															
Points – unifacial	1	1							1			1			
bifacial															
Burins															
Proto-burins (1 + scraper)															
Small scrapers															
Total	1	1							1			1			
Total	1	1							1			1			
MODIFIED TOOLS															
Trimmed chunk															
Trimmed flake – dorsal															
ventral															
Bifacially trimmed chunk															
Bifacially trimmed flake															
(Utilized)															
Total															
UTILIZED TOOLS															
Flake/blade	1	1						1						1	
Flake fragment															
Chunks															
(Cores)															
Outils esquillés															
Anvils – split cobble															
block															
Hammerstone															
Total	1	1						1						1	

TABLE 20 (*cont.*)

	Slightly abraded/weathered condition														
		Raw materials					Lengths in mm				Flake platforms				
Artifact classes	Total no.	Ch	Qz	F/Q	SSt	O	<31	31–60	61–90	>90	Pl	S/F	M/F	None	?
SHAPED TOOLS															
Large cutting/scraping															
Hand-axes															
Cleavers															
Knives															
Lanceolates															
Large scrapers															
Total															
Heavy duty															
Chisels															
Picks															
Core-axes															
Choppers															
Round-ended biface															
Core scrapers															
Spheroid															
Total															
Light duty															
Microliths															
Truncated flakes/blades															
Backed flakes/blades															
Points – unifacial	1	1						1				1			
bifacial															
Burins															
Proto-burins (1 + scraper)															
Small scrapers	1	1						1							1
Total	2	2						2				1			1
Total	2	2						2				1			1
MODIFIED TOOLS															
Trimmed chunk															
Trimmed flake – dorsal															
ventral															
Bifacially trimmed chunk															
Bifacially trimmed flake															
(Utilized)															
Total															
UTILIZED TOOLS															
Flake/blade															
Flake fragment															
Chunks															
(Cores)															
Outils esquillés															
Anvils – split cobble	1		1							1					
block															
Hammerstone															
Total	1		1							1					

TABLE 20 (*cont.*)

	Abraded/weathered condition															
		Raw materials					Lengths in mm				Flake platforms					
Artifact classes	Total no.	Ch	Qz	F/Q	SSt	O	<31	31–60	61–90	>90	Pl	S/F	M/F	None	?	Total
SHAPED TOOLS																
Large cutting/scraping																
Hand-axes	2			2						2						2
Cleavers																
Knives																
Lanceolates																
Large scrapers																
Total	2			2						2						2
Heavy duty																
Chisels																
Picks	2		2							2						2
Core-axes	1			1					1							1
Choppers																
Round-ended biface																
Core scrapers																
Spheroid																
Total	3		2	1					1	2						3
Light duty																
Microliths																
Truncated flakes/blades																
Backed flakes/blades																
Points – unifacial																2
bifacial	1	1						1								1
Burins																
Proto-burins (1 + scraper)	2		2						1	1						2
Small scrapers																1
Total	3	1	2					1	1	1						6
Total	8	1	4	3				1	2	5						11
MODIFIED TOOLS																
Trimmed chunk	1	1							1							1
Trimmed flake – dorsal	1		1							1	1					1
ventral																
Bifacially trimmed chunk																
Bifacially trimmed flake	1	1						1							1	1
(Utilized)	(1)	(1)							(1)							(1)
Total	3	2	1					1	1	1	1				1	3
UTILIZED TOOLS																
Flake/blade	1	1					1				1					2
Flake fragment																
Chunks																
(Cores)																
Outils esquillés																
Anvils – split cobble																1
block	1	1							1							1
Hammerstone																
Total	2	2					1		1		1					4

TABLE 20 (*cont.*)

		Fresh condition													
		Raw materials					Lengths in mm				Flake platforms				
Artifact classes	Total no.	Ch	Qz	F/Q	SSt	O	<31	31–60	61–90	>90	Pl	S/F	M/F	None	?
Waste pieces – flakes															
Large primary															
Two bulbar faces															
Core-axe resharpening															
Trimming – end struck	4	1	3				2	2			3			1	
side struck	2	1	1					1		1	1				1
Parallel dorsal trimming															
Short quadrilateral	2	2						1	1			1	1		
Long quadrilateral															
Short triangular	2	2						2			1		1		
Long triangular															
Total	4	4						3	1		1	1	2		
Radial dorsal trimming															
Short quadrilateral	1				1					1			1		
Long quadrilateral															
Short triangular															
Long triangular															
Irregular	1	1					1						1		
Total	2	1			1		1			1			2		
Fragments															
Totals	12	7	4		1		3	6	1	2	5	1	4	1	1
Chips and chunks	1	1													
Cores															
Bashed chunk/cobble															
Formless (?condition)															
Protobiconical															
Biconical – high-backed															
biconvex															
Pyramidal															
Angle															
'Blade' – 1 platform															
2 platforms opposing															
1 platform-triangular															
Discoid – high-backed															
lenticular															
Sub-triangular – high-backed															
lenticular															
Struck discoid – high-backed															
lenticular															
Struck sub-triangular – high-backed															
lenticular															
Total															
TOTAL	15	10	4		1		3	7	3	2					

TABLE 20 (*cont.*)

	Slightly abraded/weathered condition														
		Raw materials					Lengths in mm				Flake platforms				
Artifact classes	Total no.	Ch	Qz	F/Q	SSt	O	<31	31–60	61–90	>90	Pl	S/F	M/F	None	?
Waste pieces – flakes															
Large primary															
Two bulbar faces															
Core-axe resharpening															
Trimming – end struck	12	8	3			1 Qtz.	4	4	3	1	2	1		1	8
side struck	10	7	3				1	5	4		2		2		6
Parallel dorsal trimming															
Short quadrilateral	2	2						2					2		
Long quadrilateral	1	1							1				1		
Short triangular	2	2						1	1		1	1			
Long triangular	1	1							1		1				
Total	6	6						3	3		2	1	3		
Radial dorsal trimming															
Short quadrilateral	1	1							1			1			
Long quadrilateral	1	1								1		1			
Short triangular															
Long triangular															
Irregular															
Total	2	2							1	1		2			
Fragments	9	9									1	1	1		
Totals	39	32	6			1	5	12	12	2	7	5	6	1	14
Chips and chunks	3	2	1				1	2							
												Flakes			
Cores											Prep. plat.	Tr.	Quad.	+ Cort.	Batt. base
Bashed chunk/cobble															
Formless (?condition)	1		1							1					
Protobiconical															
Biconical – high-backed															
biconvex															
Pyramidal															
Angle															
'Blade' – 1 platform															
2 platforms opposing															
1 platform-triangular															
												Trimming			
												D>V	D/V		
Discoid – high-backed															
lenticular	1	1						1				1		1	
Sub-triangular – high-backed															
lenticular															
Struck discoid – high-backed															
lenticular															
Struck sub-triangular – high-backed															
lenticular															
Total	2	1	1					1		1					
TOTAL	47	37	9			1	6	17	11	4					

TABLE 20 (*cont.*)

	Abraded/weathered condition															
		Raw materials					Lengths in mm				Flake platforms					
Artifact classes	Total no.	Ch	Qz	F/Q	SSt	O	<31	31–60	61–90	>90	Pl	S/F	M/F	None	?	Total
Waste pieces – flakes																
Large primary	1		1							1					1	1
Two bulbar faces																
Core-axe resharpening																
Trimming – end struck	46	34	11		1		10	26	10		10	4	1	2	29	63
side struck	21	11	8	1	1		1	15	5		5	2	1		13	33
Parallel dorsal trimming																
Short quadrilateral	6	5			1			5	1		1	5				10
Long quadrilateral	5	5						2	2	1	2	3				6
Short triangular	1	1						1			1					5
Long triangular	3	3							2	1	1	2				4
Total	15	14			1			8	5	2	5	10				25
Radial dorsal trimming																
Short quadrilateral	2	1	1					2			2					4
Long quadrilateral																1
Short triangular	5	4			1			5				4	1			5
Long triangular																
Irregular	3	3						2	1			2	1			4
Total	10	8	1		1			9	1		2	6	2			14
Fragments	4	3		1				1								13
Totals	97	70	21	2	4		11	59	21	3	24	22	4	2	43	148
Chips and chunks	18	12	5		1		3	10	5							22
												Flakes				
											Prep. Plat.	Tri.	Quad.	+ Cort.	Batt. base	
Cores																
Bashed chunk/cobble																
Formless (?condition)																1
Protobiconical																
Biconical – high-backed	1	1						1								1
biconvex																
Pyramidal																
Angle																
'Blade' – 1 platform																
2 platforms opposing																
1 platform-triangular																
												Trimming				
												D>V	D/V			
Discoid – high-backed	1	1							1			1		1		1
lenticular																1
Sub-triangular – high-backed lenticular	1	1							1			?				1
Struck discoid – high-backed lenticular	2	2						2			1	2		2		2
Struck sub-triangular – high-backed lenticular																
Total	5	5						3	2		1					7
TOTAL	133	92	31	5	5		15	73	32	9						195

The increased percentage of abraded artifacts in hard quartzite should, however, be noted.[1]

Figure 24 shows that the Hillslope component from the A4 Trench consists mostly of unmodified waste with only 1·1 per cent of shaped tools and three times as many utilized pieces. The utilized category could assume greater importance if it could be shown that a greatly reduced number of formally shaped tools was a characteristic of the Polungu industry and perhaps also more generally in southern Africa at this time.

SHAPED TOOLS (36)

Microliths (3) (Plate 44: 2; Plate 45: 19)
These are clearly a poorly represented class and there is no indication from broken segments or technical evidence that microliths (backed bladelets or small backed flakes) were common tools and regularly manufactured. This could mean that the component dates to the beginning of the time in northern Zambia when microliths began to become important or, alternatively, it may simply emphasize that, their manufacture being a specialized activity, the resulting scatter was very localized. The three examples are comparatively poorly made, or unfinished; one is a lunate and the other two obliquely backed. One of the latter (Plate 44: 2) is unfinished and should, perhaps, be classed as a non-microlithic tool although its length is just under 50 mm. The retouch is characteristic of that found on the larger backed blades and microliths occurring with aggregates of 'Second Intermediate' age. It consists of many small, scaled flakes struck from the ventral face as in normal backing so that the proximal ends of the scars start to curl over onto the dorsal face. This results in a blunter, less steep appearance to the backing which still, however, generally shows a near 90° angle if the average measurement taken is that of the angle formed by the last two to three millimetres on the dorsal face with the ventral plane.

Points (5) (Plate 45: 5)
Together with the short triangular flakes with multi-faceted striking platforms, these are the most characteristic artifacts of the aggregate. All five examples are unifacial and sub-triangular in plan form. The retouch is minimal and marginal and is composed of very small scalar and some step flaking on the dorsal face, placed on one or both lateral edges towards the pointed, distal end and sometimes also at the proximal end to round off the angular intersection between the striking platform and the lateral edges. The primary flaking on the dorsal face is both one-directional/convergent and radial.

These points grade into the class of short triangular flakes or Levallois points (see also p. 189 below), some of which show marginal 'nibbling' resulting from utilization. A characteristic of these points and flakes is the thick, multi-faceted (more rarely, simple faceted) striking platform which gives the artifact a wedge-shaped section along a line from the distal point to the mid-point of the *talon*. It appears likely that this flake form is the result of design rather than simply a product of the flaking technique used, and the broad, flat butt would provide greater resistance to shattering, if the artifact were used as the point of a projectile, and a more efficient seating for the artifact when mounted for use. Most of these flakes do not show evidence of retouch or utilization, although a proportion show either or both such kinds of modification. They are considered, therefore, to represent a special kind of end-product which might subsequently be given minimal retouch to produce a more regular shape but which were normally used untrimmed.

Scrapers (17)
With the exception of the two small convex ('thumbnail') scrapers, these tools show little attempt at regularity of plan form and may be made indiscriminately on flakes, flake fragments, chunks and cores. The retouch is marginal and semi-invasive and is rarely continuous or regular along the full length of an edge. These are, therefore, mostly informal rather than formal tools. The majority have one, trimmed, lateral edge. Concave, notched and denticulate edges account for eight of these tools, the remainder having straight to convex trimming.

(i) *On flakes and flake fragments* (7) (Plate 43: 1; Plate 45: 12; and Plate 47: 9). The seven scrapers made on flakes and flake fragments have irregular plan forms and may be trimmed on one, or both lateral edges and the end. The end-scraper on the blade (Plate 43: 1) is the best made example in the

[1] Kleindienst has suggested that, since the percentage of chert artifacts in the abraded category is comparable to that of the flake samples in the top of the Red Rubble (Bed 14) and the rubble at A2, they may possibly relate to the Rubble component of the Polungu Industry though, for the present, they have not been included with this.

group. Another specimen is worked on both lateral edges at the distal end to form an asymmetric, double side or convergent scraper (Plate 47: 9). The double concave scraper (Plate 45: 12) is made on a Levallois flake with one-directional dorsal scar pattern and a simple-faceted striking platform. The angle of retouch ranges from shallow to steep.

(ii) *On cores and chunks* (8) (Plate 43: 14, 15; Plate 44: 10–12; and Plate 46: 16). It is generally cores rather than chunks that show scraper retouch. Any convenient edge appears to have been used and no particular pattern to the trimming is discernible. The steep- or core-scraper on a chunk is a class of tool present in all the industries at the Kalambo Falls and is characteristic of the cultural traditions in the woodland savanna regions of Equatoria and west Africa. The angle of retouch is generally steep and there is usually a preponderance of step flaking.

The examples at Plate 44 nos. 10 and 11 were made on chunks and leave little doubt that they were correctly classified as scrapers. A problem arises, however, with regard to those made on cores. For example, the discoid core at Plate 43: 14 shows careful convex trimming on two parts of the circumference, one of which the writer would now classify as a nosed-scraper edge. The discoid core at Plate 43: 12 shows two similar, steeply trimmed edges. The examples at Plate 43: 15 and Plate 46: 16 are, however, small blade cores, the former showing the same kind of edge trimming and the latter having the platform trimmed. That larger blade cores, in addition to the small ones, were sometimes used as scrapers is shown by the core resharpening spalls in the collection (Plate 43: 12; Plate 45: 6, 7; and Plate 47: 5). Each of these shows regular and continuous trimming of the edge of the striking platform, much of which is made up of very small step fractures. Although the trimming on these artifacts shows the characteristics of a scraper edge, it is possible, in the case of the discoids, that this represents the preparation of a platform for the removal of a flake which would, thus, have a multi-faceted platform. In the case of the blade cores, it appears more likely that this retouch represents preparation of the platform edge as a necessary preliminary to the removal of flakes by the punch technique. This is especially so in view of the recent experimental work of Crabtree[1] and Bordes (1967: 43–4) which shows the importance of this preparation for the successful removal of blades by the punch method.

(iii) *Small convex* (2) (Plate 43: 8; Plate 47: 13). In one case a flake and in the other a chunk was selected and the edge regularly retouched. It is unfortunate that no more of these tools were found as they appear to be the only 'formal' type of scraper with the collection. In particular, the example at Plate 43: 8 recalls similar small scrapers from the aggregate (described as 'Rhodesian Magosian') of terminal Pleistocene age from the Victoria Falls (Clark, 1950*a*: 102–7) and from the Pomongwan in Rhodesia (Cooke, 1963: 97–100).

Burins (3)
Two are single blow burins on snapped flake fragments; the third is a simple burin with two oblique burin facets formed on the broken half of a flake (*burin d'angle sur cassure d'éclat*). When such forms occur sporadically in larger collections they are usually considered to be fortuitous and not deliberately made. In the present case, because of the small number of shaped tools, it is not possible to be certain.

Proto-burins (7) (Plate 44: 11)
These are made on small chunks. The modification consists of two or more larger scars and several small step flakes and crushing on one face, opposed to a single fracture plane on the other, or to the thickness of an edge. Such artifacts might have been used as adze blades or chisels.

Miscellaneous (1) (Plate 46: 6)
This is a short quadrilateral flake with one-directional dorsal scar pattern and faceted striking platform, struck from a specialized core. It has been partially retouched by steep trimming and backing along the proximal half of one lateral edge. Other examples with retouch of this kind at the proximal end are known with the Polungu Industry (e.g. Plate 45: 5; Plate 49: 2) and may be considered characteristic as a preliminary to hafting. This artifact might, therefore, be classified with the points or triangular flakes but, since it is the only example from this aggregate and its form is only generally 'pointlike' it has been classified separately here.

[1] 'Blades and Pressure Flaking', 1969, University of California, Extension Media Film Unit, 16 mm film no. 744, with demonstration by François Bordes and Donald Crabtree.

UTILIZED/MODIFIED ARTIFACTS (88)

Flakes, blades and fragments (70)
These constitute the largest group of modified pieces although, again, there is no regularity in the primary form selected or in the nature of the modification. Utilization, in the form of discontinuous, minute, marginal scarring ('nibbling') is present on some flakes and blades (Plate 43: 4, 5; Plate 45: 1, 8, 9; Plate 47: 7). Modification is minimal, discontinuous and marginally distributed (Plate 44: 4). On the blades, the utilization again takes the form of marginal 'nibbling' and is restricted and never continuous either on blades (Plate 47: 2, 3) or bladelets (Plate 44: 7; Plate 46: 3; Plate 47: 6). More invasive modification is similarly restricted to a small area on one or both lateral edges (Plate 43: 2, 13). The edge angle is generally shallow.

Chunks and cores (15)
These forms, with irregular edge modification, are either made on small chunks or on blade cores that show the removal of a single flake to form a notch, further modified by marginal crushing and occasional more invasive scarring (Plate 47: 12). On the other hand, they may show discontinuous modification in one or more places on one or more edges (Plate 47: 14).

Outils esquillés (2) (Plate 46: 13, 14)
Since chert in reasonably large sizes was the predominant raw material used, it is to be expected that this class of tool would not be very common. The two examples found are made respectively on a flake fragment (Plate 46: 13) and a flake. In both cases the splintering is unifacial, though in the first example both lateral edges have been utilized.

Dimple scarred anvil (1) (Plate 45: 22)
This is an ellipsoidal pebble of hard quartzite with a circular pitted area on one face and battering at both ends, consistent with its having been used as a combined anvil and hammerstone. Although this is the only example that was found *in situ*, it is of special interest since it suggests the use of a rest technique for flake and/or blade production, in which the lower end of the core rested on an anvil. Such stones appear to have served equally as hammers and anvils, as Van Riet Lowe noted in connection with the initial description of the bipolar technique in Africa (Van Riet Lowe, 1946).

UNMODIFIED WASTE (2755)
It is from the analysis of the debitage that the Hillslope component of the Polungu Industry can best be evaluated. The ratio of cores to flakes/blades is just over 1:14. Of the specifically blade cores, three produced, in addition, short quadrilateral and some irregular flake forms. If these proportions of flakes and blades to cores can be relied on, they seem somewhat high, in view of the Kaposwa Industry ratio of 1:30. It is, therefore, possible that some of the blades may have been selected and intentionally removed from the working floor before the debitage became dispersed.

Two main flaking methods occur – one for the production of flakes/blades and bladelets from prismatic cores and the other for specialized flakes from Levallois and discoid cores.

CORES (70)

(*a*) *Prismatic cores for the production of flakes and blades* (41·4 *per cent of cores*)
These are classified according to the nature of the platform and are flaked from one or two directions only. Almost half (45 per cent) have striking platforms intentionally faceted and formed by several scars or portions of scars. This is well seen in Plate 43: 10. Although these have been classed here as blade cores, it is debatable whether they might not, in fact, better be termed diminutive Levallois blade cores. A number of them have also had the platform edge trimmed by a series of small step flakes to remove irregularities that appear as blades are detached (Plate 43: 15; Plate 46: 18). The significance of this feature has already been discussed and it is believed to indicate that a punch of some kind was used. Further evidence for punch technique is seen in the platforms and proximal ends of some of the blades and flakes and in the more acute angle formed between the platform and the flaking surface of the core.

(i) *Single platform* (21) (Plate 43: 10, 15; Plate 44: 16; Plate 46: 16). In plan form these are mostly broad and short. Some with plain platforms are diminutive and identical with the 'micro-blade' cores of the Kaposwa Industry (e.g. Plate 44: 16; Plate 46: 16). The majority have faceted platforms. There is some slight evidence, in the form of bruising on the lower ends of these cores, that, when in use, they may have been rested on some kind of anvil. Flakes and blades from these cores may show faceted, plain or point platforms.

(ii) *Two platforms* (8)

(1) *Opposed platforms* (5) (Plate 46: 17). These are not bipolar cores in the sense that they were struck by bipolar technique. They are made on tabular blocks of chert and have plain striking platforms. The two flakes at Plate 45: 14, 15 show that cores of this type may have been used more specifically for the production of long, broad, bladelike flakes.

(2) *Platforms at right angles* (3) (Plate 46: 18; Plate 47: 14). These are chunky forms and the platforms may be on the same face (Plate 47: 14) or on two faces at right-angles (Plate 46: 18); the striking platform is plain. In their form these cores anticipate the diminutive cores of this type that are one of the commonest forms with microlithic industries.

(*b*) *Specialized cores* (31) (44·4 per cent of cores)

These are all small with lengths mostly between 50 and 30 mm. There are two main forms: disc or discoid cores and Levallois point cores. Discoid cores have been classified as Levallois when they have been struck and one large flake removed. By reason of the small size of these cores, it is likely that they were all designed for the removal of a single flake only before being reprepared. It is not possible to determine if the unstruck examples were designed for the removal of one or several small flakes and they have, therefore, not been classified with the Levallois cores.

(i) *Levallois cores* (14) (Plate 44: 1, 6, 13, 15; Plate 46: 15; Plate 47: 15). The prepared release surface is generally flatter than the ventral face which may be flat (e.g. Plate 46: 15) or high-backed (e.g. Plate 44: 1). Two types are represented:

(*a*) *Radial Levallois* (5) (Plate 44: 15; Plate 46: 15; Plate 47: 15). These are more generally elliptic in plan and have the radial preparation on the dorsal face formed by a number of small, flat scars. The platform is multi-faceted and at a near right angle with the release surface and situated at the thickest end of the core. The flakes that were removed from these cores were generally small and broad.

(*b*) *Levallois point* (9) (Plate 44: 1, 6, 13). The release surface of these cores has been prepared, either by one-directional flaking from the proximal end or by opposed flaking, in which case they resemble the Nubian core (Type 1) found with the late Pleistocene industries on the Upper Nile (Guichard and Guichard, 1965: 68–9). The preparation may show a parallel or convergent scar pattern. The striking platform shows multi- or simple faceting. These cores are usually high-backed. They were designed to produce the characteristic broad, short, triangular flake, less commonly a short quadrilateral flake. The scar from the removal of the flake is deep at the bulbar end suggesting that this was done by hard hammer percussion. As stated above, some of the small blade cores might also be classed as 'unstruck' Levallois point cores. These cores are particularly interesting for the light they throw on the level of technological development of this aggregate.

(ii) *Disc, discoid* (17) (Plate 43: 14, 16; Plate 44: 12, 14, 17; Plate 46: 19, 20; Plate 47: 11). These are diminutive examples of a form of core with a long history in central Africa. Both flat and high-backed examples occur and the striking platforms are either plain or simple-faceted. The more traditional type in which the preparation is formed by several large, radially struck flakes, is present (Plate 47: 11) but more usually the prepared face shows a greater number of smaller flakes, radially removed (e.g. Plate 46: 19). In addition, there are examples which show a greater tendency for the preparation flakes to be struck from two directions. This is the case with the cores illustrated at Plate 43: 16; Plate 44: 17; Plate 46: 20. They suggest that attempts were being made at this time to adapt the specialized disc core to the production of bladelets and short quadrilateral flakes which were now becoming a preferred primary form.

Some of these flat disc cores, whether for Levallois flakes or not, show one or more areas of the circumference that have been more carefully trimmed on one or both faces. This is well seen at Plate 43: 14 and 16 and Plate 44: 15 and does not appear to be related to platform faceting or preparation. When the fact is taken into account that the industry appears to be without any heavy duty tools, it seems likely, as has previously been suggested (Clark, 1958: 149) that this retouch relates to preparation of the specimen for use as the blade of an adze or similar wood-working implement.

(*c*) *Other cores* (10) (14·2 per cent of cores)

(i) *Formless* (3). These are small, chunky cores with three or more platforms. They occur in every industry at the Kalambo Falls. Two have plain platforms and the third shows simple preparation of one platform.

Flake/blade form	No.	Platform types: Plain (%)	Faceted (S & M) (%)	Point (%)	Unrecorded (%)
Irregular – end-struck	562	56·8	27·4	14·6	1·2
– side-struck	167	53·5	31·25	15·25	—
Short quadrilateral	127	62·5	29·5	8·0	—
Long quadrilateral (blades)	74	49·25	21·25	13·25	16·25
Triangular	65	33·75	64·75	1·5	—
Total	995				

(ii) *Proto-biconical* (5). This is not a common form and represents, perhaps, the initial stage in the preparation of a discoid.

(iii) *Biconical* (2). Again, these may show a stage in the preparation of a disc core (later than that shown by the previous form). The platform is classed as faceted but in this type of core this is likely to be fortuitous.

Flakes (921) (31·8 per cent of all artifacts)
Flakes predominate over blades (74) by approximately 12:1. They are mostly irregular in plan form. Of the combined total of flakes and blades (995) side flakes comprise 16·6 per cent and short quadrilateral flakes and blades 20·2 per cent; of these 12·75 per cent are short quadrilateral flakes and 7·45 per cent true blades. Although triangular flakes comprise only 6·6 per cent of the flake/blade total they are, perhaps, the most significant form represented in the component. The striking platform types of the flakes and blades are shown in the table at the top of the page.

Blades, short quadrilateral and irregular, end-struck flakes have mostly plain striking platforms whereas the triangular flakes show predominantly simple- and multi-faceted platforms. Point platforms make up a small percentage and there are not significantly more with the blades than with the irregular flakes (or they would not have gone unrecorded). They are, however, clearly not a feature of the triangular flakes, a characteristic that must be directly related to the method of removing the flake. For a proportional sample of 100 flakes and 50 blades from Levels 1–4, the measurement details are given in the table below.

In general, therefore, both flakes and blades are of small size and lengths cluster between 30 and 50 mm. The average flake form is comparatively narrow while that of the blades and bladelets is comparatively broad. The relationship between flake form and dorsal scar patterns is shown on the following page.

Most of the irregular flakes show one- or two-directional patterns. As might be expected, short quadrilateral flakes and blades have mostly one-directional flaking from the proximal end but, also, between 23 per cent and 25 per cent have two-directional, opposed, flaking. The greatest con-

	No.	Range: Min.–Max.	Mode	Median	Mean	S.D.
Flakes						
Length	100	10–70 = 60	30	27	36·2 ± 0·13	13·1
Breadth	100	10–60 = 50	20	20	25·7 ± 0·96	9·6
Thickness	100	7·5–20 = 12·5	7·5	7·5	8·7 ± 0·23	2·3
B/L ratio	100	0·2–4·0 = 3·8	0·6	0·6	0·79 ± 0·04	0·42
Blades						
Length	50	20–80 = 60	50	50	48·6 ± 1·9	14·02
Breadth	50	10–35 = 25	20	20	17·8 ± 0·99	7·06
Thickness	50	7·5–20 = 12·5	7·5	7·5	8·4 ± 0·27	2·05
B/L ratio	50	0·2–0·5 = 0·3	0·4	0·4	0·39 ± 0·009	0·065

Percentages of dorsal scar patternings: flake blade sample from Levels 1–4

Flake/blade form	No.	One-dir.	(%)	Two-dir.	(%)	Multi-dir.	(%)	Unre-corded	(%)
Irregular, end-struck	363	171	47·0	107	29·5	68	18·75	17	4·75
Irregular, side-struck	167	68	41·5	56	33·0	37	22·0	6	3·5
Short quadrilateral	117	80	68·5	27	23·25	9	7·5	1	0·75
Blades	44	32	73·0	10	22·0	1	2·5	1	2·5
Triangular	49	38	78·0	5	10·0	5	10·0	1	2·0
Total	740	389		205		120		26	

sistency in one-directional flaking is found with the triangular flakes (78 per cent).

(i) *Irregular, end-struck flakes* (562) (56·6 per cent of flakes/blades). These include both Levallois (Plate 45: 12, 13, 20) and non-Levallois (Plate 46: 9, 10, 12, 14) flakes. Plain striking platforms appear to decrease with depth and point platforms show the reverse trend, suggesting increased use of the punch technique in Level 1. The flakes come both from blade and specialized cores.

(ii) *Irregular, side-struck flakes* (167) (16·6 per cent) (Plate 45: 21; Plate 46: 11). These tend towards forms where the length and breadth are nearly equal rather than to the very broad side-flake. They were produced from discoid, Levallois and blade cores. Plain striking platforms predominate.

(iii) *Short quadrilateral flakes* (127) (12·75 per cent). Most of these flakes show plain striking platforms and one-directional flaking (Plate 43: 4), indicating that they were mostly from single-platformed, blade-type cores. However, a smaller proportion have faceted platforms and are from Levallois cores, more usually with single direction or opposed flaking (Plate 44: 5; Plate 45: 9, 11, 17, 18; Plate 46: 7) coming from a core such as that illustrated at Plate 43: 10. Examples with radial dorsal preparation are less frequent but also occur (Plate 43: 3; Plate 44: 4; Plate 45: 16).

(iv) *Triangular flakes* (65) (6·6 per cent) (Plate 43: 5, 6, 9; Plate 45: 1–4, 8, 10; Plate 46: 4, 5, 8; Plate 47: 7, 8, 10). Although a small class, these are among the most distinctive artifacts in the component, as has been shown, and it is apparent that the specially selected primary form was intended for use with a minimal amount of further modification. The smaller examples are often wedge shaped in section along both short and long axes (e.g. Plate 43: 9; Plate 45: 2–4; Plate 46: 4, 5). Longer examples, and some smaller ones also, have a flatter cross-section and are diminutive Levallois points. In the majority of cases the platform is preserved across the full width of the flake so that the broadest part of the artifact is at the proximal end. The dorsal scar pattern is one-directional. As has been shown, these flakes are present in each of the four main levels.

(v) *Blades and bladelets* (74) (2·5 per cent of all artifacts; 7·45 per cent of flake forms). Blades over 50 mm long or greater in length are rare (Plate 46: 1; 47: 1–4) and the greater number have lengths of 50 mm and just below, so that they should be classified as bladelets (Plate 43: 7, 11; Plate 44: 3, 8, 9; Plate 46: 2; Plate 47: 6). They come from one- and two-platformed cores with parallel flaking, either from one direction or from opposite ends of a blade core. Platforms are usually plain (49·25 per cent) and often restricted or negligible (13·25 per cent). The latter group is of importance here since this is often a characteristic of punched blades.

Other waste (1690)
The total of 2,879 artifacts in the component is completed by 1,420 flake and blade fragments, mostly of chert and 270 chunks, also mostly of chert, none of which deserve any particular comment.

Discussion

Comparisons between the Hillslope component and other cultural entities from southern and east Africa falling within the estimated time range of the Polungu Industry are reserved for a later section (Chapter 8) following the description of the Rubble component. Although it occurs throughout some 2 feet (61 cm) to 2 feet 6 inches (76 cm) of red soil and sandy clay, the Hillslope component is a homogeneous aggregate and shows no cultural unconformity such as might be expected if the technology had undergone any significant changes during the time it was being made. A possible increase in blades in the top level and a possible reverse increase in specialized core forms (Levallois and disc) in the lower levels are the kind of changes to be expected if the lithic tradition had remained locally independent and unaffected by external influences, as that of the Hillslope is believed to have been. The time period covered by Beds 4 and 11 is unknown but it would not be unreasonable to expect that it may be reckoned in millennia rather than in centuries.

The component is characterized by a paucity of formal shaped tool classes and the few that are present are represented by only a small number of examples – microliths, convex, concave and end-scrapers, points and burins – all more usually informal rather than formal tools. Informality is again emphasized by the number of utilized and minimally modified pieces in the collection – flake and blade forms and chunky modified artifacts. The component consists essentially of light cutting equipment and makes use of primary flake forms which show none of the regular retouch associated with earlier traditions at the Kalambo Falls. At the same time, it is lacking in the dominant microlithic element that is a main feature of the Kaposwa Industry. Originally, this was interpreted as indicating that the component was incomplete since, because it was not derived from an occupation floor or floors but occurred dispersed throughout the cultural layer, this seemed the most likely explanation. However, the artifacts are generally in fresh condition throughout the bed and each of the four main levels contains the same artifact types. It is, therefore, necessary to suppose either that the deposit formed comparatively rapidly, the artifacts being incorporated from a single workshop area, or that the immediate locality remained in fairly constant use only as a flaking area for some considerable time. There is, however, no indication that Beds 4 and 11 formed very rapidly, rather the contrary. Moreover, it is reasonable to suppose that natural dispersal from a concentration area or areas adjacent and upslope would have produced significantly more shaped tools than are represented here if they had been present. It begins to appear more probable, therefore, that the lithic component may, in fact, be representative to a greater degree than was at first thought. That it is deficient in formal classes of retouched stone tools must not, of course, be taken as indicating that the equipment of the groups using the Kalambo basin at this time was in any way inadequate or lacking in efficiency. Rather does it suggest that stone was now being used in new and different ways and that other materials were also assuming new importance.

The tools and utilized pieces emphasize the functional importance of cutting over scraping or heavy duty equipment. Some of the flakes and blades could have been used as they are, but most of these artifacts are only some 50 mm long or less and it is difficult to see how they could have been effective unless they were mounted as the working parts of composite tools. The small blade forms might have been mounted singly or in serration but the small Levallois points and other specialized flake forms are morphologically suited to mounting on the end, rather than along one or more lateral edges of the haft. By the evidence of utilization they exhibit, some of the thin-sectioned examples might have formed effective knife blades. The triangular forms with intentionally thickened butt would, on the other hand, be more suitable for hafting and would better withstand shattering on impact. If this is so, then it raises the question of the kind of projectile they were intended for. The point at Plate 45: 5 might have served as the head of a small spear, while the small examples at Plate 43: 5 and 9 appear more suited for use as the heads of arrows. Although the earliest certain evidence for the use of the bow and arrow in central Africa belongs to the early third millennium B.C. (Fagan and Van Noten, 1971) there is, nevertheless, reason to believe that the technological changes to be seen in the local lithic industries from about the ninth millennium onwards may be related to the introduction of this new hunting weapon. Since, as has been shown, the Hillslope component is younger than 9550 ± 210 B.P. it is, therefore, not impossible that these small triangular points with minimal or no modification are among the earliest form of arrowhead in use in south central Africa. This is also consistent with the scarcity of microliths and the rather crude nature of the backing on those which do occur, indicating perhaps that the component belongs to a time when the microlith as a formal tool was just beginning to be made use of in this part of the Zambian savanna woodlands.

It is of interest that microliths mounted by means of mastic as barbs and points of arrows were used for hunting large and medium sized game and are known from actual specimens in early third millennium contexts in Egypt (with representations of these forms also in the fourth millennium) (Emery, 1961: 114). These compare very closely with examples of historic and late prehistoric arrowheads made by the Cape Bushmen in South Africa (Clark, 1959*a*), suggesting that this was one, generally universal way in which the microlith was used in Africa. If the small triangular points of the Polungu Hillslope component were, indeed, the heads of arrows, it is possible to regard them as an early form that was superseded by the more efficient methods of mounting and related traits that belong with the adoption of the arrowhead with mounted microliths.

By contrast with the light cutting and scraping equipment, heavy duty tools are conspicuous by their virtual absence. However, as has been suggested, the flat discoids with unifacial or bifacial retouch on one or more parts of the circumference, the artifacts with proto-burin modification and also the small convex scrapers and core-scrapers may, in fact, have fulfilled the role of the axe and other heavy duty equipment, if mounted as the functional ends of combination scraper/adzes and chisel tools.

The grinding equipment is represented by a single rubber but, since there is little difference between those found with the Siszya Industry in Rubble I and those with the microlithic Kaposwa Industry, its significance lies chiefly in its implications for the use that was made of seeds and grains.

Some form of applied art, if only painting of the body, is implicit in the presence of haematite and specularite.

As has been noted, the unmodified waste shows that two main techniques of flaking were in use. The one was designed to produce small, delicate flakes and triangular points made by the Levallois and disc core methods; the other was intended for the manufacture of blades and flakes from single- and double-platformed, prismatic cores. The preparation of the striking platform edge on the blade cores, the small and restricted bulb and platform and fine step scars at the proximal end on some blades and flakes, strongly suggests the use of a punch. Since broad flakes are an important percentage of flake forms, it may tentatively be suggested that a method related to that still in use in the headwaters of the Congo and Zambezi basins (see Chapter 4 and Plate 97) which produces rather similar broad flakes, may have been employed.

The Levallois flakes and points have thicker platforms and more prominent bulbs, indicating some form of direct percussion technique. In view of the composite anvil and hammerstone (Plate 45: 22) it is possible that some form of bipolar technique was used and the flake detached by resting the lower end of the core on the anvil and striking the upper, faceted, end with a small, elongate stone hammer. However, many of the platforms are both broad and thin so that it seems more probable that, if a rest method was used, the core was reversed and the striking platform was rested on the edge of the anvil and struck from above with a stone or hardwood hammer that detached the flake by indirect percussion. Conceivably, also, the flake might have been detached by a direct blow on the platform with a stone punch. Experiment is necessary to show which, if any, of these suggestions is the more likely. Previous experiment using both indirect and direct methods have resulted in the flake's fracturing as it is detached. A greater degree of success can be expected, however, if the core is wrapped before it is struck so that the force is more shallowly diffused, thus preventing the flake from shattering. The effectiveness of wrapping the hand-held core with bark when striking flakes by bipolar technique has been demonstrated by White (1968*b*) describing the practice of the aborigines of the New Guinea Highlands and it seems likely that this may have been another basic and ancient trait, independently adopted by prehistoric populations whenever the need arose.

If, therefore, the Hillslope component is generally representative of the range of stone artifacts being manufactured in the local basin in the earlier Holocene, it can be interpreted as a stage in the readjustment that followed the diffusion or invention of new technological traits relating to the development of composite tools more especially, perhaps, to the bow and arrow, and the new hunting and collecting behaviour these imply.

CHAPTER 7

The Polungu Industry: the Rubble component

The artifacts that form this component are mostly in fresh condition and are never very numerous in any of the excavations. Besides the aggregates from the base of the bedded sands that overlie Rubble I, they are found on Rubble I where it is composite, on Rubble Ia and Ib and even associated with rubble tentatively correlated with the Pits Channel Fill at the A2, 1956, Excavation, where this had been temporarily exposed by erosion and hillwash prior to the reblocking of the Spillway Gorge that raised the base level and initiated the later phase of filling when the bedded sands of the Mbwilo Member were deposited.

The identification of industrial components in Rubble I and related sands, rests upon the use of several interconnected lines of evidence, the correlation of which is sometimes complicated. In order to make clearer the criteria and the procedure used for component identification, together with the description of the individual artifact sets that constitute what has been named here the Rubble component of the Polungu Industry, the sections and sub-sections into which the discussion is divided are listed below:

A. Aggregates from the current-bedded sands over Rubble I, Mbwilo Member.

B. Aggregates from Rubble I, Mbwilo Member:

1. Mode and agencies of deposition of rubbles and artifacts.
2. Identification of artifact sets.
3. Categories of abrasion and correlation with artifact sets.
4. Direct and indirect dating evidence.
5. Basis for identification of industrial component.
6. An example in component identification: aggregates from Site B2, 1959: Rubble Ia.
7. Description of artifact sets in fresh condition from other Rubble I aggregates:

(*a*) Site A aggregates – A1, 1956, Rubble Ib; A3, 1956, Rubble Ia; A3, 1956, Rubble Ib and c composite; A4, 1959, Rubble I (composite).

(*b*) Site B aggregates – B1, 1956, Rubble I (composite); B2, 1959, Rubble Ia; B2, 1959, from bedded sands and grits between Rubbles Ia and Ib; B2, 1959, Rubble Ib.

(*c*) Site D aggregates – D1, 1956, Rubble I (composite).

C. Aggregates from Site A, Excavation A2, 1956 ?Pits Channel Rubble.

D. Definition of the Rubble component of the Polungu Industry.

A. Aggregates from the current-bedded sands (filling phase F. 6) immediately overlying Rubble I; Mbwilo Member

The next stratigraphically earlier aggregates, predating those contained in the hillslope soil and clay in the A4 Trench, are found in the base of the current-bedded sands – Bed 12 – of the Mbwilo Member, generally in association with a discontinuous pebble line. These sands are represented in all the excavations in the local basin except in the pits in the swamp at Site B and in the auger hole through the low terrace opposite Site A. The upper levels have usually been removed by erosion, as at Sites A and B, but they are preserved at Site C where the total thickness recorded was *c*. 30–32 feet (9·1–9·7 m) overlying Rubble I and, at Site D, where the measured thickness over Rubble I (composite) was *c*. 11 feet (3·3 m). Artifacts are found only in the basal levels of these sands at Sites A1, 1956; B1, 1956 and at Site C, 1956 where most of them occur in association with an intermittent scatter of small pebbles. These horizons are believed to represent the surfaces of temporary sandbanks that were seasonally exposed within the river channel at the beginning of the aggradation phase initiated by the blocking of the Spillway Gorge. The base of these pebble lines (A1, 1956: Bed 8a; B1,

TABLE 21. *Artifacts from pebble lines at base of current – bedded sands overlying Rubble Ib, Mbwilo Member, Excavation A1, 1956 (Bed 8a) and over Rubble I (composite), Excavation B1, 1956 (Beds 8 and 7′)*

		Length		Raw material						Flake platform					Length		Raw material						Flake platform					Length		Raw material						Flake platform				
Site A1, 1956	Fresh	> 100 mm	< 100 mm	Chert	H/Q	F/Q	Qz	Chal	Sil	Plain	Simple faceted	Multi-faceted	Point	Slightly abraded	> 100 mm	< 100 mm	Chert	H/Q	F/Q	Qz	Chal	Sil	Plain	Simple faceted	Multi-faceted	Point	Abraded	> 100 mm	< 100 mm	Chert	H/Q	F/Q	Qz	Chal	Sil	Plain	Simple faceted	Multi-faceted	Point	Total all artifacts
Shaped tools																																								
Cleaver																											1	1			1									1
Core-axe														1	1			1																						1
Core-axe resharpening flake														1		1		1																						1
Small scrapers														1		1	1																							1
Total shaped tools														3	1	2	1	2									1	1			1									4
Utilized/modified pieces																																								
Flakes														2		2	1					1	2				2	1	1		1	1				2				4
Chunks																																								
Total utilized/modified														2		2	1					1	2				2	1	1		1	1				2				4
Unmodified waste																																								
Flakes																																								
Irregular	7		7	6	1					5	1		1	32	1	31	32						14	16		2	28	3	25	14	7	1			6	11	13	4		67
Short quadrilateral	1		1	1						1				3		3		2				1	1	2			6		6	5		1					4	1	1	10
Triangular														1	1							1		1																1
Long quadrilateral														3		3	3						2			1														3
Cores																																								
Formless																											1		1	1						1				1
Specialized, high-backed																											1		1	1								1		1
Flake and blade fragments	41	1	40	27	11	1			2																															41
Chunks	5	1	4	2	3																																			5
Total unmodified waste	54	2	52	36	15	1			2	6	1		1	39	2	37	35	2				2	17	19		3	36	3	33	21	7	2			6	12	17	6	1	129
Total all artifacts	54	2	52	36	15	1			2					44	3	41	37	4				3					39	5	34	21	9	3			6					137
Site B1, 1956																																								
Shaped tools																																								
Core-axe resharpening flake														1		1	1									1														1
Truncated blade/flakes														1		1	1									1														1
Unifaced points	1		1	1									1																											1
Small scrapers														2		2	2									2	1		1	1									1	3
Total shaped tools	1		1	1									1	4		4	4									4	1		1	1									1	6
Utilized/modified pieces																																								
Flakes														1		1				1						1	4		4	3	1								4	5
Chunks																											1		1	1									1	1
Total utilized/modified														1		1				1						1	5		5	4	1								5	6
Unmodified waste																																								
Flakes																																								
Irregular	17	1	16	8	6	2			1	11	6			21		21	16	3			1	1	5	12		4	30		30	11	7	10	2			22	6		2	68
Short quadrilateral	5		5	4	1					3	2			4		4	2	1				1	2	2			7		7	4	1	2				7				16
Triangular	1		1			1				1				1		1			1				1				4		4	3		1				4				6
Long quadrilateral	3		3	3						2	1			2		2	2						1	1			1		1			1				1				6
Cores																																								
Biconical														1	1			1					1																	1
Opposed platform, blade	1		1	1						1																														1
Specialized, high-backed														4	1	3	3	1						4			2		2	1					1			2		6
Total waste with recorded physical condition	27	1	26	16	7	3			1	18	9			33	2	31	23	6	1		1	2	10	19		4	44		44	19	8	14	2		1	34	6	2	2	104
Flake and blade fragments																																								45
Chunks																																								129
Total unmodified waste	27	1	26	16	7	3			1	18	9			33	2	31	23	6	1		1	2	10	19		4	44		44	19	8	14	2		1	34	6	2	2	278
Total all artifacts	28	1	27	17	7	3			1					38	2	36	27	6	1	1	1	2					50		50	24	9	14	2		1					290

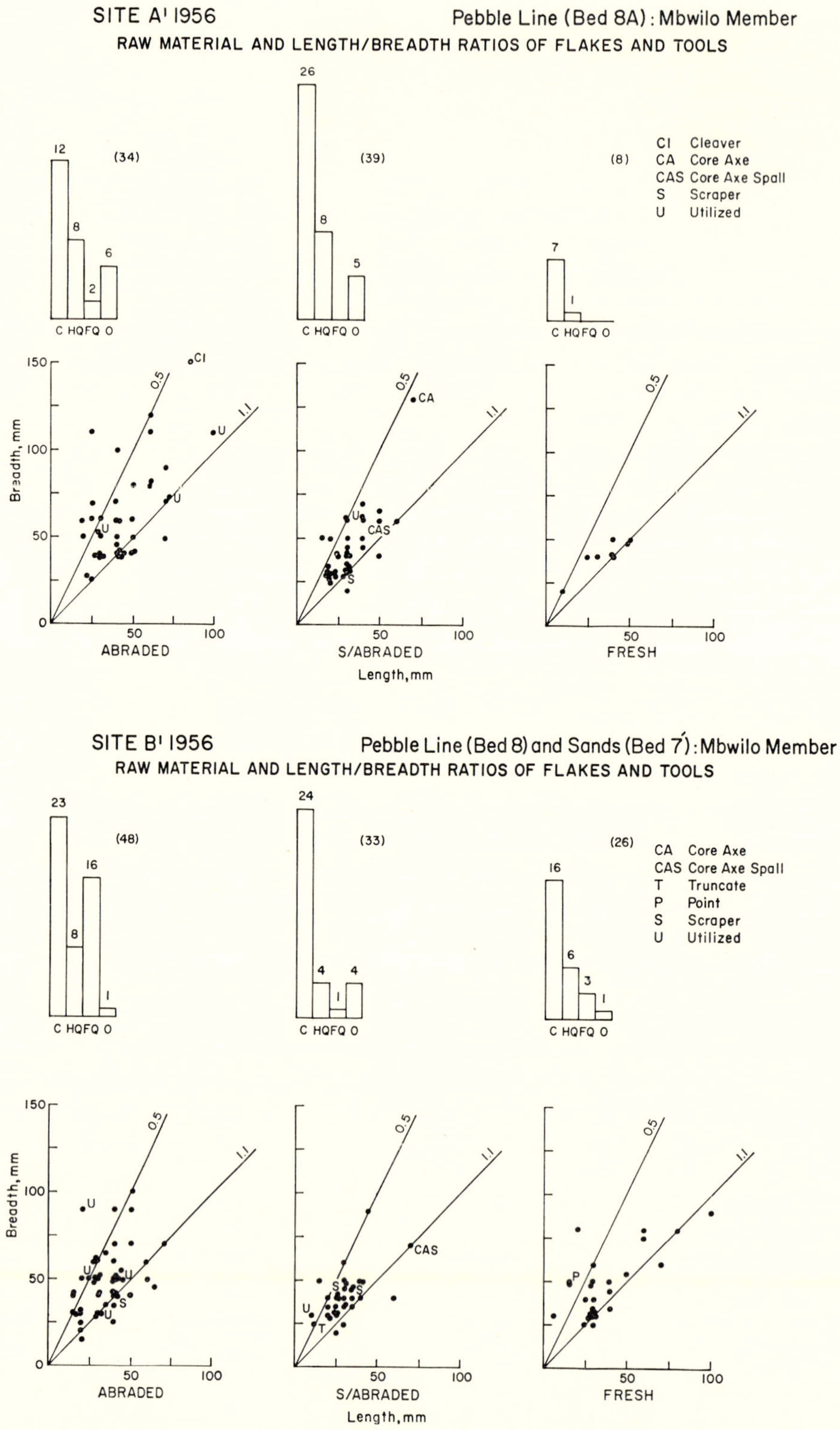

Fig. 25. Raw material and breadth/length ratios of flakes and tools from pebble lines over the base of the current-bedded sands of the Mbwilo Member, Site A1, 1956, Bed 8a and Site B1, 1956, Beds 8 and 7′.

Key:

C = Chert
HQ = Hard quartzite
FQ = Feldspathic quartzite
O = Other

1956, Bed 8) usually lie not more than 12 inches (30 cm), sometimes less above Rubble I[1] and both abraded, fresh and very slightly abraded artifacts are associated. The fresh material has clearly not been moved very far and is believed to represent the kind of scatter that would relate to transient occupation. It exhibits some primary and minimal secondary flaking that might have been executed by groups searching for raw material in the rubble exposed in the adjacent channel bed. These artifacts are likely to be very nearly contemporary with the latest occurring in Rubble I, if they are not derived from it – the most probable source also for the slightly abraded and abraded artifacts. The counts of artifacts from these sands (Beds 8 and 8a) in Excavation A1, 1956 (Volume 1: 94–5, Figure 20) and from Excavation B1, 1956 (Beds 7, 7′) (Volume 1: 157, Figure 35) are set out in Table 21.

In spite of the proximity of the Rubble and of the likelihood that some of the abraded and slightly abraded groups were directly derived from it, it is probable that the fresh and very slightly abraded artifacts on each of these horizons can be considered to be contemporary with the pebble lines, although they may be separated by only a short period of time from the latest component in the Rubble I above. In A1, 1956, only a very small part of the base of the sands between 12 feet (3·6 m) and 12 feet 6 inches (3·8 m) below the surface remained undisturbed (grid squares A/7–9) and, over the rest of the excavation, the pre-Chiungu Member channelling had cut down to and rested on Rubble Ib. The pebble line (Bed 8a) occurred 3–6 inches (7·6–15·2 cm) above the rubble.

The artifacts from Bed 8a (Table 21) show that 40 per cent of all artifacts are fresh, 32 per cent slightly abraded and 29 per cent more heavily abraded. If only whole flakes and shaped and utilized pieces are included, these figures are changed to 9 per cent fresh, 48 per cent slightly abraded and 43 per cent abraded, from which it is clear that most of the small fragments and chunks are fresh. Comparing the breadth/length ratios of the whole flakes and tools (Figure 25) it can be seen that there is little difference between the three weathering categories. Most are broad, irregular, end-flakes though flake forms with the abraded group tend to be longer and to show a greater size range than do those in the slightly abraded group, where there are also some smaller flakes. The fresh examples are too few to be significant, although the diagnosis is not at

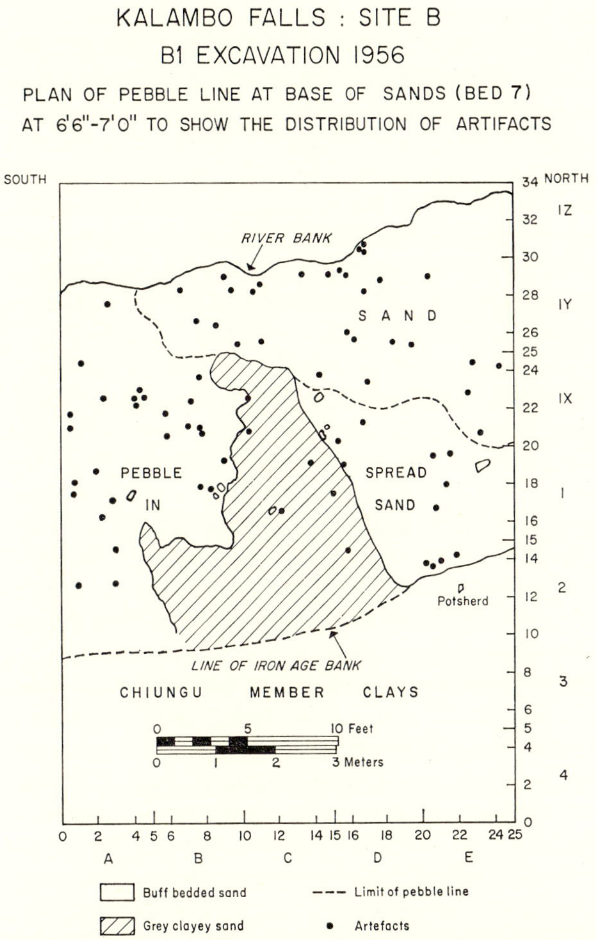

Fig. 26. B1, 1956 Excavation: to show the extent of the pebble line (Bed 8) – broken line – in the current-bedded sands (Beds 7–7′) of the Mbwilo Member and the distribution of artifacts at this horizon.

variance with the expectation that they form a unit with the slightly abraded group. There are more chert flakes in these two categories than in the abraded group, while the range of raw materials used is greater. The abraded, parallel-sided cleaver in hard quartzite, the slightly abraded, unifacial 'core-axe' on a triangular sectioned chunk of which only the distal end is worked to a straight, blunt, plano-clinal edge, and the core-axe resharpening spall were, presumably, incorporated when the channelling in which the bedded sands rest, cut through older sediments lying further upslope to the south. The small, single, concave scraper on a flake fragment is very lightly abraded.

In the B1, 1956 Excavation, the pebble line was not

[1] Rubble Ib at A1, 1956 and Rubble I (composite) at B1, 1956.

continuous over the whole area excavated but was largely confined to grid squares A–C/1x and 2. This, and the artifacts found at the level of this pebble line are shown in Figure 26. This is a very thin scatter and, as can be seen, the artifacts are not confined to the pebble area but lie equally in the sand with a few on the surface of the clay. Other artifacts occurred also sporadically in the 12 inches (30 cm) or so of sands (Bed 7′) that immediately underlie the pebble horizon, interposed between this and the rubble. Table 21 shows the counts for these artifacts.

Of the artifacts 24 per cent are fresh, 33 per cent slightly abraded and 43 per cent are abraded. These figures become 26 per cent, 30 per cent and 44 per cent, respectively, if only whole flakes and tools are included. As with the previous aggregate, the breadth/length ratios suggest that the size is more variable in the abraded group, though all three categories show the same general patterns (Figure 25). The majority in the fresh and slightly abraded groups are made of chert and there is a noticeable increase in the number of those made from feldspathic quartzite in the abraded group. The fresh group contains a diminutive, unifacial point made on a blade with marginal, stepped retouch (Plate 50: 3) together with a range of, mostly small, unmodified flakes that include four bladelets with plain or point platforms, five short quadrilateral flakes, three with one-directional and two with radial dorsal scar patterns; three of these have faceted platforms. There are also five, broad, radially prepared Levallois flakes and two with one-directional dorsal flaking; these also show prepared platforms. One triangular flake with faceted striking platform (Plate 50: 1) recalls the Levallois point forms with the Hillslope component of the Polungu Industry. A core rejuvenating flake shows parts of two platforms, one plain for the removal of small bladelets and one simple-faceted from which the spall was detached at right angles to the first. The opposed platform blade core is illustrated at Plate 50: 4. The slightly abraded group contained one truncated bladelet (Plate 50: 2) which, together with the small scrapers and very lightly abraded flakes, appears to belong to the same cultural entity as the fresh artifacts.

Although these two aggregates are both very small samples, they are very probably in primary context and they do provide a stratigraphic link between the Hillslope component of the Polungu Industry and the Rubble component, which they resemble very closely and to which they are assigned.[1]

Small flecks of charcoal, probably deriving from burned vegetation occurred in association with the pebble line and bedded sand in B1, 1956 and very small pieces were found also between rubble lines 2 and 3 in Site C, 1966. Charcoal flecks of presumably similar age also occurred in the base of the sand overlying Rubble I (composite) in Excavation A4. Unfortunately, none of these samples was sufficient for radiocarbon dating and the only date for this time range comes from the sample collected from Rubble Ia in A3, 1956.

B. Aggregates from Rubble I, Mbwilo Member

(See Volume 1, Plates 12, 18, 20, 21, 26)

1. MODE AND AGENCIES OF DEPOSITION OF RUBBLES AND ARTIFACTS

The excavations have shown that the accumulation of the rubble from which the component mostly comes, follows a phase of downcutting by the river to at least 40 feet (12 m) (Phase C. 6) and covers a wide area from Site A to Sites B, C and D at the southwestern end of the local basin, where it forms the basal deposit of the Mbwilo Member. On the upper slopes at Site A, this takes the form of a land rubble or scree accumulation (Red Rubble Bed), on an existing land surface. It is composed of boulders of large size and angular and sub-angular rock fragments derived from the slopes of the Siszya Ridge to the south, set in a fairly homogeneous, ferruginous, sandy matrix which also contains artifacts of the Lupemban Industrial Complex. The base of this colluvial rubble bed lies approximately 40 feet (12 m) above the river and the bed attains a thickness of 10 feet (3 m). It probably continued to build up throughout the time when the multiple and thinner rubble lines and gravels (Rubble I), into which it grades, were formed downslope and in the river channels. Rubble I is divisible into three main rubble lines (Rubbles Ia, Ib, Ic) and several that are subsidiary on Sites A, B and C, and they may also be composite where two or more come

[1] The aggregates from the upper two pebble lines at Site C in 1966 had not been completely analysed before the end of the excavation season. They are now in the Livingstone Museum and so, regrettably, are not available at the time of writing for inclusion here. They yielded little that was diagnostic except for a small, unifacial, triangular point from the uppermost of these pebble lines (Plate 49: 1). A similar, but asymmetric, foliate example was found at the same site in 1963. These diminutive, delicate points with marginal retouch are characteristic of others found with the Rubble component of the Polungu Industry as described below.

together. It is a sub-angular scree or rubble mixed, in the lower exposures, with some rounded cobbles and boulders set in a sorted sand matrix and contains a considerable quantity of artifacts, the great majority of which have been subjected to gentle abrasion by water carrying fine sand, silt and clay.

These rubbles do not, therefore, represent occupation floors but, rather, surfaces onto which artifacts found their way and became mixed together, both through human activities and as a result of natural agencies of transport. Rubble I and its subdivisions downslope probably accumulated fairly slowly since it is in part the equivalent of the Red Rubble Bed upslope which reaches 10 feet (3 m) in thickness in the A4, 1959 excavation, and also since it contains fresh and abraded artifacts which, on typological and technological grounds, will be shown to form three successive and distinct industrial components.

2. IDENTIFICATION OF ARTIFACT SETS

Qualitative and quantitative criteria make it possible to distinguish three separate artifact sets, in addition to some older and derived artifacts from the Mkamba Member, in each of the Rubble I aggregates examined. Comparing these artifact sets with dated developmental trends elsewhere (e.g. in the Congo basin, Zambia and Rhodesia) it becomes possible to place Kalambo Falls material in proper sequence and to check this against other lines of evidence as described below.

The artifact sets from Rubble I are each distinguished by characteristic shaped tools. In part, these are new forms making their appearance for the first time. In part they are common to more than one of the components but in that case they show clear morphological differences of a repetitive nature which distinguish them as separate sub-classes. The proportions in which these various shaped tool classes and sub-classes occur also differ in each of the artifact sets. In each case the primary flaking techniques are closely comparable and indicate traditional relationships between the sets but there is a proportional shift through time in the percentages in which flake, blade and core forms are represented. Artifacts become smaller with time and the size range is correspondingly more consistent; changes can also be seen in the preferential use of certain raw materials.

It must, however, be borne in mind that colluvial and alluvial processes will re-sort artifacts according to size and shape, so that the size differences recognized here might be due to natural rather than cultural causes. Possibly non-cultural factors may also be a cause underlying the dimensional differences shown by the aggregates from the rubbles at Sites A and B (see p. 220), but it is unlikely that natural causes were the main agencies responsible for the size differences observable in the artifact sets from Rubble I at the Kalambo Falls. The smallest and lightest flakes were most probably removed by stream activity from the rubbles that lay in the channel, for it is otherwise difficult to explain their absence and the fact that virtually none with a length less than 20 mm were recovered. While there is also evidence for a general east/west orientation of the long axes of rocks and artifacts in Rubble I, which is similar to that shown by the boulders in the bed of the Kalambo river today (Volume I, Figures 9 and 10), there is some, but no consistent, evidence of size sorting. Artifacts lie at all angles in the rubbles – small, light implements adjacent to large and heavy ones – with no regularity in the degree of abrasion each may show and there are some artifacts with the 'nibbled' edges so characteristic of natural fracture. However, the abrasion shown by these artifacts generally takes the form of smoothing and very fine polish, rather than fractured edges. This suggests that the colluvial and alluvial action to which they were subjected was not of sufficient violence to remove any but the smallest and lightest material. For these reasons, and the degree of correlation between the typological sets and the abrasion categories, we believe the size differences shown equally by flakes and cores to be due essentially to cultural rather than to natural factors.

The youngest of the artifact sets is that identified below as the Rubble component of the Polungu Industry. Although present in each of the Rubble aggregates, except those from Rubble Ic, the artifacts that comprise this component are never numerous. They are characterized by a small quadrilateral flake element with parallel scar pattern obtained from prismatic and Levallois specialized blade cores, together with flake forms derived from specialized disc, Levallois point and radial Levallois cores. Among the shaped tools, the heavy duty category, though present, is not numerically significant and the most characteristic are light duty tools delicately retouched to form points, various small backed artifacts and thin-sectioned disc knives or adzes. There is no apparent difference in the artifact sets from Rubble I and those in the base of the overlying bedded sands described above.

The great majority of the artifacts in the aggregates

from Rubble I are, however, typologically and technically representative of a later stage of the Lupemban Industrial Complex, more specifically defined here as the Siszya Industry and these are grouped into two further components. Artifacts belonging to the sets that comprise the younger, or component B, of the Siszya Industry are considerably more numerous than those distinguishing the older component (A), in each of the excavated aggregates. This may be an indication that the formation of Rubble I, as now seen in the excavations, is in general contemporary with component B. This view receives some confirmation from the fact that no group of artifacts which can with certainty be assigned to any later industrial entity, has been found in Rubble Ic and Ic(iii) – the oldest and lowest of these rubble lines in the A1, 1956 excavation. The Siszya Industry artifacts are found also in the Red Rubble upslope, but in greater numbers in the rubble lines that occur down to the present low water level in the Kalambo river between Sites A and B, as also at Site C, a fact that again emphasizes the activity association of the groups that made them with the river channels. The settlements to which this profuse scatter of artifacts relates are believed to have been either removed by later channelling or to be still, in part, present in the area upslope between A1, 1956 and the Camp Site. More detailed discussion of the earlier artifact sets in Rubble I and their related cultural remains is reserved for Volume III with the description of the Siszya Industry, since we are concerned here only with the latest component that can be separated on typological and technological grounds and which is believed to relate more to the exposed surface of this rubble than to its formation, with the possible exception of the latest of the rubble lines.

In addition to the artifacts that fall into one or other of the three sets (components) there are a smaller number of tools and debitage that are derived from the beds of the Mkamba Member where these have been cut out by the contemporary channelling in which the rubbles lie; in this way, tools of the earlier Lupemban, Sangoan and Acheulian Industrial Complexes are sometimes found incorporated within Rubble I, in particular in the lower rubble lines which relate to channels that lie at or at no great height above present water level.

3. CATEGORIES OF ABRASION AND CORRELATION WITH ARTIFACT SETS

In places there is close correlation between *état physique* and the three artifact sets recognized from Rubble I. As will be shown, most of the artifacts in the set identified as the Rubble component of the Polungu Industry are fresh or have the edges only very slightly dulled, in contrast to those belonging to the set identified as component B of the Siszya Industry which generally show a light, rather than heavy, degree of abrasion but, even in Rubble I, are rarely fresh, except in Rubble Ic and its sub-divisions in Trench A1. Those comprising component A, being older, might be expected to have been subjected to a heavier degree of abrasion. While this is sometimes the case, as at Site B, it is not always so and the preferred use of feldspathic quartzite for certain classes and sub-classes of tools and primary flakes and blades, provides a better means of distinguishing between these two components.

The various derived artifacts – earlier Lupemban, Sangoan and Acheulian – are generally more heavily, as distinct from slightly, abraded, but the degree of wear they exhibit is directly related to the previous history of the piece. Some are heavily abraded and bear the record of a long period of movement in the stream, while others, incorporated directly from the beds cut into by the erosion surface on which Rubble I rests, may be in fresh or near fresh condition. However, if it is a shaped tool, the morphological character of the specimen generally leaves no doubt as to the industry to which it belongs. While, therefore, except in Ic, the fresh category correlates with the latest artifact set (the Rubble component of the Polungu Industry) and the greater number of artifacts composing the B component of the Siszya Industry are slightly abraded, artifacts of the A component may show either light or heavy abrasion. The abraded category does not, therefore, correlate directly with any one artifact set and it also includes older and derived specimens from the Mkamba Member.

4. DATING: DIRECT AND INDIRECT EVIDENCE

No precise estimates of the length of time that the various surfaces of Rubble I remained exposed can be made. However, the general freshness of most of the artifacts that comprise the Rubble component of the Polungu Industry on each of these rubble lines, suggests that they did not remain exposed for very long before being covered. There are a number of points of resemblance between this latest component in Rubble I and the Umguzan (formerly 'Magosian') in Rhodesia (see Chapter 8). At Pomongwe Cave, the upper limit of the Umguzan Industry is dated to after 15,800 ± 100 B.P. and before 9400 ± 110 B.P. (Cooke, 1963: 148). The lower limit may be as early as 21,360 ± 280 B.P. on evidence from Zombepata Cave in Mashonaland (Cooke, 1971: 124) and 21,700 ± 400 B.P. from a charcoal sample at Pomongwe previously believed by the excavator to be associated with the Bambata ('Stillbay') Industry (Cooke, 1971: 124 and Cooke, 1963: 146). In Zambia, the Nachikufu I, dated to 10,820 ± 340 B.P., was perhaps as old as 16,715 ± 95 B.P. and, on the basis of its important microlithic element, might be presumed to be younger than the latest component in Rubble I. This last has more in common with the 'proto-L.S.A.' found in the basal occupation layer in Leopard's Hill Cave, which dates between 21,550 ± 950 and 23,600 ± 360 B.P. (Miller, 1969: 495).

However, small blade technology can sometimes be shown to have made its appearance in sub-Saharan Africa appreciably earlier than had been previously thought possible. At Zombepata an increase in bladelets and microlithic tools (crescents, small backed blades and thumbnail scrapers (Cooke, 1971: 123)) has recently been observed in two levels of a late phase of the Bambata Industry where they are associated with a radiocarbon date of 40,700 ± 400 B.P. Indeed, the increasing number of early radiocarbon dates from southern and central Africa for 'Middle' and 'Later Stone Age' aggregates indicate that technical equivalence alone should no longer be used as a basis for assessing contemporaneity (Vogel and Beaumont, 1972).

If the base of the bedded sands burying the latest accumulations of Rubble I dates to approximately 9550 ± 210 B.P. (the age of the carbon sample from the surface of Rubble I at Excavation A3) and the contained aggregates are contemporary or older, then, extrapolating from the other dates referred to above, it can be suggested that the latest component of Rubble I might date to some time between 9500 and ± 25,000 B.P. on the Rhodesian evidence, or between 16,000 and 23,000 on that from Zambia. If this is so, then areas of Rubble I may have remained exposed for potential occupation for as long as 15,000 years. It is unfortunate, therefore, that a sample of scattered charcoals from one of the upper rubble lenses at Site C, 1966, was too small for dating, and it is necessary to await the recovery of further samples from Rubble I before any more satisfactory dating can be carried out. A date of ± 15,000 B.P. would be more conventional for the latest component of this rubble but, in view of the Leopard's Hill and Zombepata evidence and the very old dates that have recently been recorded for the Howieson's Poort-type (= 'Magosian') aggregates from South Africa (Mason, 1969; Keller, 1970), an earlier dating is equally possible. Indeed, a date in the range of 20,000 years B.P. would be acceptable if the carbon sample L. 3991 giving a date of 27,500 ± 2300 B.P. is a reliable indication of the age of the oldest and lowest of these rubble horizons (Rubble Ic(iii) at Site A1, 1956.

5. THE BASIS FOR THE IDENTIFICATION OF COMPONENTS IN THE RUBBLES

The three components in these rubbles have, therefore, been identified by using four independent lines of evidence and observing how these correlate:

(i) Recognition of artifact sets by appraisal of morphological features.

(ii) Modal differences in the products of primary flaking techniques in these artifact sets.

(iii) Changes in the preferential use of certain raw materials.

(iv) *Etat physique* and its correlation with the artifact sets identified on the basis of (i) and (ii) above.

Initial qualitative assessment of shaped tools and debitage suggested a division of the Rubble I aggregates into three abrasion categories – fresh, slightly abraded and more heavily abraded. This threefold division received some confirmation also from the discernible shifts in the extent to which certain raw materials were used. For example, the increased importance of silicified mudstone (chert) and exotic materials in the fresh and youngest component and greater emphasis on the hard and feldspathic quartzites in the abraded and earlier components. Using these three abrasion categories as a basis, a quantitative study of the tools and unmodified waste shows that there are small but perceptible changes in the classes of tools represented in each category as well as shifts in the size and attributes of the products of primary flaking. As might be expected, these changes can be seen better in some of the aggregates than in others but this quantitative evidence complements fairly well the findings from qualitative and raw material studies and appears to show that these three abrasion categories have cultural significance though there are, clearly, also some anomalies. For example, the oldest artifacts recognized on typological grounds, i.e. Sangoan and Acheulian, are, for the reasons already given, not always the most heavily abraded. Also the differential weathering properties of the various raw materials present further complications – chert and feldspathic sandstone, for example, abrading more easily than hard quartzite. Generally, where such anomalies occur, they can be identified and compensated for but they are easier to recognize in the shaped tool classes than in the debitage. There, nevertheless, remains a close, though not precise, correlation between the lithic technology and *état physique* that forms, as will be shown, a valid basis for qualitative and quantitative comparison of the artifact sets in each of the rubble aggregates.

A further complication in defining discrete components arises if, as the evidence appears to indicate, Rubble I accumulated comparatively slowly over several millennia. During this time the prehistoric populations continued to occupy the exposed surfaces on which the rubble was accumulating and their artifacts became incorporated in it. These stone implements, therefore, represent a cultural continuum, not several separate and distinct entities or periods of occupation interspersed by times of non-occupation. It is important that this should not be lost sight of when the different components are described and defined. The statistical evidence also confirms that we are dealing with a continuum but with one in which technological innovation and change can best be demonstrated through the broad groupings (or components) that can be identified. These components are, therefore, convenient but artificial units which show the general composition of the stone tool-kit towards the beginning, the middle and the end of the sequence. They are thus no more than artificial units that enable us to demonstrate conveniently some of the more obviously significant changes and trends in a long cultural tradition.

The problem of distinguishing between the different components in these rubbles is, therefore, a complicated one and we have not been able to devise any really satisfactory quantitative or other method of doing so precisely and with confidence. Our analysis employs several different criteria any or all of which are open to subjective and individual error. When abrasion categories can be correlated with qualitative and quantitative data, the artifact sets can be seen to fall into several groupings which recur at different excavations in Rubble I. These groupings form the basis on which the components have been identified and their recurring nature suggests a high degree of probability that the components are valid and temporal entities. Until, however, they are found stratigraphically separated and archaeologically concentrated, their more precise composition and relationships cannot be determined.

In general, the bulk of the artifacts that comprise the most evolved component at any place in Rubble I are in fresh or very slightly abraded condition. Typologically and technically, they show a close relationship with the slightly abraded and abraded categories and it is apparent that they belong at the upper end of the cultural continuum that is represented in the rubble bed. However, at Site B, at Site A in Rubble Ia and Ib and in Trenches A2, A3 and A4 where Rubble I is higher in elevation, certain of the tool classes and flake and core forms show affinities also with the Hillslope component of the Polungu Industry.[1] On the principle that it is the latest forms represented that best establish the status of lithic aggregates, this component has, therefore, been placed in the Polungu Industry as the Rubble component.

6. AN EXAMPLE IN COMPONENT IDENTIFICATION: AGGREGATES FROM B2, 1959, RUBBLE IA

Besides the aggregates from the base of the current-bedded sands at Excavations A1, 1956 and B1, 1956, described above, the Rubble component of the Polungu Industry occurs in nine other contexts in direct association with Rubble I and in one instance in association with what may be the re-exposed surface of rubble contemporary with the sediments of the Pits Channel. However, before considering the artifact composition at each of these Occurrences and in order to demonstrate how the components were isolated, it is necessary to examine the whole content of at least one of these rubble lines. For this purpose, Rubble Ia at Site B2, 1959, has been selected, because it is not only typical and contains a representative number of artifacts in each of the abrasion categories, but also because it is the latest of these rubble lines present in this excavation and may thus be expected to be generally characteristic, so far as the latest component is concerned.

This stoneline and its relationship to the underlying Rubble Ib can be seen from the section drawings

[1] This does not seem to be the case in Rubble Ic and its sub-divisions at the A1 Excavation, however, where some small and 'evolved' artifacts do occur but where the fresh and at least part of the slightly abraded material differs from the Polungu Industry in a number of respects, including size, and is assigned to component B of the Siszya Industry.

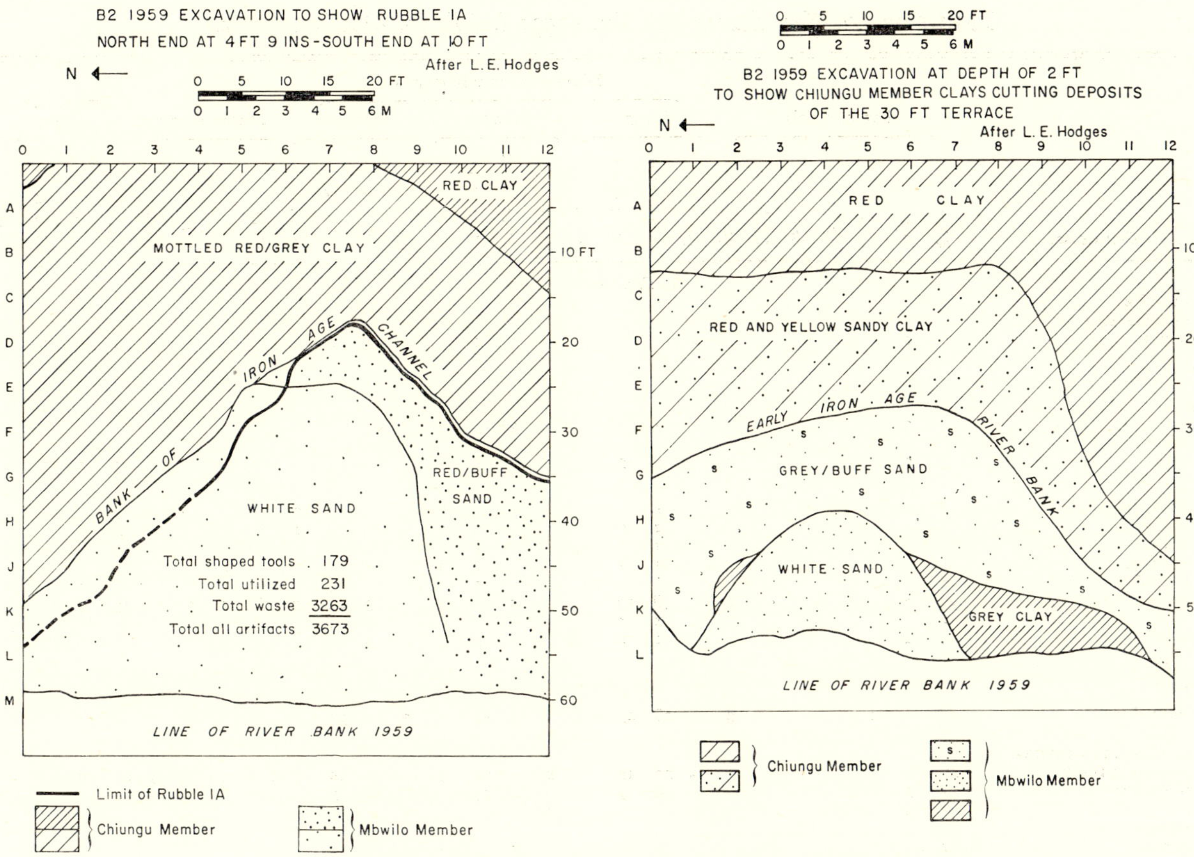

Fig. 27. Excavation B2, 1959, to show the relationship of Rubble Ia and overlying sands to the channel clays of the Chiungu Member.

of the B2, 1959, Excavation in Volume 1, Figures 36–39. The Ia and Ib rubbles can be seen to converge at both the north and south sides of the excavation. They join to form Rubble I (composite), a short distance beyond the south wall of B2, 1959, and rest on a southward sloping surface that is exposed in the river bed at low water level between Sites A and B. Immediately north of B2, 1959, the rubble has again become composite and was exposed in the 1956 excavation at this site (Volume 1, Figure 35) where it was found to cover the whole of the western half of the excavation. In the area of B2, 1959, the river had encroached further eastwards so that the line of the river bank in 1959 was separated by some 30 feet (9 m) from the clays of the Chiungu Member, the channel in which these rest having cut out the former eastward extension of the sands and clays of the Mbwilo Member. These are preserved here as a tongue that extends eastward with depth and is delimited by the profile of the Chiungu channel fill.

Figure 27 (also Volume 1, Plate 25) shows, on the right, an early stage of the excavation in which the white sand covering Rubble Ia is beginning to appear and, on the left, the plan of this rubble line after it had been exposed.

The artifacts are fairly evenly distributed among the angular and rounded rock fragments and there was no discernible pattern of concentration as might be expected if the aggregates had been in primary context. Individual specimens were mostly lying flat with one or other face horizontal but it was not uncommon to find them also lying at angles where they had become wedged between natural rocks. Although, therefore, the context is a geological one, the fresh or very slightly abraded condition of the majority of the artifacts indicates that they had not been moved very far from the place where they were made. Table 22 gives details, broken down into abrasion categories, of all artifacts found, according to raw material, size range, striking platform and

TABLE 22. *Artifact classes, Site B2, 1959: Rubble Ia, Mbwilo Member*

Artifact classes	Raw materials							Dimensions in millimetres: Length				Dimensions in millimetres: Breadth				Dimensions in millimetres: Thickness				Platform types				Dorsal scar pattern				
	Chert	H/Q	F/Q	Qz	SSt	Chal	Sil	100+	< 100 to 50	< 50 to 30	< 30	100+	< 100 to 50	< 50 to 30	< 30	50+	< 50 to 20	< 20 to 10	< 10	Plain	S/F	M/F	Point	1-Dir.	2-Dir.	M-Dir.	Cortex	Total
										Fresh series																		
SHAPED TOOLS																												
Large cutting/scraping																												
Large scrapers		2						2						2			1	1						1		1		2
Heavy duty																												
Picks																												
Core-axes																												
Choppers		2						1	1				2			2									2			2
Polyhedrals																												
Core-scrapers	3	2					1		3	3			2	4			6							3	2	1		6
Light duty																												
Truncated blades/flakes	2								1	1					2				2				2	2				2
Backed blades	4								1	3				2	2			3	1	1			3	2	2			4
Backed flakes	1								1					1				1					1			1		1
Points: unifacial	1		1						1	1				1	1			2		1	1			2				2
bifacial	1									1				1				1			1				1			1
Small scrapers	27	2					2		18	13			1	29	1		3	23	5	6	5	2		13	7	11		31
Burins	2								1	1				2			1	1										2
Proto-burins	2	1							1	2				3			3											3
Other																												
Bored stones																												
Total shaped tools	43	9	1				3	3	28	25			5	45	6	2	14	32	8									56
UTILIZED/MODIFIED PIECES																												
Flakes, blades and fragments	27	6	1					2	20	12		1	4	20	9		7	14	13	15	5	2	4	20	10	4		34
Cores and chunks	13	3	1						8	9			2	15			14	3										17
Rubbers		1						1				1				1												1
Hammerstones																												
Miscellaneous	1								1				1					1										1
Total utilized/modified	41	10	2					3	29	21		2	7	35	9	1	21	18	13									53
UNMODIFIED WASTE																												
Flakes																												
Irregular, end-struck	178	64	9	1		3	9	2	106	154	2		32	207	25		10	171	83	134	72	28	30	101	71	86	6	264
Irregular, side-struck	25	18	4			1			6	36	6	1	21	26			2	38	8	28	13	2	5	23	8	17		48
Short quadrilateral	21	6	1				2		9	21			2	24	4			18	12	14	11	3	2	14	9	7		30
Triangular	16	3				2	1		9	13				18	4			18	4	9	6	6	1	19	3			22
Long quadrilateral	42	6	1			1	2	2	29	21				20	32			19	33	25	11	9	7	39	11	2		52
Core-axe resharpening		1							1				1				1											1
Cores																												
Single platform, blade	3			1						4			1	2	1		3	1		4				4				4
Single platform, flake	3									3			1	2			3			3				3				3
Opposed platforms, blade	2									2				2			2			2					2			2
Opposed platforms, flake	1									1				1			1			1					1			1
Pyramidal																												
Formless	2									2				2			2			2						2		2
Proto-biconical	1	1							1	1				2			2								2			2
Biconical	3	1							1	3				4			4									4		4
Discoid, high-backed	5	1					1		6	1			2	5			6	1			7					7		7
Discoid, flat	16								3	13			2	13	1		3	13			16				1	15		16
Sub-triangular	3									3				3				3		3						3		3
Flake and blade fragments																												
Chunks																												
Miscellaneous																												
Total unmodified waste	321	101	15	2		7	15	4	171	278	8	1	62	331	67		39	282	140									461
Total all artifacts	405	120	18	2		7	18	10	228	324	8	3	74	411	82	3	74	332	161									570

TABLE 22 (*cont.*)

	Raw materials							Dimensions in millimetres												Platform types				Dorsal scar pattern				
								Length				Breadth				Thickness												
Artifact classes	Chert	H/Q	F/Q	Qz	SSt	Chal	Sil	100 +	< 100 to 50	< 50 to 30	< 30	100 +	< 100 to 50	< 50 to 30	< 30	50 +	< 50 to 20	< 20 to 10	< 10	Plain	S/F	M/F	Point	1-Dir.	2-Dir.	M-Dir.	Cortex	Total
								Slightly abraded series																				
SHAPED TOOLS																												
Large cutting/scraping																												
Large scrapers		1						1					1			1										1		1
Heavy duty																												
Picks		1	1					2					2			2												2
Core-axes	7							1	4	2				6	1		4	3										7
Choppers	1								1				1				1											1
Polyhedrals																												
Core-scrapers	2	4						2	3	1		1	2	3		2	4							3	1	2		6
Light duty																												
Truncated blades/flakes																												
Backed blades																												
Backed flakes																												
Points: unifacial	1									1				1				1				1			1			1
bifacial																												
Small scrapers	51	7	1					1	22	36			7	46	6		10	47	2	15	5	4		18	23	18		59
Burins	3								1	2				3			1	2										3
Proto-burins	4								1	3				4			3	1										4
Other																												
Bored stones					1			1					1			1												1
Total shaped tools	69	13	2		1			8	32	45		1	14	63	7	6	23	54	2									85
UTILIZED/MODIFIED PIECES																												
Flakes, blades and fragments	86	8	4					6	56	35	1		13	76	9		6	77	15	32	22	13	15	52	21	23	2	98
Cores and chunks	13	2		2				1	6	10			2	12	3		15	2						6	7	2	2	17
Rubbers		1							1				1				1											1
Hammerstones		2							2				1	1			2											2
Miscellaneous	1	1						1	1					2			2											2
Total utilized/modified	100	14	4	2				8	66	45	1		17	91	12		26	79	15									120
UNMODIFIED WASTE																												
Flakes																												
Irregular, end-struck	280	149	18	1			6	8	219	225	2		66	363	25		97	284	73	250	118	41	45	169	141	139	5	454
Irregular, side-struck	62	61	3				4	1	13	106	10	4	70	56			5	113	12	76	40	2	12	61	27	39	3	130
Short quadrilateral	26	10	2						16	22			3	32	3			26	12	23	7	3	5	18	15	5		38
Triangular	19	10	3					3	16	12	1		1	31				31	1	11	12	9		28	2	2		32
Long quadrilateral	47	6	3				1	3	46	8				41	16			36	21	28	15	8	6	48	8	1		57
Core-axe resharpening		1							1					1		1												1
Cores																												
Single platform, blade	2									2				2			1	1		2				2				2
Single platform, flake	14								5	9			4	10			14			13	1			14				14
Opposed platforms, blade	1	1							2				1	1			2			2					2			2
Opposed platforms, flake																												
Pyramidal	1								1				1				1			1				1				1
Formless	4	2							2	4			1	5		1	4	1		6					2	4		6
Proto-biconical	2	1							1	2				3			3								2	1		3
Biconical	5	1	3						9				3	6			9									9		9
Discoid, high-backed	17								2	15			1	15	1		9	8			17				3	14		17
Discoid, flat	23								9	14			4	19			10	13			23				1	22		23
Sub-triangular	1									1				1				1			1					1		1
Flake and blade fragments																												
Chunks																												
Miscellaneous	6																											6
Total unmodified waste	510	242	32	1			11	15	342	420	13	4	155	586	45	2	155	514	119									796
Total all artifacts	679	269	38	3	1		11	31	440	510	14	5	186	740	64	8	204	647	136									1,001

TABLE 22 (*cont.*)

Artifact classes	Raw materials: Chert	H/Q	F/Q	Qz	SSt	Chal	Sil	Dimensions in millimetres: Length: 100+	< 100 to 50	< 50 to 30	< 30	Breadth: 100+	< 100 to 50	< 50 to 30	< 30	Thickness: 50+	< 50 to 20	< 20 to 10	< 10	Platform types: Plain	S/F	M/F	Point	Dorsal scar pattern: 1-Dir.	2-Dir.	M-Dir.	Cortex	Total	Physical condition not recorded
															Abraded series														
SHAPED TOOLS																													
Large cutting/scraping																													
Large scrapers							1	1					1				1									1		1	
Heavy duty																													
Picks																													
Core-axes	3							2	1				2	1		1	1	1										3	
Choppers		1							1				1			1									1			1	
Polyhedrals		1								1				1			1											1	
Core-scrapers	4	4							3	5			2	6		2	6							4	2	2		8	
Light duty																													
Truncated blades/flakes																													
Backed blades																													
Backed flakes																													
Points: unifacial	5								4	1				5				5			3		2	1	4			5	
bifacial																													
Small scrapers	14	3							6	11			2	14	1		2	13	2	6	2		3	6	5	6		17	
Burins																													
Proto-burins	1	1							1	1				2			2											2	
Other																													
Bored stones																													
Total shaped tools	27	10					1	3	16	19			8	29	1	4	13	19	2									38	
UTILIZED/MODIFIED PIECES																													
Flakes, blades and fragments	22	13					2	2	21	14		1	7	26	3		11	20	6	12	5	3	8	15	15	6	1	37	
Cores and chunks	14	6						1	10	9			1	18	1	2	14	4						7	6	6	1	20	
Rubbers		1						1					1			1												1	
Hammerstones																													
Miscellaneous																													
Total utilized/modified	36	20					2	4	31	23		1	9	44	4	3	25	24	6									58	
UNMODIFIED WASTE																													
Flakes																													
Irregular, end-struck	168	126	27	1		1	7	8	175	146	1		70	253	7		20	281	29	184	85	21	40	113	100	114	3	330	
Irregular, side-struck	28	58	16				2	1	32	70	1	9	72	23			13	85	6	65	24	2	13	32	31	41		104	
Short quadrilateral	17	8	1				3		9	20				29			3	22	4	18	2	7	2	17	8	4		29	
Triangular	14	8	4					1	18	7			3	21	2		1	23	2	14	8	4		18	6	2		26	
Long quadrilateral	20	8	2					6	19	4	1			24	6			20	10	13	12	8	1	17	11	2		30	
Core-axe resharpening	3	1	1						5					2	3	2	3											5	
Cores																													
Single platform, blade	1						1		1	1			1	1			2			2				2				2	
Single platform, flake	3	2							2	3				5			5			4	1			5				5	
Opposed platforms, blade																													
Opposed platforms, flake																													
Pyramidal	1								1				1				1			1				1				1	
Formless	1	1							1	1			1	1		1	1			2					1	1		2	
Proto-biconical	4	1	1					1	1	4			2	4			6								6			6	
Biconical		4	2						5	1			5	1		1	5									6		6	
Discoid, high-backed	10		1				1		6	6			2	10			12				12				4	8		12	
Discoid, flat	8	1	1				1		7	4			3	8			7	4			11					11		11	
Sub-triangular	1								1				1				1				1					1		1	
Flake and blade fragments																													1,056*
Chunks																													346*
Miscellaneous		34																										34	
Total unmodified waste	279	252	56	1		1	15	17	283	267	3	9	161	382	18	4	80	435	51									604	1,402
Total all artifacts	342	282	56	1		1	18	24	330	309	3	10	178	455	23	11	118	478	59									700	1,402

* Raw material of	Chert	H/Q	F/Q	Qz	SSt	Chal	Sil
Fragments	622	351	58	2		3	20
Chunks	149	186	4	3		2	2

TABLE 23. *Site B2, 1959: measurements of flakes and cores in Rubble Ia, Mbwilo Member*

	Measurement in mm	Number in sample	Range Min.	Range Max.	Mode(s)	Median	Mean ± error	S.D.
				Fresh flakes: all raw materials				
Unspecialized								
End-struck – irregular	Length	264	20	100 = 80	50	50	53·3 ± 0·92	15·0
	Breadth	264	20	80 = 60	40	40	39	
	Thickness	264	< 10[a]	30 = *c.* 22·5	10	10	*c.* 11·7	
	B/L ratio	264	0·3	1·0 = 0·7	1·0	0·75	0·75 ± 0·035	0·56
End-struck – short quadrilateral	Length	30	30	80 = 50	50	50	50·8 ± 2·4	13·17
	Breadth	30	20	50 = 30	30	30	34	
	Thickness	30	< 10[a]	20 = *c.* 12·5	10	10	*c.* 9·8	
	B/L ratio	30	0·6	1·0 = 0·4	0·6	0·65	0·69 ± 0·09	0·52
Side struck	Length	48	20	70 = 50	40	40	40·4 ± 1·7	12·45
	Breadth	48	30	100 = 70	60	50	52·9	
	Thickness	48	< 10[a]	40 = *c.* 32·5	10	10	*c.* 13·5	
Specialized								
Long quadrilateral	Length	52	30	110 = 80	50, 60	60	60·6 ± 2·35	16·96
	Breadth	52	10	40 = 30	20	20	23·7	
	Thickness	52	< 10[a]	20 = *c.* 12·5	< 10[a]	< 10[a]	*c.* 9·2	
	B/L ratio	52	0·25	0·5 = 0·25	0·35	0·35	0·39 ± 0·009	0·065
Triangular	Length	22	30	80 = 50	50	50	51·8 ± 3·12	14·7
	Breadth	22	20	50 = 30	30	30	33·8	
	Thickness	22	< 10[a]	20 = *c.* 12·5	10	10	*c.* 9·5	
	B/L ratio	22	0·3	1·0 = 0·7	0·6	0·6	0·6 ± 0·034	0·16
	Th/B ratio	22	0·2	0·5 = 0·3	0·3	0·3	*c.* 0·3 ± 0·048	0·22
Combined specialized								
Quadrilateral and triangular	Length	74	30	110 = 80	50	60	59·3 ± 1·88	16·22
	Breadth	74	20	50 = 30	20, 30	30	26·5 ± 0·98	8·46
	Thickness	74	< 10[a]	20 = *c.* 12·5	< 10	8·75	*c.* 9·6	
	B/L ratio	74	0·25	1·0 = 0·75	0·5	0·43	*c.* 0·45 ± 0·14	0·21
All flakes								
	Length	416	20	110 = 90	50	50	52·7 ± 0·61	15·69
Cores								
	Length	44	30	70 = 40	50	50	49·7 ± 1·54	10·22
	Breadth	44	10	60 = 50	40	40	40·3 ± 1·58	10·47
	Thickness	44	10	50 = 40	15, 30	22·5	23·6 ± 1·93	12·82
				Slightly abraded flakes: all raw materials				
Unspecialized								
End-struck – irregular	Length	454	20	130 = 110	50	65	56·9 ± 0·908	19·36
	Breadth	454	20	80 = 60	40	40	42	
	Thickness	454	< 10[a]	40 = *c.* 32·5	10	10	*c.* 15·2	
	B/L ratio	454	0·3	1·0 = 0·7	1·0	0·8	0·77 ± 0·001	0·036
End-struck – short quadrilateral	Length	38	30	80 = 50	50	50	53·6 ± 2·21	13·64
	Breadth	38	20	60 = 40	30	35	39·8	
	Thickness	38	< 10[a]	20 = *c.* 12·5	10	10	11	
	B/L ratio	38	0·6	1·0 = 0·4	0·6	0·7	0·71 ± 0·01	0·063
Side struck	Length	130	20	110 = 90	40	40	40·9 ± 1·203	13·72
	Breadth	130	30	130 = 100	60	60	58·4	
	Thickness	130	< 10[a]	40 = *c.* 32·5	10	15	*c.* 14·5	
Specialized								
Long quadrilateral	Length	57	40	100 = 60	60	70	69·4 ± 1·91	14·47
	Breadth	57	20	50 = 30	30	30	29·2	
	Thickness	57	< 10[a]	20 = *c.* 12·5	10	10	*c.* 11·5	
	B/L ratio	57	0·25	0·5 = 0·25	0·4	0·4	0·42 ± 0·001	0·08

[a] Calculated at 7·5 mm.

TABLE 23 (*cont.*)

	Measurement in mm	Number in sample	Range Min.	Max.	Mode(s)	Median	Mean ± error	S.D.
				Slightly abraded flakes: all raw materials (*cont.*)				
Specialized								
Triangular	Length	32	20	100 = 80	60	60	60·6 ± 3·32	18·8
	Breadth	32	30	60 = 30	30	40	37·8	
	Thickness	32	< 10[a]	20 = *c.* 12·5	10	10	12·2	
	B/L ratio	32	0·4	1·0 = 0·6	0·6	0·6	0·62 ± 0·047	0·27
	Th/B ratio	32	0·16	0·5 = 0·34	0·33	0·33	*c.* 0·34 ± 0·055	0·31
Combined specialized								
Quadrilateral and triangular	Length	89	20	100 = 80	60	60	63·9 ± 1·55	14·63
	Breadth	89	20	60 = 40	30	30	32·3 ± 0·88	8·33
	Thickness	89	< 10[a]	40 = *c.* 32·5	10	15	*c.* 12·4	
	B/L ratio	89	0·25	1·0 = 0·75	0·5	0·45	0·49 ± 0·02	0·15
All flakes								
	Length	711	20	130 = 110	50	60	55·3 ± 0·64	17·18
Cores								
	Length	78	40	80 = 40	50	52·5	54·4 ± 1·19	10·5
	Breadth	78	20	70 = 50	40	40	44·7 ± 1·04	9·2
	Thickness	78	10	60 = 50	30	30	27·6 ± 1·12	9·9
				Abraded flakes: all raw materials				
Unspecialized								
End-struck – irregular	Length	330	20	120 = 100	50	60	59·7 ± 0·93	17·06
	Breadth	330	20	90 = 70	40	40	51	
	Thickness	330	< 10[a]	40 = *c.* 32·5	10	15	*c.* 13·9	
	B/L ratio	330	0·3	1·0 = 0·7	1·0	0·75	0·78 ± 0·009	0·159
End-struck – short quadrilateral	Length	29	30	90 = 60	50	50	56·9 ± 3·2	17·63
	Breadth	29	30	50 = 20	30	40	38·2	
	Thickness	29	< 10[a]	20 = *c.* 12·5	10	10	*c.* 12·07	
	B/L ratio	29	0·6	1·0 = 0·4	0·6	0·6	0·68 ± 0·026	0·14
Side struck	Length	104	20	100 = 80	40	50	50·8 ± 1·31	13·45
	Breadth	104	30	140 = 110	70	70	67·4	
	Thickness	104	< 10[a]	45 = *c.* 37·5	20	20	*c.* 17·4	
Specialized								
Long quadrilateral	Length	30	20	110 = 90	80	80	70·4 ± 3·3	18·29
	Breadth	30	10	50 = 40	30	30	32	
	Thickness	30	< 10[a]	40 = *c.* 32·5	10	10	*c.* 11	
	B/L ratio	30	0·3	0·5 = 0·2	0·4, 0·42	0·45	0·43 ± 0·006	0·35
Triangular	Length	26	40	110 = 70	70	70	66·1 ± 3·07	15·64
	Breadth	26	20	70 = 50	40, 50	40	41·3	
	Thickness	26	< 10[a]	40 = *c.* 32·5	10	10	*c.* 13·6	
	B/L ratio	26	0·4	0·8 = 0·4	0·6	0·6	0·62 ± 0·035	0·18
	Th/B ratio	26	0·2	0·57 = 0·37	0·25	0·33	*c.* 0·29 ± 0·051	0·263
Combined specialized								
Quadrilateral and triangular	Length	56	20	110 = 90	80	70	70·2 ± 2·09	19·66
	Breadth	56	10	70 = 60	30	40	36·3 ± 1·49	11·16
	Thickness	56	< 10[a]	40 = *c.* 32·5	10	10	*c.* 12·4	
	B/L ratio	56	0·3	0·8 = 0·5	0·5	0·5	0·53 ± 0·02	0·12
All flakes								
	Length	519	20	120 = 100	50	60	58·8 ± 0·83	18·99
Cores								
	Length	46	40	100 = 60	50	55	57·4 ± 1.98	13·43
	Breadth	46	30	80 = 50	40	50	49·0 ± 1·72	11·68
	Thickness	46	10	60 = 50	30	30	30·4 ± 1·83	12·42

[a] Calculated as 7·5 mm.

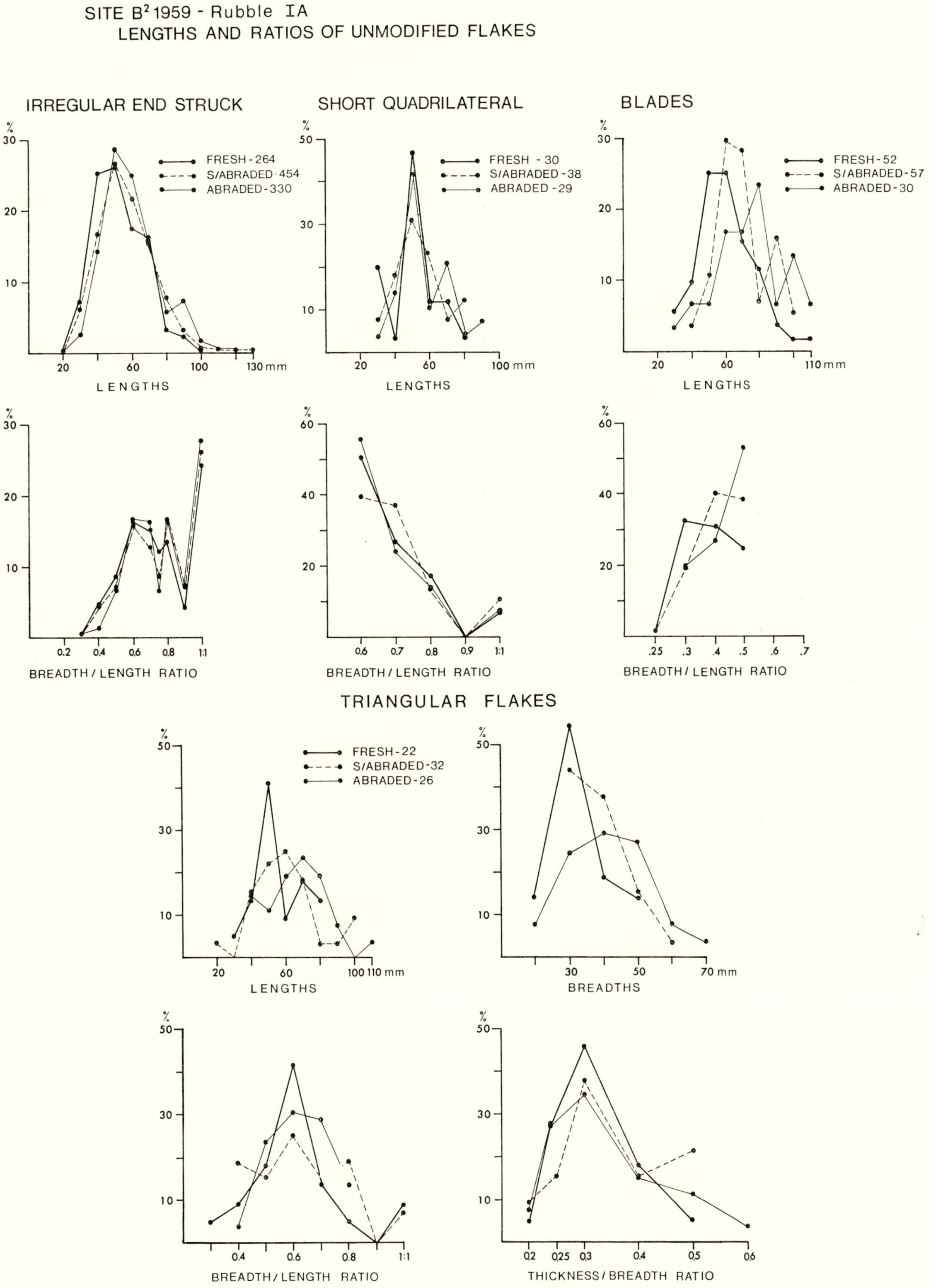

Fig. 28. Lengths, breadths and ratios of unmodified flakes from Rubble Ia, Site B2, 1959.

SITE B² 1959 : RUBELE IA — FLAKE AND BLADE DETAILS

Plan Form : Platform Type : Dorsal Scar Pattern : Raw Materials

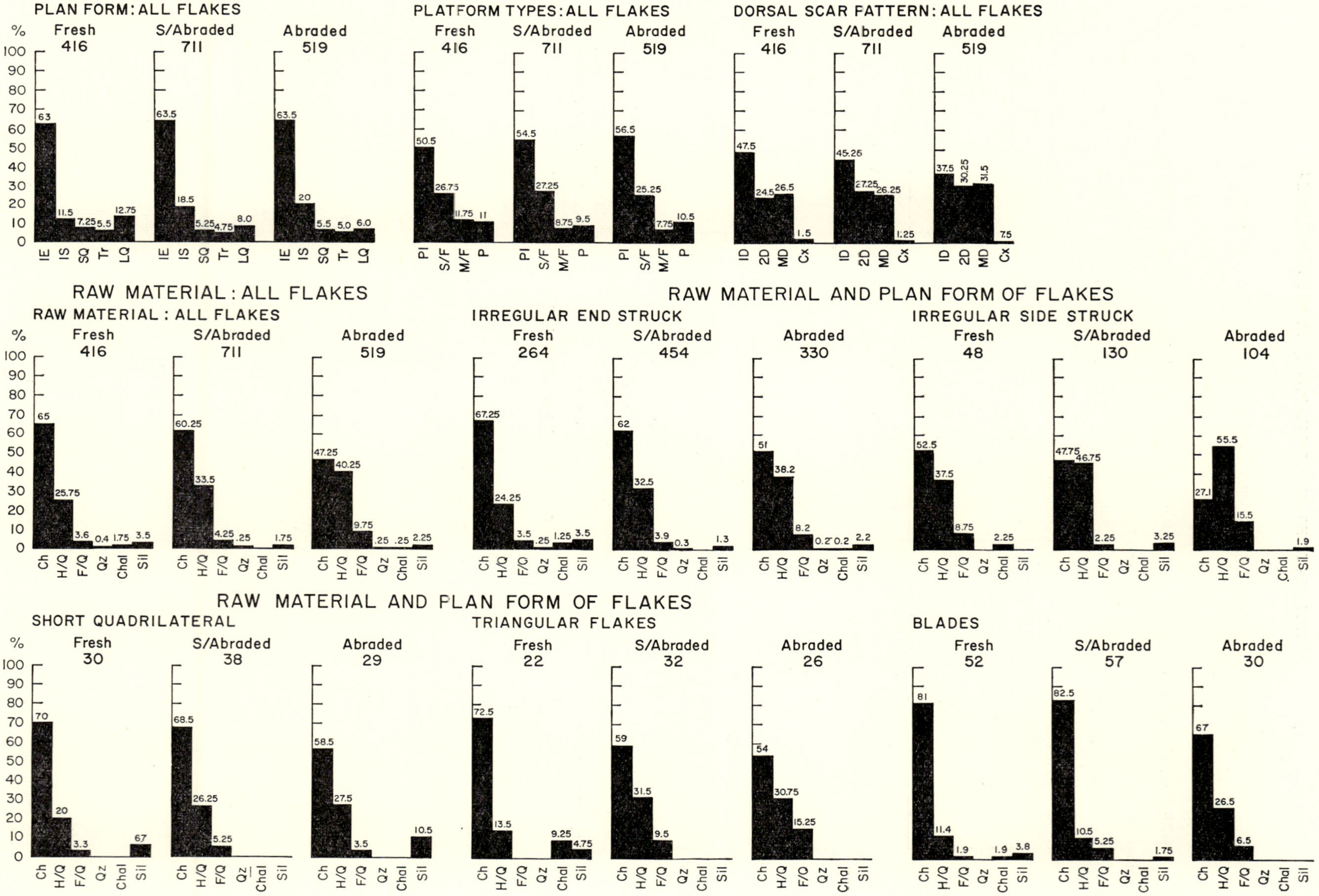

dorsal scar pattern. From this it can be seen that the slightly abraded category contains roughly twice as many as the fresh and abraded categories and, as might be expected, the greater part of the collection consists of unmodified waste and cores. Table 22 shows also that there is no appreciable difference in the small number of large cutting and heavy duty tools nor in the light duty classes, in each category, except for the backed flake and blade forms which are represented only in the fresh category. The presence or absence of these classes cannot be taken as a valid basis for separating components since such forms do occur in the slightly abraded category at other sites in the local basin. Minor size and plan form differences and qualitative characteristics, such as the nature of the secondary flaking, have been used to show some differences in the individual tool classes in each of the abrasion categories but they are not apparent from a general inventory of this kind. Since changes in flaking techniques are best reflected in the differences in the waste classes, the flakes and cores have been further analysed for comparison by abrasion categories and some differences can be discerned here.

Table 23 gives dimension details for the whole flakes and cores in Rubble Ia in B2, 1959 within the three abrasion categories. Again no dramatic changes are apparent but a gradual trend from larger sized forms in the more abraded categories to smaller in the fresh can be clearly demonstrated. The size range for irregular end- and side-struck flakes shows no difference in the minimum measurements (as was noted at p. 197, none less than 20 mm in length were recovered) but a greater number of longer examples are present in the slightly abraded and abraded categories.[1] There is no difference to be seen in the modes but the mean shows a very gradual change from shorter and thinner flakes in the fresh category to increasingly larger and thicker ones; this is also borne out by the position of the median. The same trend is demonstrated again by the short quadrilateral and blade classes but the decrease in overall dimensions is best reflected by the specialized triangular flakes and is well seen in the mode and median: fresh 50; slightly abraded 60; abraded 70 mm – as well as in the mean: fresh 51·8; slightly abraded 60·6; abraded 66·1 mm.

Turning to the breadth/length ratios, it is only in the long quadrilateral flakes with parallel dorsal scars, that any differences can be discerned and here the values for the fresh category show a small decrease from those for the other two categories, which are the same. The triangular flake abrasion categories differ only in that there are more longer and thicker examples in the abraded groups. When the specialized flakes are combined the values confirm the same general trend from longer and broader forms with the slightly abraded and abraded groups to shorter and narrower primary forms in the fresh group with the slightly abraded series falling in an intermediate position. This is borne out also for the values for the flake class as a whole. Comparing the lengths and breadth/length ratios (Figure 28) the overall similarity in the graphs of the flake percentages in the three abrasion categories becomes very apparent, but there is a clear, though not a marked, tendency for the fresh category to have a greater number of smaller flakes. The evidence from the cores, best seen in the mean values, substantiates that from the flakes and shows a corresponding diminution in size from abraded to fresh;

Fig. 29. Plan form, platform types, dorsal scar patterns and raw material of unmodified flakes and blades from Rubble Ia, Site B2, 1959.

Key:

Plan form
- IE = Irregular end-struck
- IS = Irregular side-struck
- SQ = Short quadrilateral
- Tr = Triangular
- LQ = Long quadrilateral

Platform types
- Pl = Plain
- S/F = Simple faceted
- M/F = Multi-faceted
- P = Point

Dorsal scar pattern
- 1D = One-directional
- 2D = Two-directional
- MD = Multi-directional
- Cx = Cortex

Raw material
- Ch = Chert
- H/Q = Hard quartzite
- F/Q = Feldspathic quartzite
- Qz = Quartz
- Chal = Chalcedony
- Sil = Silcrete

[1] The gradations of 10 (i.e. 20 mm, 30 mm, etc.) in many of the measurements result from the expression in millimetres of the original figure in many cases recorded only to the nearest centimetre.

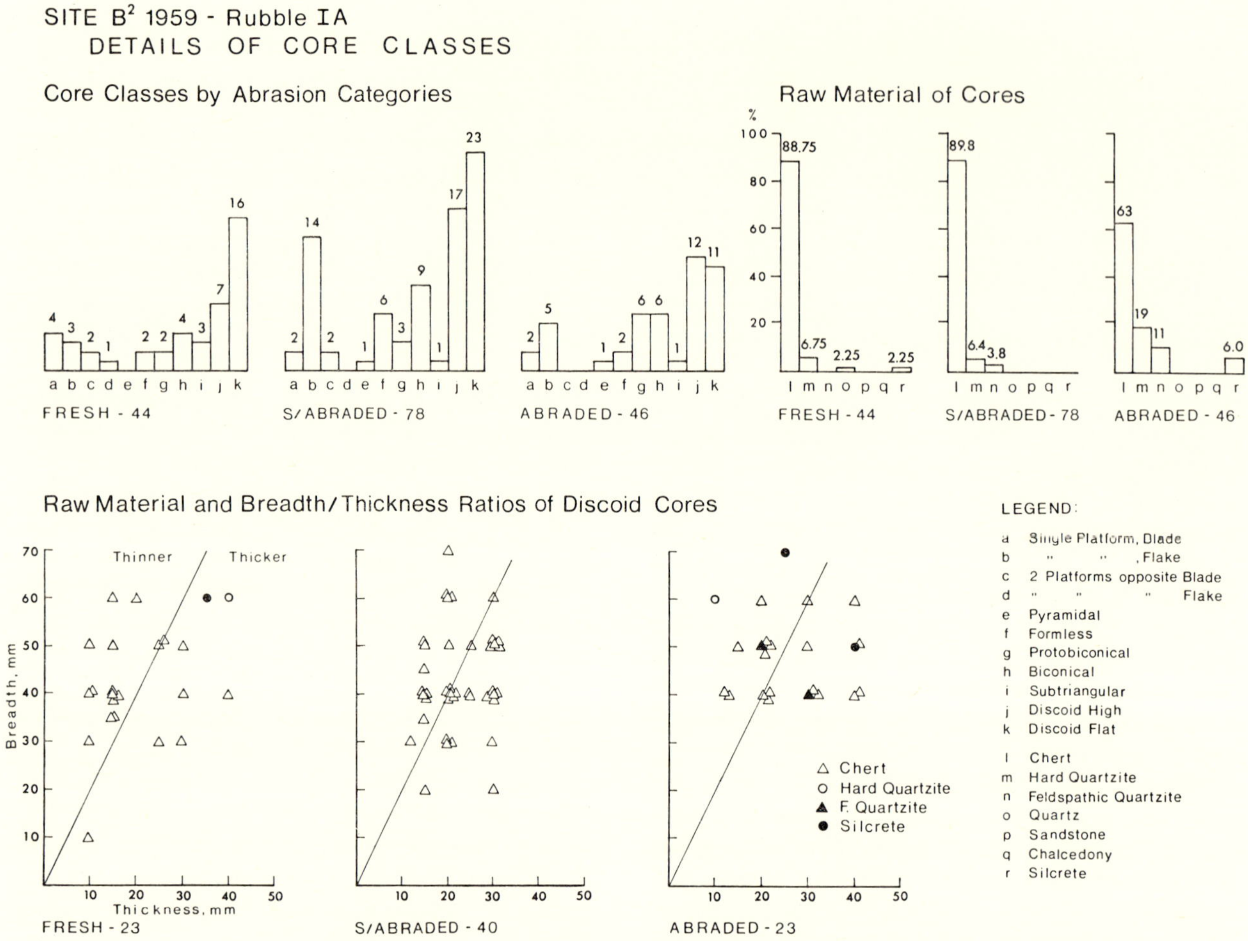

Fig. 30. Details of core classes from Rubble Ia, Site B2, 1959.

this is considered as corroboration that the agencies responsible for this dimensional shift were cultural and not natural ones.

Plan form, platform types and dorsal scar patterns of all flakes are shown in the bar diagrams at Figure 29 as well as the breakdown by raw material for each abrasion category. Irregular, side-struck flakes gradually decrease from the abraded to fresh groupings, while the incidence of blades shows a corresponding increase in the other direction from 6·0 per cent in the abraded to 12·75 per cent in the fresh group; percentages for the other forms remain virtually the same. Platform types show no essential differences. In each category over 50 per cent have plain striking platforms and point platforms, often indicative of punch technique, show appreciably the same percentage in each category. There is, however, a slight increase in the number of flakes showing multi-faceted platforms and this is probably significant in view of the importance attached to this type of platform preparation in the Hillslope component of the Polungu Industry.

In the raw material breakdown, the fresh and slightly abraded categories resemble each other more closely than they do the abraded group. There is an 18 per cent increase in the amount of chert used in the fresh category over that used in the abraded, hard quartzite shows a 15 per cent increase from the fresh to the abraded. The same trend is shown by the feldspathic quartzite artifacts though it is not so significant as there are fewer of them. The exotic materials which form only a very small percentage of the total, but which might be expected to reflect an increase in the fresh category, show no apparent change, indicating that they were also being brought into the local basin by the makers of the Siszya Industry.

Figure 29 also shows the breakdown according to flake forms which reflects a generally similar pattern.

TABLE 24. *Lengths in millimetres of specialized flakes: Sites A and B, Rubble I and ?Pits Channel Rubble (M.R.K. and J.D.C.)*

Sample	Fresh			S/Abraded			Abraded			Total		
	No.	Mean	S.D.	No.	Mean	S.D.	No.	Mean	S.D.	No.	Mean	S.D.
Total sample, whole flakes – all raw materials												
A2/II ?I or P.Ch.	22	46·2	18·1	75	47·9	13·4	31	61·55	18·8	128	50·9	16·7
A3 Rubble Ia	1			6			6			13	56·0	17·1
A3 Rubble Ib and I comp.	29	38·7	10·1	83	51·6	16·5	35	65·3	21·2	147	52·3	18·9
A4 Rubble I comp.	8	56·8	34·2	161	55·4	20·96	411	54·6	17·7	580	54·9	18·9
Chert flakes only												
A2/II ?I or P.Ch.	18	47·2	19·6	71	46·6	11·4	25	55·6	13·8	114	47·9	13·9
A3 Rubble Ia	1			5			5			11	54·4	17·3
A3 Rubble Ib and I comp.	24	37·8	8·5	72	50·99	16·9	24	61·96	21·8	120	50·5	18·4
A4 Rubble I comp.	4			120	52·9	21·1	334	53·1	16·7	458	52·9	18·0
Total sample,[a] whole flakes – all raw materials												
B2 Rubble Ia	74	59·3	16·2	89	63·9	14·63	56	70·2	19·66	219	64·89	18·0

[a] The short quadrilaterals have not been included as no record was made as to whether these were, in fact, from specialized cores. If, however, they are included, then the figures for B2 Rubble Ia would be: 104 56·6 ± 16·25 127 62·5 ± 16·97 85 65·6 ± 19·31 316 61·2 ± 17·28.

Somewhat greater use was made of exotic materials for irregular, end-struck flakes by the makers of the fresh group. Side-struck flakes in the abraded category are made mostly of hard quartzite while chert decreases as feldspathic quartzite increases in importance. The importance of chert for the manufacture of flakes from blade cores, as also of flakes from Levallois cores, is clear from the bar diagrams for short quadrilateral flakes, blades and triangular forms; 81 per cent of the fresh and 82·5 per cent of the slightly abraded blades are made from chert as against 67 per cent in the abraded group. Of the fresh triangular flakes 72·5 per cent are made from chert, 9·25 per cent from chalcedony and only 13·5 per cent from hard quartzite. In the abraded category only 54 per cent are in chert, there are none in chalcedony and the percentage of hard quartzite has more than doubled.

There were 168 cores in Rubble Ia; 44 are fresh, 78 slightly abraded and 46 abraded. Details of classes and raw materials are given in Figure 30. The breakdown by classes shows no great difference between the three categories although there is a slight increase in blade/flake cores in the fresh and slightly abraded categories: 22·7 per cent and 24·25 per cent as against 17·39 per cent. In each group the greatest number of cores are specialized discoid and subtriangular – 59 per cent fresh, 52·57 per cent slightly abraded and 52·17 per cent abraded. The nonspecialized, biconical, proto-biconical and formless cores show an interesting increase in the abraded group from 18·1 per cent fresh, 23·1 per cent slightly abraded to 30·43 per cent abraded. This probably reflects the incorporation of some derived Sangoan and Acheulian artifacts in Rubble I. In the raw material used for cores, the fresh and slightly abraded groups most nearly resemble each other, in contrast to the abraded group. Appreciably more use is made of chert in the first two categories (88·7 per cent fresh; 89·8 per cent slightly abraded) as against 63 per cent in the abraded group which records higher values for hard quartzite and feldspathic quartzite. There are, thus, more of the unspecialized classes and more quartzite used in the cores that are abraded.

In order to measure any changes in 'refinement' in the disc cores, which can be divided into those that are high-backed or thick in section relative to breadth and those that are flatter and more lenticular, the thickness/breadth ratios of these cores were plotted (Figure 30) in an attempt to determine if there had

TABLE 25. *Dimensions in millimetres of fresh flakes from Rubble I (composite), Sites A3 and A4 and from Rubble Ia, Site B2 (M.R.K. and J.D.C.)*

		Range					
	No.	Min.	Max.	Mode	Median	Mean	S.D.
			A3 and A4 Rubble I composite				
Unspecialized							
Lengths							
End-struck	97	15·5	115·5 = 100	35·5	36·3	43·7	20·9
Side-struck	40	15·5	95·5 = 80	35·5, 85·5	46·7	51·0	23·7
Specialized							
Lengths							
A3 total	29	23	66 = 43	33	36·6	38·7	10·1
A4 total	8[a]	20	121 = 101	—	50·0	56·8	34·2
Combined A3 and A4							
Lengths							
Quadrilateral (L and Sh)	15[a]	25	68 = 43	43	41·5	42·3	11·4
parallel or convergent triangular	14	23	83 = 60	33	33·3	39·1	15·1
Radial triangular	6	20	49 = 29	38	35·0	33·8	10·2
Radial other	2	66	121 = 55				
Total	37[a]	20	121 = 101	33, 43	38·1	42·6	19·0
B/L ratios							
Quadrilateral (L and Sh)	15[b]	0·16	0·79	0·555	0·54	0·54	0·141
parallel or convergent triangular	14	0·29	0·80	0·655	0·60	0·56	0·164
Radial triangular	6	0·55	0·85	0·755	0·73	0·72	0·103
Radial other	2	0·55	0·75				
Total	37[b]	0·16	0·85	0·55, 0·755	0·59	0·59	0·171
			B2 Rubble Ia				
Unspecialized							
Lengths							
End-struck	264	20	100 = 80	50	50	53·3	15·0
Side-struck	30	30	80 = 50	50	50	50·8	13·7
Specialized							
Lengths							
L/Quadrilateral	52	30	110 = 80	50, 60	60	60·6	16·96
Triangular	22	30	80 = 50	50	50	51·8	14·7
Total	74	30	110 = 80	50	60	59·3	16·22

[a] Blade tool with retouched or utilized end not included; length over 103 mm, increases means.
[b] Blade tool not included; B/L ratio of 0·39 decreases means.

been a replacement of the thick, high-backed form by flat discs. As the scatter diagrams show, there are an almost equal number of thick and thin discs in the abraded and slightly abraded categories. In the fresh category there are 14 flat discs as against 9 high-backed but the total number is too small to have much significance. The fresh category shows a greater variability in dimensions than either of the other two and there seems to be a trend from larger, abraded, to smaller, slightly abraded examples which has not been followed up in the fresh category. In all three categories, chert was the material most favoured for the making of these specialized cores.

Turning to the shaped tools, the numbers in the various classes are, with one exception, too small to show any quantitative indication of change. Only the small scraper class provides this information; the attributes of all scraper classes are given in Table 26. In each of the abrasion categories, small scrapers are made predominantly from chert with a few in hard

TABLE 26. *Attributes of scraper classes, Rubble Ia, Site B2, 1959*

	Scrapers											
	Fresh				Slightly abraded				Abraded			
	Large	Core	Small	Total	Large	Core	Small	Total	Large	Core	Small	Total
Raw material												
Chert		3	27	30		2	51	53		4	14	18
H/Q	2	2	2	6	1	4	7	12		4	3	7
F/Q							1	1				
Silcrete		1	2	3					1			1
Primary form												
Flake	1		17	18			25	25			9	9
Fragment			3	3			14	14			2	2
Chunk/core	1	6	11	18	1	6	20	27	1	8	6	15
Plan form												
Irregular	1	5	21	27	1	4	45	50	1	2	13	16
Long quadrilateral	1		3	4			1	1				
Short quadrilateral			6	6		2	7	9		2	4	6
Triangular			1	1			5	5				
Circular		1		1			1	1		4		4
Edge working												
Single side	1	2	12	15	1	2	34	37		2	10	12
Double side	1	2	11	14		1	9	10	1		2	3
Side and end		1	3	4		2	7	9			1	1
Three sides			1	1		1	1	2		1	1	2
End			3	3			6	6			2	2
All round		1		1						4		4
Butt			1	1			2	2		1	1	2
Edge form												
Straight	2		18	20		2	21	23			10	10
Convex		6	10	16		8	26	34		10	5	15
Concave			2	2			9	9			1	1
Notched	1	1	3	5	1		10	11	1		2	3
Denticulate			9	9		1	6	7			2	2
Beaked			2	2			3	3			1	1
Nosed		2	2	4			2	2	1		1	2
Convergent			1	1								
Edge angle												
Shallow			12	12			12	12			4	4
Blunt	2	1	10	13	1		30	31	1		6	7
Steep		5	9	14		6	17	23		8	7	15
Flake platform												
Plain	1		9	10			16	16			6	6
S/F			5	5			5	5			2	2
M/F			2	2			4	4				
Point			1	1							1	1
Dorsal scar pattern												
1-direction	1	3	13	17		3	18	21		4	6	10
2-direction		2	7	9		1	23	23		2	5	7
Multi-direction	1	1	11	13	1	2	18	18	1	2	6	9
Total of worked edges	3	9	47	59	1	11	77	89	2	10	22	34
Total of scrapers	2	6	31	39	1	6	59	66	1	8	17	26

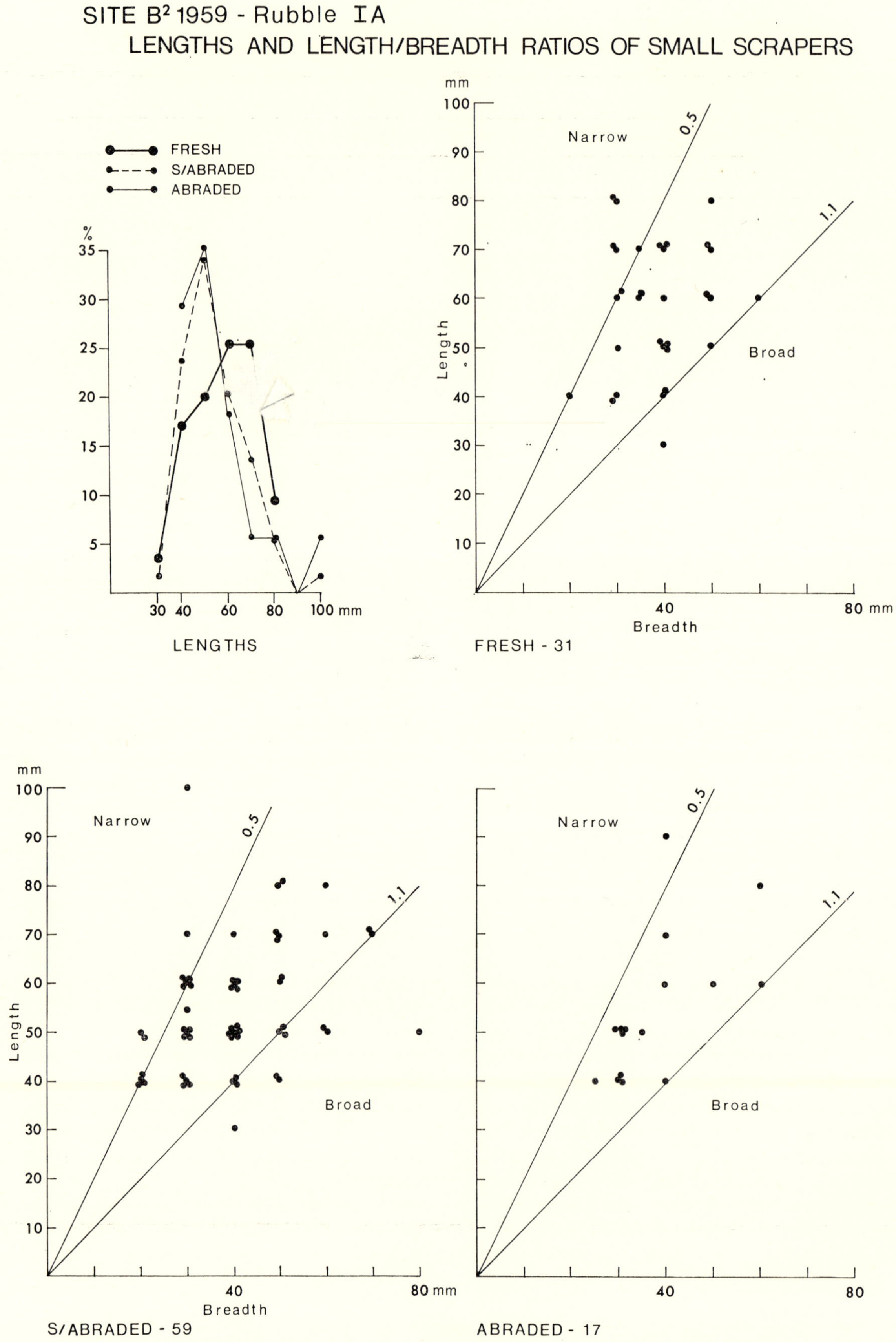

Fig. 31. Lengths and breadth/length ratios of small scrapers, Rubble Ia, Site B2, 1959.

quartzite. There appears to be no particular preference in the primary form for flakes or chunks but the number of scrapers made on fragments increases in the slightly abraded group. The great majority show no regular plan form and are small scrapers with one or more retouched edges. In the two abraded groups single edges predominate but retouch on two lateral edges assumes importance with the fresh scrapers and is equally as common as on one edge. The most frequently found edge forms in all three categories are convex and straight but there is a greater number of concave and notched edges among the slightly abraded and denticulate edges increase in this and the fresh category also. In the angle of edge retouch there is a swing from mostly steep angles in the abraded group to an increased number with shallow edges in the fresh group.[1] The platform type on the primary flake is generally plain but there is an increase in the number with multi-directional dorsal scar patterns in the fresh group. There appears to be a preference for making large- and core-scrapers in the harder, tougher rocks which perhaps indicates a different purpose from that for which the small scrapers were used; they mostly have steep or blunt retouch angles and convex working edges.

Lengths and breadth/length ratios of small scrapers are shown at Figure 31. The graph of lengths shows a greater range among the fresh scrapers whereas the abraded groups are usually between 40 and 50 mm long. The breadth/length ratios of the three categories are not very different although there is a slight increase in the number of broad forms in the slightly abraded group and a trend towards narrower forms in the slightly abraded and fresh categories. Breadth/length ratios of other light duty, large cutting and heavy duty tools are shown at Figure 32. The other small tools show no apparent difference; they are all longer than they are broad and there is, perhaps, a tendency to longer forms in the abraded group than in the other two. Burins and proto-burins are made mostly on fragments and chunks and the ratios of these can have little or no significance. It might have been thought that the points, which do show some interesting qualitative differences between the fresh and abraded groups, would have been distinguished, but this is not so, probably because the number is, unfortunately, too small. The greater length of the triangular flakes in the abraded category might be reflected by two of the points in this group and the fresh ones tend to be narrower. The only real difference is in the narrow, backed and truncated blade and flake forms. Although, again, there are too few for them to have any statistical significance, they confirm observations from the other Rubble I aggregates.

The large cutting and heavy duty classes (Figure 32) represent a small but important group. Although there are none represented in Rubble Ia at B2, 1959, some of the other Rubble I aggregates contain a few hand-axes and cleavers together with some core-axes and picks, usually made in hard or feldspathic quartzite, that are in fresh condition. Clearly, they do not belong with the main group of the artifacts in this category and, on typological grounds, they belong with earlier industrial traditions and are derived directly from the Ochreous Sands and White Sands when these were cut into by the erosion directly preceding the formation of Rubble I. Often, although not always, the dimensions of these tools are outside the observed limits for the other tools and unmodified waste and, on typological grounds, they can be distinguished from them. In the B2, 1959 Excavation the erosion surface on which Rubble Ia has formed is cut into the Ochreous Sands with the (Sangoan) Chipeta Industry but no deeper (see Volume 1, Figures 36–39). Typological comparisons show that excepting those noted above there is no reason to disassociate any of the heavy duty or large scraper forms from the components that are contemporary with Rubble I. The core-axes and picks are mostly made from chert and exhibit attributes that show them to belong with the abraded groups in the Lupemban Industrial Complex. Although a few atypical and unifacial examples of core-axes or high-backed scrapers were recovered with fresh material from other Rubble I aggregates (see p. 167), the evidence suggests that the typical, bifacial Lupemban-type of core-axe was no longer being manufactured at the time the makers of the latest and fresh component in Rubble I occupied the local basin. It is to be expected, however, that some heavy duty equipment would have been required in the more thickly wooded savanna at the close of the Pleistocene so that the few large scrapers, choppers and core-scrapers are not out of place here. As Figure 32 shows, their dimensions exhibit no essential difference from the equipment types in the abraded categories.

Apart from the unmodified waste, the most numerous artifacts in the B2, 1959 Excavation are the informal utilized/modified pieces with discontinuous

[1] Shallow trimming may become less recognizable with abrasion, however.

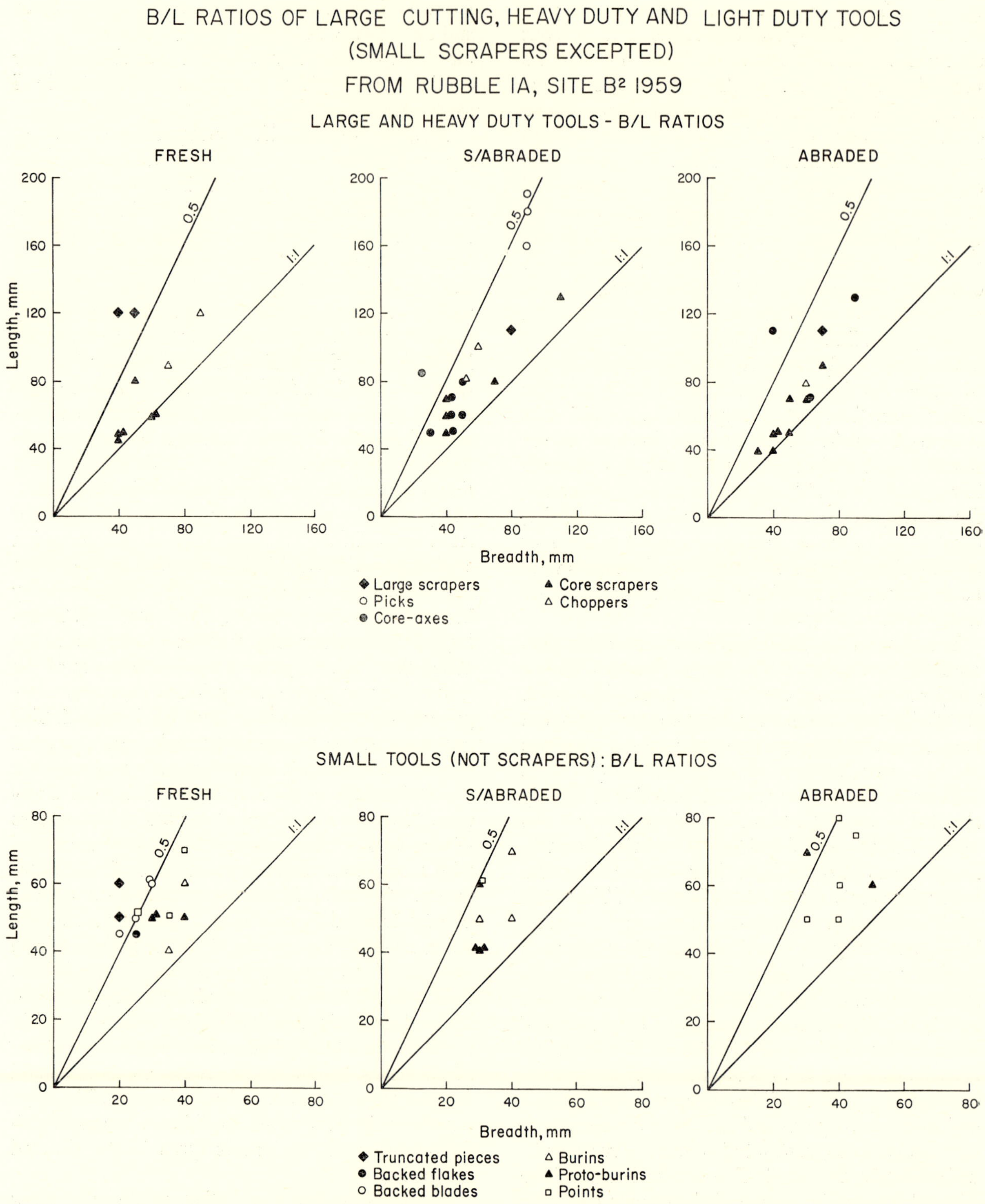

Fig. 32. Breadth/length ratios of large cutting, heavy duty and light duty tools (small scrapers excepted) from Rubble Ia, Site B2, 1959.

retouch and utilization, usually marginal. There is little difference between the attributes of these pieces in the three categories and those of the small scraper forms. Chert was the predominant raw material; they are mostly between 60 and 90 mm in length and have a plain striking platform and one-directional flaking on the dorsal face. Abrasive agents have resulted in some marginal nibbling but this has been taken into account in deciding whether an artifact should be classified as utilized or not and these pieces generally show one or more small areas of discontinuous trimming. They apparently represent a common element in the tool-kits of the later Pleistocene at the Kalambo Falls as, indeed, they do in other 'Middle Stone Age' aggregates from southern Africa as, for example, at Montagu Cave at the Cape (Keller, 1970: 192).

Reviewing the evidence set out above, it will be apparent that there is a close resemblance in most attributes between the artifacts in the fresh and the abraded categories. There is more resemblance between the fresh and slightly abraded groups than between the fresh and the abraded categories, as might be expected if these lie in temporal relationship to one another and all form part of a long and developing tradition. The fact that the slightly abraded category shows in general more uniformity in the attributes of its artifacts than do either of the other groups while trending sometimes towards the fresh group and sometimes towards the abraded, is more likely to reflect its medial position than that it includes artifacts which properly belong in one of the other groups. Although some mixing of this kind must surely exist where one of the main criteria for separation is based on *état physique*, the available data make it unlikely that this has resulted in any serious distortion of the components.

The component represented by the fresh and latest artifacts in Rubble Ia at Site B2, 1959, can be distinguished from the next oldest component, having in general slightly abraded artifacts, on the following criteria:

1. A greater range in artifact form with correspondingly less uniformity within the artifact classes.

2. An increase in narrower, more blade-like forms and a tendency for these to be smaller. At the same time broad, multi-faceted platforms become more common.

3. More exclusive use is made of chert as material for artifacts with only small percentages of hard quartzite and exotic materials such as chalcedony and quartz.

4. The shaped tool-kit combines small numbers of traditional forms of large chopping and scraping tools (but without the Lupemban (Siszya Industry) core-axe) with a more significant small tool element.

5. Traditional forms of Siszya Industry tools that continue to be represented are the burins and proto-burins, backed flakes, points and small scrapers. New forms are represented by the backed blades, the bored stone and others such as *outils esquillés*, not present in the Rubble Ia at B2, 1959.

6. The small scrapers show an increase in the number with two worked lateral edges and with shallower retouch angles of the working edges. Denticulate edges also increase in importance. Finally, the size range is greater and some specimens are narrower than those in the other components.

7. DESCRIPTION OF ARTIFACT SETS IN FRESH CONDITION FROM OTHER RUBBLE I AGGREGATES

An examination of the aggregates from the Rubble I excavations (excepting Rubble Ic) showed that the same characteristics distinguished the fresh series from the remainder while also adding some new artifact forms. In spite of the small number of shaped tools, we believe that the common affinities shown by all the fresh artifact groups in each of these aggregates indicate a valid cultural entity which forms a link between the Siszya Industry (Lupemban) and the Hillslope component of the Polungu Industry. Because of the new artifact forms and the shift, slight though it is, in the dimensions of the unmodified waste, these aggregates have for the present been referred to the Polungu Industry and are identified here as the Rubble component. This is here described on the basis of the aggregates from eight excavated areas in addition to that from Rubble Ia at Site B examined in detail above. Analysis of the fresh artifact group in each aggregate is presented in Table 27 and a representative series of tools and unmodified waste is illustrated at Plates 48–54. Since the greatest number of artifacts in each of these aggregates from Rubble I can be shown to belong to the Siszya Industry, the tables showing the breakdown by abrasion categories will be reserved for reproduction in Volume III where that industry is described and only the details of the fresh category forming the Rubble component of the Polungu Industry, are given here.

TABLE 27. *Artifact classes of the Rubble component of the Polungu Industry and other fresh artifacts from excavations at Sites A, B, and D, Kalambo Falls*

	A1, 1956		B1, 1956		A1, 1956		A2, 1956	A3, 1956		A4, 1959	B2, 1959			D, 1956	
	Base bedded sands		Base bedded sands		Rubble Ib		?Pits channel Rubble (F)	Rubble Ia (F)	Rubble I b and c (F)	Rubble I (composite) (F)	Rubble Ia (F)	Between Ia and Ib (F)	Rubble Ib (F)	Rubble I (composite) (F)	
Artifact classes	F	S.a.	F	S.a.	F	S.a.									Total
SHAPED TOOLS															
Large cutting/scraping															
Hand-axes									1				1		2[a]
Cleavers									1						1[a]
Large scrapers										1	2		2		5
Total large cutting/scraping tools									2	1	2		3		8
Heavy duty															
Picks										2		1	1		4[b]
Core-axes		1				2	1			1		1	11		17[c]
Core-scrapers						1			2		6		12		21
Choppers											2		3		5
Chisels					1								2		3
Bored stones											1				1[d]
Total heavy duty tools		1			1	3	1		2	3	9	2	29		51
Light duty															
Microliths									1						1
Truncated flakes/blades				1							2		2		5
Backed flakes/blades							1			1	5	3	5	1	16
Points: unifacial			1								2	3	3		9
bifacial											1	4	2		7
Burins											2	1	2		5
Proto-burins										1	3	1	6		11
Small scrapers		1		2		1		1	4	1	31	4	32	2	79
Discoid/adzes							1			1			1		3
Borers							1			1					2
Total light duty tools		1	1	3		1	3	1	5	5	46	16	53	3	138
Total all tools	—	2	1	3	1	4	4	1	9	9	57	18	85	3	197
UTILIZED/MODIFIED PIECES															
Flakes/blades		2		1					3	2	34	2	81	2	127
Cores/chunks					1		(1)		2		17		24		44
Outils esquillés												2	2		4
Hammerstones							1			4					5
Rubbers											1		1		2
Anvils													2		2
Miscellaneous rubbed											1		1		2
Total utilized/modified pieces	—	2	—	1	1	—	1	—	5	6	53	4	111	2	186

TABLE 27 (*cont.*)

Artifact classes	A1, 1956 Base bedded sands F	A1, 1956 Base bedded sands S.a.	B1, 1956 Base bedded sands F	B1, 1956 Base bedded sands S.a.	A1, 1956 Rubble Ib F	A1, 1956 Rubble Ib S.a.	A2, 1956 ?Pits channel Rubble (F)	A3, 1956 Rubble Ia (F)	A3, 1956 Rubble I b and c (F)	A4, 1959 Rubble I (composite) (F)	B2, 1959 Rubble Ia (F)	B2, 1959 Between Ia and Ib (F)	B2, 1959 Rubble Ib (F)	D, 1956 Rubble I (composite) (F)	Total
UNMODIFIED WASTE															
Flakes															
Irregular: end	7	28	8	16	12	8	7	5	74	23	178		128	1	495
side		3	3	1	3	4	10	7	30	8	31		42	1	143
Specialized: parallel dorsal trimming															
Short quadrilateral	1	3	5	4	1	1	7		9	2	23		66	3	125
Long quadrilateral		3	3	2	2	2	9		4		50		52		127
Short triangular			1	1			1	1	8	1	13		21		47
Long triangular		1							3	2	9		13		28
Specialized: radial dorsal trimming															
Irregular		1	6	4		5	3[e]		1		103		71		194
Short quadrilateral							4			1	7		19		31
Long quadrilateral											2		2		4
Short triangular							2		4	2			1		9
Long triangular													3		3
Core-axe resharpening		1		1							1		4		7[a]
Total waste flakes	8	40	26	29	18	20	43	13	133	39	417	—	422	5	1,213
Cores															
Blade – Single platform							1		4	2	7		5		19
2 platforms: opposing			1						2	2	3	1	3		12
2 platforms: two planes													2		2
Pyramidal													2		2
Proto-biconical/angle/bashed chunk									1		2		6		9
Biconical				1						2	4		9		16
Discoid				4		1		1	1	1	21	1	27		57
Sub-triangular								1			3		4		8
Struck – discoid (Levallois)							(1)		1	1	2		14		18
sub-triangular (Levallois)										1			5		6
Formless							1		3		2		5		11
Total cores			1	5		1	2	2	12	9	44	2	82		160
Flake fragments	41						7	3	32	2					85
Chunks	5					1		6				1	1		14
Total unmodified waste	54	40	27	34	18	22	52	24	177	50	461	3	505	5	1,472
Total all artifacts	54	44	28	38	20	26	57	25	191	65	571	25[f]	701[g]	10	1,855

[a] Not included in Rubble component.
[b] 1 only included in Rubble component but additional 2 from A4 Rubble I (composite) and 1 from B2 Rubble Ib, possible.
[c] 2 only included in Rubble component but additional 2 from A1 Rubble Ib, 1 from A4 Rubble I (composite) and 1 from B2 between Rubbles Ia and Ib possible.
[d] Slightly weathered. [e] Includes 2 broad/elliptical flakes.
[f] Incomplete count as abrasion categories recorded only for shaped tools.
[g] Sample of unmodified waste only: all flakes and cores from grid squares E6–K12.
* F = fresh; S.a. = slightly abraded.

(a) Aggregates from Site A; Rubble I excavations
The aggregates from the various exposures of Rubble I at Site A have been analysed by Kleindienst and the artifact lists and other details of these excavations that follow have been prepared by her. Before proceeding to examine the individual aggregates, however, it is first necessary to see how the dimensions of the flake content from the rubbles at Site A compare with those from Rubble Ia at Site B. Table 24 compares the mean lengths of all the specialized flakes in the three abrasion series, both separately and combined, as well as those for the chert flakes only, from the Site A rubbles. The values for the chert flakes within each aggregate are generally comparable with those for all raw materials combined. Comparing the four aggregates from the Site A rubbles, the variation in the mean length is seen to be greater but none of them vary among themselves to the degree that they all do from the mean length of the flakes from the Site B rubble where the mean from the fresh category is more comparable to that from the two abraded series from the A Site rubbles. The same degree of variability can be seen also in Table 25 where the further comparisons are made between different flake classes within the fresh series. While the values are generally consistent between the Site A rubbles, as they are within the Site B rubble, those for the latter are invariably higher by about 15 mm. The only instance where there is comparability between the two sites is with the specialized flakes from A4 but here the number on which the figure is based is too small to be statistically significant. One chert blade (> 103 mm long) with utilized and trimmed end has been intentionally omitted from the length measurements since, if it were included, the mean for the A4 total would be increased from 56·8 to 61·9 mm and the long quadrilateral mean from 42·3 to 46·1 mm.

We can give no certain explanation for this difference without further study of the original material. Qualitatively, no actual difference was observed and we believe these aggregates to be technically similar and broadly contemporary. There are several possible reasons to account for these differences in dimensions that were not observed in the field. They could be due to raw material preferences and selection and/or idiosyncratic differences in the by-products of flaking as between different individuals or groups among contemporary populations. They might also reflect behavioural differences as between activities on the hillslope and those by the river bank. Such variation might be expected to be accentuated if time differences of the magnitude of one or two thousand years were involved and this cannot, of course, be discounted until some more precise dating techniques become available and African industries can be more accurately dated. The agencies for natural sorting that distributed the artifacts in Rubble I at the Site A exposures, somewhat higher up the valley slope to the south than those at Site B, may have been such that a greater proportion of the smaller artifacts was not preserved. Some of this variance might also be due to procedural differences in data recording as between individual workers or to a percentage of the smaller unmodified pieces' either not having been recorded or not having been preserved. While these last possibilities cannot be excluded, we do not believe they could be sufficient to account for the dimension difference shown by the Rubble I aggregates from the two sites. Possibly we have been too ready to assume that dimensional differences of the degree shown by the aggregates from Site A and Site B do not occur among contemporary populations and perhaps the most likely causes are idiosyncratic. However, until more comparative evidence for radiometrically contemporary and closely adjacent aggregates is forthcoming from other localities, the degree of 'conformity' that can be expected in the dimensions of the by-products of stone flaking by 'contemporaneous' groups, still remains to be assessed.

Excavation A1, 1956: *Rubble Ib* (see Volume 1, Plate 12). Rubble line Ia has been cut out here by later channelling (Volume 1, Figure 32) and the truncated rubble preserved over the northern half of the excavation is correlated with Rubble Ib in the A5, River Face section. The rubble was some 4–6 inches (10–15 cm) thick and lay at a depth of 12 feet 6 inches to 13 feet 6 inches (3·8–4·1 m) below the surface. The following fresh and very slightly abraded artifacts, numbering 46 specimens, were associated with 280 slightly and more heavily abraded implements.

The two very slightly abraded core-axes are made of hard quartzite; they measure 210 × 90 × 60 mm and 170 × 100 × 80 mm, respectively. The one is parallel sided and unifacially worked with convex distal end, while the second has convergent lateral edges, a convex distal end and untrimmed butt, it is high-backed in section and worked on the dorsal face only. These tools probably belong with the Rubble component though they would not be out of place

Shaped tools	
Core-axes	2
Chisel	1
Core-scrapers	1
Small scrapers	1
Utilized/modified	
Chunks	1
Unmodified waste	
Unspecialized flakes	
Irregular end-struck	20
Irregular side-struck	7
Specialized flakes	
Parallel dorsal pattern –	
Long quadrilateral	4
Short quadrilateral	2
Radial dorsal pattern – irregular	5
Cores	
Prepared, discoid high-backed	1
Chunk	1
Total	46

with the included Siszya Industry component. They are less likely to group with older, abraded core-axes and two hand-axes that can only be derived from the Ochreous Sands bed of the Mkamba Member on which Rubble I rests upslope to the south and west. The remaining artifacts conform to the Rubble component as it can be seen in Rubble Ia, B2, 1959. The core-scraper is cuboid in shape and of hard quartzite. The chisel is formed on a crudely bifacial triangular fragment and shows edge damage on the chisel edge at the distal end. The small scraper, in chert, has concave trimming on the end of a flake fragment. It is of interest that 20 per cent of the irregular, end-struck flakes and blades are of microlithic proportions (i.e. less than 30 mm).[1]

Excavation A3, 1956: *Rubble Ia* (see Volume I, Plate 18). This thin rubble line was present over the southern part of the excavation. At the south end it was separated from Rubble Ib and c by 12 to 14 inches (30–35 cm) of white, unbedded sand. Northward it dipped down to join with the underlying rubble at grid line 2/3. The total number of artifacts was 121 of which 67 were slightly abraded and 29 abraded; only 25 of the artifacts – mostly unmodified waste – were fresh and are discussed here. One small scraper n hard quartzite is the only tool. This has the end obliquely retouched by steep, straight trimming and falls into the 31–60 mm length range. There are no utilized/modified pieces and the waste flakes are mostly irregular – end-struck (5) and side-struck (7). One short, triangular flake shows sub-parallel to convergent dorsal scars. Eight are in chert, 4 in hard quartzite and 1 in sandstone. One of the specialized, unstruck fresh cores is sub-triangular and high-backed, of quartzite and 48 × 55 × 25 mm in size; the other is of chert, is radially trimmed, sub-rectangular in plan with a cortex platform and measures 49 × 31 × 20 mm. It is possible that some or all of the slightly abraded artifacts should be included with the fresh series from this rubble as part of the Rubble component, as it is identified here. (Full details of artifact counts will be given in Volume III.)

Excavation A3, 1956: *Rubble Ib and c* (*composite*) (see Volume I, Plate 18). This is the main rubble with which Rubble Ia also merges and it contains considerably more artifacts – 1,044 of which 191 are fresh, 633 slightly abraded and 220 abraded. (There were also 9 heavily abraded and 1 that was not recorded.) Artifacts in the fresh category are listed overleaf.

The elongated, convergent edged hand-axe and the cleaver (possibly a side scraper on a flake with cleaver bit (M. R. K.)) in hard quartzite and sandstone, respectively, are clearly out of place here and can be presumed to be derived, as also can probably one of the trimmed quartzite cobble core-scrapers; all are forms found in Rubble II. The small tools are made in chert. The microlith[2] is made on a bladelet segment, 25 × 17 × 3 mm in size and has been obliquely retouched only on one end; the longer lateral edge has been utilized, with two small notches, one at either end. In this respect it resembles the single trapeze recovered from Rubble Ic in Excavation A1 (to be illustrated in Volume III) and suggests that these may have been utilized in some specific way. The small scrapers show the usual irregular plan form (one is retouched on the end and the others on one lateral edge) but, again, some could have come from Rubble II. The blade cores are quite typical and produced small, irregular, end-struck flakes, short quadrilaterals, blades and sub-triangular forms. All are small in size, ranging from 35 to 67 mm in length, yielding mainly flakes and bladelets less than

[1] Although in the aggregate from Rubble Ia, Site B2, 1959, there are exceedingly few end-struck flakes and blades with lengths less than 30 mm, some 33 per cent of them have lengths less than 50 mm.

[2] Kleindienst suggests that it is possible that microliths formed a more important element in the Rubble I components than has been preserved since blade snapping seems to have been practised at least as early as component B of the Sisya Industry and smaller material appears to have been removed from the rubbles by natural agencies.

Shaped tools	
Large cutting	
Hand-axe/core-axe	1
Cleaver/scraper	1
Heavy duty	
Core-scrapers (trimmed cobbles)	2
Light duty	
Microliths	1
Small scrapers	4
Total	9
Utilized/modified	
Flakes/blades	3
Chunks	2
Total	5
Unmodified waste	
Flakes	
End-struck	74
Side-struck	30
Short quadrilateral (parallel dorsal pattern)	9
Blade (parallel dorsal pattern)	4
Triangular (parallel/convergent dorsal pattern)	11
Triangular (Levallois) (radial dorsal pattern)	4
Broad/elliptical (Levallois) (radial dorsal pattern)	1
Total	133
Cores	
Prismatic, single platform	4
Prismatic, 2 platforms, opposed	2
Bashed chunk	1
Discoidal, unstruck	1
Struck Levallois flake	1
Formless	3
Total	12
Fragments and chunks	32
Total waste	177
Total artifacts	191

50 mm long with some blades less than 30 mm. Two show battering on the lower end; none have faceted platforms. Of the flakes/blades, 34 are under 30 mm; 77 lie between 30 and 60 mm, 20 between 60 and 90 mm and 2 are over 90 mm. The great majority (92) are made from chert; there are 34 of hard quartzite, 10 of sandstone, 3 of chalcedony, 2 of quartz and 1 of dolerite. The majority of the striking platforms of the specialized, parallel and radially prepared flakes are plain (15), only 4 show multi-faceting and 2 have point platforms. The unstruck core of chert measures 42 × 40 × 32 mm and the struck core 54 × 44 × 20 mm. Both are radially trimmed. The struck Levallois flake core produced a broad/elliptical flake, about 30 × 30 mm in size, with a 3-faceted, inclined platform and 7 radial dorsal scars.

Excavation A4, 1959: *Rubble I* (*composite*) (Plate 49) (see also Volume 1, Plate 20). The rubble was exposed in this excavation from grid line 21 northwards to grid line −2. It sloped down, at first steeply and then more gently, from south to north, intersecting Rubble II at about grid line 16 (Volume 1, Figures 28 and 29). It contained a large number of artifacts, the majority (2,664) being abraded. Only 65 artifacts are classified as fresh and comprise the following:

Shaped tools	
Large cutting	
Large scraper (nosed)	1
Heavy duty	
Pick, unifacial	2
Core-axe	1
Light duty	
Backed blade	1
Proto-burin	1
Discoid-adze	1
Small scraper	1
Borer	1
Total	9
Utilized/modified	
Flake	1
Blade/blade scraper	1
Hammerstone	4
Total	6
Unmodified waste	
Flakes	
Irregular, end-struck	23
Irregular, side-struck	8
Short quadrilateral (parallel dorsal pattern)	2
Short quadrilateral (radial dorsal pattern)	1
Triangular – short (parallel/convergent dorsal pattern)	1
long (parallel/convergent dorsal pattern)	2
short (radial dorsal pattern; 1 of chalcedony)	2
Total	39
Cores	
Bladelet, prismatic, single platform	2
Bladelet, prismatic, 2 platforms opposed	2
Biconical (1 in quartz)	2
Discoid, unstruck, high-backed (in chalcedony)	1
Levallois point, struck	1
Levallois, struck (unsuccessful) (in chalcedony)	1
Total	9
Fragments[1]	2
Total waste	50
Total artifacts	65

[1] Chips and chunks (flake fragments and chunks) were discarded in the field; the fresh/mint and slightly abraded categories were not differentiated.

There are more artifacts (excluding the two fragments) in hard quartzite (29) than in chert (26) which is unusual; chalcedony was used for one Levallois flake and two specialized cores and one side-struck flake and one biconical core are in vein quartz; one artifact was in feldspathic quartzite and two in sandstone. The picks, core-axe and scraper (> 100 mm) are all large and made in hard quartzite; with the possible exception of the two picks (?or scrapers) these must be considered to be derived. The large (> 100 mm) scraper is a round, end-scraper (165 × 130 × 40 mm) on a side-struck cobble flake which might, but need not necessarily be derived from Rubble II.

Most of the fresh material came from north of grid line 6, with the exception of 10 irregular flakes (6 of quartzite), the quartz biconical core (from grid square B/11), 1 bladelet core (B/9), 1 hammerstone (A/14) and the borer (B/11). The area of thicker rubble accumulation on the northern end of the trench is adjacent to the previous A3 excavation where material in general was in fresher condition. The two unifacial picks (150 × 95 × 50 mm and 180 × 85 × 90 mm), the core-axe made on a flat cobble (146 × 118 × 48 mm) and the large end-scraper (165 × 130 × 40 mm), together with 15 end-struck and 4 side-struck, irregular flakes and 2 specialized flakes of quartzite, plus one Levallois flake in sandstone, could all be derived from Rubble II or the Red Rubble in the immediate vicinity. However, they might also suggest that some heavy equipment is still part of the Rubble component. Unifacial picks (or ?specialized, high-backed scrapers) also are found in Excavation A1, Rubble Ib and in Excavation B2. The disc-adze (or core) is a relatively large example, made of chert (74 × 41 × 20 mm) with fine secondary retouch round the circumference on both faces but with the dorsal face trimmed last and with cortex retained in the centre of the ventral face, as is the case with many prepared cores. It is slightly asymmetrically biconvex in section and an attempt may have been made to remove a larger flake which hinged out; the opposite edge shows step-flaking on both faces which may be related to the striking or be use damage.

The utilized chert blade, or end-scraper, is longer than most of the fresh quadrilaterals (103 × 40 × 12 mm); it has nibbling and some step-flaking on both lateral edges on the dorsal face, with larger, thin, stepflaking and scalar flaking on the nosed end which may be either retouch or use damage. The collection includes only 8 specialized flakes (9 if the utilized blade is included): 4 have plain platforms, 3 are simple-faceted, 1 is multi-faceted and 1 is a point platform. They show a greater size range than do those from Excavation A3. The short quadrilateral or broad, Levallois flake of sandstone is the longest in the fresh group from either excavation (121 × 82 × 20 mm); a somewhat smaller example is found in A3 (66 × 52 × 8 mm). In this soft material, these can hardly have been transported but they could come from adjacent Rubble II or be manuports. The 4 prismatic cores are all small (26 × 26 × 10 mm, 35 × 35 × 32 mm, 35 × 25 × 25 mm, 62 × 39 × 23 mm) and of chert; none have faceted striking platforms. The smallest bladelets produced would have been about 15 × 7 mm in size and none are found in either A4 or A3. The two biconical cores are also small (65 × 50 × 40 mm and 60 × 45 × 35 mm).

A small series of artifacts from this rubble is illustrated at Plate 49 to show some of the characteristic artifacts of the Rubble component of the Polungu Industry.[1] They are all in chert and comprise a blade backed at the distal end (Plate 49: 3), truncated blades (Plate 49: 4 and 5) and a utilized/modified, short quadrilateral flake with parallel dorsal pattern and simple-faceted platform showing minimal retouch at the distal end of one lateral edge (Plate 49: 6); a triangular-sectioned borer on a chunk, possibly atypical but a very similar tool was found on the re-exposed ?Pits Channel Rubble at the A2, 1956, trench. Two examples of specialized cores are illustrated (Plate 49: 8 and 9). These are both small and high-backed and both have faceted striking platforms. In the one (no. 8) two irregular flakes have been struck from platforms at opposing ends; in the other, two short, triangular flakes have been struck from the side of the core and it might, therefore, be classified as a para-Levallois core. The discoid/adze at Plate 49: 10 is fairly typical of this kind of tool. It is lenticular in section and has areas of the circumference on one or both faces where fine, semi- and fully-invasive retouch shows preparation for some special purpose. It might be considered to demonstrate a morphological development of these tools from the lenticular-sectioned disc core, but it seems likely that these finely made specimens with the

[1] Some of these were classed as slightly abraded or abraded by M. R. K. The length distribution of specialized flakes in the slightly abraded category in A4 is bimodal, suggesting that probably Polungu material is incorporated (modes at 33·5 and 48·5); the bimodality is less marked in the A3 excavation but, here also, some smaller material has been slightly abraded.

Rubble component were never intended for use as cores. Although more often than not they have had one fairly insignificant, thin flake removed from one face (e.g. Plate 48: 9) this appears to be more probably the result of use or perhaps to facilitate hafting.

(*b*) *Site B aggregates*

Excavations B1, 1956 *and B2*, 1959: *Rubble Ia and Rubble I* (*composite*). The manner of occurrence of this rubble in the 1959 excavation and its relationship to that in the 1956 excavation has already been discussed, as also has the analysis of the artifacts. Rubble I composite in the B1, 1956, excavation yielded a considerable concentration of artifacts (4,221 in some 500 square feet (46·4 m^2)) but very few artifacts in completely fresh condition. However, when the analysis was carried out the artifacts from this floor were not broken down by abrasion categories so that it is, regrettably, not now possible to give precise figures for these without re-analysing the collections in Livingstone. The only artifacts specifically distinguished as fresh are one poorly-made microlith, a small scraper, a triangular flake and one *outil esquillé*. The backed blades, blade cores, burins, points, dimple-scarred rubbers as well as the heavy duty and large cutting tools all belong to earlier industrial entities, mostly to the Siszya Industry, and are variously abraded.

The small scraper (Plate 54: 11) is made on an irregular, end-struck flake and shows alternate retouch on two edges. A notched or concave edge has been formed on the ventral face and is opposed to a steeply trimmed edge on the dorsal face. These trimmed edges converge to a blunt, *bec*-like point. The short, triangular flake (Plate 54: 18) shows a parallel to convergent scar pattern on the dorsal face and a broad, simple-faceted striking platform consistent with having been struck from a specialized core; it is made from chalcedony.

A representative collection of the Rubble component from Rubble Ia in B2, 1959, is illustrated at Plates 51 and 52. Blade forms (Plate 51: 1–8) show one-directional flaking and plain, simple or point platforms, which are usually restricted. Plate 51: 9 is a resharpening flake from a blade core with two platforms at right angles. Plate 51: 19–23 show examples of the short, triangular flakes, generally with convergent and one-directional flaking, and faceted striking platforms; several of them have been utilized. A blade and irregular, end-struck flakes with marginal 'nibbled' utilization are illustrated at Plate 51: 10–12 and 17. Broad, radially prepared flakes with faceted platforms from specialized Levallois cores are represented at Plate 51: 28 and 29. A typical opposed platform core for small blades is illustrated at Plate 51: 33; one of the platforms is plain and the other faceted. The diminutive, single platform core on a quartz pebble for detaching micro-flakes and blades (Plate 51: 27) is interesting. It is one of the smallest cores in the collection and emphasizes the writer's general observation from several parts of sub-Saharan Africa that raw material can significantly affect the form and dimensions of the primary product. In localities where the common and preferred material is not quartz and comes in large sizes so that the primary and secondary products are correspondingly larger (as with *grès polymorphe* in the Congo basin or chert at Kalambo Falls), the small bladelet cores on quartz pebbles sometimes used at this time level appear strikingly out of place. In such a milieu they suggest the possibility that the correlation which certainly exists between the use of pebbles of quartz or other siliceous rocks and microliths, may relate as much to the material selected as it does to the tradition of the selectors.

The specialized disc cores that range from true discs to elliptic in plan form and show radial dorsal preparation for the removal of several small flakes, may be both high-backed (Plate 51: 32 and Plate 52: 2) or flat (Plate 52: 5, 7, 12). Those with sub-triangular plan form (Plate 51: 31) may be designed more specifically for the removal of a single, Levallois flake but, unless they have been struck, it is not possible to be certain. Plate 52: 6 is a radially prepared, struck core, relatively flat, which yielded a broad, Levallois flake. Plate 52: 8 is a typical small, Levallois point core from which one triangular and one blade-like flake have been struck. Plate 52: 10 is another such core, more correctly, perhaps, a para-Levallois core, with convergent flaking and markedly high-backed in section.

In addition to the utilized flakes referred to above, an example of a utilized/modified blade fragment with marginal retouch is illustrated at Plate 51: 25 and two modified chunks at Plate 52: 1 and 4. The first of these shows notching to form a *bec* and a nose has been formed on another area of the circumference by steep retouch. The second has been modified by notching with step-flaking and, on the opposite end, a proto-burin edge. Among the utilized/modified tools is also the rubber (Plate 52: 11) made from a cobble of hard quartzite which has four rubbed and smoothed faces with a dimple scar in the middle of one of them. It is difficult to determine whether these kinds of tools are fresh or abraded, for obvious reasons, and most of those associated with Rubble I have been placed in the slightly abraded category.

Among the shaped tools, the only heavy duty example illustrated is the bored stone fragment which came from grid square M/12, Rubble Ia at the south-west corner of the excavation (Plate 52: 13). There can be absolutely no doubt that it belongs in this rubble line where it is overlain by some 2 feet 6 inches to 3 feet (76–91 cm) of current-bedded, buff sands of the Mbwilo Member and the specimen has been stained by iron, as have many other artifacts in Rubble I. It provides further conclusive proof of the antiquity of this implement in central Africa where, on the evidence from Pomongwe Cave in Rhodesia and Leopard's Hill in Zambia, it is dated to the later part of the Upper Pleistocene. This specimen is made of sandstone and the fractured edges show rounding and light abrasion but whether from water action or

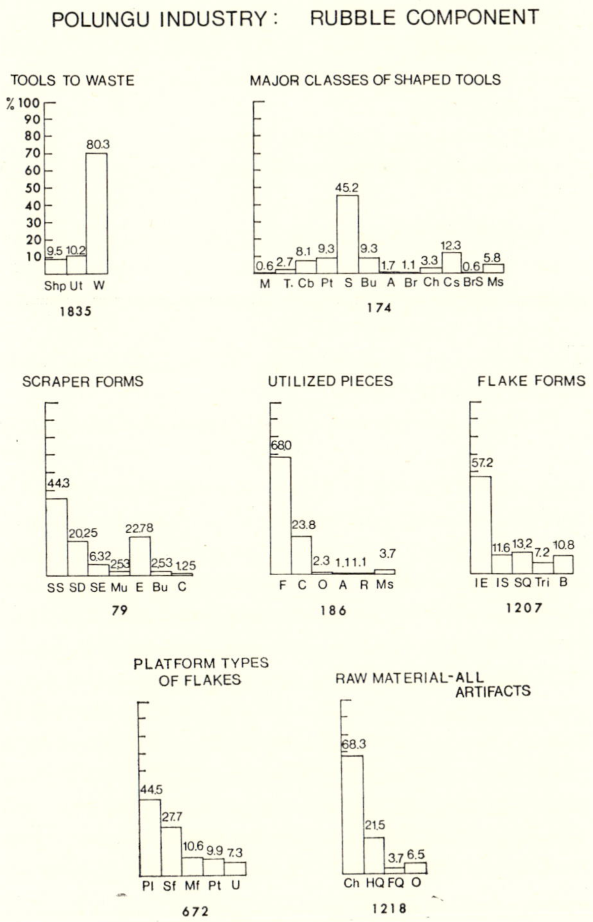

Fig. 33. Polungu Industry, composition of Rubble component.

Key:

Major artifact classes
Shp = Shaped tools
Ut = Utilized/modified
W = Unmodified waste

Scraper classes
SS = Single side
SD = Double side
SE = Side and end
Mu = Multiple edges
E = End
Bu = Butt
C = Circular/all round

Utilized pieces
F = Flake/blade and fragments
C = Chunk
O = *Outil esquillé*
A = Anvil
R = Rubber
Ms = Miscellaneous

Platform types
Pl = Plain
Sf = Simple faceted
Mf = Multi-faceted
Pt = Point
U = Unclassified

Major Classes of shaped tools
M = Microlith
T = Truncated flake/blade
Cb = Convex backed flake/blade
Pt = Point
S = Small scraper
Bu = Burin/proto-burin
A = Discoid/adze
Br = Borer
Ch = Chopper
Cs = Core-scraper
Brs = Bored stone
Ms = Miscellaneous large tools

Flake forms
IE = Irregular end-struck
IS = Irregular side-struck
SQ = Short quadrilateral
Tri = Triangular
B = Long quadrilateral/blade

Raw material
Ch = Chert (silicified mudstone)
HQ = Hard quartzite
FQ = Feldspathic quartzite
O = Other

weathering cannot be determined. It is approximately circular in plan form, shows hour-glass perforation and the external surface has been shaped by rubbing. In the light duty category of shaped tools, the backed flake and blade forms (Plate 51: 13–15; Plate 54: 9) from Rubble Ia are mostly thick with rather crude, normal, vertical backing. The small scraper forms are illustrated by one example with a single, straight edge (Plate 51: 16), two double edge, denticulate, side-scrapers (Plate 51: 18, 30) and a circular, denticulate or notched scraper on a chunk (Plate 51: 26). The burin (Plate 51: 24) is double ended, one end being dihedral and the other having a single blow burin scar.

Excavation B2, 1959: *from the bedded sands and grits separating Rubbles Ia and Ib.* The maximum thickness of the sands separating these rubble lines is *c.* 5 feet (152 cm) narrowing to *c.* 1 foot (30 cm) at the south wall. They contain a considerable number of artifacts (4,667) which are found in association with discontinuous lenses and lines of fine gravel interbedded with the sands and are, therefore, most likely to have been redeposited by the stream. Large tools are rare in these sands and, as might be expected, most of the artifacts are abraded, though generally lightly. However, a precise breakdown by abrasion category was not undertaken though an estimate showed that less than 20 per cent of all artifacts were fresh and those consisted mostly of unmodified waste, most of which was under 50 mm in greatest dimension. The tools specifically recorded as fresh or only very slightly abraded are as follows and some of them are illustrated at Plate 53.

Shaped tools	
Heavy duty	
Pick	1
Core-axe	1
Light duty	
Backed flake/blade	3
Points: unifacial	3
bifacial	4
Burins	1
Proto-burins	1
Small scrapers	4
Total shaped tools	18
Utilized/modified	
Flakes	2
Outils esquillés	2
Total utilized	4
Unmodified waste	
Blade core – two platforms, opposed	1
Flat disc core, radial preparation	1
Chunk	1
Total waste	3
Total artifacts	25

Both the core-axe and the pick are unlike those associated with either the Siszya or the Chipeta (Sangoan) Industry and, in view of their fresh condition, they can be presumed to belong with the Rubble component. The core-axe might better, perhaps, be termed an adze. It is made on a flat chunk, roughly triangular in plan form with the working edge forming the base of the triangle. It measures 47 × 40 × 12 mm. The straight, distal end at right angles to the long axis has been trimmed along the full length of the edge and intersects at a blunt angle with the ventral plane which shows marginal scarring due, probably, to use. The pick is illustrated at Plate 53: 11. It might equally be classified as a large, convergent scraper and is made on a thick unprepared flake of hard quartzite. The two lateral edges show blunt to steep retouch angles and converge at a blunt point. The ventral plane is the main release surface and the section is plano-convex.

Backed blade forms are illustrated at Plate 53: 3, 4 and 6. No. 6 is 60 mm long and is a Levallois blade with one-directional dorsal flaking and a multifaceted striking platform. The convex, normal backing is steep but rather irregular. The opposite lateral edge shows marginal scalar retouch and utilization. This specimen is representative of the 'heavy' form of backed blade or flake such as make their first appearance in the Siszya Industry. Nos. 3 and 4 are made on thin blades obtained by the punch method of flaking. No. 3 shows oblique, vertical truncation on a blade broken by snapping at the proximal end. No. 4 shows typical punch technique bulb, platform and scarring of the platform edge on the dorsal face. The backing is straight and the retouch angle shallow to blunt. The opposite lateral edge shows marginal scarring due to use. The points associated with the Rubble component are small, rarely above 60 mm in greatest dimension and elongate rather than broad. They are either unifacial, bifacial or parti-bifacial. The bifiacial examples are generally foliate in plan form while the unifacial specimens are more often triangular. With the backed blades they are the most characteristic tools of the Rubble component. Plate 53: 9 is an example of the foliate, bifacial form with lenticular section. The retouch is fully invasive and scalar and special care has been given to the margins to give the tool a regular edge form and profile. Plate 53: 10 has been retouched over the whole of the dorsal face and shows also some trimming on the ventral face, although it has the triangular form of the unifacial type of point. Of the remaining examples from these sands, two of the unifacial forms are sub-triangular with the retouch concentrated on the margins of the distal half of the two lateral edges (they measure 50 × 30 and 30 × 25 mm respectively). The plan form of the third is regular foliate and the lateral edges show some attempt at denticulation. The third bifacial example is a broad, asymmetric foliate (70 × 40 mm) lacking the distal point. The fourth is the proximal half of a bifacial foliate point in chalcedony.

The burin is a single blow example (*d'angle sur cassure*) on a flake fragment. The proto-burin is double ended, made on a small blade core. The four fresh scrapers comprise one small, convex example in quartz (35 × 25 mm); two side-scrapers, one with straight and one with convex trimmed edges on a flake and fragment, respectively; and one larger, angled or convergent scraper on a concavo-convex, side-flake with marginally retouched, denticulate edges. This specimen, made in silcrete, is illustrated at Plate 53: 12.

Classified as utilized are two short, triangular flakes (Plate 53: 1, 2) with broad, multi-faceted striking platforms with some discontinuous marginal scarring. One shows one-directional the other two-directional flaking and they appear to have been struck from small Levallois cores. The two *outils esquillés* are illustrated at Plate 53: 5 and 7. The first is made in chert and is single ended on a bipolar core while the second is double ended on a small, bipolar core of quartz crystal. Among the unmodified waste only two examples have been specifically recorded as fresh. The one is a small bladelet core in chert with two opposed platforms. The other is a diminutive, flat, radially prepared disc core (Plate 53: 8) from which several small flakes have been struck. This shows well the general size range of the almost microlithic flaking waste found with the Rubble component.

Excavation B2, 1959: *Rubble Ib* (Volume 1, Plate 26). Rubble Ib is the main rubble line and rests on an erosion surface cut into the buff, bedded sands of the Mkamba Member. Reference should be made to Volume 1: 167–9 and Figures 38 and 39 for details of the occurrence of this Rubble. It was continuous from north to south across the excavation and lies immediately beneath Rubble Ia with which it merges in the B1, 1956, excavation upslope as also again immediately downstream and downslope from B2, 1959.

Rubble Ib is thickest over the northern half of the excavation where it is composed of sub-angular rocks (often larger than those found in Rubble Ia) that have accumulated to a depth of 4 to 5 inches (10–13 cm). It yielded 11,157 artifacts of which just over 700 are fresh or only very slightly abraded. The artifacts seem in part to have been resorted since some clustering of large and small artifacts in different parts of the rubble occurs and would appear to have been the work of natural agencies. The fresh artifacts show no particular accumulations and the occurrence is more like that to be expected over the floor of a shallow stream course. Especially is this so over the southern half of the excavation. The fresh or only very slightly abraded artifacts are listed below and in Table 27 and representative forms are illustrated at Plate 50: 5–12 and Plate 54: 1, 2, 4–8, 10, 12–17, 19. It is apparent from the list that some of the large tools and probably also some of the unmodified flakes, especially those made in hard quartzite, are derived from the bedded Ochreous Sands and gravel lines of the Mkamba Member since the rubble line rests on an erosion surface cut into this bed. The hand-axe, a double pointed form in hard quartzite, belongs either with the Acheulian or the Sangoan. The two large scrapers are also probably derived and the same is the case with the large, convergent edged pick in hard quartzite. The core-axes also, mostly convergent and parallel-sided, are made in hard quartzite and feldspathic quartzite and typologically and technically they belong with the Siszya Industry and the Sangoan. Some, if not all, of the core-scrapers can be associated with the Rubble component of the Polungu Industry and the same is the case with the choppers and chisels.

The same range of light duty tools as occurred on the other Rubble I sites is present here. The truncated blades are illustrated at Plate 54: 1 and 2. No. 1 is punch struck and the truncation on both is vertical and normal. Backed flake forms are shown at Plate 54: 4 and 5 and Plate 50: 8. No. 4 is a broad, irregular flake with the backing on the proximal half of the edge only. No. 5 is a triangular flake from a Levallois core and the backing shows a shallow to blunt retouch angle. Plate 50: 8 is a punched bladelet, again with shallow to blunt marginal backing in the manner considered characteristic of aggregates formerly called 'Magosian'. The fresh points recovered from Rubble Ib

Shaped tools	
Large cutting	
Hand-axe	1
Large scraper	2
Heavy duty	
Pick	1
Core-axe	11
Core-scraper	12
Chopper	3
Chisel	2
Light duty	
Truncated blade	2
Backed flake/blade	5
Points: unifacial	3
bifacial	2
Burins	2
Proto-burins	6
Small scrapers	32
Discoid/adze	1
Total shaped tools	85
Utilized/modified	
Flakes/blades	81
Chunks/cores	24
Outils esquillés	2
Rubber	1
Anvil	2
Rubbed pigment	1
Total utilized/modified	111
Unmodified waste (sample only)	
Flakes	
Irregular, end-struck	128
Irregular, side-struck	42
Short quadrilateral (parallel dorsal flaking)	66
Blade (parallel dorsal flaking)	52
Irregular (radial dorsal flaking)	71
Triangular, short (parallel dorsal flaking)	21
Triangular, long (parallel dorsal flaking)	13
Short quadrilateral (radial dorsal flaking)	19
Blade (radial dorsal flaking)	2
Triangular, short (radial dorsal flaking)	1
Triangular, long (radial dorsal flaking)	3
Core-axe resharpening spalls	4
Total flake classes	422
Cores	
Blade, one platform	5
two platforms, opposing	3
two platforms, two planes	2
pyramidal	2
Discoid	27
Sub-triangular	4
Struck discoid (Levallois)	14
Struck sub-triangular (Levallois)	5
Proto-biconical	6
Biconical	9
Formless	5
Total cores	82
Chunks	1
Total unmodified waste	505
Total all artifacts	701

are again characteristically either foliate or sub-triangular. The three unifacial examples are all sub-triangular – one long and narrow (Plate 50: 10), the others shorter and broader (Plate 50: 11 and 12). No. 11 in particular shows, at the distal end, some fine small scaled retouch which could have been done by pressure. No. 12 is made of chalcedony. All three were probably produced from Levallois point cores. The bifacial forms are foliate but have the distal ends broken. Plate 50: 5 is made from hard quartzite, carefully retouched over the whole of both faces; it shows a lenticular section. Plate 50: 6 is irregular and probably unfinished but otherwise similar.

The burins again are single blow examples and probably can be classed as technical; the proto-burins are on chunks and fragments. The 32 small scrapers are mostly side-scrapers with one (16) or two (5) retouched edges. One double side-scraper on a punched blade is illustrated at Plate 54: 14 and Plate 50: 7 is the only side-scraper with inverse retouch of Kasouga-type. The remainder are end and side (3), end (7) and nosed (1) scrapers. The scraper at Plate 54: 10 has the distal end modified by only 4 main scars to form a straight, notched working end and which also shows marginal step-flaking and crushing from use. Plate 54: 8 is a finely retouched discoid/adze with an asymmetric lenticular to biconvex section. The specimen has been thinned by the removal of a number of thin, often parallel, short quadrilateral flakes radially round the circumference, the margins of which show areas where a number of very small flakes have been removed. This is a characteristic example of what has been termed a discoid/adze or knife, since the care with which the tool has been thinned and the retouch are surely beyond what is necessary for discs designed only as cores.

The utilized flakes and flake and blade fragments and chunks show the usual form with irregular retouch, minimal modification or utilization on one or more edges, similar to those already described and illustrated. Mostly, they have informal plan forms but a few more regular examples occur. The artifact at Plate 50: 9 is a short blade with convergent dorsal flaking, having the whole of the ventral surface at the proximal end retouched by flat, invasive flaking to reduce the striking platform and bulb; it might also be classed as an unfinished foliate point. Plate 54: 6 is an example of the characteristic Levallois flakes, marginally trimmed on one or both lateral edges at the proximal end, such as are present also in the Hillslope component of the Polungu Industry (e.g. Plate 46: 6; Plate 49: 2). The *outils esquillés* (Plate 54: 7) are both double-ended examples made in chert on small bipolar cores.

One lump of kaolin clay with rubbing facets and striations over a large part of both faces was found in the course of stepping back the excavation over the south side, associated with Rubble Ib. This is soft material and it seems probable that it belongs with the latest artifact component of the rubble since abrasion would be expected to have removed the evidence of utilization. It was possibly used for making white pigment (Plate 54: 17).

The unmodified waste follows the usual pattern of that seen in Rubble Ia. The full range of blade forms is represented as also is that of the specialized cores with radial and parallel or convergent preparation. The commonest of all forms are the discs and Levallois disc cores. Plate 52: 9 is an example of one of these flat discoid cores which has been modified by a notch at the distal end on the ventral face, showing crushing and marginal utilization. Examples of the flakes struck from these cores are illustrated at Plate 54. Nos. 12 and 13 are flakes from small blade cores, one showing a radial dorsal scar pattern, the other a parallel pattern from two opposed ends. Nos. 15 and 16 are irregular, broad flakes from small discoid cores and have radial dorsal scar patterns. No. 19 is an example from a triangular Levallois point core with one-directional flaking and a multi-faceted striking platform.

(*c*) *Site D aggregates*

Excavation D, 1956: *Rubble I composite*. The composite rubble line here is some 4 inches (10 cm) thick and the usual sub-angular rock fragments are set in a brown to grey, sandy clay matrix. Rubble I here rests on an erosion surface cut into a white to light grey clay sand (Mkamba Member) sloping very gently from south to north. Some alignment can be distinguished in the long axes of the larger artifacts which suggests that they have been moved by stream or colluvial action (see Volume 1: 186–8). The rubble here contained only a comparatively few artifacts – a total of 225 – and most of these (155) are abraded, 60 being more lightly abraded and 10 only being fresh. These last consist of:

Shaped tools	
Light duty	
Backed blade	1
Small scraper	2
Total	3
Utilized/modified	
Flakes	2
Unmodified waste	
Flakes	
Irregular, end-struck	1
Irregular, side-struck	1
Short quadrilateral	3
Total	5
Total artifacts	10

The convex backed blade in chert (Plate 54: 3) is typical of the larger forms found with 'Second Intermediate' industries. The specimen is thin in section and measures 50 × 16 mm. The backing is normal and continues along the whole length of the left edge; the retouch angle is steep to blunt. Both the small scrapers are made from chert. One (35 × 35 mm) is a short end-scraper with a straight edge and blunt retouch angle on an older flake. The other (70 × 40 mm) is a double notched scraper on a tabular chunk; the edge angle is steep. One of the two irregular flakes is in chert and has been modified by two scars on the ventral face to form a shallow notch; the second is in hard quartzite and shows denticulation on one lateral edge. The unmodified irregular flakes show a one-directional dorsal scar pattern, plain platforms and are made from silcrete and chert, respectively. Two of the short quadrilateral flakes are in chert and one in chalcedony. One shows multi-directional flaking and a simple-faceted platform; the remainder have plain platforms and one-directional flaking.

C. Aggregates from Site A, Excavation A2, 1956 ?Pits Channel Rubble

(Volume 1, Plate 17)

The main rubble line exposed in the A2 Excavation in 1956 was originally believed to be the Rubble I composite horizon. In 1963, however, further excavation in the A4 Trench showed the existence of the Pits Channel and fill, intermediate in age between Rubbles I and II. The same year, further excavation at the west end of A2 suggested that the sands that here overlie the rubble are probably the same as those filling the Pits Channel. Considering the late aspect of the included artifact aggregate, however, and the differences in elevation of the rubbles in Trench A2 from that of both Rubble II and Rubble I in Trench A4, or on the River Face, the stratigraphic placement of Trench A2 is not certain and further clarification by excavation is needed here. The most probable hypothesis that can now be advanced is that it may represent the Pits Channel rubble which has been re-exposed by later erosion and re-used by man (see Volume 1: 109–13 and 131). The sample obtained from this rubble in 1956 contained a total of 332 artifacts of which 57 are fresh, 223 slightly abraded and 52 abraded. In the fresh category, 46 are in chert, 6 in hard quartzite, 1 in sandstone, 3 in chalcedony and 1 in dolerite. The latter is taken as an indication that the fresh material has not been exposed to weathering for any length of time and has not been transported. The greatest dimensions of the artifacts (excluding the 7 fragments) are:

under 30 mm	9
between 31 and 60 mm	33
between 61 and 90 mm	5
more than 90 mm in length	3

The fresh series is listed below and representative artifacts are illustrated at Plate 48. This small series is closely similar to the aggregates from Rubble I that form the Rubble component of the Polungu Industry. Plate 48: 2 is a small chert blade showing blunt, normal backing along the distal half of one lateral edge. The discoid/adze (Plate 48: 9) is a quite typical, flat disc thinned on the dorsal face by flat, radial invasive scars and with marginal scalar retouch on both faces to give the tool a straight biclinal edge profile. The one larger, flat, irregular scar on the dorsal face is probably fortuitous and not by design. The borer (Plate 48: 8) recalls the example from

Shaped tools	
Heavy duty	
Core-axe/core	1
Light duty	
Backed blade	1
Discoid/adze	1
Borer	1
Total	4
Utilized/modified	
Hammerstone	1
(Core)	(1)
Total	1
Unmodified waste	
Flakes	
Irregular, end-struck	7
Irregular, side-struck	10
Short quadrilateral (parallel dorsal scars)	7
Long quadrilateral/blades (parallel dorsal scars)	9
Triangular (parallel/convergent dorsal scars)	1
Levallois	
Irregular, radial dorsal scars	1
Short quadrilateral, radial dorsal scars	4
Triangular (radial dorsal scars)	2
Broad/elliptical (radial dorsal scars)	2
Total	43
Cores	
Prismatic, single platform	1
(Struck Levallois flake)	(1)
Formless (utilized)	1
Total	2
Flake fragments	7
Total waste	52
Total artifacts	57

Rubble I in the A4 Trench (Plate 49: 7) and is made on a rhomboid chunk of chert, the original shape being determined by joint planes. These tools show no evidence of rough usage at the distal ends such as would result from pecking stone and were thus, probably, used on soft materials.

The utilized/modified core (Plate 48: 10) is a specialized Levallois core with radial preparation and is elliptic in plan form with one large flake struck from it. The bifacial flaking for the initial preparation of the core is preserved at the end opposite the striking platform but the aretes that separate the scars are rounded unlike the remainder of the specimen where the scars are quite fresh. Either, therefore, this is a tool of which the proximal two thirds were protected by hafting, or it is a derived implement that was reworked as a core. Plate 48: 1, 3–5 are examples of light blades and bladelets struck from blade cores and specialized, one-directional,

Levallois cores. Plate 48: 6 and 7 are characteristic of the short, broad, triangular flakes with faceted striking platforms and with one-directional or radial scar patterns, found with the Rubble component.

This completes the review of the aggregates on which the knowledge of the Rubble component of the Polungu Industry is based and on which it may now be defined.

D. Definition of the Rubble component of the Polungu Industry

1. STRATIGRAPHIC POSITION

Within the Mbwilo Member of the Kalambo Falls Formation in the following stratigraphic positions:

(*a*) associated with discontinuous pebble lines in the base of the current-bedded sands immediately overlying Rubble I at Site A, Excavation A1, 1956; Site B, Excavation B1, 1956 and Site C, 1963 and 1966;

(*b*) within Rubbles Ia, Ib, Ia and b composite and I composite at Sites A, B, C and D, in Excavations A1, A3, 1956; A4, 1959 and 1963; B1, 1956; B2, 1959; C, 1963 and 1966; D, 1956;

(*c*) on the surface of rubble tentatively identified with the Pits Channel rubble, where this had been re-exposed at the northeast end of Excavation A2, 1956.

2. DATING

Older than 9950 ± 210 B.P. and younger than 27,500 ± 2300 B.P. Extrapolation on the basis of typological comparisons with assemblages from other localities suggests that the greater part of Rubble I may have formed *c.* 20,000 years B.P.

3. CLIMATIC EVIDENCE

Pollen spectra from clay layers interstratified with current-bedded sands lying between Rubble Ib and Rubble Ic at Excavation A1, 1956, indicate an open type of vegetation and cool conditions such as prevail today near the upper limit of the *Brachystegia* woodland up to 2,000 metres. Conditions are considered to have been cool, humid and misty with a temperature *c.* 4° C lower than now (see Van Zinderen Bakker, Volume I: 70, 74). It is difficult to assess the effect of this lowering of temperature on the biome in the local basin but it probably did not significantly affect the availability of traditional food sources there; the pollen assemblage from Ishiba Ngandu (Livingstone, 1971) only 175 miles (282 km) to the south at an altitude of between 4,000 and 5,000 feet (1,219–1,524 m) remains unchanged at the generic level over this period and would also seem to confirm that *Brachystegia* woodland was the climax vegetation and that the habitat was not greatly different from today.

4. ARTIFACT COMPOSITION AND ATTRIBUTES

The composition and main features are summarized in Table 27 and Figures 34 and 35. The following classes of artifacts are represented and examples are illustrated at Plates 48–54:

Shaped tools

Large cutting (5). With the exception of a few large scrapers (5), generally in hard quartzite, this category of tools is absent.

Heavy duty (33). Artifacts in this category comprise: choppers (5); chisels (3); an atypical core-axe or adze (Plate 48: 10); unifacial pick or core-axe-like tools (3, with a possible additional 7) (Plate 53: 11) which, as already stated, may be some form of large nosed scraper with parallel or convergent retouch along the lateral edges; core-scrapers (21) and a bored stone (52: 13). They are reminiscent of the 'heavy duty' element associated with some of the industries from southern Africa that have been dated to the later Pleistocene or earliest Holocene (e.g. Nachikufu I Industry) and are appropriately usually made from hard, tough stone.

Light duty (138). These are the artifacts that best characterize this component. They consist of:

Microliths. There are only two examples of microlithic proportions. These are not lunates but bladelets that have been obliquely truncated. That from A3, Rubble I (composite) is a snapped section of blade, retouched at one end and Kleindienst draws attention to its similarity to the trapeze from Rubble Ic in Excavation A1, 1956, to be described and illustrated in Volume III. The second example, from the base of the bedded sands over Rubble I (composite) in B2, 1959, has been classified here as truncated and illustrated at Plate 50: 2. It is probable that small, retouched artifacts of this kind will be found to be a more common element of the Rubble component than this insignificant sample suggests, since bladelets from which they could have been made are present in most of the aggregates grouped here as the Rubble component.

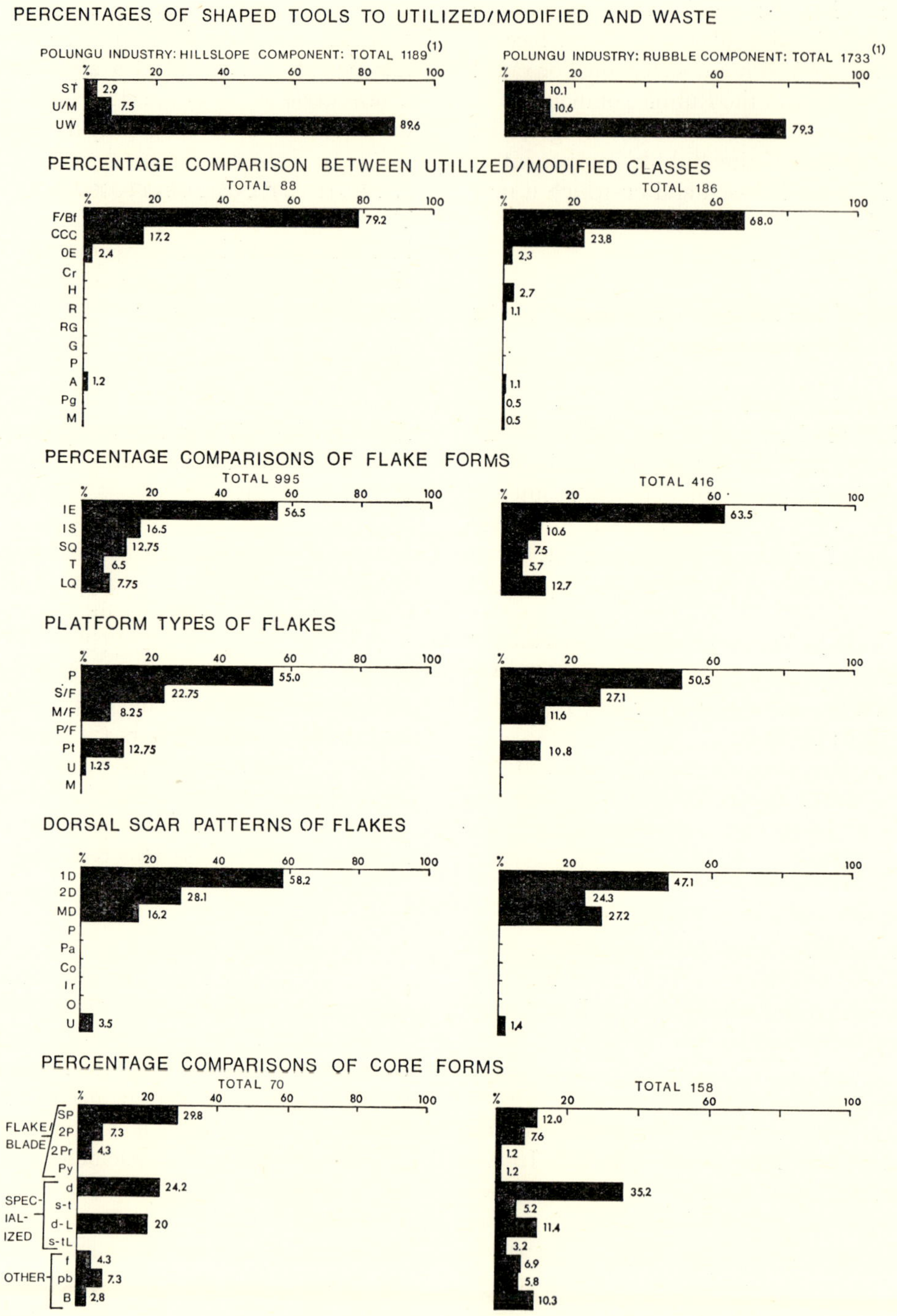
PERCENTAGES OF SHAPED TOOLS TO UTILIZED/MODIFIED AND WASTE
POLUNGU INDUSTRY: HILLSLOPE COMPONENT: TOTAL 1189(1)
POLUNGU INDUSTRY: RUBBLE COMPONENT: TOTAL 1733(1)
% 20 40 60 80 100
ST 2.9
U/M 7.5
UW 89.6
10.1
10.6
79.3
PERCENTAGE COMPARISON BETWEEN UTILIZED/MODIFIED CLASSES
TOTAL 88
TOTAL 186
F/Bf 79.2
CCC 17.2
OE 2.4
Cr
H
R
RG
G
P
A 1.2
Pg
M
68.0
23.8
2.3
2.7
1.1
1.1
0.5
0.5
PERCENTAGE COMPARISONS OF FLAKE FORMS
TOTAL 995
TOTAL 416
IE 56.5
IS 16.5
SQ 12.75
T 6.5
LQ 7.75
63.5
10.6
7.5
5.7
12.7
PLATFORM TYPES OF FLAKES
P 55.0
S/F 22.75
M/F 8.25
P/F
Pt 12.75
U 1.25
M
50.5
27.1
11.6
10.8
DORSAL SCAR PATTERNS OF FLAKES
1D 58.2
2D 28.1
MD 16.2
P
Pa
Co
Ir
O
U 3.5
47.1
24.3
27.2
1.4
PERCENTAGE COMPARISONS OF CORE FORMS
TOTAL 70
TOTAL 158
FLAKE/BLADE
SP 29.8
2P 7.3
2Pr 4.3
Py
SPEC-IAL-IZED
d 24.2
s-t
d-L 20
s-tL
OTHER
f 4.3
pb 7.3
B 2.8
12.0
7.6
1.2
1.2
35.2
5.2
11.4
3.2
6.9
5.8
10.3

Fig. 34, part 1

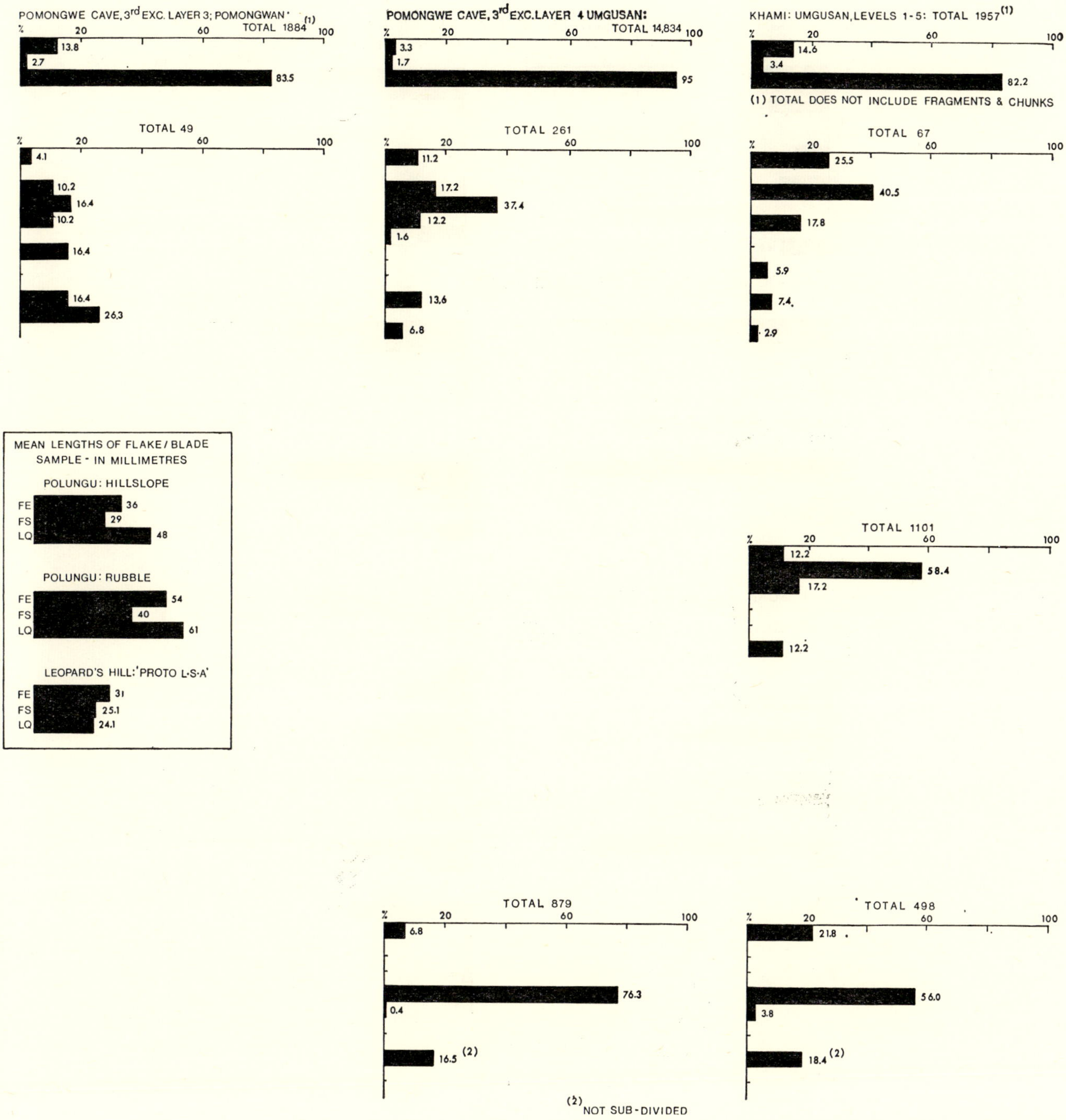
POMONGWE CAVE, 3rd EXC. LAYER 3; POMONGWAN (1)
TOTAL 1884
%
20
60
100
13.8
2.7
83.5
POMONGWE CAVE, 3rd EXC. LAYER 4 UMGUSAN:
TOTAL 14,834
3.3
1.7
95
KHAMI: UMGUSAN, LEVELS 1-5: TOTAL 1957 (1)
14.6
3.4
82.2
(1) TOTAL DOES NOT INCLUDE FRAGMENTS & CHUNKS
TOTAL 49
4.1
10.2
16.4
10.2
16.4
16.4
26.3
TOTAL 261
11.2
17.2
37.4
12.2
1.6
13.6
6.8
TOTAL 67
25.5
40.5
17.8
5.9
7.4
2.9
MEAN LENGTHS OF FLAKE / BLADE SAMPLE - IN MILLIMETRES
POLUNGU: HILLSLOPE
FE
FS
LQ
36
29
48
POLUNGU: RUBBLE
54
40
61
LEOPARD'S HILL: 'PROTO L·S·A'
31
25.1
24.1
TOTAL 1101
12.2
58.4
17.2
12.2
TOTAL 879
6.8
76.3
0.4
16.5 (2)
TOTAL 498
21.8
56.0
3.8
18.4 (2)
(2) NOT SUB-DIVIDED

Fig. 34, part 2

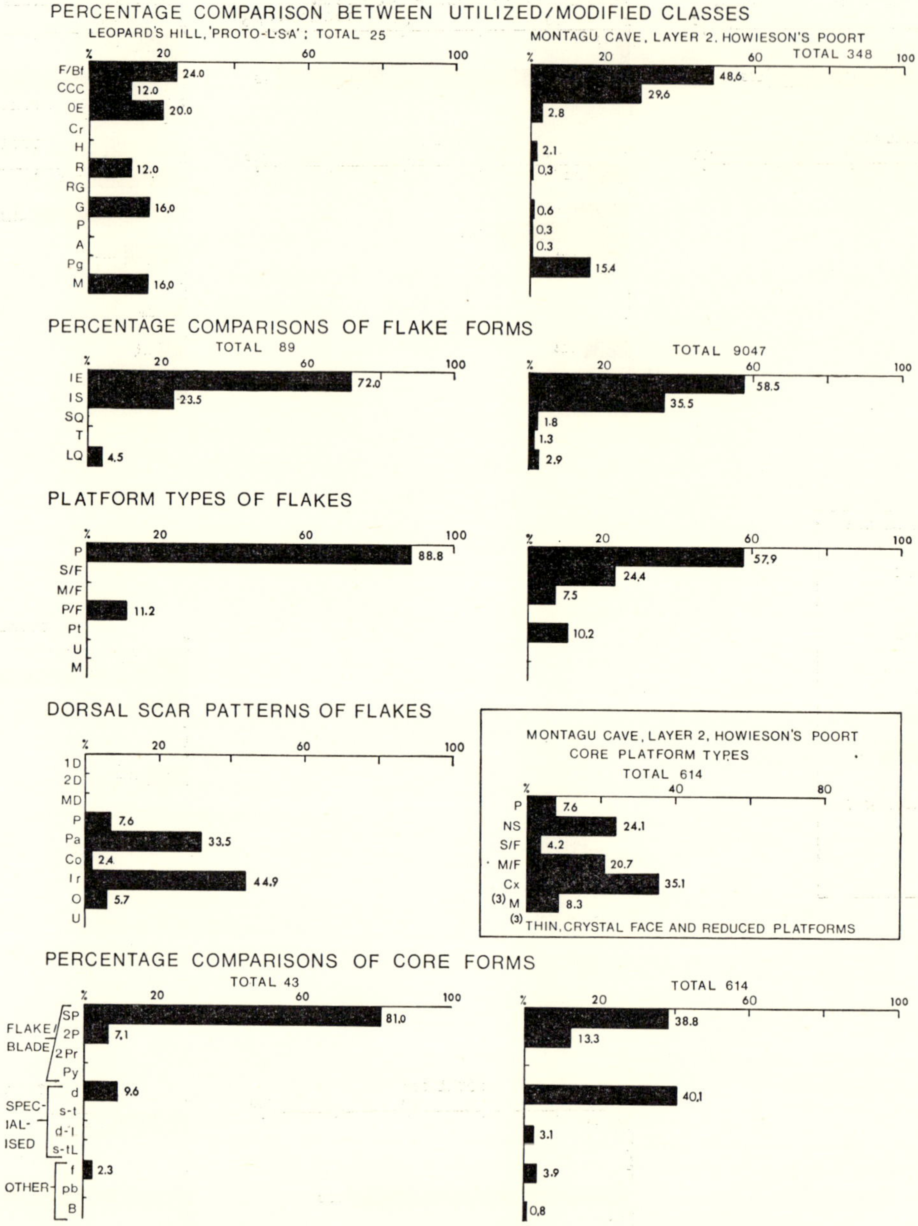
PERCENTAGE COMPARISON BETWEEN UTILIZED/MODIFIED CLASSES
LEOPARD'S HILL, 'PROTO-L·S·A' ; TOTAL 25
MONTAGU CAVE, LAYER 2, HOWIESON'S POORT
TOTAL 348
F/Bf
CCC
OE
Cr
H
R
RG
G
P
A
Pg
M
PERCENTAGE COMPARISONS OF FLAKE FORMS
TOTAL 89
TOTAL 9047
IE
IS
SQ
T
LQ
PLATFORM TYPES OF FLAKES
P
S/F
M/F
P/F
Pt
U
M
DORSAL SCAR PATTERNS OF FLAKES
1D
2D
MD
P
Pa
Co
Ir
O
U
MONTAGU CAVE, LAYER 2, HOWIESON'S POORT
CORE PLATFORM TYPES
TOTAL 614
P
NS
S/F
M/F
Cx
(3) M
(3) THIN, CRYSTAL FACE AND REDUCED PLATFORMS
PERCENTAGE COMPARISONS OF CORE FORMS
TOTAL 43
TOTAL 614
FLAKE/BLADE
SP
2P
2Pr
Py
SPEC-IAL-ISED
d
s-t
d-l
s-tL
OTHER
f
pb
B

Fig. 34, part 3

Backed blades/flakes (16). These are of two kinds (*a*) those made on thin blades from prismatic cores which show regular, fine scalar retouch along part or all of one lateral edge (Plate 48: 2; Plate 49: 3; Plate 50: 8; Plate 53: 3, 4; Plate 54: 3); and (*b*) those made on thicker flakes or blades, some struck from specialized cores. The backed edge usually shows a more irregular profile and vertical or steep, step-flaking to produce the back. The chord has sometimes been modified by marginal retouch and use (Plate 51: 13–15; Plate 53: 6; Plate 54: 4, 5, 9). These two forms were presumably used for two different purposes. The first is new, the second is a form characteristic of the Siszya Industry.

Truncated blades/flakes (5). A small but distinctive class that includes both diminutive (Plate 49: 4; Plate 50: 2) and larger (Plate 49: 5; Plate 54: 1, 2) examples. The latter are a form that is found also with the Siszya Industry.

Points (16). These are (*a*) unifacial (9), generally triangular in plan form and with the retouch confined largely to the margins and distal ends (Plate 48: 1; Plate 50: 3, 10–12) and (*b*) bifacial (7). These are foliate, less usually triangular, in plan form, the retouch being either fully invasive over both faces or parti-bifacial on the release face where it may be confined to the proximal end to remove the bulb and platform (Plate 50: 5, 6; Plate 53: 9, 10). The lenticular sectioned, 'tear drop' form (e.g. Plate 53: 9) is new and not known from the earlier Siszya Industry component. The retouch on these tools appears to be by some form of controlled percussion, though the very small and regular marginal retouch on some examples (e.g. Plate 50: 11) may result from pressure flaking.

Fig. 34. Percentage comparisons of shaped tool classes of Polungu and selected industries.

Key:

Shaped tools to unmodified waste
ST = Shaped tools
U/M = Utilized/modified pieces
UW = Unmodified waste

Utilized/modified categories
F/Bf = Flakes/blades and fragments
CCC = Chunks, cores and chips
OE = *Outils esquillés*
Cr = Crystals
H = Hammerstones
R = Rubbers
RG = Rubbed and grooved pieces
G = Grindstones
P = Pestles
A = Anvils
Pg = Pigment
M = Miscellaneous

Flake forms and attributes
IE = Irregular end-struck
IS = Irregular side-struck
SQ = Short quadrilateral
T = Triangular
LQ = Long quadrilateral

Mean lengths of flakes/blades
FE = Flakes – end
FS = Flakes – side
LQ = Long quadrilateral

Platform types – flakes
P = Plain
S/F = Simple faceted
M/F = Multi-faceted
P/F = Pseudo-faceted
Pt = Point
U = Unclassified
M = Miscellaneous

Platform types – cores
P = Plain
NS = Negative scar
S/F = Simple faceted
M/F = Multi-faceted
Cx = Cortex
M = Miscellaneous

Dorsal scar patterns
1D = One-directional
2D = Two-directional
MD = Multi-directional
P = Plain
Pa = Parallel
Co = Convergent
Ir = Irregular
O = Other
U = Unclassified

Core forms
Flake/blade – Sp = Single platform
2p = Two platforms, opposed
2pr = Two platforms at right-angles
Py = Pyramidal
Specialized – d = Discoid
s-t = Sub-triangular
d-L = Discoid (Levallois)
s-tL = Sub-triangular (Levallois)
Other – f = Formless
pb = Proto-biconical (angle)
B = biconical

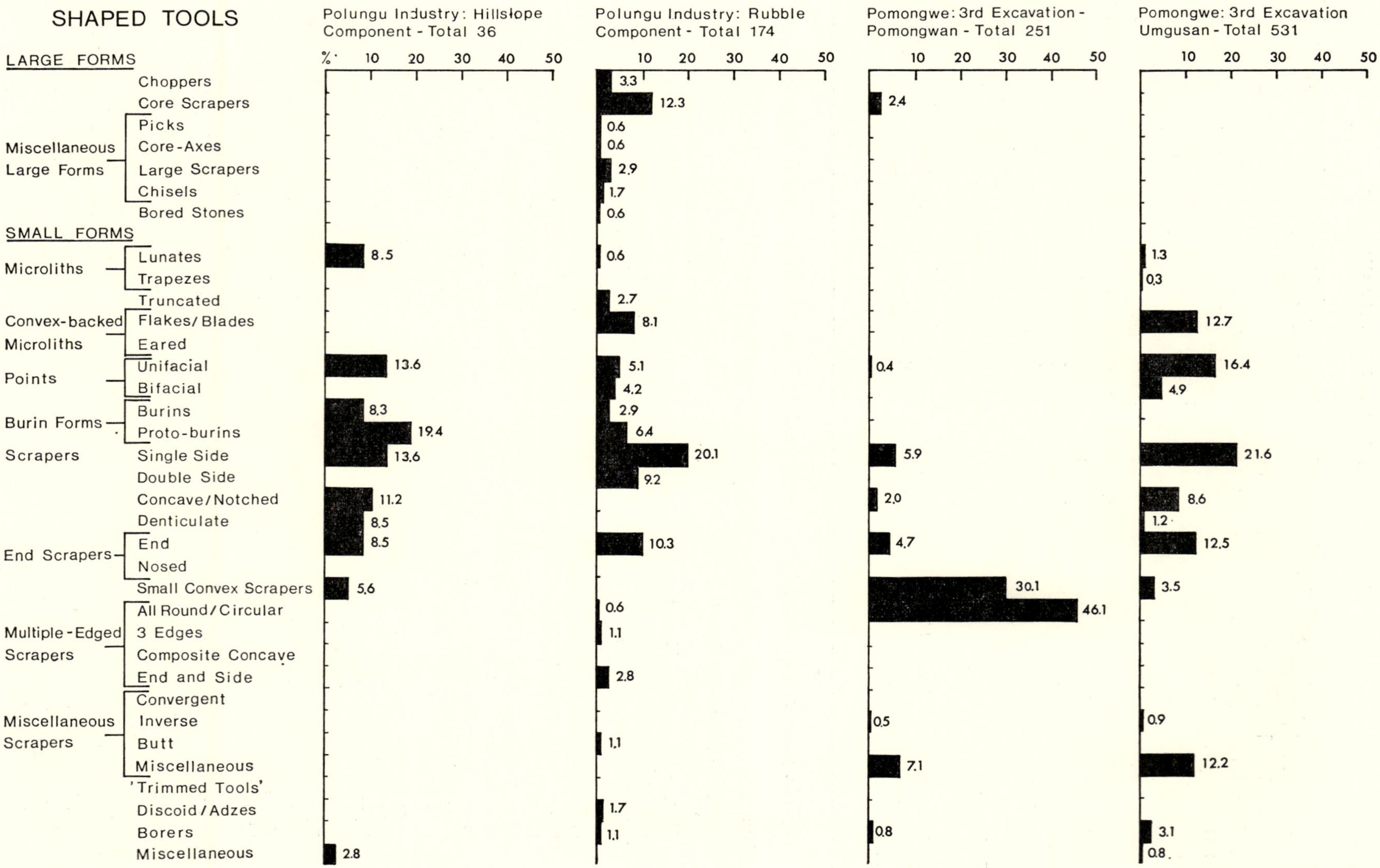
SHAPED TOOLS
LARGE FORMS
Choppers
Core Scrapers
Miscellaneous Large Forms
Picks
Core-Axes
Large Scrapers
Chisels
Bored Stones
SMALL FORMS
Microliths
Lunates
Trapezes
Truncated
Convex-backed Microliths
Flakes/Blades
Eared
Points
Unifacial
Bifacial
Burin Forms
Burins
Proto-burins
Scrapers
Single Side
Double Side
Concave/Notched
Denticulate
End Scrapers
End
Nosed
Small Convex Scrapers
Multiple-Edged Scrapers
All Round/Circular
3 Edges
Composite Concave
End and Side
Miscellaneous Scrapers
Convergent
Inverse
Butt
Miscellaneous
'Trimmed Tools'
Discoid/Adzes
Borers
Miscellaneous
Polungu Industry: Hillslope Component - Total 36
Polungu Industry: Rubble Component - Total 174
Pomongwe: 3rd Excavation - Pomongwan - Total 251
Pomongwe: 3rd Excavation Umgusan - Total 531
%

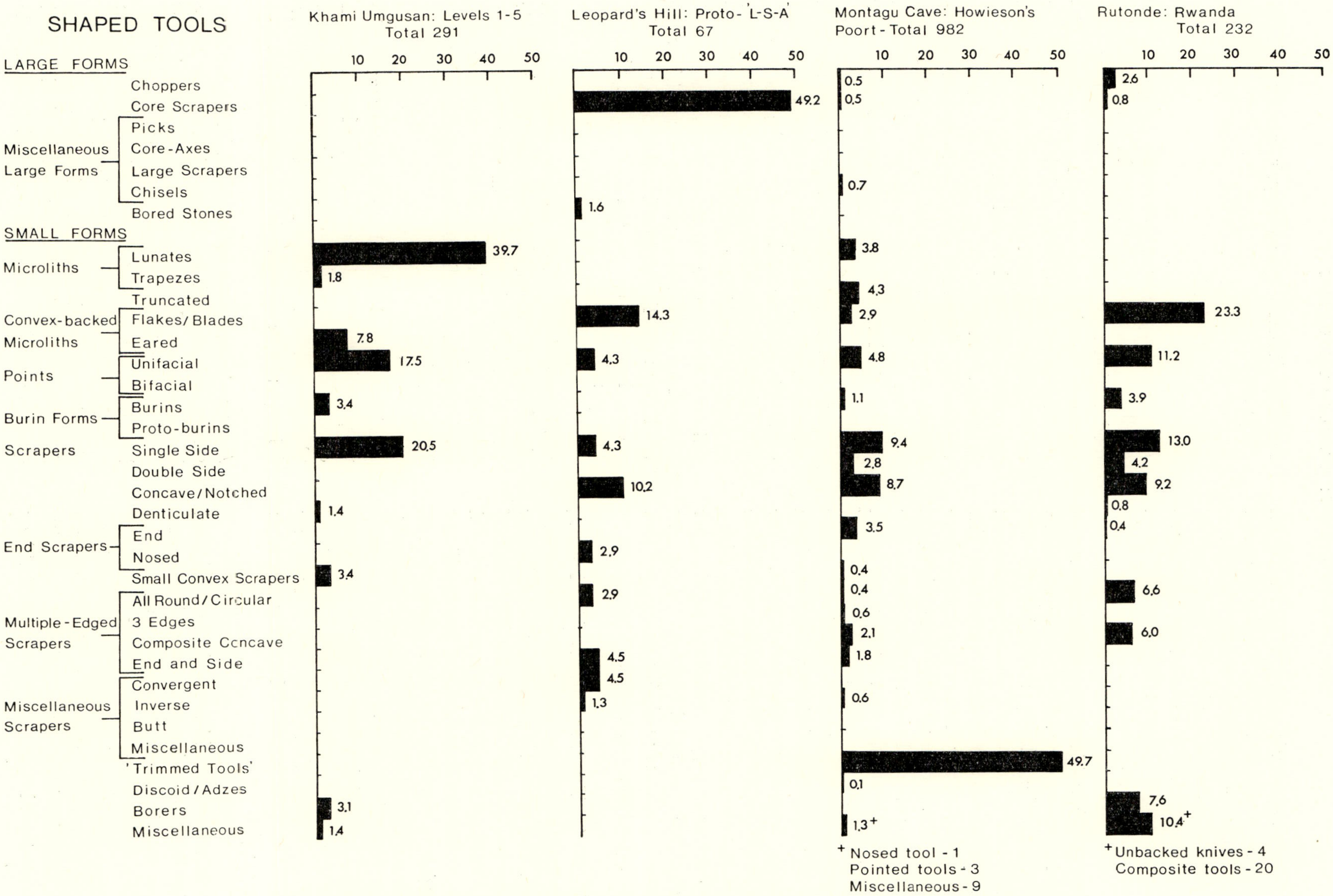

Fig. 35. Percentage comparisons of shaped tool classes of the Polungu Industry – Hillslope and Rubble components – with certain other selected industries.

Burins (5) *and proto-burins* (11). There are no burins on truncations or dihedral forms, the five examples being single blow burins (*burins d'angle sur cassure*) usually with one burin facet. Plate 51: 25 is a double burin on a fragment. The proto-burins show typically modified straight edges on the face of a fragment or chunk (Plate 52: 4).

Small scrapers (79). These are the largest class of shaped tools. No regular plan form is recognizable, any convenient flake (Plate 51: 18; Plate 54: 10), blade (Plate 50: 7), fragment (Plate 54: 11; Plate 51: 30) or chunk (Plate 51: 26; Plate 52: 3) was used. The retouch angle is generally blunt to steep. A few more regularly retouched examples with regular edge form occur (e.g. Plate 53: 12; Plate 54: 14) but these are the exception rather than the rule. Plate 50: 7 is an example of inverse or Kasouga retouch, the rarity of which indicates that this was not a significant form of artifact with the Polungu Industry. The breakdown by sub-classes according to edge plan is given in the bar diagrams at Figure 33. That for the form of the edge retouch shows 32·2 per cent straight edges, 15·2 per cent convex, 9·4 per cent concave and 9·5 per cent notched, 20·8 per cent denticulate, 3·8 per cent with opposed notches to produce a *bec*, 7·5 per cent nosed and 1·9 per cent convergent.

Discoid/adze (3). Together with the bifacial points, this is the class that shows the most extensive amount of retouch. This retouch is sufficiently flat and scalar to suggest that it may have been executed by means of a punch. Any larger flakes that may have been removed from one or other face are generally of an insignificant nature and look more like the result of use than an attempt to remove a Levallois flake. Alternatively, they might result from resting a punch on too broad a platform. The disc/adze blade or knife is a form that makes its appearance with the Siszya Industry but those with the Polungu Industry are generally smaller and more lenticular in section (Plate 48: 9; Plate 49: 10; Plate 54: 8).

Borers (2). These would probably be considered atypical in a larger collection but the only two examples of this class of tool are so similar, made on rhomboidal chunks of chert, that it is probable they represent a specific type. It is probable that the manner of cleavage of the Plateau Series chert has predetermined the form, for the writer is not aware of similar tools with other Archaeological Occurrences from Zambia. They resemble Tixier's *grand perçoir capsien* (Tixier, 1963: 66).

Utilized/modified (186)

Flakes, blades, fragments and chunks (171). Like the small scrapers, these show no regular plan form. Edge modification may take the form of notching with attendant crushing and marginal step fracture, discontinuous retouched areas and fine nibbled edges; in fact, the same general pattern that is present with the earlier Siszya and later Polungu aggregates. Flakes (Plate 49: 6; Plate 51: 11, 12, 17, 19–23; Plate 54: 18, 19), blades, fragments (Plate 51: 26) and chunks (Plate 52: 1, 4) were selected for modification. That on the flakes and fragments is more often shallow or blunt and that on the chunks is steep or blunt.

Of further note are the small flakes with marginal retouch at the proximal end on one or both lateral edges, the flakes themselves often being the product of specialized cores. These artifacts are characteristic of the Polungu Industry and the retouch presumably follows from a need to mount the flakes in some kind of handle or haft (Plate 49: 2; Plate 54: 6). The same need may underlie the invasive scar pattern at the proximal end of the ventral face of the blade at Plate 50: 9.

Outils esquillés (4). These are new forms, the chief significance of which lies in the evidence they provide for the use of bipolar flaking; all four examples are probably to be considered as cores that may have received further modification from use (Plate 53: 5, 7; Plate 54: 7).

Edge wear and rubbed aretes are present on the unique utilized core (Plate 48: 10) as also on a small chunk with one rubbed edge, classed as miscellaneous. The faceted and striated lump of white pigment (Plate 54: 17) also belongs in the rubbed group.

Hammerstones, rubbers and anvils (9). All five hammerstones are of hard quartzite with one or more battered areas. The rubbers (2) are characteristic of those found with the Siszya Industry as also with the later lithic industries at the Kalambo Falls (Plate 52: 11). They show smooth and striated plane surfaces, sometimes with a dimple pecked into the centre of one face. The anvils (2) are made from similar sized quartzite cobbles and, while they exhibit the dimple scar associated with the hammers and anvils used in bipolar flaking, they do not have the rubbing planes that distinguish the rubbers.

Unmodified waste (1,480)
Several core forms are found giving, in general, different kinds of primary flakes. There are three main sub-classes:

(*a*) *Blade and small flake cores* with one or two striking platforms. The opposed platform blade core is characteristic, the platforms being sometimes plain and sometimes faceted. Both microlithic (Plate 51: 27) and larger (Plate 50: 4; Plate 51: 33) forms occur. The blades and bladelets from these cores are often thin and ribbon-like; they exhibit one-directional flaking and plain, point or, sometimes, faceted platforms (Plate 51: 1–10). Plate 54: 13 is an example of an 'overpass' flake from a two-directional, opposed platform blade core.

(*b*) *Specialized discoid and sub-triangular cores.* These are mostly discs or elliptics, either high-backed or flat, for the removal of several small flakes from the dorsal face. The preparation on the face is usually radial (Plate 51: 32; Plate 52: 2, 5, 7, 9, 12; Plate 53: 8) but is sometimes from two directions, opposed or at right angles (Plate 49: 8; Plate 52: 3).[1] The flakes removed from these cores are generally broad, show multi- or two-directional flaking on the dorsal face and have plain, dihedral or simple-faceted platforms (Plate 51: 22; Plate 54: 15, 16). Discoid and sub-triangular cores designed for the removal of one large flake at a time by the Levallois method show both radial (Plate 48: 10; Plate 51: 31; Plate 52: 6) and one- (more rarely two-) directional (Plate 49: 9; Plate 52: 8, 10) dorsal preparation, the latter being either parallel or convergent. The former class yielded broad Levallois flakes with radial preparation and faceted platforms (Plate 51: 28, 29) while the latter produced irregular (Plate 51: 11, 12; Plate 54: 12) and short quadrilateral (Plate 49: 6), long triangular (Plate 50: 1, 10) and short triangular flakes, generally with faceted striking platforms (Plate 48: 6, 7; Plate 49: 2; Plate 51: 19–21, 23; Plate 53: 1, 2; Plate 54: 18, 19).

(*c*) *The formless, proto-biconical and biconical* cores make up the third main group. The last two classes may be unfinished or aberrant forms of discoids. These classes are present in small percentages in most later Pleistocene industries; they carry no particular significance in the Polungu aggregates at the Kalambo Falls.

The Rubble component of the Polungu Industry emerges from the comparisons of the mixed components of Rubble I as an archaeological entity showing close relationship with the Siszya Industry while, at the same time, incorporating innovations that link it also with the aggregates from the Hillslope soil and sandy clays in the A4, 1959, Excavation. While some uncertainty must remain, this Rubble component has been treated here as an earlier expression of the industrial tradition named from Polungu Hill, rather than as the final stage of the Siszya Industry, both because of the additional and apparently new artifact forms and because of its persistence within the base of the overlying sands after the formation of Rubble I at Sites B and C. Whether this interpretation is the right one will depend for confirmation on the discovery of a homogeneous assemblage such as may exist within the upslope sediments on the south side of the local basin.

[1] In cases where one larger flake has been removed from each end of the dorsal face of opposed platform cores (e.g. Plate 49: 8) we believe it possible that these may have been simultaneously removed by bipolar or rest technique rather than that they were individually struck. Experiment shows that it is only rarely that bipolar technique produces usable flakes simultaneously from each end of the core, rather does one or other flake split or hinge out. Some of the larger cores do, in fact, show just such snapping.

CHAPTER 8

Comparisons and relationships of the Polungu industrial components

As has been shown, there is reason to believe that the Polungu Industry components were being made during the closing stages of the Pleistocene and early Holocene – the Rubble component, most probably, from *c.* 20,000 B.P. but not later than 9000 B.P.; and the Hillslope component between some time after 9000 B.P. and before 4000 B.P. In part, therefore, they fall within the broad time range of what has been described as the 'Second Intermediate period' (Clark and Cole, 1957) and may thus be considered to be in part contemporary with those Archaeological Occurrences which typologically and technologically would appear to belong within this period, previously envisaged as one of industrial transition. Certainly, they have many characteristics in common. Recently, however, surprisingly early dates have been reported for some of these Occurrences from southern and central Africa. The available descriptions of the aggregates contained in these Occurrences indicate that morphologically they are comparable to others that date mainly from the later Pleistocene. This may show, therefore, that technical comparability is no longer as reliable a chronological indicator as it was once thought to be. Alternatively, it may be that the inference of comparability is still being made from a level of data and descriptive detail that is too general and so masks the significant differences between these seemingly much earlier Archaeological Occurrences and those which have been conventionally dated. There can, however, be little doubt that at the Kalambo Falls the Polungu Industry components belong within the conventional time range. The most meaningful comparisons can, therefore, be expected from other Archaeological Occurrences that fall within this range of time. In a few cases statistical comparisons can be made while in others only more general, qualitative comparisons are possible.

Comparison of the Hillslope and Rubble components

The two components can be compared in Figures 34 and 35. While the composition is broadly similar, there are also differences, although these are more in degree than in typologically exclusive elements. In the percentages of tools to waste, the bar diagrams (Figure 34) show only 2·9 per cent tools with the Hillslope component against 10·1 per cent with that from the Rubble. Possibly this is a significant difference, indicating that by the time of the later component, the formal tools representative of evolved 'Middle Stone Age' aggregates had ceased to be made, while the formal microlithic element had not yet been developed. On the other hand, the Rubble component may reflect some incomplete recording of unmodified waste (e.g. of the small flake/blade element (see p. 221 footnote 2)) though this is unlikely to be sufficient to account for the more than 7 per cent difference between tools and waste in the two components. Perhaps the best indicator of relationship is the unmodified waste (Figure 34). The bar diagrams of flake form show a generally similar composition, though it might have been expected that the Hillslope component would have contained the higher percentage of blades. Possibly, if the sample available from the Rubble component had been greater, it might have provided better evidence as to this seeming reversal in the quadrilateral forms. The mean flake lengths are, however, consistently longer with the earlier component and the later swing to microlithic proportions is what could be expected. The percentages of platform types are not greatly different but there is a slight increase in plain platforms and fewer faceted ones with the later component.

The core forms of both components exhibit the same general range of classes (Figure 34) but greater differences are apparent than was the case with the flakes. Blade cores, especially single platform types, show a significant increase with the Hillslope component as do also small, discoid, Levallois cores. By contrast, there are more ordinary disc cores, subtriangular and biconical cores with the Rubble component. In the utilized category (Figure 34) there are closely comparable numbers of flakes, fragments and chunks and, in each case, there is a small percentage of *outils esquillés*. There are no real differences in the classes of large, utilized pieces for the 1963 excavation at Site A4, Pit 3, Bed 11, also yielded a rubber.[1]

The chief differences between the two components appear in the shaped tool classes (Figure 35). There are no heavy tools with the Hillslope component and the choppers, core-scrapers and large scrapers of the Rubble component represent a significant element that has, apparently, disappeared by the time of the later component. They do not appear, either, with the later Kaposwa Industry, although occasional, atypical examples are known. The same cannot be said for the bored stone, however, and it is clear that it would have been known to the makers of the Hillslope component. In the light duty category, the larger backed and truncated flake and blade forms with the Rubble component are missing from the Hillslope. On the other hand, for what it is worth, there are three, as opposed to one microlith with the latter. The points show a significant difference in that the Hillslope examples are all unifacial and exhibit minimal evidence of retouch. The examples with the Rubble component are much more carefully retouched and the bifacial forms show a degree of flat, invasive retouch that is quite lacking in the later component. It is doubtful if the percentages of burins and protoburins have any significance, but the value of 45·2 per cent of small scrapers with the Rubble component as against 13·6 per cent with the Hillslope certainly has. The breakdown by edge type of the 79 small scrapers shows: single side 44·3 per cent; double side 20·25 per cent; side and end 6·32 per cent; three edges 2·53 per cent; end-scrapers 22·78 per cent; butt 2·53 per cent and circular 1·25 per cent. There are 106 worked edges and notches of which 27·26 per cent are straight; 16·30 per cent are convex; 10·26 per cent are concave; 12·25 per cent are notched; 20·75 per cent are denticulate; 2·82 per cent are *becs* (with opposed notches); 0·94 per cent are convergent; 5·66 per cent are nosed and 3·76 per cent are irregular.

The discoid/adzes, as also, perhaps, the borers, show that bifacial retouch was a significant method of trimming with the Rubble component that had, apparently, fallen out of use by the time of the Hillslope component.

In sum, therefore, these two components can best be seen as representing two temporarily distinct stages of a continuing cultural tradition which, sometime after *c.* 15,000 B.P., underwent a fairly rapid modification, with the adoption of innovative techniques of which the most significant may have been the development of composite tool technology and the accompanying adjustments in social behaviour intimately connected with the new equipment.[2] The only other Archaeological Occurrence from the vicinity of the Kalambo Falls that shows technical relationship with the Polungu Industry from the local basin, comes from a now silted basin south of the Chulungoma stream about 3½ miles (6 km) southeast of Mbala at an altitude of *c.* 5,400 feet (1,646 m).

Chulungoma

A contractor had opened several pits for building sand; these went down to a depth of 8 to 10 feet (2·4–3 m) and had exposed two archaeological horizons. In 1958 the site was found by Mr John Carlin to whom the writer is indebted for his visit the following year. Carlin collected a number of artifacts both *in situ* in the sections and from the bottom of the pits.

Chulungoma basin appears formerly to have been a shallow pan, now silted up, with an outlet at the south end. The basin, which today contains no standing water, is oval and measures 300 by 150 yards (274 × 137 m) and is surrounded on all sides by *Brachystegia* woodland. Towards the edges, the higher sections show *c.* 2 feet (60 cm) of light to dark grey sand with some organic matter nearer the centre of the basin. This is underlain by a thin layer, 3 to 4 inches (76–102 mm) of white clay which in turn rests unconformably on a brown to grey sand of medium texture and with no apparent bedding planes. This brown sand has an average thickness of *c.* 4 feet (122 cm) and at a depth of 3 feet (91 cm) within it

[1] Not included in the total here which is based on the 1959 excavation.

[2] The snapped blades found with the Siszya Industry aggregates may possibly indicate that the first experiments in composite tool technology took place at an even earlier period.

occurs the upper Archaeological Horizon. This horizon has no thickness but is distinguished by a sparse scatter and bunching of flakes of chert, chalcedony and quartzite, together with occasional lumps of weathered quartzite and sandstone, all of which must have been carried onto the site. The sand beneath this horizon is noticeably yellower and becomes buff to white in colour with depth. This colour change of brown, to yellow to buff is not accompanied by any non-sequence or noticeable texture change and the section is interpreted as a weathering profile which preserves evidence of a short episode of human occupation. Some finely comminuted organic fragments, vegetation or charcoal, were sometimes present and may be evidence for a temporary halt in accumulation of the sand. At a depth of 8 feet (2·4 m) below the surface in one pit, a lower horizon with a very few artifacts was located in the buff sand. The base of this sand was not exposed. Nearer the centre of the basin, prospect pits dug by Mr Carlin exposed sections showing *c.* 6 inches (15 cm) of peaty soil, 6 inches (15 cm) of a barely moist friable white clay and black peaty clay to a depth of more than 2 feet (61 cm).

Without systematic study no certain interpretation of this sequence can be made. Tentatively, it may be suggested that two climatic episodes may be represented at Chulungoma: an earlier encroachment and filling of the swampy basin by colluvial and, perhaps, wind blow sands from the surrounding woodland slopes, with evidence of two separate periods of human occupation; the second towards the closing stages of the episode when sand accumulation ceased and soil formation began on the slopes. The second episode might then be represented by the white clay which could bc an indication that the basin had become a shallow pan once again, with open water, the episode being brought to an end by the beginning of the present cycle of soil forming processes. Whether this interpretation is tenable only further work will show.

The Chulungoma artifacts are now in the Livingstone Museum and they have not been analysed. The writer had the opportunity to examine Mr Carlin's collection among which were several small, short and elongate triangular, unifacial points in chalcedony, chert and quartz, with marginal retouch, which are comparable to those found with the Rubble component of the Polungu Industry at the Kalambo Falls. The unmodified waste also confirms the use of both blade and specialized core technologies. In addition, Mr Carlin recovered five whole or fragmentary bored stones that had been dug out by the contractors. It is not known whether these came from the horizon with the Polungu-type artifacts or whether they are later but, in view of the discovery of the bored stone fragment from Rubble Ib at Site B at the Kalambo Falls, there is no reason to dissociate them from this horizon at Chulungoma.

This area is important for its possible association with the Kalambo Falls. The buff to brown sands might be equated with the formation of Rubble I and the sandy layers that separate the various manifestations of this rubble complex at the Kalambo Falls. The brown/grey sand overlying the upper Archaeological Horizon at Chulungoma would then be the equivalent of the current-bedded sand (Bed 12) of the Mbwilo Member. The white clay, therefore, may, perhaps, have formed during the more humid conditions of the post-Pleistocene hyperthermal.

Comparisons with occurrences from other areas in east and southern Africa

It is of interest to compare the Polungu Industry components with certain other aggregates from sites in east and southern Africa which, by reason of a common level of technology and/or temporal relationships, may help to a better understanding of the place and significance of these Polungu components at the Kalambo Falls. Three problems arise in any general comparisons of this kind and need to be taken into account.

Firstly, since there is no single terminology and classificatory system in general usage among African archaeologists and precise comparability cannot be established between the different systems, it is not always possible to be absolutely sure that the artifact classes being compared are really the same. Usually there is no problem where the major categories and classes are concerned and what, for example, is classified as a 'thumbnail scraper' by one author can with confidence be identified as the small convex scraper of another. For the purpose of the comparative discussion that follows, therefore, and for Figures 34 and 35, the terminology has been adjusted, where necessary, to conform to the system used in this volume. Where, however, typological equivalence is dubious or relates to more than one class of artifact in one of the collections or, for other reasons, could not be established as, for example, for the 'trimmed tools' with the Howieson's Poort at Montagu Cave, the excavator's own classification has been retained. Secondly, dimension details of flakes can be given only for a few of the collections and, if these were more generally available for comparative purposes, they might help to distinguish finer shades of similarity or difference. Thirdly, where comparisons are based, as they sometimes are, on very different numbers of artifacts, any implications should be treated with reserve.

Magosi Rock Shelter I, Uganda

Since the Polungu components have been likened to the entities formerly known as 'Magosian', it might be thought that they would show a number of common characteristics with the aggregate from the Magosi Rock Shelter in northeastern Uganda. This has been re-examined recently by Cole (1967*a*) and by Cole and Posnansky (1963). Cole found at least two periods of occupation at the shelter (Magosi I) excavated by Wayland. The earlier, normal rock shelter occupation had subsequently been dug out by a later prehistoric group in order to construct a water cistern. The greater part of the cultural material from the original excavation (Wayland and Burkitt, 1932) belongs with this later occupation which, in this shelter, is associated with a radiocarbon date of 13,870 ± 130 (11,920 B.C.) (S.R. 92. Sheppard and Swart, 1967: 383), although typologically and technically this is not a 'Second Intermediate' period Occurrence. The earlier aggregate, from the rock shelter deposit, which had become heavily impregnated with calcium carbonate, may, however, be more comparable in age with one or other of the Polungu components since it would seem to be related typologically. Bone from this deposit has given a date of 6510 ± 180 B.P. (Sheppard and Swart, 1971: 428) but there is reason to think that this may be contaminated or intrusive from the overlying horizon.[1] The aggregate from the lower horizon is nearly 79 per cent quartz and has yielded very few tools. There are stated to be 6 crescents, a dozen or so backed bladelets and small scrapers, 20 bifacial points and point fragments and a few burins as well as a few radially prepared Levallois cores and one dimple-scarred hammerstone (Cole, 1967*a*: 157–8). Through the courtesy of Dr Cole the writer was able to examine the points which are small, delicately made forms, several of them sub-triangular and showing affinities with those from the Rubble component at the Kalambo Falls.

East African Sites – Kisese II

In central Tanzania, the rock shelter at Kisese II, about 40 miles (64 km) north of Kondoa Irangi, excavated by Inskeep (1962*a*), provided a long, stratified sequence 20 feet (6·1 m) deep. The uppermost IX to X spits contained a series of ('Later Stone Age') aggregates with some nine classes of microliths and small convex scrapers. These overlay, in the lower eighteen spits, aggregates that have been described as 'Second Intermediate' in technology. Statistical data are not yet available so that no detailed comparisons can be made. The industry is, however, a small blade one made in quartz and it has a high percentage of *outils esquillés* from which it can be inferred that bipolar flaking was a usual technique. All microlithic classes are extremely rare though lunates and triangles are not totally absent. The two main tool forms are numerous convex and concave scrapers, a small number of burins and tools known as 'sinew frayers' which are artifacts showing inverse retouch, usually across the short axis at one end of a flake, fragment or blade.

The middle levels of this industry have been dated to 31,480 ± 1350–1640 (29,530 B.C.) (NPL-38) and the radiocarbon age of the transition (spits IX–X) into the microlithic is dated to 18,190 ± 300 (16,240 B.C.) (NPL-38). These dates (on ostrich eggshell) were at first considered to be too early but they are not inconsistent with the appearance of microlithic elements in the culture sequence in Uganda and Zambia. This suggests that the introduction of small blade technology must now be considered as beginning more generally in central Africa about 16,000 B.C. while the large blade element is probably twice as old in the 'Middle Stone Age' traditions of south-central and southern Africa. At Munyama Cave on Buvuma Island, the industry in quartz dated between 9780 ± 160 B.P. and 14,950 ± 80 B.P. is fully microlithic. It

[1] The Magosi II shelter excavated by Posnansky has also provided two dates from depths of between 1 and 2 feet (30–60 cm) in the upper layers of compact grey earth. Charcoal from a depth of 1 foot 4 inches (40·6 cm) gave a date of 700 ± 100 (A.D. 1250) (Sheppard and Swart, 1967: 382–3). Another sample from 1 foot 10 inches (58·9 cm) and believed to date the 'Wilton' in Uganda, gave an age of 6080 ± 130 (4130 B.C.) (Sheppard and Swart, 1966: 423). Because of the discrepancies, little reliance can be placed on any of these dates without further checks.

consists of backed bladelets and some geometric forms, many small, convex end-scrapers, core-scrapers, borers, *outils esquillés*, dimple-scarred anvils, grindstones and ochre. The borer illustrated (Van Noten, 1971) is on a triangular flake and shows marginal retouch over the distal half of the two converging lateral edges. It is reminiscent of, but not identical with, the small triangular points found with the Hillslope component of the Polungu Industry at the Kalambo Falls. Again, only a preliminary report has been published so that no detailed comparisons can be made.

Rutonde, Rwanda

An aggregate from the Rutonde site in Rwanda, which has been ascribed to the 'Magosian' was excavated by Nenquin (1967*a*: 96–119). The site is a hillslope talus adjacent to the Nyabarongo river, near Kigali, and appears to be a workshop and occupation area. The artifacts have been redistributed in a brown hillslope soil, 30 to 45 centimetres thick, with small gravel elements, and resting on a sterile sandy clay. The secondary, geological, nature of this occurrence can be seen in the illustrations that depict the notched and steep modification exhibited by many of the primary forms. The composition of the shaped tool category (Figure 35) shows a high percentage of small scrapers (27·6 per cent), mostly single side and concave and 12·6 per cent of composite scrapers with multiple edges. There are 23·3 per cent of backed blades and flakes; 11·2 per cent of points, mostly unifacial but some also bifacial (4 specimens), the triangular form being dominant. They are between 30 and 50 mm long and a few examples with short tangs also occur. There are a small number of choppers, core-scrapers and burins, as at the Kalambo Falls, but the class of small, awl-like borers (7·6 per cent) is not reflected there. Among the cores, 15 are discoid, radially prepared and 4 are formless (polyhedral). No blade cores are specifically mentioned and the basic primary form for tools appears to be flakes.

Zambian sites

Belonging to this time range also, as has been mentioned, is the Nachikufu I Industry, on the evidence of a date of 16,715 ± 95 (S.R.-138) for this aggregate at Leopard's Hill Cave in Zambia. It combines both a microlithic element in quartz, mostly marginally retouched and utilized bladelets, with a large scraper element made often in hard quartzite and other tougher, coarse grained rocks. At Mwela Rocks rock shelter, the assemblage ascribed to the Nachikufu I Industry and dated to 10,820 ± 340 B.P., produced one unifacially trimmed point in quartzite and one smaller, bifacial example in chert, associated with the characteristic microliths and scrapers (Miller, 1969).

Nsalu Cave

Beneath the Nachikufu I Industry in Nsalu rock shelter, the red, lower cave earth produced an assemblage showing characteristics in common with the Rubble component of the Polungu Industry. However, because of the shallowness and limited extent of the deposit, it is clearly incomplete. The aggregate is in quartz and has been partially analysed by Miller (1969: 203–6). Amongst the finds are included three short, triangular points and one double pointed tool. Three of these are parti-bifacial, one is unifacial and all are small (maximum length between 24 and 38 mm). They are associated with a few microliths, straight backed flakes and bladelets, small convex and concave scrapers, a bored stone, a spheroid, a dimple-scarred anvil and a fair amount of pigment. The unmodified waste includes disc cores, approximately 50 per cent struck to remove a single, specialized flake, with size ranges between 20 and 40 mm. Many of the flakes show faceted, some multi-faceted, striking platforms. However, while there are a small number of short quadrilateral flakes and bladelets, single platform and bladelet cores are almost entirely absent.

The lower occupation at Nsalu Cave, therefore, does show affinities with the Polungu Industry but it is not possible to be more specific. On the evidence of the ± 10,000 B.P. date for the Nachikufu I Industry at Mwela Rocks, it seems more likely that the lower occupation at Nsalu Cave overlaps in time with the Rubble component.

LEOPARD'S HILL CAVE

The Nachikufu I Industry at Leopard's Hill Cave in central Zambia is separated from the underlying aggregate by a stalagmitic layer of breccia and, if the radiocarbon date can be accepted, a time period of some 5,000 years. The earliest occupation in this cave occurs in a thin, grey earth layer and an underlying red earth resting on decomposing bed rock and both are sealed by the breccia. The aggregate, mostly in quartz, has been analysed by Miller (1969: 307–30) and is as yet unnamed, being referred to as 'proto-L.S.A.' Dates for the aggregate indicate that it is between 21,000 and 23,000 years old so that it may antedate even the Rubble component at the Kalambo Falls.

The composition of this 'proto-L.S.A.', as given by Miller, when compared with that of the Polungu Industry components (Figures 34 and 35) shows a number of features in common with the Rubble component, as well as a number of differences. Heavy duty scrapers on cores and small chunks comprise 49·2 per cent of the tools as opposed to 12·3 per cent of core-scrapers at the Kalambo Falls, though the other heavy duty equipment, which there constitutes 9·1 per cent of the tools, is absent from Leopard's Hill. Both aggregates have the bored stone and both are also comparable in the virtual absence of microliths and they have similar percentages of backed flakes and blades (14·3 per cent and 8·1 per cent). The Rubble component has more points and some burins as well as the discoid/adze but there is again a resemblance in the small scraper classes – 30·5 per cent at Leopard's Hill and 45·2 per cent with the Rubble component. Side scrapers comprise *c.* 47 per cent of the small scraper class at Leopard's Hill and 64·5 per cent in the Rubble component at the Kalambo Falls. Of these, *c.* 58 per cent are concave and notched forms at Leopard's Hill and 22 per cent at the Kalambo Falls. Leopard's Hill has also no end-scrapers, 23 per cent composite forms (including circular and end- and side-scrapers) and 19 per cent convergent and miscellaneous. The corresponding values of the Rubble component are: end-scrapers 23 per cent, composite 10 per cent and convergent and miscellaneous 2·5 per cent.

In the utilized/modified category there are further differences, although mostly in degree (Figure 34). Many more utilized flakes, fragments and chunks are recorded with the Rubble component and, as might be expected where quartz is the raw material, there is a sharp increase in *outils esquillés* at Leopard's Hill (20 per cent as against 2·3 per cent). Leopard's Hill also has more grinding and rubbing equipment but this may relate to the fact that the Occurrence is in primary context in a cave.

It is difficult to compare the unmodified waste flakes (Figure 34) but no short quadrilateral or triangular flakes are recorded from Leopard's Hill while there are almost twice as many side-flakes. Comparison of the mean lengths of flakes and blades shows that Leopard's Hill resembles the Hillslope component here more closely than it does the Rubble component, where in every instance the artifacts are longer. It may be suspected that this is in large part due to the difference in form and properties of the raw materials used. At Leopard's Hill 33·5 per cent of the flakes have a parallel dorsal scar pattern; at the Kalambo Falls most of the 47·1 per cent of flakes with one-directional flaking show a similar parallel pattern. Faceted platforms are not represented at Leopard's Hill though in part, perhaps, the 11·2 per cent of pseudo-faceted platforms, possibly from discoid cores, may overlap with the faceted group at the Kalambo Falls. Even with this proviso, however, there is a preponderance of plain platforms at Leopard's Hill. The core forms show some startling differences although, if a greater number had been available from Leopard's Hill, some modification of conclusions might have been called for. Most of the flake forms suggest derivation from unspecialized or discoid cores and there are very few blades, but the core forms show a complete reversal with 81 per cent being small blade cores and only 9·6 per cent discoids. This is difficult to explain unless the small area excavated is not a true sample of the overall activities of the makers of the lithic artifacts in this horizon or unless the disc cores were being reworked for the production of bladelets. The Polungu Industry components both contain a higher percentage of specialized disc and Levallois cores and a lower percentage of blade cores.

It is also of importance that at Leopard's Hill there are seven bone awls and, although no bone has survived at the Kalambo Falls, it may be assumed that the working of bone was a general practice in southern Africa by this time, when occasion dictated.

Although the differences are, perhaps, over-emphasized by the samples available, it is apparent that the 'proto-L.S.A.' and the Polungu Rubble component are more alike than dissimilar. Both show the blending of an evolved discoid core technique with a small blade element but, whether due to the raw material or to other cause, it is the 'proto-L.S.A.' – believed to be the older of the two – that is more fully developed towards a microlithic blade technology.

VICTORIA FALLS

No other primary context aggregates falling within this time range have yet been described from Zambia. At the Victoria Falls, on both sides of the river, aggregates are eroding from camping and workshop sites on the sand scarps. Although these have, as yet, been described only in general terms (Clark, 1950*a*: 101–7), the typology is closely comparable and nearly all the forms present in the Polungu components are represented also at the Victoria Falls where the artifacts are made almost entirely in chalcedony. The small collection (total – 750) made by the writer in 1963 on Jafuta Farm has been analysed by Gifford and Williamson and the following summary, which shows the general composition of these upper Zambezi aggregates, is taken from their unpublished account (Gifford and Williamson, University of California, Berkeley, Laboratory Research Paper, 1970). Chalcedony is the raw material used for 97 per cent of the artifacts, the remainder being made from silcrete (2 per cent) and basalt (1 per cent). Shaped tools comprise 22 per cent, utilized/modified 15 per cent and unmodified waste 63 per cent; clearly, the waste can be expected to reach higher percentages in unselected collections. The shaped tool category consists of 10 per cent microliths (backed bladelets, lunates and truncated forms and two larger backed flakes); points 12 per cent, almost all unifacial with minimal, marginal retouch; scrapers 61 per cent, mostly small; discoid adzes or knives 4 per cent; discontinuously trimmed pieces 5 per cent; *outils esquillés* 3 per cent and miscellaneous 4 per cent including two chunks with crude, bifacial trimming, eight technical and one dihedral burins, two *becs* and one awl. There are nearly twice as many convex, small end- and nosed scrapers (46 per cent) as concave, notched and denticulate forms (24 per cent); 14 per cent are core- and large end-scrapers and the remaining 16 per cent are convergent and end- and side. Grinding and pounding equipment is represented by two lower grindstones, three rubbers, one dimple-scarred rubber and a striated pebble chunk. In the unmodified waste, 52 per cent of the cores are struck Levallois flake cores, 12 per cent are disc cores, 10 per cent are single platform of which nearly two-thirds are for blades, 10 per cent have two opposed platforms almost all for producing blades; the remaining 5 per cent are unspecialized cores either formless or with two platforms at right angles. Among the waste flakes 27 per cent are Levallois and 25 per cent are bladelets. As might be expected, the Jafuta aggregate has much in common with those described below from the western part of Rhodesia.

Rhodesian sites

The excavated assemblages belonging in this time range from the open site at Khami (Cooke, 1957) and Pomongwe Cave (Cooke, 1963), both in Matabeleland, show best the characteristics of the cultural entity which the original 'Magosian' from Magosi was thought to be. These sites are both stratified with a long cultural sequence, carefully excavated and recorded and the industrial entities at Pomongwe are well dated. The aggregates previously described as 'Rhodesian Magosian' have now been renamed as the Umguzan (Cooke, Summers and Robinson, 1966). At both sites the Umguzan is found stratigraphically between the Bambata Industry (formerly Rhodesian Stillbay) and the 'Later Stone Age' aggregates. The dates for the Umguzan from Rhodesia lie between 27,000 B.P. and an age earlier than 9400 ± 110 B.P. have already been referred to (p. 199).

When the shaped tool category of the Umguzan aggregates from Khami and Pomongwe are compared, close similarities are apparent except for one important difference, namely the higher percentage of microliths (41·5 per cent) at Khami as against 1·6 per cent, or 14·3 per cent at Pomongwe if the larger, backed class is added (Figure 35). There is little difference in the numbers of blades and crescents in each of the five excavated levels so it is not the case that these tools occur only at the end of the occupation. Whether this difference between the aggregates is due to temporal or activity differences or to the limitation that partial excavation of a site imposes is unknown but Cooke has shown a sharp distinction between the activities carried out at the front and back parts of the cave at Pomongwe, so far as these can be interpreted from artifact distribution patterns.

Its chronological position suggests that the Umguzan might be expected to be closest typologically and technically to the Rubble component of the Polungu Industry. In view of the distance that separates them, the observed differences between the Khami and Pomongwe Occurrences, which are only some 50 miles (80 km) apart, and that from the Kalambo Falls in a different ecological zone, are not outstandingly great and, in fact, they compare fairly well. In the shaped tool category (Figure 35) the Umguzan lacks the large, heavy duty tools which can be seen to be related more to a closed vegetation pattern.[1] Both the Pomongwe Occurrence and the Rubble component lack the high value for microliths observed at Khami although all three contain closely similar values for the larger backed tools. Points are more common at the Rhodesian sites but the forms that occur are generally similar and the small, triangular examples are an important type if they do not predominate. Pomongwe has the highest percentage of small scrapers and in this respect is closest to the Kalambo Falls with 45·2 per cent than to Khami with 25·3 per cent. Although small, the borer class is present in all three Occurrences. Discoids with areas of flat, semi-invasive retouch occur at both the Rhodesian sites but have not been specifically distinguished by the excavator. Pomongwe has yielded also a bone point and beads of ostrich eggshell.

In the utilized/modified category (Figure 34) there are appreciably more flake and chunk forms with the Kalambo Falls Occurrences, but both the Rhodesian sites have significantly higher values for *outils esquillés*. The quartz crystals with bruised ends at Pomongwe are utilized manuports. The range of pounding and grinding equipment is much the same in all three Occurrences and it should be noted that an earlier excavation at Khami yielded a bored stone with the Umguzan (Cooke, 1957: 31).[2] Details of flake forms are not available for Khami or Pomongwe but the platform types from Khami show a preponderance of faceted over plain forms (Figure 34). This will be repeated in the core classes if, as is generally believed, intentional faceting is to be associated with specialized core preparation. The value for discoid cores is particularly high at Pomongwe (76·3 per cent). If, however, at the Kalambo Falls, the discoids giving Levallois flakes are added then values between Khami (56·0 per cent) and the Rubble component (46·6 per cent) are not very different. In the small blade cores, the Rubble component value falls between that of the two Rhodesian aggregates. Khami has 21·8 per cent of these cores and is, thus, somewhat closer to the Hillslope component with 29·8 per cent. The Rubble component has the highest percentage of sub-triangular cores (8·4 per cent) as against 3·8 per cent at Khami and 0·4 per cent at Pomongwe; other core forms show little difference.

There is a closer level of agreement between the Pomongwe Umguzan and the Rubble component, and both of the Rhodesian Occurrences appear to be different from the Hillslope component except in the products of small blade technology where Khami and the Hillslope component are closest.

POMONGWAN

Stratified above the Umguzan in Pomongwe Cave is an aggregate that represents a break with the long tradition of which the Umguzan appears to be the final expression. It is characterized by a dearth of retouched tools with the exception of scrapers, and, since it is associated with a white ash deposit towards the back of the cave, it might be thought to represent some special activity variant of an Umguzan or later industrial entity. The existence of similar industries with large scraper forms in other parts of southern Africa, some of which have comparable radiocarbon ages – the 'Smithfield A' in the Orange Free State (Sampson, 1967); the Occurrences in the lower levels at Matjes River Cave, Cape (Louw, 1960); at the Windhoek park butchery site, South West Africa (MacCalman, 1967 and personal communication); the Smithfield aggregate from Layer 1 at Uitkomst Cave, Transvaal (Mason, 1962: 308–10; Mason and Van der Merwe, 1964) as well as an aggregate excavated by Inskeep and the writer but as yet undescribed, from Lukanda in the Gwembe Valley of Zambia, now under Lake Kariba – confirm that this technological and typological break took place in certain regions *c.* 9000–11,000 B.P. It is therefore of interest to compare the Hillslope component of the Polungu Industry with the large scraper industry from Rhodesia named Pomongwan from the site where it was first identified and defined (Cooke, 1963).

The Pomongwan occurs in Layer 3 (Third Excavation) at Pomongwe Cave. In the shaped tool category (Figure 35) there is a heavy core-scraper element (2·4 per cent) that has not yet been found with the Hillslope component but which might well be expected to occur. There are no microliths or other backed forms with the Pomongwan and only a single point is recorded. Almost all the tools are well retouched scrapers, the most significant being the large circular forms on broad flakes and chunks (46·1 per cent) and small convex (thumbnail) scrapers (30·1 per cent). The Hillslope component scrapers are not comparable, being in the main informal tools, and they comprise only 47·4 per cent of the tools. The edge forms are also different – the characteristic circular

[1] At Zombepata Cave rare examples of heavy duty tools ('cleaver', hand-axe, chopper) are found associated with the Umguzan, and this is clearly related to its location in the high rainfall *Brachystegia* woodland zone of Mashonaland (Cooke, 1971: 108–9).

[2] Pigment is also present at the Rhodesian sites but is not shown in the bar diagrams.

scrapers are missing at the Kalambo Falls where, on the other hand, occurs a higher percentage of concave and denticulate forms (19·7 per cent as against 2·0 per cent). Small convex scrapers occur in both aggregates and, although there are only two with the Hillslope component, their presence nonetheless is significant. Also with the Pomongwan are a number (10) of bone points and worked pieces of bone, wood and shell, preserved by the dryness of the cave deposits. In the utilized/modified category (Figure 34) it is the increased importance of the rubbing, grinding and pounding equipment with the Pomongwan that is, perhaps, the most significant difference, though the value for utilized flaked pieces is also much higher at the Kalambo Falls. A detailed breakdown of flake and core forms for the Pomongwan is not available but a total of 1,563 flakes, 6 disc and 1 polyhedral core are recorded. It would, therefore, appear that the Pomongwan has very little in common with either of the Polungu Industry components.

South African sites

A number of sites are referred to in the literature as yielding 'Magosian' assemblages but few of these have been published in a form to give any precise knowledge of their lithic composition. The Howieson's Poort Industry from the type site has recently been re-studied from a further excavated sample by H. and J. Deacon and a date of 18,704 B.P. (Keller, 1970: 193) for the Occurrence obtained. Personal observation, for which the author is indebted to Dr Hilary and Mrs Jeanette Deacon, shows that this aggregate is comparable but by no means identical with the Rubble component of the Polungu Industry at the Kalambo Falls.

The Rose Cottage Cave, Ladybrand, is another stratified sequence that has yielded at least three levels of 'Magosian' under a 'pre-Wilton' (Malan, 1952). The present writer can confirm from personal observation, thanks to Malan, that *typologically* this is a late or final expression of 'Middle Stone Age' technology which combines a small blade element and microliths. However, a sample of the 'Upper Magosian' obtained from a recent excavation there gave a date of more than 50,000 years B.P. (Mason, 1969). Unless, therefore, the association of the C14 date is in error, the concept that technological stages necessarily imply chronological contemporaneity must now be abandoned.

The only South African aggregates that have been described as 'Howieson's Poort' or 'Magosian' and for which full statistical data exist, come from Montagu Cave in the Cape Province (Keller, 1966 and 1970). The five dates obtained from carbon samples from Layer 2 at Montagu Cave range from 19,100 ± 100 B.P. to more than 50,800 B.P. but some of these are out of sequence. The 'Howieson's Poort' Industry from Montagu combines the use of hard quartzite or Table Mountain sandstone for the larger tools primarily made on flakes, with small pebbles of chalcedony and other fine grained rocks which produced very small near-microlithic artifacts. The larger element is not inconsistent with an earlier age but the small backed artifacts, though rare, look to be late rather than early in the Upper Pleistocene.

Bar diagrams at Figures 34 and 35 show the artifact classes and attributes of the Montagu 'Howieson's Poort' adjusted for comparison with the Polungu Industry. It is apparent that there is little resemblance with the Hillslope component. The Montagu Industry does, however, have more in common with the Rubble component, in particular in regard to the number of casually trimmed/modified pieces that are one of the main features of both. However, if the classification system used here were applied to the Montagu class of 'trimmed tools', it is certain that some of these would be regarded as scrapers with shallow angle of edge retouch and others as utilized/modified pieces. Most of the same tool classes are represented at both sites and there is general comparability between the unmodified flake forms, although the Rubble component has a higher percentage of blades (12·7 per cent as against 2·9 per cent) and there is much greater variability in size, form and raw material at Montagu. The platform types also show general agreement. Among the core types (Figure 34), Montagu has 52·1 per cent of blade and flake cores with single and opposed platforms as against 22 per cent of blade and flake cores at the Kalambo Falls. The values for discoid cores are much the same (40·1 per cent and 35·2 per cent) but there are rather more cores classified as Levallois with the Polungu. Similarities are, therefore, at the general rather than at the specific level but there are no immediately outstanding differences which might be expected if the time differences were as great as the radiocarbon dates suggest them to be.

Conclusions

The Rubble component of the Polungu Industry belongs in time somewhere between 10,000 and 20,000 B.P. when there was considerable variability in the stone industries being made by the prehistoric inhabitants of the sub-continent, if the radiocarbon chronology can be relied on. Some of these industries (e.g. Munyama Cave, Lake Victoria) have a fully microlithic tool-kit with formal microliths by 15,000 B.C.; others (Kisese Rock Shelter) have mostly informal equipment based on small core forms; or combine microlithic and heavy duty forms (e.g. Nachikufu I; Leopard's Hill 'proto-L.S.A.'). Others again combine in varying proportions the products of a small flake/blade technology with those from disc and Levallois core forms (Pomongwe and Khami Umguzan; Montagu Cave; Rutonde). Still others (e.g. the Pomongwan from Pomongwe Cave) appear to represent a break with the previous tradition of the locality and, although these 'scraper industries' might seem at first sight to reflect only part of the full range of flaked stone tools that were being made by the local population, such 'incompleteness' is more probably an indication that significant new equipment, using other materials, amongst which were wood and bone, had replaced older traditional kinds of tools.

At present it does not appear that these different industrial patterns fall into any kind of chronological order but only more dated Archaeological Occurrences will show whether this, in fact, is so. This disparate pattern might more satisfactorily be explained as due to behavioural differences dictated by local ecological factors and cultural selection. Thus, in the tool classes, the heavy duty equipment appears to be associated more with the higher rainfall, tropical savanna sites (Kalambo Falls, Leopard's Hill and Rutonde) and the considerable antiquity for the use of the bored stone in both woodland and park savanna is confirmed (Kalambo Falls, Leopard's Hill, Khami). Linked, most probably, with the pattern of variation in the core forms, the importance of the microlith and point classes is very variable and could equally reflect cultural preferences as environmental causes. Microliths are important in the Khami Umguzan but not so significant as points in that from Pomongwe; these are in parkland and, by contrast, the microlith is also important in the woodlands in northern Zambia and on Lake Victoria. However, it is possible that there may be a more certain relationship between environment and the higher percentages of concave, notched and denticulate scrapers in the tropical woodland (Kalambo Falls, Leopard's Hill, Rutonde) and the importance of the circular and small convex scrapers in the parkland sites (Pomongwe, Khami). The expectation that greater variability rather than comparability would exist between the prehistoric tool-kits of this time appears, therefore, to find some confirmation from the limited comparisons it has been possible to make here.

In the utilized/modified category, *outils esquillés* form small but sometimes significant percentages of the artifact aggregates, as at Pomongwe, Khami and Leopard's Hill, but are of negligible importance at the other sites. In the industries from the caves – the Pomongwan and Umguzan at Pomongwe and the 'proto-L.S.A.' at Leopard's Hill – the pounding, rubbing and grinding equipment is a small but significant factor as it is also with the Umguzan Occurrence at the open site at Khami. The unmodified waste shows no particular pattern. Sometimes there are more cores with parallel flaking (for example *c.* 88 per cent at Leopard's Hill), at other sites it is the discoid cores that predominate (Pomongwe Cave Umguzan *c.* 76 per cent). The flake forms are broadly the same although there is a greater range in size at some sites than at others, probably attributable to the use of different raw materials.

Comparisons of the Hillslope and Rubble components of the Polungu Industry with the other components in Rubble I at the Kalambo Falls indicate the likelihood that, in general, greater similarity may be expected between succeeding industries from the same locality with similar ecology, than will be the case between 'contemporary' occurrences several hundred miles apart in localities with differing ecological conditions. The greater the ecological differences of the habitat, the greater, it may be suggested, will be the degree of variability between the tool-kits. We are not yet in a position, however, to judge the truth or otherwise of the converse – that the more alike are the environment and the resources exploited, the closer will be the resemblances that can be anticipated between the lithic assemblages. There are too many cultural and geographic variables that can control prehistoric flaking traditions and so few detailed locality studies that, if any general pattern exists, there are few, if any, regions of the continent where it can, as yet, be demonstrated.

This review of industrial entities from other parts of sub-Saharan Africa which, for various reasons – general typological/technical equivalence, stratigraphic position or radiocarbon dating – might be thought to show affinities with the Polungu Industry components, raises a number of questions that are unlikely to be answered except by further research.

Firstly, typological/technical equivalence is not confined to those entities that are generally contemporary. If the radiocarbon dating is not in error, then aggregates far separated in time and space appear sometimes to have more in common than do those for which contemporaneity is established.

Secondly, all of these Occurrences, except, perhaps, the Pomongwan, combine a small blade element with an evolved and specialized flake core technology. However, the relative importance of the blade element may be very different, appearing much earlier in some localities than in others. The same is the case with the formal microlithic classes which are sometimes only found in the later aggregates while in others they are remarkably early (e.g. at Nachikufu and Leopard's Hill).

Thirdly, with the exception of the Pomongwan, each of these industries can be seen to show close affinities with the antecedent regional industries of 'Middle Stone Age' tradition.

Fourthly, the technological changes that can be seen to be taking place in these 'Second Intermediate' industries are changes that relate to the adoption through invention, stimulus diffusion or other cause, of new forms and the falling out of old ones as a gradual process through time and not as a complete and sudden technological break. Again, in this regard the Pomongwan appears to be distinctive.

These technological innovations are viewed here as the means and products of readjustment by the local hunting populations to various kinds of long- and short-term pressures, the effects of which were the primary causes of social and economic change. For example, climatic and ecological changes had their effect on the availability and variety of plant and animal resources and so on which of these were selected as primary food sources; or, again, increases or decreases in human population density dictated the depth to which available resources were exploited and the extent to which previously by-passed environments were brought into use and also necessitated readjustment in the regional distribution of population. These can all be seen to be major sources of change in prehistoric society. Changes in social relationships which are reflected in the settlement pattern and in the economic efficiency which can be inferred from the technological products of the group may be the result of long-range stimulus or more direct diffusion as, up to now, it has been generally supposed. On the other hand, the new radiocarbon evidence lends support to the likelihood that these behavioural changes may equally well have come about quite independently of any external stimuli. Given the existence of a generally similar technological background, we now believe there to be valid reasons for suggesting that the technological innovations we have been considering may be the direct outcome of independent experiment by the exponents of the individual African regional traditions.

When such fundamental improvements as concern us here first began to make their appearance in southern Africa, is, as yet, uncertain. However, the disparity in technical levels recently indicated by the radiocarbon chronology, suggests that the most significant controls that determined whether these innovations were late or early in making their appearance may have been directly related to the immediate or long-term economic and social advantages that they were able to offer.

The advantages of a small blade technology probably relate to the use of composite weapons and tools. This manifests itself earlier in east and central Africa than in the south if we leave out of the discussion for the present the enigmatic dates for Montagu and Rose Cottage Cave. Nevertheless, there is little close comparability between the various industries and it is becoming increasingly clear that each has a comparatively restricted range. While, therefore, comparisons between adjacent regions are often close at the general level, it becomes increasingly unlikely that they will be seen to be so at a more detailed level. Indeed, if we are dealing with the artifacts of relatively isolated population groups, as we believe, then what we are comparing are not the products of closely related peoples but the results of locally adaptive processes operating in generally similar ecological niches. If this is so, then the greatest similarities for the Polungu components might be expected with those entities that are closest in time and space and/or in eco-systems similar to that pertaining at the Kalambo Falls. If, on analysis, these are not generally comparable, then it becomes necessary to look for other variables such as special local pressures and preferences, which may have been factors in occasioning some of the differences.

It is hard to judge, except from primary context sites, the significance of the grinding and pounding equipment or of the bored stone. A more intensive use of grains and seeds is implied by the former while the latter suggests also that some new or more efficient use was being made of other resources, possibly connected, as has been suggested earlier (p. 147) with the development of trapping. The shaped bone tools, awls and points, and the use of ostrich eggshell are also innovations that carry with them important social and economic implications. Although at the Kalambo Falls bone tools were not preserved, the probability that they would have been known to the local population there is indicated by their occurrence earlier in time at Leopard's Hill.

The Polungu components would, therefore, appear to be crucial, albeit incomplete indications of those technological changes whereby the Upper Pleistocene 'Middle Stone Age' technology was replaced by one in which the most important flaked stone tool was the microlith.

Volume I Errata

p. 47, Table 1, lines 1–2, right hand column: read 'red sandy clay' (i.e. not capitalized).
line 5: under ''Alluvial facies', read 'sandy clay' (not capitalized).
line 6: read 'sands or' (not capitalized).

p. 52, lines 3–4: for 'bed nos. 5, 6, 7 and 8' read '6, 6′, 7′, 8 and 8′'.

p. 103, paragraph 1, line 11: for '(Plate 14)' read '(Plate 13)'.

p. 150, Table 2: under 'Named geological units', for 'Rubble Bed (Ia)' read '(rubble Ia)' and for 'Rubble Bed (Ib)' read '(rubble Ib)'.

Under 'Elevations' for phase F5 add 'Base *c.* +32 feet'.

p. 179, Table 1: under 'Named geological units', for 'Rubble Bed (Ia)' read '(rubble Ia)'.

p. 194, line 9: read ''Older Boulder Beds' (Chitambala Gravel Beds)'.
line 36: read ''Younger Boulder Beds' (Chisya Gravel Beds)'.

p. 236, Appendix J: Sample Grn–3196, under Site A, for '6 in. below Rubble II' read '6 in. below Rubble I'.

BIBLIOGRAPHY

Allan, W. (1967). *The African Husbandman.* New York. Barnes and Noble.

Ansell, W. F. H. (1960). *Mammals of Northern Rhodesia.* Lusaka.

Balout, L. (1955). *Préhistoire de l'Afrique du nord.* Paris. Arts et Métiers graphiques.

Bishop, W. W. and J. D. Clark (eds.), (1967). *Background to Evolution in Africa.* Chicago University Press.

Boileau, F. F. R. (1899). The Nyasa–Tanganyika Plateau – I. *Geographical Journal,* Vol. XIII (6), pp. 577–94.

Bordes, F. (1961). *Typologie du Paléolithique ancien et moyen.* Bordeaux.

Bordes, F. (1967). Considérations sur la typologie et les techniques dans le Paléolithique. *Quatär,* **18**: 25–55.

Brelsford, W. V. (1938). *Handbook to the collections in the Livingstone Museum.* Lusaka.

Brelsford, W. V. (1956). *The Tribes of Northern Rhodesia.* Lusaka.

Breuil, H. (1944). Le Paléolithique au Congo Belge d'après les recherches du Docteur Cabu. *Trans. Roy. Soc. South Africa,* **30**, II: 143–67.

Brézillon, M. N. (1968). La dénomination des objets de pierre taillée. Supplément 4, *Gallia Préhistoire,* C.N.R.S. Paris.

Brock, Beverly (1966). The Nyiha of Mbozi. *Tanganyika Notes and Records,* 65: 1–30.

Brock, B. and P. W. G. (1965). Iron working amongst the Nyiha of southwestern Tanganyika. *South African Archaeological Bull.* 20 (78): 97–100.

Brothwell, D. R. (1971). The population: skeletal remains. In B. M. Fagan and F. Van Noten, *The Hunter-gatherers of Gwisho.* Musée royal de l'Afrique centrale, Tervuren. Annales, Séries in-8°, Sciences humaines, no. 74.

Brothwell, D. and T. Molleson (In press). A study of the human skeletal remains of Late Stone Age date from Fingira Rock Shelter, Malawi. In J. D. Clark (ed.), *Report on Palaeoanthropological Investigation in the Lake Malawi Rift.*

Bruwer, J. P. (1956). Note on the Njazi rock shelter site in the Eastern Province of Northern Rhodesia. *Northern Rhodesia Journal,* III (1): 87–90.

Busson, F. (1965). *Plantes alimentaires de l'Ouest africain: Etude botanique, biologique et chimique.* Centre national de coordination des études et recherches sur la nutrition et l'alimentation. Marseille.

Cabu, F. and P. van den Brande (1938). Contribution à l'étude de la répartition des kwés au Katanga. *Annales du Musée royal du Congo Belge,* D. Sér. 1, 1 (4): 141–244.

Cambell, J. S. (1950). I knew Lewanika. *Northern Rhodesia Journal* 1 (1): 18–23.

Capart, A. (1949). *Sondages et carte bathymétrique.* Institut royal national belgique, Exploration hydro-biologique du Lac Tanganyika (1946–7). Résultats scientifiques 2 (2).

Capart, A. (1952). *Le milieu géographique et géophysique.* Résultats scientifiques 1.

Chaplin, J. H. (1961). Notes on traditional smelting in Northern Rhodesia. *South African Archaeological Bulletin,* **16** (62): 53–60.

Chapman, J. D. & F. White (1970). *The Evergreen forests of Malawi.* Oxford. Commonwealth Forestry Institute.

Chavaillon, J. (1964). *Classification des pièces présentant un biseau terminal.* Tableau multigraphié, Bellevue, Laboratoire de Géologie du Quaternaire, C.N.R.S.

Clark, J. D. (1942). Further excavations (1939) at the Mumbwa Cave, Northern Rhodesia. *Trans. Roy. Soc. South Africa.* XXIX: 133–201.

Clark, J. D. (1950*a*). *The Stone Age Cultures of Northern Rhodesia.* Cape Town.

Clark, J. D. (1950*b*). A note on the pre-Bantu inhabitants of Northern Rhodesia and Nyasaland. *South African Journal of Science,* **47** (3): 80–5.

Clark, J. D. (1954). *The Prehistoric Cultures of the Horn of Africa.* Cambridge.

Clark, J. D. (1958*a*). Certain industries of notched and strangulated scrapers in Rhodesia: their time range and possible use. *South African Archaeological Bull.* **13** (50): 56–66.

Clark, J. D. (1958*b*). Some Stone Age wood-working tools in southern Africa. *South African Archaeological Bull.* **13** (52): 144–51.

Clark, J. D. (1959*a*). *The Prehistory of Southern Africa.* Penguin Books.

Clark, J. D. (1959*b*). The rock paintings of Northern Rhodesia and Nyasaland. In R. Summers (ed.), *Prehistoric Rock Art of the Federation of Rhodesia and Nyasaland.* Salisbury, pp. 163–230.

Clark, J. D. (1959*c*). Further excavations at Broken Hill, Northern Rhodesia. *J.R.A.I.* **89** (II): 201–32.

Clark, J. D. (1963). *Prehistoric Cultures of Northeast Angola and their Significance in Tropical Africa.* Museu do Dundo, Lisbon, Pub. Cult. no. 62.

Clark, J. D. (1964). *The Sangoan Culture of Equatoria: The Implications of its Stone Equipment.* Diputación Provincial de Barcelona, Instituto de Prehistoria y Arqueologia, Monografias, **9**: 309–25.

Clark, J. D. (1966). *The Distribution of Prehistoric Culture in Angola.* Museu do Dundo, Lisbon. Pub. Cult. no. 73.

Clark, J. D. (1968). *Further Palaeoanthropological Studies in Northern Lunda.* Museu do Dundo, Lisbon, Pub. Cult. no. 78.

Clark, J. D. (1969). Further excavations (1965) at the Middle Acheulian occupation site at Latamne, northern Syria; general results, definitions and interpretations. *Quaternaria,* **10**: 1–71.

Clark, J. D. (1971). Problems of archaeological nomenclature and classification in the Congo basin. *South African Archaeological Bull.* **26**: 69–78 and plates 9–13.

Clark, J. D., G. H. Cole, G. Ll. Isaac and M. R. Kleindienst (1966). Precision and definition in African Archaeology. *South African Archaeological Bull.* **21** (3): 114–21.

Clark, J. D. and S. Cole (eds.), (1957). *Proceedings of the third Pan-African Congress on Prehistory, Livingstone, Northern Rhodesia* (1955). London.

Clark, J. D. and B. M. Fagan (1965). Charcoals, sands and channel-decorated pottery from Northern Rhodesia. *American Anthropologist,* **67** (2): 354–71.

Clark, J. D., C. Vance Haynes, Jr., J. E. Mawby and A. Gautier (1970). Interim report on Palaeoanthropological investigations in the Lake Malawi Rift. *Quaternaria,* **13**: 305–54.

Clarke, D. L. (1968). *Analytical Archaeology*. London.

Cline, Walter (1937). *Mining and metallurgy in Negro Africa.* General Series in Anthropology, no. 5. Wisconsin.

Cole, G. H. (1967*a*). A reinvestigation of Magosi and the Magosian. *Quaternaria,* **9**: 153–68.

Cole, G. H. (1967*b*). The Later Acheulian and Sangoan of southern Uganda. In W. W. Bishop and J. D. Clark (eds.), *Background to Evolution in Africa,* Chicago. Pp. 481–526.

Cole, G. H. and M. Posnansky (1963). Recent excavations at Magosi, Uganda: A preliminary report. *Man,* **63** (132): 104–6.

Colson, E. (1964). The Little People of Rhodesia. *Northern Rhodesia Journal,* v (6): 567–8.

Cooke, C. K. (1957). *The Waterworks site at Khami, Southern Rhodesia: Stone Age and Proto-historic.* Occ. Papers, Nat. Museums of Southern Rhodesia. (Human Sciences), **3** (21A): 1–43.

Cooke, C. K. (1963). Report on excavations at Pomongwe and Tshangula Caves, Matopos Hills, Southern Rhodesia. *South African Archaeological Bull.* **18** (71): 73–151.

Cooke, C. K. (1968). What does the future hold for the amateur archaeologist? *S. Afr. Arch. Bull.* **23** (89): 3–8.

Cooke, C. K. (1971). Excavation at Zombepata Cave, Sipolilo District, Mashonaland, Rhodesia. *South African Archaeological Bull.* **26**: 104–26.

Cooke, C. K., R. Summers and K. R. Robinson (1966). *Rhodesian Prehistory re-examined: Part I, the Stone Age.* Arnoldia (Rhodesia) Misc. Pub. Series. Nat. Museums Southern Rhodesia **2** (12): 1–8.

Cornwall, J. W. (1929). The survey of the Kalambo Gorge. *Geographical Journal,* **74**: 33–8.

Crabtree, D. E. (1964). *Notes on Experiments in Flint Knapping: I, Heat Treatment of Silica Minerals.* Tebiwa, Idaho State University Museum, **7** (1): 1–6.

Crabtree, D. E. (1970). Flaking stone with wooden implements. *Science,* 169: 146–53.

Cunnison, I. (1959). *The Luapula Peoples of Northern Rhodesia.* Manchester.

Deacon, H. J. (1970). The Acheulian occupation at Amanzi Springs, Uitenhage District, Cape Province. *Annals of Cape Provincial Museums,* **8** (2).

Dunn, E. J. (1931). *The Bushmen.* London.

Ellis, H. H. (1957). *Flint-working Techniques of the American Indians: An Experimental Study.* Ohio Historical Society, Columbus.

Elton, J. F. (1879). *Travels and Researches among the Lakes and Mountains of Eastern and Central Africa.* London.

Emery, W. B. (1961). *Archaic Egypt.* London.

Fagan, B. M. (1961). A note on pot making among the Lungu of Northern Rhodesia. *Man,* **61** (104): 87–8.

Fagan, B. M. (1963). The Iron Age sequence in the Southern Province of Northern Rhodesia. *Journal of African History,* **4** (2): 157–77.

Fagan, B. M. (1965). *Southern Africa during the Iron Age.* London, Thames and Hudson.

Fagan, B. M. (1966). *Iron Age Cultures of Zambia,* Volume I. London.

Fagan, B. M. (1967). Iron Age peoples of Zambia and Malawi. In W. W. Bishop and J. D. Clark (eds.), *Background to Evolution in Africa.* Chicago: 659–85.

Fagan, B. M. (1969*a*). Radiocarbon dates for sub-Saharan Africa. *Journal of African History,* **10** (1): 149–70.

Fagan, B. M. (1969*b*). Early trade and raw materials in south central Africa. *Journal of African History,* **10** (1): 1–13.

Fagan, B. M., D. W. Phillipson and S. G. H. Daniels (1969). *Iron Age Cultures in Zambia,* Volume II. London.

Fagan, B. M. and F. van Noten (1964). Two channel-decorated pottery sites from Northern Rhodesia. *Man,* **65** Article 8.

Fagan, B. M. and F. van Noten (1971). *The Hunter-Gatherers of Gwisho.* Musée royal de l'Afrique centrale, Tervuren, Séries in-8°, no. 74.

Fagan, B. M. & J. E. Yellen (1968). Ivuna: Ancient saltworking in southern Tanzania. *Azania,* III: 1–44.

Fagan, B. M. and J. E. Yellen (In preparation). The Pot-makers of Ivuna.

Foran, W. R. (1937). *African Odyssey.* London.

Fülleborn, Friedrich (1906). *Deutsch Ost-Afrika, Band IX: Das Deutsche Nyassa- und Ruwuma-Gebiet: Land und Leute, nebst Bermerkungen über die Schire-Länder.* Berlin.

Gabel, C. (1965). *Stone Age Hunters of the Kafue: The Gwisho A Site.* Boston University African Research Studies, no. 6.

Galloway, A. (1959). *The Skeletal Remains of Bambandyanalo.* Johannesburg.

Gardner, G. A. (1963). *Mapungubwe,* Volume II. Pretoria.

Gifford, D. and K. Williamson (1970). Analysis of the Jafuta aggregate. University of California, Berkeley, Laboratory Research Paper. Unpublished.

Giraud, V. (1890). *Les lacs de l'Afrique Equatoriale.* Paris.

Goodwin, A. J. H. (1945). Some historical Bushman arrows. *South African Journal of Science* XLI: 429–43.

Goodwin, A. J. H. (1953). *Method in Prehistory.* South African Archaeological Society Handbook Series, no. 1. Second edition.

Goodwin, A. J. H. and C. van Riet Lowe (1929). Stone Age cultures of South Africa. *Annals of the South African Museum,* Cape Town, no. 27.

Gould, R. (1968). Chipping stones in the outback. *Natural History,* **77** (2): 42–9.

Gould, R. A. (1969). *Yiwara: Foragers of the Australian Desert.* New York.

Gouldsbury, C. and H. Sheane (1911). *The Great Plateau of Northern Rhodesia.* London.

Greig, R. C. H. (1937). Iron smelting in Fipa. *Tanganyika Notes and Records,* **4**: 77–81.

Guichard, J. and G. Guichard (1965). The Early and Middle Palaeolithic of Nubia: A preliminary report. In F. Wendorf (ed.), *Contributions to the Prehistory of Nubia.* Fort Burgwin Research Center and Southern Methodist University Press, pp. 57–166.

Gulliver, P. H. (1959). A tribal map of Tanganyika. *Tanganyika Notes and Records,* **52**: 61–74.

Haldemann, E. G. (1969). Geology, Part I: Geological and Physiographical setting of the Kalambo Falls Prehistoric Site. In *Kalambo Falls Prehistoric Site,* Volume I, pp. 20–46.

Harding, J. R. (1963). A note on holed stones and 'rain stones' in the Lake Rukwa District of Tanganyika. *Man,* **63** (245): 194.

Harwood, A. (1970). *Witchcraft, Sorcery and Social Categories among the Safwa.* London.

de Heinzelin de Braucourt, J. (1962). *Manuel de typologie des industries lithiques.* Institut royal des sciences naturelles de Belgique, Brussels.

Hiernaux, J. (1960). Cultures préhistoriques de l'âge des métaux au Ruanda-Urundi et au Kivu (Congo Belge). *Mémoires Acad. roy. des sciences d'outre-mer.* x (2).

Hoch, E. (1963). Know your home – Rhodesia. (Privately circulated.)

Holmes, W. H. (1919). Handbook of Aboriginal American Antiquities, Part I. *Bulletin of the Bureau of American Ethnology*, **60**.

Howell, F. C., G. H. Cole and M. R. Kleindienst (1962). Isimila: An Acheulian occupation site in the Iringa Highlands, Southern Highlands Province, Tanganyika. In G. Mortelmans and J. Nenquin (eds.), *Actes du IVe Congrès panafricain de Préhistoire et de l'étude du Quaternaire.* Tervuren. Mus. roy. de l'Afrique centrale, Sér. in-8°, Sciences Humaines, no. 40: 43–80.

Huffman, T. N. (1970). The Early Iron Age and the spread of the Bantu. *South African Archaeological Bull.* xxv (97): 3–21.

Inskeep, R. (1962*a*). The age of the Kondoa rock paintings in the light of recent excavations at Kisese II rock shelter. In G. Mortelmans and J. Nenquin (eds.), *Actes du IVe Congrès panafricain de Préhistoire et de l'étude du Quaternaire.* Tervuren. Mus. roy. de l'Afrique centrale, Sér. in-8°, Sciences Humaines, no. 40: 249–57.

Inskeep, R. R. (1962*b*). Some Iron Age sites in Northern Rhodesia. *South African Archaeological Bull.* xvii (67): 136–80.

Isaac, G. Ll. (1968). The Acheulian site complex at Olorgesailie, Kenya: A contribution to the interpretation of Middle Pleistocene Culture in East Africa. Doctoral dissertation, University of Cambridge. Unpublished.

Isaac, G. Ll. and C. M. Keller (1968). Note on the proportional frequency of side- and end-struck flakes. *South African Archaeological Bull.* **23** (89): 17–30.

Isaac, G. Ll., H. V. Merrick and C. M. Nelson (1972). Stratigraphic and archaeological studies in the Lake Nakuru basin, Kenya. In E. M. van Zinderen Bakker (ed.), *Palaeoecology, of Africa*, 6. Balkema, Cape Town. In press.

Kay, G. (1964). *Chief Kalaba's Village.* Rhodes–Livingstone Institute Papers, 32. Manchester.

Keller, C. M. (1966). Archaeology of Montagu Cave. Doctoral dissertation, University of California, Berkeley. In press, 1972.

Keller, C. M. (1970). Montagu Cave: A preliminary report. *Quaternaria*, xiii: 187–204.

Keller, C. M. and G. Ll. Isaac (1971). Reports on two short conferences of archaeologists working in Africa. In Bulletin No. 4 of the Berkeley Office of the Commission on Nomenclature and Terminology, Pan-African Congress on Prehistory and Quaternary Studies, pp. 36–9.

Kleindienst, M. R. (1961*a*). Variability within the Late Acheulian assemblage in eastern Africa. *South African Archaeological Bull.* **16** (62): 35–52.

Kleindienst, M. R. (1961*b*). Note on bored stones. *South African Archaeological Bull.* **16** (64): 150.

Kleindienst, M. R. (1962). Components of the east African Acheulian assemblage: An analytic approach. In G. Mortelmans and J. Nenquin (eds.), *Actes du IVe Congrès panafricain de Préhistoire et de l'étude du Quaternaire.* Tervuren. Mus. roy. de l'Afrique centrale, Sér. in-8°, Sciences Humaines, no. 40: 81–112.

Kleindienst, M. R. (1967). Questions of terminology in regard to the study of Stone Age industries in eastern Africa: 'Cultural stratigraphic units'. In W. W. Bishop and J. D. Clark (eds.), *Background to evolution in Africa.* Chicago: 821–57.

Kootz-Kretschmer, E. (1929). *Die Safwa.* Berlin.

Leakey, L. S. B. (1931). *The Stone Age Cultures of Kenya Colony.* Cambridge.

Leakey, L. S. B. (1942). The Naivasha Fossil skull and skeleton. *Journal of east African Nat. History Soc.* xvi (4, 5): 169–77.

Leakey, L. S. B. and S. Cole (eds.) (1952). *Proceedings of the Pan-African Congress on Prehistory, Nairobi*, 1947. Oxford.

Leakey, M. D. (1967). Preliminary survey of the cultural material from Beds I and II, Olduvai Gorge, Tanzania. In W. W. Bishop and J. D. Clark (eds.), *Background to Evolution in Africa.* Chicago: 417–42.

Leakey, M. D. and L. S. B. (1950). *Excavations at the Njoro River Cave.* Oxford.

Leakey, M. D., W. E. Owen and L. S. B. Leakey (1948). *Dimple-based pottery from central Kavirondo, Kenya.* Coryndon Memorial Mus. Occasional Paper no. 2.

Lechaptois, Mgr. (White Father) (1932). *Aux rives du Tanganyika.* 2nd Edition. White Fathers' Press, Maison Carrée, Algiers.

Lee, R. B. (1968). What hunters do for a living or How to make out on scarce resources. In R. B. Lee and I. DeVore (eds.), *Man the Hunter.* Chicago: 30–48.

Lee, R. B. (1969). !Kung Bushman subsistence: Input–output analysis. In A. P. Vayda (ed.), *Human ecology: An Anthropological reader.* New York. Pp. 47–79.

Livingstone, D. A. (1971). A 22,000-year pollen record from the Plateau of Zambia. *Limnology and Oceanography*, **16** (2): 349–56.

Logsdon, R. L. (1971). The bipolar stone-working technique: An experiment and partial analysis. Sponsored undergraduate research project, University of California, Berkeley. Unpublished report.

Lopes Cardoso, C. (1967). 'Ovatjimba' em Angola. *Cadernos de Etnografia*, Second Series, 1. Museu Regional de Cerâmica. Barcelos.

Louw, J. T. (1960). *Prehistory of the Matjies River Rock Shelter.* National Museum, Bloemfontein, Memoire 1.

MacCalman, R. (1967). The Zoo Park Elephant Site, Windhoek (1964–5). In E. M. van Zinderen Bakker (ed.), *Palaeolecology of Africa*, 2: 102–3. Cape Town.

MacCalman, H. R. and B. J. Grobbelaar (1965). *Preliminary report of two stone working OvaTjimba groups in the northern Kaokoveld of South West Africa.* Cimbebasia, State Museum, Windhoek, no. 13.

MacCalman, H. R. and A. Viereck (1967). Peperkorrel, a factory site of Lupemban affinities from central South West Africa. *South African Archaeological Bull.* **22** (86): 41–50.

Malan, B. D. (1952). The final phase of the Middle Stone Age in South Africa. In L. S. B. Leakey and S. Cole (eds.), *Proceedings of the Pan-African Congress on Prehistory, Nairobi*, 1947. Oxford: 188–94.

Marks, A. E. (1971). *The recognition and description of archaeological assemblages.* Bulletin of the Berkeley Office of the Commission on Nomenclature and Terminology: Pan-African Congress on Prehistory and Quaternary Studies, no. 4: 13–19.

Marshall, L. (1960). !Kung Bushman Bands. *Africa* xxx (4): 325–55.

Mason, R. J. (1957). The Transvaal Middle Stone Age and statistical analysis. *South African Archaeological Bull.* **12** (48): 119–43.

Mason, R. (1962). *Prehistory of the Transvaal.* Johannesburg.

Mason, R. J. (1969). Tentative interpretations of new radiocarbon dates for stone artifact assemblages from Rose Cottage Cave, Orange Free State and Bushman Rock Shelter, Transvaal. *South African Archaeological Bull.* **24** (94): 57–9.

Mason, R. J. and N. J. van der Merwe (1964). Radiocarbon dating of Iron Age sites in the southern Transvaal: Melville Kopjies and Uitkomst Cave. *South African Journal of Science*, 60: 142.

Miller, S. F. (1969). The Nachikufan Industries of the Later Stone Age in Zambia. Doctoral dissertation, University of California, Berkeley. Unpublished.

Moffett, J. P. (1939). A strategic retreat from Tsetse fly. *Tanganyika Notes and Records*, 7: 35–8 and plates.

Mortelmans, G. (1947). A propos de quelques pierres percées remarquables du Katanga central. *Bull. de la Soc. roy. belge d'Anthrop. et de Préhist.* **58**: 151–71.

Mortelmans, G. (1962). Vue d'ensemble sur la Préhistoire du Congo occidental. In G. Mortelmans, and J. Nenquin (eds.), Actes du IVe Congrès panafricain de Préhistoire et de l'étude du Quaternaire. Tervuren. Mus. roy. de l'Afrique centrale. Sér. in-8°, sciences humaines, no. 40: 129–64.

Nelson, C. M. and M. Posnansky (1970). The stone tools from the re-excavation of Nsongezi Rock Shelter. *Azania*, V: 119–72.

Nenquin, J. (1959). Dimple-based pots from Kasai, Belgian Congo. *Man*, **59**, no. 242.

Nenquin, J. (1963*a*). *Excavations at Sanga*, 1957. Mus. roy. de l'Afrique centrale. Ann. Sci. humaines, 45. Tervuren.

Nenquin, J. (1963*b*). Notes on some early pottery cultures in Northern Katanga. *Journal of African History* IV (1): 19–32.

Nenquin, J. (1967*a*). *Contributions to the study of the prehistoric cultures of Rwanda and Burundi.* Mus. roy. de l'Afrique centrale, Tervuren. Annales, sér. in-8° Sciences humaines, no. 59.

Nenquin, J. (1967*b*). Notes on the proto-historic pottery cultures in the Congo-Rwanda-Burundi region. In W. W. Bishop and J. D. Clark (eds.), *Background to Evolution in Africa.* Chicago: 651–8.

Newcomer, M. H. (1971). Some quantitative experiments in handaxe manufacture. *World Archaeology*, **3** (1): 85–93.

Nurse, G. T. (1967). The name 'Akafula'. *Journal of the Society of Malawi*, XX (2): 17–21.

O'Brien, T. P. (1939). *The prehistory of Uganda Protectorate.* Cambridge.

Oliver, R. and B. M. Fagan (In Press). The emergence of Bantu Africa. In R. Oliver and J. D. Fage (eds.), *Cambridge History of Africa*, Volume II, ed. J. D. Fage.

Phillipson, D. W. (1968*a*). The Early Iron Age in Zambia – regional variants and some tentative conclusions. *Journal of African History*, IX (2): 191–212.

Phillipson, D. W. (1968*b*). The Early Iron Age site at Kapwirimbwe, Lusaka. *Azania*, III: 87–106.

Phillipson, D. W. (1969*a*). Gun-flint manufacture in northwestern Zambia. *Antiquity*, XLIII: 301–4.

Phillipson, D. W. (1969*b*). The prehistoric sequence at Nakapapula, Zambia. *Proceedings of the Prehistoric Society*, XXXV: 172–202.

Phillipson, D. W. (1970*a*). Excavations at Twickenham Road, Lusaka. *Azania*, V: 77–118.

Phillipson, D. W. (1970*b*). Notes on the later prehistoric radiocarbon chronology of eastern and southern Africa. *Journal of African History*, XI (1): 1–16.

Phillipson, D. W. (1971). Fieldwork in Eastern Province, 1970. *Archaeologia Zambiana*, 13: 5–6.

Phillipson, L. and D. W. Phillipson (1970). Patterns of edge damage on the Late Stone Age Industry from Chiwempula, Zambia. *Zambia Museum's Journal*, I: 40–76.

Popplewell, G. D. (1937). Notes on the Fipa. *Tanganyika Notes and Records*, 3: 99–105.

Posnansky, M. (1961*a*). Pottery types from archaeological sites in Uganda. *Journal of African History* II (2): 177–98.

Posnansky, M. (1961*b*). Iron Age in east and central Africa – points of comparison. *South African Archaeological Bull.* **16** (64): 134–6.

Posnansky, M. (1967). The Iron Age in east Africa. In W. W. Bishop and J. D. Clark (eds.), *Background to Evolution in Africa.* Chicago: 629–48.

Posnansky, M. and C. M. Nelson (1968). Rock paintings and excavations at Nyero, Uganda. *Azania*, III: 147–66.

Rangeley, W. H. J. (1963). The earliest inhabitants of Nyasaland. *Journal of the Society of Malawi*, XVI (2): 35–42.

Read, J. G. (1951). The Ila Buffalo Drive. *Northern Rhodesia Journal*, I, 4: 62–6.

Reynolds, B. G. R. (1968). The material culture of the peoples of the Gwembe Valley. *Kariba Studies*, III. Manchester.

Robertson, E. (1961). Use of bored stones – a suggestion. *South African Archaeological Bull.* **16** (64): 151–2.

Robinson, K. R. (1959). *Khami Ruins.* Cambridge.

Robinson, K. R. (1961). An Early Iron Age site from the Chibi District of Southern Rhodesia. *South African Archaeological Bull.* **16** (63): 75–102.

Robinson, K. R. (1963). Further excavations in the Iron Age deposits at the Tunnel site, Gokomere Hill, Southern Rhodesia. *South African Archaeological Bull.* **18** (72): 155–71.

Robinson, K. R. (1966). A preliminary report on the Recent Archaeology of Ngonde, northern Malawi. *Journal of African History*, **7** (2): 169–88.

Robinson, K. R. (1968). An examination of five Iron Age structures in the Umguza valley, 14 miles north of Bulawayo, Rhodesia. *Arnoldia*, **3** (35): 1–21.

Robinson, K. R. (1970). *The Iron Age of the Southern Lake Area of Malawi.* Department of Antiquities, Zomba, Malawi, Pub. No. 8.

Robinson, K. R. and B. H. Sandelowsky (1968). The Iron Age of northern Malawi: Recent work. *Azania* III: 107–46.

Sampson, C. G. (1967). *Zeekoegat* 13: *A Later Stone Age Open-site near Venterstad, Cape.* Researches of the Nat. Museum, Bloemfontein, **2** (6): 211–37.

Sampson, C. G. and M. Sampson (1967). *Riversmead Shelter: Excavations and analysis.* Nat. Museum, Bloemfontein, Memoire 3.

Sandelowsky, B. H. and K. R. Robinson (1968). *Fingira: Preliminary Report.* Department of Antiquities, Zomba, Malawi. Pub. No. 3.

Sankalia, H. D. (1964). *Stone Age tools: Their Techniques, Names and Probable Functions.* Poona.

Scudder, Th. (1962). *The Ecology of the Gwembe Tonga.* Manchester.

Sheppard, J. G. and E. R. Swart (1966). Rhodesian Radiocarbon Measurements II. *Radiocarbon*, 8: 423.

Sheppard, J. G. and E. R. Swart (1967). Rhodesian Radiocarbon Measurements III. *Radiocarbon*, 9: 382–6.

Sheppard, J. G. and E. R. Swart (1971). Rhodesian Radiocarbon Measurements IV. *Radiocarbon*, **13** (2): 420–31.

Shorter Oxford Dictionary (1964).

Smolla, G. (1956). Praehistorische Keramik aus Ostafrika. *Tribus*, VI: 35–46.

de Sonneville-Bordes, D. and J. Perrot (1954–6). Lexique typologique du Paléolithique supérieur. *Bull. Soc. Préhist. française.* **51** (7): 327–35; **52** (1–2): 76–9; **53** (7–8): 408–12; **53** (7–9): 547–59.

Soper, R. C. (1967*a*). Kwale: An Early Iron Age site in south-eastern Kenya. *Azania*, **2**: 1–18.

Soper, R. C. (1967*b*). Iron Age sites in northeastern Tanzania. *Azania*, **2**: 19–36.

Stayt, H. A. (1931). *The Bavenda.* Oxford.

Stefaniszyn, B. (1964). *The Material Culture of the Ambo of Northern Rhodesia.* Occasional Papers of the Rhodes-Livingstone Museum, 16.

Summers, R. F. H. (1958). *Inyanga.* Cambridge.

Summers, R. F. H. (1961). The Southern Rhodesian Iron Age. *Journal of African History*, II (1): 1–13.

Summers, R. F. H. (1967). Iron Age industries of southern Africa with notes on their chronology, terminology and economic status. In W. W. Bishop and J. D. Clark (eds.), *Background to Evolution in Africa.* Chicago: 687–700.

Summers, R., K. R. Robinson and A. Whitty (1961). *Zimbabwe excavations*, 1958. Occasional Papers of the Nat. Mus. of Southern Rhodesia, 23A.

Sutton, J. E. G. (1968). Archaeological sites in Usandawe. *Azania*, III: 167–74.

Sutton, J. E. G. (1969). 'Ancient civilisations' and modern agricultural systems in the southern highlands of Tanzania. *Azania*, IV: 1–13.

Sutton, J. E. G. and A. D. Roberts (1968). Uvinza and its salt industry. *Azania*, III: 45–86.

Thomson, D. F. (1964). Some wood and stone implements of the Bindibu tribe of central western Australia. *Proceedings of the Prehistoric Society*, XXX: 400–22.

Tixier, J. (1957). Le hachereau dans l'Acheuléen nord-Africain. *Congrès préhistorique de France, 15e session (1956) Compte rendu*: 914–23.

Tixier, J. (1963). *Typologie de l'Epipaléolithique du Maghreb.* C.R.A.P.E. Memoire 2. Paris.

Tobias, P. V. (1958). Skeletal remains from Inyanga. In R. F. H. Summers, *Inyanga*. Cambridge. 159–72.

Tobias, P. V. (1961). New views on the evolution of man in Africa. *South African Journal of Science*, **57** (2): 25–38.

Toerien, M. J. (1955). The Skeletal Remains. In J. D. Clark, Human skeletal and cultural material from a deep cave at Chipongwe, Northern Rhodesia. *South African Archaeological Bull.* **10** (40): 114–16.

Twiesselmann, F. (1958). Les ossements humains du gîte Mésolithique d'Ishango. Explorations du Parc nat. Albert, Mission J. de Heinzelin de Braucourt, 1950. Vol. 5. Inst. des parcs nats. du Congo belge, Brussels.

Trapnell, C. G. (1953). *The Soils, Vegetation and Agriculture of Northeastern Rhodesia*. Lusaka.

Turner, V. W. (1953). *Lunda Rites and Ceremonies.* Occasional Papers of the Rhodes–Livingstone Museum, 10.

Van Noten, F. (1971). Excavations at Munyama Cave. *Antiquity*, **45** (177): 56–8.

Van Riet Lowe, C. (1946). The coastal Smithfield and bipolar technique. *South African Journal of Science* XLII: 240–6.

Van Riet Lowe, C. (1952). *The Pleistocene Geology and Prehistory of Uganda: Part II: Prehistory*. Uganda Geological Survey, Memoire VI.

Vansina, J. (1966). *Kingdoms of the Savanna.* University of Wisconsin Press, Madison.

Van Zinderen Bakker, E. M. (1969). The Pleistocene vegetation and climate of the basin. In *Kalambo Falls Prehistoric Site*, Volume I: 57–84.

Vogel, J. C. and P. Beaumont (1972). Revised radiocarbon chronology for the Stone Age in South Africa. *Nature*, **237**: 50–51.

Watson, W. (1958). *Tribal Cohesion in a Money Economy.* Manchester.

Wayland, E. J. (1923). *Some Primitive Stone Implements from Uganda*. Government Press, Kampala, Uganda.

Wayland, E. J. and M. C. Burkitt (1932). The Magosian Culture of Uganda. *J.R.A.I.* **62**: 362–90.

Wells, L. H. (1950). Fossil man in Northern Rhodesia. Appendix C, pp. 143–52, in J. D. Clark, *The Stone Age Cultures of Northern Rhodesia*. Cape Town.

Wells, L. H. (1957). Late Stone Age human types in central Africa. In J. D. Clark and S. Cole (eds.), *Proceedings of the Third Pan-African Congress on Prehistory, Livingstone*, 1955. London: 183–5.

White, P. J. (1968*a*). Ston Naip bilong Tumbuna: The living Stone Age in New Guinea. In D. de Sonneville Bordes (ed.), *La Préhistoire: Problèmes et Tendances*, Paris. Pp. 511–16.

White, P. J. (1968*b*). Fabricators, *outils écaillés* or scalar cores? *Mankind*, **6** (2): 658–66.

Willey, G. R. and P. Phillips (1958). *Method and Theory in American Archaeology*. Chicago.

Williamson, J. (1955). *Useful Plants of Nyasaland*. Zomba.

Willis, R. G. (1966). *The Fipa and Related Peoples of Southwest Tanzania and Northeast Zambia*. R.A.I. Ethnographic Survey of Africa.

Willett, F. (1967). *Ife in the History of West African Sculpture.* London.

Willoughby, W. C. (1928). *The Soul of the Bantu*. London, Student Christian Movement.

Wilson, M. (1957). *Rituals of Kinship among the Nyakyusa.* International African Institute, London.

Wilson, M. (1958). *The Peoples of the Nyasa–Tanganyika Corridor*. School of African Studies, University of Cape Town, Communication no. 29.

Wilson, M. (1964). Traditional art among the Nyakyusa. *South African Archaeological Bull.* **19** (75): 57–63.

Wilson, M. (1972). Reflections on the early history of north Malawi. In B. Pachai (ed.), *The Early History of Malawi.* Longmans: 136–47.

Wise, R. (1958). Iron smelting in Ufipa, Tanganyika. *Tanganyika Notes and Records*, **50**: 106–11.

Woodburn, J. (1968*a*). An introduction to Hadza ecology. In R. B. Lee and I. DeVore (eds.), *Man the Hunter*. Chicago: 49–55.

Woodburn, J. (1968*b*). Stability and flexibility in Hadza residential groupings. In R. B. Lee and I. DeVore (eds.), *Man the Hunter*. Chicago: 103–10.

Woodburn, J. (1970). *Hunters and Gatherers: The Material Culture of the Nomadic Hadza*. British Museum, London.

Worsley, P. M. and J. P. Rumberger (1949). Remains of an earlier people in Uhehe. *Tanganyika Notes and Records*, **27**: 42–6.

The plates

1 MODERN LUNGU POTTERY

1 Large rimsherd from a shouldered pot or bowl, with zigzag channelled or grooved decoration. A slight carination, grey surface colour, black paste. Modern Lungu. Rim diameter (reconstructed): 12·2 inches (30·75 cm); height (reconstructed): *c.* 6·0 inches (15·25 cm).

2 Fragmentary shouldered pot with everted rim decorated with a band of obliquely hatched coarse incision on the neck, and a cross-hatched incised motif on the shoulder. Grey colour. Modern Lungu. Rim diameter (reconstructed): 7·5 inches (19 cm); height (reconstructed): 7·6 inches (19·25 cm); maximum width: 7·8 inches (19·75 cm). B2 1959: surface.

3 Fragmentary shouldered pot with everted rim and a line of square stamping below the rim. A zigzag line and a panel of similar stamping occur on the shoulder. Grey colour. Modern Lungu. Rim diameter: 6·4 inches (16·25 cm); height: 7 inches (17·75 cm); maximum width: 6·8 inches (17·25 cm).

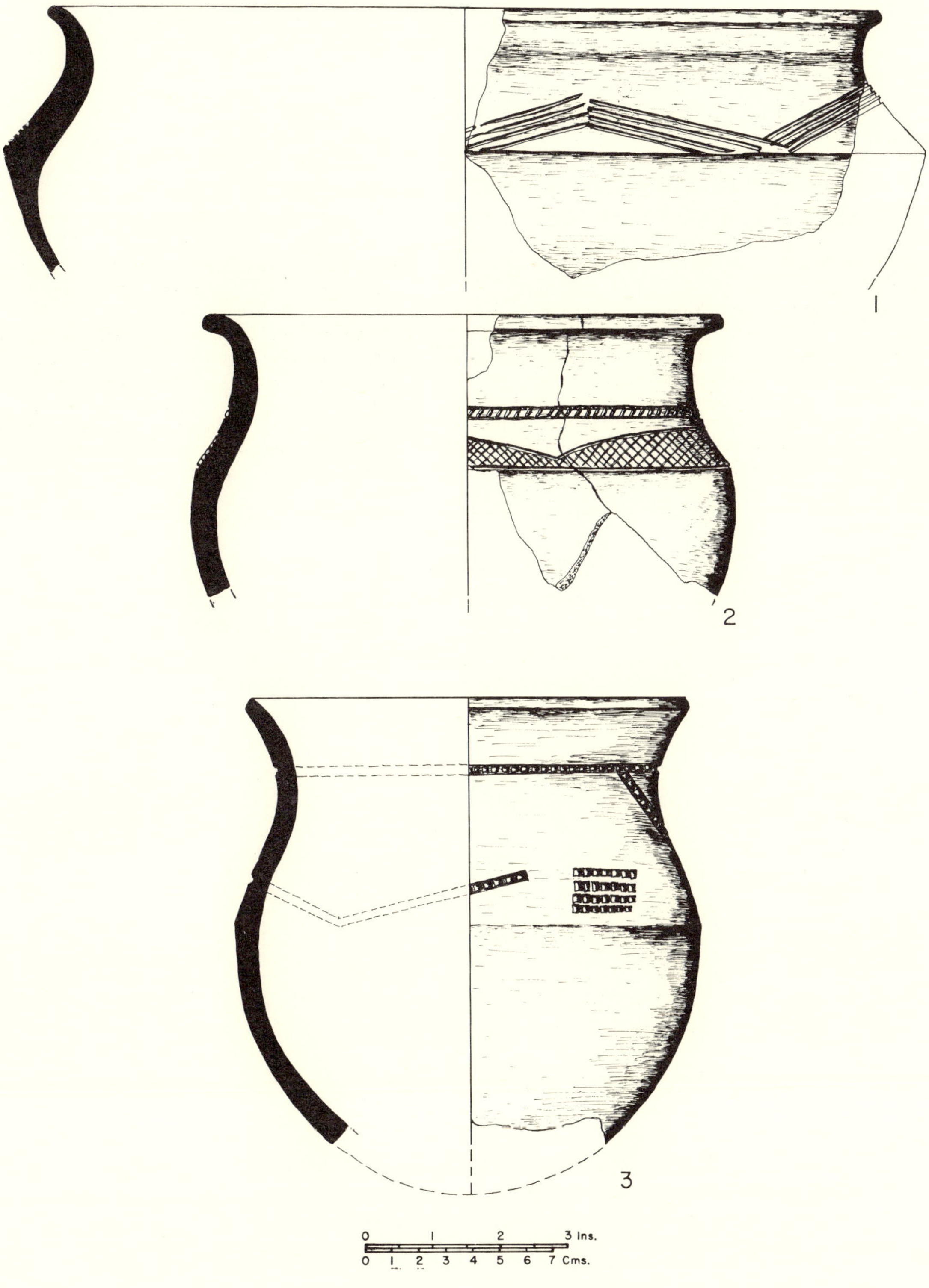
1
2
3
0 1 2 3 Ins.
0 1 2 3 4 5 6 7 Cms.

2 MODERN LUNGU POTTERY

1 Fragmentary shouldered pot with two bands of triangular stamping, the one on the shoulder giving a false relief effect. Grey colour. Modern Lungu. Rim diameter: 6·5 inches (16·5 cm); height (reconstructed): 5·5 inches (14 cm); maximum width: 6·7 inches (17 cm). On surface, from a modern grave.

2 Complete shouldered pot with nearly vertical neck and slightly everted rim. Four bands of diagonal comb-stamping on the neck. Grey/brown colour. Modern Lungu. Possibly an imported ware. Rim diameter: 6·3 inches (16 cm); height: 6·1 inches (15·5 cm); maximum width: 7·6 inches (19·25 cm). Modern, from grave near the excavation camp.

3 Complete shouldered undecorated pot. The rim bears a line of nicks. Grey paste. Modern Lungu. Rim diameter: 6 inches (15·25 cm); height: 4·2 inches (10·75 cm); maximum width: 5·9 inches (15 cm).

4 Rimsherd from an undecorated bowl. Grey colour. Modern Lungu or possibly Kalambo Falls Industry. Site C2, surface, 1959.

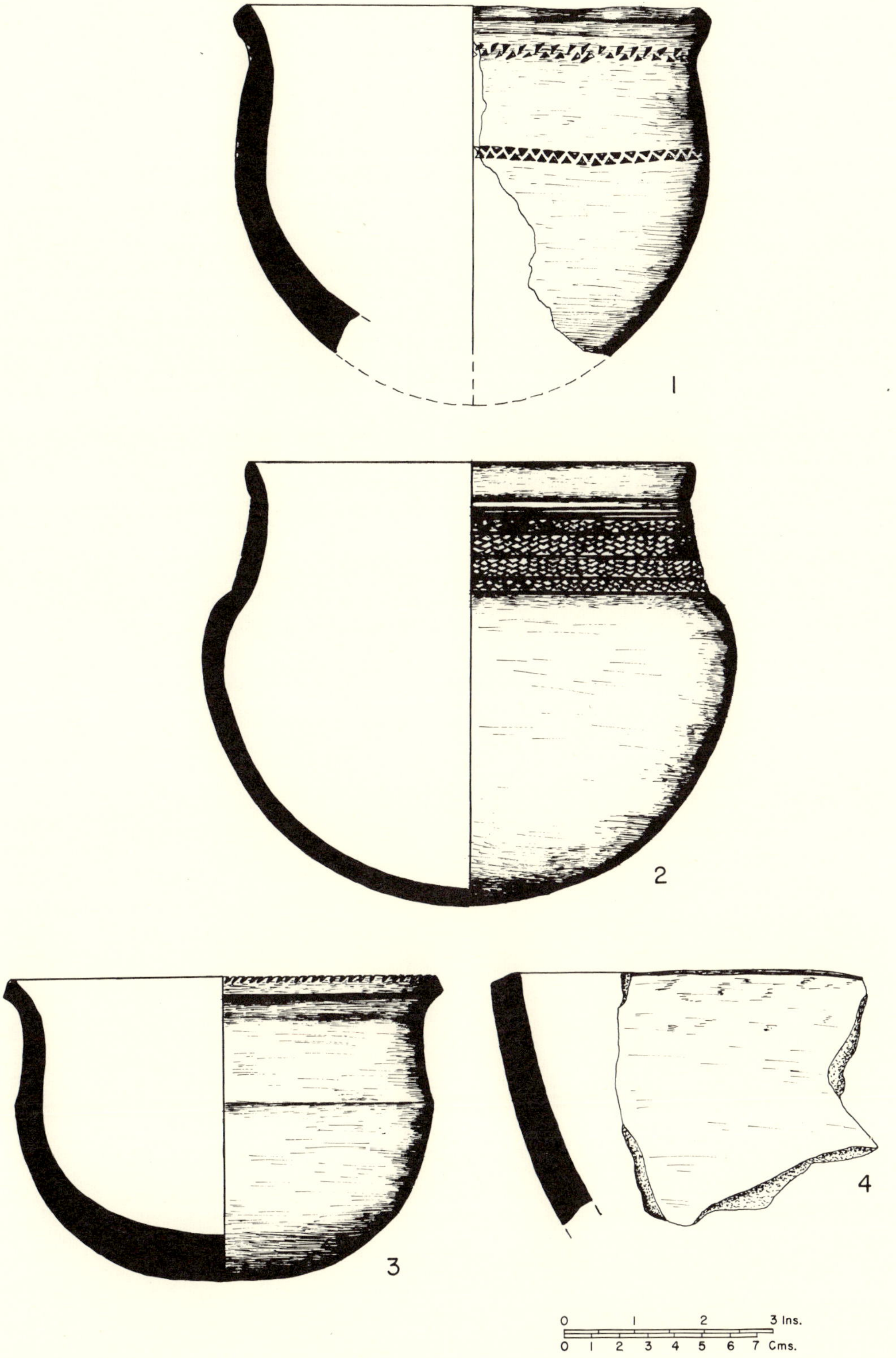
1
2
3
4
0 1 2 3 Ins.
0 1 2 3 4 5 6 7 Cms.

1 Rimsherd from a deep hemispherical bowl. The outside of the rim is decorated with a band of oblique incision. Below it two zigzag channelled lines. Patchy burnish; buff exterior colour, black paste. Diameter (reconstructed): 4·8 inches (12·25 cm); height (reconstructed): 3·8 inches (10 cm). C2, 1959: surface C/12/59.

2 Rimsherd from an undecorated, shallow hemispherical bowl. Grey; buff exterior colour, black paste. Diameter (reconstructed): 6·8 inches (17·25 cm); height (reconstructed): 3 inches (7·75 cm). B2, 1959: 3–4 feet (91 cm–1·21 m). J. 1/2. B2/368/59.

3 Sherd from a circular undecorated flat platter or pot cover. Buff exterior colour. Possibly placed on fire and used to roast fatty foods such as caterpillars, grubs and locusts or seeds, as potsherds are used today by Zambian peoples, e.g. the Ambo. B2, 1959: 6–12 inches (15·25–30·5 cm). B2/16/59.

4 Rimsherd from a hemispherical bowl with convex sides. A band of oblique comb-stamping at the rim is bounded by a band of oblique incised lines. Reddish-orange exterior colour and paste. Diameter (reconstructed): 5·4 inches (13·75 cm); height (reconstructed): 3·8 inches (10 cm). B2, 1959: 4 feet 9 inches–5 feet (1·45–1·52 m). B2/79/59.

5 Rimsherd from an undecorated hemispherical bowl. Buff exterior colour and paste. A1, 1956: Sect. 7. 8–10 feet (2·44–3·05 m). A1/45/56.

6 Rimsherd from an elaborately decorated shallow bowl; the rim itself is bevelled with two channelled lines. A line of oblique comb-stamping is underlain by a band of parallel channelled lines with a zigzag motif. Buff/red exterior colour and paste. A1, 1956: B2–4, 13–14 feet (3·96–4·11 m). A1/55/56.

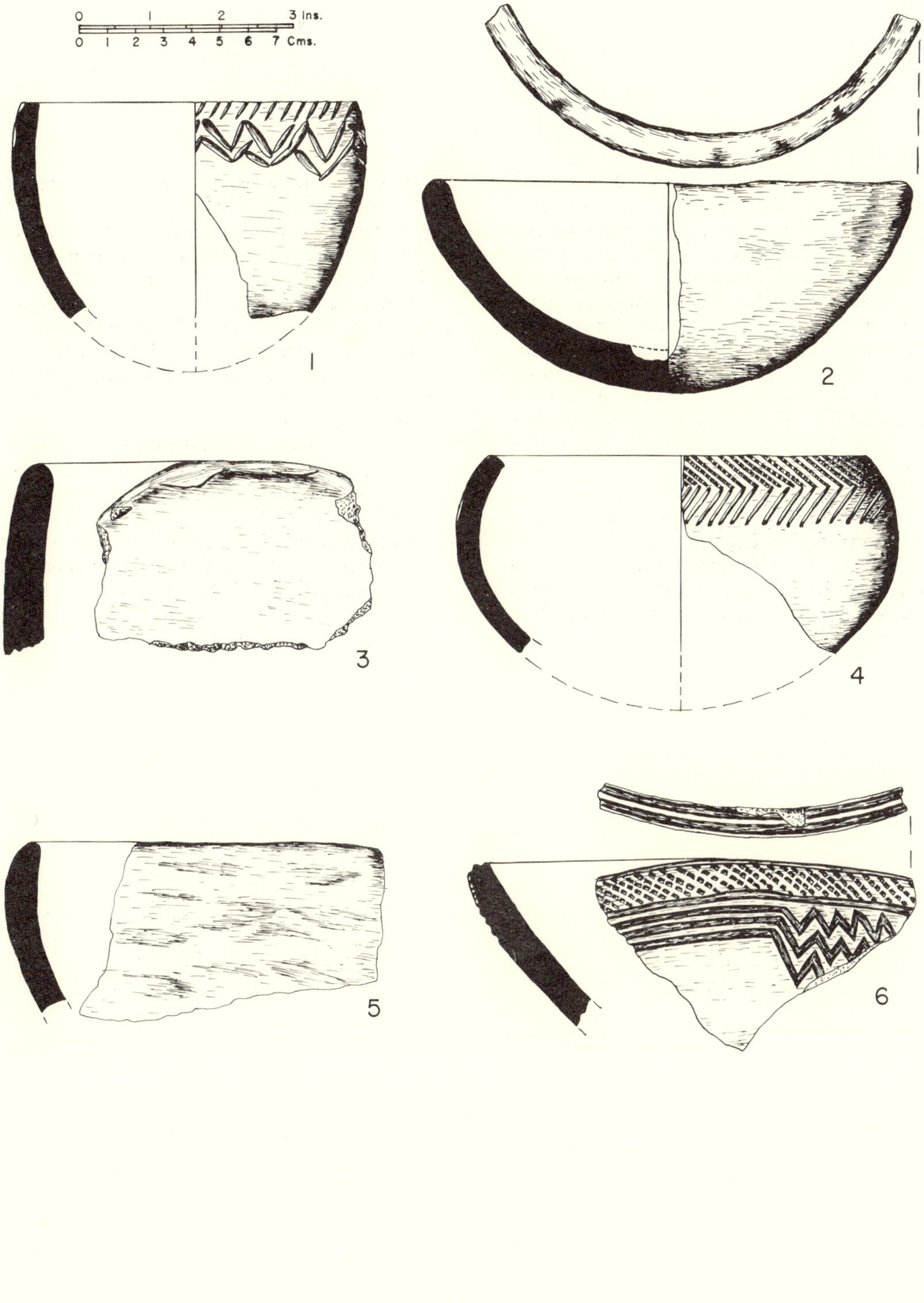
0 1 2 3 ins.
0 1 2 3 4 5 6 7 Cms.
1
2
3
4
5
6

1 Rimsherd from a hemispherical bowl with 2 parallel channelled lines immediately below the rim. Buff exterior colour and black paste. A1, 1956: 9 feet 6 inches–10 feet (2·9–3·05 m). A1/39/56.

2 Rimsherd from a hemispherical bowl with elaborate decoration. A zone of 'false relief' stamping and a stamped line are above a 1·5 inch band of channelled lines, with a zigzag motif. Buff exterior colour and paste. B2, 1959: 2 feet 6 inches–3 feet (76–91·5 cm). B2/40/59.

3 Rimsherd from a hemispherical bowl with three channelled lines below the rim. Brown exterior colour, possible burnish. A1, 1956: 10 feet–10 feet 6 inches (3·05–3·20 m). A1/41/56.

4 Rimsherd from a spheroidal bowl with a zigzag channelled design. Buff exterior colour, grey paste. A1, 1956: 8 feet–8 feet 6 inches (2·44–2·59 m). A1/33/56.

5 Rimsherd from a (?) spheroidal bowl. A band of channelling, one series of lines starting against another, is associated with a line of triangular impressions. Buff exterior colour and paste. A1, 1956: 11 feet 6 inches–12 feet (3·5–3·65 m). A1/48/56.

6 Rimsherd from a (?) spheroidal bowl. Two rows of triangular stamped decoration occur immediately below the rim. Buff paste and exterior colour. B2, 1959: 3 feet 6 inches–4 feet (1·06–1·21 m). B2/12/59.

7 Rimsherd from a spheroidal bowl with a rimband. Two channelled lines adorn the latter, a zone of cross-hatched incision and channelled bands occurring below it. A4, 1959: B/1–7, 5 feet–6 feet 6 inches (1·52–1·98 m). A/62/59.

8 Bodysherd from an unidentifiable vessel bearing a grooved meander motif. Buff exterior colour, black paste. A1, 1956: 6 feet 6 inches–7 feet (1·98–2·13 m). A1/25/56.

9 Rimsherd from a spheroidal bowl with a band of four channelled lines below the rim. Buff colour. B2, 1959: 2 feet–3 feet (61–91·5 cm). B2/212/59.

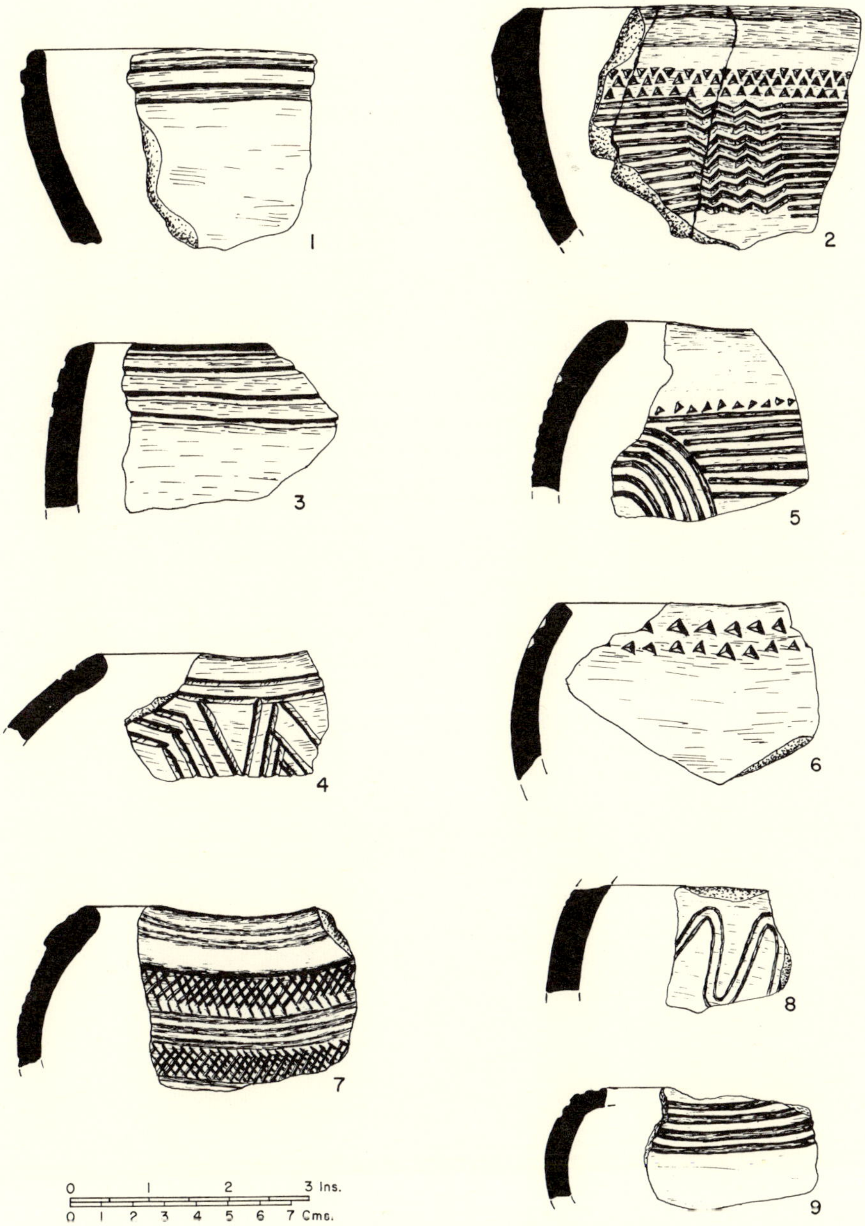
1
2
3
5
4
6
8
7
9
0 1 2 3 Ins.
0 1 2 3 4 5 6 7 Cms.

5 KALAMBO FALLS INDUSTRY: EARLY IRON AGE

1 Rimsherd from a spheroidal bowl with a rimband. A zone of cross-hatched incision and channelled lines lies below the band. Buff exterior colour. A1, 1956: 8 feet 6 inches–9 feet (2·59–2·74 m). A1/35/56.

2 Rimsherd from a shouldered pot. A zigzag incised line on the outside of the rim. Below it three stamped lines, rectangular and triangular impressions, and two channelled lines. Grey/buff exterior colour. B2, 1959: 2 feet–3 feet (61–91·5 cm). B2/212/59.

3 A nearly complete shouldered pot with bevelled and inclined rim. (See also Plate 86.) On the neck is a zone of cross-hatched incision and channelled lines. The latter are backed up against each other. Brick red exterior colour and paste. Rim diameter: 8·8 inches (22·75 cm); height: *c.* 13 inches (33 cm); maximum width: 13·3 inches (33·75 cm). A site, A5 River Face. Found with one undecorated pot, one fragment of another decorated pot (see Plate 9, no. 8) and a flat grindstone in the base of the red clays of the Chiungu Member *c.* 40 m east of A4 trench, 1959. A/184/59.

4 Rimsherd from a shouldered pot with rimband. Bevelled rim, and a zone of class 3 decoration. Buff exterior colour. A1, 1956: 12 feet–13 feet (3·66–3·96 m). From floor of Chiungu Member channel. A1/51/56.

5 Rimsherd from an unidentified vessel, perhaps a shouldered pot. Incised decoration on the rim and a band of oblique cigar-shaped impressions below it. Buff colour. B2, 1959: 3 feet–6 feet (91 cm–1·83 m). Stepping back. B2/213/59.

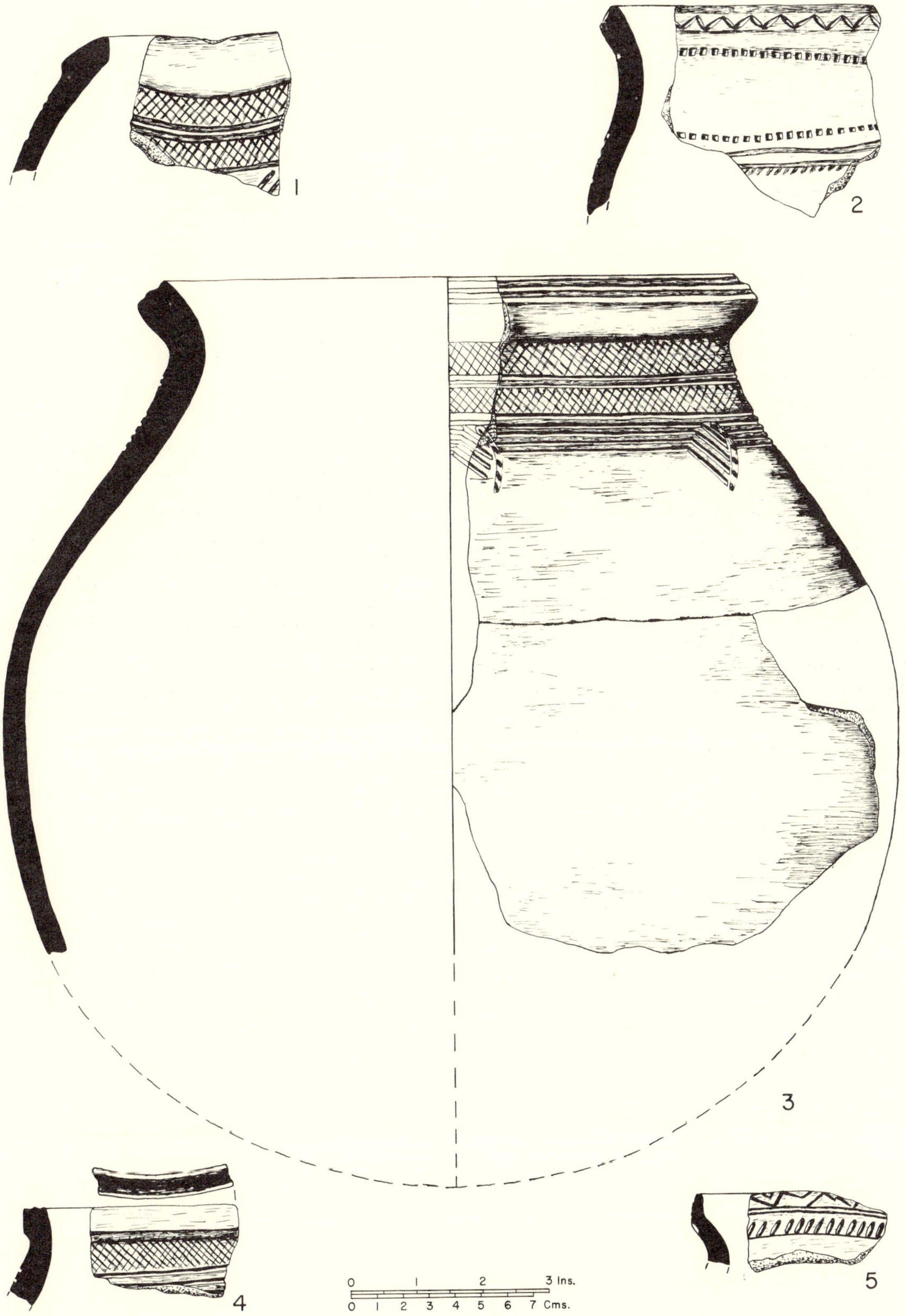
1
2
3
4
5
0 1 2 3 Ins.
0 1 2 3 4 5 6 7 Cms.

1 Large rimsherd from a globular shouldered pot with rolled over and bevelled rim. A band of rough cross-hatched incised decoration is underlain by two channelled lines adorned with a semicircular 'loop' motif. Buff exterior colour and paste. Rim diameter (reconstructed): 4·6 inches (11·25 cm); height (reconstructed): *c.* 6·4 inches (16·25 cm). B2, 1959: 0–6 inches (0–15 cm). B2/10/59.

2 Bodysherd from a shouldered pot, bearing zigzag and horizontal channelled lines and a zone of cigar-shaped stamps. Buff exterior colour. Some burnish. A1, 1956: Sect. 7. 8 feet–10 feet (2·44–3·05 m). A1/45/56.

3 Rimsherd from a shouldered pot, bearing bands of oblique comb-stamping and horizontal channelled lines with a zigzag motif. Buff/red exterior colour. B2, 1959: 3 feet–6 feet (91 cm–1·83 m) stepping back. B2/213/59.

4 Bodysherd from a shouldered pot with incised and channelled decoration. The lowest channelled zone is executed in a filled triangle motif. Buff/red exterior colour and paste. A1, 1956: Sect. 7 & 8. 10–11 feet (3·05–3·35 m). A1/46/56.

5 Rimsherd from a shouldered pot with a row of triangular stamps on the slightly everted rim. Two crude rows of the same on the neck are delimited by channelled lines. Grey/buff exterior colour. B, 1956: 1–2 feet (30·5–61 cm). B/23/56.

6 Complete shouldered pot with a rolled over rim. The body is adorned with an exotic circular motif incised after firing and possibly representing a burial in a grave. Red exterior colour. Rim diameter: 5 inches (12·75 cm); height: 6·3 inches (16·25 cm); maximum diameter: 6·7 inches (17 cm). 2 feet 6 inches–3 feet 6 inches (76 cm–1·06 m). D2, 1956. D2/a3/1956.

7 A closely similar undecorated vessel, represented by a large rimsherd. Rolled over rim; buff colour. A1, 1956: B/2–4. 13–14 feet (3·96–4·11 m). A1/55/56.

8 Rimsherd from a shouldered pot with inclined rim. Channelled and incised decoration, buff colour. A1, 1956: 9 feet 6 inches–10 feet (2·9–3·05 m). A1/39/56.

1
2
3
4
5
6
7
8
0 1 2 3 Ins.
0 1 2 3 4 5 6 7 Cms.

1 Large rimsherd from a shouldered pot with everted and bevelled rim. Bands of chevron comb-stamping and channelled lines are on the neck. The lowest band of channelling is somewhat irregular and bears a lozenge motif. Buff colour, traces of burnish. Rim diameter (reconstructed): 6·8 inches (17 cm); height (reconstructed): 9·5 inches (24·25 cm); body width (reconstructed): 10·4 inches (26·5 cm). B2, 1959: 2 feet–2 feet 6 inches (61–76 cm). B2/33/59.

2 Large rimsherd from a shouldered pot with rolled over and bevelled rim. The neck bears a zone of chevron comb-stamping and a band of channelled decoration with angular motif. Red/buff colour. Rim diameter (reconstructed): 6·9 inches (17·5 cm); height (reconstructed): 9 inches (23 cm); body width (reconstructed): 9·4 inches (24 cm). A1, 1956: 9 feet 6 inches–10 feet (2·9–3·05 m). A1/39/56.

3 Large rimsherd from a shouldered pot with everted and bevelled rim. The neck bears lines of circular and hooked stamping and irregular channelling. Buff colour. Rim diameter (reconstructed): 7·0 inches (17·75 cm); body width (reconstructed): 9 inches (23 cm). B2, 1959: 0–6 inches (0–15·25 cm). B2/59/N 10.

1

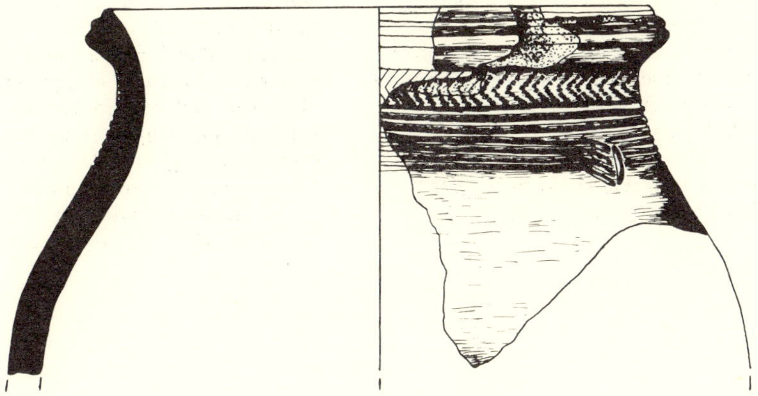

2

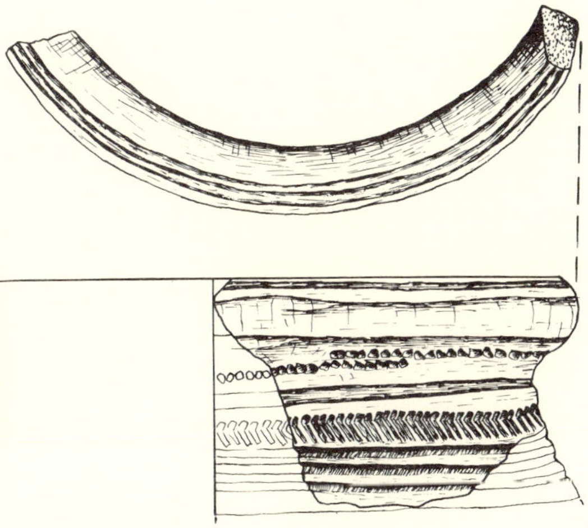

3

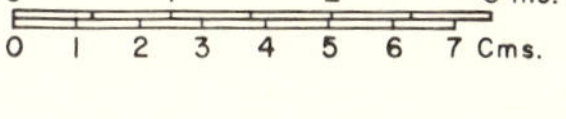

1 Rimsherd from an undecorated shouldered pot with slightly everted rim. Buff exterior colour. Rim diameter (reconstructed): 9 inches (23 cm). A1, 1956: Floor of 'Older Channel', 12–13 feet (3·66–3·96 m). A1/52/56.

2 Rimsherd from an undecorated vessel, which is probably an extreme example of either class 1 or class 3. Thin walls, grey exterior colour. A4, 1959: B/50–32/ 9–12 inches (23–30·5 cm). A/13/59.

3 Bevelled rimsherd from a shouldered pot with a band of oblique incision below the rim. A1, 1956: Sect. 7 & 8. 11 feet–11 feet 6 inches (3·35–3·50 m). A1/47/56.

4 Bevelled rimsherd from a shouldered pot with a band of oblique comb-stamping and channelled lines below the rim band. A1, 1956: 10 feet 6 inches–11 feet 6 inches (3·20–3·50 m). A1/43/56.

5 Large rimsherd from a gourd-shaped vessel with a band of parallel vertical or oblique incised lines on the outside of the rim. Buff exterior colour. Rim diameter: 8·2 inches (21 cm). D2, 1956: stepping back; 9 inches–1 foot 6 inches (23–45 cm). D2/56/1.

6 Large rimsherd from another undecorated, possibly gourd-shaped pot with everted rim. Buff exterior colour. A4, 1959: B/50–32, 9–12 inches (23–30·5 cm). A/13/59.

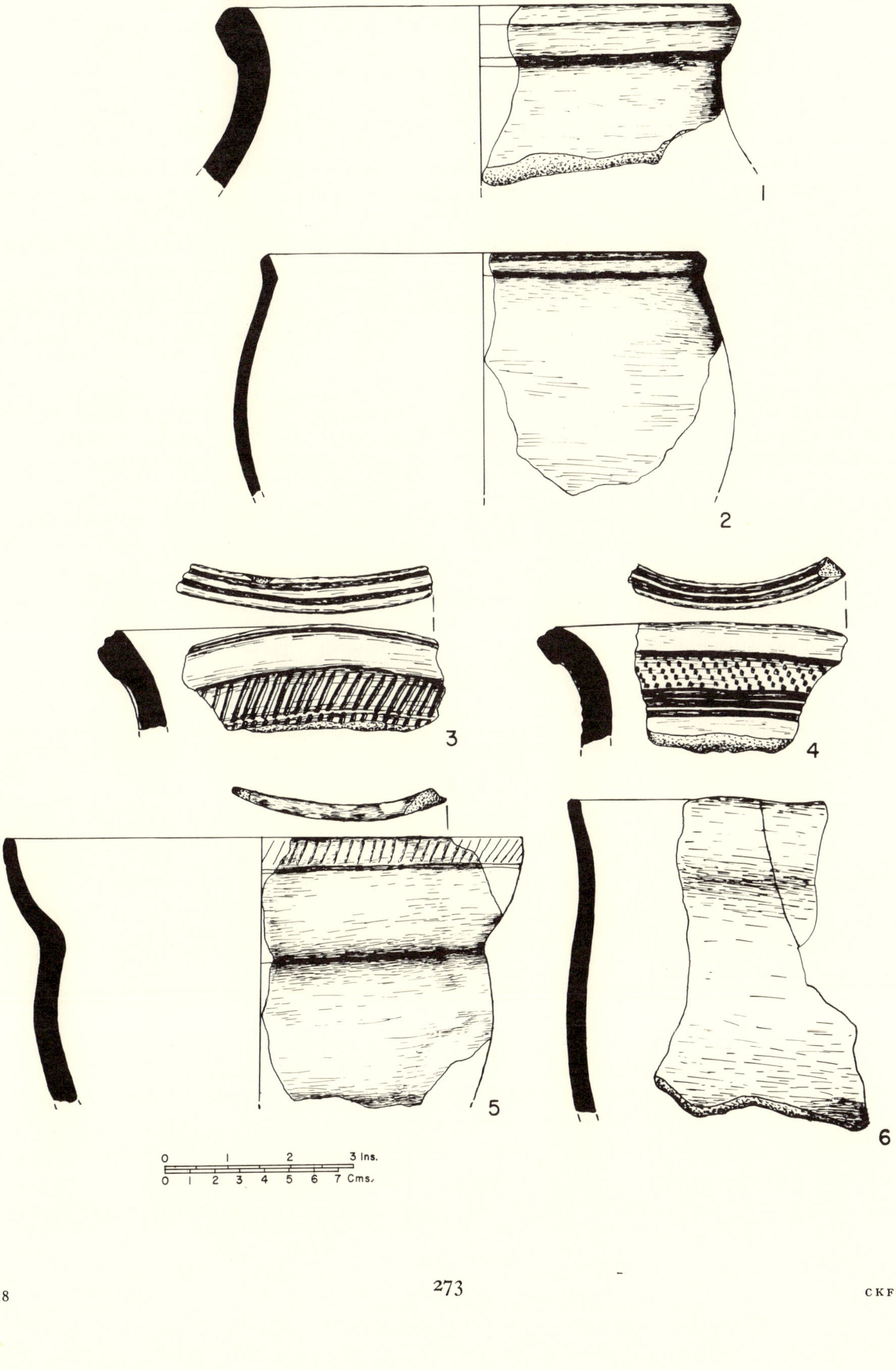
2
3
4
5
6
0 1 2 3 Ins.
0 1 2 3 4 5 6 7 Cms.

9 KALAMBO FALLS INDUSTRY: EARLY IRON AGE

1 Rimsherd from a (?) globular pot with a concave neck. May equally be a shouldered vessel. Coarse incised and channelled decoration on the neck, and a bevelled rim. Red to buff exterior colour. A1, 1956: 10 feet–10 feet 6 inches (3·05–3·20 m). A1/41/56.

2 Rimsherd from an unidentifiable vessel. The rim is decorated with short incised nicks, and the neck with coarse criss-cross incision. Buff colour. C2, 1959: surface. C2/5/59.

3 Rimsherd from another unidentifiable vessel, bearing an irregular meander decoration. A1, 1956: stepping back. 1 foot 6 inches–2 feet (45–61 cm).

4 Rimsherd from a vessel with a straight neck, bearing at least three parallel bands of vertical impressed decoration. Buff colour. A4, 1959: stepping back. 0 inches–3 feet (0–91 cm). A/132/59.

5 Rimsherd from an undecorated globular pot with a bevelled rim caused by false relief stamping. Buff colour. C2, 1959: surface. C2/9/59.

6 Rimsherd from an unidentifiable, but probably globular, vessel with a slightly everted rim, which is decorated by a coarse band of criss-cross incision and a broad channelled line. Buff colour. B2, 1959: 0–6 inches (0–15 cm). B2/9/59.

7 Rimsherd from a straight sided vessel bearing a band of triangular stamping and a channelled line or rimband. Thin walls, brown colour, A4, 1959: stepping back. 0 inches–3 feet (0–91 cm). A/132/59.

8 Rimsherd from a globular pot with bevelled rim. Channelled and incised decoration with the addition of a line of stamping. Red/buff exterior colour. Site A River Face; with Plate 5, no. 3. A/184/59.

9 Rimsherd from a globular pot with bevelled rim. A zone of vertical impression is associated with two channelled lines and another probable band of impressions. Buff colour. A1, 1956: Sect. 7 & 8. 10–11 feet (3·05–3·35 m). A1/46/56.

10 Rimsherd (one of two) from a straight sided vessel with slightly everted rim. A fine comb-stamped motif of two rows of filled triangles and attendant lines. Light brown/buff exterior colour. A1, 1956: 12–13 feet (3·66–3·96 m). A1/51/56.

11 Rimsherd from an undecorated, straight sided vessel. Buff colour. A1, 1956: 11 feet 6 inches–12 feet (3·5–3·66 m). A1/48/56.

12 Enigmatic object of clay, perhaps the base of a pedestalled pot, more probably a potstand. It is decorated with two channelled lines. A4, 1959: B (50–32) 9–12 inches (23–30·5 cm). A/13/59.

13 Fragment of another unidentified object. A smoothed edge of a possible hole is found on one side. A1, 1956: 8 feet 6 inches–9 feet (2·59–2·74 m). A1/35/56.

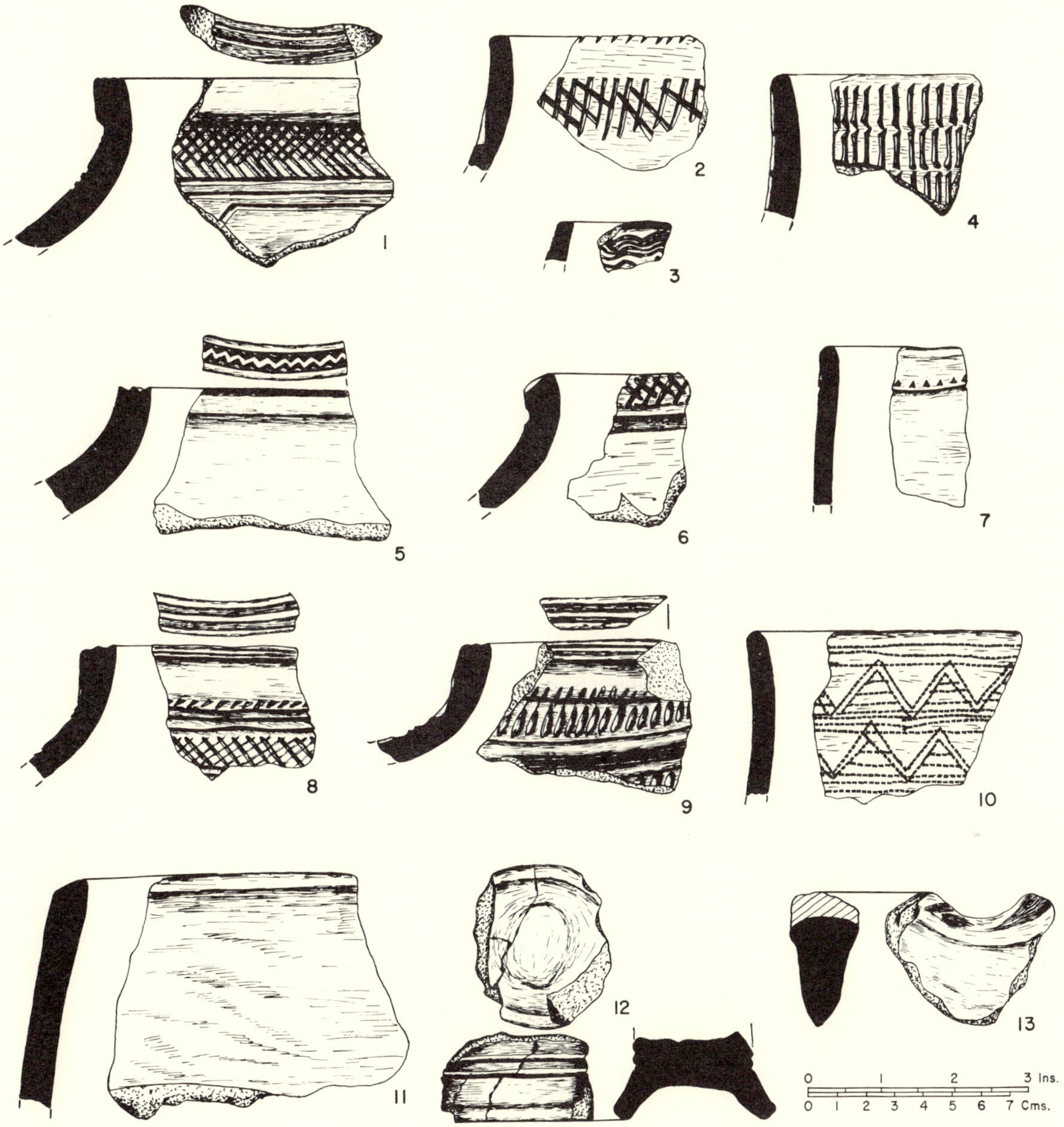
1
2
3
4
5
6
7
8
9
10
11
12
13
0 1 2 3 Ins.
0 1 2 3 4 5 6 7 Cms.

10 KALAMBO FALLS INDUSTRY: EARLY IRON AGE

1 Rimsherd from a hemispherical bowl, with unidentified decoration, including incision and channelling. Buff colour. Site C, 1963: Midden. 2 feet–2 feet 6 inches (61–76 cm). C/63/63.

2 Rimsherd from a hemispherical bowl with bevelled rim. On the outside of it a zigzag comb-stamp motif and a series of channelled lines with a chevron motif. Site C, 1963: Midden F4. 1 foot 6 inches–2 feet (45–61 cm). C/63/90.

3 Rimsherd from a shouldered pot with a band of criss-cross incision on the shoulder. Buff colour. Site C, 1963: Midden H1. 1 foot 6 inches–2 feet (14–61 cm). C/63/20.

4 Rimsherd from a shouldered pot. Bevelled rim, and coarse channelled lines on the neck. Reddish colour. Site C, 1963: Midden H2. 1 foot 6 inches–2 feet (45–61 cm). C/63/21.

5 Rimsherd from a hemispherical bowl. Three channelled lines and panels of incised lines from an unidentifiable motif. Buff colour. Site C, 1963: Midden D6. 1 foot 6 inches–2 feet (45–61 cm). C/63/21.

6 Rimsherd from a spheroidal bowl with irregular stamped decoration under the rim. Buff colour. Site C, 1963: Midden H2. 1 foot 6 inches–2 feet (45–61 cm). C/63/21.

7 Rimsherd from a gourd shaped vessel with an inturned rim. Two channelled lines near the lip. Buff colour. Site C, 1963: Midden D2. 2 feet–2 feet 6 inches (61–76 cm). C/63/55.

8 Rimsherd from a spheroidal bowl with an irregular channelled motif. Reddish colour. Site C, 1963: collapsed Midden. River Face. C/63/4.

9 Rimsherd from a spheroidal bowl with a band of criss-cross incision and a zone of channelling with zigzag motif. Reddish colour. Rim diameter (reconstructed): 7·1 inches (18 cm); maximum width (reconstructed): 9 inches (23 cm). Site C, 1963: collapsed Midden. River Face. C/63/4.

10 Rimsherd from a hemispherical bowl, with a criss-cross incised band and a zone of irregular channelling beneath it. Buff colour. Site C, 1963: Midden. 2 feet 6 inches–3 feet (76–91·5 cm). C/63/46.

11 Rimsherd from an undecorated hemispherical bowl. Buff colour. Site C, 1963: collapsed Midden. River Face. C/63/4.

12 Small rimsherd from a shouldered pot with two lines of triangular stamping below the rim. Buff colour. Site C, 1963: Midden H1. 1 foot 6 inches–2 feet (45–61 cm). C/63/20.

13 Rimsherd from an undecorated, hemispherical bowl with flared sides. The illustrated side is perforated with an hour-glass perforation on the flared portion of the wall. Buff colour. Site C, 1963: collapsed Midden. River Face. C/63/4.

14 Bodysherd from an unidentified vessel with irregular channelled lines on it. Reddish colour. Site C, 1963: Midden C1. 0 inches–1 foot 6 inches (0–45 cm). C/63/60.

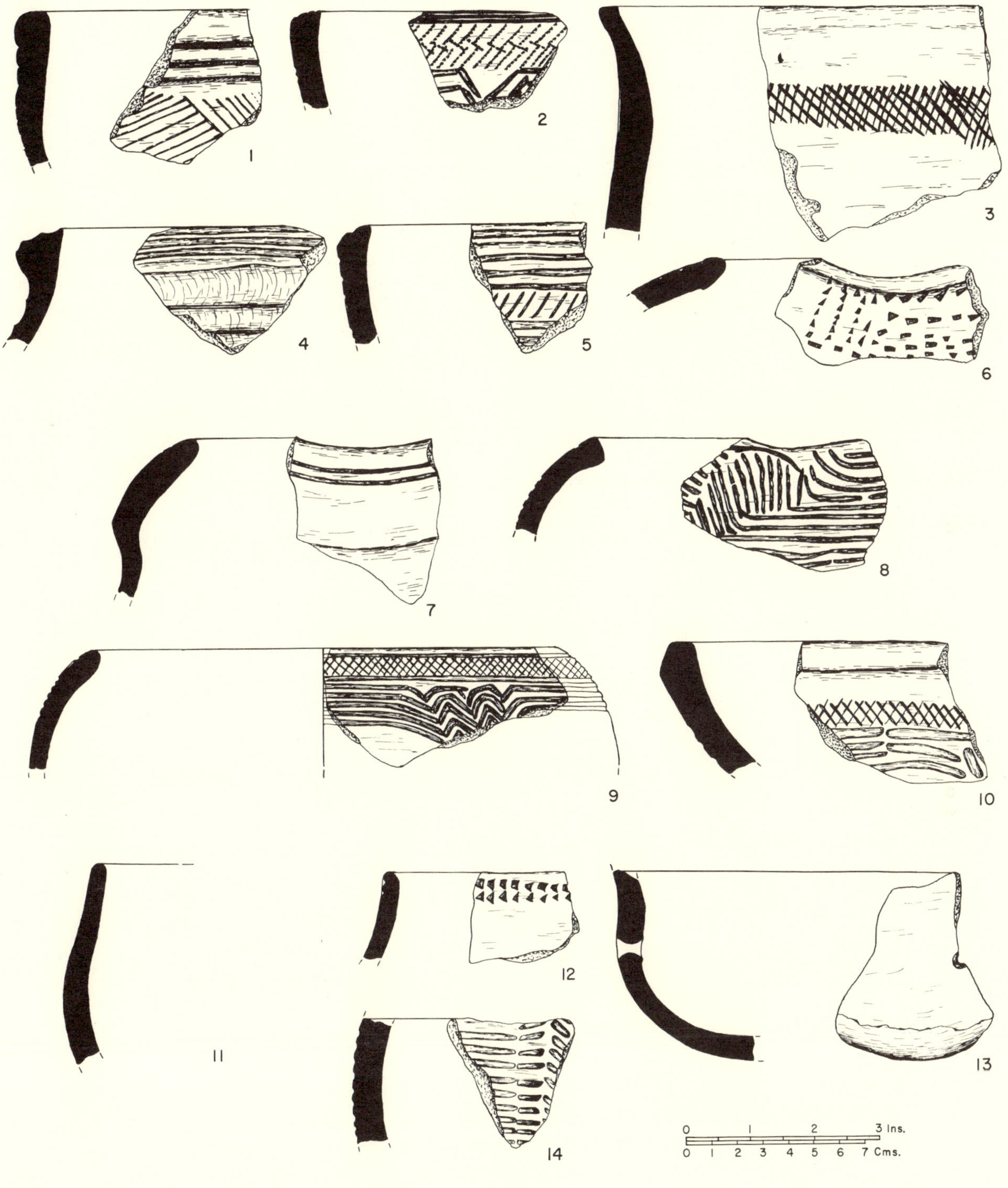
1
2
3
4
5
6
7
8
9
10
11
12
13
14
0 1 2 3 Ins.
0 1 2 3 4 5 6 7 Cms.

1 Complex 3. Reconstructed shouldered pot with everted rim. A zigzag line on the outer edge of the rim is associated with a line of 'false relief' triangular stamping. A similar line is associated with a band of four channelled lines associated with a chevron motif. Buff colour. Rim diameter (reconstructed): 12·8 inches (32·5 cm); height (reconstructed): 9·1 inches (23·25 cm); maximum width (reconstructed): 13·2 inches (33·5 cm). Site C, 1963: C1/2. 3 feet–3 feet 6 inches (91 cm–1·06 m). C/63/32.

2 Rimsherd from a hemispherical bowl with convex sides. The outer edge of the rim is decorated with a band of false relief triangular stamping. Five bands of channelled decoration with a broken, almost zigzag motif under this. Buff colour. Rim diameter (reconstructed): 6·3 inches (16 cm); height (reconstructed): 3·9 inches (10 cm); maximum width (reconstructed): 7·5 inches (19 cm). Site C, 1963: collapsed Midden. River Face. C/63/4.

3 Complete coarse shouldered pot of irregular shape with crude channelled decoration, including a zigzag line. Brown colour. Rim diameter: 4·4 inches (11·5 cm); height: 5·2 inches (13·5 cm); maximum diameter: 5·4 inches (14 cm). Site C, 1963: collapsed Midden. River Face. C/63/1.

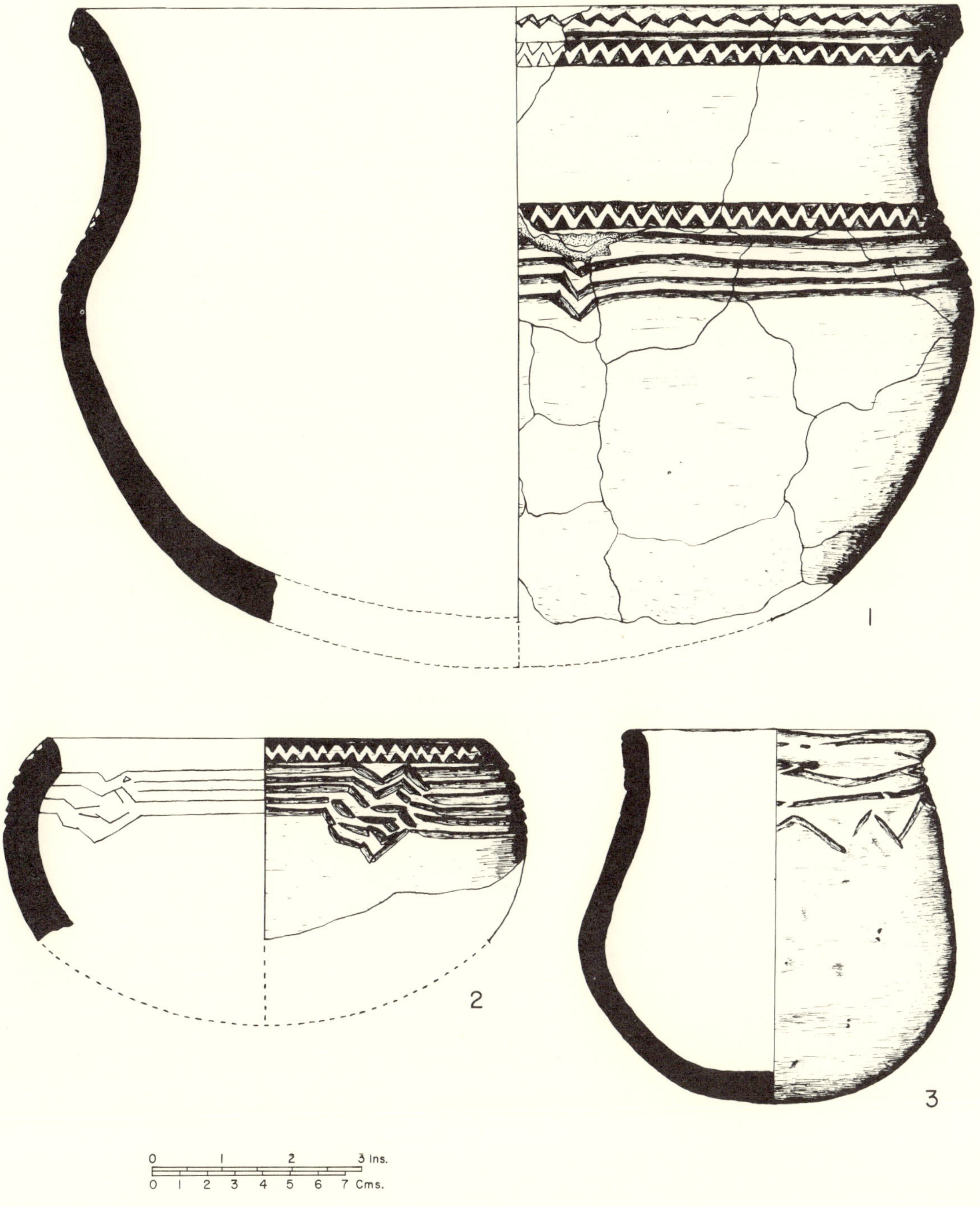
1
2
3
0 1 2 3 Ins.
0 1 2 3 4 5 6 7 Cms.

12 KALAMBO FALLS INDUSTRY: EARLY IRON AGE:

Site C, Complex 1

1 Shouldered pot with bevelled rim and two bands of criss-cross incision, separated by channelled lines. On the shoulder a zone of channelled lines with zigzag motif. Buff exterior, pale red interior. Rim diameter: 6·4 inches (16 cm); height: 9·9 inches (25·15 cm); maximum width: 10·1 inches (25·6 cm). C/63/25.

2 Undecorated deep bowl with two holes in it. Well burnished, buff exterior colour. Rim diameter: 8·7 inches (22·1 cm); height (reconstructed): 4·6 inches (11·7 cm). C/63/22.

3 Bodysherd from a shouldered pot with zones of oblique comb-stamping and channelling. A chevron motif is probably part of the lowest zone of channelling. Pale red exterior colour. C/63/25.

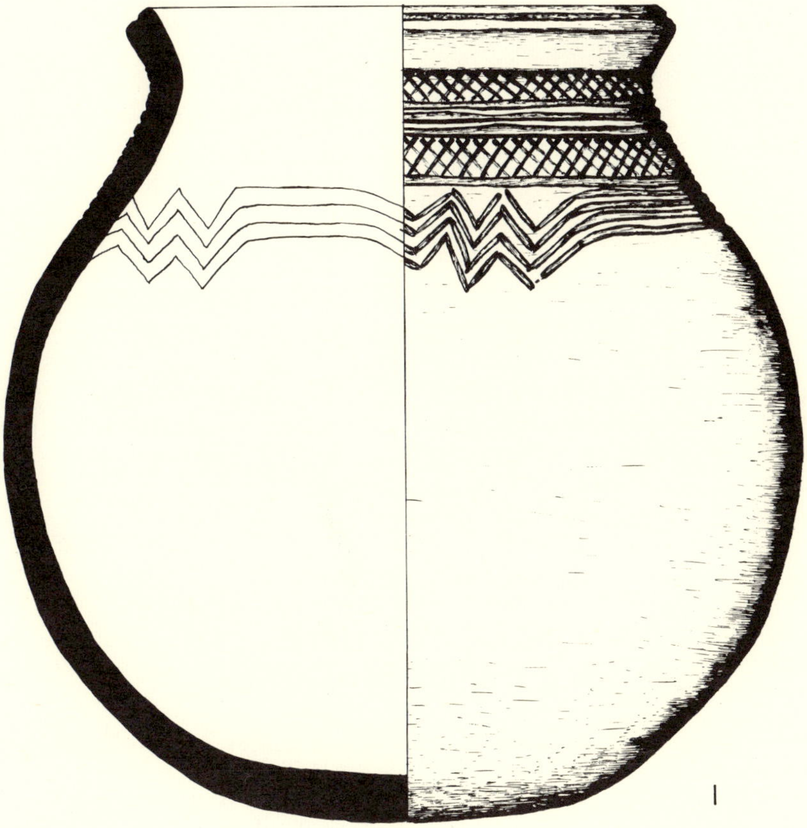

1

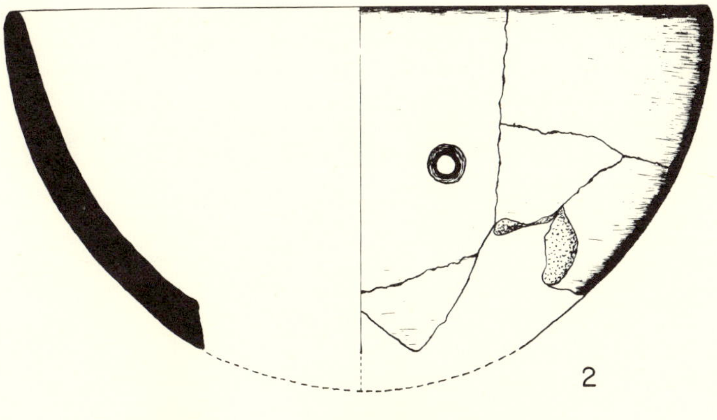

2

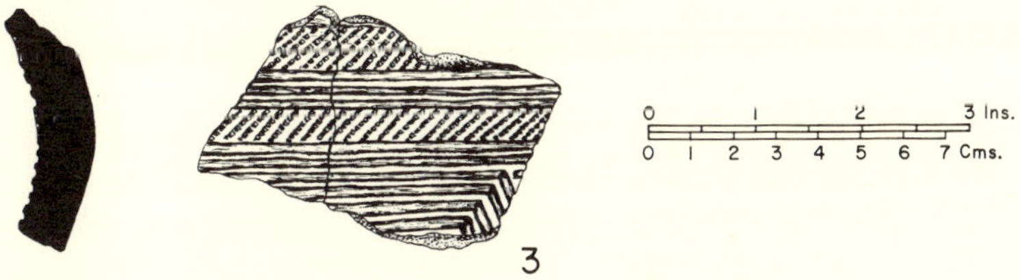

3

13 KALAMBO FALLS INDUSTRY: EARLY IRON AGE:
Site C, Complex 2

1 Shouldered pot with bevelled and rolled over rim. A band of cross-hatched incision on the neck is bounded by a band of channelling with a chevron motif. Pale red surface with black patches. Rim diameter: 5·5 inches (14 cm); height: 6·2 inches (16 cm); maximum width: 7·1 inches (18 cm). C/63/29.

KALAMBO FALLS INDUSTRY: EARLY IRON AGE:
Site C, Complex 4

2 Rimsherd from a globular pot with a bevelled rim and a line of coarse stamping on the neck. Buff exterior colour. Rim diameter: 5·3 inches (13·75 cm). C/63/113.

3 Rimsherd from a shouldered pot with a well-defined neck; and bevelled rim. The outside of the rim bears diagonal comb-stamping; below it are two rows of triangular impressions. Buff to pale red colour. Rim diameter (reconstructed): 7·0 inches (17·75 cm). C/63/113.

4 Rimsherd from an undecorated shallow bowl. Rim diameter (reconstructed): 12·2 inches (31 cm); height (reconstructed): 4·7 inches (12 cm). C/63/113.

5 Rimsherd from a small shouldered pot. Decoration is confined to panels of short channelled lines on the shoulder. Buff exterior colour. Rim diameter (reconstructed): 5·5 inches (14 cm); height (reconstructed): 4·2 inches (11 cm); maximum width: 5·5 inches (14 cm). C/63/113.

6 Rimsherd from an undecorated shallow bowl. Buff colour. C/63/113.

7 Rimsherd from a shallow bowl. The rim bears diagonal incision or impressions. Buff colour. Rim diameter (reconstructed): 10 inches (25·5 cm); height: 3·2 inches (8 cm). C/63/113.

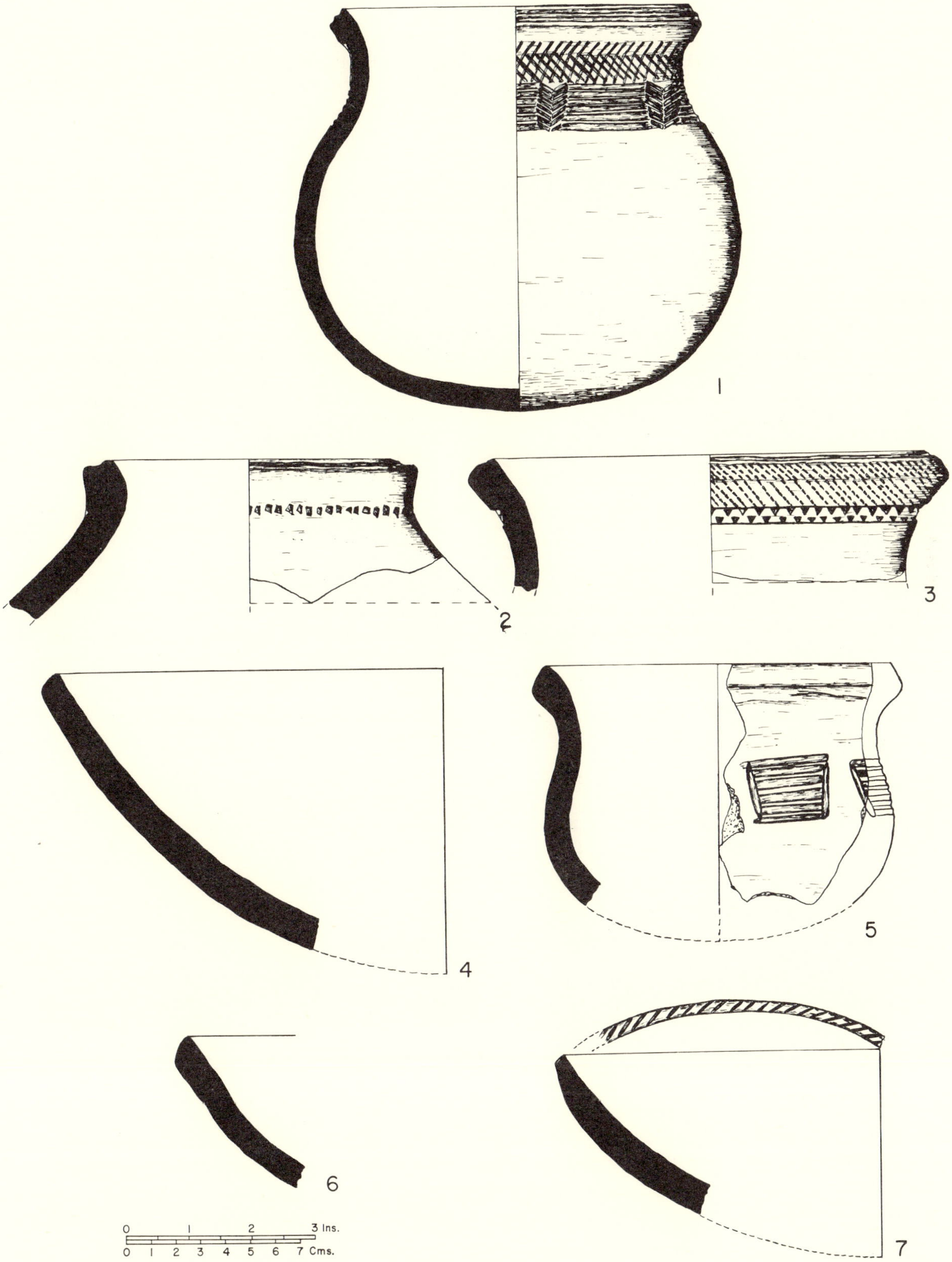
1
2
3
4
5
6
7
0 1 2 3 Ins.
0 1 2 3 4 5 6 7 Cms.

14 KALAMBO FALLS INDUSTRY: EARLY IRON AGE:
Site C, Complex 4

1 A shouldered pot with everted rim, decorated with criss-cross lines. A zone of 'false relief' on the neck. At the shoulder a grooved line and a zone of light cross-hatched incision, well burnished. Buff exterior colour. Rim diameter: 7·4 inches (19 cm); height (reconstructed): 7·4 inches (19 cm); maximum width: 8·7 inches (22·25 cm). C/63/113.

2 Rimsherd from a shouldered pot with a line of triangular stamping on the rim. Two further lines of coarse stamping adorn the neck. Buff colour. Rim diameter (reconstructed): 6·2 inches (16 cm). C/63/113.

3 Rimsherd from a globular pot, with a stamped zigzag effect on the rim. Two lines of stamping on the neck. Red colour. C/63/113.

KALAMBO FALLS INDUSTRY: EARLY IRON AGE:
Site C, Complex 5

4 A shouldered pot with a zigzag decoration on the rim. On the neck a zone of channelling bounded by elongated impressions and cross-hatched incision. Buff exterior colour. Rim diameter: 6·5 inches (16·75 cm); height: *c.* 12 inches (30·5 cm); maximum width: 12 inches (30·5 cm). C/63/114.

5 A shouldered pot with everted rim decorated with triangular impressions. The neck bears two lines of elongated triangular stampings; on the shoulder three irregular channelled lines and panels of triangular stamping. Rim diameter: 8·9 inches (22·75 cm); height (reconstructed): *c.* 10 inches (25·5 cm); maximum width: 11·7 inches (29·75 cm). C/63/114.

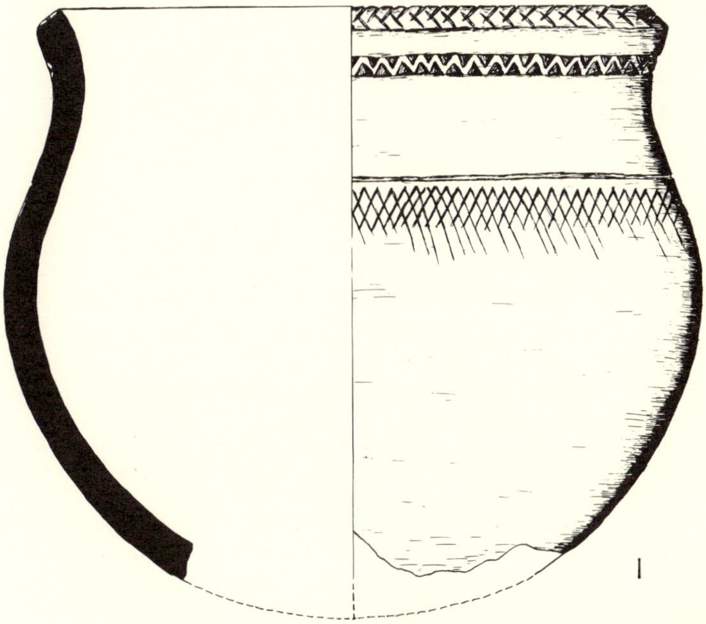

1

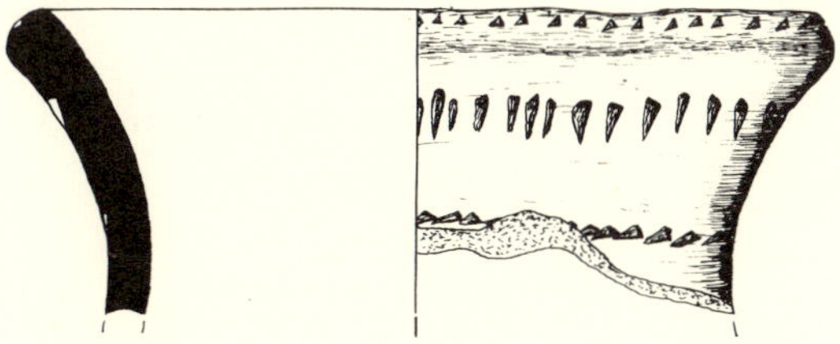

2

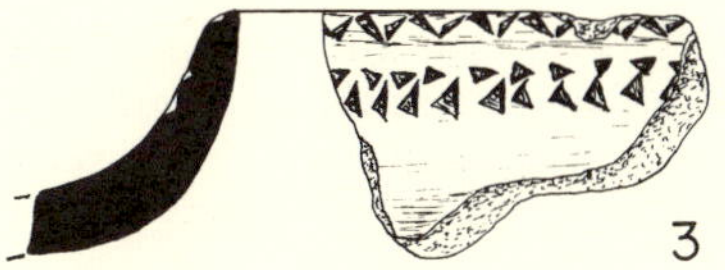

3

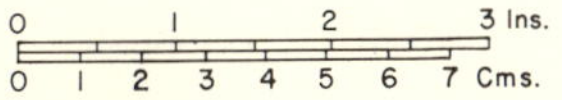

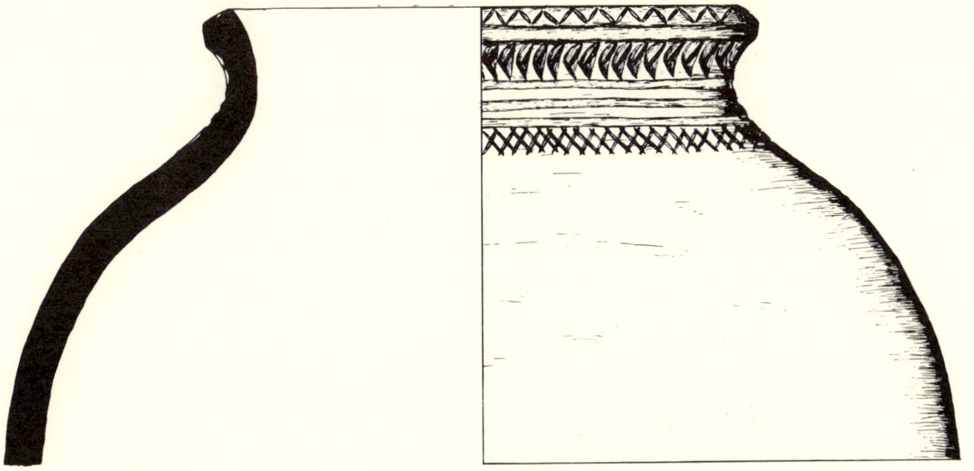

4

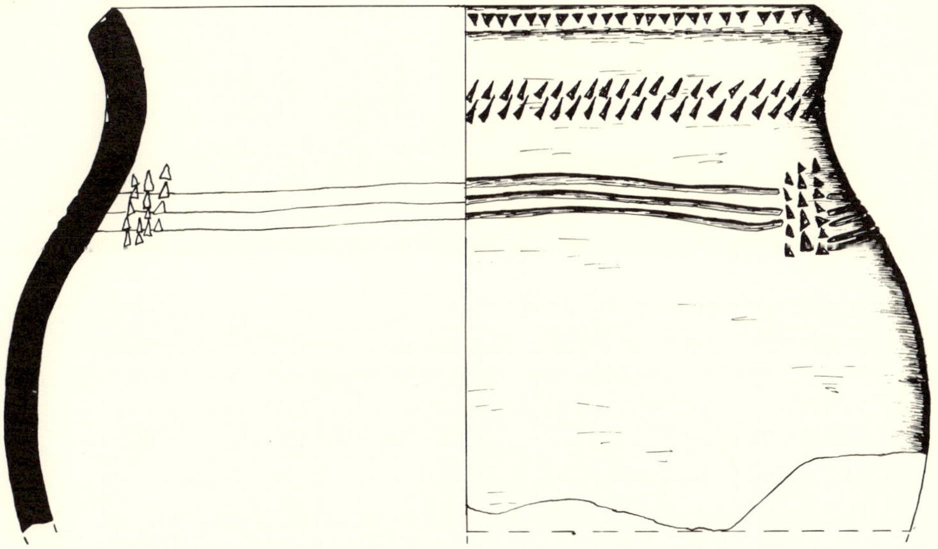

5

15 KALAMBO FALLS INDUSTRY: EARLY IRON AGE:
Site C, Complex 5

1 Bodysherd from a shouldered pot with cross-hatched, incised and channelled decoration. On the shoulder a line of triangular stamps, two vertical lines of which occur on the body. Orange exterior, red interior. C/63/114.

2 Rimsherd from an undecorated shallow bowl. Buff exterior colour. Rim diameter (reconstructed): 8 inches (20·25 cm); height (reconstructed): 3·4 inches (8·25 cm). C/63/114.

3 Bodysherd from a shouldered pot with a band of channelled lines on the shoulder. These are broken, and overlain by a zone of semicircular channels and triangular stampings. Buff colour. C/63/114.

4 Rimsherd from a shouldered pot with bevelled, everted rim. On the rim is zigzag stamped decoration between two irregular lines of triangular stamping and below this five lines of channelling. Pale red exterior colour. C/63/114.

5 Large rimsherd from a shouldered pot with a line of stamping on the rim and a line of 'false relief' stamping on the neck. Buff surface. C/63/114.

6 Rimsherd from a shouldered pot with two lines of stamping and an incised line on the rim. Buff colour. C/63/114.

7 Rimsherd from a shouldered pot with simple, but slightly flattened rim. A zone of crude, elongated, triangular impressions at the base of the rim. Cross-hatched impression on shoulder. Buff colour. Rim diameter (reconstructed): 7·5 inches (17·25 cm); height (reconstructed): 6·3 inches (16·25 cm); maximum width: 8·7 inches (22 cm). C/63/114.

KALAMBO FALLS INDUSTRY: EARLY IRON AGE:
Site C, Complex 6

8 Globular pot with a rim decorated with a zigzag line. Buff exterior surface. Rim diameter: 6·3 inches (16 cm); height (reconstructed): 12 inches (30·5 cm); maximum width: 15 inches (38·25 cm). C/63/115.

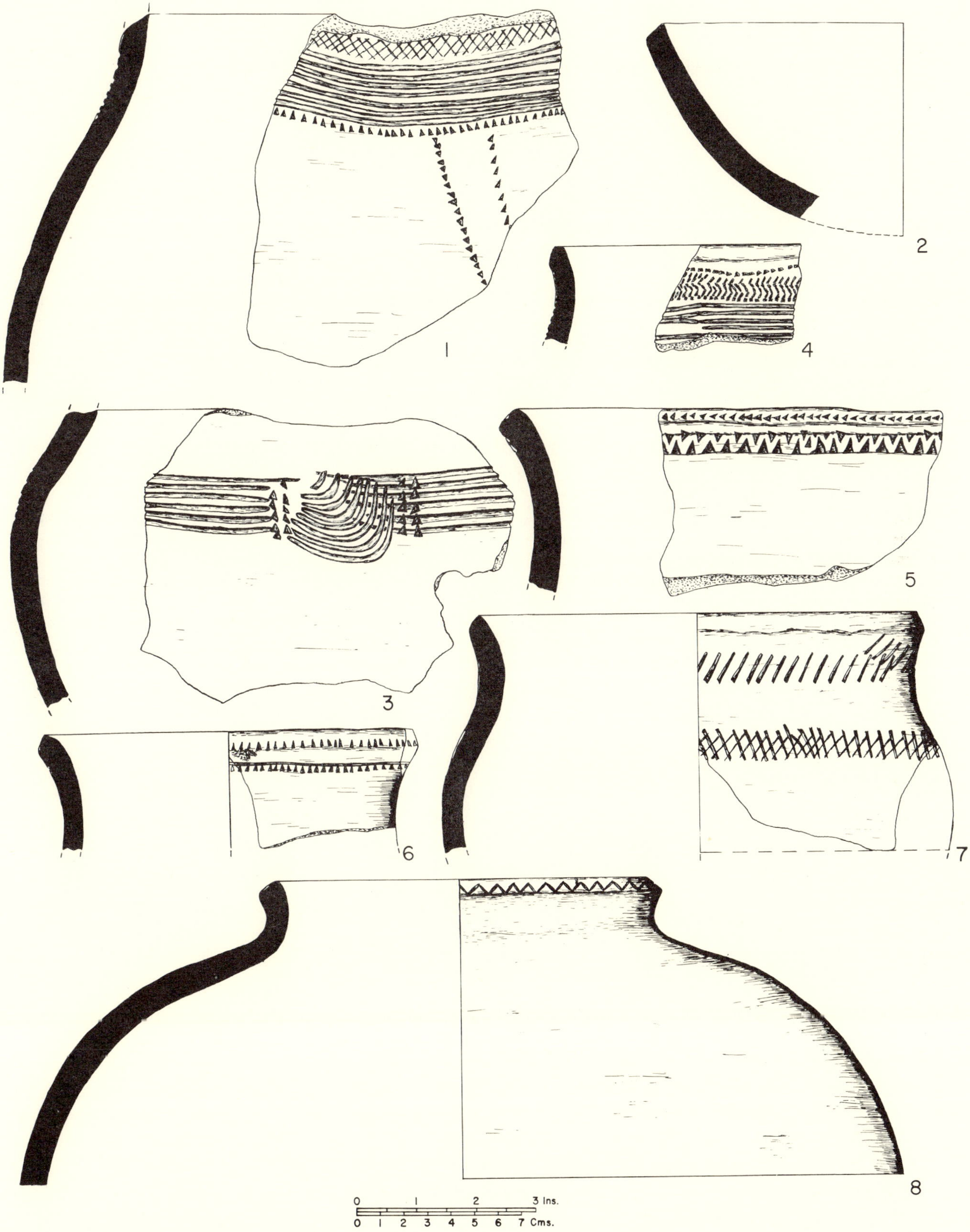
1
2
3
4
5
6
7
8
0 1 2 3 Ins.
0 1 2 3 4 5 6 7 Cms.

16 KALAMBO FALLS INDUSTRY: EARLY IRON AGE:

Site C, Complex 6

1 Rimsherd from a shouldered pot with an everted rim, which is bevelled with a zigzag line. Alternating zones of cross-hatched incision and channelling lie above three meandering channelled lines on the shoulder. Pale red exterior colour. C/63/115.

2 Rimsherd from an undecorated shallow bowl. Buff exterior colour. Rim diameter (reconstructed): 9·0 inches (23 cm); height: 2·9 inches (7·25 cm). C/63/115.

KALAMBO FALLS INDUSTRY: EARLY IRON AGE:

Site C, Complex 8

3 Rimsherd from a shouldered pot with three rows of rectangular stamping and a channelled line on the neck. Buff exterior colour. Rim diameter (reconstructed): 4·7 inches (12 cm); height (reconstructed): 5·5 inches (14 cm); maximum width: 5·5 inches (14 cm). C/63/116.

4 Rimsherd from an undecorated deep bowl. Buff exterior colour. Rim diameter (reconstructed): 7·4 inches (19 cm); height (reconstructed): 4·5–5 inches (11·25–12·75 cm). C/63/116.

5 Rimsherd from an undecorated shallow bowl. Rim diameter (reconstructed): 6·2 inches (16 cm); height: 2·9 inches (7·25 cm). C/63/116.

6 Rimsherd from a shouldered pot with an everted and bevelled rim. A chevron comb-stamped motif on the rim. Rim diameter (reconstructed): 9·1 inches (23·25 cm). C/63/116.

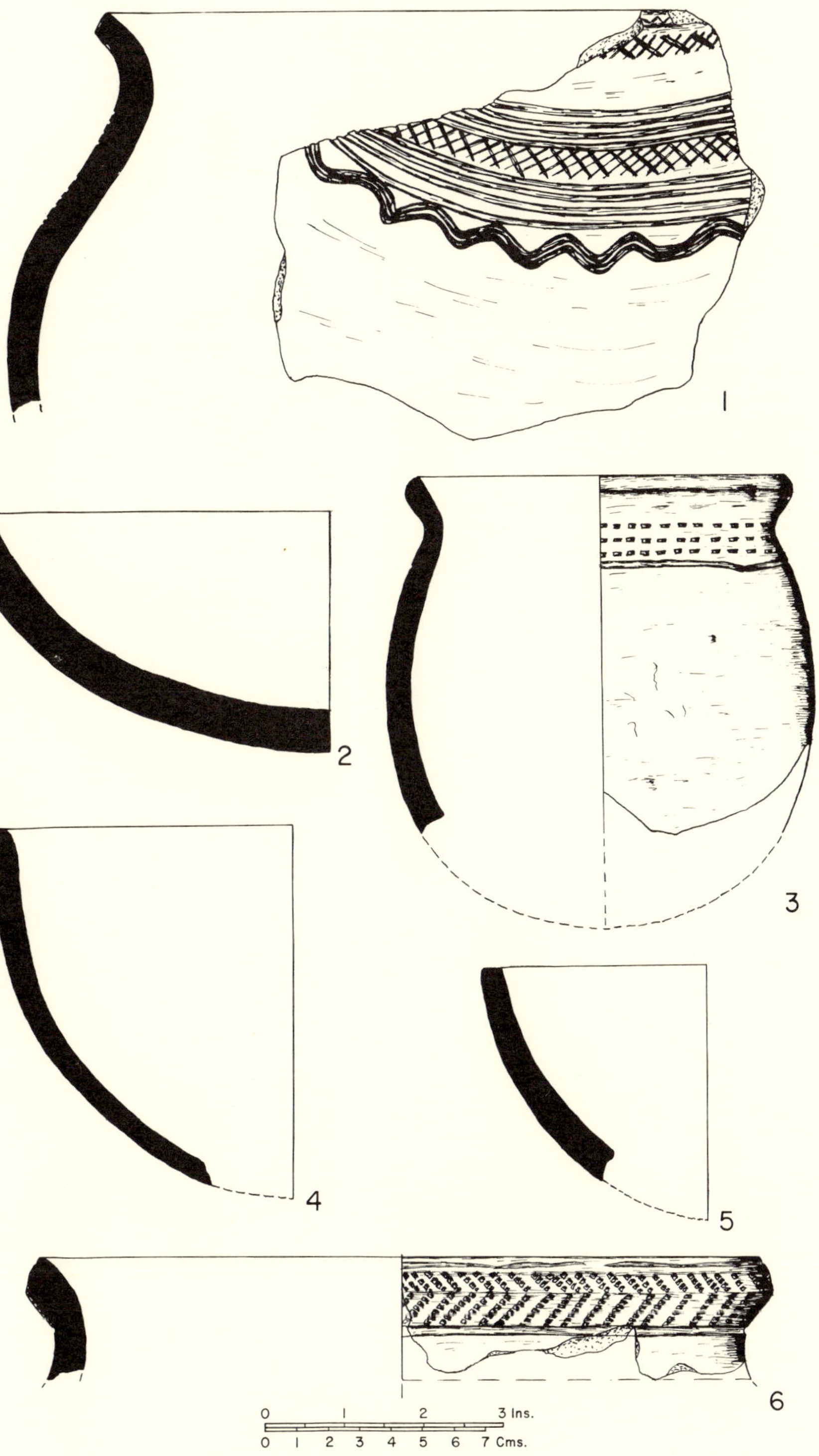
1
2
3
4
5
6
0 1 2 3 Ins.
0 1 2 3 4 5 6 7 Cms.

17 KALAMBO FALLS INDUSTRY: EARLY IRON AGE:
Site C, Complex 8

1 Shouldered pot with bevelled rim and incised and channelled zones on the neck. The lowest zone of channelling has a chevron motif. Buff exterior colour. Rim diameter: 6·6 inches (17 cm); height (reconstructed): 8·6 inches (22 cm); maximum width: 9·6 inches (24·25 cm). C/63/116.

2 Undecorated shouldered pot with roughly bevelled rim. Pale red exterior colour. Rim diameter: 8·0 inches (20·25 cm); height (reconstructed): 13·3 inches (33·75 cm); maximum width: 11·7 inches (29·5 cm). C/63/116.

3 Rimsherd from a shouldered pot with a bevelled rim. A band of cross-hatched incision below the rim. Buff exterior colour. C/63/116.

4 Rimsherd from a slender, shouldered and undecorated vessel. Buff exterior colour. Rim diameter (reconstructed): 2·5 inches (6·5 cm); maximum width (reconstructed): 3·8 inches (9·75 cm). C/63/116.

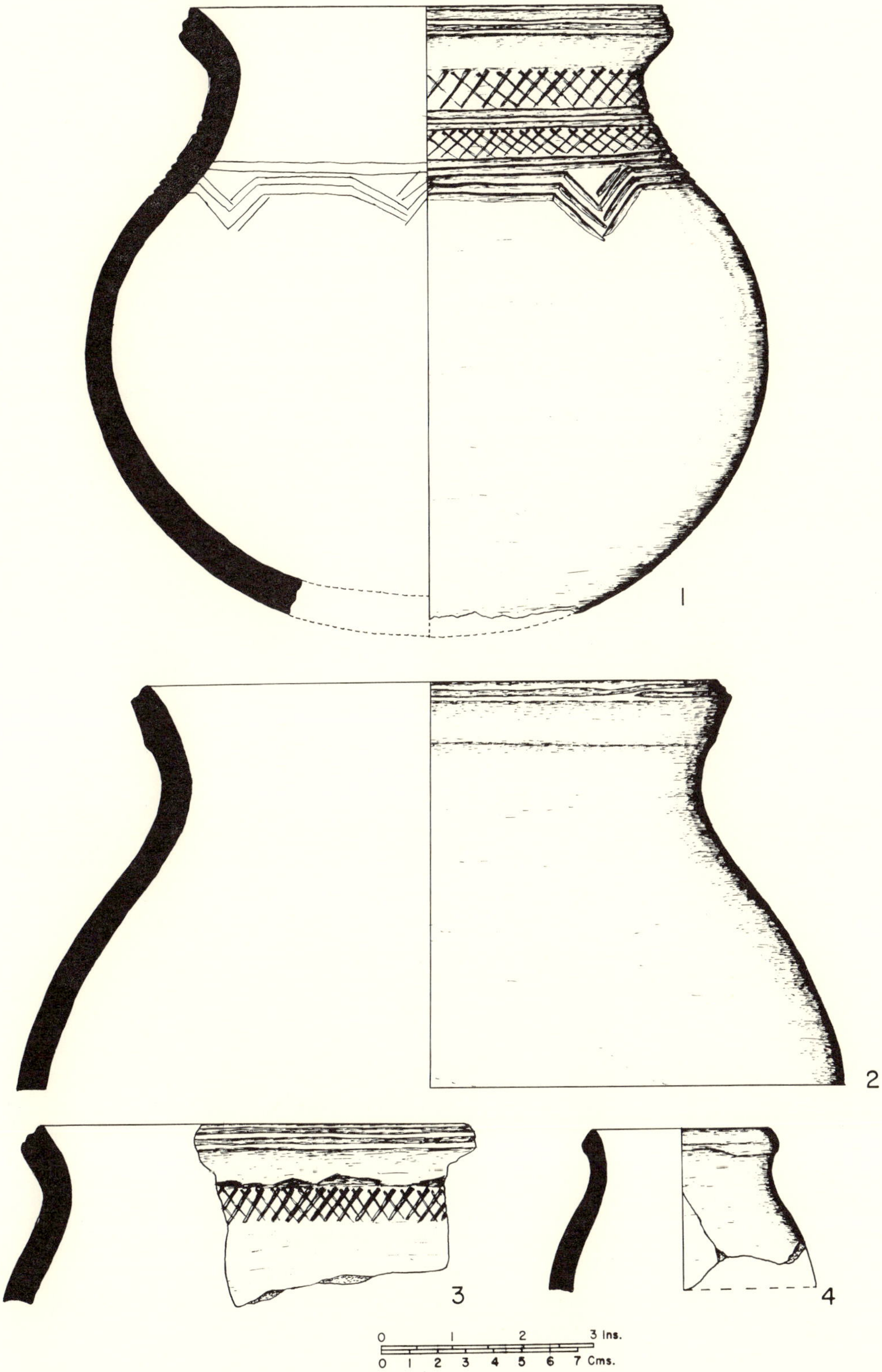
1
2
3
4
0 1 2 3 Ins.
0 1 2 3 4 5 6 7 Cms.

18 KALAMBO FALLS INDUSTRY: EARLY IRON AGE:
Site C, Complex 8

1 Shouldered pot with everted and bevelled rim. The neck is decorated with bands of channelling and stamping. The shoulder bears a chevron channelled motif. Buff exterior colour. Rim diameter: 6·7 inches (17 cm); height (reconstructed): 10 inches (25·5 cm); maximum width: 9·5 inches (24 cm). C/63/116.

2 Undecorated shallow bowl, buff exterior colour slightly, inverted rim. Rim diameter: 12·1 inches (30·75 cm); height: 5·3 inches (13·25 cm). C/63/116.

3 Shouldered pot with everted and bevelled rim. A crude, cross-hatched, incised band below the rim. Buff to pale red exterior colour. Rim diameter: 7·8 inches (20 cm); height (reconstructed): 6·3 inches (16·25 cm); maximum width: 8·1 (20·75 cm). C/63/116.

4 Rimsherd from a shouldered pot with a bevelled rim. A band of cross-hatched incision is associated with a zone of channelling 1·2 inches (3 cm) wide. Three lines of looped channelling are on the shoulder. Buff to yellow exterior colour. Rim diameter (reconstructed): 6·4 inches (16·5 cm); maximum width: 7·5 inches (19 cm). C/63/116.

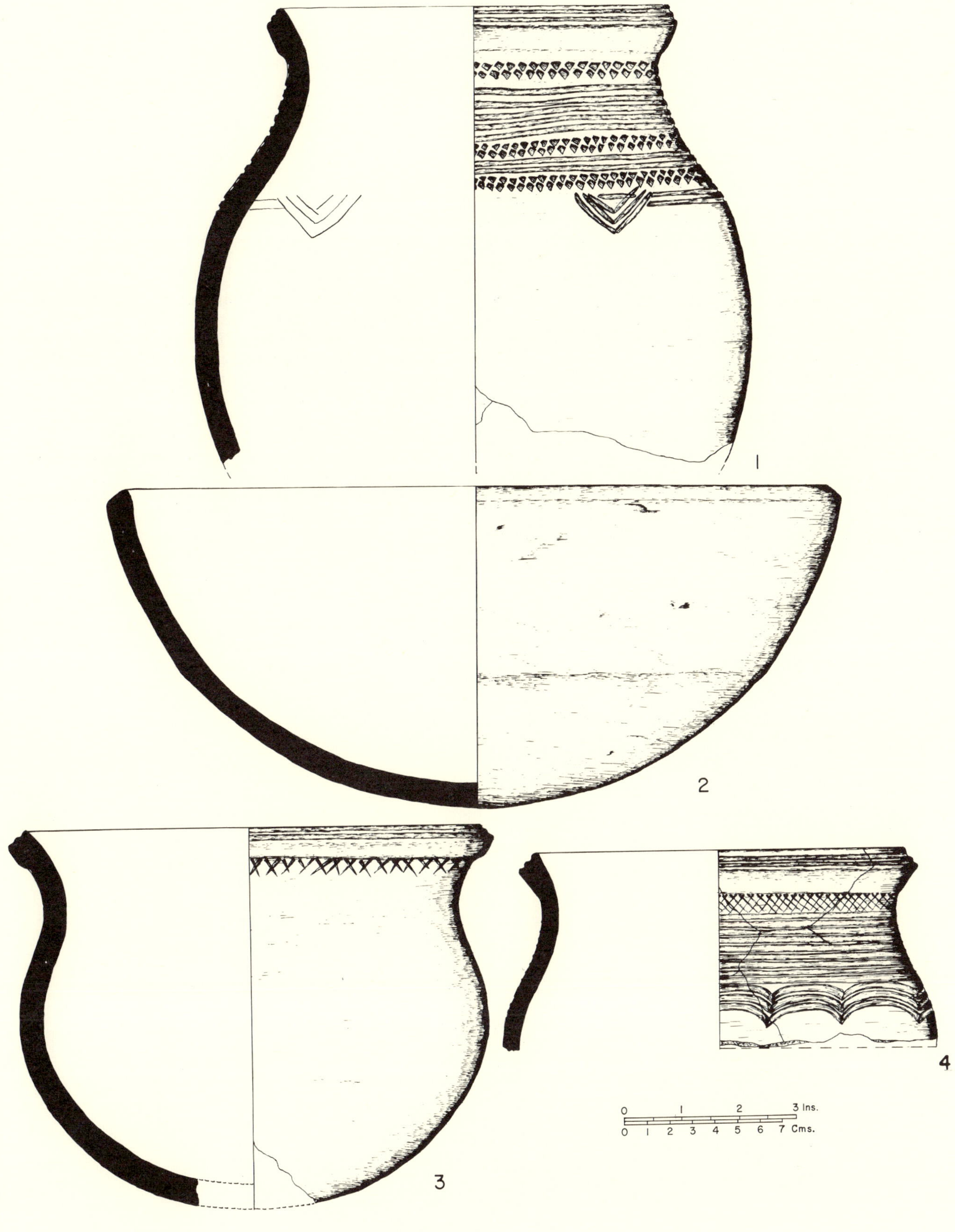
1
2
3
4
0 1 2 3 Ins.
0 1 2 3 4 5 6 7 Cms.

19 KALAMBO FALLS INDUSTRY: EARLY IRON AGE:
Site C, Complex 8

1 Rimsherd from a shouldered pot with everted rim. A band of oblique impressions, below the rim, and a zone of cross-hatched incision associated with a looped, channelled line. C/63/116.

2 Rimsherd from a shouldered pot with a bevelled rim; two channelled lines below it, and a line of stamping and two channelled lines with an oblique motif at the shoulder. Buff colour. Rim diameter (reconstructed): 6·4 inches (16·26 cm); height (reconstructed): 7·8 inches (20 cm); maximum width: 7·9 inches (20·25 cm). C/63/116.

3 Rimsherd from an undecorated shouldered pot with an everted rim. Buff colour. Rim diameter (reconstructed): 5·2 inches (13·25 cm). C/63/116.

4 Rimsherd from a shouldered pot with a bevelled rim and a line of triangular impressions below the rim. Rim diameter (reconstructed): 7·5 inches (19 cm). C/63/116.

5 Rimsherd from an unidentifiable vessel with three rows of semicircular impressions and two channelled lines. Bevelled rim, buff exterior colour. C/63/116.

6 Unidentifiable bodysherd with a band of channelling with zigzag motif. Buff colour. C/63/116.

7 Unidentifiable bodysherd with a band of channelling on the body with oblique variation. Buff colour. C/63/116.

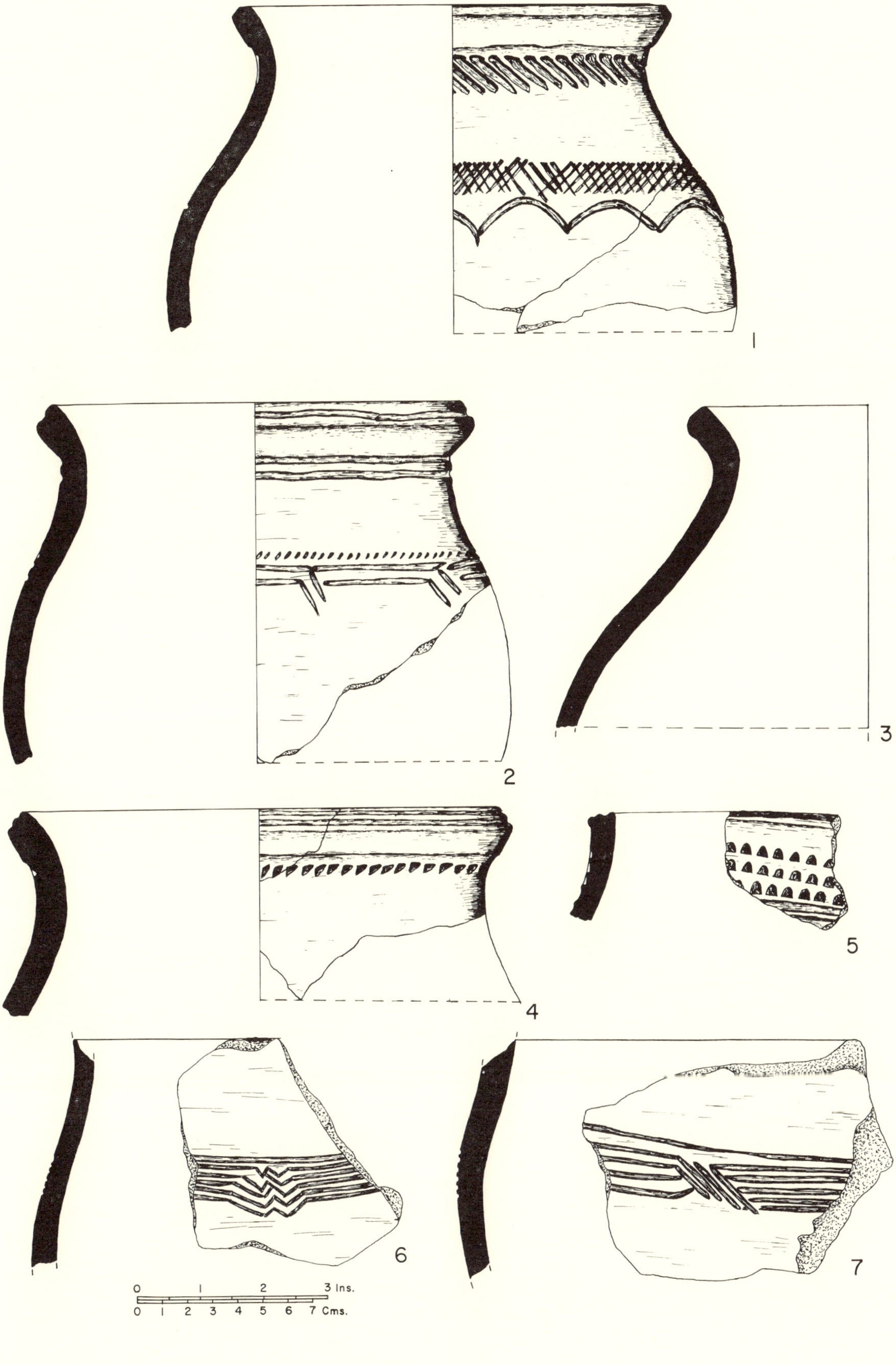
1
2
3
4
5
6
7
0 1 2 3 Ins.
0 1 2 3 4 5 6 7 Cms.

20 KALAMBO FALLS INDUSTRY: EARLY IRON AGE:
Site C, Complex 9

1 Undecorated shouldered, or globular pot with a slightly rolled over rim. Pale red exterior colour. Rim diameter: 8·4 inches (21·75 cm); height (reconstructed): 15·6 inches (39·6 cm); maximum width: 16·2 inches (41·25 cm). C/63/118.

2 Rimsherd from a shouldered pot with a bevelled rim, bearing a zigzag incised line on its outer edge. Below it are two horizontal rows of triangular stamps, two similar but vertical lines adorn the neck. The shoulder bears three channelled lines and further rows of triangular stamping. Buff exterior colour. Rim diameter (reconstructed): 12·4 inches (31·15 cm); height (reconstructed): 11·6 inches (29·5 cm); maximum width: 13·3 inches (33·75 cm). C/63/118.

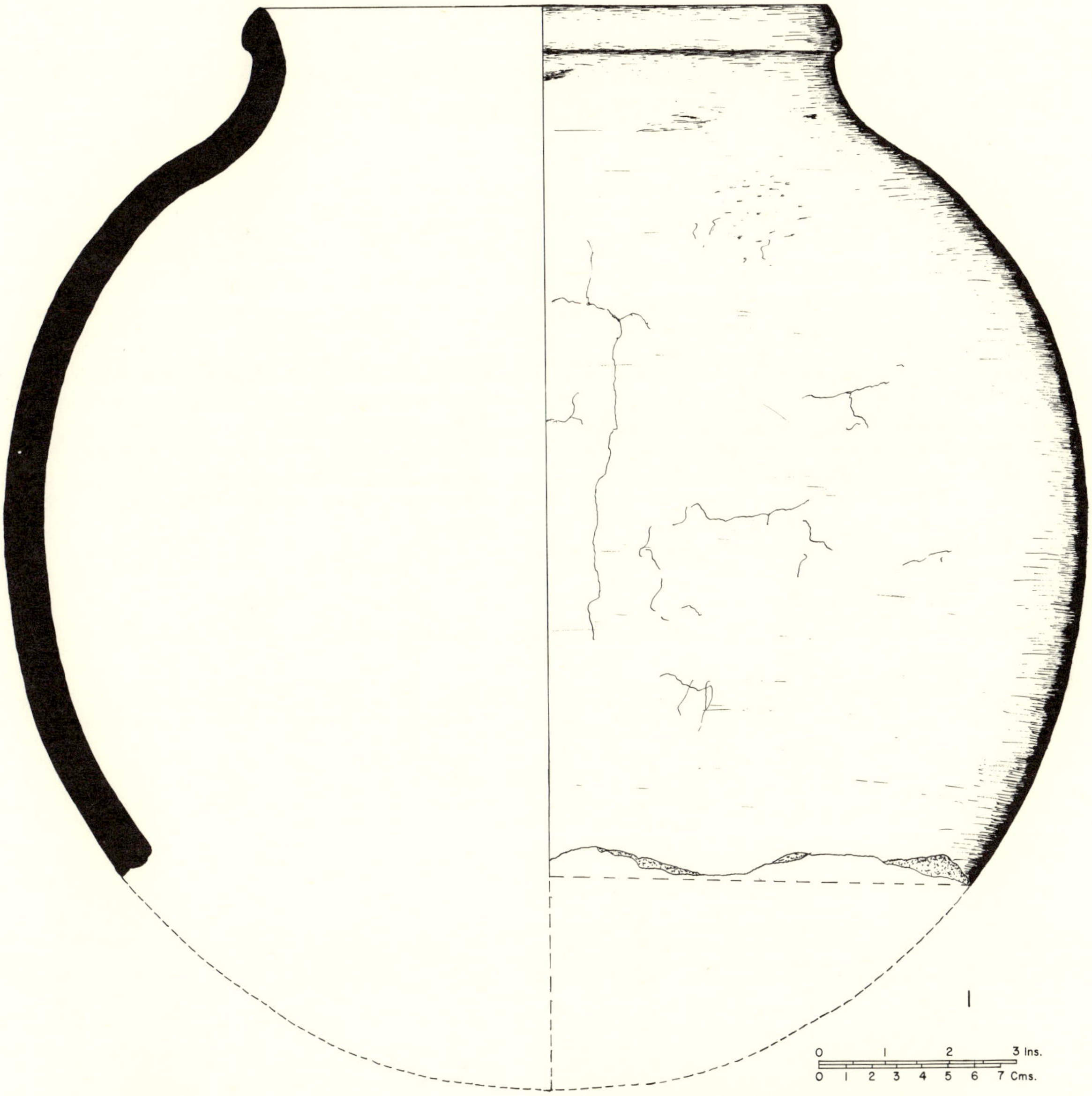

1

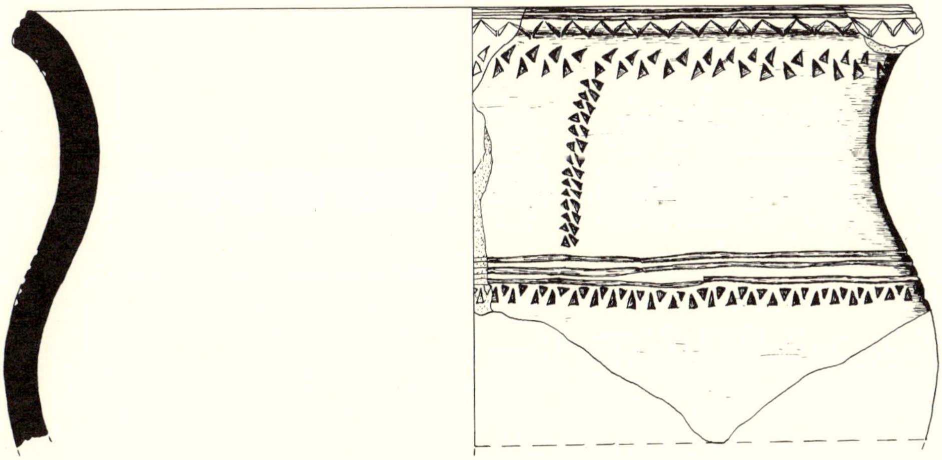

2

21 KALAMBO FALLS INDUSTRY: EARLY IRON AGE:

Site C, Complex 9

1 'Dimple base' thumb impression on the base of a pot. Pale red colour. C/63/118.

2 Rimsherd from a shouldered pot, nearly straight sided. Two lines of triangular decoration at the rim. Buff colour. Rim diameter (reconstructed): 6·3 inches (16·25 cm); height (reconstructed): 4·4 inches (11·25 cm); maximum width: 6·3 inches (16·25 cm). C/63/118.

3 Rimsherd from an undecorated, straight sided vessel. Buff colour. C/63/118.

4 Bodysherd from a shouldered pot with a line of 'false relief' and a band of channelling with a chevron motif. Buff colour. C/63/118.

5 Rimsherd from an undecorated shallow bowl. Buff colour. Rim diameter (reconstructed): 5·8 inches (14·75 cm); height (reconstructed): 3·4 inches (8·75 cm). C/63/118.

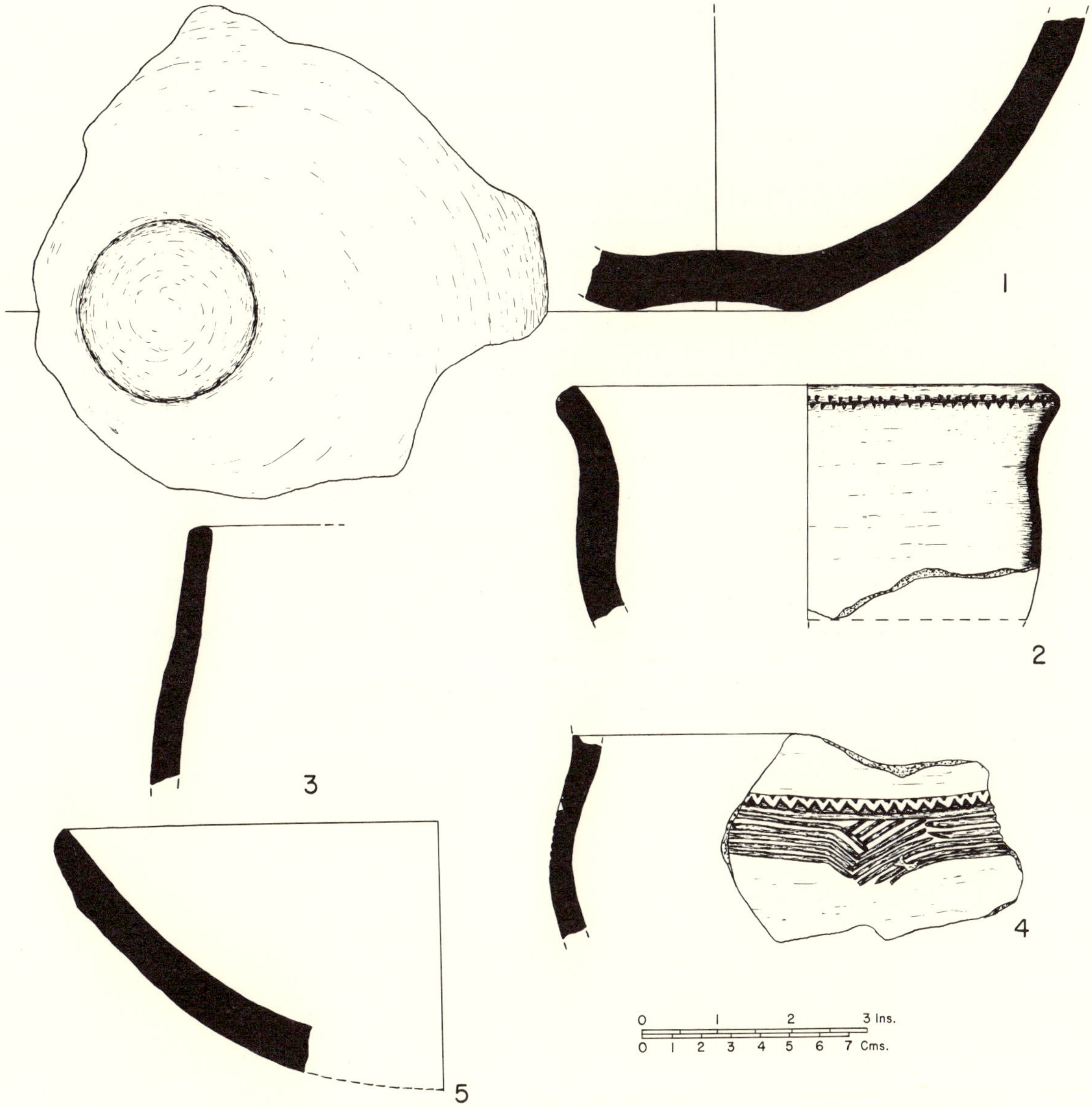
1
2
3
4
5
0 1 2 3 Ins.
0 1 2 3 4 5 6 7 Cms.

22 KALAMBO FALLS INDUSTRY: EARLY IRON AGE:
Site C, Complex 10

1 Incomplete globular pot with flattened and slightly everted rim. No decoration. Rim diameter: 6·8 inches (17·3 cm); height (reconstructed): *c.* 15 inches (38·25 cm); maximum width: 17·7 inches (44·75 cm). C/63/117.

2 Rimsherd from a shouldered pot with zigzag incised motif on the rim. Two lines of coarse zigzag incision on the shoulder. Buff exterior colour. C/63/117.

3 Rimsherd from a shouldered pot with a line of stamping. On the shoulder a line of stamping with vertical lines of triangular stamping under it. Buff exterior colour. Rim diameter: 6·7 inches (17 cm); height (reconstructed): 7·4 inches (19 cm); maximum width (reconstructed): 8·6 inches (22 cm). C/63/117.

4 Rimsherd from a shouldered pot with sharply everted and bevelled rim, decorated with two lines of triangular stamping. A band of cross-hatched incision on the rim, and two lines of triangular impressions below it. A band of channelling delimited by two lines of 'false relief' on the shoulder. Brown to red outside, pale red inside. Rim diameter (reconstructed): 6·7 inches (17 cm); height (reconstructed): 4·0 inches (10·25 cm); maximum width: 6·6 inches (16·8 cm). C/63/117.

5 Rimsherd from a shouldered pot with a line of rectangular impressions on the rim. Lines of triangular stamping adorn the neck and shoulder. Buff exterior colour. Rim diameter (reconstructed): 6·2 inches (16 cm); height (reconstructed): 5·3 inches (13·5 cm); maximum width (reconstructed): 6 inches (15·25 cm). C/63/117.

6 Rimsherd from a globular pot, probably undecorated. Buff colour. C/63/117.

7 Rimsherd from an undecorated shallow bowl. Buff colour. Rim diameter (reconstructed): 10 inches (25·5 cm); height (reconstructed): 2·8 inches (7 cm). C/63/117.

8 Rimsherd from a shouldered pot, bearing irregular lines of stamping. Buff colour. C/63/117.

9 Rimsherd from a shouldered pot. A band of oblique incised lines on the rim, and an irregular motif on the neck. Buff colour. Rim diameter (reconstructed): 5·9 inches (15 cm). C/63/117.

10 Rimsherd from an undecorated shallow bowl. Buff colour. C/63/117.

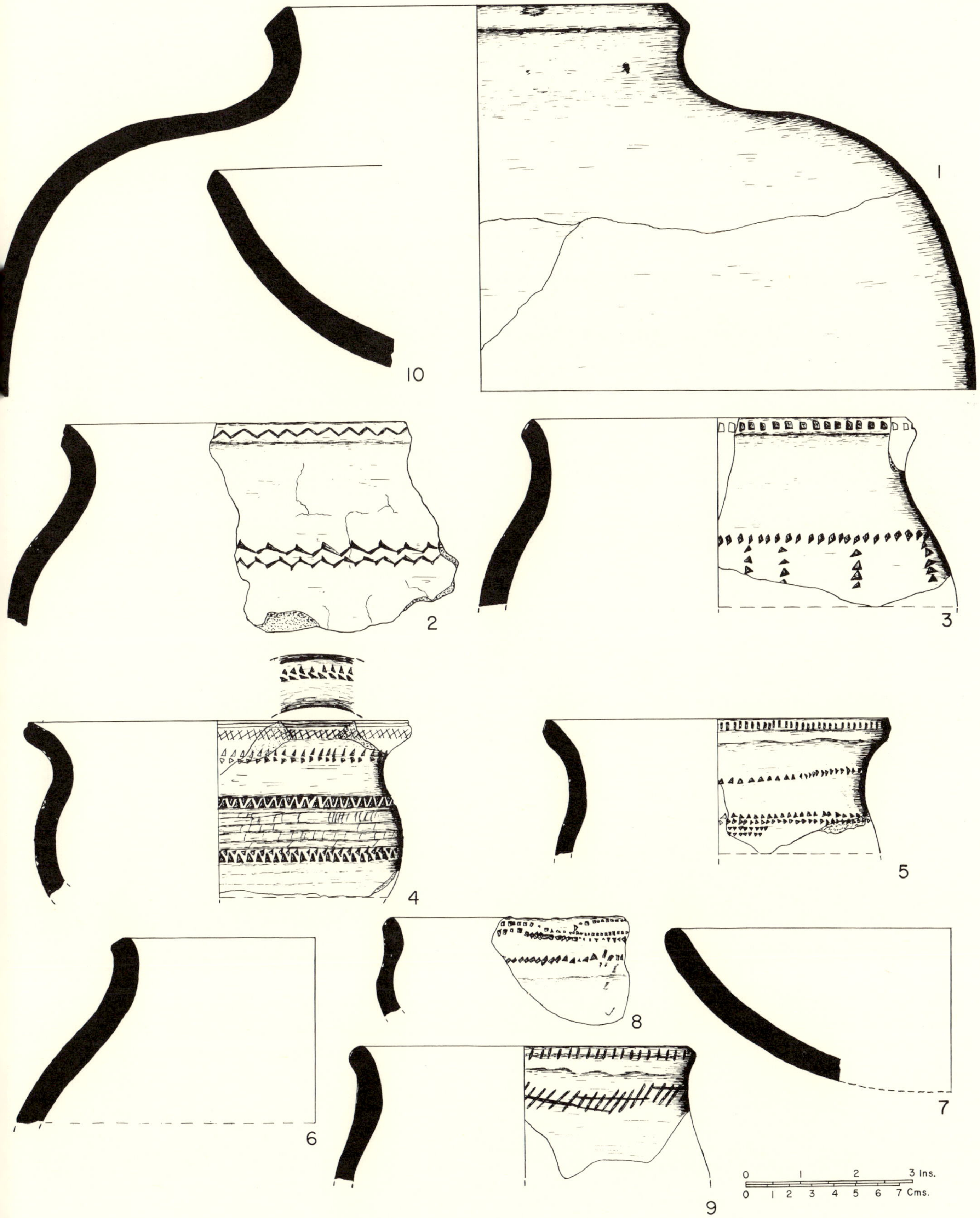
1
10
2
3
4
5
6
7
8
9
0 1 2 3 Ins.
0 1 2 3 4 5 6 7 Cms.

23 KALAMBO FALLS INDUSTRY: EARLY IRON AGE:
Site C, Complex 11

1 Large, undecorated shouldered pot with a bevelled and everted rim. Buff exterior colour. Rim diameter: 5·6 inches (14·25 cm); height (reconstructed): 13·5 inches (34·3 cm); maximum width: 13 inches (33 cm). C/63/139.

2 Large undecorated shouldered pot with a slightly everted rim. Buff exterior colour. Rim diameter: 6·8 inches (17 cm); height (reconstructed): *c.* 16 inches (40·75 cm); maximum width: 15 inches (38·25 cm). C/63/139.

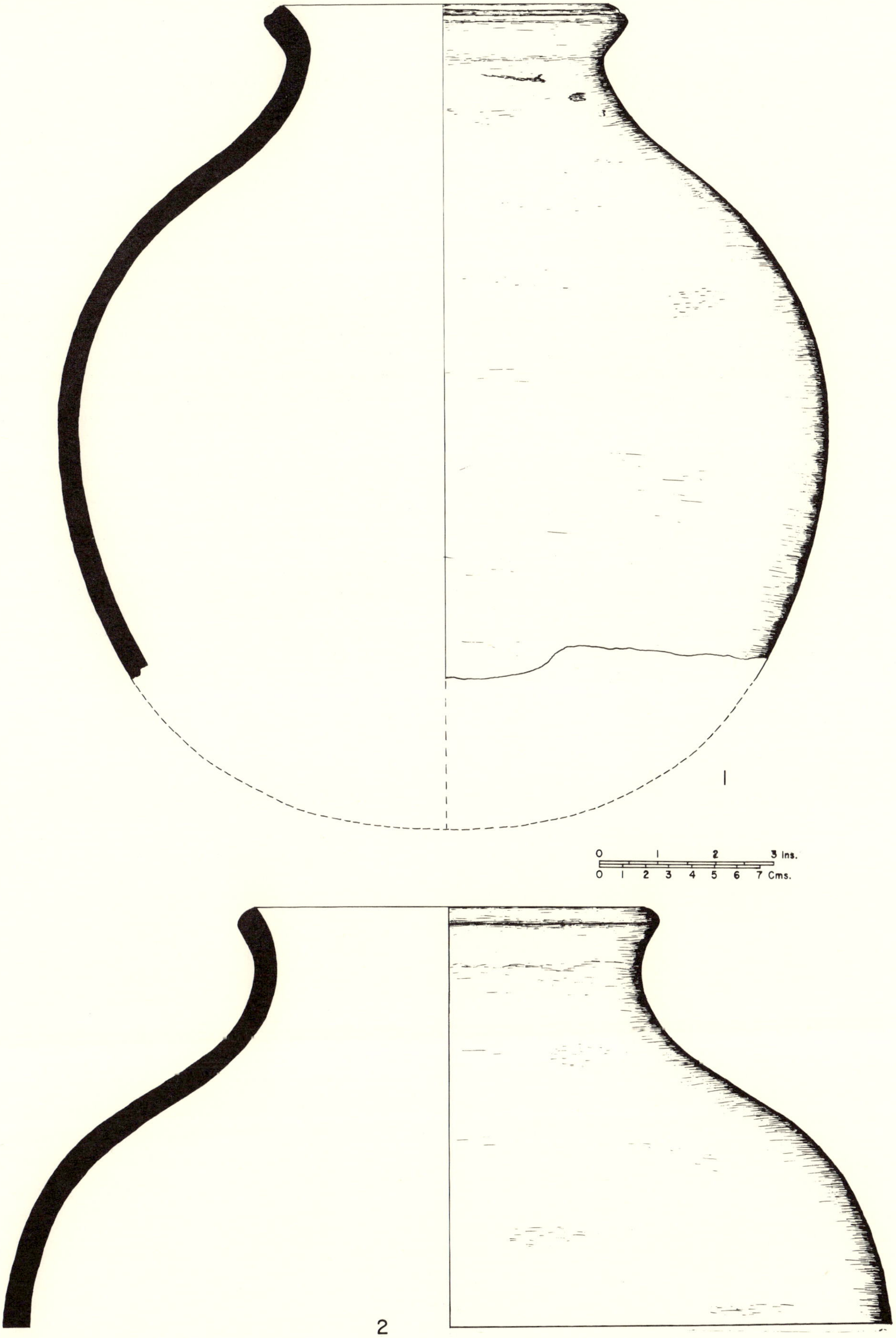
1
0 1 2 3 Ins.
0 1 2 3 4 5 6 7 Cms.
2

24 KALAMBO FALLS INDUSTRY: EARLY IRON AGE:

Site C, Complex 11

1 Rimsherd from a shouldered pot with a bevelled rim. A zone of bands of oblique comb-stamping and channelling on the rim. Buff exterior surface. Rim diameter (reconstructed): 6·3 inches (16 cm); height (reconstructed): 7·3 inches (18·5 cm); maximum width: 8·3 inches (21 cm). C/63/139.

2 Rimsherd from a shouldered pot with bevelled rim; below it a band of vertical impressions, a line of rectangular stamped decoration, and a band of channelling with an angular or circular motif. Pale red and black outside, red inside. Rim diameter (reconstructed): 5 inches (12·75 cm); height (reconstructed): 5·8 inches (14·75 cm); maximum width: 6·1 inches (15·5 cm). C/63/139.

3 Rimsherd from a shouldered pot with bevelled rim. Two bands of crude cross-hatched incision are separated by a channelled zone. Below them, a band of channelling with chevron motif. Buff and pale red colour. Rim diameter: 7·3 inches (18·5 cm); height (reconstructed): 8·8 inches (22·5 cm); maximum width: 9·1 inches (23·25 cm). C/63/139.

4 Rimsherd from a shouldered pot with fine, cross-hatched incision and channelled decoration. Buff and pale red colour. Rim diameter: 5·3 inches (13·5 cm); height (reconstructed): 4·3 inches (11 cm); maximum width: 6·0 inches (15·25 cm). C/63/139.

5 Rimsherd from an undecorated spheroidal bowl. Buff colour. Height: 3·7 inches (9·5 cm). C/63/139.

6 Rimsherd from a shouldered or nearly spherical pot with bevelled rim and two lines of stamping below the rim. Buff colour. Rim diameter: 5·7 inches (14·5 cm); maximum width: 10·8 inches (27·5 cm). C/63/139.

7 Rimsherd from a shallow bowl with bevelled rim. Buff exterior colour. Rim diameter (reconstructed): 11·7 inches (29·75 cm); height (reconstructed): 4·2 inches (10·75 cm). C/63/139.

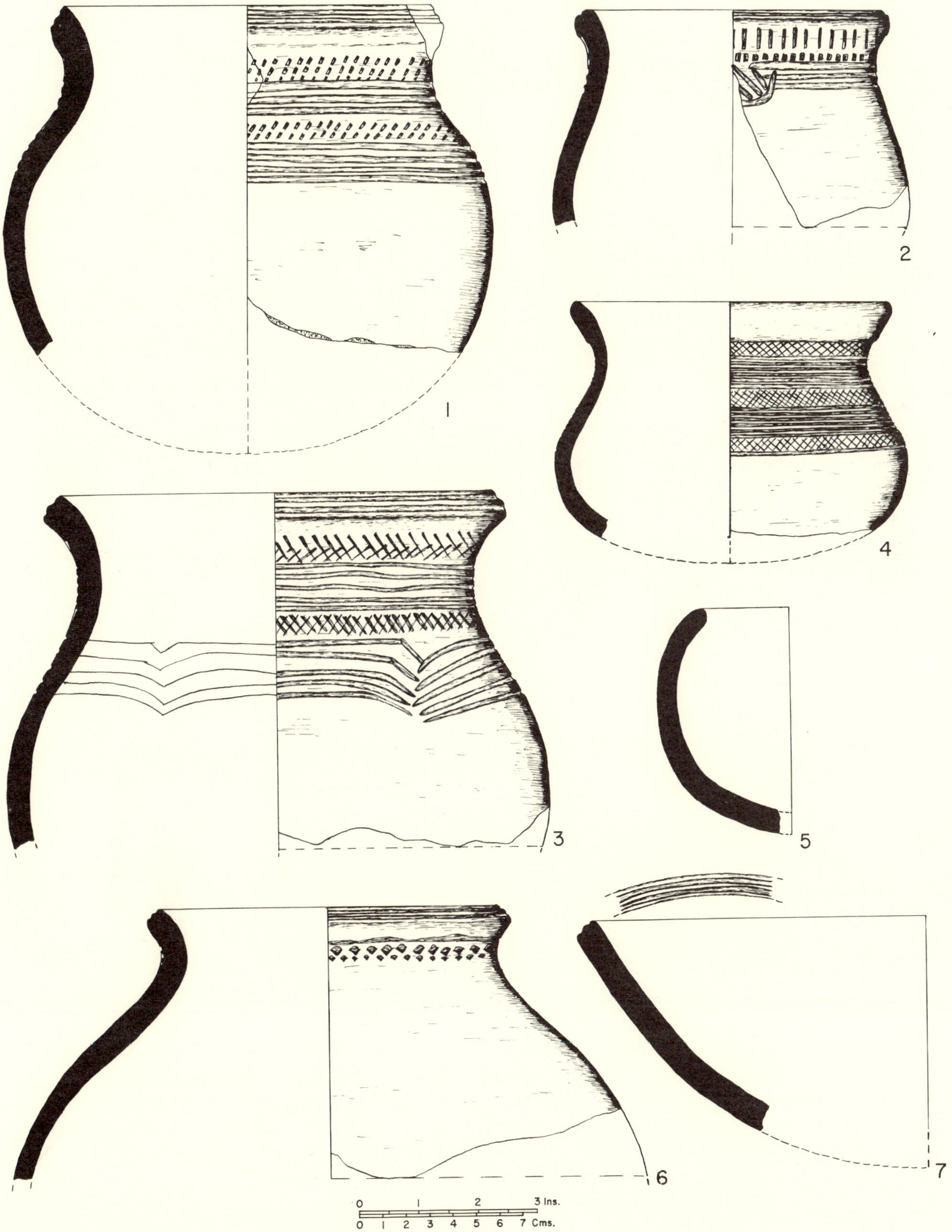

305

CKF

25 KALAMBO FALLS INDUSTRY: EARLY IRON AGE:

Site C, Complex 11

1 Large fragment of a shouldered pot with a bevelled rim. A line of criss-cross incision and a broad band of channelling on the neck. Reddish colour. Rim diameter (reconstructed): 7·3 inches (18·5 cm); maximum width: 9·6 inches (24·25 cm). C/63/139.

2 Rimsherd from a shouldered pot. A band of criss-cross incision on the neck, and a band of channelling on the shoulder with angular motif. Buff colour. Rim diameter (reconstructed): 8·7 inches (22·25 cm); maximum width (reconstructed): 10·8 inches (27·5 cm). C/63/139.

3 Rimsherd from an unidentified vessel with a broad band of channelling at the rim. Buff colour. C/63/139.

4 Rimsherd from an undecorated, shouldered pot. Buff colour. C/63/139.

5 Rimsherd from a shouldered pot with bevelled rim with everted profile. A band of comb-stamped chevrons on the rim itself. Reddish colour. C/63/139.

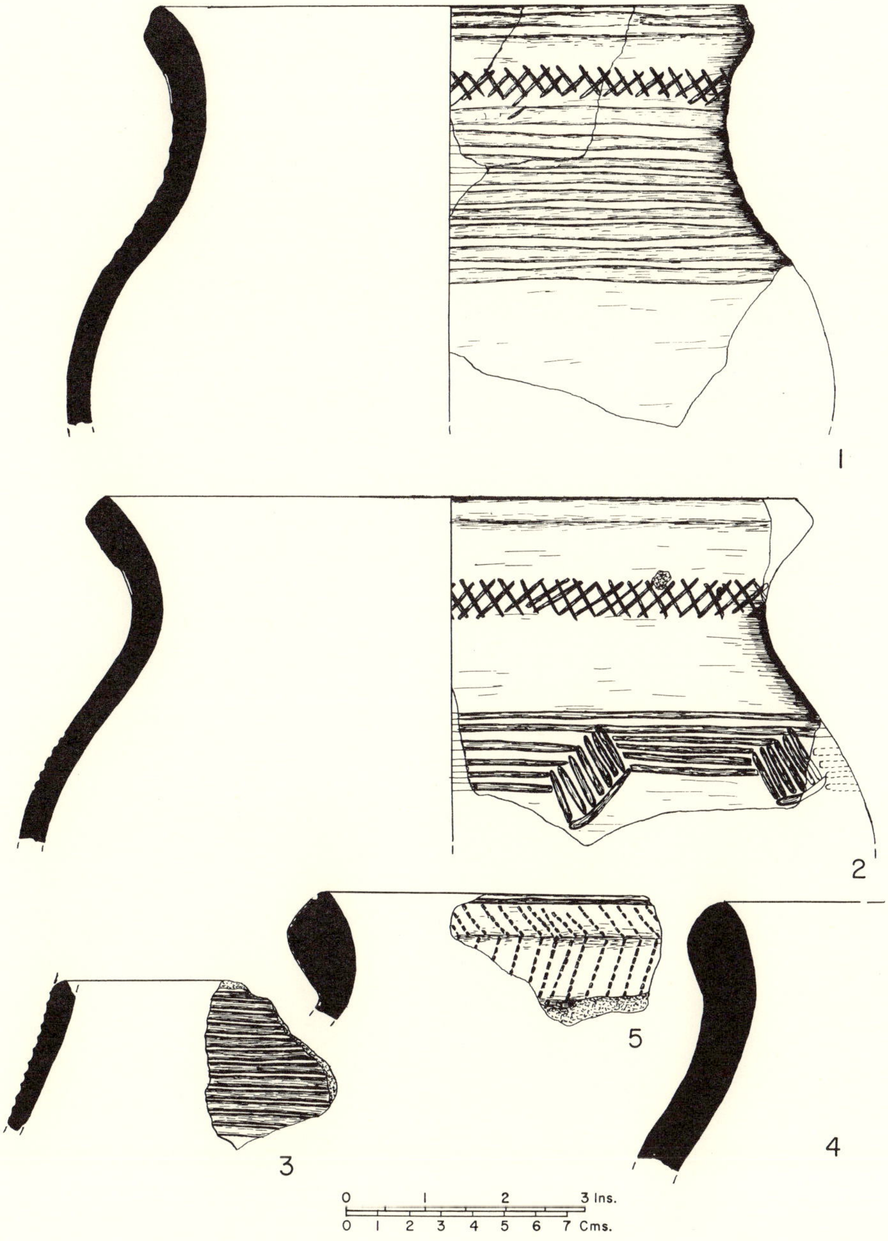
1
2
3
4
5
0 1 2 3 Ins.
0 1 2 3 4 5 6 7 Cms.

26 KALAMBO FALLS INDUSTRY: EARLY IRON AGE:
Site C, Complex 12

1 Rimsherd from a shouldered pot with a band of criss-cross incision immediately below the rim. A band of the same and of straight and wavy channelled lines at the shoulder. Buff colour. Rim diameter (reconstructed): 10·4 inches (26·5 cm); maximum width (reconstructed): 11·9 inches (30·25 cm). C/63/146.

2 Large fragment of a shouldered pot with a band of criss-cross incision on the shoulder and rim. Buff colour. Rim diameter (reconstructed): 8·6 inches (22 cm); maximum width (reconstructed): 9·2 inches (23·5 cm). C/63/146.

3 Rimsherd from a shouldered pot with a line of triangular impressions on the rim. Two lines of similar stampings are on the shoulder and panels of the same on the neck. Buff colour. Rim diameter (reconstructed): 9·9 inches (25·25 cm); maximum width (reconstructed): 11·8 inches (30 cm). C/63/146.

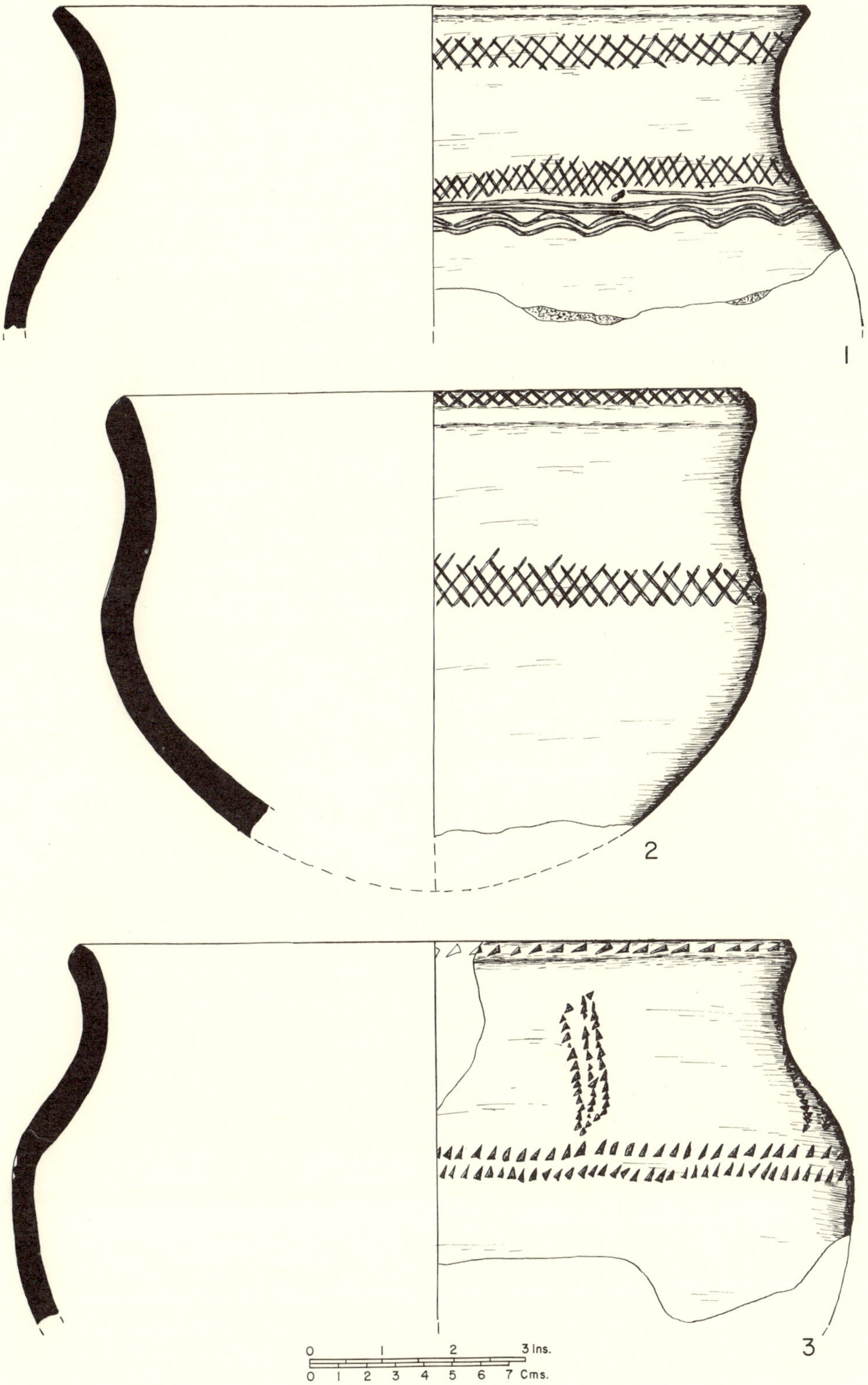
1
2
3
0 1 2 3 Ins.
0 1 2 3 4 5 6 7 Cms.

27 KALAMBO FALLS INDUSTRY: EARLY IRON AGE:

Site C, Complex 12

1 Rimsherd from a shouldered pot with zigzag, incised motif on the rim, a zone of irregular stamping below it, and four parallel, channelled lines on the shoulder. Buff colour. Rim diameter (reconstructed): 8·8 inches (22·5 cm); maximum width (reconstructed): 9·6 inches (24·25 cm). C/63/146.

2 Rimsherd from a shouldered pot with criss-cross incision on the rim, a line of stamping and an irregular channelled line below it. A crude 'false relief' effect at the shoulder, together with a zigzag stamped line. Buff colour. Rim diameter (reconstructed): 5·9 inches (15 cm); height (reconstructed): 5·1 inches (13 cm); maximum width (reconstructed): 7·2 inches (18·25 cm). C/63/146.

3, 5, 7 and 8. Undecorated shouldered pots. Buff or reddish colour. C/63/146.

4 Undecorated, hemispherical bowl fragment. Red colour. C/63/146.

6 Rimsherd from a deep, hemispherical bowl with a bevelled rim. Reddish colour. C/63/146.

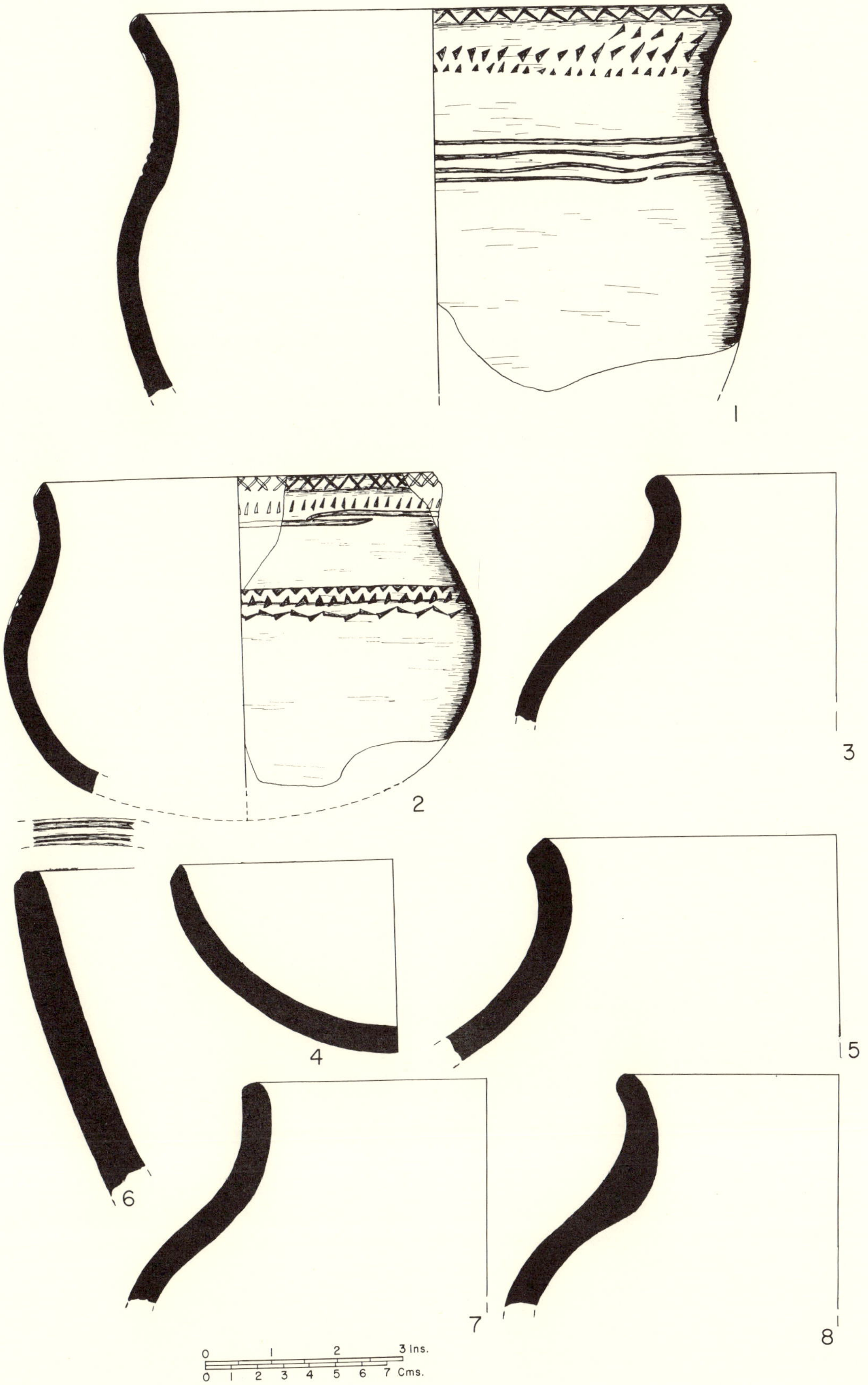
1
2
3
4
5
6
7
8
0 1 2 3 Ins.
0 1 2 3 4 5 6 7 Cms.

28 KALAMBO FALLS INDUSTRY: EARLY IRON AGE

Nos. 1–3, Site C, Complex 12; nos. 4, 5, Site C, River Face; no. 6, Site A.

1 Complete, undecorated, shouldered pot. Grey to buff in colour. Rim diameter: 5 inches (12·75 cm); height: 5·2 inches (13·25 cm); maximum width: 5·6 inches (14·25 cm). C/63/146.

2 Fragmentary spheroidal bowl with a 'nicked' rim and two lines of irregular stamping below it. Reddish colour. Rim diameter (reconstructed): 4·2 inches (10·75 cm); height (reconstructed): 5·4 inches (13·75 cm); maximum width: 7 inches (17·75 cm). C/63/146.

3 Rimsherd from an undecorated, shouldered pot. Buff colour. C/63/146.

4 Fragmentary tuyère or bellows pipe with slag adhering. Diameter: 1·2 inches (3 cm). Collapsed midden, River Face. C/63/4.

5 Fragmentary tapered tuyère pipe. Diameter at orifice: 1·5 inches (4 cm). Collapsed Midden, River Face. C/63/4.

6 Fragment of tuyère pipe. Diameter: 2·4 inches (6 cm). From A1 Site, 1956 at a depth of 10 feet 6 inches–11 feet (3·2–3·35 m). A1/43/56.

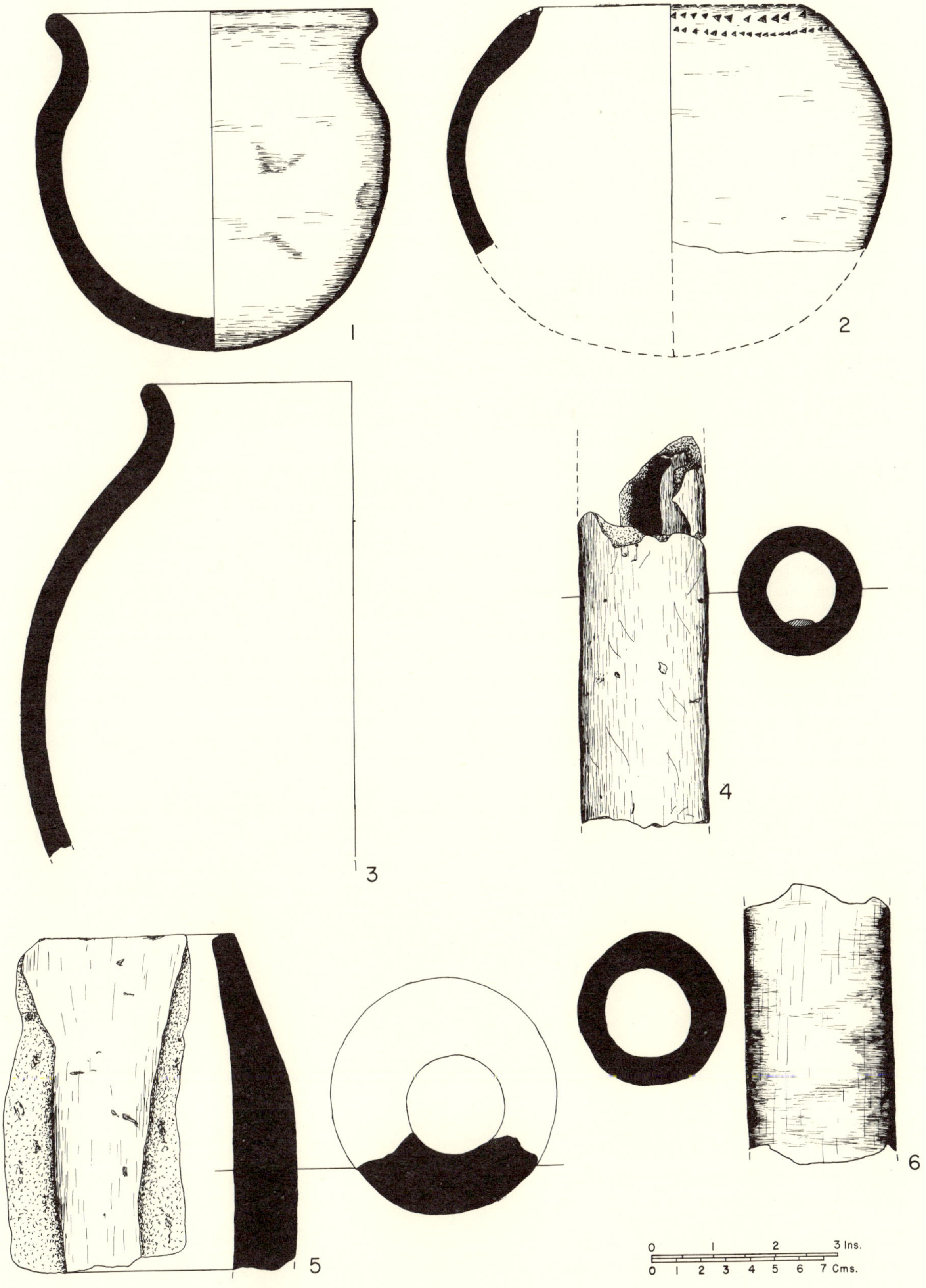
1
2
3
4
5
6
0 1 2 3 Ins.
0 1 2 3 4 5 6 7 Cms.

29 KALAMBO FALLS INDUSTRY: EARLY IRON AGE:

Site A, Excavation A7, 1966

1 Everted rimsherd from a shouldered pot with two lines of comb stamping on the lip, made with a stamp with round-ended teeth. Grey exterior colour; weathered. Thickness at base of rim 9 mm. CE/66:B3:0/6.

2 Sherd from the lower part of the neck of a large, shouldered pot. Decoration formed by five, narrow, grooved lines below several rows of similarly formed short, wavy lines. Dull red burnished exterior colour. Thickness 12 mm. CE/66:A3:6/1.0.

3 Rimsherd from a shouldered pot. The rim is square or flattened and decorated with two shallow parallel channels. Decoration immediately below the rim is formed by a band of oblique comb stamping. Grey exterior colour; weathered. Thickness at base of rim 10 mm. CE/66/A3:6/1.0.

4 Undecorated rimsherd from a shouldered pot. The rim has been squared with faint traces of narrow bevelling. Red brown burnished exterior colour. Thickness at base of rim 5 mm. CE/66:B3:6/1·0.

5 Undecorated sherds from a shouldered pot with straight neck and rounded rim; trace of a narrow, shallow, dragged line at the base of the rim. Dark grey to buff colour with traces of external and internal burnish. Some weathering. Thickness at base of rim 9 mm. CE/66:B3:6/1·0.

6 Rimsherd from shouldered pot with everted and rounded rim. Decoration below the rim consists of a band of oblique, parallel, incised lines. Red/brown colour. Very weathered. Thickness at base of rim 7 mm. CE/66:A1:1·0/1·5.

7 Rimsherds from large, shouldered pot with short, straight neck and rounded rim. Decoration, at the base of the rim, consists of three lines of punctate impressions made with a wedge shaped tool rather carelessly applied. Red exterior colour. Thickness at base of rim 11 mm. (From rubbish pit, depth 1 foot 5 inches to 2 feet 3 inches (43–68 cm).)

8 Sherd from a large pot or deep bowl with black burnished exterior colour and decoration of loops formed by three narrow, grooved lines. Thickness 10 mm. CE/66:B3:2·5–3·0.

9 Incomplete, small hemispherical bowl with thick rim-band, externally inclined; undecorated. Red/brown exterior and interior colour. Little or no attempt to smooth either surface, the interior preserving what are probably dragged finger impressions. Reconstructed dimensions: internal diameter at rim 64 mm; height 71 mm; maximum width 84 mm. Thickness below rim 6 mm, at base *c.* 15 mm; some weathering. CE/66:B3:2·5–3·0.

10 Rimsherd from large, undecorated, shouldered pot. Straight, squared rim with trace of shallow, narrow grooving on outer edge. Red/brown ?burnished exterior. Thickness at base of rim 9 mm. CE/66:A3: 2·5–3·0.

11 Rimsherd from large, undecorated, shouldered pot. Gently everted and rounded rim with trace of shallow, narrow grooving on outer edge. Red/brown exterior colour. Thickness at base of rim 5 mm. CE/66:B3: 2·5–3·0.

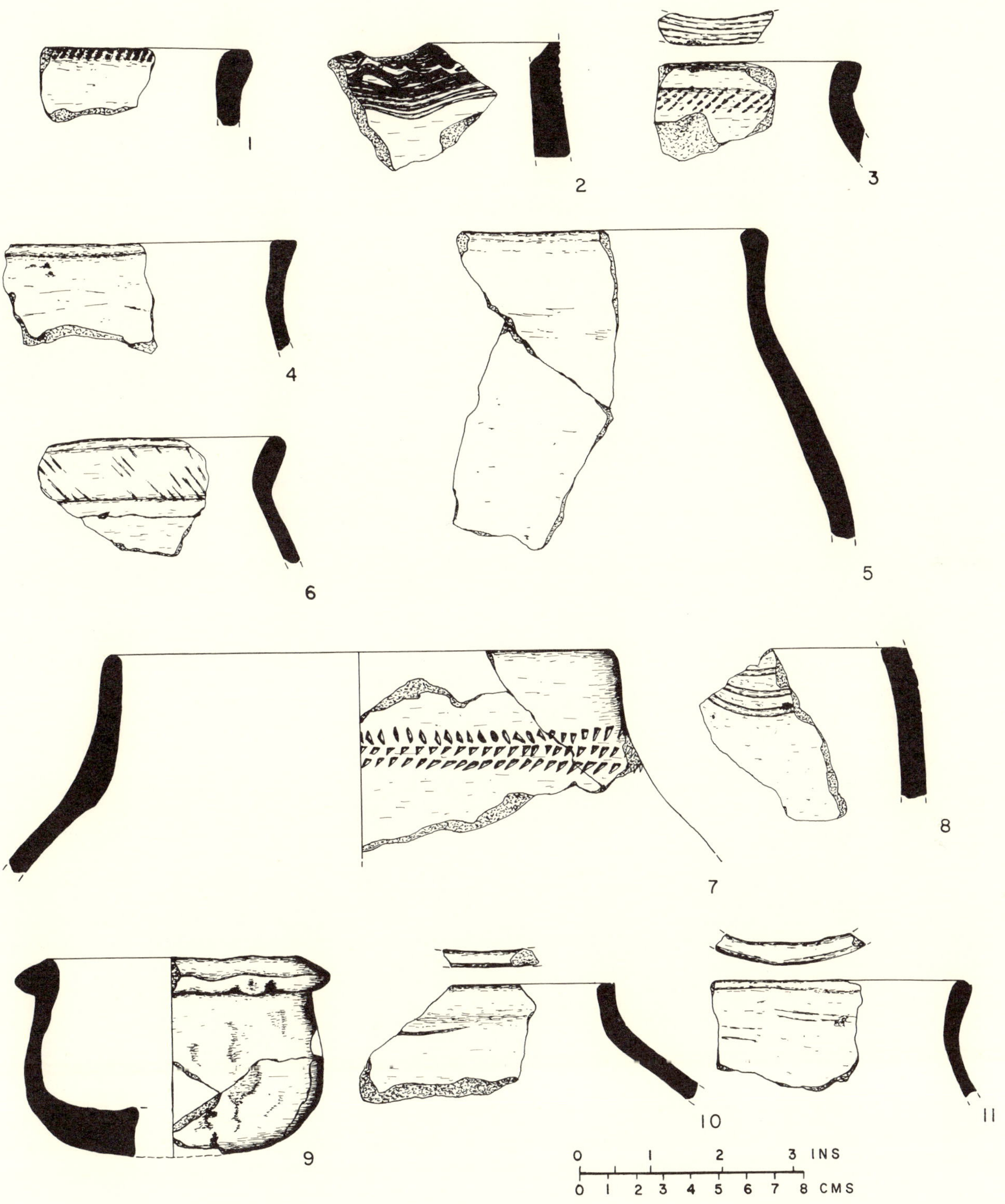
1
2
3
4
5
6
7
8
9
10
11
0 1 2 3 INS
0 1 2 3 4 5 6 7 8 CMS

30 LUNGU AND EARLY IRON AGE KALAMBO FALLS INDUSTRY–WORKED IRON, COPPER AND BEADS

Nos. 1–3: *Lungu*

1 Triangular arrowhead with tang formed by twisting a length of iron rod. When in use, poison is attached to the tang. Found in surface soil at Site B2 in 1963.

2 Oblate trade bead of violet blue, translucent glass of nineteenth century European origin. Diameter: 9 mm. D2/1956. 0·9 inches (0·23 cm).

3 Annular trade bead of dark blue translucent wound glass of nineteenth century European origin. Diameter: 1·4 cm. A4/1959. B/22–21. 1 foot 6 inches–2 feet (45·75–61·0 cm).

Nos. 4–18: *Kalambo Falls Industry*

4 Fragment of arm or leg ring formed by bending a thin, sub-rectangular sectioned iron rod. Estimated internal diameter: 4·6 cm. C/63/114. From shaft of Complex No. 5. Site C settlement.

5 Fragment of arm or leg ring formed in the same way as 4 above. Estimated internal diameter: 7·8 cm. C/63/116. From shaft of Complex No. 8. Site C settlement.

6 Arm or leg ring of thin copper rod with semicircular section formed by bending with the ends left unjoined. Estimated diameter: 6–8 cm. From red hillwash soil A4/1959 in grid square B/49. 2 feet–2 feet 6 inches (61·0–76·25 cm).

7 Finger or toe ring of sub-rectangular iron strip bent into a circle with the ends left unjoined. Diameter: 2·2 cm. C/63/116. From shaft of Complex No. 8. Site C settlement.

8 Half a finger or toe ring of thin sub-rectangular iron strip. Estimated diameter: 2 cm. C/63/116. From shaft of Complex No. 8. Site C settlement.

9 Tang or piece of circular sectioned iron rod. Length: 6·6 cm; diameter: 0·6 cm. D2/1956. 0–2 feet (0–61 cm) stepping back.

10 Lower, pointed, end of a spike anvil or heavy iron spear. Length: 5·6 cm; average diameter: 1·3 cm. A1/1956. From clays 9–12 feet (2·74–3·66 m) stepping back.

11 Fragment of a thin iron blade 4·3 cm long and 2·0 cm wide. C/63/114. From shaft of Complex No. 5. Site C settlement.

12 Arrowhead (?) made from a circular sectioned piece of iron flattened at the point and sharpened on one edge. Presumably this type of head was used in connection with poison. Length: 17·4 cm; average diameter: 0·5 cm. C/63/139. From shaft of Complex No. 11. Site C settlement.

13 Barbless, leaf shaped iron arrowhead. Length: 10·6 cm; width of head: 1·8 cm. C/63/116. From the shaft of Complex No. 8. Site C settlement.

14 Incomplete tang of iron. Length: 8·5 cm. C/63/113. From shaft of Complex No. 4. Site C settlement.

15 Incomplete tang of iron. Length: 6·5 cm. C/63/139. From shaft of Complex No. 11. Site C settlement.

16 Fragment from a thin iron blade preserving part of one concave edge. Length: 6·8 cm. C/63/114. From shaft of Complex No. 5. Site C settlement.

17 Leaf shaped spearhead or knife blade of iron with simple tang (point missing). No midrib. Length of surviving section of blade: 15·5 cm; width of blade: 3·7 cm. C/63/27. C1, 1 foot 6 inches–3 feet (45·75–91·5 cm). From Site C settlement midden.

18 Incomplete flat blade, tanged and asymmetric without midrib. Possibly an adze or axe blade. Existing length 114 mm. Estimated maximum breadth of blade at cutting edge 44 mm. Maximum thickness of tang 15·5 mm. Found in collapsed block of midden deposit, Site C, 1966.

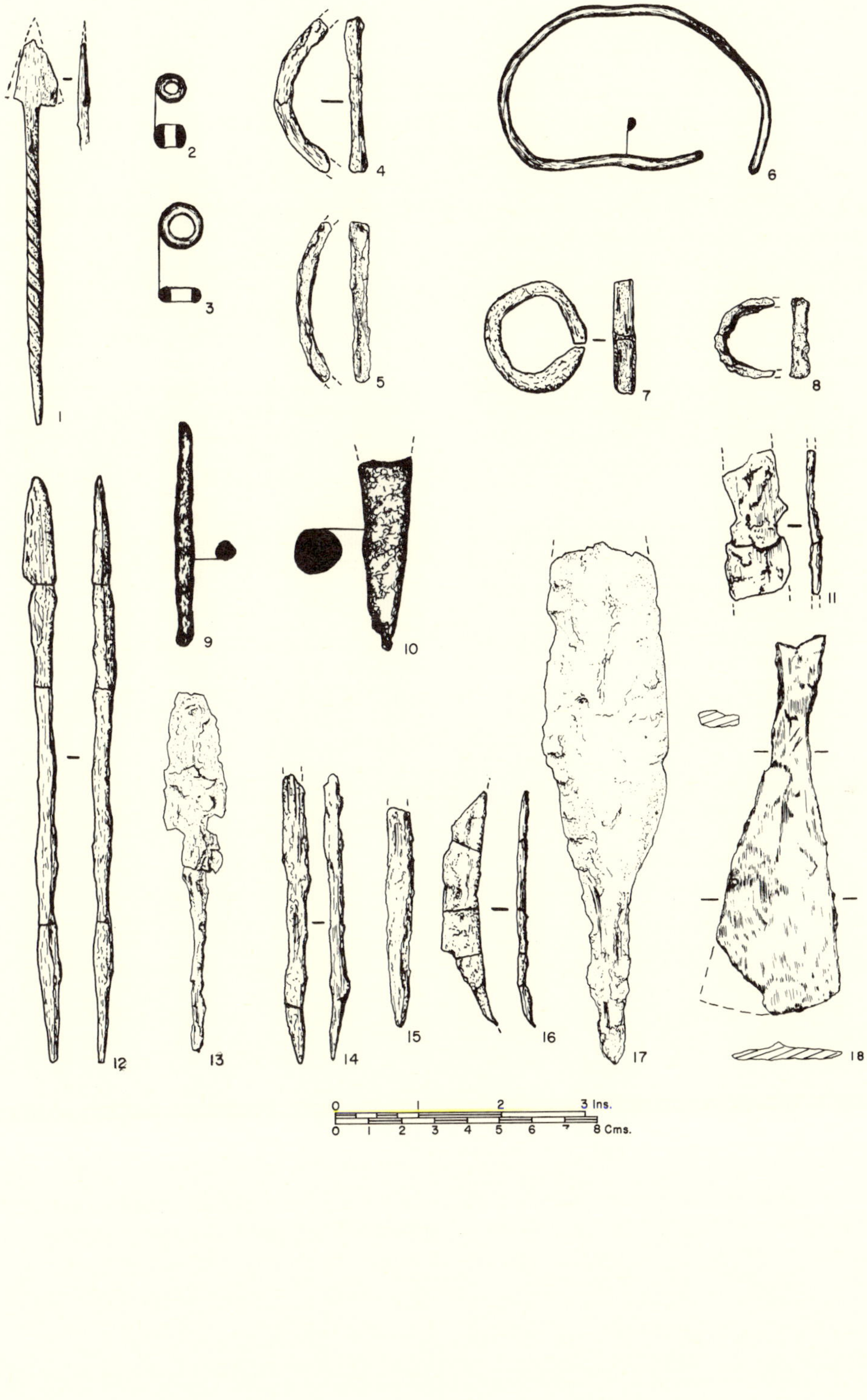
1
2
3
4
5
6
7
8
9
10
11
12
13
14
15
16
17
18
0 1 2 3 Ins.
0 1 2 3 4 5 6 7 8 Cms.

31 UTILIZED STONE ARTIFACTS ASSOCIATED WITH THE EARLY IRON AGE KALAMBO FALLS INDUSTRY

From the settlement midden, Site C, 1963. All fresh and unpatinated.

1 Short, irregular end flake of hard quartzite with utilized notch. C/63/27. C1, 1 foot 6 inches–3 feet (45·75–91·5 cm).

2 Long quadrilateral spall of chert, utilized down one edge and showing some shallow serration. C/63/19. G2, 0–1 foot 6 inches (0–45·75 cm).

3 Short quadrilateral end flake of chert with one straight, serrated edge. Probably a Kaposwa Industry artifact reused. C/63/19. G2. 0–1 foot 6 inches (0–45·75 cm).

4 Irregular chunk of hard quartzite with sub-triangular section. The pointed end and main ridge between the fracture planes on the upper face have been rubbed smooth by use. C/63/31. D2. 1 foot 6 inches–3 feet (45·75–91·5 cm).

5 Chopping tool on an irregular, fire fractured, chunk of hard quartzite; the convex edge shows minute percussion scars, blunting and bruising due to use. C/63/18. G1. 0–1 foot 6 inches (0–45·75 cm).

6 Flat irregular chunk of fire fractured quartzite bruised from utilization along the edges. C/63/19. G2. 0–1 foot 6 inches (0–45·75 cm).

7 Irregular end-struck flake of hard quartzite. The convex edge is blunted and scarred from utilization. C/63/31. D2. 1 foot 6 inches–3 feet (45·75–91·5 cm).

8 Heat spall of hard quartzite utilized along one concave edge. C/63/19. G2. 0–1 foot 6 inches (0–45·75 cm).

9 Irregular side flake of hard quartzite showing utilization of both edges. C/63/57. D4. 1 foot 6 inches–2 feet (45·75–61 cm).

10 Small lump of haematite with one rubbed facet showing fine striations resulting from grinding for pigment. C/63/87. F3. 1 foot 6 inches–2 feet (45·75–61·0 cm).

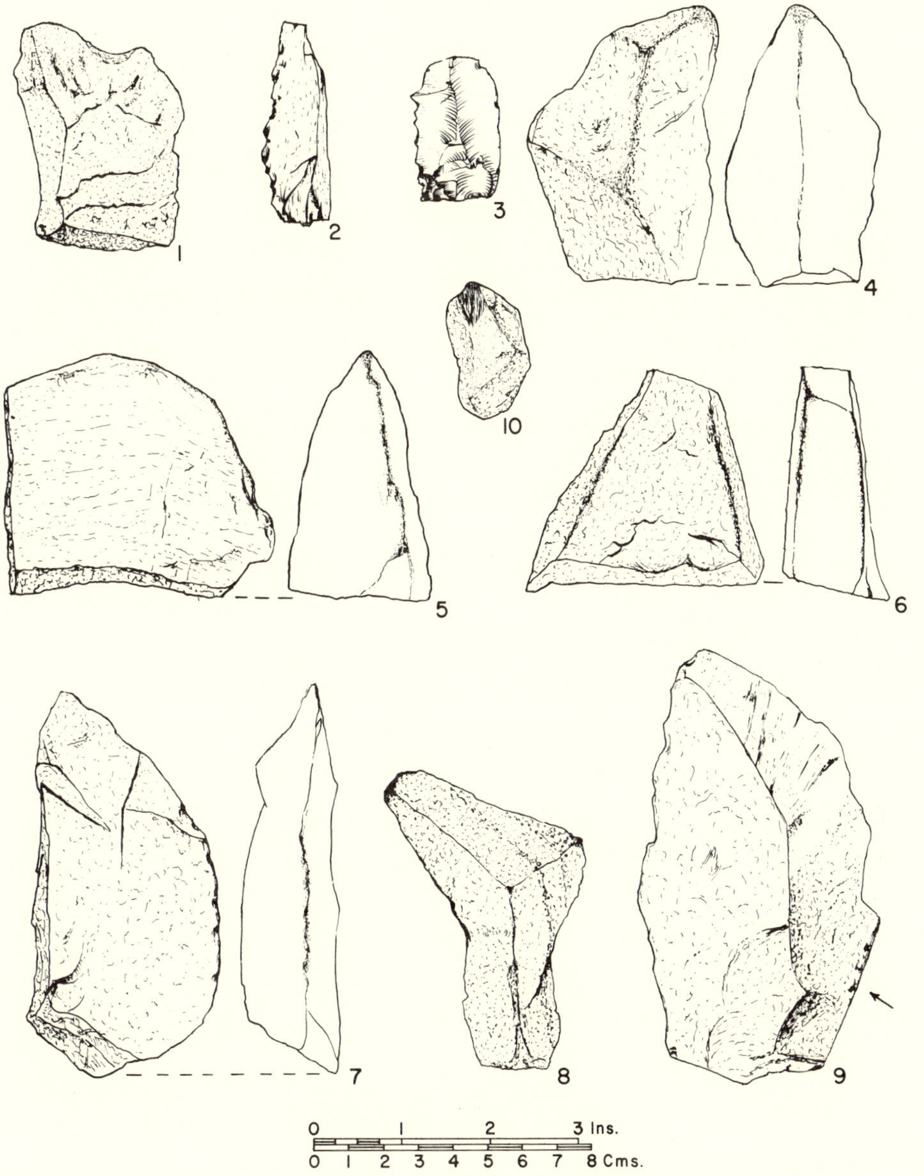

1
2
3
4
10
5
6
7
8
9
0 1 2 3 Ins.
0 1 2 3 4 5 6 7 8 Cms.

32 WORKED AND UTILIZED STONE ARTIFACTS ASSOCIATED WITH THE EARLY IRON AGE KALAMBO FALLS INDUSTRY

From the clays of the Chiungu Member, Sites A and B.

1 Irregular, end-struck flake of patinated chert with plain platform that has been utilized or re-utilized in Early Iron Age times. Retouched bifacially on one straight edge and unifacially on one concave edge and at the butt to form a scraping tool. Fresh. A/54/D.3/1956. 12 feet–12 feet 6 inches (3·66–3·81 m) in clays.

2 Thick chunk of hard quartzite trimmed to a notch and utilized on one edge. Fresh. B2/70/59. 4 feet–4 feet 9 inches (1·22–1·45 m) in clays.

3 Patinated tabular chunk of chert retrimmed down one edge by steep retouch to form a straight scraping edge. Fresh. A1/44/1956. 5–6 feet (1·52–1·83 m) in clays.

4 Irregular flake fragment or heat spall of hard quartzite trimmed down one edge to form a scraper. Blunt angle of retouch. Fresh. B1/29/1956. 6 feet–7 feet (1·83–2·13 m) in clays.

5 Flake fragment of indurated chert with utilized edge and end. Fresh. A4/16/59. 1 foot–1 foot 6 inches (30·5–45·75 cm) in hill wash soil.

6 Irregular chunk of indurated chert with steep trimming and battering along two irregular edges and the butt and with a steeply trimmed notch at the upper end. Fresh. A1/1956. In clays.

7 Patinated and weathered chunk of chert with triangular section. Notched and utilized along both edges and across the end. Fresh. B1/3/1956. 1 foot–2 feet (30·5–61·0 cm) in clays.

8 Spheroid cobble of hard sandstone with a shallow groove worn in the top by use as a rubber on some round sectioned object. The edges of the groove also show polishing due to use. Fresh. A1/41/1956. 10 feet–10 feet 6 inches (3·05–3·20 m) in clays.

9 Irregular chunk of chert with two steeply trimmed edges. Fresh. B1/23/56. 1–2 feet (30·5–61 cm) in sandy clays.

10 Flat, spherical pebble of hard quartzite, probably used for burnishing. A1/55/1956. 13–14 feet (3·96–4·27 m) in gritty clays.

11 Elongate pebble used at both ends as a hammer stone; probably also a burnisher. B2/6/59. Surface of Early Iron Age bank.

12 Irregular block of hard quartzite roughly square in section and crudely split on all four faces. The lower end has been worked by rotating to form a smooth pestle end, probably for fine grinding of some vegetable product. The upper end has been similarly used but is not so smooth. One face shows that the specimen was also used as a rubber. Perhaps a snuff, relish or pigment grinder. Fresh. A3/3/56. 1 foot 6 inches–2 feet (45·75–61 cm) in sandy soil over clays.

13 Flat, triangular fragment of haematite with rubbed faces and edges showing striation in some places. Presumably used for pigment. Fresh. D2/0/56. 0–9 inches (0–23 cm) in sandy soil.

14 Small rubber made from a flat pebble of hard quartzite used as a hammer stone at one end and perhaps also employed for burnishing. A4/17/59. 1 foot–1 foot 6 inches (30·5–45·75 cm) in sand of Early Iron Age bank.

15 Spherical grindstone sharpener made from dolerite. Well pecked and smoothed surface. B2/5/59. Surface of Early Iron Age bank.

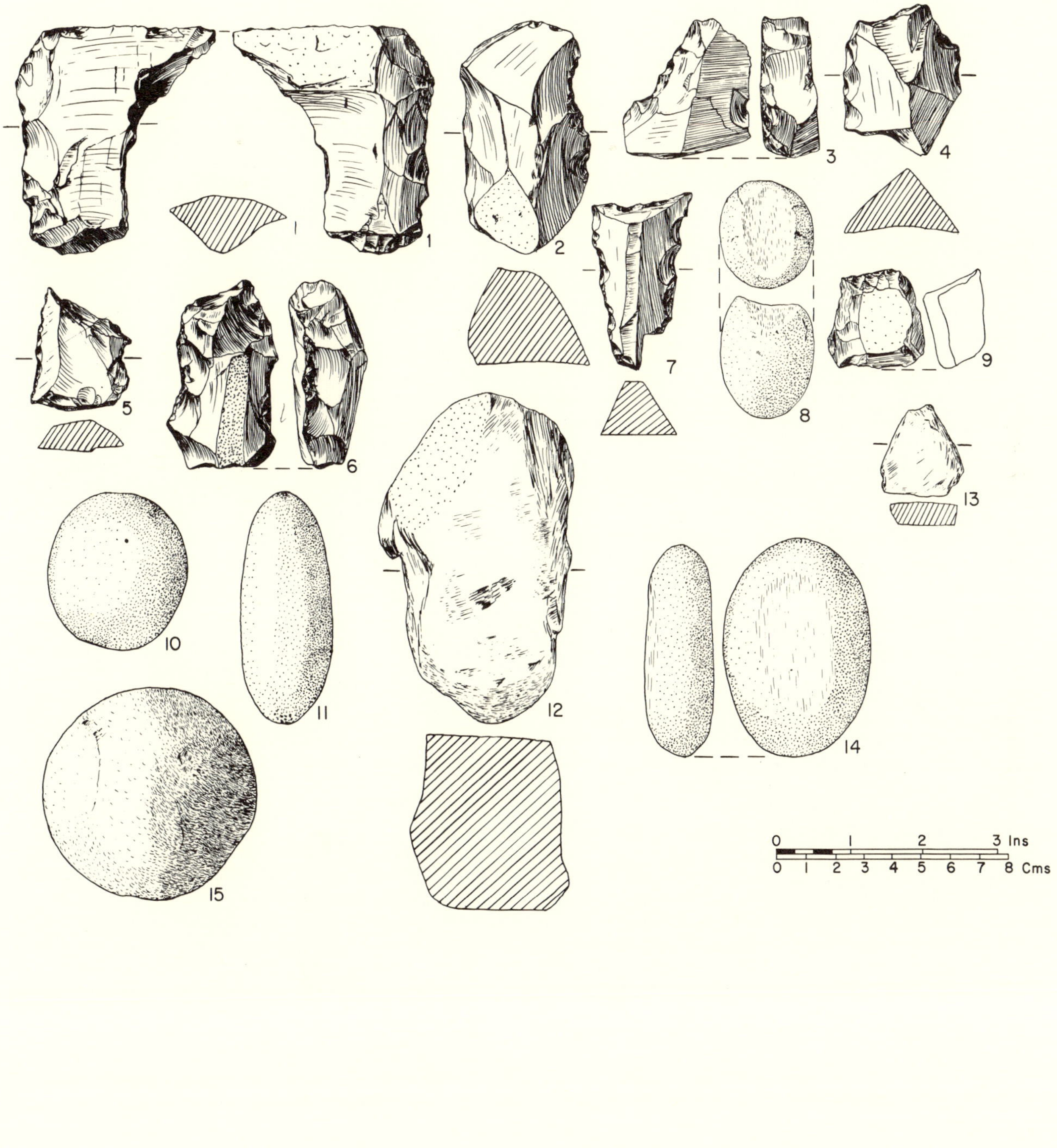
1
2
3
4
5
6
7
8
9
10
11
12
13
14
15
0 1 2 3 Ins
0 1 2 3 4 5 6 7 8 Cms

33 MICROLITHIC AND LARGER STONE TOOLS OF THE KAPOSWA INDUSTRY

From the Chiungu Member clays associated with Kalambo Falls Industry pottery.
From Sites A and B except no. 24 from Site C, 1966.

1 Chunky, prismatic core of chert with two plain platforms at right angles for the removal of short quadrilateral and irregular flakes. Fresh. B2/76/59.

2 Single, plain platformed, pyramidal-type core of chert for microlithic blades and flakes. Platform edge shows utilization or preparation for punch. Fresh. A1/43.

3 Single, plain platformed, pyramidal-type core of chert for microlithic blades. Platform edge prepared for punch or utilized. Fresh. A/9/59.

4 Chunky, prismatic, bipolar core of chert with platforms at opposite ends in the same plane. For micro-flakes and blades. Fresh. B/18/59.

5 Single, plain platformed, pyramidal core of chert for microlithic flakes and blades. Edge of platform prepared or possibly utilized. Fresh. A/14/59.

6 Short, irregular, end-struck flake of hard quartzite with plain, inclined platform, possibly utilized. Fresh. A/14/59.

7 Short quadrilateral end-struck flake of chert with narrow, restricted, plain platform. Distal retouch on one lateral edge. Reddened – possibly from fire. Fresh. B/22/59.

8 Short quadrilateral, end-struck flake of chert. Bulb and platform removed and marginal retouch and utilization at both ends and down one edge. Fresh. B/5/59.

9 Short quadrilateral end-struck flake of chert with narrow, restricted, plain striking platform and one utilized lateral edge. Fresh. B/22/56.

10 Small, irregular end flake with no bulb or platform. Retouched on one edge. Fresh. A1/51/b/4.

11 Dihedral (angled) burin on an irregular, end-struck flake with plain, inclined platform. Fresh. B/2/56.

12 and 13 Micro-blades in chert. Fresh. A1/48 and A1/41.

14 Triangular sectioned blade of chert, distally trimmed from the ventral face by steep backing. Fresh. D2/3/56.

15 Chert lunate with steep, unifacial backing for half the length of the convex edge. Fresh. B/4/59.

16 Straight backed microlith (lower tip broken) of chert. Fresh. B/11.

17 Chert trapeze made from a section of blade with normal backing. Fresh. B/24.

18 Chert lunate backed from both faces. Fresh. A/14/59.

19 Proto-biconical core with steep, marginal retouch forming a semi-circular core scraper. Fresh. D2/3/56.

20 Oval cobble of hard quartzite showing pitting on both flat faces perhaps from use as an anvil. One face shows possible artificial smoothing. Fresh. A/17/59.

21 Thick flake of hard quartzite with plain, inclined platform and broken distal end. Edges show notching and utilization. Fresh. A/19/59.

22 Half a flat bored stone made of mudstone. Both faces of the tool are uneven but have been reduced by rubbing. Little attempt appears to have been made to round that part of the circumference that remains and two notches have been subsequently worked on the dorsal face to form a blunt nose – presumably after the specimen had been broken. The bore is hour-glass and shows fine vertical striations. The probable external diameter of the stone was 12·5 cm and the thickness 7·4–4·4 cm. The maximum diameter of the bore is 4·5 cm and the minimum diameter of the bore 3·0 cm. The broken edges are very little abraded for such a soft stone. Some ferruginous incrustation on the ventral face suggests that it is not impossible that the specimen could be derived in the first instance from the ferruginous surface of Rubble IA which yielded another bored stone fragment *in situ*. It is, however, more likely to have come from the Kaposwa Industry horizon at the top of the 30 foot (9·1 m) terrace. B/14/56.

23 Circular chopper made from a cobble of hard quartzite. The bifacially trimmed edges show battering and utilization in several places. Fresh. A/15/59.

24 Flat, sub-rectangular bored stone with hour-glass perforation. An attempt has been made to produce a more regular shape with percussion flaking and battering round the circumference. Measurements 111 × 82 × 32 mm. Maximum diameter of bore 45 mm and minimum diameter 16 mm. Mudstone. Found in 1966 in collapsed talus on the cliff slope at Site C. Believed to be derived from the Kaposwa Industry occupation floor at the top of the cliff.

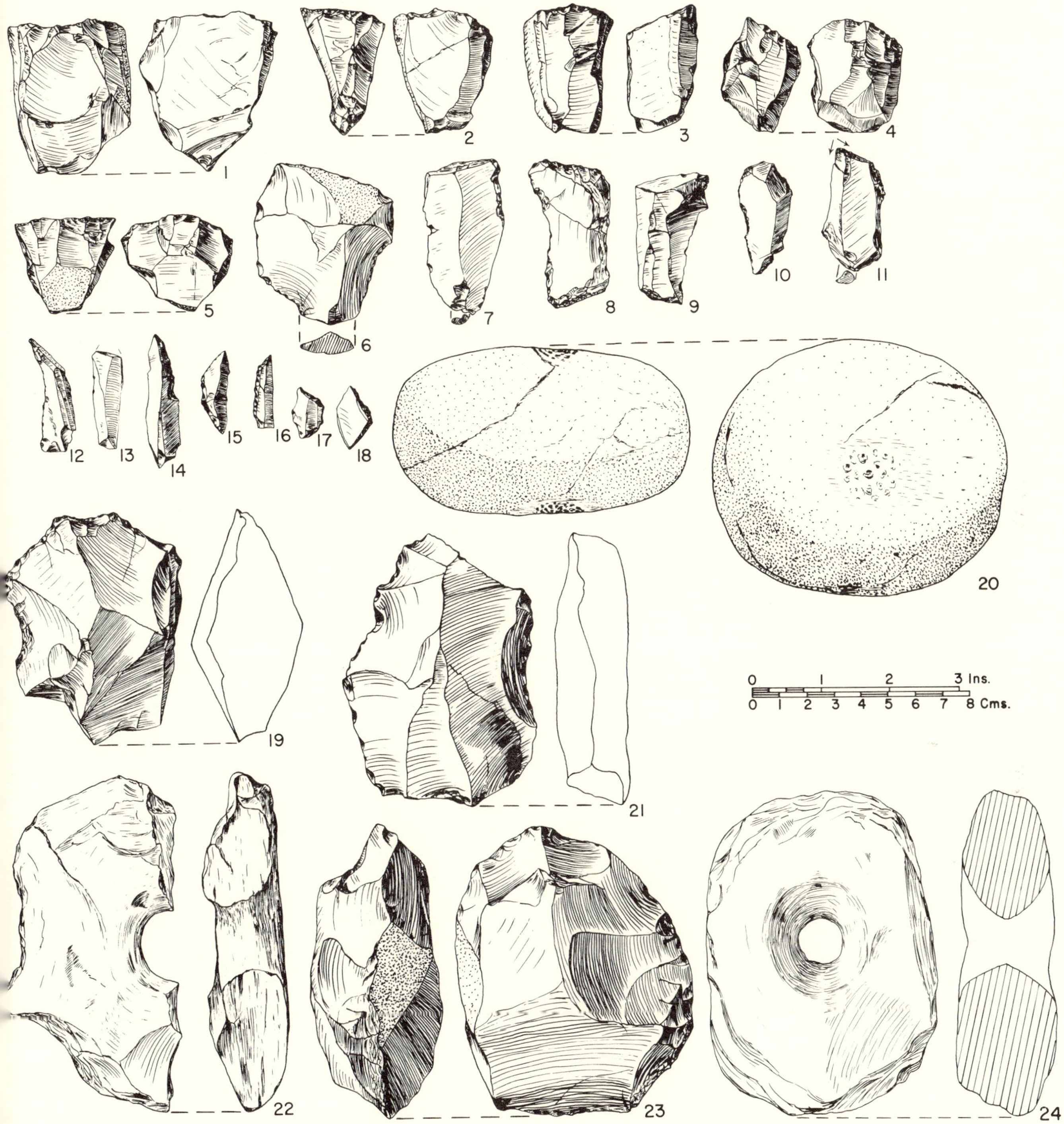
1
2
3
4
5
6
7
8
9
10
11
12
13
14
15
16
17
18
19
20
21
22
23
24
0 1 2 3 Ins.
0 1 2 3 4 5 6 7 8 Cms.

34 LARGE TOOLS FROM THE KAPOSWA INDUSTRY OCCUPATION FLOOR

Site C, 1963, except no. 2 which was found derived in the overlying Iron Age Layer.
All fresh unless otherwise stated.

1 Edge ground axe made from a large side-flake of dolerite which has first been shaped by percussion. Only the working edge of the specimen shows polish. Weathered with ochreous brown patina. C/63/131. 3 feet 6 inches–4 feet (1·06–1·22 m). 160 × 73 × 48 mm.

2 Half an edge ground axe made from a fragment of dolerite flaked by percussion prior to grinding and polishing. This specimen was associated with the pot and potsherds of Complex No. 1 but it is believed to have been derived from the underlying Later Stone Age horizon. C/63/25.B1. 2 feet 8 inches (81·25 cm).

3 The finely polished working end of a ground and polished axe in dolerite. Weathered and with ochreous brown patina. C/63/160. D6. 3 feet 6 inches–4 feet (1·06–1·22 m).

4 Ground and polished axe or adze of dolerite. Elongate ovate in plan form with thick butt. Made from a pebble which was reduced by percussion flaking on both faces before polishing. Asymmetric edge profile. C/63/163. F4. 3 feet 6 inches–4 feet (1·06–1·22 m). 153 × 85 × 45 mm.

5 Broken percussion flaked axe in dolerite. The upper working end is missing and may, therefore, have been ground and polished. Weathered with ochreous brown patina. C/63/151. F6. 3 feet 6 inches–4 feet (1·06–1·22 m).

6 Combined rubber and dimple-scarred anvil in hard quartzite. Three rubbing faces show striation and smoothing and two show dimple scarring. C/63/130. F1. 3 feet 6 inches–4 feet (1·06–1·22 m).

7 Dimple-scarred anvil on a sub-rectangular pebble of hard quartzite. Shows scarring in five places. Also used as a rubber on one face. C/63/128. F3. 3 feet 6 inches–4 feet (1·06–1·22 m).

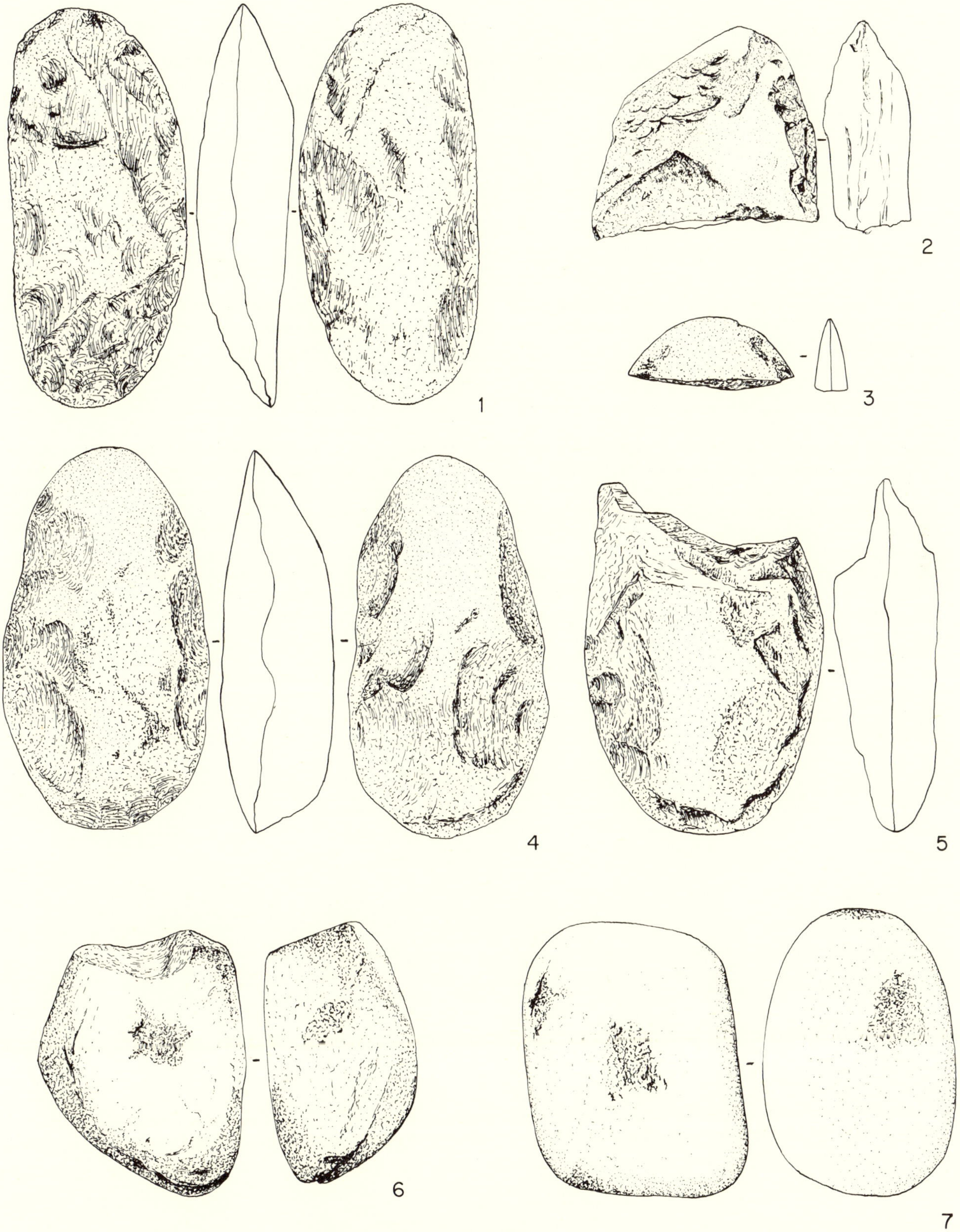
1
2
3
4
5
6
7
0 1 2 3 Ins.
0 1 2 3 4 5 6 7 8 Cms.

35 LARGE TOOLS FROM THE KAPOSWA INDUSTRY OCCUPATION FLOOR

Site C, 1963. All fresh unless otherwise stated.

1 Pestle stone on a long, rectangular pebble of chert, used at both ends. C/63/138. G2. 3 feet 6 inches–4 feet (1·06–1·22 m).

2 Abrader. Flat, sub-rectangular sectioned fragment of sandy quartzite. The straight edge on one end is rubbed and abraded by use on both faces. C/63/162. F2. 3 feet 6 inches–4 feet (1·06–1·22 m).

3 Abrader. Irregular chunk of sandy quartzite from a large cobble. One end has been rubbed and abraded on both faces and the straight ridge on the dorsal face formed by the intersection of a flake scar and cortex shows similar utilization. C/63/125. D6. 3 feet–3 feet 6 inches (91·5 cm–1·06 m).

4 Hammerstone made on a pebble of hard quartzite bruised and battered over one end. One face shows use for rubbing. C/63/66. E1. 3 feet–3 feet 6 inches (91·5 cm–1·06 m).

5 Dimple-scarred anvil on a cylindrical pebble of hard quartzite. Dimple scarring occurs on three faces and both ends are well bruised and battered by hammering. C/63/137. H1. 3 feet 6 inches–4 feet (1·06–1·22 m).

6 Oval pebble of semi-crystalline quartz used as an edge-type anvil. One directional battering and flaking from the upper face extend round most of the circumference. C/63/39. C2. 4 feet (1·22 m).

7 Chunk of chert. The lower end has been worked by steep retouch to form an end scraper. The upper end is bifacially retouched forming a chopper edge. C/63/132. G1. 3 feet 6 inches–4 feet (1·06–1·22 m).

8 Side chopper made from a rolled flake or weathered fragment of greenstone (Dyke rock), flaked on both faces. Perhaps a roughout for a polished axe. C/63/53. D2. 3 feet 6 inches–4 feet (1·06–1·22 m).

9 Edge anvil on a cuboid pebble of hard quartzite flaked and battered along one straight edge and bruised by hammering on other rounded edges. C/63/137. H1. 3 feet 6 inches–4 feet (1·06–1·22 m).

10 Side chopper on a cuboid block of hard quartzite. One edge shows bifacial flaking and battering from use. C/63/133. H2. 3 feet 6 inches–4 feet (1·06–1·22 m).

11 Side chopper on an irregular chunk of hard quartzite. One edge shows bifacial retouch and bruising from use. C/63/125. D6. 3 feet–3 feet 6 inches (91·5 cm–1·06 m).

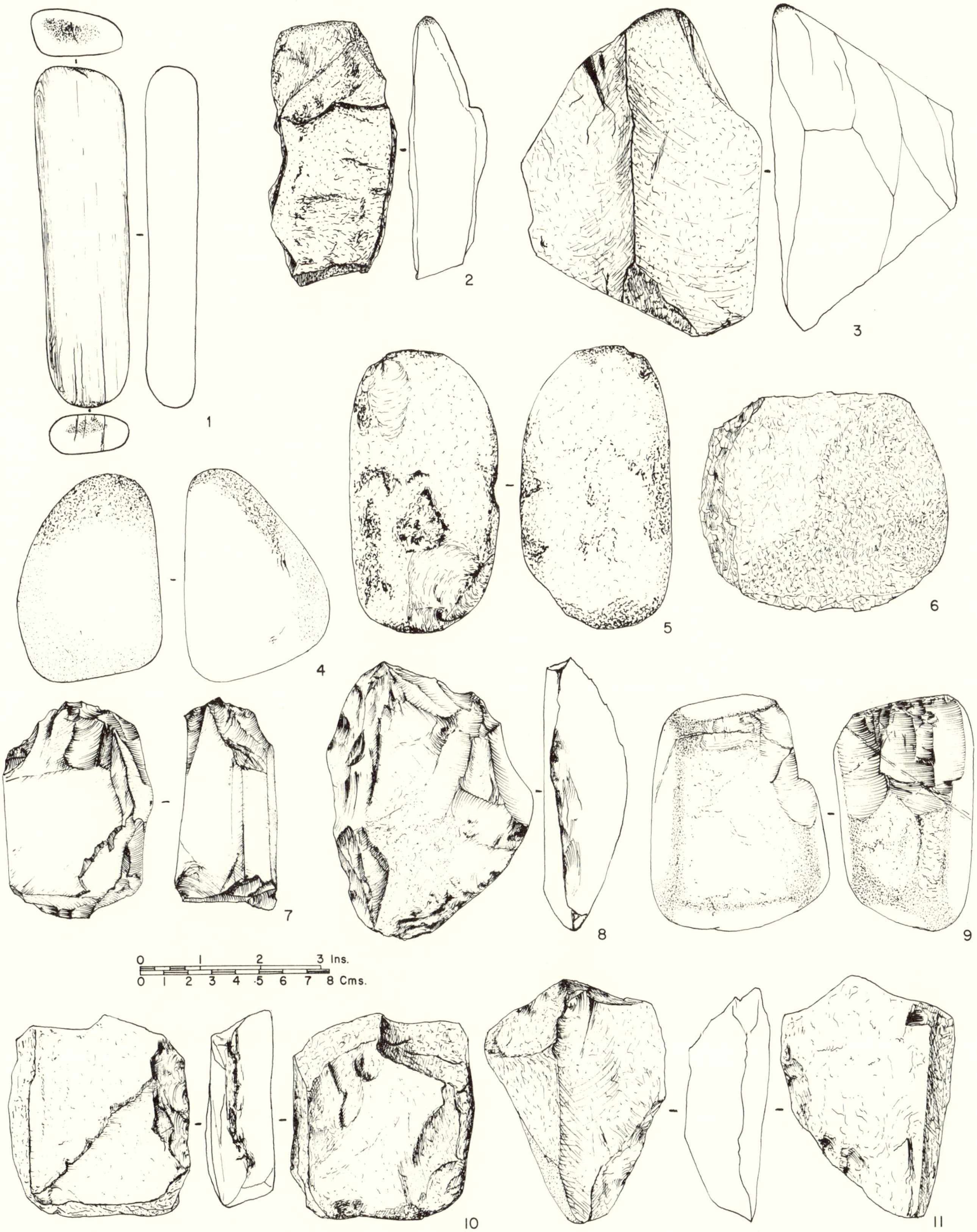
1
2
3
4
5
6
7
8
9
0 1 2 3 Ins.
0 1 2 3 4 5 6 7 8 Cms.
10
11

36 MICROLITHS FROM THE KAPOSWA INDUSTRY OCCUPATION FLOOR

Site C, 1963, except nos. 77 and 78 which are from Site C, 1959.

1–30 Lunates.
31–47 Triangles.
48–51 Shouldered microliths.
52–56 Trapezes.
57–60, 62, 64–68 Backed blades – convex backing.
61, 63, 77, 78 Backed blades – straight backing.
69–72, 76 Obliquely truncated bladelets.
73 Diminutive, worked out bipolar core.
74 Quartz burin on a crystal.
75 *Lamelle à piquant trièdre.*
All fresh and all chert except no. 38 in chalcedony and no. 74 in crystalline quartz.

Location of specimens by grid squares: All from a depth of 3 feet 6 inches–4 feet (1·06–1·22 m) except nos. 77 and 78.

C/37 B2	nos. 17, 61
C/52 D1	72
C/157 D3	20, 60
C/134 E1	10, 62
C/170 E2	18
C/127 E2	15, 42, 50, 63
C/128 E3	14, 25, 38, 67
C/135 E4	64
C/165 E6	4
C/130 F1	3, 33
C/131 F2	26, 37, 44, 54
C/106 F3	46
C/129 F3	21
C/136 F3	51, 58, 65
C/163 F4	6, 40
C/151 F6	7, 22, 24, 75
C/132 G1	2, 23, 29, 30, 45, 56
C/133 G2	41, 55, 59
C/153 G3	9, 13, 28, 43
C/154 G3	36
C/158 G3	73
C/167 G3	12
C/169 G4	31
C/137 H1	5, 39, 47, 53, 66, 70, 71, 76
C/138 H2	1, 8, 11, 16, 19, 27, 32, 34, 35, 49, 52, 57, 69, 74
C/156 H4	48, 68
C/3/1959	Surface of mound garden 77, 78

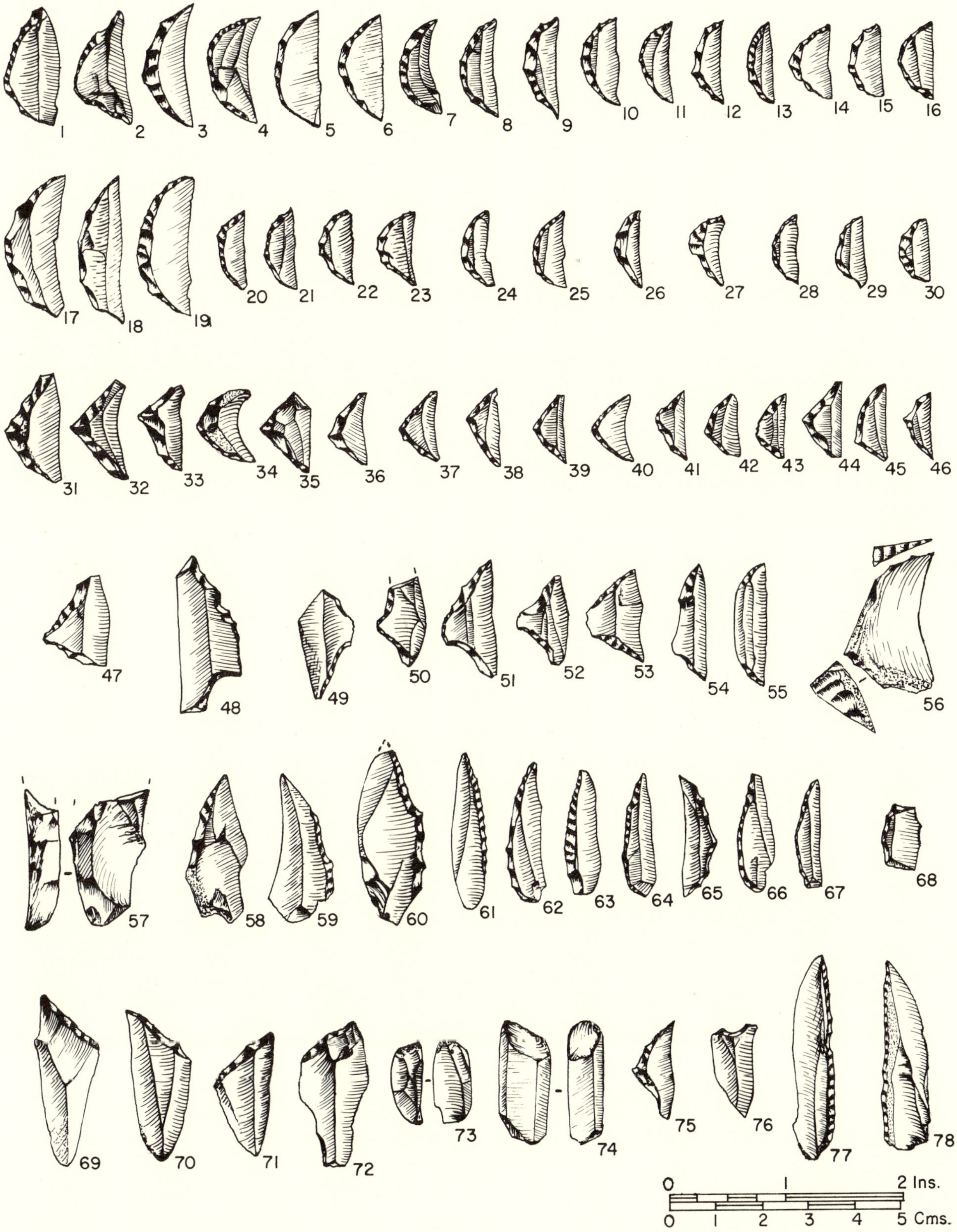
1 2 3 4 5 6 7 8 9 10 11 12 13 14 15 16
17 18 19 20 21 22 23 24 25 26 27 28 29 30
31 32 33 34 35 36 37 38 39 40 41 42 43 44 45 46
47 48 49 50 51 52 53 54 55 56
57 58 59 60 61 62 63 64 65 66 67 68
69 70 71 72 73 74 75 76 77 78
0 1 2 Ins.
0 1 2 3 4 5 Cms.

37 SCRAPERS FROM THE KAPOSWA INDUSTRY OCCUPATION FLOOR

Site C, 1963

1–8, 16 Small end scrapers on flakes and flake fragments.

9, 11–15 Core scrapers: end (13), end and side (9, 12, 15), side (14) and round (11).

10 Flake with bifacially retouched convex edge (flat, scalar, inverse retouch) and minute scarring due to use on the opposite lateral edge. Broad, plain, inclined striking platform.

All fresh and in chert. All from a depth of 3 feet 6 inches to 4 feet (106–122 cm) except no. 8 (grid square G/3) from 4 feet to 4 feet 6 inches (122–135 cm).

Location of specimens by grid squares:

C/53 D2	No. 11	C/127 E2	No. 9
C/135 E4	12	C/130 F1	2, 4, 6, 13
C/163 F4	14	C/136 F3	15
C/151 F6	16	C/132 G1	1, 5, 7
C/155 G3	8	C/137 H1	10
C/156 H4	3		

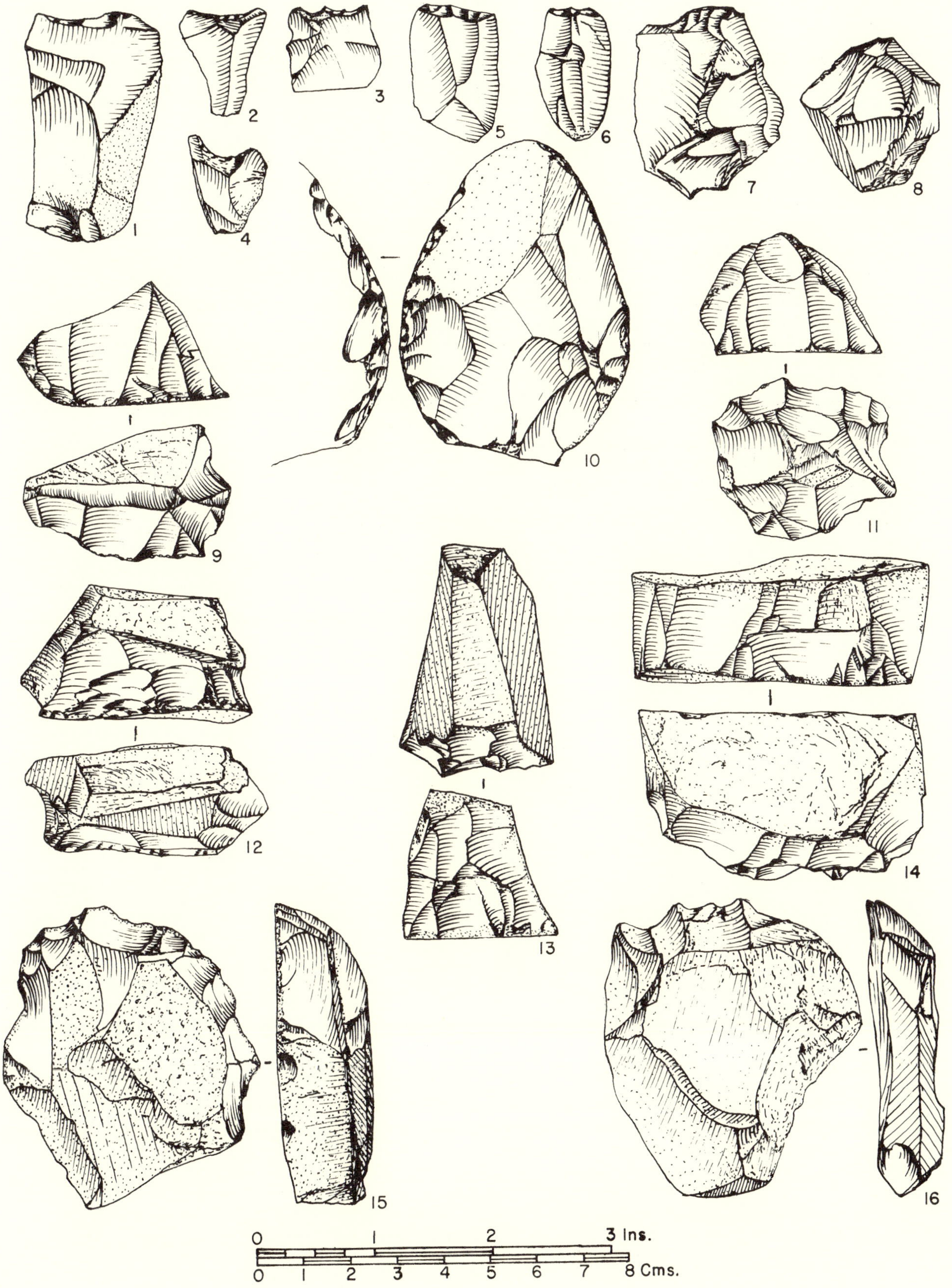
1
2
3
4
5
6
7
8
9
10
11
12
13
14
15
16
0 1 2 3 Ins.
0 1 2 3 4 5 6 7 8 Cms.

38 UTILIZED ARTIFACTS FROM KAPOSWA INDUSTRY OCCUPATION FLOOR

Site C, 1963. All fresh and all chert, except nos. 16 in hard quartzite; 6 and 8 in quartz.

1, 2, 4, 9, 10, 12, 14 Utilized flakes: single lateral edges – nos. 1, 2, 4, 10, 12; end – no. 9.

3, 11, 15 Utilized bladelets. No. 3 notched: no. 11 one lateral edge; no. 15 both edges.

5–8 *Outils esquillés*, both ends used.

13 Flake with shallow inverse retouch on one lateral concave edge.

16 Irregular chunk with two edges dulled by rubbing.

17 Pyramidal utilized chunk with steep notching on one edge and flat, straight inverse retouch along the opposite lateral edge of the ventral face.

18 Discoid chunk showing steep end-scraper retouch and utilization at the proximal end and a convex, bifacially worked edge at the distal end.

19 Technical burin on a chunk.

Location of specimens by grid squares: All from a depth of 3 feet 6 inches to 4 feet (106–122 cm) except no. 6 (grid square E/2) which is from a depth of 3 feet to 3 feet 6 inches (91–106 cm).

C/52 D1	No. 1	C/67 E2	No. 6
C/127 E2	7, 8	C/135 E4	12
C/165 E6	14	C/130 F1	9
C/131 F2	15	C/133 G2	5
C/158 G3	13	C/167 G3	3
C/152 G4	2	C/137 H1	4, 10
C/138 H2	11, 16, 17, 19	C/156 H4	18

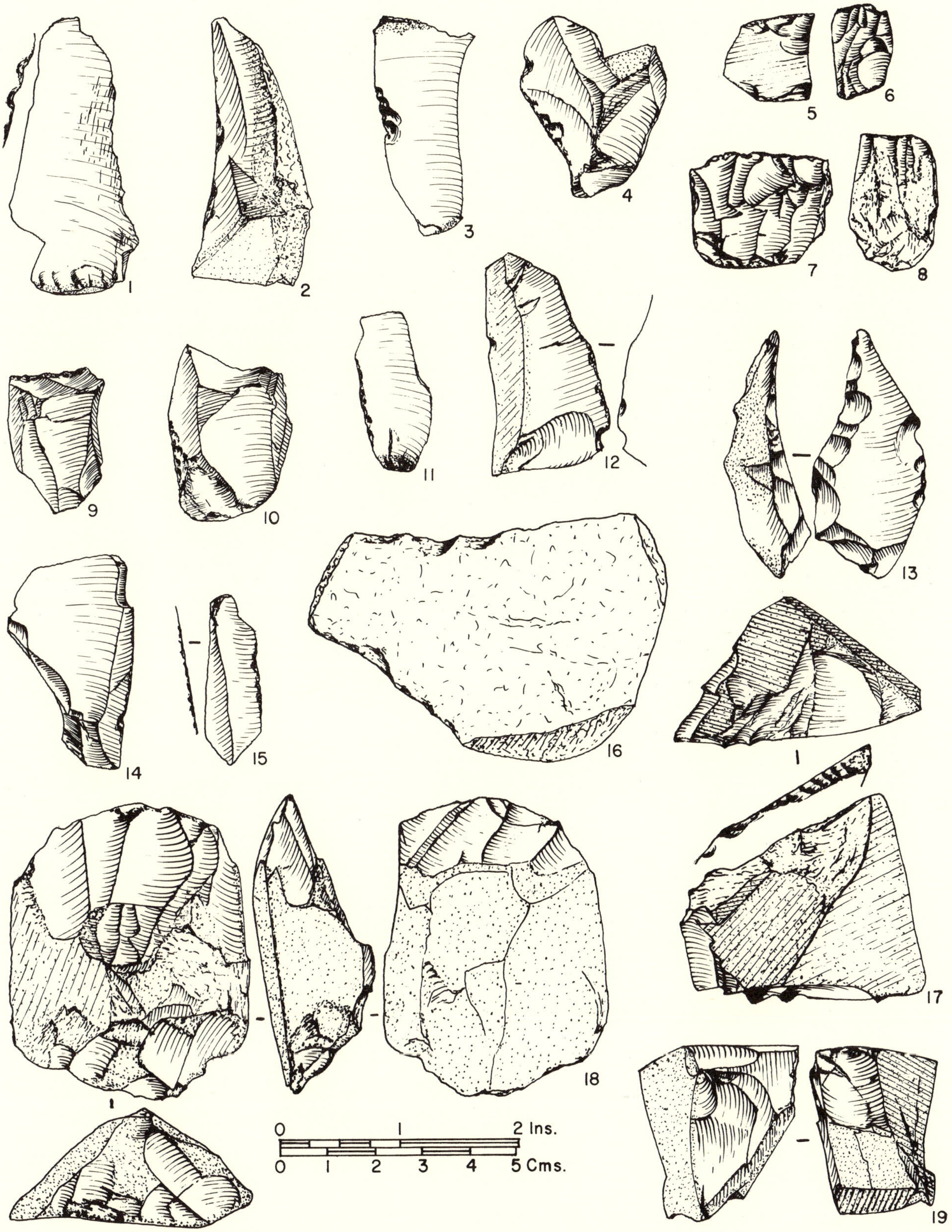
1
2
3
4
5
6
7
8
9
10
11
12
13
14
15
16
17
18
19
0 1 2 Ins.
0 1 2 3 4 5 Cms.

39 FLAKES AND BLADES FROM THE KAPOSWA INDUSTRY OCCUPATION FLOOR

Site C, 1963.

1–12 Blades and bladelets.

13, 14, 16, 19, 20, 22, 23, 25, 26–28, 31, 32, 35 Irregular flakes, end-struck.

15 Irregular, side-struck flake.

17, 18, 23, 34 Short quadrilateral flakes.

21 Triangular flake.

24 Core resharpening flake, broad. From the platform edge of a single platformed or pyramidal blade core.

29 Short quadrilateral flake fragment such as was used for the production of end-scrapers and microliths.

30 Core resharpening flake, broad. Probably from the platform edge of a single platformed core.

36, 37 Core resharpening flakes, long. From the platform edge of a chunky core with two platforms at right angles and in different planes.

38 Core resharpening flake, long. From the platform edge of a broad single platformed core.

All fresh and in chert.

Location of specimens by grid squares: All from a depth of 3 feet 6 inches to 4 feet (1·06–1·22 m) except nos. 7, 11 and 21 (grid square G3) which are from a depth of 4 feet to 4 feet 6 inches (1·22–1·37 m).

C/150	C5	nos. 23
C/52	D1	1
C/160	D6	18
C/134	E1	2, 13, 27
C/170	E1	4
C/127	E2	14, 17, 34
C/128	E3	26, 28, 37
C/135	E4	29, 36
C/130	F1	3, 22, 32
C/129	F3	12
C/136	F3	24
C/151	F6	19
C/132	G1	8, 9, 38
C/133	G2	5, 6, 10
C/155	G3	7, 11, 21
C/137	H1	25, 30
C/138	H2	15, 16, 20, 31, 33, 35

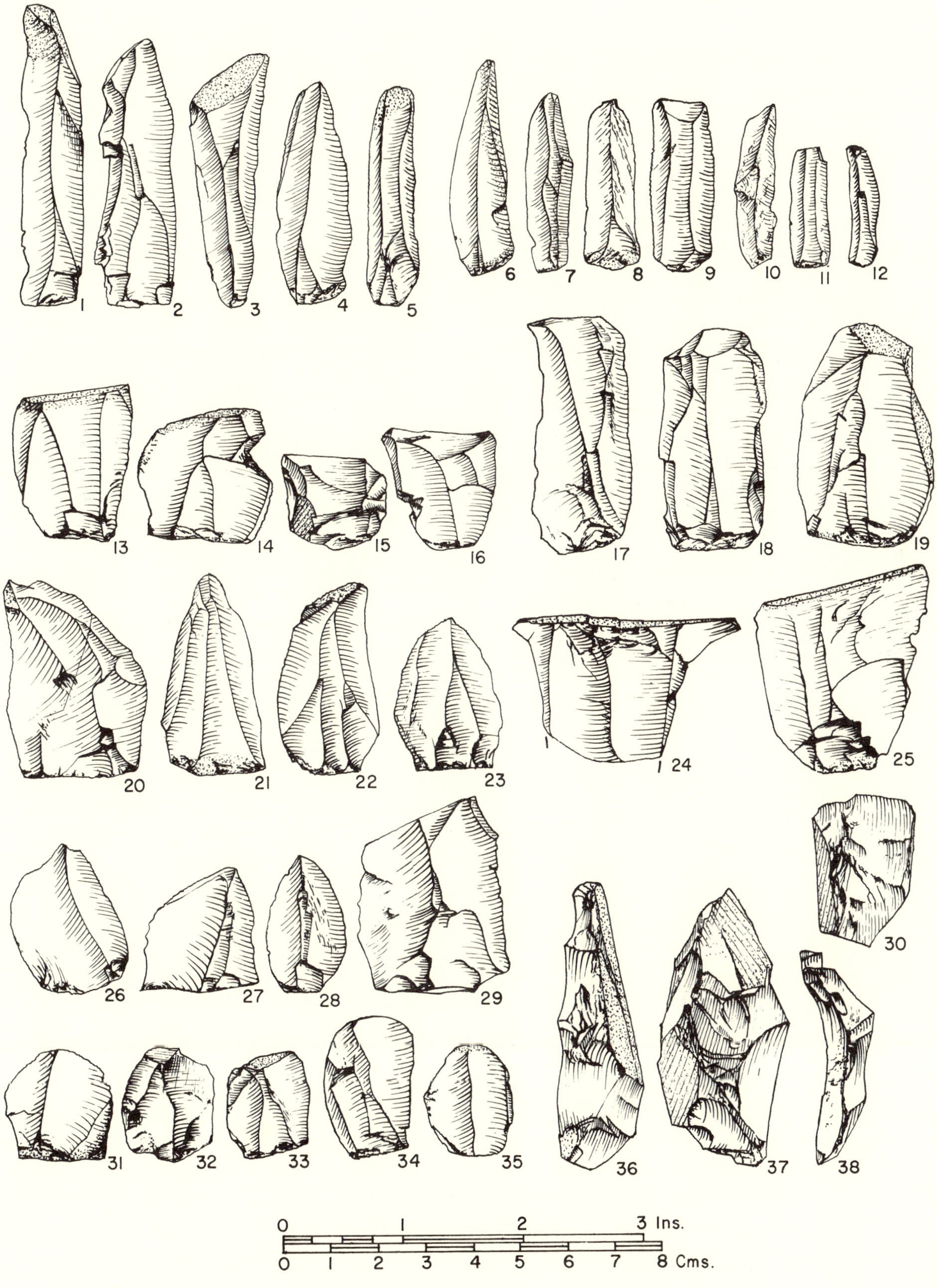

1
2
3
4
5
6
7
8
9
10
11
12
13
14
15
16
17
18
19
20
21
22
23
24
25
26
27
28
29
30
31
32
33
34
35
36
37
38
0 1 2 3 Ins.
0 1 2 3 4 5 6 7 8 Cms.

40 CORES FROM THE KAPOSWA INDUSTRY OCCUPATION FLOOR

Site C, 1963. All fresh and in chert.

1 Single platform, long, prismatic.
2 Single platform, broad, prismatic.
3 Double platformed core with platforms at opposite ends (bipolar type).
4, 7 Chunky, prismatic cores with two platforms at right angles and on different faces.
5 Biconical core.
6, 9–11 Pyramidal, prismatic cores.
8 Flat discoid core worked only on the upper face and simulating a prepared core from which one long flake has been detached.

Location of specimens by grid squares: All from a depth of 3 feet 6 inches to 4 feet (1·06–1·22 m).

C/39	C2	nos. 2
C/130	F1	1, 4
C/129	F3	8
C/132	G1	3, 5
C/133	G2	6
C/153	G3	7
C/171	G3	9
C/137	H1	10
C/138	H2	11

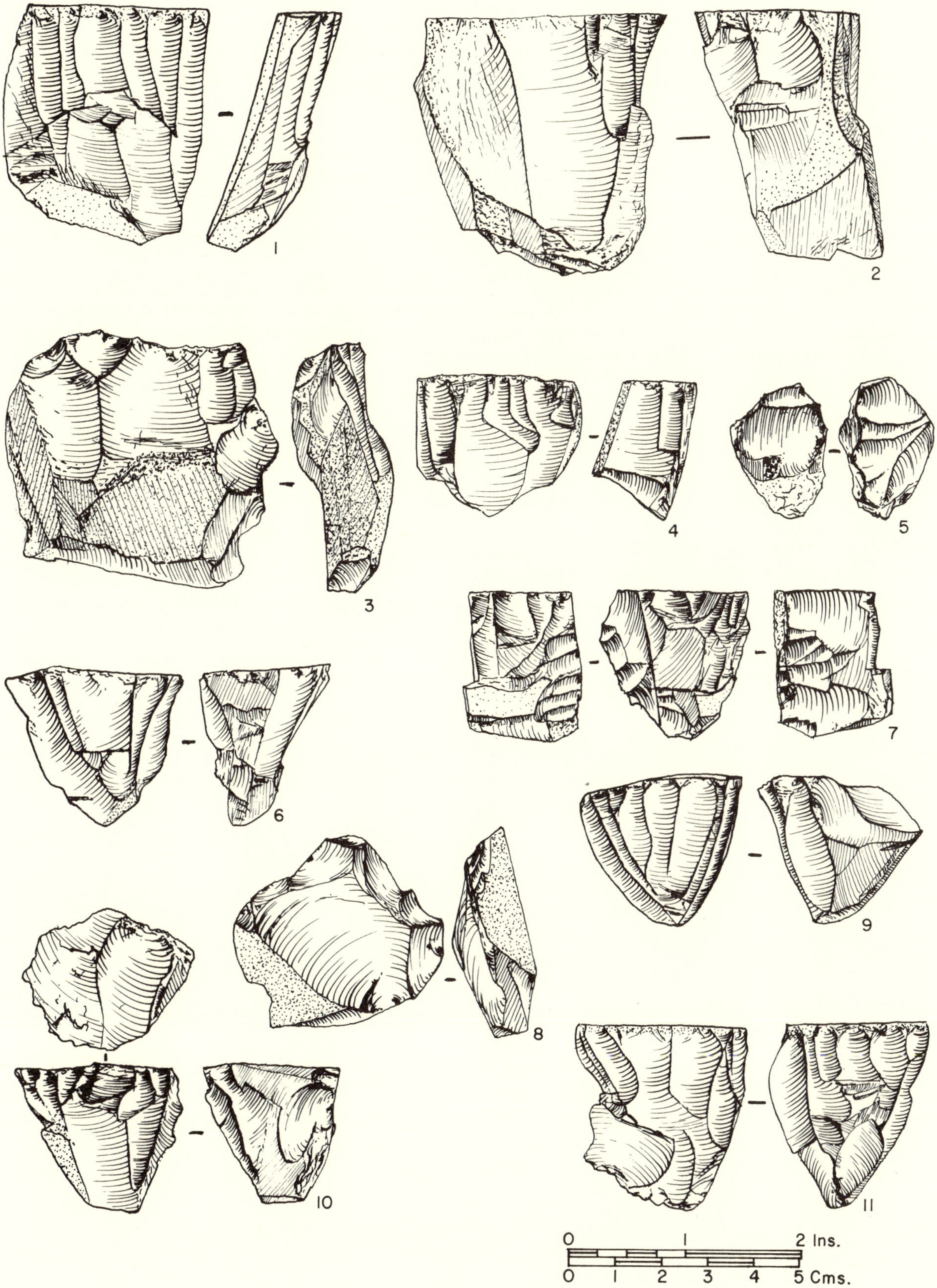
1
2
3
4
5
6
7
8
9
10
11
0 1 2 Ins.
0 1 2 3 4 5 Cms.

41 ARTIFACTS FROM THE KAPOSWA INDUSTRY OCCUPATION FLOOR

Site C, 1963, except no. 1 which is from River Face Site C, 1963. All fresh.

1 Broken half of an incompletely bored pebble of sandstone, probably broken in process of boring. Hour-glass perforation done by pecking, well seen on reverse side, and by rotary grinding. Found in collapsed earth immediately adjacent to the excavation and presumed to come from the Kaposwa Industry occupation floor.

2, 3, 6 Lumps of pigment: no. 2 haematite; no. 3 yellow ochre and no. 6 white ?kaolin. Show rubbing facets and striations.

4 Double ended (bipolar) core with opposed platforms on the same face. Chert.

5 Formless core with three platforms. Chert.

7 Anvil (edge type) on a flat chert fragment battered from use on two edges and across the thickness at one end.

Location of specimens by grid squares: All from a depth of 3 feet 6 inches to 4 feet (106–122 cm) except no. 1.

C/127 E2	no. 5	C/151 F6	no. 2
C/132 G1	3, 4, 7	C/138 H2	6
River Face	1		

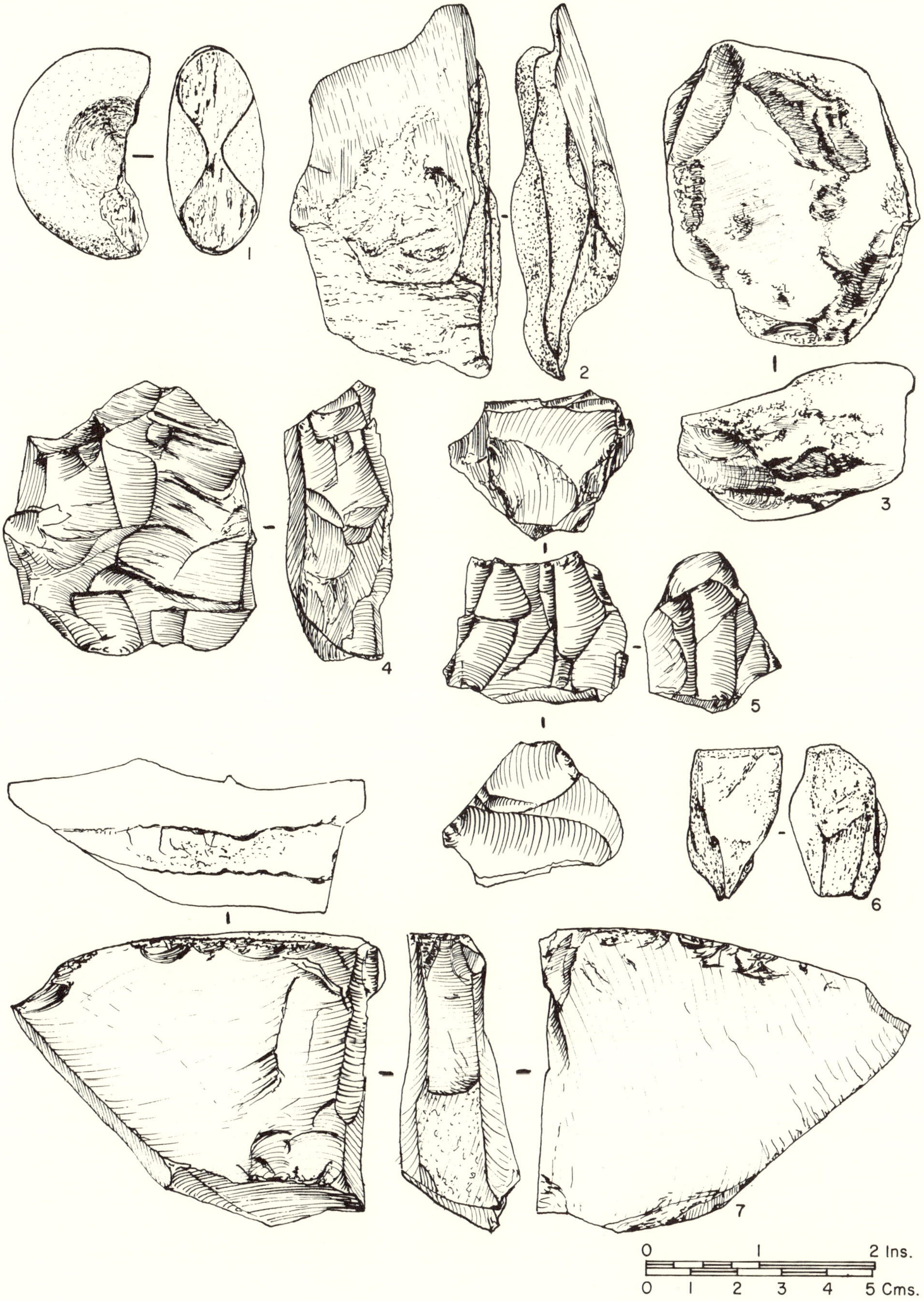
1
2
3
4
5
6
7
0 1 2 Ins.
0 1 2 3 4 5 Cms.

42 WASTE FROM A MODIFIED MICRO-BURIN TECHNIQUE, KAPOSWA INDUSTRY OCCUPATION FLOOR

Site C, 1963. All fresh and in chert.

1 Butt end of a snapped short quadrilateral flake or blade. The distal portion (here missing) of such snapped flakes or blades would sometimes be used for the manufacture of microliths.

2–4 Butt ends of flakes which have been notched and broken across to detach the upper end. No. 4 is a proximal micro-burin, nos. 2 and 3 are *micro-burins ratés*.

5–9 Upper ends of flakes and bladelets detached from the butt ends by notching and breaking: distal micro-burins.

10–13 Upper ends of bladelets ready to be made into microliths by the completion of the backing already begun in the initial notching: ?*lamelles à piquant trièdre ratées*.

14 Obliquely truncated bladelet with notching for detaching the butt end by the micro-burin technique.

15–19 Spalls resulting from striking the edge of a previously retouched flake or blade: 'Krukowski burins'.

20, 22, 23, 25 Distally trimmed flakes and bladelets with transverse 'burin-like' facets that have detached half the retouched edge. These forms are sufficiently numerous to indicate a special modification of the micro-burin technique, the detached segments already having one trimmed edge being made into microliths.

21, 24 The spalls removed from the above distally trimmed forms prior to final backing.

Location of specimens by grid squares: All from a depth of 3 feet 6 inches to 4 feet (106–122 cm) except nos. 2 and 20 (grid squares E3 and G2) which are from 3 feet to 3 feet 6 inches (91–106 cm).

C/134 E1	nos. 10, 19	C/103 E3	2
C/128 E3	6	C/130 F1	16, 25
C/131 F2	17, 21, 23	C/136 F3	4, 8, 14
C/163 F4	15	C/151 F6	1
C/132 G1	3	C/100 G2	20
C/137 H1	13, 22	C/138 H2	5, 7, 9, 11, 12, 18, 24

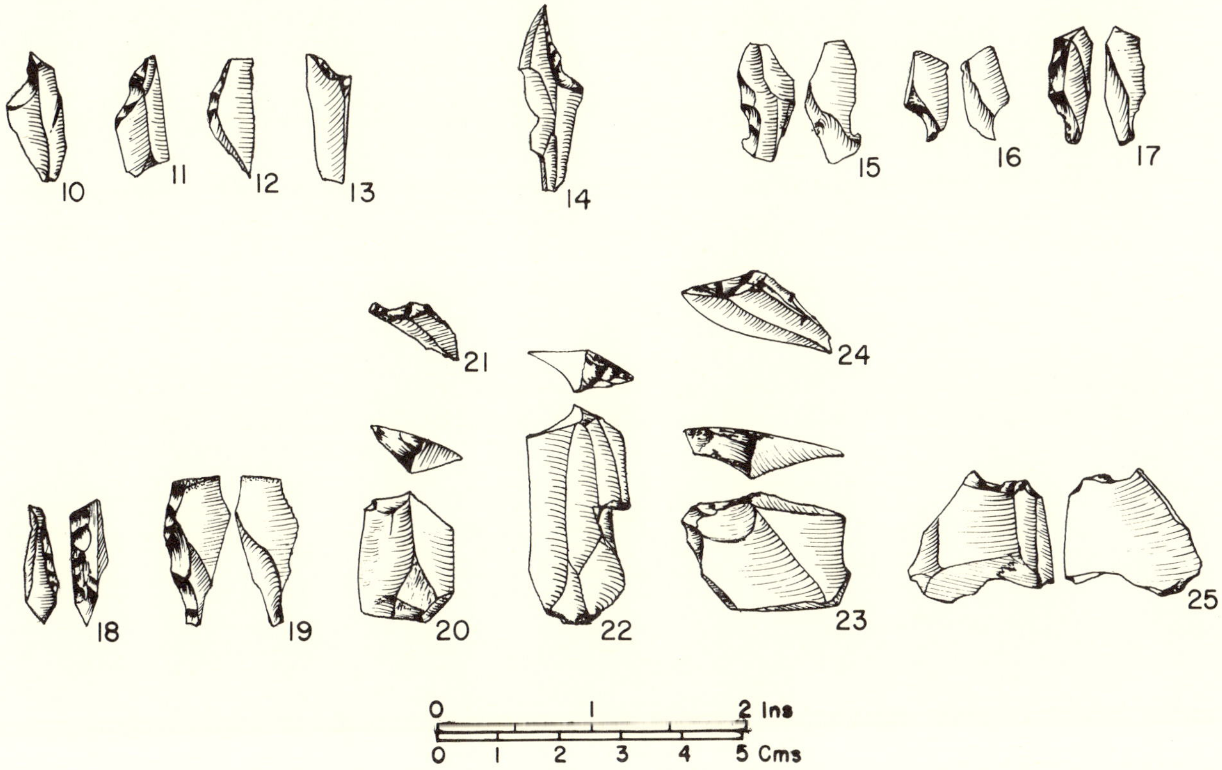

1
2
3
4
5
6
7
8
9
10
11
12
13
14
15
16
17
18
19
20
21
22
23
24
25
0 1 2 Ins
0 1 2 3 4 5 Cms

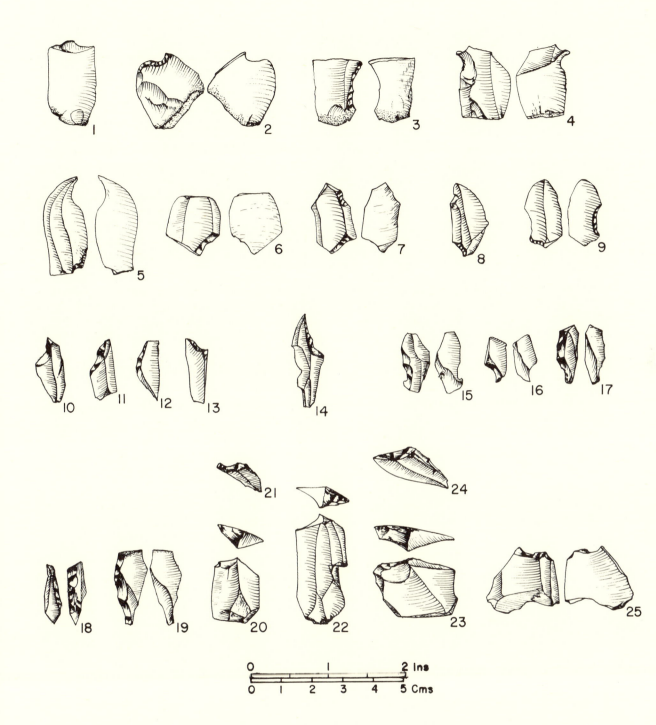

43 ARTIFACTS OF THE POLUNGU INDUSTRY

Hillslope component from depth of 3 feet to 3 feet 6 inches (91–106 cm) in Bed 4, A4 Excavation, 1959, Sections 21–37. (A/32/59–A/35/59.) All chert and fresh and mostly thinly patinated.

1 Long quadrilateral flake partially trimmed to form an oblique end-scraper. Marginal utilization on right hand edge on main flake surface.

2, 7, 11, 13 Bladelets, nos. 2 and 13 utilized/modified.

3, 4 Short quadrilateral flakes, no. 3 Levallois point type with faceted striking platform and struck from specialized Levallois core; no. 4 with plain platform struck from blade-type core shows utilization.

5, 6, 9 Short, broad, sub-triangular flakes with multi-faceted platforms struck from small, specialized cores; no. 5 is utilized.

8 Small convex scraper made on a chunk. Blunt angle of retouch.

10 Single platformed core for small blades and triangular flakes, the platform being faceted. This example might also be classified as an unstruck Levallois point core.

12 Resharpening spall from a single platformed core, perhaps used as a core scraper prior to the removal of the rejuvenating flake.

14, 16 Discoid, specialized cores. No. 14 is very slightly abraded and may, therefore, be derived. It shows radial preparation of the dorsal face and two small areas of the circumference show careful retouch for further use as a core scraper. No. 16 shows two directional preparation of the dorsal face.

15 Single platform prismatic core for small blades. Lower end shows trimming to form a steep scraper edge.

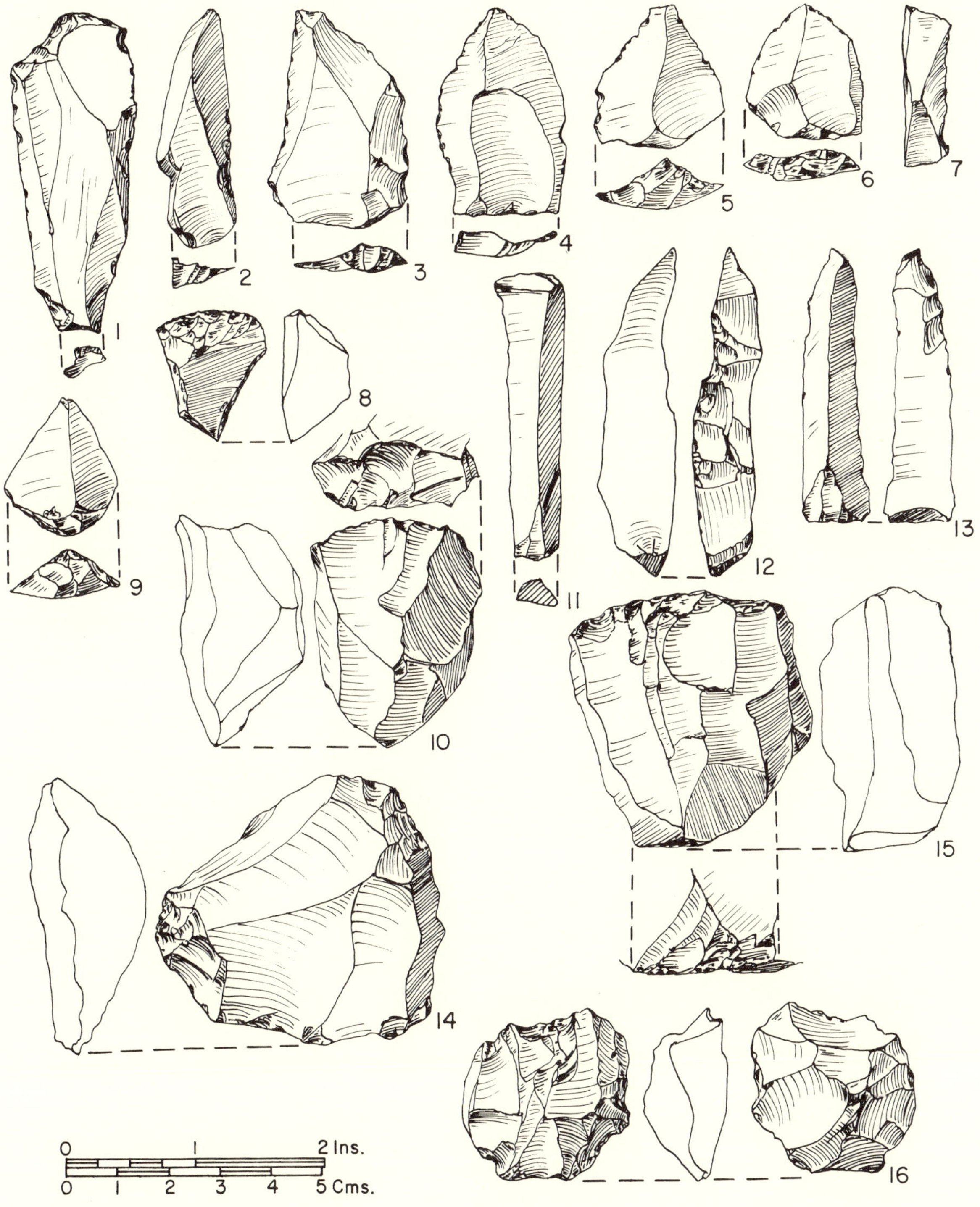
1
2
3
4
5
6
7
8
9
10
11
12
13
14
15
16
0 1 2 Ins.
0 1 2 3 4 5 Cms.

44 ARTIFACTS OF THE POLUNGU INDUSTRY

Hillslope component, from a depth of 3 feet 6 inches to 4 feet (106–122 cm) in Bed 4, A4 Excavation, 1959, Sections 21–50. (A/36/59; A/37/59; A/43/59; A/44/59.) All fresh and thinly patinated and all in chert except no. 17 in silcrete.

1, 17 Sub-rectangular specialized cores with opposed, two directional dorsal preparation and faceted striking platforms. For the removal of Levallois points, triangular flakes and blades. A flake of Levallois point type with simple faceted striking platform has been removed from no. 1. Ferricrete concretions adhere to no. 17.

2 Irregular backed bladelet with oblique backing on both edges at the distal point: probably unfinished.

3, 7–9 Bladelets, no. 7 utilized.

4, 5 Short quadrilateral flakes from specialized Levallois cores; no. 5 with multi-faceted platform and no. 4 with minimal modification on one edge.

6, 13 Small specialized cores for the removal of triangular Levallois point flakes with faceted striking platforms.

10 Core scraper with notched edge and steep angle of retouch made on a chunk.

11 Notched scraper with steep retouch angle and proto-burin modification; made on a chunk.

12 Small specialized disc core with two steeply trimmed scraping edges.

16 Small blade core with single, straight, unprepared platform. The angle between the platform and the flaked face is between 84° and 93°.

14, 15 Disc cores, radially prepared for the removal of one or more small flakes. No. 15 has had a single flake removed and is thus classifiable as a diminutive Levallois core.

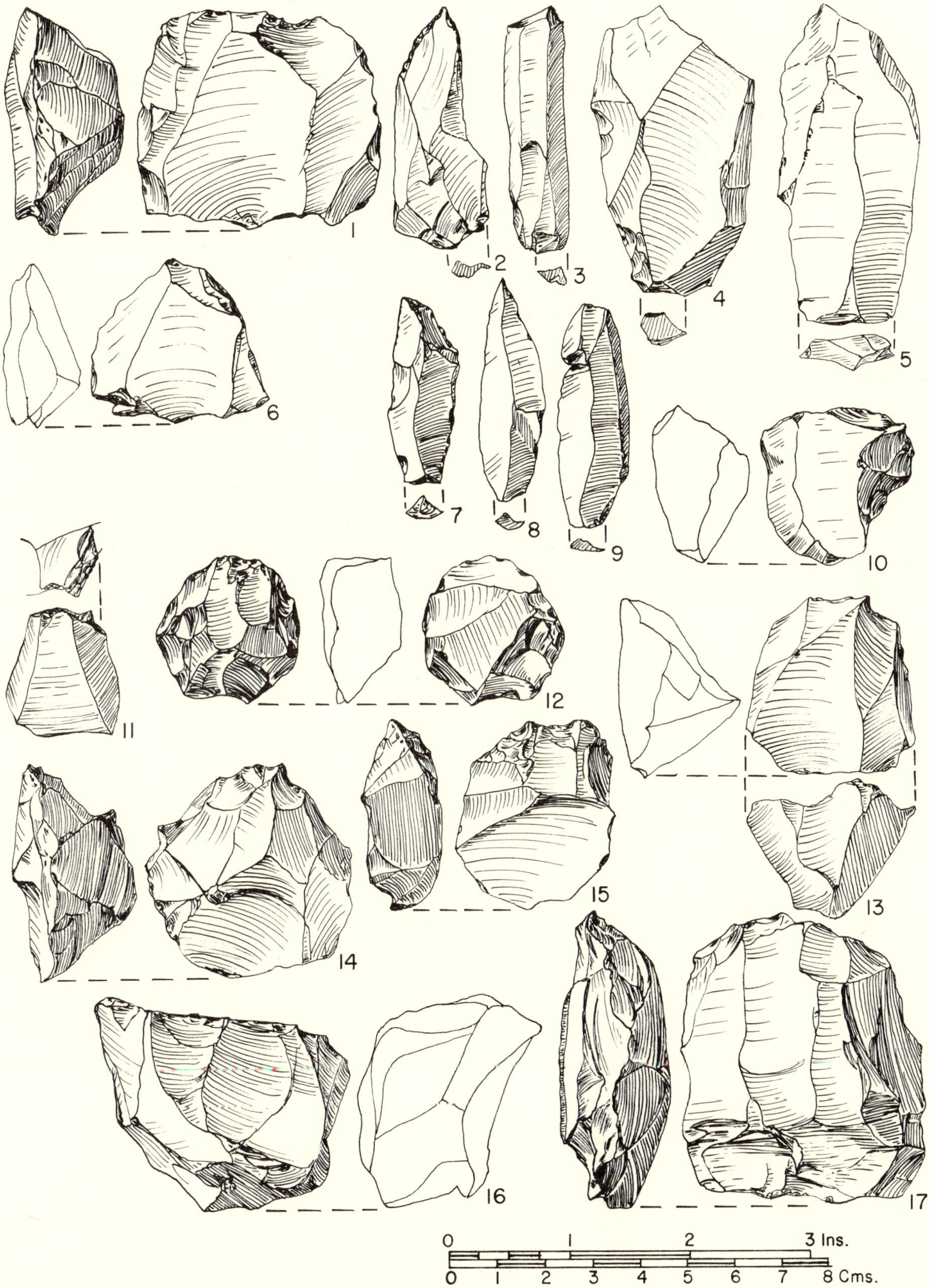
1
2
3
4
5
6
7
8
9
10
11
12
13
14
15
16
17
0 1 2 3 Ins.
0 1 2 3 4 5 6 7 8 Cms.

45 ARTIFACTS OF THE POLUNGU INDUSTRY

Hillslope component, from a depth of 3 feet 6 inches to 4 feet (106–122 cm) in Bed 4, A4 Excavation, 1959, Sections 21–50. (A/36/59; A/37/59; A/43/59; A/44/59.) All fresh and all chert except no. 22 in hard quartzite.

1–4, 8, 10 Triangular flakes with multi-faceted striking platforms; nos. 1, 8 and 9 utilized.

5 Flake marginally retouched on the butt and discontinuously on the left lateral edge to form a unifaced point.

6, 7 Resharpening spalls from plain, single platformed cores. Retouch on the platform edges suggests possible use as core scrapers before detachment from the core, or edge preparation in connection with the use of a punch.

9, 11, 16–18 Short quadrilateral flakes struck from specialized Levallois cores with simple and multi-faceted striking platforms.

12, 13, 20, 21 Irregular flakes with plain and faceted platforms struck from cores mostly prepared by radial flaking; no. 21 from a disc core, the remainder from Levallois cores. No. 12 has been retouched on both edges to form a double concave or notched scraper.

14, 15 Trimming or plunging flakes from double ended blade cores. No. 14 shows an inclined, multi-faceted and restricted platform indicative of punch or some rest method of flake release. The butt end of no. 15 has been snapped off.

19 Microlithic blade backed to form a lunate and showing also retouch on the cord at the proximal end.

22 Ellipsoid cobble with bruising at top and bottom ends and on one face; a combined dimple-scarred anvil and hammerstone.

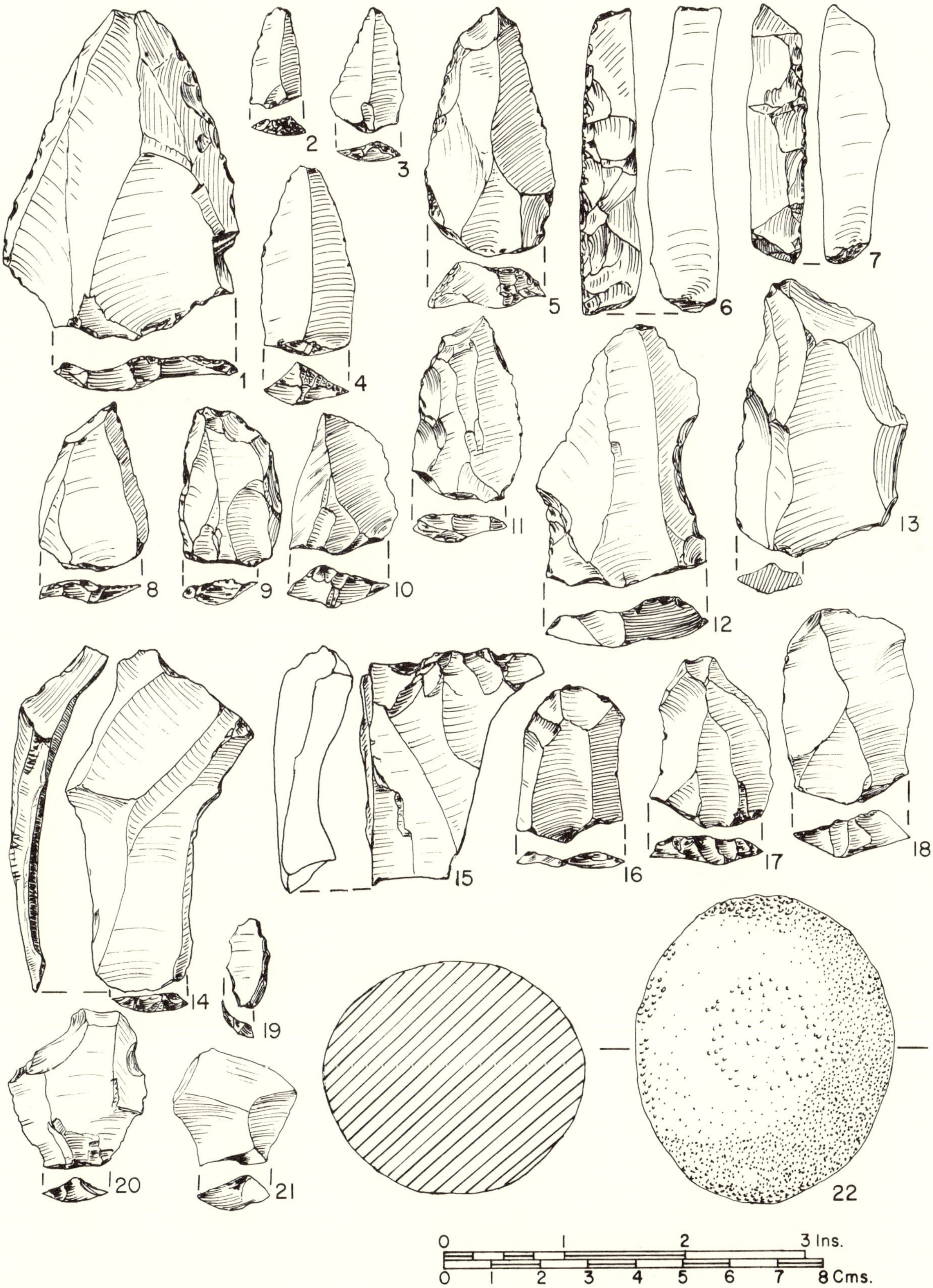
1
2
3
4
5
6
7
8
9
10
11
12
13
14
15
16
17
18
19
20
21
22
0 1 2 3 Ins.
0 1 2 3 4 5 6 7 8 Cms.

46 ARTIFACTS OF THE POLUNGU INDUSTRY

Hillslope component, from a depth of 4 feet to 4 feet 6 inches (122–137 cm) in Bed 4, A4 Excavation, 1959, Sections 20–43. (A/38/59; A/39/59; A/40/59; A/47/59.) All chert and fresh and mostly thinly patinated.

1–3 Blade and bladelets with faceted platforms; no. 3 utilized.

4, 5, 8 Small, triangular flakes from small specialized Levallois point cores.

6 Parti-backed flake with normal retouch on the proximal half of the left lateral edge; faceted platform.

7 Short quadrilateral flake with faceted platform from a Levallois blade core.

9, 10, 12 Short irregular end-struck flakes; probably all from specialized cores.

11 Irregular side-struck flake from Levallois core.

13 Double ended *outil esquillé* on flake fragment.

14 Short, thick, irregular flake with esquillé utilization on part of left lateral edge on the main flake surface.

15 Flat, sub-triangular, radially prepared core; three small flakes have been struck from the proximal end.

16 Pyramidal, micro-blade, prismatic core with plain, convex striking platform; perhaps retouched as a steep core scraper or as preparation for using a punch.

17 Double ended, prismatic blade core with plain striking platforms, made on a patinated quadrilateral chunk.

18 Double platformed prismatic core for micro-blades and flakes. The platforms are at right-angles to each other, the flaked surfaces being one on the dorsal and one on the ventral face. One platform is prepared for using a punch.

19, 20 Small, irregular, discoid cores, no. 19 with radial preparation and no. 20 flaked from two directions at right-angles.

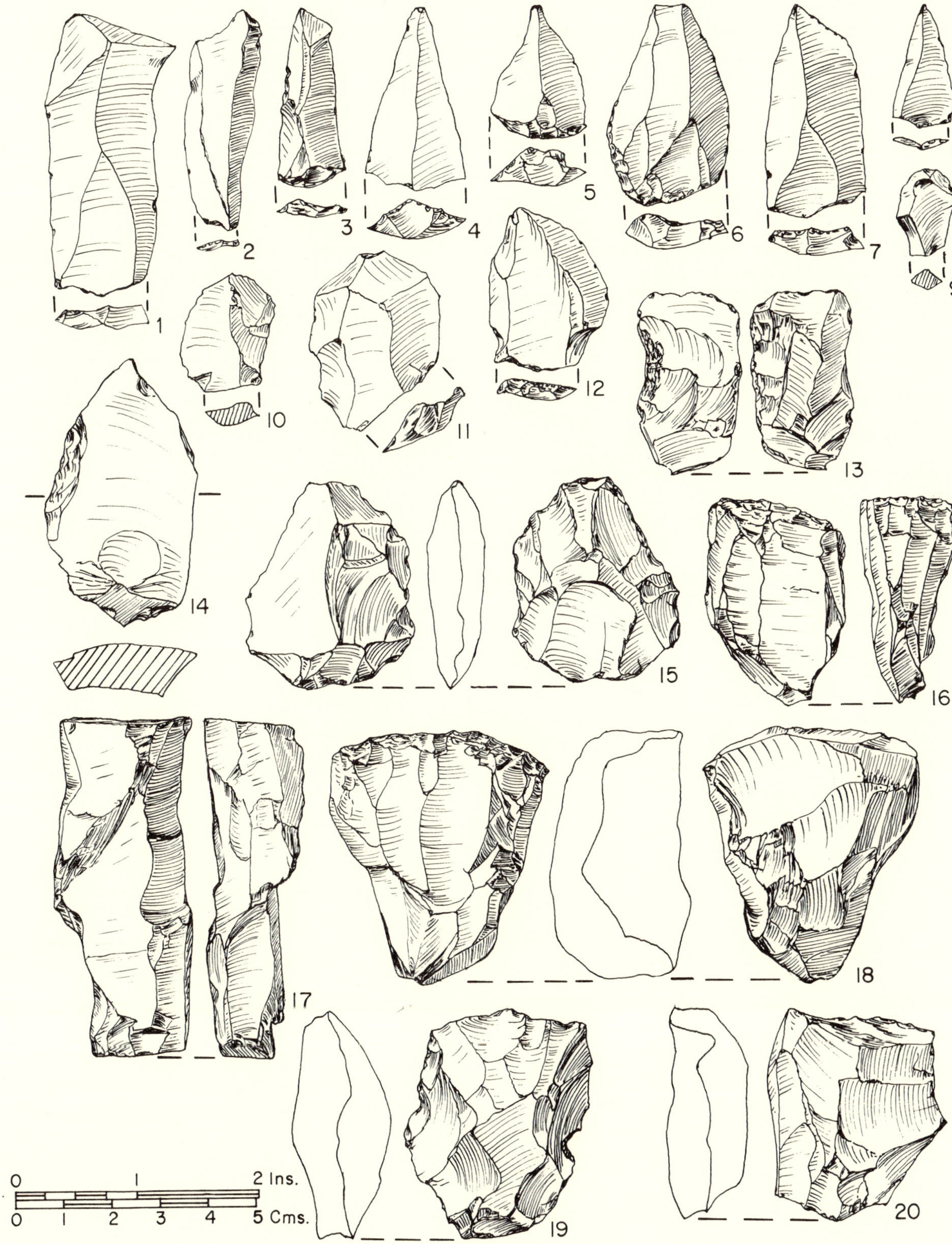
1
2
3
4
5
6
7
8
9
10
11
12
13
14
15
16
17
18
19
20
0 1 2 Ins.
0 1 2 3 4 5 Cms.

47 ARTIFACTS OF THE POLUNGU INDUSTRY

Hillslope component, from a depth of 4 feet 6 inches to 5 feet (137–152 cm) in Bed 4, A4 Excavation, 1959, Sections 20–34. (A/41/59; A/42/59; A/49/59; A/50/59.) All chert and fresh and mostly thinly patinated.

1–4, 6 Blades and bladelet; nos. 1–3 from Levallois blade cores. Nos. 2, 3 and 6 utilized.

5 Core resharpening spall showing platform edge preparation for using a punch.

7, 8, 10 Small, triangular Levallois point flakes from specialized cores: no. 7 utilized.

9 Short, irregular flake with faceted platform, retouched at the distal end to form a double sided/convergent scraper.

11 Specialized core for the removal of several small flakes.

12 Utilized/modified chunk or core with steep, modified edge at the distal end and double notch and *bec* at the proximal end.

13 Short convex scraper made on the butt end of an older, brown patinated flake.

14 Core with two unprepared platforms at right angles, utilized as a steep, two edged scraper.

15 Diminutive, elliptic Levallois core from which one short quadrilateral flake has been struck.

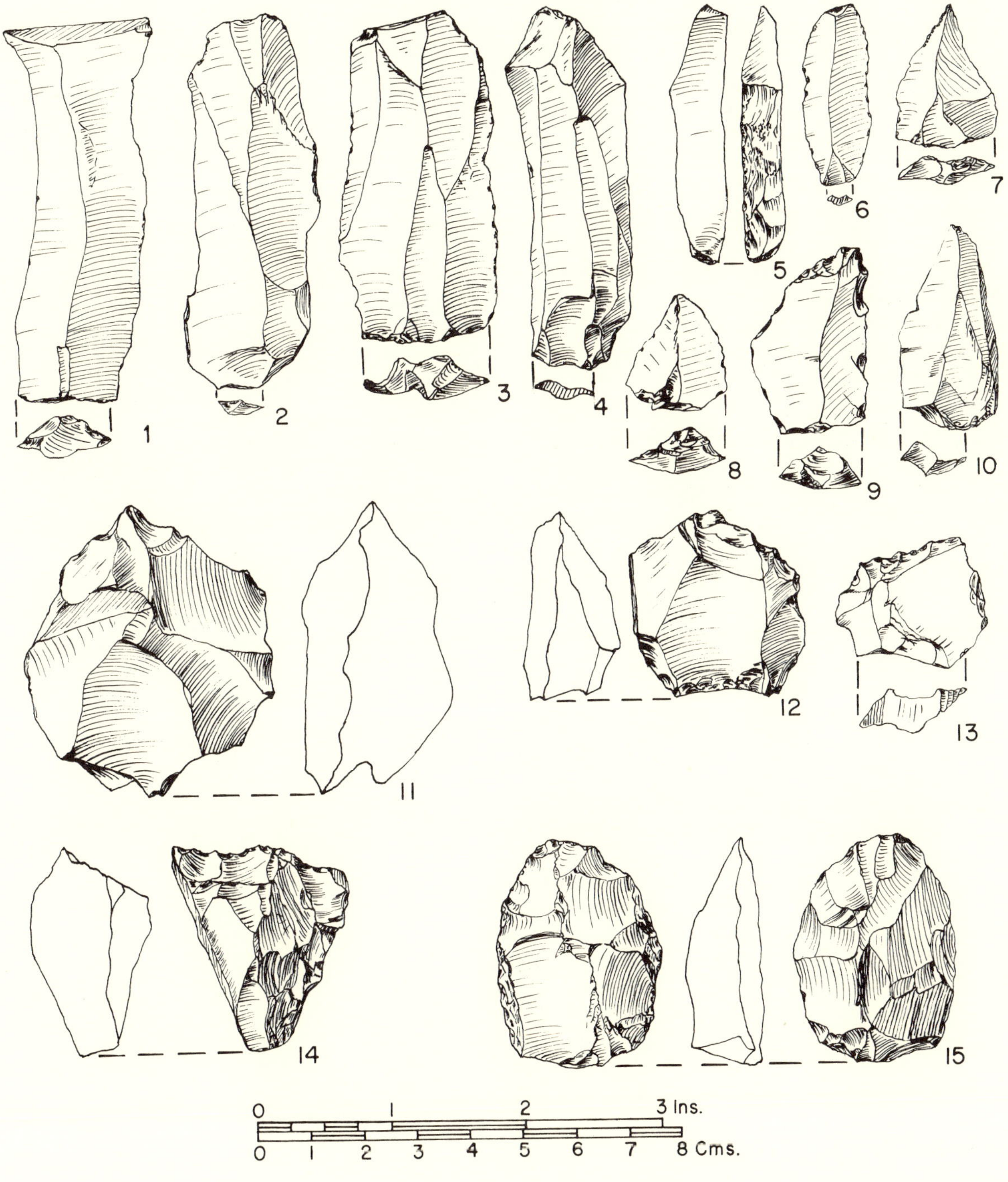
1
2
3
4
5
6
7
8
9
10
11
12
13
14
15
0 1 2 3 Ins.
0 1 2 3 4 5 6 7 8 Cms.

48 RUBBLE COMPONENT OF THE POLUNGU INDUSTRY

Artifacts from rubble probably contemporary with the 'Pits Channel' and intermediate in age between Rubble I and Rubble II, Excavation A2, 1956. All of chert except no. 10 in sandstone or soft, feldspathic quartzite.

1, 3–5 Bladelets, fresh. Nos. 1 and 3 from punched cores; no. 5 from Levallois blade (var.) core.

2 Partially trimmed and backed bladelet; fresh.

6, 7 Broad, triangular flakes with multi-faceted platforms. Fresh to very lightly abraded.

8 Borer with parti-bifacial retouch made on a rhomboidal sectioned chunk of chert; fresh.

9 Flat, bifacially flaked discoid/adze with finely retouched edge; one small flake only removed from one face, probably for resharpening or to facilitate hafting. Fresh.

10 Elongate Levallois core with high back; one large flake has been struck and the top end of the core has been worked to a core-axe edge. The scar ridges over the upper half of the tool on both faces have been dulled while those at the lower end are still fresh. The specimen may either be a Sizya Industry core that has been reworked or, possibly, a core that was hafted and used as a core-axe, the mounting material having protected the lower half of the tool. In the latter case the thinning of the proximal end may have been intentional to facilitate hafting. Sandstone or soft feldspathic quartzite.

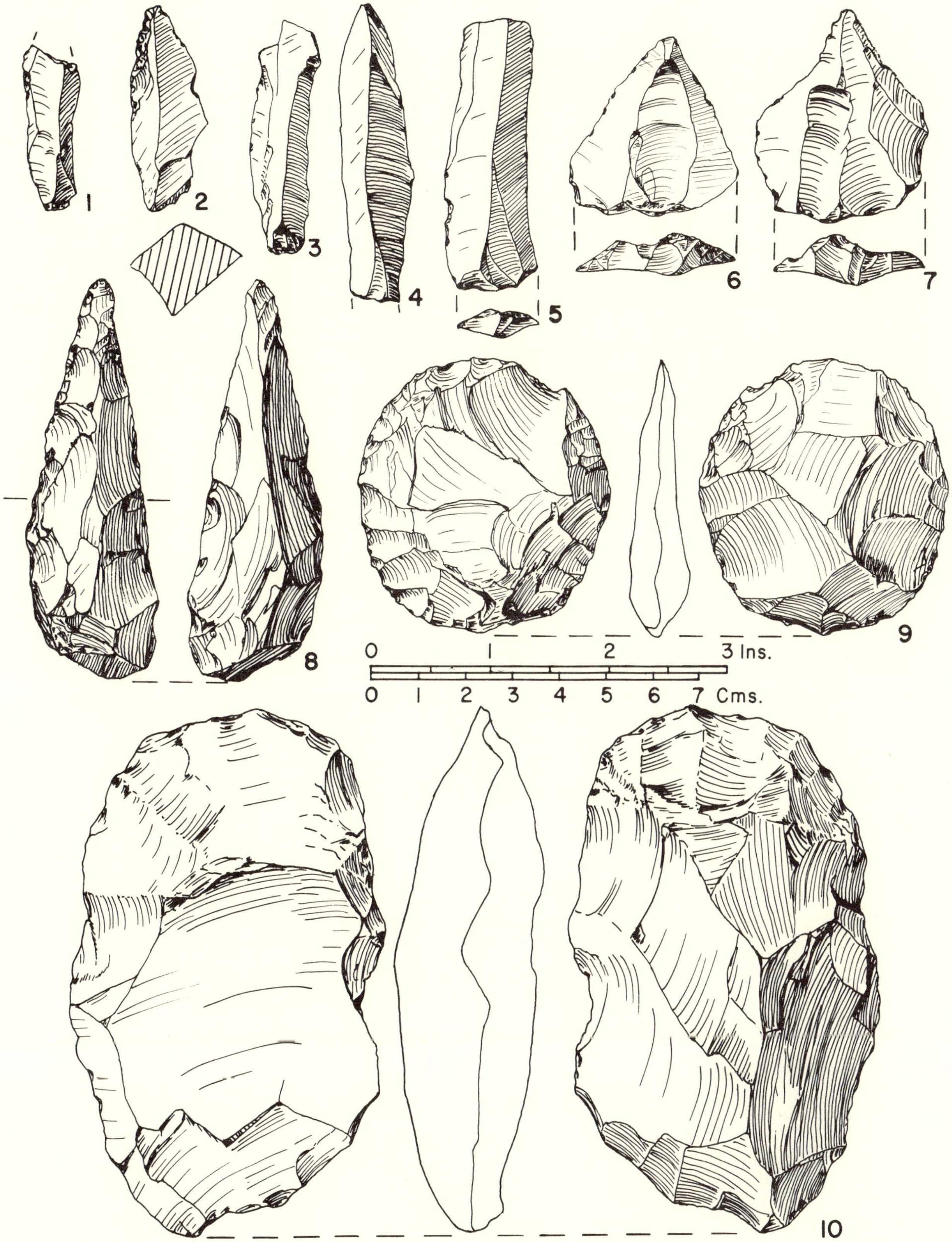
1
2
3
4
5
6
7
8
9
0 1 2 3 Ins.
0 1 2 3 4 5 6 7 Cms.
10

49 RUBBLE COMPONENT OF THE POLUNGU INDUSTRY

Artifacts from rubble I (composite) (nos. 1 and 4) Site C, 1963 and 1966 Excavations; also from Grey Sandy Clay (Bed 7) and sands (Bed 9) overlying Rubble I (nos. 2 and 3) and from Rubble I (composite) (nos. 5–12), Excavation A4, 1959. All represent the Rubble component of the Polungu Industry except possibly nos. 2 and 3 which may belong with the Hill-slope component.

1 Short, triangular, unifacial point on a chert flake with one-directional convergent dorsal scar pattern and broad, multi-faceted striking platform. Flat, shallow, semi-invasive and marginal retouch on the lateral edges. Fresh. C/66, Trench 4, uppermost rubble line.

2 Asymmetric, unifaced point with fine retouch by ?pressure along both lateral edges. Shallow and blunt angles of edge retouch. Chert; fresh; from Bed 7. A/64/59.

3 Diminutive, sub-triangular flake of chert with simple-faceted striking platform and marginal retouch on the dorsal face at the proximal end on both lateral edges. Fresh. From fine brown sand (Bed 9), A4 Excavation, 1959, grid square 0/2. A/117/59.

4 Asymmetric, foliate, unifacial point on a chert flake with parallel, one-directional dorsal scar pattern. The platform has been removed and the butt and both lateral edges modified by marginal to semi-invasive retouch; retouch angles shallow to blunt. Fresh. Site C, 1963, Rubble I (composite), here close to river level.

5 Partly backed blade. Chert; fresh/very slightly abraded. A/171/59–B/6.

6, 7 Abruptly truncated chert blades; fresh/very slightly abraded. A/128/59–A/1; A/145/59–A/2.

8 Utilized, short quadrilateral flake of chert struck from a specialized core. Fresh/very slightly abraded. A/163/59–A/9.

9 Unifacially trimmed borer made on a triangular-sectioned fragment of chert with flat flaking on the dorsal face. Fresh/very slightly abraded. A/157/59–B/11.

10 Specialized disc core from which two flakes have been struck from two opposed platforms. Chert; fresh/very slightly abraded. A/105/59–A–B/21.

11 Diminutive, high-backed and sub-triangular, specialized core from which two small, triangular flakes have been struck; these would have had multi-faceted platforms. Chert; fresh/very slightly abraded. A/174/59–B/1.

12 Discoid/adze, finely retouched by flat scalar flaking all round the circumference. Chert; fresh/very slightly abraded. A/147/59–A/13.

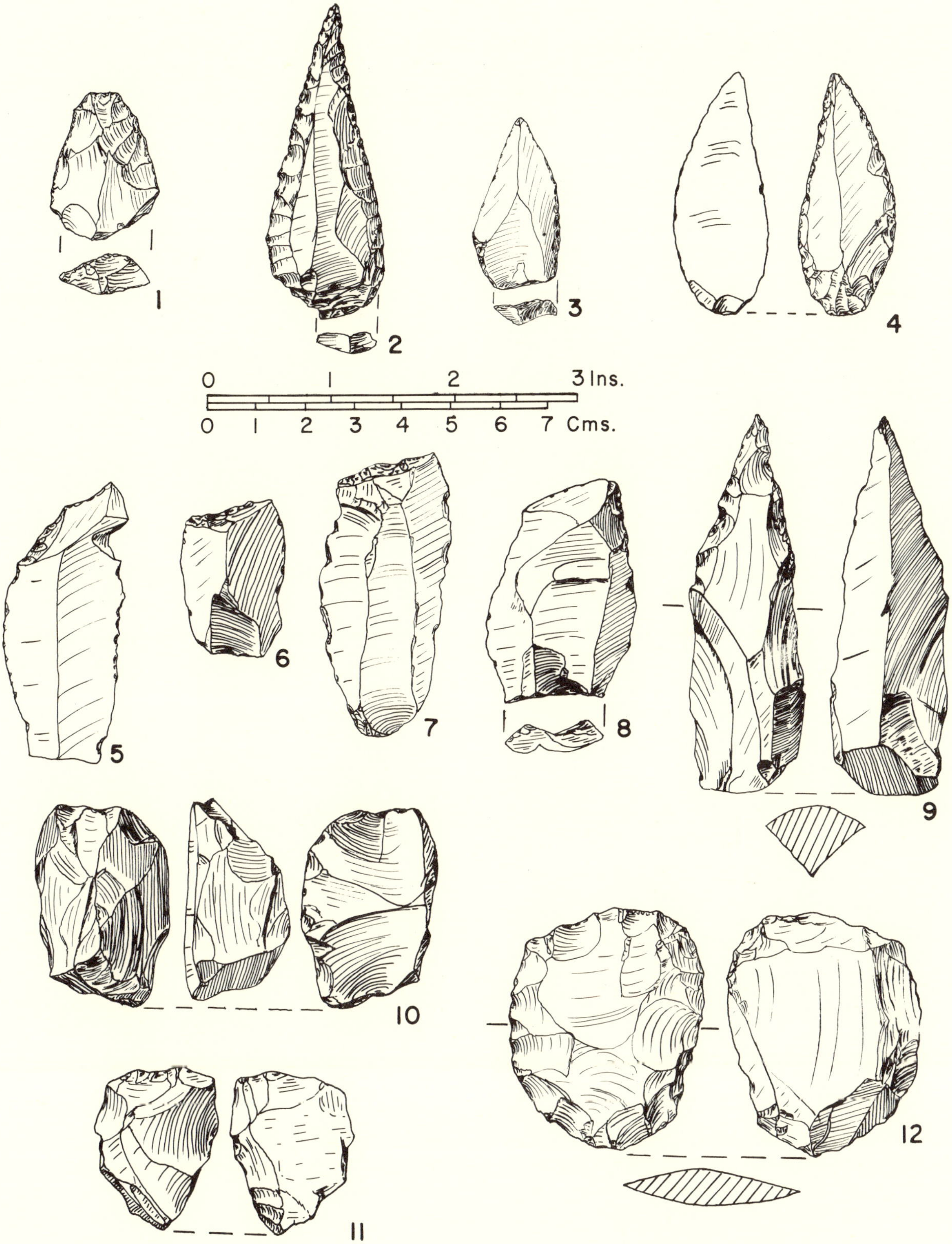
1
2
3
4
0 1 2 3 Ins.
0 1 2 3 4 5 6 7 Cms.
5
6
7
8
9
10
11
12

50 RUBBLE COMPONENT OF THE POLUNGU INDUSTRY

Artifacts from pebble line near the base of the yellow sands overlying Rubble I (composite), B1 Excavation, 1956 (nos. 1–4) and from Rubble Ib, B2 Excavation, 1959 (nos. 5–12).

1 Triangular flake with multi-faceted platform. Chert; fresh. B1/56.

2 Truncated bladelet. Chert; very lightly abraded. B1/56.

3 Double backed blade or unifaced point. Chert; fresh. B1/56.

4 Double ended, prismatic blade core on a square sectioned piece of chert. Fresh. B1/56.

5 Bifacial foliate point with distal end missing, made on a flake of hard quartzite. Bifacially trimmed by flat, invasive and step flaking over the whole of both faces. Fresh. B2/II/H7.

6 Bifacial point (distal end broken) made on an end-flake of chert with plain, inclined platform. Poorly retouched. Fresh. B2/II/H6.

7 Chert bladelet backed at both ends and with flat, inverse (Kasouga-type) retouch and utilization of one, straight lateral edge. B2/II/H6.

8 Chert bladelet with blunt backing down the upper half of one edge on the dorsal face. The distal end is broken and shows *esquillé* utilization on the main flake surface. Fresh. B2/II/1959/L3.

9 Long quadrilateral flake with modified invasive retouch at the proximal end to remove bulb and platform. Silcrete; fresh. B/134/59.

10 Unifaced point made on a long quadrilateral flake of chert from which the bulb and platform have been removed by snapping. Shallow, convergent, marginal retouch along the greater part of both lateral edges. Fresh. B2/II/1959/G6.

11 Sub-triangular, unifaced point made on a chert flake with multi-faceted striking platform. Finely retouched at the point, perhaps by pressure. Fresh. B2/II/1959/L2.

12 Sub-triangular, unifaced point made on a flake of chalcedony with broad, multi-faceted striking platform. Minimal marginal retouch on both edges. Fresh. B2/II/1959/K12.

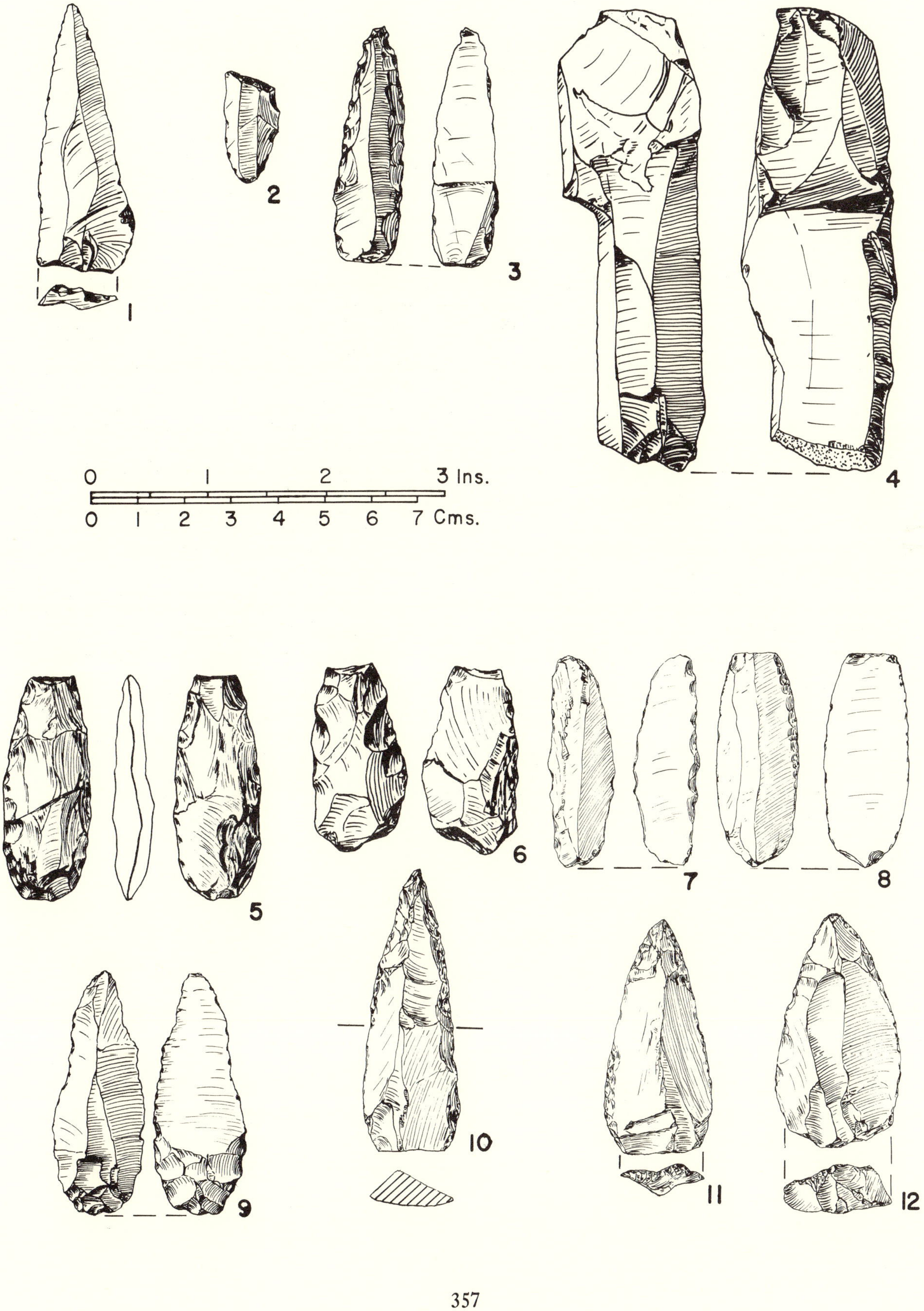
1
2
3
4
0 1 2 3 Ins.
0 1 2 3 4 5 6 7 Cms.
5
6
7
8
9
10
11
12

51 RUBBLE COMPONENT OF THE POLUNGU INDUSTRY

Artifacts from Rubble Ia, B2 Excavation, 1959.

1–8 Bladelets; chert; fresh. Nos. 1, 2, 5, 6 and 8 with simple faceted butts; nos. 3 and 4 with plain butts and no. 7 with point platform. B/128, 126, 127, 131, 181, 163, 132/63/59.

9 Trimming flake from small blade core having two platforms in different planes. Plain platform. Chert; fresh. B/65/59.

10 Blade with simple faceted platform; probably utilized. Chert; fresh. B/158/59.

11, 12 End flakes with multi-faceted platforms; utilized. Chert; fresh. B/132/59; B/128/59.

13 Flake backed down length of one lateral edge. Bulb and platform removed by retouch. Chert; fresh. B/128/59.

14 Blade or large lunate backed by steep retouch. Chert; fresh. B/128/59.

15 Backed flake with basal concave retouch and utilized cutting edge. Chert; fresh. B/132/59.

16 Straight, single edged side-scraper. Chert; fresh. B/158/59.

17 Utilized flake of chert. Fresh. B/131/59.

18 Denticulated scraper; retouch on both lateral edges and distal end. Shallow angle of retouch. Chert; fresh. B/126/59.

19–23 Short, triangular flakes with convergent dorsal scar pattern. Fresh. Nos. 19–21 with multi-faceted butts; no. 22 simple faceted and no. 23 plain. Most show utilization and no. 23 has been retouched at the proximal end of the right, lateral edge. B/133, 163, 163, 131, 131/59.

24 Double ended burin, dihedral (multiple facets) at distal end; single blow (angle burin on a break) at proximal end. Made on a chert fragment; fresh. B/163/59.

25 Marginally retouched blade fragment. Chert; fresh. B/163/59.

26 Denticulated, circular scraper with chisel edge worked on the distal part of the circumference. Made on a chert chunk; fresh. B/131/59.

27 Single platform, micro-blade core, made on a quartz pebble. Fresh. B/129/59.

28, 29 Broad flakes with radial preparation of the dorsal face, struck from ?Levallois cores; no. 28 with simple and no. 29 with multi-faceted platform. Chert: fresh. B/100/59; B/165/59.

30 Double edged, denticulated side-scraper on the broken proximal end of a long quadrilateral flake of chert. Plain platform; fresh. B/127/59.

31 Specialized, sub-triangular, radially prepared core of chert, flat backed. Fresh. B/163/59.

32 Specialized, radially prepared core, ovate, high backed. Silcrete; fresh. B/132/59.

33 Core with opposed platforms for the production of small blades by punch technique. Shows preparation of the striking platform which forms an angle of 58° with the flake surface. Chert; fresh. B/131/59.

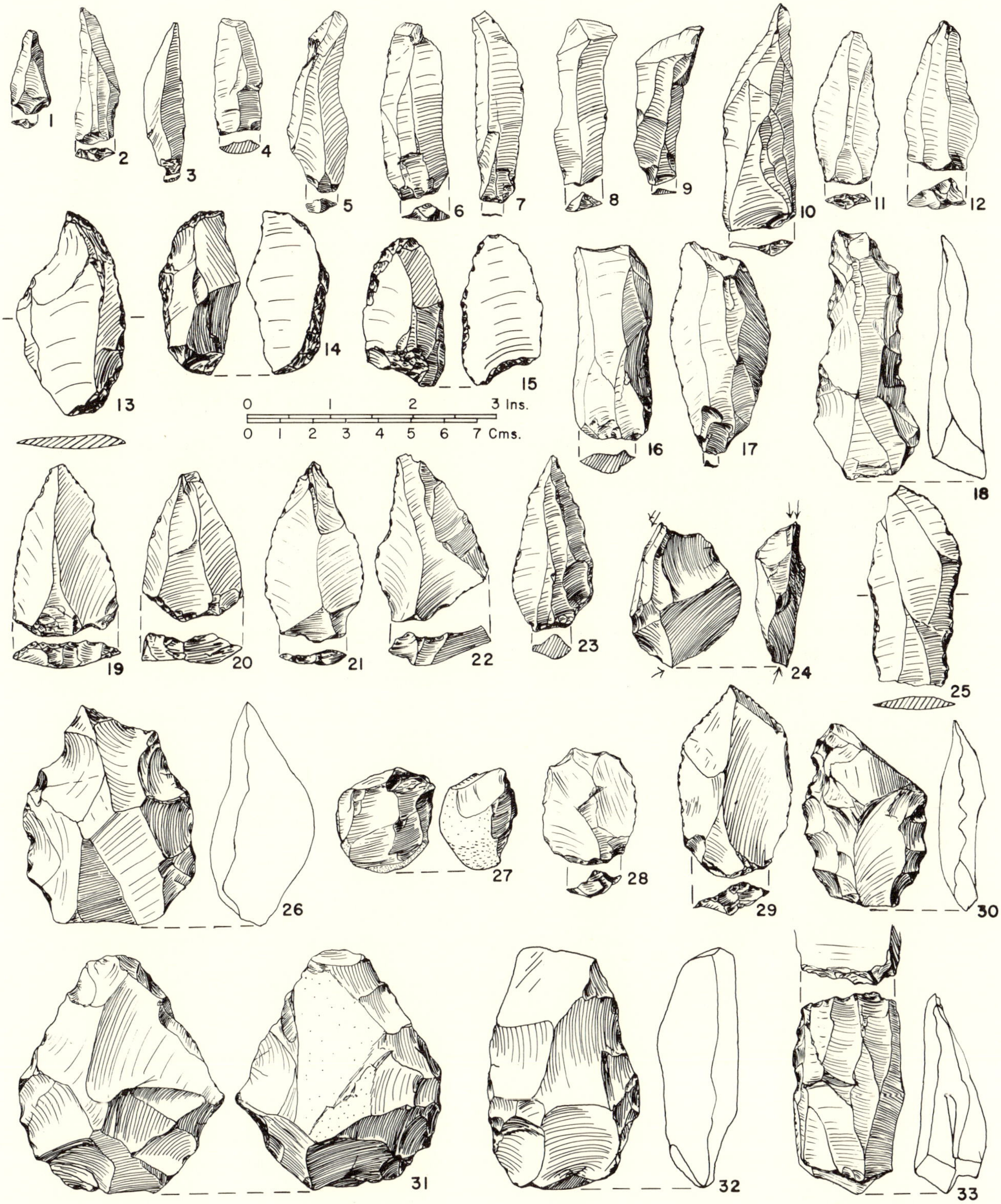
0 1 2 3 Ins.
0 1 2 3 4 5 6 7 Cms.

52 RUBBLE COMPONENT OF THE POLUNGU INDUSTRY

Artifacts from Rubble Ia, B2/1959, except no. 9 from Rubble Ib, B2/1959.

1 Chunk of chert worked by notching and with utilized beak and nosed areas. Fresh. B/133/59.

2 Discoid, high backed, specialized core in chert; fresh. B/127/59.

3 Diminutive, specialized core with one-directional flaking, trimmed to form a beaked scraping edge at the distal end. Chert; fresh. B/131/59.

4 Chunk of chert with notch (steep angle of retouch) and two proto-burin edges. Fresh. B/105/59.

5–6 Specialized cores, discoid, radially trimmed, flat backed. Chert; fresh. B/132, 131/59.

7 Specialized, radially prepared Levallois core: one large flake removed. Chert; fresh. B/132/59.

8 Specialized, sub-triangular core with convergent flaking for Levallois points; flat backed. Fresh; chert. B/131/59.

9 Discoid/adze, with utilization of *esquillé* type in the concavity at the distal end. Hard quartzite. Fresh/very lightly abraded. Rubble Ib. B/174/59.

10 Specialized discoid core with convergent dorsal scar pattern; high backed. Hard quartzite. Fresh. B/131/59.

11 Rubber made from a cobble of hard quartzite with four flat faces, one of which shows dimple scarring in the centre. The opposite face is polished by rubbing and grinding and shows incipient scarring, probably the result of use. B/126/59.

12 Specialized discoid core with radial dorsal scar pattern and flat back. Chert; fresh. B/163/59.

13 Half a bored stone made of sandstone. Diameter: 124 mm. Minimum diameter of bore: 26 mm; maximum diameter of bore: 44 mm; maximum thickness: 8·5 mm; minimum thickness: 6·5 mm. The external surface of the stone appears to have been carefully pecked smooth. The section through the bore shows asymmetric, hour-glass perforation due to uneven pecking and reaming from both faces. Weathered edges to the fracture faces which are also ferruginized. B/158/59.

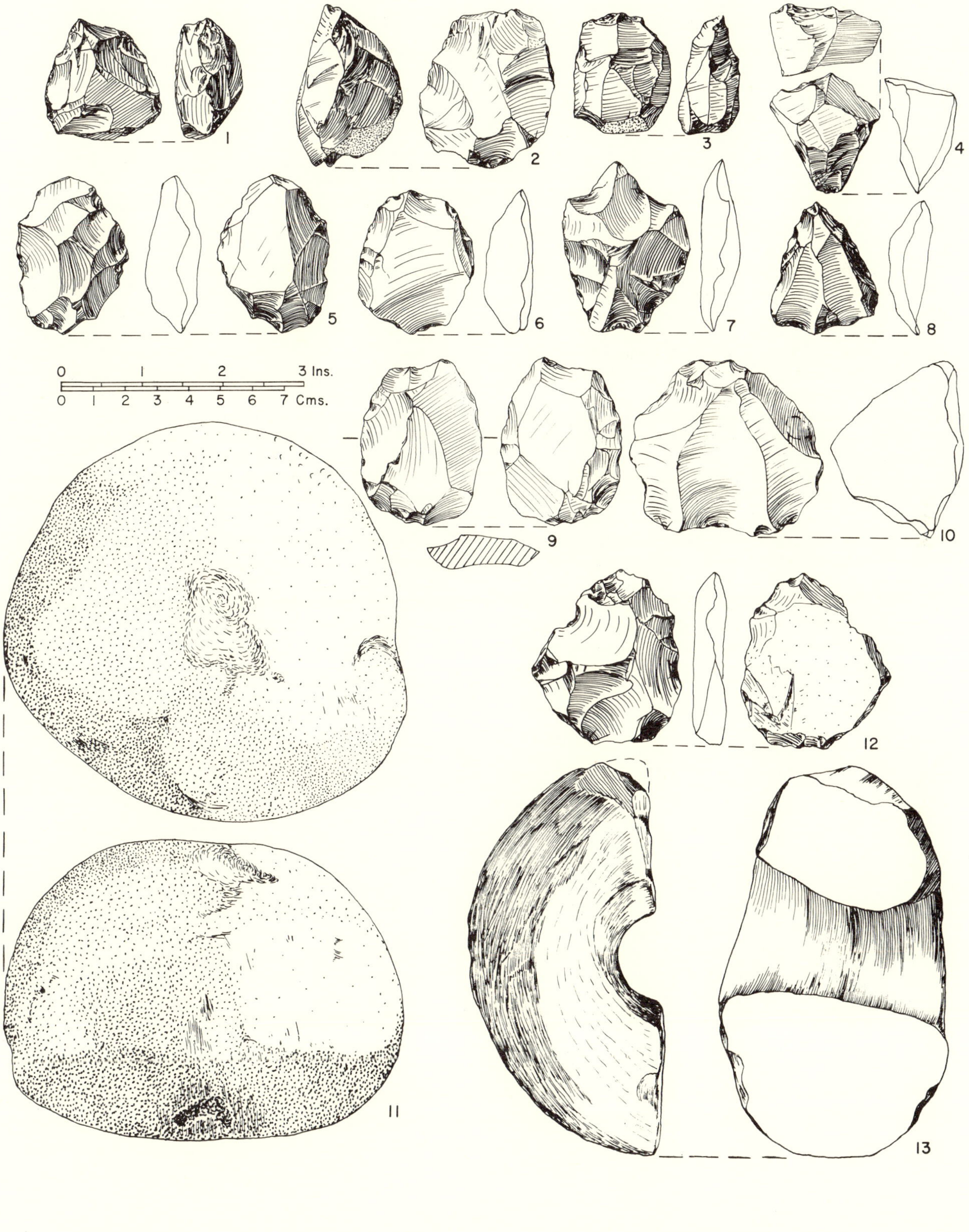
1
2
3
4
5
6
7
8
0 1 2 3 Ins.
0 1 2 3 4 5 6 7 Cms.
9
10
11
12
13

53 RUBBLE COMPONENT OF THE POLUNGU INDUSTRY

Artifacts from pebble lines and sands between Rubbles Ia and Ib, B2 Excavation, 1959.

1 Short, sub-triangular flake with multi-faceted striking platform. Edges utilized. Chert; very lightly abraded. B/104/59.

2 Short, asymmetric, sub-triangular flake with right angled, multi-faceted striking platform, two directional flaking on the dorsal face and utilized edges. Chert; very lightly abraded. B/116/59.

3 Obliquely truncated bladelet snapped across at the proximal end. Blunt angle of retouch. Chert; very lightly abraded. B/104/59.

4 Punched bladelet with straight, shallow backing down the left lateral edge. The right lateral edge shows utilization. Chert; very lightly abraded. B/96/59.

5 *Outil esquillé* on a ?bipolar core. Chert; fresh. B/111/59.

6 Large backed blade with steep angle of edge retouch. Multi-faceted striking platform. The straight cutting edge also shows shallow retouch and utilization. Chert; fresh. B/118/59.

7 Double ended *outil esquillé* on a bipolar core of crystalline quartz. Fresh/very lightly abraded. B/110/59.

8 Diminutive, specialized discoid core, radially prepared for the removal of more than one small flake; flat. Multi-faceted striking platform prepared at the proximal end. Chert; fresh. B/110/59.

9 Bifacial, lanceolate point with asymmetric, lenticular cross-section. Completely flaked over both faces by controlled percussion retouch. Silcrete; fresh. B/96/59.

10 Sub-triangular, parti-bifacial point with triangular cross-section. Made on a chert flake by controlled percussion retouch. Fresh. B/110/59.

11 Large, convergent scraper or asymmetric, unifaced pick made from a thick, plain platformed, primary flake of hard quartzite. Blunt angle of edge retouch. Fresh/very lightly abraded. B/99/59.

12 Angled or convergent scraper on an unprepared, concave–convex, side flake of silcrete. Regular, serrated, convex retouch on the main edge. Blunt angle of retouch. Fresh. B/110/59.

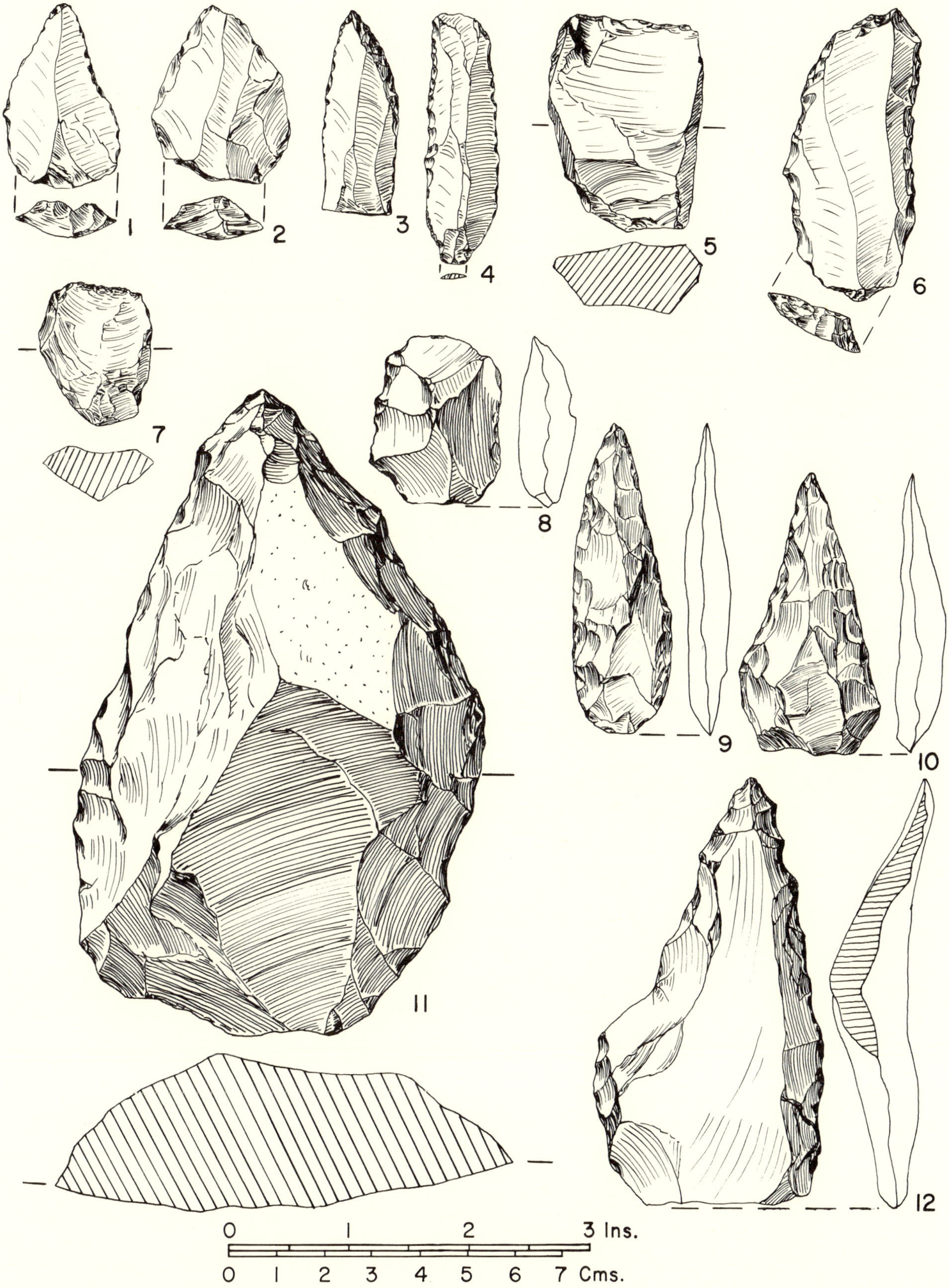
1
2
3
4
5
6
7
8
9
10
11
12
0 1 2 3 Ins.
0 1 2 3 4 5 6 7 Cms.

54 RUBBLE COMPONENT OF THE POLUNGU INDUSTRY

Artifacts from Rubble I, B1 Excavation, 1956 (nos. 11 and 18); from D, 1956 Excavation (no. 3); from Rubble Ia, B2 Excavation, 1959 (no. 9); and from Rubble Ib, B2 Excavation, 1959 (nos. 1, 2, 4–8, 10, 12–17, 19).

1 Punch struck blade with steep, oblique truncation. Chert; grey patina; fresh. B2/II/L5.

2 Obliquely truncated blade with steep angle of retouch. The truncation is on the proximal end and has removed the bulb and platform. Chert with white patina. B/142/59.II/59/J6.

3 Bladelet backed down the whole of one lateral edge. Blunt to steep angle of retouch which is directed from the ventral surface. Chert; fresh. D2/56/II/a/1.

4 Backed, side-struck flake of chert. Fresh/very lightly abraded. B2/II/M6.

5 Backed flake or asymmetric, unilaterally retouched point, made on a sub-triangular flake with multi-faceted, right-angled striking platform. Backing from the ventral surface and with shallow to blunt retouch angle. Chert; fresh. B2/II/L5.

6 Short quadrilateral flake with proximal retouch on both lateral edges and simple faceted striking platform. Chert; very lightly abraded/fresh. B2/II/M9.

7 Double ended *outil esquillé* with typical utilization scars on both faces. Chert; fresh/very lightly abraded. B/15/59.II/H5.

8 Discoid/adze of chert, bifacially worked by flat radial flaking. Straight edge in profile. Asymmetric, biconvex section. Fresh. B2/II/L1.

9 Backed blade (proximal end broken). Sub-triangular in plan form. Blunt retouch from the ventral face. Chert; very lightly abraded. B2/I/59. B/163/59. Rubble Ia.

10 End-scraper on a short quadrilateral flake with plain, inclined striking platform and blunt to steep angle of retouch. Fresh/very lightly abraded. Chert. B/138/59. K4.

11 Convergent scraper or *bec*, straight edged on a short, irregular, end-struck flake of chert; blunt retouch angles. Plain, inclined striking platform. The retouch is alternating: notched on the ventral and straight on the dorsal face. Fresh/very lightly abraded. B/56/II/biy.

12, 13 Flakes struck from double ended bladelet cores. Chert; fresh/very lightly abraded. B/134/59; B/113/59.

14 Straight edged, double side-scraper made on a chert blade. Narrow, restricted striking platform with platform scarring at the proximal end on the dorsal face; probably struck by punch technique. Retouched by step flaking; shallow angles. Fresh. B2/II/H12.

15 Short, irregular quadrilateral flake with plain platform, struck from a disc core. Chert; fresh. B/143/59.

16 Flakelet with simple faceted platform (two scars), struck from a disc core. B/163/59. A/9.

17 Sub-rectangular lump of kaolin from which white pigment was obtained, shaped by rubbing, possibly in the process of obtaining the pigment. The main, broad, rubbed surface is oblique to the main axis of the lump. Found in stepping back. B/211/59.

18, 19 Examples of triangular flakes struck from specialized cores. Broad, faceted striking platforms; edge utilization. No. 18 in chalcedony and no. 19 in chert; fresh. B56/e2/II; B/209/59.

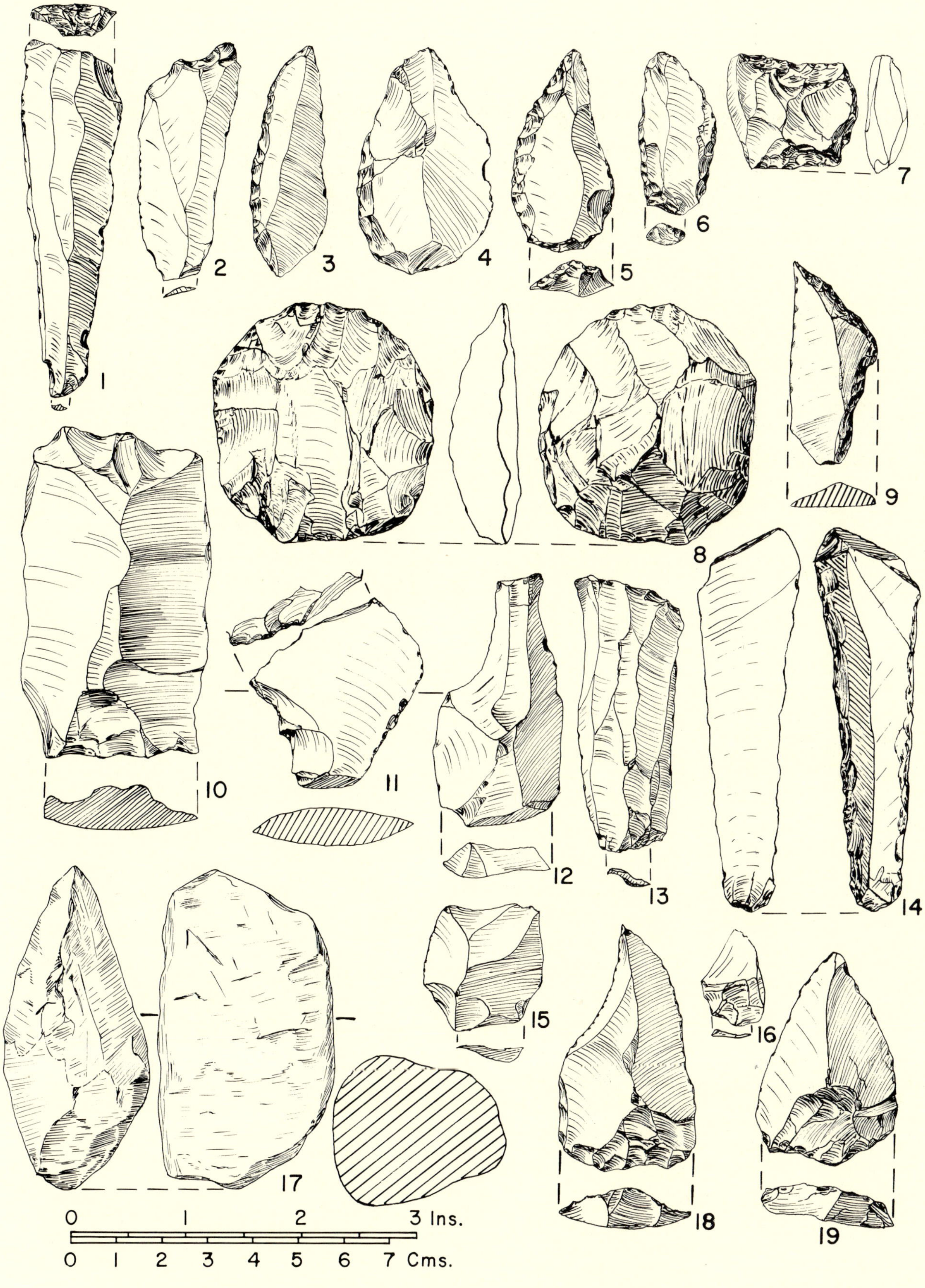
1
2
3
4
5
6
7
8
9
10
11
12
13
14
15
16
17
18
19
0 1 2 3 Ins.
0 1 2 3 4 5 6 7 Cms.

55 The Ichianga Swamp (1956), a small local basin formed by impeded drainage between the junction of two feeders of the Chianga stream, 14 miles (22·5 km) southeast of the Kalambo Falls. Grass and swamp vegetation cover the central parts which flood, with limited areas of open water, following a succession of good rainy seasons (e.g. in 1963). A small patch of swamp forest with raphia palms is prominent at left and the surrounding *Brachystegia-Julbernardia* (*miombo*) woodland is well seen in the middle distance. The vegetation of the Kalambo basin was probably not unlike this during the Early Iron Age before the woodland and forest were cut out by many years of cultivation.

56 The central valley from Mkamba Village, showing the eroded remnant of the 30 foot (9 m) terrace (middle distance, right) formed by the Mbwilo Member of the Kalambo Falls Formation. Site C and the Early Iron Age (Kalambo Falls Industry) settlement are located on this terrace, now a finger millet garden, between the small garden hut (centre right) and the footpath (right). Site B lies behind the trees (centre) and Site D on the extension of the terrace off the photo to the right. In the background is Siszya Ridge with Polungu Hill at right. Mound and ridge gardens can be seen in the low-lying centre part of the basin (left and centre) and Chiungu Village in the trees at left (middle distance).

57 A MuLungu hunter from the Kalambo Falls showing the method of arrow release and shooting with the bow. The bow, *ulapwa*, is made from *mukole* wood (*Thespesia garckeana*) and bound at each end with bark string (*mwando*) or thong. The bowstring is made from twisted hide, *lusienga*. The typical arrow, *lucheto*, has a triangular iron head with barbs and a long tang. The shaft of *Phragmites* reed, *itete*, is bound with wire, *lusambe*, where the head fits into the shaft, to prevent splitting. Poison, *mwambane*, (*Strophanthus* sp.) in the form of a malleable paste, is applied to the whole length of the tang. In the hand grasping the bowstave, the hunter holds a bird arrow with conical wooden head. Other arrows are contained in the quiver, *munengo*, slung from the left shoulder and made from a gourd, *nembo*, with greenhide, *mpapa*, covering the base and forming a band round the mouth.

58 A MuLungu from Mkamba Village demonstrating the method of smoothing a bowstave with a piece of bottle glass. Note the steep angle made by the wood and the working edge of the glass scraper which is drawn over the surface towards the body. Before glass became available, sharp fragments of stone were used and are still sometimes so employed today.

59 Modern Lungu hut, Mkamba Village, showing wall construction of poles with mud plastered on both faces, thatched roof, verandah and raised floor level; pots and baskets. Just visible at the right is a drying rack for cassava, etc.

60 Pile of burned and disintegrating *daga* and bases of charred wall poles – all that remains after the destruction of a hut on the death of its owner. Kaporo area, northern Malawi.

61 Small *tutu* beehive hut built of bent branches and thatch by Fipa men at the Kalambo Falls in 1966. The framework may be thatched, covered with sods or mud plaster as circumstances or purposes dictate.

62 Traditional *mwende* huts of poles, banked earth and thatched apex built by Nyiha in Ufipa (Lechaptois, 1932) are still sometimes constructed today in remoter parts of the plateau.

63 The only surviving example of a group of several iron smelting furnaces of the tall upright variety situated approximately half a mile (805 m) north of Mkamba Village, Kalambo Falls. This furnace is said to have been in operation in 1914. A pile of discarded tuyères and slag is visible at the left behind Professor G. Bond.

64 Large, vertical kiln for smelting iron in use in Ufipa in the 1930s (Lechaptois, 1932). In the left foreground is the pit made in the side of a termite mound from which the clay to construct the furnace was taken. The kiln is stacked from the scaffolding with alternate layers of iron ore (centre right) and charcoal (in baskets). Tuyères (*tewels*) pipes for admitting air to the furnace stand against the wall ready to be set in the holes left at intervals round the base of the kiln. The smelt takes between two and three days to complete.

65 Small refining furnace in use in Ufipia in the 1930s (Lechaptois, 1932), necessary after initial smelting in the tall furnace when the ore is of poor quality. Three goat skin bellows provide the blast through tuyères set in the furnace wall. Note the *tutu*-type hut at left. This smelting takes *c.* 45 hours to complete.

66 Smith and assistants operating bellows and using heavy stone hammer to beat out iron metal on stone anvil. Note the large stone to hold the nozzle of the bellows firmly in position; iron hammers for finishing work; a large hoe blade leaning against the wall and a hafted hoe (right rear). Framework of *tutu*-type hut in background. (Lechaptois, 1932.)

67 Line of stones and fine gravel at depth of 6 to 7 feet (1·8–2·1 m) that separates the red clay of the 'Younger Channel' fill (F″) (right) from the grey silty clay of the 'Older Channel' fill (F′) (left) with Early Iron Age pottery of the Kalambo Falls Industry. The stones are probably naturally accumulated along the line of the channel bank (C7″) though the line may possibly be in part artificial. Site A, Excavation A1, 1956.

68 Circular area (diameter *c.* 4 feet (1·2 m)) of reddened and hardened clay with stone surround found at a depth of 9 feet 3 inches (2·8 m) in 'Older Channel' fill and overlain by the red clays of the 'Younger Channel' (Phase F7″). Possibly the floor of a field hut set in the bottom of the channel as in the broad gully immediately north of the excavation where bananas were under cultivation. Grid squares B/1–2, Site A, Excavation A1, 1956.

69 Site C, looking south. General view of the eastern half of the 1963 excavation in the Early Iron Age settlement on the top of the 30 foot (9·1 m) terrace, Kalambo Falls. The excavation cuts through the occupation midden into the stratified, yellow sands (Phase F6) of the Mbwilo Member of the Kalambo Falls Formation. Occupation debris of the Kalambo Falls Industry occurs throughout the ±3 feet (91 cm) of grey, ashy midden. The microlithic ('Later Stone Age') aggregate occurs in the top few inches of the underlying yellow sand. Several of the shaft complexes dug by the Early Iron Age inhabitants into the yellow sands are clearly visible as darker circles, some marked by collections of pottery and stones. Left foreground – part of Complex 4, Complex 5, Complex 6 (by break in River Face wall), Complexes 11 and 8 adjacent to rear wall. River level is 34 feet (10·4 m) below the cliff top immediately beyond the east wall. See Volume 1, Plate 31 for view of the cliff face at Site C (1966).

70 Site C, looking east. General view of 1963 excavation showing Complexes 10, 9 and 5 to left and Complex 8 to right.

71 Group of stones and broken pottery in the top of the shaft of Complex 4. Note the darker colour of the fill in the centre pit and surrounding ring. Grid squares A/1–2 and B/1–2, Kalambo Falls Industry settlement excavation, Site C, 1963.

72 Close up of the three large grindstone fragments, broken shouldered pot, sherd from an undecorated bowl and smaller sherds in the fill of the central shaft of Complex 4, Kalambo Falls Industry settlement excavation, Site C, 1963.

73 The concentration of pottery in the mouth of the shaft of Complex 8; Grid squares F/4–5 to G/4–5, Kalambo Falls Industry settlement excavation, Site C, 1963.

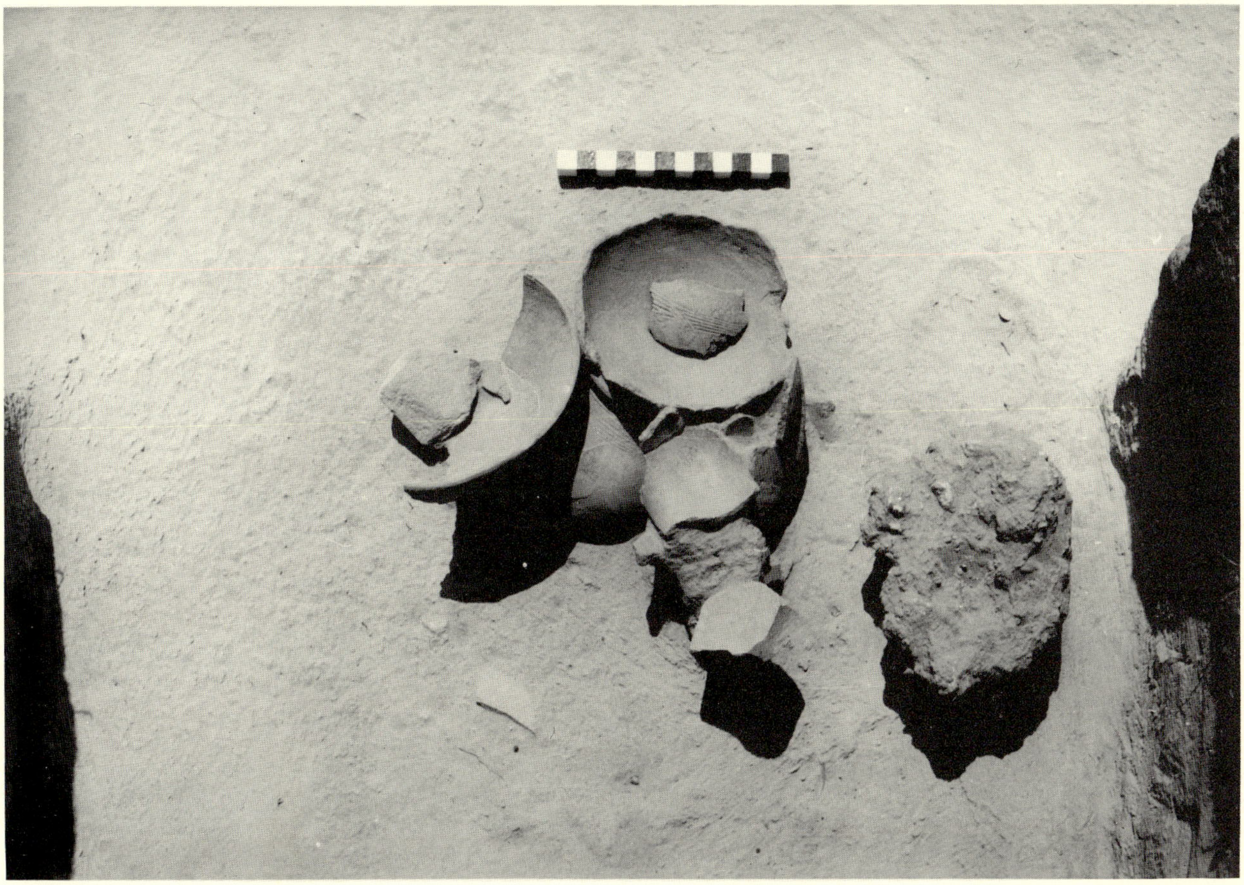

74 Large slab immediately underlying the concentration seen in Plate 73, Complex 8, Kalambo Falls Industry settlement excavation, Site C, 1963.

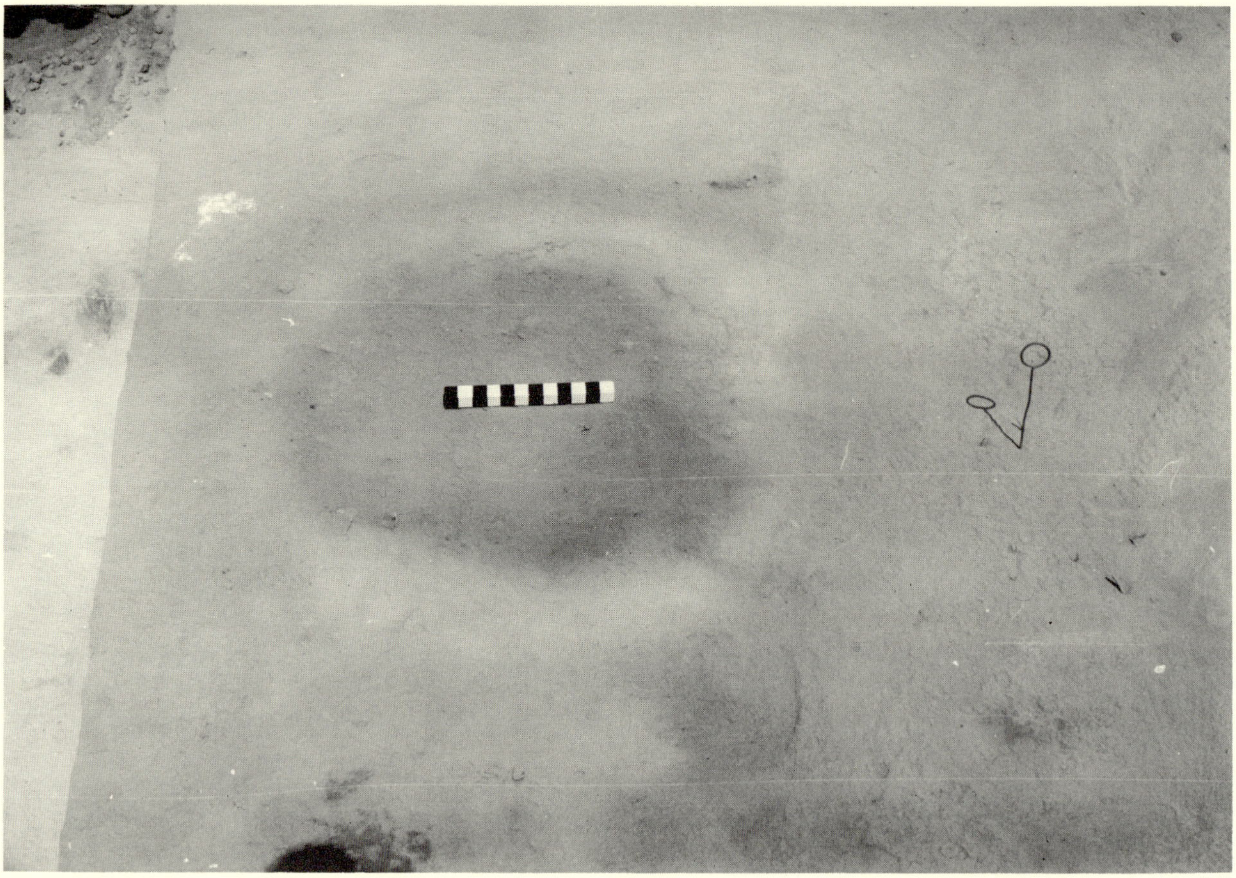

75 The dark fill in the mouth of the shaft of Complex 9, separated by a ring of light coloured sand from an outer ring of darker, sandy fill probably marking the circumference of a shallow footing trench to support a wall. Grid squares C/3–D/3, Kalambo Falls Industry settlement excavation, Site C, 1963.

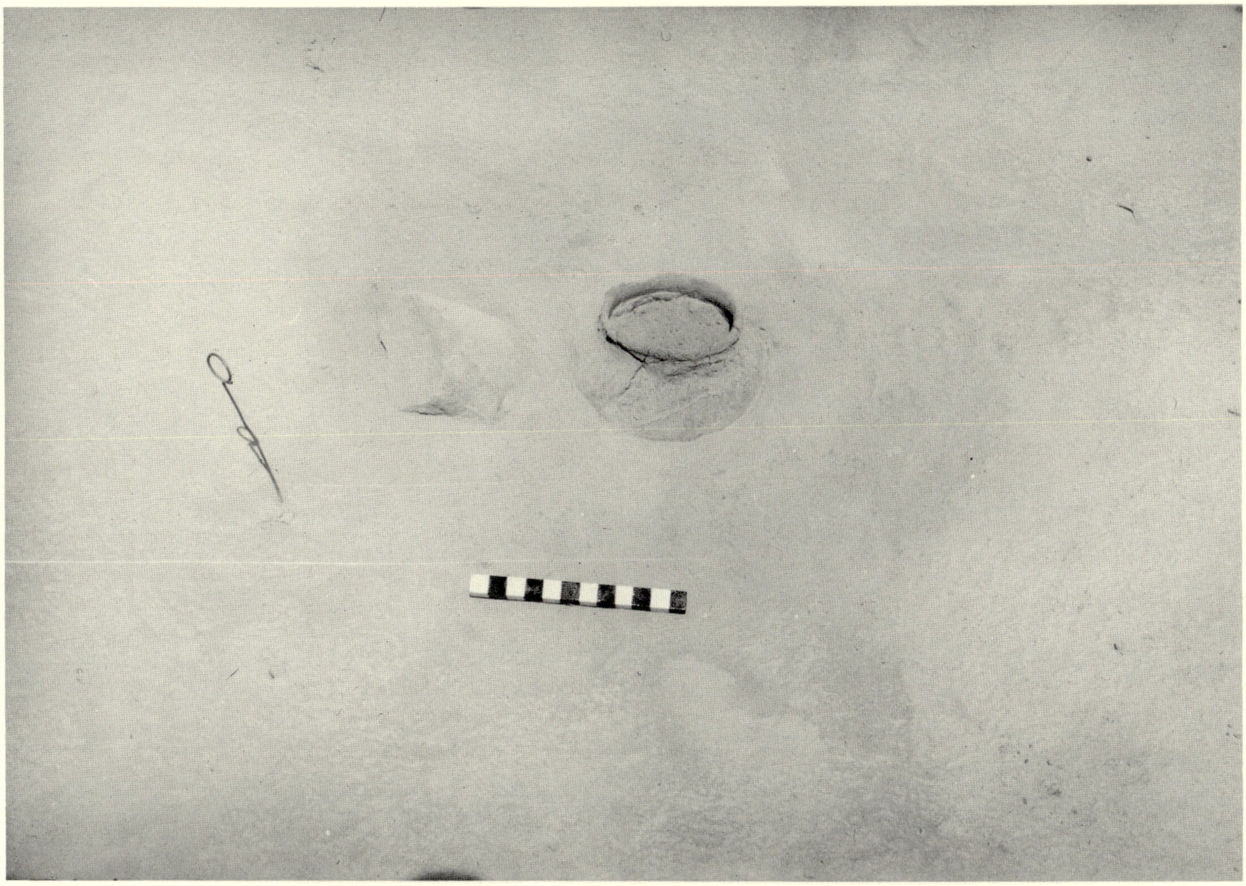

76 The upper part of the large, shouldered pot and one of two grindstone fragments at a depth of 4 feet 10 inches (1·5 m) in the upper part of the shaft of Complex 9, Kalambo Falls Industry settlement excavation, Site C, 1963.

77 Complex 7 belonging to the beginning of the Early Iron Age occupation and comprising a grinding stone, three further fragments of grinders, *daga* and potsherds not associated with a shaft or pit. Possibly the base of a grain store or a grinding place. Grid squares E/4–F/4, Kalambo Falls Industry settlement excavation, Site C, 1963.

78 The saucer shaped bloom of iron metal and slag from the base of an iron smelting furnace adjacent to an irregular area of reddened and hardened clay floor 2 feet (61 cm) below the surface in the Early Iron Age midden and lying one foot (30 cm) above the mouth of the shaft of Complex 10. Grid squares C/4–5 to D/4–5, Kalambo Falls Industry settlement excavation, Site, C, 1963.

79 The top of the shaft and outer ring of Complex 10 with potsherds and stone, after the removal of the bloom and floor in Plate 78. The shaft and ring of Complex 9 can be seen towards the top of the picture. Kalambo Falls Industry settlement excavation, Site C, 1963.

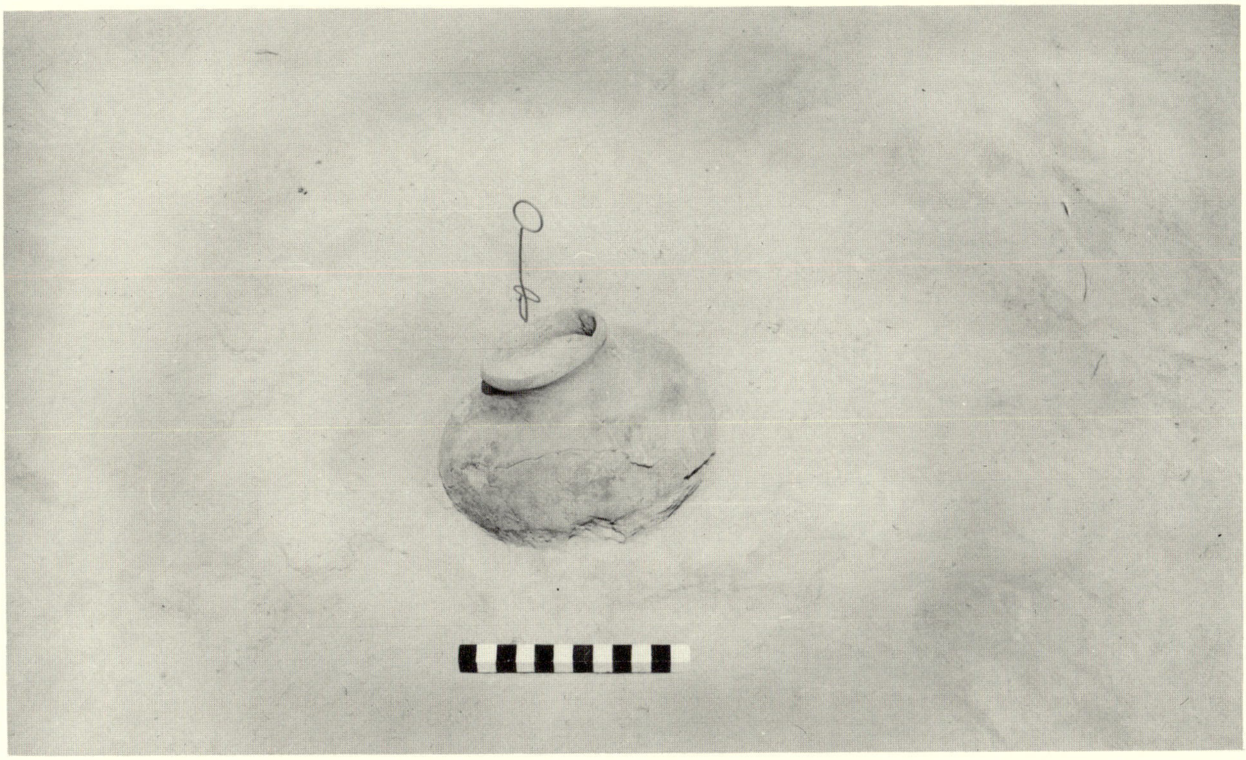

80 The upper part of a large, shouldered pot *c.* 10 inches (25·4 cm) below the top of the shaft of Complex 10, Kalambo Falls Industry settlement excavation, Site C, 1963.

81 Section through the shaft of Complex 11 showing one of the large pots and concentrations of stones and potsherds in the lower part of the fill. The thin, post-depositional clay lenses can be seen to dip but to continue across the shaft filling. Grid squares G/3–H/4, Kalambo Falls Industry settlement excavation, Site C, 1963.

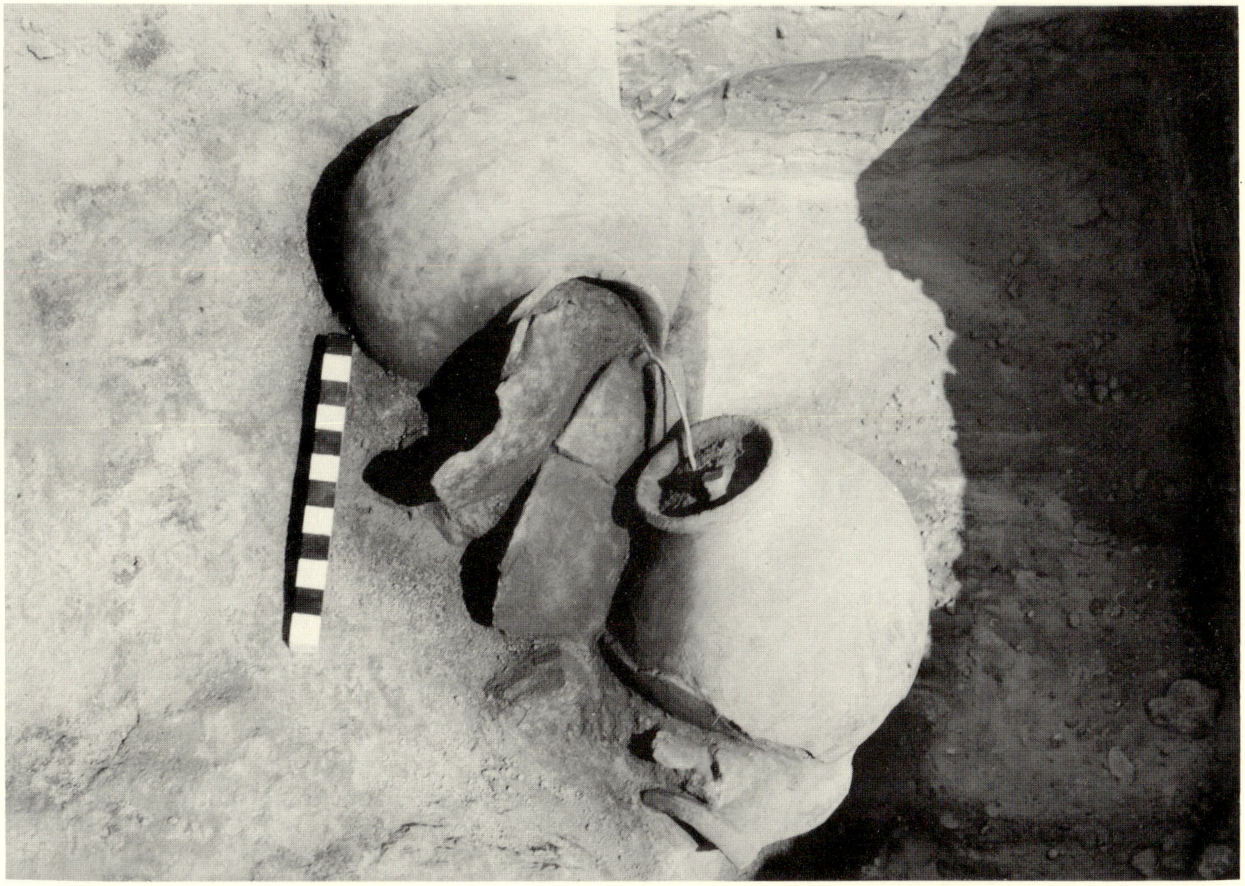

82 The two large shouldered pots without bases and bowl sherds at a depth of 5 feet 6 inches (1·7 m) in the shaft of Complex 11. The white line joining the mouths of the two pots is a root. Kalambo Falls Industry settlement excavation, Site C, 1963.

83 Showing the nearly complete, large, shouldered pot, stone and sherds (pedestalled) in the top of the shaft of Complex 6; also sherds on end in the base of the shaft, the dimensions of which show clearly against the light coloured sand through which the shaft is dug. Note also the way in which the irregular lenses of clay run right across the shaft showing them to be a post depositional feature of the site. Grid square E/1, Kalambo Falls Industry settlement excavation, Site C, 1963.

84 Concentration at a depth of 4 feet 6 inches (137 cm) of stone fragments and large sherds from a shouldered pot and undecorated bowl in the shaft of Complex 12; grid squares B/2–C/3, Kalambo Falls Industry settlement excavation, Site C, 1963.

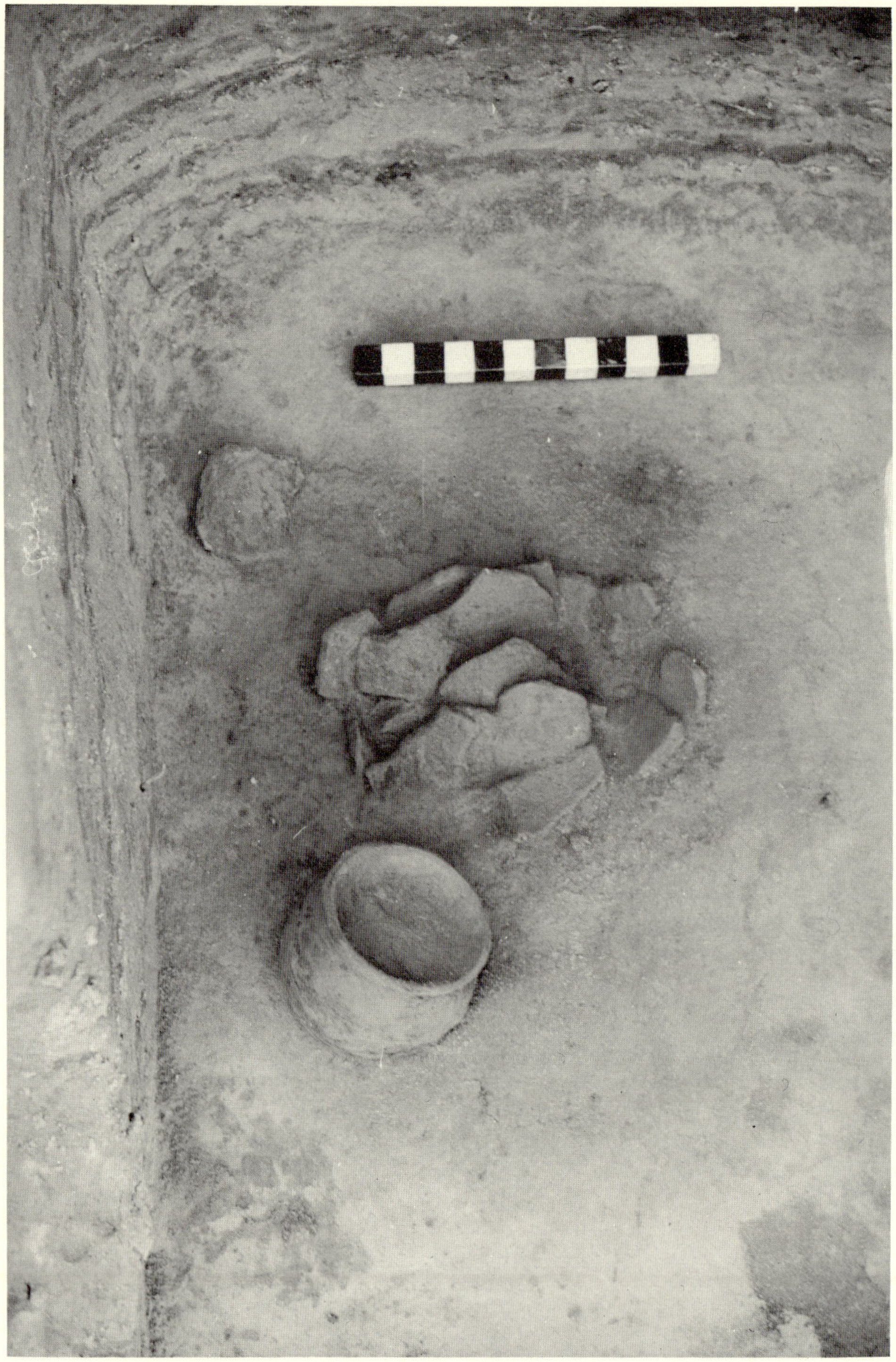

85 Concentration of sherds and complete, unbroken pot in the bottom of the shaft of Complex 12. Kalambo Falls Industry excavation, Site C, 1963.

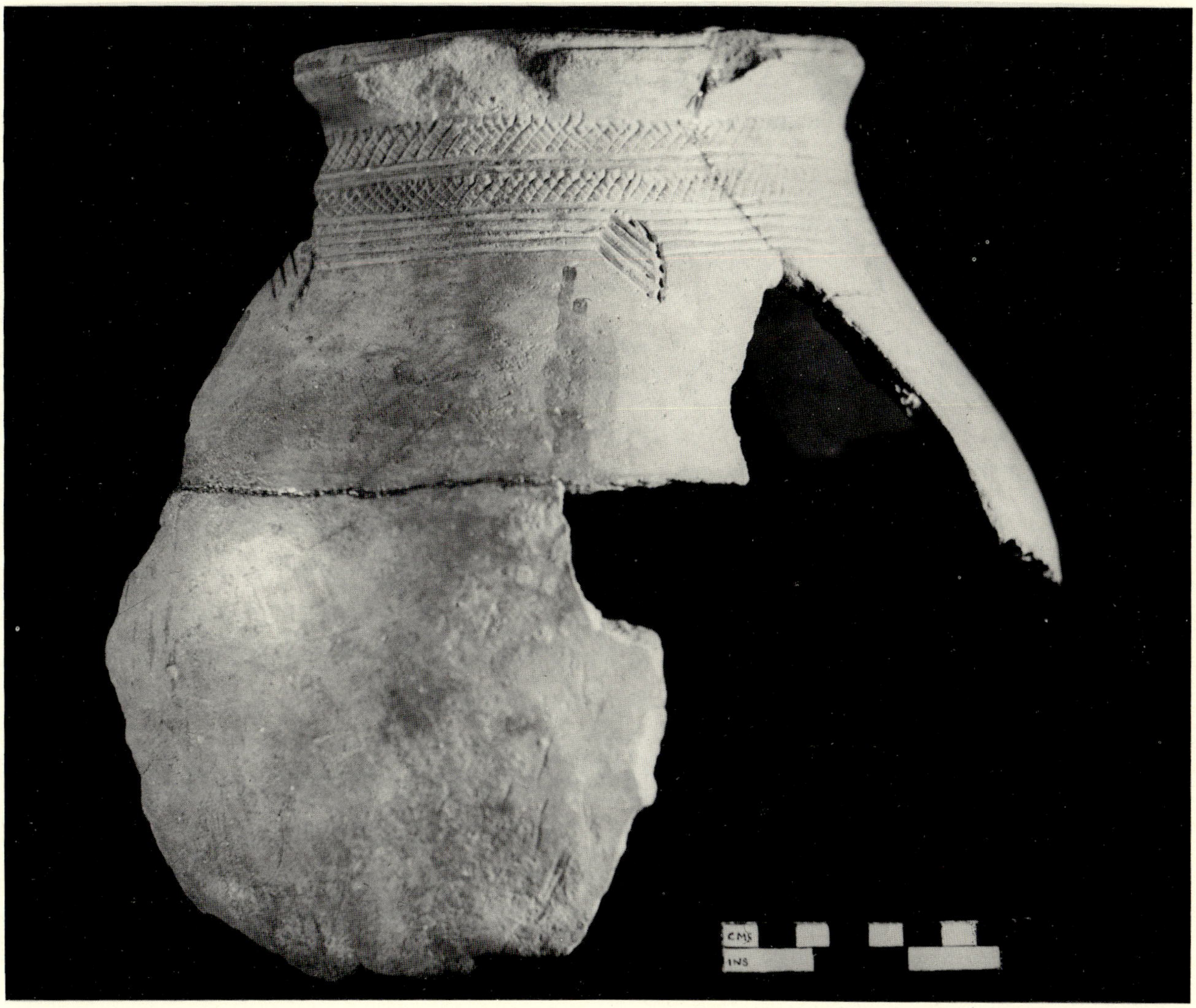

86 The large, incomplete, shouldered pot (Plate 5, no. 3) with grooved and bevelled rim and with the typical channelling and cross-hatched decoration of the Kalambo Falls Industry wares. Found broken into a number of large pieces, with sherds of two other pots and a grindstone (Plate 91, left) in the top of the grey brown clay (Bed 9) near the base of the 'Older Channel' fill (F7) (Chiungu Member) *c.* 40 metres east of A4 trench. Site A, River Face, 1959 (A/184/59).

87 Shouldered pot with bevelled rim, cross-hatching and channelling with zigzag motif. Site C, Kalambo Falls Industry. Found at the base of the occupation midden with Complex 1, associated with bowl sherds possibly buried into a shallow pit dug into the midden soil from a depth of 1 foot 6 inches to 2 feet (45–61 cm).

88 Kalambo Falls Industry shouldered pot with rolled over rim; undecorated except for a motif incised on the outside wall after firing and thought, perhaps, to represent a body in a grave. From a depth of 2 feet 8 inches (81 cm) in grey sand of the Early Iron Age midden. Grid square A/3; Site D2, 1956. (Photograph by L. Titchener. Copyright Zambia Information Department.)

89 Sherds showing examples of channelled decoration, incised hatching, chevron decoration and stamping. From 'Older Channel' fill clays, Site A1, 1956. Depths, respectively from left to right: top row – 9 feet 6 inches to 10 feet (2·0–3·1 m), 12 feet to 13 feet (3·6–3·9 m), 8 feet to 10 feet (2·4–3·1 m); bottom row – 11 feet to 11 feet 6 inches (3·3–3·5 m), 10 feet to 11 feet (3·1–3·3 m), 13 feet to 14 feet (3·9–4·3 m). (Photograph by L. Titchener. Copyright Zambia Information Department.)

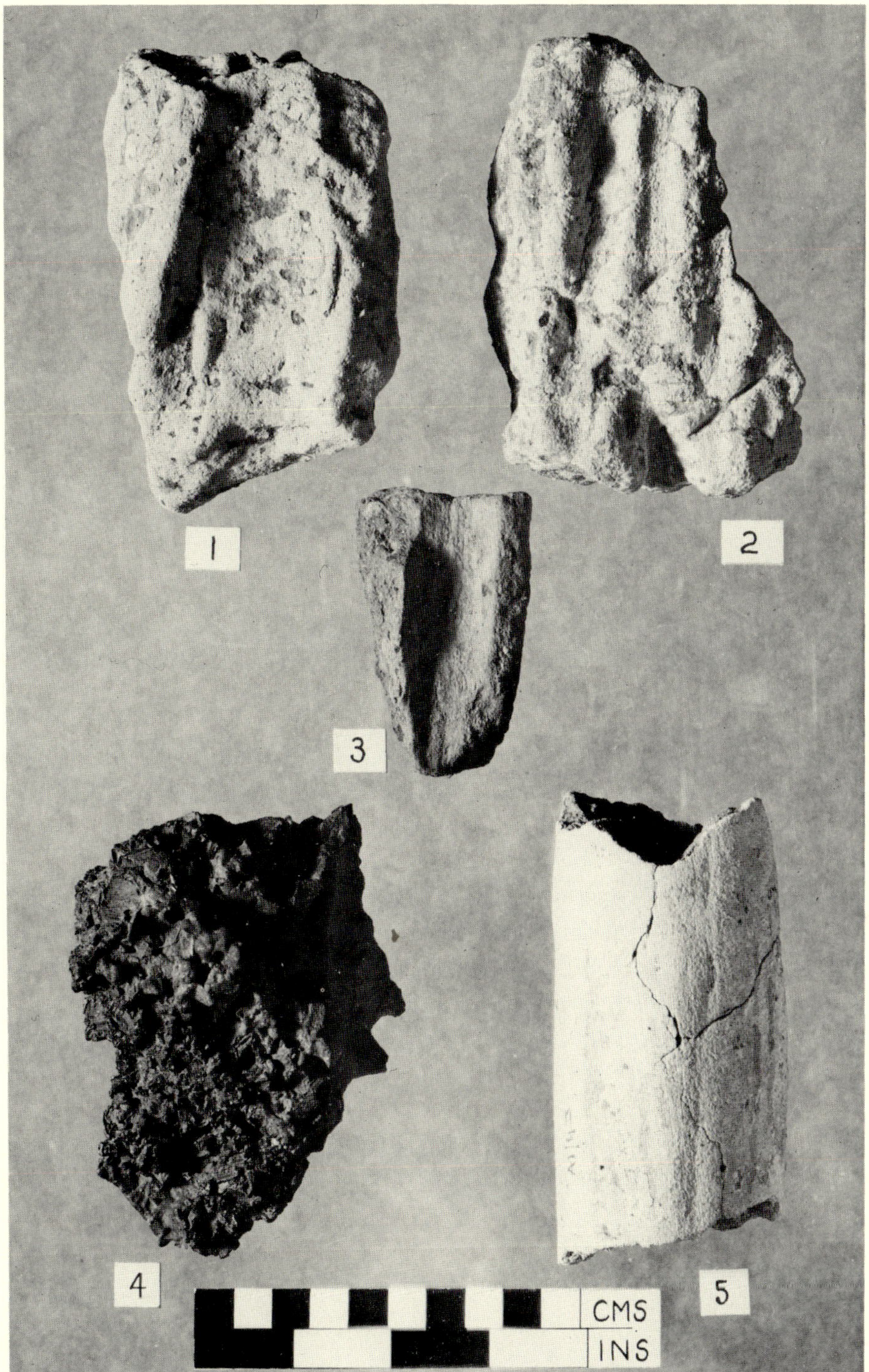

90 I and 2 – Hut *daga* showing pole and stick impressions. 3 and 5 – *tuyère* fragments and 4 – iron slag; from the 'Younger Channel' fill clays, Kalambo Falls Industry, Site A1, 1956 (A1/9) 3 feet 6 inches to 4 feet 6 inches (107–137 cm). (Photograph by L. Titchener. Copyright Zambia Information Department.)

91 *Left:* Upper grindstone of 'bun rubber' type. Both faces show extensive use for grinding and side edges for pounding. Found at the same level and in proximity to the lower grindstone (right). In 'Older Channel' fill (F7) (Chiungu Member). Grid square F/4 (no. A25). Sandstone, $15 \times 15 \times 7 \cdot 5$ cm. Site A, excavation A1, 1956.

Right: Lower grindstone of sandstone, $31 \times 26 \times 11$ cm. Both faces show striated grinding surfaces but shallow, elongate dishing on the upper face only. Found in association with possible upper grinding stone (left) at depth of 6 feet 10 inches (2·0 m) in 'Older Channel' fill (F7) (Chiungu Member) Grid square F/4 (no. A25), Site A, excavation A1, 1956.

92 *Left:* Flat (?upper), grindstone, well striated and used on both faces; fractured on one edge. Found in association with the large channel decorated pot (Plate 86) in the top of the grey brown clay (Bed 9) near base of the 'Older Channel' fill (F7) (Chiungu Member) *c.* 40 metres east of A4 trench. Site A, River Face, 1959. Sandstone, 12 × 8 × 2 cm. (A/184/59).

Right: Flat grindstone fragment of sandstone (20 × 13 × 8 cm) with two utilized, very slightly concave surfaces at right angles. The main striated surface is uneven and bears several sharply incised cut marks at the right edge, probably made with a metal blade. Probably a whetstone. From depth of 7 feet to 7 feet 6 inches (2·1–2·3 m) in 'Older Channel' fill (F7) (Chiungu Member), A27, Site A, excavation A1, 1956.

93 Pot of inferior workmanship found on the Ufipa plateau 6 miles (9·7 km) south of Upper Muse Village in 1966. Note the interrupted band of oblique impressions on the neck and, on the shoulder, a grooved, irregular chevron pattern made by dragging a double pointed stick across the wet clay. The base has been pressed in to form a broad 'dimple', possibly to secure seating on the floor or bench.

94 Group of Lungu pots made from the locally dug grey to white clays in the Mkamba Member of the Kalambo Falls Formation, ready for firing, on the low terrace (8 feet (2·4 m)) on the Tanzania side of the river, opposite Site A. Firing is completed in *c.* 30 minutes and the oxidized outer surface is immediately blackened by the application of water in which bark strips have been steeped.

95 An example of a threshing floor for finger millet (*Eleusine coracana*) with earth mortars and pestles. Bemba temporary village built at the site of the gardens, near Chitambo Mission, south of Mpika, Zambia, close to the Great North Road, 1958.

96 Temporary windbreak of two mats supported by sticks, showing traditional position of the hearth and activity area; Hukwe Bushman group at Domba Waterhole, 1951; *c.* 15 miles (24 km) south of Ngwezi Pools, Sesheke district, southwest corner of Western Province (Barotseland), Zambia. (Photograph by Nigel Watt. Copyright Zambia Information Department.)

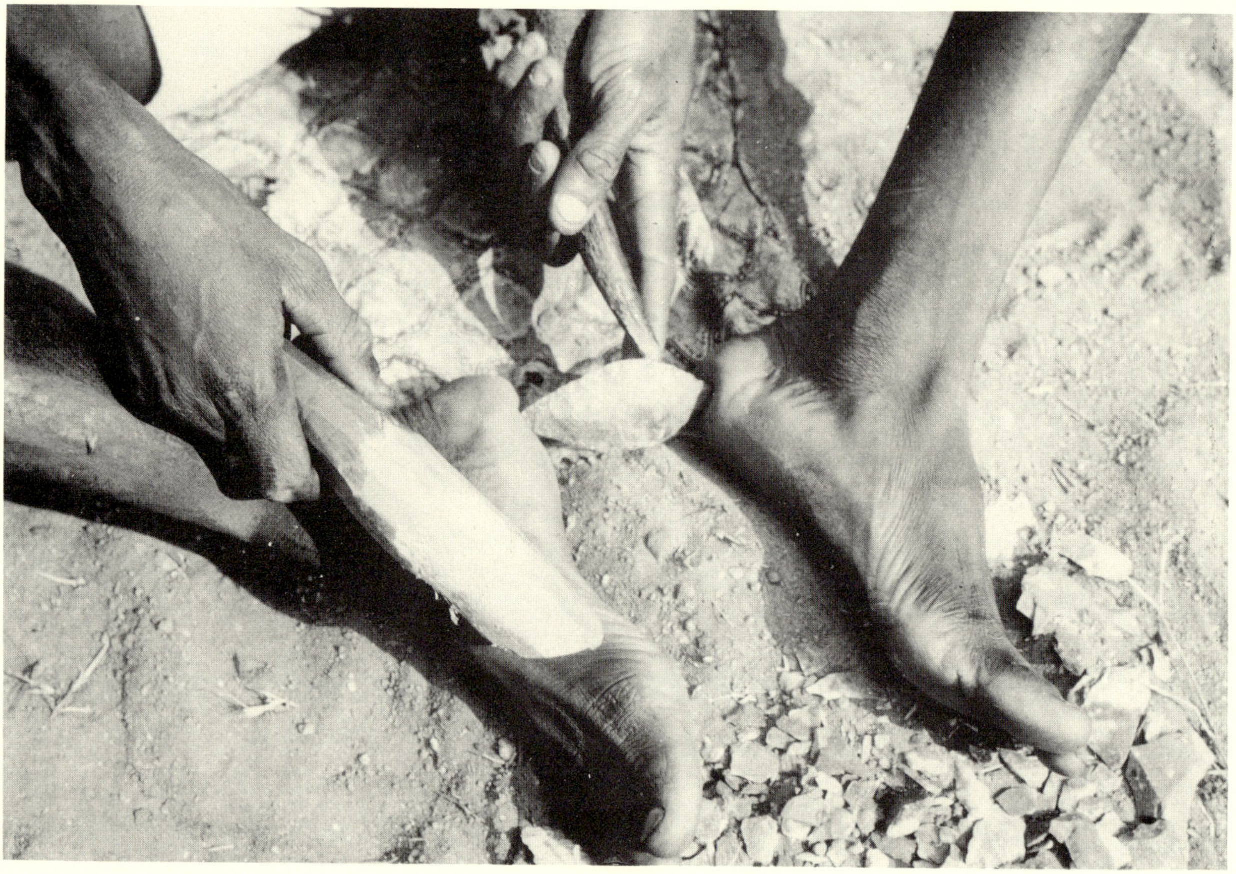

97 Punch technique for the manufacture of gunflints, demonstrated by Chokwe specialist at Dundo, Lunda Province, northeast Angola. The hammer and punch are normally of soft iron but Lupemban and Tshitolian artifacts can be copied equally well by using a wooden hammer and horn punch. The flakes are removed from the under face of the tool when the punch is struck approximately 6 cm up from the point.

98 West wall of A4 trench, 1959, between pegs 40 and 38 to show the pebble and grit horizons in compact, red, sandy soil containing the Hillslope component of the Polungu Industry. Sherds of the Kalambo Falls Industry (Early Iron Age) are contained within the upper 2 feet (61 cm) or so and the dark grey earth immediately below and to the right of peg 39 (centre) is a Later Iron Age pit dug prior to the formation of the present humic soil.

INDEX